Peter Mandelson was born in London in 1953 and educated at Hendon County Grammar School and Oxford University. At the age of thirty-two he became Labour's Director of Campaigns and Communications, and he was elected as MP for Hartlepool in 1992. During Tony Blair's premiership he was Minister without Portfolio, Secretary of State for Trade and Industry, and Secretary of State for Northern Ireland. He stood down as an MP in 2004 to become EU Trade Commissioner, before returning to the government under Gordon Brown as Secretary of State for Business, Innovation and Skills, First Secretary of State, and Lord President of the Council. He remains in Parliament as a member of the House of Lords.

THE THIRD MAN

Life at the Heart of New Labour

PETER MANDELSON

Harper
Press

HarperPress

An imprint of HarperCollins*Publishers*

77–85 Fulham Palace Road,

Hammersmith, London W6 8JB

www.harpercollins.co.uk

Published by HarperPress in 2010

2

The author asserts the moral right to be identified as the author of this work

A catalogue record for this book is available from the British Library

ISBN HB 978-0-00-739528-6
ISBN PB 978-00-739529-3

Set in Minion

Printed and bound in Great Britain by Clays Ltd, St Ives plc

To my parents, Mary and Tony,
who gave me my values and the
best upbringing anyone could
wish for

Contents

List of Illustrations

(© John Stillwell / PA Archive/Press Association Images)
With a group of school children in Hartlepool.
With guest speaker Mo Mowlam and friends at a constituency
summer barbeque in Hartlepool.
With Prince Charles at a reception in St James's Palace.

Planning the 1997 general election campaign with Margaret
Beckett, Alastair Campbell, Tony Blair and Gordon Brown.
(© Tom Stoddart/Getty Images)
New Labour's kings of spin: with Alastair and David Hill prior
to our 1997 election manifesto launch. *(© Fiona Hanson/PA
Archive/Press Association Images)*
A new dawn: the election victory party at the Royal Festival Hall on
the morning of 2 May 1997. *(© Brian Harris/Rex Features)*
Minister without Portfolio: outside the Cabinet Office on my first
day at work.
At the Millennium Dome site with Chris Smith, Michael Heseltine,
Tony Blair and John Prescott. *(© John Stillwell/PA Archive/Press
Association Images)*
John Prescott in conversation with his mate 'Peter'. *(© Ben Curtis/
PA Archive/Press Association Images)*
Relaxing in the company of Sabrina Guinness and Mick Jagger.
With Bobby and Jack on the steps of Hillsborough Castle.
At Stormont with Tony and Bill Clinton, December 2000.
The Queen visits Hillsborough. Housekeeper Olywn McCarthy
keeps hold of Bobby.
Making my resignation statement outside Number 10 after leaving
the government for the second time, January 2001. *(© Alastair
Grant/AP/Press Association Images)*
With Tony in Hartlepool, September 2001. This was the first time
we had been photographed together since my second resignation.
(© Owen Humphreys/PA Wire/Press Association Images)
Supporting the campaign for justice for the families of the victims
of the Omagh bombing, 2000. *(© Topfoto.co.uk)*

With my constituency agent, Steve Wallace, in Hartlepool.

Anxiously awaiting the result at the Hartlepool count on the night of the 2001 general election. (© *Carl Rutherford/PA Archive/Press Association Images*)

Jubilation with my supporters after my victory is announced. (© *Ian Hodgson/Reuters/Corbis*)

At the Progressive Governance Conference in London, 2003 with President Lula of Brazil, Tony and President Thabo Mbeki of South Africa.

With Tony at the EU–China political summit in the Great Hall of the People in Beijing. (© *Kirsty Wigglesworth/AP/Press Association Images*)

Arriving at the WTO talks in Geneva, July 2008. (© *Fabrice Coffrini/ AFP/Getty Images*)

Irish farmers protesting in Dublin against the proposed WTO deal. (© *Collins Photo Agency, Dublin*)

'Cashmering my way into Number 10' on my return to government for the third time, October 2008. (© *Fiona Hanson/PA Wire/Press Association Images*)

At the Cabinet table with Alan Johnson, David Miliband, Alistair Darling, Douglas Alexander and Ed Balls. (© *Anthony Devlin/AP/ Press Association Images*)

Gordon and I see the funny side during a question-and-answer session with local business people in Kent on 21 October, shortly after I rejoined the government. (© *Gareth Fuller/PA Wire/Press Association Images*)

Resplendent in my robes on the occasion of my introduction to the House of Lords, with Roger Liddle. (© *Gary Lee/ Photoshot*)

On a return visit to Brussels, with the President of the European Commission, José Manuel Barroso.

In a military aircraft during my visit to Iraq, April 2009. (© *Peter Nicholls/The Times*)

Comeback kid: delivering my speech to the Labour Party
conference, September 2009. *(© Mirrorpix)*

The *Mirror* headline the next day summed up the mood of
delegates in the hall. *(© Mirrorpix)*

Dancing with Hannah Rita-Mackenzie in the Blackpool Tower
Ballroom during the general election campaign, April 2010.
(© Graeme Robertson/Guardian News & Media Ltd 2010)

On our final day in Downing Street with Douglas Alexander,
Alastair, Gordon and Ed Balls. *(© Martin Argles/Guardian
News & Media Ltd 2010)*

Acknowledgements

When I first embarked on writing this book some years ago, I wrongly assumed that to get what was in my head onto paper would be a relatively straightforward exercise. One false start later, I realised that a project like this is far from simple. I could not have crossed the finishing line without the support of four people in particular.

The first is Robert Harris, who for the last twenty years of my political career has repeatedly urged me both to keep a diary, and to write a book based on it. I decided to hide from him, and from everyone else, the fact that for many years I have been an inveterate note-taker and sporadic diary-keeper. This book is the result, and I am grateful to Robert for his persistence, and for so many other acts of kindness from him and Gill and their family.

The second is Ned Temko, former chief political correspondent of the *Observer*, who persuaded me that the physical undertaking of writing a book was not beyond me, and provided the initial drive to get the project off the ground with insights and support which he maintained throughout.

The other two people who proved equally indispensable were Benjamin Wegg-Prosser and Patrick Loughran, my special advisers at either end of my ministerial career between 1997 and 2010. They are exceptional individuals, and I was never sure with either Ben or Patrick whether I was in charge or they were, but we got there in the end. I relied on their judgement about many matters relating to this book, but needless to say, I take full responsibility for its content. I am especially grateful to Yulia Wegg-Prosser and Victoria O'Byrne for allowing me to benefit from so much of Ben and Patrick's time.

I am grateful to my friend and spokesman Peter Power for reading the book at proof stage and for giving me his frank views on it, as he has on so many other things in recent years.

My agent, Eddie Bell, has encouraged me throughout in writing the book, and I benefited greatly from his wisdom. At HarperCollins, I will always remember and be grateful for the integrity and utter dedication to their work of Martin Redfern and Robert Lacey. They enabled me to complete the book in record time, and gave up much of their own in the process. I would like to thank Helen Ellis as well, and of course Vicky Barnsley, the chief executive, who took this book on in good faith without my actually signing a contract until the end of May 2010.

Throughout my life in politics to date I have been supported by some quite remarkable staff, especially including Maree Glass, and her husband, Nick Gold. There are few aspects of my life that remain untouched, or unimproved, by Maree's capable hands. Derek Draper has been a source of both inspiration and irritation from the time I was first elected to the House of Commons in 1992.

I would like to thank Clive Russell, who helped me out in my Commons office before 1997, as did Sarah Hunter; Joe Dancey, who was my researcher, media handler and all-round support from 2001 to 2004; and Simon Latham, who worked diligently for me during the 2010 general election campaign. Patrick Diamond was my special adviser at the Northern Ireland Office. He, along with Roger Liddle, has never ceased encouraging and helping me in all my political endeavours. Geoffrey Norris was an invaluable special adviser to me at the Business Department when I returned to government.

I am grateful for the unfailing courtesy and mutual support of the Number 10 political staff and civil servants I worked with under both Tony Blair and Gordon Brown. I hope they feel that I gave as much to them as they did to me.

I would like to thank and pay tribute to all those officials, both in private office and in the departments, whose professionalism and good company I relished and relied upon. It is a privilege to work with the British civil service, and I am only sorry that I cannot identify every single individual to whom I owe thanks. I should, however, make particular mention of my successive principal private secretaries since 1997 – Rupert Huxter, Anthony Phillipson, Nick Perry and Richard Abel.

In Brussels, I would like to thank other members of my cabinet in addition to those mentioned in the book: Per Haugaard, Peter Hill, Hiddo Houben, Renate Nikolay, Eric Peters and Catherine Wendt, as well as my driver Johnny Melkebeek, and Katherine Mixture and Fiona Kitson who worked in my personal office. Stephen Adams holds a special place in my gratitude as my speechwriter both in Brussels and London.

I cannot thank every individual member of the Labour Party's staff with whom I have worked so closely and enjoyably since 1985, but they all have my undying admiration for what they achieved. In the 2010 election campaign, Marianna Trian, Roger Baker, Torsten Henricson-Bell, Sam White, Sue Macmillan, Mary Doherty, John Stolliday and his team in media monitoring were all amongst the most notable troupers, along with those referred to in the book. Mark Lucas, as ever, made an exceptional contribution in the election films he produced.

Mentioned also in the book are a number of friends who have carried me through my highs and lows. I would like to thank some for their particular kindness over the years, including Waheed Alli, Bridget Brody, Peter Brown, Matthew Freud, Philip Goelet, Waring Hopkins, B.S. and Christina Ong, James Palumbo, Evelyn and Lynn de Rothschild, Roland Rudd, Dennis Stevenson, Linda Wachner, and Stephen and Vicki Wegg-Prosser.

Of the many protection officers who looked after me during my time in Northern Ireland and after, I would like to thank Duncan Johnson and Mick Hickin in particular, and also remember their colleagues, and my friends, the late Alec VanderPool and Ami Sanghera. They were among the best.

Last of all I would like to thank Reinaldo and his family for their commitment to me, and my brother Miles and his wife Valerie and their children. All his life, Miles has overlooked my shortcomings and continued to love and support me. I could not have wished for a better friend in need.

Introduction

This may seem an odd admission from someone who once embodied New Labour's reputation for spin and control freakery, but almost everything about this book is different from what I had imagined it would be.

Alongside Tony Blair and Gordon Brown, I helped to found the modernising project that became New Labour, and to win the party an unprecedented three terms in government. I was not just a witness to, but a participant in, the highs and the lows of those years. In the early days of our modernising project, journalists dubbed us 'The Three Musketeers', and the remarkable bond that linked Tony, Gordon and me was at the heart of all that we achieved, and failed to achieve.

When I decided to call this book *The Third Man*, it was not out of feigned modesty. No matter how influential each of us was, at different times and in different circumstances, in the creation and achievements of New Labour, there is an obvious distinction between us. Tony, and then Gordon, became leader of our party and Prime Minister of our country. By contrast, through much of our time in government, my influence was exercised largely behind the scenes, sometimes even in the shadows – another reason why the title's echo of Graham Greene's story of post-war Vienna seemed appropriate.

I first met Tony and Gordon in 1985, when I started work as Labour's youthful campaign director at the party headquarters in Walworth Road and they were recently-elected MPs. I have a clear recollection of when I first brought the three of us together as a team.

I was looking ahead to the coming general election in 1987, and had already identified both of them as very gifted politicians – they shared an appetite for hard work, a deftness for identifying political opportunities, and an ability to communicate with an electorate that was still very sceptical about Labour. Above all, they were attuned to voters' feelings rather than simply to what our activist base wanted to hear. The role I had in mind for them was to work with me to develop campaign grenades for us to lob at the Tories when the election was called.

The two of them needed little encouragement. In the coming months we prepared our lines of attack, and when the election starting pistol was fired, I scheduled a press conference to enable them to release the first salvo. It turned out to be both the first and the last such occasion. Chaired by the sometimes acerbic but media-savvy frontbencher Gerald Kaufman, the event was organised so that Gordon would launch the initial attack on the Tories, before Tony stepped in to finish them off. Instead, he came close to finishing off his own political career almost before it had begun. Momentarily departing from the prepared script, he described Mrs Thatcher as 'unhinged'. The journalists' ears pricked up at the sound of the Prime Minister, then at the height of her powers, apparently being described as deranged or worse. To his credit, Tony's antennae, even then, were in full working order. He quickly spotted the danger, and glanced at me from the platform with a pained expression that I was to become very familiar with in the years to come. It was ITN's super-sharp political editor at the time, Michael Brunson, who leapt on the gaffe. 'That's a good line to lead the Ten with,' he said, smiling, to me when I went over to the press pack to see what story they were likely to report. I managed to get Tony off the hook, telling Michael firmly that 'unhinged' did not mean mad, that it was Mrs Thatcher's policies that Tony was describing, not her mental state, and that anyway, it would not be fair to embarrass a newcomer who was sure to be going places, and was therefore someone Michael would want to befriend.

This was the sort of incident that helped establish my reputation as Britain's original 'spin doctor', someone who could 'fix' the news, or write the next day's headlines. The Conservatives feared me, and inside the Labour Party some revered me, while others loathed me, depending on their political standpoint. It was no secret which side of the modernising argument I was on. Unfortunately, transforming the Labour Party would prove an altogether much harder and lengthier process than squaring hard-nosed political journalists, but at least from that time the identities of those who would lead the modernising pack began to be established.

From the outset, I knew that much of this book would centre on the defining relationships of my political life, with Tony Blair and Gordon Brown. As I wrote, and relived my life in the Labour Party, I found myself recalling some of the despair I occasionally felt during the 1980s: the lurking, ever-present thought that our party might never form a government again, and the sheer hunger and drive this instilled in me to ensure that it did not happen.

I found that same hunger in Tony and Gordon, the two people who gave me most hope in those wilderness years that Labour's best days might yet be ahead of it. It was not a hunger for office for its own sake, but for a modernised Labour Party that would build a more humane, tolerant and socially just country than the one we were living in during the 1980s and early 1990s.

The three of us became like brothers. The force of our personalities, and the desire for change that we shared with the team of political professionals we built together – people like Philip Gould and Alastair Campbell – would help to take us back into government and keep us there for a longer period than any in Labour's history. We transformed our party's attitudes to the economy, to markets, to state ownership, to defence, to business, to the trade unions, to tax and spending, to public service reform, and to individual rights and responsibilities. In doing so, we defined New Labour, and reconnected the party with the broad mainstream of modern Britain.

In government, this modernising project helped create the fairer, more generous, more open-minded Britain that will be our legacy. We have a record that I am proud of. Our public infrastructure – the essential services we all rely on – was rebuilt: the days of winter crises and longer waiting times in our National Health Service, and the crumbling school buildings that we inherited on coming into office, now seem like something from another era. Faster treatment for serious diseases such as cancer has saved lives, and the NHS is more patient-focused than at any time since its birth. Our unprecedented investment in schools and universities was combined with far-reaching reform to widen educational opportunity at every level, in particular during the crucial early years. We irreversibly improved attitudes to the work–family balance, acted successfully to bring about peace in Northern Ireland, significantly reduced crime, increased support for families with children, and promoted more tolerant attitudes on race, gender and sexuality. All of these achievements were possible only because of the project to which Tony, Gordon and I dedicated our political lives: fundamental change to the Labour Party.

In writing this book, I knew there would be no way to avoid describing the occasional soap-opera aspects of our relationship. I am conscious that my diaries and contemporaneous notes, on which this account is based, have focused disproportionately on the frustrations, arguments and disagreements we had, rather than on those areas on which we did agree and which, as a government, were the basis of our long-term achievements. Inevitably with such a close-knit group of strong personalities, there were family feuds, tensions and differences of opinion – sometimes of epic proportions, sometimes, in retrospect, far too petty. These were magnified and fed by the burgeoning twenty-four-hour news culture, the development of which accelerated during our time in office. But more often than not, particularly in the earlier years, the tensions between us were a source of strength for New Labour. And in the end, through all the strains, we held together – unlike Thatcher, Howe and Lawson, unlike the SDP's Gang of Four, and even, going back further, the Labour trio of Crosland, Jenkins and Healey.

If any of us had reason to split from the others and break up the team, it was me. I became the meat in the sandwich in the struggle that developed between the other two. My falling-out with Gordon after John Smith's death, when Tony rather than Gordon became party leader, would lead to my exclusion from government for lengthy periods, blighting my ministerial career. Yet I remained close to Tony, and I finally made up with Gordon.

Whatever my other failings, I am a loyal person, and I rate loyalty above all other qualities. There were many times in my political life when it would have been simpler for me either to keep my head down, or to change sides at an opportune moment. It would have been advantageous for me to desert Tony when he was battling for survival against Gordon's drive to accelerate his departure and succeed him as Prime Minister. And I would have been applauded by many in my party if, later on, I had deserted Gordon when it was clear that he could not win re-election. Perhaps it is a fault to cling too dogmatically to an idea or a policy, but not, in my view, to a person to whom you have made a commitment.

The reason I did not waver in my support for Tony is that I believed in him, his political outlook and his skills as a leader. The more pressure he came under, the more steadfast I became, overcoming my feelings that at times he had let me down. Tony was not perfect. Notwithstanding the steel he showed towards me, he did not always enforce his will sufficiently with others to get the policy changes he wanted. But his personal conviction, and sense of right and wrong, were unflagging. He had great leadership qualities, and it was always impressive to see how he would manage to defeat his opponents more often than not by means of intelligent planning and calculation, rather than employing less subtle tactics.

The reasons I came back to Gordon in late 2008, rejoining the government even though I was enjoying my life and my fulfilling job as the EU's Trade Commissioner, were that he needed me – always a nice feeling to have – and that I wanted to serve the country I love. I felt that I could make a difference when the financial crisis struck, and I strongly supported the policies Gordon was pursuing. I know that, later on, some people in the party felt that by bolstering Gordon's position and keeping him in place, I contributed to our electoral defeat. One reason I did not take action was partly selfish: I did not want to be accused of 'treachery' all over again. But also, I was never convinced, so near the election and in the absence of an obvious consensual alternative, that a change of leadership could have been easily, bloodlessly or quickly achieved, or that having three different Prime Ministers in a single Parliament would have been an electoral asset. And I never gave up the hope that Gordon would be rewarded at the polls for his efforts in preventing a painful economic recession from turning into something far worse.

One of the things for which I have attracted criticism from the media is my circle of friends. I admit that I am drawn to individualists, to people whose achievements and strong personalities make them interesting company. I am more interested in what people do and think than their ideologies, and I judge them by their character, by their personal qualities, rather than by how they are perceived. There is no escaping the fact that people who are successful in politics, business, journalism, fashion or the arts give off energy, have thought-provoking insights and attract dynamic company around them. I enjoy this, and have a wide range of friends and acquaintances, mostly outside politics. I make no apology for that. I am a restless soul.

As I began writing this book during my final period in Brussels, I was uncertain about how much personal and political detail I should, or could, include. New Labour was, after all, still in power, and I was keen to avoid anything that might harm or embarrass the government, or Gordon or Tony. Or, frankly, myself. But the book I have written turned out to be neither trimmed nor self-censored. For one thing, I recognised that doing so would have made it not only less truthful, but also less rounded and less compelling. My time in Brussels changed the tone and the breadth of the book I have written. Away from the pressure-cooker of Westminster, I was able to establish a new distance from the events of which I had been a part. I also became more relaxed personally, more self-confident politically, and much less interested in the spin and the message-control which, for both good and ill, had defined my early years as a Labour moderniser.

The result is that I have ended up by writing what I believe to be a frank and truthful account of my political life. Unlike those in politics who appear able to go with the flow, I am not a neutral figure. I do not remember a moment when I have not been fighting for something or against something, or simply fighting back against the tumult engulfing me. While I am capable of changing my views, I am rarely without a view. Ever since I entered politics, I have stood for certain principles, and I have had a particular political outlook. I am on the centre-left, but I have always been open to fresh ways of implementing the progressive values I hold. The more involved I became in writing this account, the more I realised that I am anything but a mere fence-sitting chronicler of New Labour, or of the characters and relationships at its core.

The main sense, though, in which the book has turned out differently from what I had anticipated has less to do with my own choices or judgements than with what Harold Macmillan famously described as the determining force in politics: 'Events, dear boy, events.' As I began writing in earnest, I felt oddly liberated by no longer being directly part of the story I was setting out to tell. Tony had left office. Gordon was in Number 10. I was in Brussels, out of front-line British politics altogether. But then, suddenly and astonishingly, events took an unexpected turn. Not only did I find myself returning as a participant, rather than an observer. Once again I was at the heart of the story.

1

'Can You Help Me?'

The most fateful four hours of my political life were also the most surreal. They began on the afternoon of the first Thursday of October 2008, across a tray of sandwiches, yoghurt and slightly over-ripe bananas, with Gordon Brown in 10 Downing Street. They culminated in my return to the heart of government, at the behest of a Prime Minister who for much of the previous decade had denounced and denigrated me.

Our first quiet step towards reconciliation, the rekindling of a deep if damaged friendship, came seven months earlier and two hundred miles away. It was a crisp late-February morning in Brussels, my base as European Trade Commissioner since I had left front-line British politics in 2004. Gordon was on his first full-dress visit to the European Commission as Prime Minister. Before making his way to the imposing, glass-fronted headquarters of the Commission on the Schuman roundabout, he had arranged for us to talk briefly in the office of our permanent representative to the EU, Kim Darroch, down the road. It would be the first time Gordon and I had met since his truculent takeover from Tony Blair in Downing Street the year before. I was intrigued, expectant. And apprehensive. From the moment in 1994 when Tony had emerged as the irresistibly obvious choice to succeed John Smith as Labour Party leader, Gordon had convinced himself that I had schemed behind his back to deny him the job. As he surely must have recognised, that was unfair, and untrue. Yet in more recent years, as he and his allies waged their insurgency against Tony, he had come to view me as Tony's staunchest defender and as a siren voice of alarm over how and where he was likely to lead New Labour.

I had spent the early months of Gordon's premiership trying to keep my head down. But I was goaded during a *Today* programme interview shortly before he took over to observe a bit mischievously that while this might 'come as a disappointment to him', the new Prime Minister couldn't actually fire me from my Commission post, because I had been appointed by the government to a full, five-year term. Yet I hastened to add a note of reassurance. I said I did not intend to seek a second term once my time in Brussels ended in November 2009. I assumed the new guard in Number 10 would recognise that I was playing an important role in delicate negotiations for a world trade agreement. I also knew that my ability to do the job well, and to finesse the interests of individual EU states along the way, would suffer if I were seen to lack the confidence of my own government. The more I could stay off Gordon's political radar, the better, and my *Today* interview was a maladroit first move in achieving this.

Privately, I was still upset over the way he had treated Tony, and me. I not only resented the personal pain caused to me by his behaviour, and that of his parliamentary foot-soldiers and media briefers; in addition to their part in ending my own cabinet career, I felt they had kept Tony from delivering on key areas of New Labour's policy promise to Britain. They had acted to weaken his room for manoeuvre and his legacy in government, well beyond the huge damage caused by the aftermath of the war in Iraq. But Gordon was now leader. I did not want to become a sulking, resentful presence, desperately clinging on to past bad feelings and finding fault in everything he did. At his first party conference as Prime Minister, in Bournemouth at the end of September 2007, I used an address to the modernisers' policy group Progress not just to praise him for his part in the transition from one New Labour government to another, but to extol him as the man incomparably qualified to tackle the new challenges facing our country in the twenty-first century.

I spoke with more certainty than I actually felt – though neither I nor anyone else could have anticipated the vertiginous decline in

Gordon's fortunes that would begin within days of the conference ending. Still, the message of support was genuine. It was rooted not only in political calculation, or a desire to ward off trouble for myself in Brussels. Though my earlier doubts about Gordon's fitness as Prime Minister remained, I wanted to be proved wrong. Before our spectacular falling-out, he had been my closest friend and ally in politics. I was intimately familiar not only with Gordon's weaknesses, personal and political. I knew his strengths: intelligence, iron determination, and above all a grasp of the economic challenges that were increasingly threatening our country and the world.

By the time Gordon arrived in Brussels, the seriousness of the world economic crisis for Britain was becoming clearer. Fully-fledged recession was some months ahead, but the American sub-prime banking meltdown had claimed its first UK victim. The previous autumn, a run on the Newcastle-based bank Northern Rock had brought it to the brink of collapse. It was saved only by financial support from the Treasury. In the months that followed, Gordon and his Chancellor, Alistair Darling, tried desperately to find a private buyer for the bank. Only days before Gordon came to Brussels, they had given up, and taken Northern Rock into public ownership. I happened to believe they were right both to have worked for a private deal as the better option, and to have chosen nationalisation when that proved impossible.

The immediate problem for the Prime Minister was that he was now mired in a political crisis as well as an economic one. It had begun at party conference. While I was publicly on my best behaviour, I had seen it coming. For days, Gordon's inner circle had been stoking up speculation that he was about to call an early general election. His first three months in power had gone extraordinarily well. He was confronted with a cattle-disease scare, but the effects had been less severe than at first appeared likely. Two attempted terror bombings had mercifully resulted in only a single death, of one of the terrorists. A spate of summer flooding was of course bad for those affected, but turned out to be less serious than feared. He had dealt with these potential crises in an assured way, and his supporters were hailing his strength and statesmanship. Going into conference, he was riding high in the opinion polls. But he was also an *unelected* Prime Minister – not just because our 2005 general election campaign had been under Tony's banner and not his, but because he had not even faced a challenge for the succession inside Labour. Now, here was a chance for a mandate of his own.

But from the moment I'd seen the first of the media hype, I was almost sure it wouldn't happen. Gordon – the Gordon I had known so well and worked with so closely since the 1980s – was a risk-averse politician. In 1992, he had shied away from fighting John Smith for the party leadership. After John's death – in fairness because Gordon had finally realised he couldn't possibly win – he had stepped back from challenging Tony for the leadership. Most of all, Gordon was cautious when it came to Britain's voters.

As the pre-conference election speculation intensified, a number of the old Blairite stalwarts had phoned me in Brussels. What did I think? Would there be a snap election? 'I've known Gordon for more than twenty years,' I replied. 'I can tell you when the date of the election will be – May 2010.' Yet, by the time I arrived in Bournemouth a snap election was being touted as a foregone conclusion. When a reporter asked me to comment, I said the minimum I felt I could get away with. 'I can see no reason,' I replied, 'why he shouldn't call an election.'

Within days, it all went horribly wrong. I was back in Brussels, and the Tories were holding their own conference in Blackpool, when I suddenly saw TV pictures of the Prime Minister pitching up in Iraq, where he let out news of plans to begin reducing British troop levels. It immediately worried me. I had no way of knowing – at least until later – of the thinking behind Gordon's visit to the front line. I did, however, know what it would look like: a publicity stunt during David Cameron's conference, with our troops used as pre-electoral wallpaper. Then things got worse. Cameron's Shadow Chancellor, George Osborne, used the Tory conference to unveil a proposal to ease inheritance tax, trebling the threshold to £1 million. This was tailor-made to appeal to the aspirational voters of Middle England, who were not alone in feeling over-taxed as the signs of world recession intensified. They were the very voters who, by buying into Tony and New Labour, had helped give us three election victories. They were the voters Gordon needed, too. But they were the voters he understood least well, always a particular frustration for him because Tony connected with them so instinctively and so easily. To top it off, Cameron used his closing conference address to taunt the Prime Minister into action. Go on, he said. Call an election.

Gordon was torn. First, he ham-fistedly decided to steal Osborne's inheritance-tax trick. Then, even before Alistair Darling had unveiled our version of it in the Pre-Budget Report – the series of government finance announcements made in the autumn prior to the spring budget – he announced that there would be no election after all. As if that were not damaging enough, he insisted that he had never been minded to call one in the first place. Having looked so assured as Prime Minister at the start of his time in office, Gordon was now portrayed – by Cameron, of course, but also by the media – as hapless and a ditherer. All the controversies and embarrassments that bedevil any government were fed into that narrative. Not only the serious issues that arose in the weeks after the party conference, like improperly declared Labour donations, or the loss of a set of computer disks containing millions of Revenue and Customs records, but even the frankly farcical. In December, European heads of state gathered in Lisbon to approve the amended EU constitutional treaty. Gordon, apparently fearing the political toxicity of the issue, at first feinted at staying away. He ended up managing not to have his cake or to eat it either. He went to the ceremony, but showed up only after the other heads of government had done their signing.

There was a further awkward moment when he arrived at Kim Darroch's office some months later, at the end of February 2008, for what both of us must have feared could be a tense reunion. I was with Kim and a handful of aides when Gordon strode into the outer office. At first my old friend and more recent foe did not see me at all. After he had greeted everyone else in the room, I finally had to take the initiative. 'Hello,' I said. Gordon quickly replied: 'Oh. Hi,

Peter, hi. How are you doing?' We made our way to Kim's office, and settled into a pair of plush chairs in the centre of the room. I had expected that we would begin with trade, and we did. That was my job, after all. Our only real conversation since Gordon had moved into Number 10, a telephone call four months earlier, had been about the world trade talks. I was also fairly sure that both of us – by instinct, and from a sense of familiarity and partner-ship that went too far back to have disappeared entirely – would be unable to keep from talking about politics. Within barely a minute, we were not only discussing the big-picture issues Britain faced, we were talking about Gordon, about his government, and about the nose-dive in public support they were both suffering. It would be wrong to suggest that it was like the old days, as if the rift between us had not happened. But the conversation was easy, calm, and at times extraordinarily forthright – on both sides.

Gordon's main concern, a theme to which he would return repeat-edly in the months ahead, was that he was 'not getting the communi-cations right' – not with the media, nor with the British people. My reply was that good communications required not just good, confi-dent people and organisation, but clear, bold policy. 'I've got all the policy, all the ideas,' Gordon insisted. 'I just can't communicate it.' I told him that was not always my impression. His policies had to be thought through. They had to be 'prepared, bottomed out, agreed and owned by relevant ministers'. Instead, it seemed to me, he had been seduced by the idea that a constant stream of media announce-ments could take the place of hard policy. I told him he had to wean himself off these 'announceables'. Policy was tough going, espe-cially when it involved changing or reforming anything. You had to keep pushing uphill. Then people would start noticing that some-thing serious was happening. That was where 'communications success' would come from. I was at pains to reassure him that there was still a real opportunity for him to regain the political initiative. The key, I said, was the economy. 'You've got to present yourself as the guy with the experience, the big brain, to deal with the big prob-lems,' I told him. 'That is your USP.' The point I sought to make, as subtly as I could, was that David Cameron *did* have natural communications skills. Gordon's task, one to which he ought to be genuinely well-suited, was to make it clear that his grasp and determination in dealing with the economic crisis stood in contrast to Cameron. He had to be able to portray the Tory leader as 'the guy in short trousers, who's good enough perhaps to lead a student protest, but certainly not to lead a country'.

Our talk had been scheduled to last for twenty minutes. By the time Gordon left for the Commission headquarters, behind schedule for his meeting with the Commission's President, José Manuel Barroso, we had been talking for well over an hour. Gordon seemed more upbeat when we'd finished talking, and more focused on how to get a new hold on government. I felt oddly buoyed too. I realised that despite all that we had gone through, I still cared about him. I wanted him to succeed. And, if I'm honest, I was pleased he was seeking my views and advice on how to help rescue and repair the New Labour project that he and I and Tony had begun. It was also puzzling that he should start opening up to me in the way he had. Given all that had happened between us, he had reason to doubt whether he could trust me. Surely he had people around him in London he could rely on, without needing to talk to me?

Within days of Gordon's return to London, leaving me in Brussels to wrestle with my trade negotiations, there were signs that our meeting had at least begun to repair our relationship – but also of how difficult it might be to break long habits of misunderstanding and mistrust. A first hint at reconciliation came just forty-eight hours later, when he phoned me from Number 10. It was ostensibly to say that he had enjoyed our talk, but mostly to discuss a speech he was giving a few days later, at Labour's Spring Conference in Birmingham. I told him he needed to identify his strengths and play to them. People felt threatened by the economic storm clouds. He had had a decade's experience as Chancellor. He was seen as having a command of economic policy. His task now, and his opportunity as well, was to explain what was really going on, and how he and his government would enable Britain to deal with the storm and to come to terms with the new economic order more widely, and indeed benefit from it. 'People think GB is brainy, so he should turn it to his advantage,' I scribbled on my notepad when we had finished speaking. 'He should identify our national strengths and position, and set out an agenda to maximise these to our lasting gain.' That, essentially, is what I said to him. It was also what he went on to say in Birmingham – sort of. The speech began well. Then it faded out. It started on the theme of 'fulfilling our national ambitions', then meandered, without any real emotional connection, into a patch-work of policy examples and occasionally catchy phrases. It lacked a central, driving political message, a coherent story of the difficulties Britain faced, how Gordon proposed to lead us past them, and why he was best-placed to do so. It would be several weeks before I next talked to Gordon. By that time, there would be a reminder of the old days, and the old mistrust as well.

After our meeting in Brussels, my press spokesman Peter Power, who had learned very adeptly to pick his way on my behalf between the shoals and currents of trade policy and UK domestic politics, was besieged by questions from the media. He fended them off with an admirably straight bat. The Prime Minister and Britain's European Commissioner, he said, had had a 'friendly' discussion – about the world trade talks, about Britain's place in Europe, and about domestic politics. When asked whether this meant I might now hope to stay on for a second EU term, Peter was understandably keen to find a way to dodge the issue. He opted not to be drawn, rather than re-affirming my *Today* programme pledge not to seek a further term. His reticence invited speculation that I was fishing for an invitation to stay on. When Gordon was asked to comment a few days later, he replied that I *had done* a good job in Brussels. His choice of tense unleashed a new spate of headlines. 'Mandelson's Hopes of Serving Second EU Term Crushed by Gordon Brown', blared the *Daily Mail*. It seemed that old habits – mine, Gordon's, the media's – would die hard.

Gordon's political problems were clearly on a downward spiral. Partly, as he had insisted to me, it was an image problem. Once the 'iron' Chancellor, and then briefly a breath of fresh air in Downing Street, he was now seen as a 'dithering' Prime Minister in political freefall. Worse, he had become not only a figure of disdain, but of ridicule. This sense was summed up by Vince Cable, then acting leader of the Liberal Democrats, standing up at Prime Minister's Questions and deadpanning: 'The House has noticed the Prime Minister's remarkable transformation in the last few weeks – from Stalin. . .to Mr Bean.'

There were problems of policy substance, too. By far the most pressing was a legacy of Gordon's final budget as Chancellor, three months before he had moved in next-door. As part of an eye-catching announcement reducing the standard tax rate to 20p, beginning in April 2008 – which meant now – he had axed the entry-rate 10p bracket. The unintended, and clearly unanticipated, effect was to damage those at the very bottom of the ladder just as the economic crisis was beginning to bite. The immediate result was the worst back-bench rebellion Gordon had faced as Prime Minister. That subsided – only just – when he promised a package to compensate those who stood to lose out from the tax changes. This was the last thing we needed in the run-up to local elections across England and Wales on 1 May, and the results were disastrous. In the most high-profile con-test, for Mayor of London, even Ken Livingstone could not stave off defeat to the Conservatives' Boris Johnson. I won't claim to have shed many tears for Ken. With an ego the size of the London Eye, and what I always felt was a facile populism, he had delighted in stirring up 'real Labour' opposition to Tony during our first years in government. Still, I recognised that his defeat was bad news. Even Ken's image as a maverick, untainted by ordinary party constraints, had not saved him from falling victim to our declining fortunes. Nationally, we were not only outpolled by the Tories – by a margin of 44 per cent to 24 – we finished in third place, behind the Liberal Democrats.

I felt conflicted. Not about the results, of course. I was no less shaken than if Tony had still been in charge by our diminishing pros-pects of keeping David Cameron, short trousers or not, from usher-ing in a period of Conservative rule. Yet despite the renewed warmth

I had felt for him in Brussels, I began to wonder whether even a more focused Gordon Brown, playing to his strengths, could really succeed in turning things round. I was by now intermittently back in touch with him by phone. Perhaps equally surprisingly, given Gordon's role in hastening him out of Downing Street, so was Tony. Although now absorbed in his work on the Arab–Israeli conflict, his faith foundation and his business activities, Tony retained a train-spotter's interest in British politics, however much, publicly, he wanted to keep out of it. He also cared about his own legacy, and how Labour was going to secure it and build on it. Like me, he wanted to offer support to Gordon, and I encouraged him to do so.

Tony phoned him in Downing Street the day after the local elections. He told him he had to push back, not to sound defeated, not to beat himself up. Yes, he said, he had to listen to what the public were saying. But what he really had to do – a message I was also conveying – was to reassert what government was doing, why it was doing it, and how it would improve Britain. He had to provide a clearer sense of direction, a strong reform programme. If he looked and sounded wounded, Tony told him, he would invite further attacks: 'Be careful of what scent you give off.' We both agreed, however, that Gordon was beginning to look bad, physically. Sleepless and grey. Fearful. On the ropes. No wonder everyone assumed that he was all of those things.

A few days after he had spoken to Gordon, Tony called me from the Middle East at my small, quirky Brussels flat, whose large windows I liked staring out of as I worked or talked on the telephone. He said he felt that while Gordon had the intelligence and the ideas, the drive and determination, to make a success of government, 'none of that is the most important thing for a politician. It is intuition – what to do, when to do it, how to say it, how to bring people along.' That, he felt, was Gordon's problem. I agreed. Intuition, of course, was a political gift that Tony himself had in spades, and it had helped guide every step the three of us had taken in the long campaign to make Labour a party of government again.

After the local elections, Gordon scrambled to steady the wheel of what was beginning to look very much like a sinking ship. He brought forward his announcement of the government programme for the next Parliament. It proved to be a mishmash of the already known and the small-fry, and it was picked to pieces by the opposition, and even by some of the media pundits who at the height of Gordon's war against Tony had cheered him on as Labour's messiah-in-waiting. Nor was there any respite from Alistair Darling's panicked 'mini-budget' in mid-May, in which he was forced to borrow £2.7 billion to cushion the effect of the 10p rate axe on at least some of the lowest-paid workers. In late May, Gordon faced a further electoral test, and a further body-blow. The death of one of my own early political allies, the indomitable Labour backbencher Gwyneth Dunwoody, forced a by-election in Crewe. The Tories cruised to victory in what should have been one of the safest of Labour seats, defeating Gwyneth's own daughter by 8,000 votes. Gordon's early contrast between his premiership and Tony's was wearing perilously thin. The Brownite promise to an unsettled party had been that the Blair rollercoaster would be replaced by a calmer ride. Now it appeared we were going nowhere. Or very possibly off the rails.

In early June, Gordon called me again in Brussels. We agreed that I would come and see him at Downing Street when I was in London in the middle of the month. My role, if you could call it that, remained strictly informal. As far as I could tell, very few people knew I was back in touch with the Prime Minister. Sue Nye, Gordon's office 'gatekeeper' and one of my oldest friends in politics, was in the loop. As for others in the inner circle, even those who knew Gordon and I were talking seemed puzzled about where this latest twist in our relationship was headed. That was understandable: so was I.

When I went to London, I arranged to have lunch with Jeremy Heywood the day before I was to meet Gordon. I wanted to bring myself up to date with how things were running in Number 10, and to see what I could do to help. Jeremy was now Permanent Secretary, Gordon's top civil servant. In the early days of the Blair government he had been with Gordon at the Treasury, and before that, private secretary to Conservative chancellors. I had got to know him well when he moved to Number 10 and worked with Tony in 1999. When he arrived at the restaurant in the Royal Festival Hall, he was smiling. As he had been on his way out of Number 10, he said, Gordon had asked to see him. When he had explained that he was going to a lunch appointment, to meet me, Gordon had said he would join us – only to find that he couldn't scramble his protection officers quickly enough. 'The reason I made a point of mentioning you is that I'm still not sure just what your status is these days,' Jeremy said. 'I was afraid what Gordon might say if he found out. Now he says he wants to meet you this afternoon.' I told him I had arranged to see Gordon the following day, but Jeremy replied: 'He says he wants to meet you today, too.' Looking back on it, I suppose that was when our real sense of reconnection began.

'I've just been talking to Tony,' Gordon said as I arrived in the upstairs study at Number 10 – Mrs Thatcher's favourite room – from my lunch with Jeremy. I couldn't help but chuckle. 'Are things really that desperate?' I asked.

'Come on,' Gordon replied with a broad smile. He told me he had read a speech I'd recently given in New York, on the need for new policies and institutions to address the challenges of the global economy, and said he wanted to find a time to talk further about what that meant not just for the EU, but for Britain. I felt flattered, which, I suspect, was his intention. Then, after only a short pause, he turned to a more immediate worry – his own political crisis. And he uttered four extraordinary words: 'Can you help me?'

'How?' I asked, taken aback by his directness, and still feeling my way in this revived relationship.

'By giving me your strategy,' he said. 'Only a few people in politics are strategists, and you are one of them. I need that. I need to know what you think of my situation.'

I had an instant in which to make up my mind how honest to be with him. I didn't want to damage his confidence further, or put him off talking to me, but nor did I want to miss the chance to offer the kind of blunt advice I suspected he might not be getting from others. 'Look, people have stopped listening to you,' I said. 'They've tuned out. They don't know what you believe. They don't know what your government is for. You have policies, but they don't seem joined up.' Gordon took this well, considering my directness, and replied by returning to his Brussels refrain. He did have ideas, he insisted. What he lacked was strategy. And he couldn't communicate. 'It seems,' he sighed, 'that you can be a good Prime Minister or a popular one, preferably both. But I'm neither.'

'You're a better Prime Minister than people think,' I told him. I meant it, just as I genuinely felt that a Cameron government would be no better, and very likely worse, for Britain.

We spoke for well over an hour. It was not so much about what Gordon should do next. As I'd said in Brussels, the solution to that seemed to be straightforward, if not necessarily easy to achieve. It came down to developing the strong policy programme, and coherent message, his government seemed to lack. Mostly, however, we talked about how he had ended up where he was. 'A lot of your problems,' I said, 'stem from not calling the election when you led everyone to think you were going to do so. It has meant everything you do is viewed through that negative lens.' Gordon said he now realised he should have gone ahead. The political timing had been right, and with the economic crisis worsening, the opportunity was now gone. But he had been unsettled by last-minute poll figures in marginal constituencies. 'They showed a very different picture from the national polls,' he said. 'They hadn't presented it properly to me before.' And the Tory inheritance-tax initiative had scared him off, too. He now saw that his copying of Osborne's idea, and even more so his visit to the troops in Iraq, had made things worse.

But he had started so well in Downing Street that he had felt the run would never end. 'I thought, because of my first few months, I was being seen as above politics,' he said. 'You inhaled your own propaganda,' I replied. The image his media team had created around him at the start was bound to unravel. 'All that stuff about single-handedly turning back the biblical plagues, the floods, the cattle disease and the terror bombers. Your people went around saying how strong you were, what a great, statesmanlike Prime Minister. They took their eye off what was happening in the real world.' I felt almost cruel saying it.

Gordon was quiet for a few moments, and so was I. Finally, I said, with what I am sure he sensed was a genuine desire to help: 'If you could start all over again, you would do things differently. You need a different way of working, a different rhythm, a different approach.' I was not absolutely sure what that approach would be, but I was sure that the problem was not simply a matter of Gordon lacking the communications skills for modern politics, although that was what he always came back to. 'I'm good at what politics used to be, about policies,' he said. 'But now people want celebrity, and theatre.'

'Only up to a point,' I replied. 'Actually, it's a lot simpler than that: they just want someone to make their lives better, someone they can believe, and believe in. If you can do that, they can dispense with celebrity.'

Gordon nodded. Then, after another period of silence, he turned to me quietly with the same four words with which he had begun. 'Can you help me?'

'Yes,' I replied. 'We can try and work it out together.' At that moment, I could feel my old sense of commitment to him welling up inside me. Suddenly it was nice to feel wanted, needed again.

The question was how to help. I think I had forgotten, over the years of estrangement, how extraordinarily complex a man Gordon was. He had huge strengths, and sometimes debilitating weaknesses. That was simply to say that, like the rest of us, he was human. With Gordon, however, the balance on both sides of the ledger had never quite been captured in the public image which ossified around him. Some bits of the caricature were accurate. Yes, he was bright. He was intensely, obsessively, political. He was fiercely ambitious – for himself, certainly, as his single-minded pursuit of Tony's job had made clear, but also for the people of Britain. Yet all that was only part of the picture. At the height of the Brown–Blair civil war, I used to laugh at the media's contrast between Blair as the headline-driven tactician and Brown as the 'big-picture' man, the strategist who looked beyond day-to-day trivialities and spin and focused on the issues that counted. As those who knew Gordon best and had worked with him closest could attest – and I had done both for as long as anyone in active politics – the truth was much more nuanced than that. Gordon did see the big picture, but he tended to create tactical opportunities, rather than a strategy to advance it. Tony, by contrast would conceive his strategy at the outset, and then paint a big picture in order to carry people with him.

It is true that Tony cared about the media. Both of us came to realise, the longer he was in power, that we had probably cared too much about what the daily papers and the TV news bulletins were saying. But even – indeed, particularly – in times of crisis, he never lost sight of the issues that mattered. He kept in mind the longer-term goal. Gordon, from the time I first started working with him in the 1980s, was transfixed by the media. He was also transfixed by the Tories. Tony, of course, also took on the Conservatives. The difference was that Gordon wanted to pulverise them, whereas Tony was more often content to outmanoeuvre them. Gordon's life revolved too keenly around looking for opportunities to grab a front-page headline or top billing on the evening news with some carefully calibrated announcement or initiative. In some ways, he was a more innate politician than Tony. But he was also a more old-style politician. He had grown up in machine politics, in Scottish Labour. For him, politics was always a battle. He plotted a probing advance here, a flanking operation there. It was all planned to weaken rivals or enemies – sometimes in his own ranks, but ultimately the enemy that mattered most to him, and still did, was the Tories.

Yet it was Gordon the person, not Gordon the politician, who would matter most if he, our party and the government were to be pulled out of their tailspin. Despite my closeness to Tony, I had been much closer, much earlier, to Gordon when the three of us began the reforming crusade that would lead to New Labour. Gordon was the older of the two. He had deeper roots in Labour. He was the more driven political operator, the more obviously ambitious. He was the natural leader. That was one reason why Tony's later ascendancy so hurt him, and so damaged the relationship between all three of us.

On a human level, however, Gordon was buttoned up, less sure of himself – not of his political views, but of how he should handle himself in public. Tony was never clubbable in party-political terms. But he had a natural ease about him, a charm, an enjoyment of human contact. Gordon did not possess this easy manner.

I think Gordon's uneasiness and vulnerability was part of what was now drawing me back to his side, part of what made me genuinely want to keep my word to him and to do what I could to help. It was not out of pity, though it did pain me to see him so bruised. Nor was it merely out of loyalty to New Labour, or my conviction that if Gordon and the government crashed to defeat it would be bad for Britain, although I felt both of these things. It was a sense of fellow-feeling. I had taken my share of knocks along the way as well.

Unlike Gordon, and much more like Tony, I was comfortable in social situations. I enjoyed other people's company. I was at ease with most of them. Most of the time I was at ease with myself. I had interests and a life outside politics, especially now that I was in Brussels. But I too had had my periods of private doubt and private pain. I had endured, and only very slowly recovered from, the humiliation of being forced to leave the cabinet table not just once, but twice. The second exile had been particularly hard, because I had felt let down by colleagues, by Tony in particular. There had been other tough times as well. Over the years, I had become more thick-skinned. But what I had been through gave me an insight into Gordon's crisis. He had reached out for help. The truth was that I had no idea whether that was something I, or anyone, could deliver.

When we met again in Downing Street the next day, I tried to get him to focus on the one area where the country clearly needed new policy certainty, and new leadership, and where he was well-placed to deliver. 'It's the world economy, stupid,' I said, borrowing the Clinton campaign quip. 'Your message has to be that we are steering through the worst and equipping people to benefit from the upturn, to make sure they, and the country as a whole, are not the losers.'

Almost as if a switch had been tripped, Gordon's mood brightened. He spoke non-stop for five minutes, reeling off the challenges posed by the economic crisis, and the range of programmes – job creation, infrastructure, energy, education, science – needed to make Britain stronger when we got to the other side. He spoke of a redefined, less dominant role for government, providing a safety net for those in need, but above all encouraging aspiration and providing the skills and the conditions for all who worked hard to succeed. An empowering government. This was the Gordon I remembered from the 1980s, full of ideas, full of passion. It was also, I couldn't help noting, remarkably similar to Tony's policy agenda, which because of his deep frustration at his wait to take over, Gordon had done much to undermine, and had spent his early months in Number 10 distancing himself from.

'You could have done all of this without dumping on the government of which you were a member for the last ten years,' I said.

'I never did that,' he insisted.

'Yes, you did. You couldn't resist it. It was all that neurosis and pent-up anger about Tony, fanned by the people around you.'

He insisted that he had moved beyond all that now. I think we both knew, and Tony too, that some of the scars would always remain. But I sensed that he was right. The terrible political knocks he had taken, and the crisis facing the party to which all three of us had devoted our lives, made the old battles seem somehow irrelevant. As I left, Gordon put his hand on my shoulder. 'The main thing,' he said, 'is that I want us to work together. I want to rebuild our friendship.'

Still not quite sure where all this was leading, I agreed to have dinner the following week with three of Gordon's aides: his Europe adviser Stewart Wood, the long-standing Number 10 business policy adviser Geoffrey Norris, and his trusted former Treasury adviser Shriti Vadera, who had now become a minister. Knowing that Gordon wanted me to provide input from Brussels as their recovery project began, they urged me to do all I could to help. By the end of the evening I felt there was a real understanding of the problems Gordon faced, and a commitment to help turn things round, at least amongst some of those around him. He had changed, they insisted. 'He realises how bad things are. He realises it's personal, that he is the problem,' one of them said. 'He's calmer than you would have expected. He's mellowed a lot – maybe because of the children.' They felt that Gordon's strengths had yet to come through, above all his grasp of the economic crisis and his understanding of what had to be done. 'But he doesn't communicate easily, and the public aren't responding.' That may be, I said. 'But if he hopes to get people to like him, or even listen, he has to speak in a language people understand, and to be seen as acting for the national interest, not party or political interest. He has to lead.'

With Parliament breaking up for the summer, Gordon's first real shot to show that kind of leadership would come in the run-up to the party conference in the autumn, and that was what I urged him to focus on, especially as his problems steadily increased. The economy continued to worsen. Unemployment was rising. The property market was heading south. The political picture was, if anything, more discouraging. The ill-health and subsequent resignation of the Labour MP for Glasgow East, David Marshall, presented Gordon with a nightmare scenario: an end-of-July by-election not only in a safe Labour seat, but a *Scottish* Labour seat, in his own political back yard. Labour initially struggled even to find a candidate. When the votes were counted, we lost, on a massive 22 per cent swing, to the Scottish Nationalists.

Gordon was by then ostensibly on holiday by the Suffolk seaside. In fact, he was in nearly constant contact with aides, and increasingly with me. His mood was bleak. That was nothing compared to the rest of the party. A few days after the by-election defeat, Foreign Secretary David Miliband wrote a piece in the *Guardian*. The party must not succumb to 'fatalism', he said. Yes, we were down. We had made mistakes. We had waited too long to reform the NHS. We had won the war but lost the peace in Iraq. We had held power too tightly in Westminster, rather than devolving it to the people affected by what we decided. But we had accomplished much as well, and should not be shy of saying so. The next election was winnable, if we embarked on a new stage of New Labour to confront challenges that were different from those we had faced when we had first come to power. We had to deal with the economic crisis and equip people to emerge stronger when recovery came. We had, David argued, to give more control over the public services to those who used them. We had to build a sense of local empowerment and local society. David Cameron, he said, 'may be likeable and sometimes hard to disagree with', but he had no competing vision. He was 'empty'.

On the face of it, the article was simply an elegantly argued rallying cry. It did not directly criticise Gordon, but it did something that was immediately over-interpreted: it did not mention him at all. When one front-page headline screamed 'Labour at War', David had himself photographed with a copy of the paper, on which he had scribbled the word 'not'. His article was not, he insisted, the start of a leadership challenge.

Inevitably, however, with Labour's poll ratings so low, media speculation began to build about Gordon's prospects for hanging on as leader. The subject was becoming not just a source of speculation within the party, but a national talking point. When I next spoke to Tony, he was sombre about the chances for a political recovery. 'It's all very sad,' he said. 'We've got to help him, but without letting him lead us to disaster.' He also left me with a request to keep in touch with David Miliband. I texted David. 'How are you?' I asked. He replied: 'Large mountain ahead. Orienteering/climbing/planning skills much needed.' I texted back: 'Guides, sherpas available.'

David was aware how difficult it would be for the government to recover public support, and I wanted to lend my experience in helping to achieve this. But both of us were in difficult positions: David because, before deciding not to stand, he had been the one credible challenger to Gordon as leader when Tony left Number 10; and I because although I still had my taste for domestic politics, I wanted to tread very carefully, and not to interfere.

I was close to David, having first worked with him when he was a very young, and fearfully bright, policy adviser in the run-up to the 1997 election. I was certain that his newspaper article was at most an attempt to put down a marker, to open up a debate and inject new purpose into the government. I shared his hope that this would happen – it was what I had been talking to Gordon about. David and I shared something else, as well: alarm at the drift and decline since Gordon's first few months in Downing Street. In this, he was reflecting a wider concern, in the party and in cabinet, over whether Gordon could lead a recovery. He told me he feared the *Guardian* piece had made him look divisive, but he still felt it had been the right thing to do. He had provided a 'coherent message' that many ministers felt was sorely lacking. He said there was no move to push Gordon out, but there was a lot of unease in the cabinet.

Tony was getting the same message. When we next spoke, he said his sense was of a fatalism enveloping Labour MPs: some thought Gordon was unsalvageable and should go, while others thought he was unsalvageable, but that they just had to accept it. I couldn't help replying that if that was true, history might be tough on Tony: 'You saved your own skin by constantly stringing Gordon along, and then landed him on the rest of us when you went.' He said he was afraid that might be true. When he added that his real fear was that the British public had simply given up on Gordon, and that the party would sooner or later follow suit, I pointed out that he'd been there too. 'The same would have been true of you after Iraq. The people stuck with you, but only just. That saved you. Otherwise, it would have been curtains.' He replied: 'I know.'

But I think both of us felt a desire, a duty, to help Gordon if we could. The key would be the party conference in September. Tony felt his chances of pulling through were not high, and that if he failed, a leadership change would become inevitable. I thought this judgement was right. 'It's not about loyalty to one man,' he said. 'It's about loyalty to the Labour Party. It's about saving the Labour Party. He has to completely rethink and reconnect. If he fails, it's hopeless. He cannot stagger on. The public aren't going to elect him for another five years.' If Gordon failed, there was at least David. 'He's not perfect,' Tony said, 'but he has matured. He's humble enough to listen. He has to keep going, be strong, show decisive leadership.'

Tony and David talked several times as the summer wore on. Tony became ever more impressed by David's strength and political instincts. Gordon, he believed, had about a 20 per cent chance of pulling off an escape act and leading a real recovery in the autumn. Both of us had a duty to help him take that one last shot, but if he stumbled, Tony felt, there would have to be a leadership challenge.

In contrast to the last time David had been in the frame for a leadership challenge, when Tony stepped down, I had no intention of publicly expressing a view. When he phoned me in mid-August, I said that he appeared to be in a very different state of mind from the year before. 'Not quite,' he said. 'I didn't bottle it in 2007. I never intended to stand.' What about other members of the cabinet, I asked. He said no one seemed in the mood to speak out unless they were sure others were going to join in: 'There's a lot of "After you, Claude" going on.' David said there was no way of knowing how things would develop. He was anticipating the main argument Gordon and his allies would make to forestall a move: that the public wouldn't wear a second unelected Labour Prime Minister. 'If we do replace Gordon,' he said, 'we have to go for an election four to six months later. The moment you appear frightened of the voters, you're finished.'

Whatever Gordon's chances, I knew that he faced a steep climb, and that only by clearing his head and investing all his energies in an autumn recovery would he have any real chance of success. He was frustrated. He felt wronged. He was also obviously unsettled by the newspaper chatter about coups and conspiracies, and about David Miliband too. I tried to get him to put all that out of his mind. I was about to go on holiday myself, departing by easyJet for Naples to join Italian friends whose company I had enjoyed on Capri every summer since my first years in Brussels. When I called Gordon before leaving, to try to lift his spirits a bit, he was preoccupied with the party conference, above all with what we both knew could be his make-or-break speech. Though we spoke only in general terms at first, I told him the key was that it had to contain a personal appeal, to connect emotionally in a way he had so far been failing to do. It would have to provide the definition he had failed to offer when he moved into Number 10. I also urged him to seize the moment before conference by giving a few interviews in which he could set up his relaunch. He had to explain the lessons he had learned over the past few months, how his approach to the job would change, and how he would lead the government and the country forward. In other words, there had to be a genuine sense of reflecting and learning, almost of starting again.

During August, he became more and more anxious. He began to include me in daily, hour-long conference calls involving a tightly-selected group. How my participation did not become public, I will never know. I am also not sure how much help these calls were. Every morning on Capri I would sit in the shade, mobile pinned to my ear, and run through an array of ideas and themes for Gordon to put in his conference speech, and an accompanying policy document that would be published at the conference. As I later discovered, whatever we agreed in the morning would often be unravelled by further conference calls, with different participants, during the course of the day. So when we spoke again the next morning, we would often go back to square one and cover the same ground all over again. It was a cycle with which I became more and more frustrated, with nobody taking charge of the process on his behalf.

Gordon became jittery when I said that in his pre-conference interviews he would have to explain to people how his views of government, and his approach to it, had changed as a result of the difficulties he found himself in. 'You mean *Mea culpa*?' he asked, something we both knew would not come easily to him. No, I said. Just be honest. Give an account of why things had gone wrong. His message should be: 'I have been able to reflect about what the country is going through, and about our response. These are real challenges, and I think we have to strengthen how we cope with them. This is what the government is going to do about it – this is where I was, and this is where I am now going.'

I also tried to steer him away from falling back on an urge to build the speech around a nuclear assault on David Cameron and the Tories – the 'dividing-line' approach he had first drummed into both me and Tony in the 1980s in his ceaseless quest for the killer opportunity to wrong-foot the Conservatives. 'Dividing lines with the Tories can't be your priority now,' I said. 'If you have any dividing line, it's between the easier, simpler, original politics of New Labour when first elected, and the new politics of the economic crisis that we have to deal with now, and where the Tories offer nothing.' He also had to be personal. Not soppy, not apologetic, but he had to reach out to the public, draw them in, and help them understand him better. Gordon warmed to that. He even drew a comparison between his past 'struggles' and those of Barack Obama – a parallel that I hoped, for his sake, would end up on the cutting-room floor.

Still, he was right to believe he had a compelling story to tell. He *had* struggled. With the loss of his eye. With the death of his and Sarah's first child, Jennifer, in January 2002, ten days after her birth. And four years later, with the news that their youngest son, Fraser, had cystic fibrosis. 'I have overcome setbacks and tests which I've had to struggle with,' Gordon said. 'My health, and my daughter, and my son.' I sensed that this might indeed provide the emotional connection Gordon had so often lacked. It would ring true, because it was.

Gordon also called me separately at times to share his fears that moves were afoot to drive him out. During one call, he said he had heard that the former Blair cabinet heavyweight Charles Clarke was 'putting pressure' on David to 'reveal his hand, be a candidate – saying he must do so or be discounted. They're getting a letter together to say there must be change. They're getting signatures for a coup.' 'Sounds familiar,' I teased him, thinking back to previous attempts by Gordon's own supporters to drive Tony from office. I told him there were no plots for a coup as far as I could tell, and there wouldn't be as long as he focused on September and the conference, and got everything right.

He agonised, too, about his staff – and they about him. Now that I was in fairly regular contact with Gordon and his aides, I got both sides of the story. Gordon felt alone. He felt he needed to do too much – and very often, all – of the policy-making himself. He said, surprisingly, that was partly why it had occurred to him to bring me back into the mix, and that he had even toyed with contacting me much earlier, in May 2007, the month before he moved into Number 10, but had concluded that it would not have worked. Now he wished he had done.

In fact, as even his closest aides made clear to me, Gordon himself was a big part of the problem. At the Treasury he'd had a well-oiled machine, a group of experienced and gifted civil servants under the direction of a unique political ally, Ed Balls. Ed was so close to Gordon – so seamlessly identified not only with his thinking, but his ambitions – that he was Deputy Chancellor in everything but name. Now Ed was Children, Schools and Families Secretary. He was still very much part of the inner circle, but he was not based in Downing Street. He had a day job, and legitimate ambitions of his own. Running the government and the country was simply harder than running the Treasury. Shorn of Ed, Gordon lacked, or at least had not yet acquired, the new set of skills and staff members he needed. One of his closest advisers put it best: 'Gordon is a hub-and-spoke operator. He's the hub, and he works through lots of separate spokes, rather than an integrated machine.' Another member of the team said: 'He only trusts people in boxes, silos. He listens to them in that particular context, like he would use an electrician or bring in a plumber. He's not geared to run a group that interacts, communicates with one another.' They all agreed that there was no one – no Ed Balls – to pull things together for him, and that was the chief loss.

The more I spoke to Gordon, and to those around him, the more convinced I became that the key to any recovery was Gordon himself. With all his ideas, with all his passion, he seemed so distracted, so distressed, that I wondered whether he would be able to rise to the occasion at the party conference. It wasn't just the politics he had to get right, I told him. Not even just the speech, though that would obviously be crucial. He had to *look* revived as well. I kept urging him to rest, spend time in the sun, exercise, eat well. 'You've got to take care of yourself so that people get a different picture of you, as on top of the job rather than struggling with it,' I said on one occasion. 'If you look better on the outside, people will feel you're more in control of things.' I think he realised I was right.

Very quietly, he said: 'It was all so wretched between us all – you, me, Tony. It was so wasteful! We could have achieved so much more. We still did a lot, though. Perhaps surprisingly.'

'I agree,' I replied. 'What on earth were we doing? We doubted each other. We read everything into each other's motives and actions.'

He was right, I said. 'You saw everything we did through the prism of "We want to destroy you." We saw everything you did through the prism of "You want to get Tony out." It was a sort of mutually assured destruction.'

For my part, I couldn't help but reflect on how different, and how much more fulfilling, my life had become since I had left front-line British politics. For a long time after my second defenestration, I had felt angry and resentful. Before I finally accepted that a third return to government was impossible, I had been fixated on finding a way back. I felt unfairly exiled. I felt incomplete without a seat at the cabinet table. That was no longer true. The new job had transformed me. On an unfamiliar and much wider stage, I had found myself bartering, bargaining and seeking common cause across over two dozen European states, and, in my role in the world trade talks, across the globe. I was still doing politics, but not politics as I'd known it. In the formative years of New Labour, 'concession' and 'compromise' had been almost dirty words. Rather than shying away from confrontation, we had sought it out, even orchestrated it. We were convinced that head-on battle was the only way the Labour Party would really change – and be seen to have changed. Our time in government should have altered that. In some ways, it did. Yet almost everything we accomplished in government, and the great deal we failed to achieve, was forged in combat – this time, between Gordon and Tony. My job in Brussels, in contrast, revolved around building relationships, alliances, coalitions. That was what had made it initially so challenging, and now so satisfying.

But the main reason I had come to enjoy my European 'exile' was personal. For the first time I could remember, I was out of the Westminster spotlight. For the best part of two decades, I had been defined by an increasingly malign media image. I was Machiavelli with a red rose. The Prince of Darkness. I had managed over time to come to terms with Mandelson the Media Caricature. I also realised that I had played a part in its creation. What had hurt most was the unbridled aggression with which the media sought out 'stories' to burnish the caricature, and to propel their narrative of what kind of politician and person I was. This had had a real and damaging effect on my career. It was certainly a central factor in my second resignation. Still, the media storm that had hastened my departure, however inaccurate or misleading, could at least have been seen as the press doing its job. The reporters and headline-writers were sinking their teeth into an issue relating to a public figure performing public duties. That was not the case with intrusion into my personal life, or the licence that reporters and photographers felt they had to stalk my every step, pick away at my every social engagement, home in on my every friendship and – as I could hardly help but recall on Capri – every holiday. I reflected, with a relief that would have been unimaginable in my higher-octane years in Westminster, that I was no longer news.

For equally unimaginable reasons, by the time my holiday was over, that assumption would turn out to be wrong. Three days remained before I was due back in Brussels. On the way, I was making a stop-over on the Greek island of Corfu. Two months earlier I had received a phone call from Matthew Freud, the PR supremo married to Rupert Murdoch's daughter Elisabeth. Matthew had been one of the key advisers during my challenging stewardship of the Millennium Dome, and had become a good friend. I had also got to know Elisabeth well. Matthew was calling because he wanted me to come to Corfu for Elisabeth's fortieth birthday party, which was being organised at the house there of my friends Jacob and Serena Rothschild. I imagined that it would be fun, and looked forward to spending a few days on the waterside estate, which I recalled with fondness and gratitude from the time I had spent there with Jacob and Serena after my first ejection from government. I looked forward too to seeing their son Nat, with whom I had also become close.

By the time I arrived it was Friday evening, just before the party was due to begin. The other guests – an array of yacht-borne Murdochs, and friends of both generations of Rothschilds – were already there. There was not a bed to sleep in at the Rothschild home. In part, as Nat explained to me with a smile, this was because one of his old Oxford friends was staying there: George Osborne, David Cameron's closest political ally and Shadow Chancellor. Nat arranged for me to be billeted on a yacht belonging to another of his friends, the Russian industrialist Oleg Deripaska. I also knew Oleg, though not well, having met him previously through Nat. I was intrigued by his rags-to-riches story. Having begun life in a poor corner of rural Russia, he trained as a physicist, and had become a major businessman during the entrepreneurial free-for-all that followed the collapse of the Soviet Union. Not only had he become wealthy, he was also well-read, and voraciously interested in a constellation of social and economic ideas, as well as Russia's future, which dominated his conversation. Despite later media suggestions that I had gone to Corfu to join Oleg for a holiday on his yacht, I barely saw him, except for an amusing episode in which, during an early-morning wander around his boat, I stumbled across a yoga session he and his wife were taking, and I happily joined in under the instruction of their teacher.

I knew George Osborne, too. We had never exchanged much beyond social pleasantries and that is all we did at the birthday party. It was not until the following evening, with repercussions that would emerge only later, that this changed. The remaining guests, about thirty of us in all, had arranged to assemble at a seaside taverna down the road from the Rothschilds' house. I had fallen asleep in the evening sun, and arrived late. When I showed up, there were two vacant seats, one at each end of the table, and two simultaneous shouts of welcome. One was from Rebekah Wade, then editor of Rupert Murdoch's *Sun*. The other was from George. I planted myself next to him, as he'd seemed the more insistent. For the next fifty minutes or so, we talked. By the time our remarks, or a skewed version of them, surfaced in the press a couple of months later, a central point would be lost.

Yes, we talked frankly, on both sides. But it was the kind of conversation political colleagues on opposite sides of the party fence have far more often than is sometimes realised. I had been one of the creators of New Labour, and the repositioning David Cameron and George were attempting with the Conservatives was in many ways being modelled on that. I was sceptical that they had learned the real lesson of New Labour: that it was not just about creating a new image, but required making tough policy changes and bringing the party behind them. But it was a fascinating and not unenjoyable chat, a bit like two golf pros comparing their swings. In fact, George did most of the talking. He spoke animatedly, initially about the Prime Minister. It was not just that he disliked Gordon Brown; he seemed consumed by his interest in what the *Observer* had once famously called Gordon's 'psychological flaws'. George recited a litany of slights he said he had suffered at Gordon's hands in the months while he was shadowing him as Chancellor: Gordon had blanked him whenever they met; he had denied him the courtesy of advance copies of Treasury statements; on one occasion, George had phoned him only for Gordon to put the receiver down, or so he said. He was especially fascinated by the tensions between Gordon and Tony, saying that the 'TB-GBs' had made both him and David Cameron aware of the importance of sustaining their own relationship.

I listened. On occasion, I nodded. And yes, I added a brush-stroke or two to the psychological portrait George had obviously spent many months assembling. But I said nothing I hadn't said to others at one time or another before. Nothing, in fact, I hadn't said to Gordon. So it was difficult not to smile when, in George's leaked version of our discussion which subsequently appeared in the press, I was said to have poured 'pure poison' about Gordon into his ear.

If anyone's ear was scorched that evening, it was mine, as George expounded on what he saw as his and Cameron's Conservative equivalent of our New Labour project. They had drained the Thatcher-era ideology from the Tories, detoxified the party, he said, to make it electable. I said it had always been my understanding that the rising generation of Tory MPs and the current activists had grown up under Thatcher, and their thinking had been formed under her leadership. George said this was true only up to a point. The party was mainly made up of old people, not young people, most of whom were involved more for social than political reasons. In his own constituency, there were lots of divorcees, widows and widowers whose interest in the party was as a place to find companionship, or a partner. 'They're not interested in ideology,' George said. 'They're interested in a Conservative Party that wins.' His, and David Cameron's, interest was also in a Tory Party that won.

When I returned to Brussels, I spoke to Tony on the telephone again. We both wondered whether Gordon had it in him to turn things round. My view was that neither of us could tell but that he had to be given the chance to try. Tony reflected on the messy way his own time in office had ended and Gordon's had begun. It was not just the absence of the long-advertised 'orderly transition'; what most upset him was that one result of Gordon's final coup had been to short-circuit the ambitious policy review Tony had put in train to give a post-Blair government a fresh, but still New Labour, agenda. 'It wasn't my fault, the way he behaved,' Tony grumbled. 'I would have gone in 2004 if he'd worked with me, and if I didn't believe the whole thing would be pulled apart by him and his people.' He said he still felt Gordon had a great brain and energy. But, he added, 'These have got to be directed at the right things. He's got to go back to being New Labour.'

I don't think either of us had any doubt that Gordon would return to London after the summer recess with a new determination to turn things round, but at the beginning, events did not help him. The trouble began, at least in Gordon's mind, with the closest thing he had to an old friend, except for Ed Balls, in the cabinet. Alistair Darling – a Scot, a long-time admirer of Gordon, and his Chief Secretary at the Treasury after the 1997 election – was evidently feeling increasingly pessimistic about where the country was heading, from an already obvious economic downturn to something far worse, and, it seemed, frustrated at being constantly second-guessed by Number 10. He gave a long, and extraordinarily frank, interview to the *Guardian* writer

Decca Aitkenhead at his holiday cottage in the Outer Hebrides. His remarks were not personally unkind towards Gordon, but he felt the country was 'pissed off' with the government: 'We patently have not been able to get across what we are for, and what we are about.' And he said he believed the recession would be 'more profound and more long-lasting than people thought'. The economic straits Britain found itself in were 'arguably the worst they've been in sixty years'.

The word 'arguably' disappeared from the quotes picked up by other newspapers and broadcasters when Alistair's interview appeared. George Osborne had a field day, launching an assault on Gordon's legacy as Chancellor and his 'truthfulness' as Prime Minister. Gordon was furious, because he felt Alistair's comments were yet one more distraction from his hoped-for September recovery. When he called me, he was seething. I probably didn't help things by questioning how he had allowed his media briefers to leak his plans to 'go personal' at the party conference – a bizarre theft of his own headlines that risked detracting from the impact of his speech when he made it. 'I didn't do that!' he protested. 'Well, somebody did,' I said calmly, to which he replied: 'OK. But we're going from one improvisation to another. It's ridiculous. I've got all these things to do, all this policy in my mind, but no means of communicating it.' Then he got to what was really upsetting him. 'That *fucking* Darling interview! It fucked up everything, absolutely everything, I wanted to do last week.'

None of us reckoned, however, on a series of events about to erupt five time zones away from Downing Street. They were hugely significant, an economic shock so seismic that they made Alistair's interview seem understated. They began with the news that one of America's most venerable investment banks, Lehman Brothers, might be going to the wall. Over the weekend, the US authorities scrambled to find a buyer. On Monday, Lehmans filed for so-called Chapter Eleven protection. It was the biggest bankruptcy in American history. World stock markets tumbled. Another British bank, HBOS, was soon showing signs of being in serious trouble. This was staved off by Gordon, who with a word in the ear of the Lloyds chairman

Victor Blank encouraged a mega-merger between Lloyds and HBOS. By the end of the week, with the Labour conference convening in Manchester on Sunday, the economic news was becoming ever more worrying.

Gordon phoned me on Friday night. He said he had been trying to get me for two days – I had been at a climate change conference in Oslo, and had not been returning messages. He started by talking about his conference speech. It was clear the political ground had shifted. 'Now,' I told him, 'you actually have something big to talk about in your speech. It really is the global economy, stupid.'

This was what we had been talking about since the summer. But now it was well and truly dramatised. The terrible crisis meant it was not just a theoretical and not just a political argument, but a real, immediate challenge. If Gordon got his message right, he had an opportunity to break through in a way he simply would not have been able to do before.

He agreed. 'It's not just about individuals and society. It must be markets as well,' he said. His only doubt, one Tony would have found reassuringly New Labour, was how far he could go in attacking the markets. I reassured him that it wasn't about attacking the markets, but individuals within them who had been acting irresponsibly, and that he should have no compunction about attacking them. But mostly what I told him was to put all his extraneous worries to one side: the so-called coups, Alistair's interview. 'Don't, for God's sake, let yourself get sidetracked,' I said. 'And don't stop being prime ministerial.'

I was fairly certain now that, given the economic turmoil, Gordon had every chance of turning in a performance sufficient to save his job. Only a frontal assault from David Miliband was likely to spur rebellion, and that was not going to happen. For the media, however, the conference was shaping up as a tale of two speeches: David's on the Monday, and Gordon's on the Wednesday. David spoke eloquently, and ranged far beyond his brief as Foreign Secretary. In parts, he sounded very much like a leader-in-waiting. He echoed his July call for the party to choose hope, energy and new ideas over 'fatalism'. But even without his unfortunate ambush by a photographer outside the conference hall, who snapped him grinning and holding a banana, David was not pushing for the leadership. Besides, there was no vacancy. Unless, of course, Gordon unravelled when he strode onto the stage.

He did the opposite. By some distance, it was the most powerful performance, the most effective message, he had delivered since his descent had begun a year earlier. It was personal. It connected. It had touches of self-deprecating humour. It played to his strengths. Galvanised by the magnitude of the new economic and financial crisis, he managed to produce what he had so far been failing to do. He offered a coherent reply to questions left unanswered for so long: What were the challenges Britain faced? What were the policies, vision and leadership needed to rise above them? And why was he the man to provide them? His most effective line, aimed at David Cameron, was: 'I'm all in favour of apprenticeships. But let me tell you that this is no time for a novice.' It was clever, it was simple, and it was what people wanted to hear.

I was back in Brussels when Gordon gave his speech, and was preoccupied with preparing for a trip to China and a speech of my own when I got there. Especially with the economic crisis deepening, I was keen to encourage expanding business and trade ties between the EU and the Chinese. But I was determined to press Beijing on our concerns about protectionist barriers, and China's lacklustre attitude to enforcing intellectual-property rights. I watched Gordon's address on television, however, and saw that it had gone well. I got two text messages that evening. The first was from one of the team at Number 10, saying very kindly that I'd made a 'profound difference' to Gordon's performance. The second was from Sue Nye. 'Gordon,' it read, 'says "thank you" for your help.' As always with big set-piece speeches, especially Gordon's, I was just one of many who had contributed. But it had been worth the effort. I told Gordon I felt it had been a good speech, the right message, effectively delivered, at the right time. What I didn't say, in part because I was sure Gordon already knew and feared it, was that he had cleared only the first hurdle on the road to recovery.

By the time we next spoke, I was in Singapore, on my way home from Beijing. The call came in the early hours of the morning. He was upset by continued signs of discontent among an assortment of back-benchers, echoed by several former Blair cabinet ministers. There was a 'plot' to drive him out, he insisted: 'The plotters are the problem.' He singled out three former ministers as the alleged culprits: Stephen Byers, Alan Milburn and John Reid. 'They are steering it,' he said. 'They had a plan, it misfired, and they failed. They wanted to wreck the conference, and they didn't succeed.'

In fact, as far as I could tell, neither they nor anyone else had had some grand plan for conference Armageddon. At least for now, Gordon was safe. 'You're getting this out of proportion,' I told him. 'I don't know why you're so wound up.' He was not wound up, he replied. But he was obviously distracted, and if he stayed that way, his conference escape could turn out to be no more than a very brief respite. 'What you have to focus on now is the fact that we don't have a strategy to win the next election,' I told him. 'The other stuff doesn't matter. New Labour 1997 is not going to win it for us in 2010. It has to be renewed, reinvented. Nobody is doing that, and you have to focus on it.'

'Can't *you* do that?' he asked, returning to a theme I thought we had finally got beyond in the summer. 'I've got it intellectually,' he said. 'I've got the policies. I accept it's different from 1997, and that now we've got to say what we're doing next. But I just can't turn it into a strategy.'

I put it to him directly: 'You need a government team to do this. Perhaps you should wonder whether you may have contributed to making people feel less of a team. You have to rebuild it.'

'I realise some in the cabinet feel ambivalent about me,' he replied. 'But others have got to show a lot more maturity.'

Sensing that we had taken this as far as we could for now, I said: 'I have to show some maturity, and go to sleep.'

'Why? Where on earth are you?' asked Gordon, genuinely surprised.

'Singapore,' I said. 'And it's after 2 a.m.' Gordon, profusely apologetic, and I, very tired, agreed to talk the following day.

When he phoned he was, at least briefly, in a brighter mood. 'If it's not after midnight, I guess I'm calling too early,' he joked. But he remained unsettled. He was some distance from getting a hold on the team effort I'd been urging him to make his priority.

'You get wound up about the wrong things and the wrong people,' I said. I advised him not to make a big mistake in the cabinet reshuffle the press was now anticipating. I was worried about reports that he was planning to replace Alistair Darling with Ed Balls, which in the gathering economic crisis struck me as perverse. No matter how upset Gordon had been over his Chancellor's interview, a vote of no-confidence in the Treasury was hardly going to help. 'Some may think it odd,' I said.

'We'll have to talk on a landline,' Gordon replied, with a sudden air of mystery. 'But I have a bigger plan than that – one which everyone will eventually say is good.'

'A tactical nuclear explosion?' I asked. At which, for the first time in ages, he laughed. He would say nothing more, beyond a suggestion that we talk again.

I was worried. From my experience, Gordon's 'big plans' had a habit of creating as many problems as they solved. His conference speech would not in itself ensure that he and the government could recover, but it was a start. He had had one last chance at survival, and he had taken it. One more 'big plan' gone wrong would risk not just ending his short and unhappy premiership, it could leave the government, and the party, in even deeper crisis.

The next call from Downing Street came two days later. It was not from Gordon, but Jeremy Heywood. It began encouragingly enough, with an assurance that I would have an opportunity to weigh in with my views before the reshuffle warheads were launched. 'I think Gordon will want to see you to discuss the reshuffle,' he said. But then he too added, 'He wants to do something quite big.'

'In what way big?' I pressed. He said that was something I would have to discuss with the Prime Minister. Apparently, Gordon wanted to do something that would affect me. This was getting more puzzling, and more worrying. I took it to be a suggestion of some root-

and-branch reworking of the cabinet, with my job in Brussels offered as consolation prize to one of the victims. The prospect of my entering a truly final political exile came as a shock. It also seemed an odd way for Gordon to recognise the help I had tried to give him in his darkest hours. I did take comfort from the fact that I was better equipped to deal with being cast into the wilderness this time round. With my EU term ending in barely a year, I had begun to adjust to the notion of life beyond politics. But it was unsettling, and I said so. 'He'd better not muck around with my job,' I told Jeremy. 'If this "big plan" involves getting rid of someone with a promise of my job, you should know I'll be furious.'

'It's not that,' he said. 'We'll talk again.'

The next call, on Wednesday, 1 October, was no more illuminating. This time it was from Gordon. 'I'm going to do this reshuffle,' he began. 'I need to talk to you about it. I want to put an idea to you – something I hope you'll go along with.' He asked if I could come to see him in Downing Street the following morning. I said I would be in London anyway, for a briefing at the Treasury on the financial crisis, and I could see him after that. He seemed satisfied, but before hanging up he added very sternly: 'Do not discuss this with anyone.'

'Discuss what?' I asked.

'Nothing,' he replied. 'Just don't discuss it.' Since I had no idea what he was on about, that was easy enough to agree to.

Maybe my famed political antennae were not as good as they have been cracked up to be. Maybe Brussels had dimmed my Westminster instincts. Maybe, despite our recent rapprochement, I simply assumed that Gordon and I had fought so many battles that some sense of estrangement would always survive. In any case, when I discreetly entered Number 10 on the afternoon of Thursday, 2 October 2008 through the french windows at the back, near the Foreign Office, I was anticipating a conversation about the other potential jigsaw pieces in Gordon's grand scheme. I took his and Jeremy's hints at some role for me to mean, at most, another attempt to get me to play a part in forging the 'strategy' he desperately wanted. I had difficulty in seeing quite how that would work, but I was willing to listen, and to help if I could.

We met in the small wood-panelled dining room on the first floor. Gordon took a spoonful of yoghurt and unpeeled a banana. 'I don't like sandwiches,' he said when I offered him the plate. Then he got down to business.

'I need to do something big. I need you to join the government. I want you to help get us through the economic situation. You would do it at the Business Department, from the House of Lords.'

For a moment, I was stunned. I was also seized by panic at the prospect, even if Gordon genuinely felt he could make it work, of a return to the political jungle, and an end to a European sojourn that had turned out even better than I had expected. 'Thanks,' I said, 'but I actually like my present job. I have things I want to finish. And I have my comfort zone.' I had my work. My life. The protection I now felt I had from the frequent ghastliness of Westminster politics as I had come to know it. I had my travel, my friends. I was now on top of the Trade Commissioner's job, and trying against all odds to play my part in rescuing hopes for a world trade deal, not to mention the intractable negotiations to update our trade relations in Africa, or the never-ending talks on Russia's membership of the World Trade Organisation.

Gordon would not be dissuaded. He said the world trade deal was going nowhere fast – he had just been in Washington, and he was sure of that. I was pretty sure of it as well: its prospects were looking about as dire as Gordon's before his conference speech.

'Think of what you would be able to achieve back in the government,' he persisted. 'It's a great opportunity.' And he added: 'We need you. We could work together.'

'Well, it would certainly be a surprise for everyone,' I laughed. Yet, except for the undeniable satisfaction I would take from an unlikely – more nearly, impossible – third return from the cabinet dead, I still found the idea unsettling. Gordon left me to ponder.

When he returned to the room, it was with Sue Nye in tow. He suggested that she and I speak. This was the start of a carousel of conversations, first with Sue, then with Jeremy Heywood, as Gordon departed and reappeared, joined the discussion and left the other two to urge me to see the logic of his proposal. It made sense from every angle, they insisted. It would be the right thing for Gordon, for the government, and for me. I was tempted. It was not merely the idea of returning to cabinet. At a time when Gordon and New Labour were in political crisis, and the country was facing an economic one, I did feel that I could play a part in making things better.

But for other reasons, I was still reluctant. Even in our resumed, long-distance relationship, I had been reminded that Gordon could be hair-raisingly difficult to work with. 'It's all too difficult,' I told him. 'I'll have to talk to Reinaldo about it. He'll hate the whole idea of becoming involved in British politics again – and the media. He's suffered enough.' Gordon replied that by all means I should call my partner, then hurriedly added: 'If you want, *I'll* talk to him.' The moment passed. Gordon's suggestion, like so much else when he was at his best, had been genuine, and generous. So too was his invitation to me to return to the top ranks of government.

I would not say no outright, I told him finally. I had to think it through. I also needed counsel from someone who knew both me and Gordon well, and whose instincts I had learned to trust. I said I wanted to discuss it with Tony. Gordon said that was fine, and we agreed that I would return by the end of the afternoon.

As soon as I left, I phoned Reinaldo. His reaction was not just surprise, but more nearly disbelief. Who could blame him? Yet as we talked through the obvious pitfalls, he came to the view that what mattered was whether the contribution I could make by returning to cabinet outweighed them. If I felt it did, I should do it. 'But you're right,' he said, 'to talk to Tony.'

When I arrived at Tony's office in Grosvenor Square, he was in a meeting. As he ushered me in a few minutes later, it was apparent that Gordon had phoned ahead. Tony grasped my hand and laughed out loud. 'You could not make it up!' he said. But he added: 'On the other hand, it has a certain logic. It's a no-brainer. You belong in the government. The economic crisis is real. If the Prime Minister asks you to serve your country, you have to. It certainly wouldn't look good if people got to know that you'd turned him down.'

'He's a nightmare to work with. It might be awful,' I said.

'It might be,' Tony replied, 'or it might not be. You don't know. In the end, people will just say that you did your best.'

When I returned to Number 10, Gordon was waiting. 'OK,' I told him. 'I'll do it. I'm still not sure it's the right thing for me to do. But I'll do my best.'

'It *is* the right thing,' Gordon said. 'I'm sure. You'll see.'

As I left, I was in a daze. I did feel a sense of excitement, the surge of adrenalin I had almost forgotten in the gentler political climate of Brussels. The role Gordon had mapped out for me might turn out to be the most important and fulfilling of my political life. My new cabinet job would take me back to the now-renamed Department of Trade and Industry. It was the place where I'd cut my departmental teeth, where with a team of impressive civil servants I had done well, only to leave long before I had expected or hoped to. It meant that along with whatever 'strategic' role Gordon clearly wanted me to play, I would be at the heart of framing the government agenda where it mattered most: the economy.

I couldn't help but smile at imagining what the media would make of my return. Outrageous? Astonishing? It was certainly both of those. But also risky? Ill-advised? Insane? I could only hope not. There was just one thing of which I was sure as I returned to my home off Regent's Park, beyond the gaze or interest of reporters, at least until the news of the reshuffle became public. As so often when conflicting issues had to be weighed and a difficult decision made, Tony had been right. If the Prime Minister asks you to serve your country, you have to.

But I also knew that the reasons I had decided to come back, the reasons that in some ways I *wanted* to come back, were more complex than that. They had less to do with Gordon, or Tony, than with me. It is true that everything I had become as a politician had been marked by my relationship with New Labour's two, very different, Prime Ministers. But the roots went back much further: to my time with Neil Kinnock, and with London Weekend Television's *Weekend World* programme in the 1980s; to my experience in local government, the trade unions and youth politics in the Old Labour heyday of the 1970s; to my time at university. And to a bright white family home ten miles up the Northern Line from the Houses of Parliament, on a suburban street called Bigwood Road.

2

Born into Labour

Big Wood seemed much bigger to me as a child than it does now. It began at the top of our road, three minutes' walk from our door. At the other end was an even larger expanse of green, the extension to Hampstead Heath, which bordered the neighbourhood where I spent the first two decades of my life. Hampstead Garden Suburb was the creation of Dame Henrietta Barnett, a Christian social reformer who believed that mixed communities with the feel of a country village would soften and ultimately heal the hostility of urban life. At the turn of the last century, after many years of charity work in the East End of London, she enlisted the architect Sir Edwin Lutyens and the utopian town planner Raymond Unwin to make her vision a reality.

The Suburb was less posh and intellectually self-important than Hampstead proper, which lay just over a steep incline and a mile or two nearer the centre of London. Under the Suburb's original planning rules, there were no fences or walls between properties, only hedgerows. No shops were permitted within its boundaries. And no pubs. While the social activist in Dame Henrietta must have understood the attraction of a comradely pint at the end of a working day, the Christian in her could not abide the idea. The roads were wide, and trees were everywhere, bursting with white and pink and purple in springtime. It was a place designed for walking, and letting one's eyes tilt skywards. The Suburb was centred on a lovely church square – St Jude's C of E on one side, the Methodists opposite – and the adjacent girls' school Dame Henrietta created, and which bears her name. For families, the Suburb was ideal. As a child, I loved it – an

40

ardour that briefly dimmed when, as a teenager, I found it a bit too quiet and confining, but which I have since rediscovered. It was in London, yet not quite of it.

It was, however, very much a part of Labour London. Hampstead was home to Hugh Gaitskell and Michael Foot, but we had our share of luminaries too, notably Harold and Mary Wilson. They were near neighbours, just around the corner, and good friends. Their boys, Robin and Giles, were a little older than me and my elder brother Miles – Mary very kindly passed Giles's rather scratchy Cub Scout jersey on to me when it was time for me to join the local pack attached to the Methodist church. My most vivid early political memory is from a few days before my eleventh birthday, when I watched the Wilsons negotiate a gaggle of camera crews and reporters, including the famous American broadcaster Walter Cronkite, as they left for Downing Street after the 1964 election.

A year later, the Wilsons invited us to Number 10 to watch Trooping the Colour. It would be ridiculous to suggest that as I walked wide-eyed through the famous black door I imagined I would return forty-five years later to watch the same ceremony as a senior minister, alongside another Labour Prime Minister. But I can't deny that I was dazzled. Marcia Williams, Harold's trusted political secretary, fed me large quantities of triangular smoked-salmon sandwiches and asparagus rolls. She even took my hand and led me into the Cabinet Room, and briefly planted me in the Prime Minister's chair. I was conscious of feeling somehow special. Conscious, too, that part of that feeling had to do with the fact that my bond with Labour really began with my family. My mother was the only child of Herbert Morrison, the founding General Secretary of the Labour Party in London, a minister in Ramsay MacDonald's 1929 government, and the first Labour leader of the London County Council in the 1930s. He served as Home Secretary in Churchill's wartime cabinet, and was the organising force behind the manifesto and the election campaign that delivered Labour's startling 1945 landslide, becoming Deputy Prime Minister and later Foreign Secretary in the Attlee government. As we left the Cabinet Room, Marcia introduced me to another guest sitting in the hallway, Clement Attlee himself. 'This is Herbert's grandson, Clem,' she said. The former Prime Minister, either through advanced age or because he and my grandfather had not exactly been bosom buddies, looked at me briefly before grunting something inaudible.

My mother cared passionately about the *issues* that drove politics: I remember joining her on a march against Enoch Powell's 'rivers of blood' speech when I was fourteen. But her experience of the way politics had come to dominate her father's life, often crowding out both her and her mother, left her with a lifelong dislike of the exposure that goes with public life. As a young girl, she told her father to keep her out of his 'beastly politics'. My father's connection with Labour was less genetic than my mother's, but in many ways stronger. Unlike her, he was fascinated by politicians, and by the bustle of energy and argument that surrounded them. By the people who surrounded them, too. He was good friends with Marcia Williams, and became especially close to the quiet, stoical Mary Wilson, as she and I have always recalled whenever our paths have crossed since.

His own starting point was traditional, Old Labour politics. Maybe this was because his views were formed in the post-war years, when the division between Labour and the Tories was starker and simpler than it has since become. Maybe part of it came from his own DNA. He was born in Pinner, an outer London suburb not exactly famous for politics, or much of anything else. But his ancestral roots went back to the nineteenth-century Jewish community in Poland, then under Russian rule. His great-grandfather Nathan was said to have been involved in an anti-tsarist plot, and to have escaped retribution only by fleeing one step ahead of the secret police.

There is a temptation to suggest that my father inherited Nathan's streak of rebelliousness and Jewish activism. Somehow, though, I suspect not. He never hid his Jewishness – indeed, he could hardly have done so. He spent nearly all of his working life as the legendarily smooth, gregarious and popular advertising manager of London's *Jewish Chronicle*, the world's oldest Jewish newspaper. Yet he remained a strident non-believer. I cannot recall his ever walking the short distance to Hampstead Garden Suburb synagogue, even on the Jewish

New Year or at Yom Kippur; he certainly never took me there. Religion never figured in our lively dinner table discussions, although politics invariably did.

I suppose I was, however, dimly aware of my refracted Jewishness. Most Fridays I would have dinner with my friend Caroline Wetzler and her family, observing a form of Jewish family routine. Another of my closest childhood friends was Keren Abse, daughter of the poet and playwright Dannie Abse and niece of the outspoken Jewish Labour MP Leo Abse. I would occasionally go with my father to the offices of the *Jewish Chronicle* in Furnival Street, just off Holborn. His army of advertising salesmen and administrators were unfailingly deferential to him, and unfailingly kind to me. But my main *Jewish Chronicle* memory was when the man in charge of ad layout, Nat Goldstein, took Miles and me to the Hammersmith Odeon one evening shortly after my twelfth birthday, for a Beatles concert. I did not enter a synagogue until more than three decades later, for the wedding of my wonderfully loyal long-time executive assistant, Maree Glass. The ceremony was extraordinarily beautiful. I also found it oddly, and a bit regretfully, alien.

My mother and Miles, but especially my father and I, followed Labour's internal debates and its battles with the Tories the way football fanatics would fixate on Cup runs or local derbies. Labour was not just our 'team', however. That does not capture the depth of the attachment: among our happy quartet of atheists at 12 Bigwood Road, Labour was more nearly a religion.

From childhood, it was certainly mine. Even before Harold Wilson left for Downing Street, I remember rushing home from school to listen to the results of the final ballot from which he emerged as Labour leader after Hugh Gaitskell's death, then racing into the kitchen to tell my mother the good news. She never became carried away by such things. At election time, I would set out on canvassing missions around the Suburb – beginning, I am told, by tricycle at the tender age of six. Once, I even embarrassingly knocked on the door of Manny Shinwell, Defence Minister alongside my grandfather in the post-war government, to remind him to vote.

What I most absorbed from both of my parents was their love for each other, and for Miles and me. Both my mother and father had been married before. They met after the war at the London advertising agency Dorlands, where my mother, who had worked with the Quaker refugee service in the war years, had a job as a secretary, while my father was on one of the ad account teams. It appears to have been love at first sight, but it was complicated by the fact that my father was still married. My mother had divorced her first husband, the son of the Agriculture Minister alongside Herbert Morrison in the cabinet. My grandfather had been unhappy enough about that first marriage, feeling that my mother, then only nineteen, was far too young. She and my father kept their liaison pretty much secret until he was divorced from his first wife.

Even then, however, the idea of my mother having married as a teenager, divorced soon afterwards, and then married another divorcee did not exactly please her father, to put it mildly. I don't know whether he had moral objections, but what is clear is that he did not relish the possibility of any gossip or criticism that might encroach on what mattered most to him: his political career. As a young boy, I would come to feel pride, respect and sometimes awe at my grandfather's political status and accomplishments. Those feelings never entirely left me as I made my own way into national politics, but as I approached my teens, I also became aware of the effects of his all-consuming political ambition on those around him, above all on my mother. He visited us when he was able to drive himself across London from his home in Eltham, but his second wife did not make it easy, as she wanted to cut him off from his family and past friends. When he died in March 1965, a few months after I turned eleven, the first we knew of it was from a newsflash that interrupted the Saturday-evening film on ITV. My mother tried not to show her hurt, but I am sure she felt it as acutely as I did. She arranged for me to be excused from school to attend my grandfather's funeral: my abiding memory of the occasion is of George Brown, then Labour's voluble deputy leader, telling me off for my politically inappropriate dress sense – I was wearing a blue tie.

The authority in our family came from my mother. She was by far the quieter of my parents, but she was a source of unquestioned support for all of us. She had an elegance, almost a regality about her: my childhood friends and I called her 'Duchess'. That is how I remember her to this day. But she had steel. Never raising her voice, she instilled in Miles and me a sense of good manners, of propriety, right and wrong. Her silent opprobrium when we strayed beyond the boundaries was far more effective than any scolding or punishment would have been.

My father was in many ways her opposite. Though his real name was George, he was universally known as Tony, ever since he had served as an officer in the Royal Dragoons during the war. He dressed impeccably, and had the bearing of a City gent rather than an advertising salesman. He had a wonderful, waspish sense of humour and fun, and revelled in being with people, until he shut the front door behind him each evening and propped himself up on his bed, smoking his pipe, surrounded by his books and newspapers. In his later years he became a Suburb personality as chairman of the residents' association. He sallied forth almost daily, walking stick in hand, sometimes with his wartime binoculars around his neck, to ensure that Dame Henrietta's sylvan planning restrictions were surviving the era of two-Volvo families and paved-over front gardens.

As a child, I remember feeling slightly embarrassed at times by the showman in my father. As an adult, however, I would come to recognise that much of my own political passion and public personality came from him. My brother Miles, who is four years older than me, and was always more tranquil and reflective, saw this earlier and more keenly than I did. Having gone on to qualify as a clinical psychologist, he contributed his insights into how each of our family jigsaw pieces fitted together for a biography the journalist Donald Macintyre wrote about me in the 1990s. They were striking and, I am sure, accurate. Miles was always much more like my mother, he observed, while I am more like my father. But growing up, the attachments we formed with our parents were a mirror image of this. I was much closer to my mother, rather doting on her, and Miles to my father.

Perhaps because my father and I were alike in so many ways, there was a certain friction between us. Especially where politics was concerned – and more than ever when my first-hand experience of Labour in the 1980s convinced me that the party had to take on the hard left if it was to survive. Even before then, it was clear that his view of Labour and mine were likely to diverge. I remember the two of us visiting a Suburb neighbour named Hans Janitschek on a bright Sunday morning in 1972. Janitschek was an Austrian writer who was then Secretary General of the Socialist International. A modern European Social Democrat, I remember him saying that he feared Labour was risking a 'dangerous' swerve to the left. Harold Wilson had lost the 1970 general election, and Tony Benn and his allies had led a successful campaign to get Labour's National Executive Committee to adopt a leftist policy programme. Harold evidently concluded that since the party wasn't going to re-enter government anytime soon, there was no particular urgency about taking them on. Janitschek was convinced – rightly, of course – that this inaction would come back to haunt Labour, and that sooner or later a battle over policy and ideology would have to be fought. I listened intently as my father not only defended Harold's apparent insouciance, but said that he felt the socialist ideologues should be given latitude and tolerance. For him, that was part of what being Labour was all about.

I loved both of my parents dearly. Even now, two decades after my father's death and four years after my mother's, there is barely a day when I don't think of them. My mother's memory, especially, still lives with me. But my father's too. Events in my life, in politics, the places I go, often rekindle recollections of them. In the waning days of Gordon Brown's government, I was in Regent's Park for an early-morning stroll when I saw a man with a cane trying to make his way up one of the paths. My mind instantly flashed back to the array of walking sticks my father kept in the front hall, and the old army greatcoat he used to throw over his shoulders as he ventured out in his role as one-man Suburb conservation force. I smiled at the image. He was so full of life and energy and élan, so passionate about what he believed in. He was such a presence. And, as Miles still reminds me, so much like the person and politician I became.

In many ways, we led a charmed childhood. My Euro-enthusiasm as a politician grew from roots planted then. From the time I was a small child, my parents took us on summer holidays in Europe. Every August we would go somewhere new: Ibiza, Brittany, Italy and Elba. We would stay either on campsites or in an inexpensive *pension* or hotel. I remember one year we camped in the grounds of a monastery in Tuscany. A group of monks stood watching the silhouette of my mother inside her tent as she combed her waist-length hair. For a few years we shared our holidays with an American family we had met, from San Francisco. They had three boys, and together the two families travelled round in a – very crowded – VW camper van.

When I was ten, we settled into a pattern of going to Spain's Costa Brava every summer. It was nowhere near as built-up then as it is now. We stayed a few miles down the coast from Rosas, at a place called Almadraba which consisted of a few dozen very basic chalets tucked away from the beach. Over dinner, my mother and father would give Miles and me a half-glass of wine, and very occasionally a tiny portion of Cointreau with ice as a nightcap. If I remember rightly, I drank more than Miles. Perhaps in part because of this distinctly Continental introduction to alcohol, I now drink only in moderation: wine and whisky.

Another effect of our Spanish summers proved slightly more painful. With light-coloured skin like my mother, and the more cavalier attitude towards such things that I got from my father, I would invariably neglect the sun lotion and quickly burn to a bright red. I still do when I'm not careful. Nor was my immersion in the sporting life of the Costa Brava especially successful. For two years running I tried – and failed – to learn how to water-ski, as everyone on the beach watched my repeated humiliation. I finally abandoned my efforts.

While the summers on the Costa Brava were idyllic for me as a child, politically, of course, Spain was no idyll. Franco was in power, and I am not sure how my parents reconciled our holidays there with their solid Labour sympathy for the republican side in the civil war. I do remember that we mollified my grandfather by bringing him a box of his favourite cigars after each holiday. He would drive over for Saturday lunch to collect them on our return.

The Suburb may have been created as a socially mixed urban utopia, but by the time I was born half a century later, it was decidedly middle-class. The more thrusting families aspired to send their children to the nearby four-hundred-year-old Highgate School, or to University College School in Hampstead. Although my parents might have been able to afford the fees, it would not have occurred to them to enrol us anywhere but at a state school. Anyway, they preferred to spend their money on our budget summer holidays in Europe. After Miles and I left Garden Suburb Primary, a short walk away on the other side of Big Wood, we moved on to Hendon County Grammar School. Under its dauntingly traditionalist head teacher, E.W. Maynard Potts, it was intellectually rigorous, and very strict. I did well academically. I enjoyed learning from, and on occasion jousting with, most of my teachers, especially about politics. I remember bringing a geography lesson to a standstill as our teacher, Mr Chapman, and I argued about the implications of the collapse of Barbara Castle's trade-union reform White Paper, *In Place of Strife*. He said the retreat was a political disaster. I knew he was right, of course, but loyally defended the government's corner.

I made some extraordinarily close friendships at school, above all with Keren Abse and a Hendon boy named Stephen Howell, who shared my teenage enthusiasm for all things political, and who remains close to me today. The two of them used to kid me about being something of a Labour anorak. Not only was I by now thoroughly conversant with the policy debates in the party, but particularly on long car journeys, I played what we called the 'constituency game'. Boringly, and at length, I would try to name the sitting Labour MP for every constituency they could think of. Nevertheless, we became an inseparable trio. When we were sixteen, Steve's grandmother and aunt, both Hendon Labour activists, suggested that we rekindle the dormant local branch of the Young Socialists. I became chairman,

Steve the secretary, and Keren the slightly less politically obsessive glue that held our founding cell together. By the time of our inaugural meeting in March 1970, we had cajoled two dozen others to enlist in the cause. My mother no doubt shuddered at the thought that I might end up joining the breed she so disliked, and become a politician. If so, she didn't show it. She provided a warm welcome to my comrades in arms, complete with egg-and-tomato sandwiches and hot chocolate, for our after-school meetings. She typed out our slightly overblown screeds for the monthly YS newsletter, and remained unruffled when the three of us were summarily thrown out of Hendon Town Hall during the 1970 election campaign for heckling the Conservative candidate. After the election, which ended in a Tory victory and brought Edward Heath into Downing Street, she even joined us on a demonstration against the new government's Industrial Relations Bill. Mr Potts was less sanguine, threatening to expel me for my unruly activism. He was deterred only by the intervention of a strong-willed, and thoroughly Labour, school governor.

My politics began spilling into my school life, to Mr Potts's alarm. In common with other grammars, Hendon County had found itself caught up in the Labour government's campaign to end the 11-Plus examination and move to comprehensive secondary schooling. Mr Potts was dead against this, and was horrified when Steve, Keren and I joined with our YS comrades in campaigning for an end to selection and a merger with a nearby secondary modern. He denounced us to a school assembly as 'industrial militants trying to tear apart the fabric of our school community' – before taking early retirement, possibly to escape the spectre of the advancing Communist hordes.

When Steve and I became prefects in the lower sixth, we found ourselves at odds with the new head teacher. This time it was over our support for a move to open up the prefects' room to all sixth-formers, liberalise the school-uniform rules and abolish the prefects system in favour of an elected school council. For me, like my parents, the joy of politics has always been in battles of principle. In this case, it meant the dilemma of abandoning the prospect of my becoming Head Boy, with all its attendant privileges. I did end up as the first head of an elected school council instead. I confess that this brought out a less attractive aspect of my future political personality, a quality Tony Blair would call my 'imperiousness'. I was quite the disciplinarian, sometimes unbearably bossy towards pupils in the lower forms. Still, my wider political focus remained on the world of Labour politics. In one of my more portentous YS editorials, I even sounded a clarion defence of Clause IV – the socialist economic creed that I would back Tony in ditching a quarter of a century later. I did say, however, that such high-sounding words were pointless unless our brave band of student socialists was organising and acting in the real world. We all actively supported the campaign against apartheid and subscribed to Amnesty International, and in two summer holidays I volunteered in the offices of the National Council for Civil Liberties, the forerunner of Liberty, dealing with cases usually arising from allegations of rough justice at the hands of the police.

Midway through the sixth form, Keren, Steve and I opted for a distinctly unreal world: the Young Communist League. Keren went first. The Young Communists appealed to her rebelliousness, with the added attraction, she said, that the boys were cuter. Steve and I agreed to join her at what turned out to be their annual meeting, in a rambling house in West Hampstead. As we started going to occasional branch meetings, we wound down our YS branch early in 1971. Our main formal YCL activity was to try, with indifferent success, to flog the *Morning Star* on Friday evenings outside Kilburn tube station. Steve and I did become stewards at the YCL national congress, at which Keren was a delegate, and was denounced as a bourgeois turncoat for speaking out against the Soviet invasion of Czechoslovakia.

The biggest impact the YCL made on my life was when news got round that a local youth club was losing its premises in a church, and was eyeing a disused four-storey Victorian pub, the Winchester Arms in Swiss Cottage, as a replacement. The pub had been purchased by Camden Council years before, and left empty. I volunteered to join

the members of the youth club in occupying this wonderful building and setting to work on converting it, while I negotiated with the
council for a short-term lease. The project consumed the attention
of my whole family. The youth leader, Graham Good, and his partner Brenda, took up residence in my parents' home, and my father
became the project's legal trustee. The refitted building survives as a
popular youth club, under voluntary rather than Communist management, to this day.

As A-levels approached, I turned my mind to life after Hendon
County. With Mr Potts barely acquiescent, I had been encouraged by my
economics master, Mr Brown, to apply for a place to read Philosophy,
Politics and Economics at St Catherine's College, Oxford. Much to
my surprise, I succeeded. But the closer the prospect of starting there
became, the more nervous I was. There was little university, much less
Oxbridge, background in my family – although Miles had broken the
mould by excelling at Nottingham, and going on to Liverpool. I felt too
young, too Hampstead Garden Suburban, to go up to Oxford straight
away, and persuaded the college to allow me to delay a year, convincing
them that I would benefit from living and working in Tanzania, where
Julius Nyerere was championing a distinctly African system of village-
based socialism which he called *Ujamaa*.

Finding a placement was not easy. Over a period of many months,
I wrote dozens of letters to the government, charities, churches
and voluntary organisations, all to no avail. Eventually, luck struck.
One evening I heard a radio interview with the Bishop of Stepney,
Trevor Huddleston, previously a bishop in southern Tanzania, and
a Nyerere enthusiast who as a young pastor had been booted out of
South Africa for his stand against apartheid. I wrote to him, and he
invited me to see him at his home in Commercial Road. We talked
for nearly an hour, during which I imagine I impressed him more
by my enthusiasm than by any special knowledge or qualifications
I might bring to rural Tanzania. But he generously arranged for me
to work with Anglican missions in the north of the country – and
even more generously, I would later discover, to pay for my room
and board.

In September 1972 I boarded a flight to Nairobi, from where I would make the short turbo-prop hop to Musoma in north-western Tanzania, with a feeling of adventure and excitement. When I arrived at the Buhemba rural aid station, amid rolling hills and sweeping valleys hundreds of miles from Tanzania's coastal capital of Dar es Salaam, I was struck by the simple beauty of my new, very un-Suburb, breeze-block home. I shared it with a VSO and a Canadian volunteer. It was lit by kerosene lamps, and we had a small gas cooker and an outdoor latrine.

Soon, however, a sense of loneliness and isolation set in. I wondered how on earth I was going to survive a year of this. Even if I were one of life's great natural linguists, which I am not, mastery of Swahili would have been a stretch. Over time, I did acquire a rudimentary competence, but thankfully most of the Tanzanians in the mission spoke English. They helped me, and teased me, over my initial difficulties. I had no obvious common ground with the assortment of New Zealand missionaries who ran the station, kind as they were. Nothing in my upbringing had prepared me to embrace the bedrock of religious belief and purpose that defined their lives. With each passing week, however, I began to feel more a part of things. When I was not working, I wrote scores of letters home to Bigwood Road, to Steve and Keren and other friends, and of course to Bishop Huddleston. They replied with letters of their own and an endless supply of books.

We started work early each morning, and finished in mid-afternoon, amid the heat of the approaching southern hemisphere summer. I planted endless gum trees, determined to stay one step ahead of the rabbits as they devoured the saplings. I built chicken coops. I painted houses. I helped in the mission office, sorting the huge pile of unfiled invoices. I also spent hours talking, and listening, to the Tanzanians with whom I was working. I travelled to Nairobi to buy agricultural spare parts and, nearer home, to Musoma to stay with a charming if slightly eccentric missionary couple, the aptly named Merry and Beatrice Hart.

After four months, I left to work at the missionary-run Murgwanza Hospital in Ngara, on the far side of Lake Victoria near the border with Rwanda and Burundi. A typical day would begin at the concrete slab that served as an operating table for the ebullient English missionary doctor, Arthur Adeney. I would pump anaesthetic ether from a cylinder into a patient with a torn limb, a broken bone, or a burst appendix. If things got complicated, Arthur would have me read him the relevant passages from his university anatomy textbook while I tried to maintain my attention on the pump. The rest of my day was devoted to the dozens of young children in the hospital's orphanage. I can still almost feel the two young sisters who waited for my arrival every afternoon clinging to me, and vividly remember their wailing when it was time for me to leave.

I thought, read and wrote a great deal during my time in Tanzania. Much of what preoccupied me was politics. This was long before the era of the internet or the mobile phone. What news we got came from the BBC World Service, the beginning of my love affair with the BBC. I read books and pamphlets by Nyerere and his TANU party thinkers, as well as other African authors. I read political novels, like Emile Zola's *Germinal* and William Morris's utopian socialist fantasy *News from Nowhere*. I read about Christianity, and remember being especially moved by the theologian Michael Green's passionate statement of belief in Christ's resurrection, *Man Alive*. It helped me to understand, and even at times to feel a part of, the fervency, commitment and simple goodness of the missionaries whom I was working and living with, and coming to admire. In my letters home, I tried to come to terms with what this new wash of knowledge and experience meant about the easier life I had lived, and the easier choices I had made, before living in Africa. There were times when I felt caught up in the promise of Nyerere's Tanzanian socialism. At others, I felt swept away by the shared purpose of the missionaries – almost, but never quite, fetching up in the arms of the organised Church.

My final work in Tanzania was at the Isamilo primary school in Mwanza. It was the hardest and most demanding of all. I taught every subject to a class of forty youngsters. Teaching had seemed so easy when I was on the receiving end, but now, no matter how hard I tried, I felt there was always a child I could not reach, or a bit of knowledge

I could not convey. It left me with an undying admiration for those who have a natural talent for teaching.

In the end, I also learned something else about myself. Africa would for ever be a part of my life, including but beyond the campaigning against apartheid that involved my whole family. But I knew my real home was in Britain – the country, the culture, the politics in which I had grown up. I ended my eleven months away more rounded, wiser, more grown-up – and with far more questions than answers. One of my many long letters to Steve, written shortly before my return, probably captured this best: 'Sometimes, I reason that Tanzanian socialism is tremendous, and the only hope for development, but that socialism in England would be wholly impractical. And that we are living in an ideological cloud-cuckoo land in which England no more has a socialist future than it will fly in the air. . . And then I think there is a lot wrong; much injustice and unnecessary poverty and human suffering, and that something must be done about it. But how? Through the Labour Party in Parliament. . .or yet more words and demonstrations?' All I knew for sure was that, anxious though I was to get home, I would feel very different when I got there from when I had left.

I was certainly no less confused when I arrived at St Catherine's in the autumn. But the tug of politics was stronger than ever, now with a pulsating African and international dimension. Whatever I had seen and written home about to Steve and the others, it never seriously occurred to me that my political home could be anywhere other than the Labour Party. This was reinforced by the influence of a small group of second-year PPE friends with whom I soon became close. Like them, I was uneasy about taking the predictable path for a would-be Labour politician at Oxford: the Union, or the Labour Club. The first of these I neither joined nor attended. It seemed full of self-serving careerists and preening would-be Cabinet ministers – although none of them, in fact, would end up fulfilling their ambitions. The Labour Club was going through one of its periodic periods of tension between right and left, social democrats and traditionalists. This time, the right was winning. Strange as it may seem in the light of the battles I would later fight, my heart was with the traditional-ists. Rather than join, I helped set up an alternative Oxford Labour Students Association. Yet although I was a member of the executive, I spent fairly little time there. With my PPE friends – Michael Attwell, who went on to a career in television; Dick Newby, who would leave Labour to join the SDP and become a Liberal Democrat peer; and the future international trade unionist David Cockroft – I became much more involved in matters overseas. I joined the United Nations Youth and Students Association, as well as a group called Young European Left. In my first year I was especially active in the political causes of southern Africa. Every week, without fail, I would travel to London, helping to organise campaigns in support of the SWAPO insurgents in Namibia, even raising £12,000 to buy a Land Rover for them.

Academically, I rather lost my footing. I suppose I assumed I would always be able to muddle through. But at the end of year one I actually failed my preliminary exam in politics, to the amazement of my tutor, Wilfrid Knapp. To this day, I am not quite sure how I managed to pass philosophy and economics; certainly my tutors, John Simopoulos and Nicholas Stern, later of climate-change fame, were not confident that I had applied myself sufficiently to their sub-jects. I was suddenly faced with the prospect of not only failing to excel at Oxford, but failing to clear the first hurdle. I returned early in the autumn to retake the politics exam, and for all of September I had the best time of my life at Oxford, thoroughly immersed in all the books I was supposed to have read the previous year. I was espe-cially engrossed by analytical tomes and biographies from post-war French politics.

I passed my prelim, but while the chastening fear of being tossed out of Oxford made me conscious of needing to rein in my political activities, I never really learned that lesson completely. In my second year I became president of the Junior Common Room, which took up considerable time, though it also marked the beginning of an enduring friendship with the college's Master, the historian Alan Bullock. Through the Young Fabians I became involved in the British Youth Council, an umbrella organisation of voluntary youth and student organisations. Each of these experiences played a role in how I did politics, and what I did in politics, after Oxford. But if I had it to do over again, there is no doubt that I would concentrate on academic matters. Every time I speak to someone who is about to go up to Oxford, or any other university, I try to pass on that lesson. Forget the politics, I tell them. And the socialising. Forget stuff like the JCR. Forget student activism. The academic opportunity – the chance to read and write, think and learn – in this artificial laboratory of the mind is the one thing that will not come your way again.

I did socialise, but not in the conventional Oxford way – the fancy-dress dinners and large college balls. I would sometimes go out with one or all of my trio of PPE friends to eat and to talk. I also became close to a lovely, warm and, to me, exotic girl named Venetia Porter, one of the first intake of young women at St Catherine's. Venetia was studying Arabic. She had grown up in Beirut, and then moved to London, where she had gone to the French Lycée. Her parents, whom I would sometimes visit with her, were separated, and also fascinatingly different. Her father, Robert Porter, was chief economist at the Ministry of Overseas Development, and was not only good company but an occasional source of rescue and support during my economics revision. Her mother was the famous, and delightfully unconventional, dress designer Thea Porter. It was she who gave me my first taste of London Bohemian life, at the Colony Room Club in Soho, where she was a member. Venetia and I were more curious observers than participants, but the Colony included an extraordinary cast of characters, and was a world away from Junior Common Room.

For a year I shared a house with Venetia and an Arabic Studies friend. It had that special, run-down quality of Oxford student lets, but it was cosy in its own way, and Venetia's company always brightened things up. During study breaks for her, or political breaks for me, we would cook dinner, eat out or go to parties, where we danced and danced. We even enrolled in a rock 'n' roll class at a dancing studio across from Balliol, on Broad Street. In my final period in government thirty years later, I would cause considerable media mirth by suggesting myself as a candidate for *Strictly Come Dancing*. Had the producers taken me up on the idea, I suppose I would have had to come clean about my formal training.

At the end of year two, an opportunity arose to visit Venetia's childhood city, and the wider Middle East. In my study of economics and politics, I was spending a lot of time focusing on the region. Through my UN Association work I met Lord Caradon, Britain's UN Ambassador in the 1960s, and he organised a sponsored fact-finding trip through the Middle East during the summer. I almost didn't make it. As term was ending, I suddenly fell ill with a form of sleeping sickness. As far as the doctors could surmise, I had probably picked it up in Africa, perhaps while rashly swimming in Lake Victoria, a notorious incubator for bilharzia, or when, in Ngara, I had waded through a swamp, swatting off tsetse flies, into Rwanda. Whatever the cause, I found myself in bed in Bigwood Road, unable to get up for nearly a month. At the suggestion of Venetia's mother, my father took me to see a homeopath in Welbeck Street. It seemed to help, a bit. But it was mainly my determination not to miss the Middle East trip that gave me the energy to make my way to Heathrow.

As I set off, I carried with me the echoes of my father's emotional ties with Israel. Even the most unobservant or deracinated British Jew felt a bond with the Jewish state. Especially having lived through the period of the Holocaust and Israel's post-war creation, my father was no exception. The only time during my childhood when I can recall him being explicitly, overtly Jewish was when I was thirteen – during the pre-emptive Six-Day War that Israel launched against Egypt, Jordan and Syria after Nasser's forces had begun massing on the Sinai border. In October 1973, just as I was starting at Oxford, Syria and Egypt joined in a surprise attack on Israel timed to coincide with the Jewish festival of Yom Kippur. Israel prevailed again, but this time it was a much more costly and close-run battle. My own views were broadly pro-Israel, but my St Catherine's PPE friends had exposed me to the Arab side of the argument, and especially to the Palestinian cause.

My first stop was Egypt, followed by Lebanon, Syria, Jordan and finally Israel. Since the Arab League had helped set up the tour, I managed to see a range of government officials, and King Hussein of Jordan's brother, the then Crown Prince Hassan. But the most memorable part of the trip was in Beirut, shortly before the civil war broke out between right-wing Christian militias and the pro-Palestinian Muslim left. Since their expulsion from Jordan after the 1970 civil war there, the political seat of Yasser Arafat's Fatah and the other Palestinian military groups had been in Lebanon. I had a fascinating lunch with the *Guardian*'s Beirut correspondent, the quietly spoken yet passionately pro-Palestinian David Hirst. I also visited one of the Palestinian refugee camps along the road to Beirut airport, just inland from the Mediterranean.

That evening I wrote home: 'The conditions are as gruesome as reported. Thousands of people living in unbearably cramped conditions. . . Of course, they will not leave the camps until they are given the opportunity to return to Palestine. It is the middle-aged and younger ones who seem most committed to return to Palestine. They are good-humoured, patient and with a will of steel. It is a desperate situation.' I recognised that Israel's situation was not easy either. I certainly did not take a 'return to Palestine' to mean the end of Israel, any more than my father did. But that the Palestinians had a national identity, and national cause, of their own seemed to me unarguable. When I returned to England I wrote an article for the *Jewish Chronicle*. Its message seems pretty unexceptional now, but it was less so then, especially for an Anglo-Jewish community audience. It was that until there were two states, one Israeli and the other Palestinian, there would never be peace for either people.

Back at Oxford, I again found myself practising politics as much as studying it. Labour had returned to power, as a minority government, the previous year, and although I was not yet sure exactly what I would do after university, I knew I wanted a future that involved working with Labour – or ideally *in* Labour – and shaping its policy. Having become more deeply involved in the British Youth Council, I became its vice-chairman in early 1976, and national chair two years later. Beyond the invigorating policy work we did, the BYC brought me into contact with a number of people who would influence me in one way or another throughout my political life. None was more dazzling to me at the time than Shirley Williams, Education Secretary in Jim Callaghan's government, who had been a political protégée of my grandfather and who I first met at a conference on 'young people in post-industrial society' at Ditchley Park in Oxfordshire. Shirley was bright, attractive, and had the extraordinary talent of both talking and listening to young would-be politicians as if they were the fully finished article. She was also a modern, outward-looking, pro-European Labour politician who knew where and how elections were won – by appealing to mainstream voters on the centre ground. When I had shied away from joining the Labour Club on arriving at Oxford, it was because of the sterile stand-off between careerists on the 'right' and 'left' of the party. Shirley was no conventional right-winger. She seemed to epitomise a liberal, thinking core in the party that recognised a need to combine our traditional values with policies that were relevant to a changing world.

As BYC head, I also met and worked with leaders of the National Union of Students. The NUS chair when I first got involved was a burly lad who had grown up down the road from me in Hampstead Garden Suburb. I had known Charles Clarke and his brothers, but not to speak to: they were Highgate School boys. The more I worked with Charles in my BYC role, the more I liked him. I worked even more closely with one of his NUS colleagues, the then-Communist and future journalist David Aaronovitch. He was engaging, funny, and obviously clever enough to accomplish anything he set his mind to. But it was Charles with whom I would interact most often and most closely in later years: first, by Neil Kinnock's side in the 1980s, and then in government, in New Labour.

My first job after university was in a distinctly Old Labour environment. I knew that if I wanted a future in the Labour Party, the most realistic route was through the trade union movement. Without the help of Alan Bullock, I would not have got the post

I did six months after leaving Oxford. At the time, he was chairing a government inquiry on industrial democracy. It is hard to say whether it was behind or ahead of its time. One of the less fruitful concessions made to the trade unions, it proposed installing union representatives on the boards of British companies. The idea never caught on. But one of the inquiry panel's members was the head of the TUC's economic department, David Lea, and Alan successfully put in a word for me.

Congress House in Great Russell Street was more than just a union headquarters, and the economic department was more than a policy talking-shop. Listening as my new department bosses peremptorily demanded to talk with this Labour Cabinet minister or that, or acting as designated note-taker in an endless series of bargaining meetings between trade union general secretaries and senior ministers, I had a crash course in how power was then wielded inside Labour. It left an indelible impression on me, and a lesson in how not to run the country. The process was a product of a 'corporatist' approach in which government, business and trade unions carved up the decision-making and attempted to run the economy – investment, prices and incomes – among themselves. It was an idea whose time had gone, if it ever arrived.

The government was struggling, not least with controlling wages and inflation. It was a battle that had already seen Denis Healey forced to go to the IMF for a bailout, and that would end two years later in the Winter of Discontent and the arrival in Downing Street of Mrs Thatcher. Congress House routinely demanded policy trade-offs for any government move to put the economy in order. Almost invariably, it got them. The TUC–Labour Liaison Committee was effectively the executive committee of government. Great Russell Street virtually shared sovereignty with Downing Street. More often, it seemed to be calling the shots.

This might have been heady stuff had I seen my future as a trade union power-broker. But the claustrophobic life of the TUC was not for me. Although I worked hard, my heart was in my role with the BYC. I had researched and written a BYC policy report called 'Youth

Unemployment: Causes and Cures', and was a founding member of a pressure group we helped set up called Youthaid, which was intent on getting the government to do more to help the young unemployed. We called for more intervention to ensure that school-leavers had relevant training and skills, and that the national economy prioritised securing them jobs.

The beginning of the end of my glittering career in the trade union movement came when I and two colleagues were asked by the Prime Minister's political adviser, Tom McNally, now a Liberal Democrat peer and government member, to come to Number 10 to discuss the BYC report with Jim Callaghan. This was my first visit to the Cabinet Room since I had strayed into it during my youthful excursion to view Trooping the Colour, and the Prime Minister and the other ministers with him were polite and receptive to our proposals. It was also my first encounter with Albert Booth, then the Employment Secretary, who would later employ me as his research assistant. My invitation to Number 10 put the TUC headquarters into a major tailspin. If anyone went to talk policy in Downing Street, they made it clear, it should be the top union brass, certainly not some young scribe from the economic department. Responsibility for youth unemployment policy belonged to the TUC's Organisation Department. Before long, it was clear that I would have to choose between my union job and youth politics.

With the approach of the World Youth and Student Festival in Cuba in the summer of 1978, I handed in my notice. The idea of lending the presence of the flower of British youth to a transparent Soviet-bloc propaganda exercise was always going to be controversial, and we debated for months whether or not to attend. In the end we decided that our independent, Western, non-Communist voice should receive a hearing, although the Conservatives on the BYC voted against. There was considerable media criticism of our plans to participate, but the Foreign Secretary, David Owen, gave us a nod of approval, and Charles Clarke, freshly graduated from the NUS, took up residence in Havana as a member of the preparatory committee. I headed the national delegation with an NUS leader who soon became a friend, Trevor Phillips.

We went. We saw. We did not exactly conquer. Yet Trevor and I did manage to cajole, convince, outmanoeuvre or outvote a sizeable pro-Soviet – in some cases, pro-Stalinist – core in the British delegation, whose fervour was being whipped up by a slightly older 'visitor' to the festival, the Yorkshire miners' union leader Arthur Scargill. Cuba was also my first experience of dealing with the press. The term 'spin doctor' did not exist then, and even if it had, I could hardly have imagined that one day I would come to embody it. Yet each day I would go to the Havana Libre hotel to brief British journalists on our pro-freedom, pro-human-rights agenda. It was there that I learned three basic rules of spin-doctoring that remained with me. Don't overclaim. Be factual. And never arrive at a briefing without a story.

Most of the critics back home ended up being supportive, and not a little surprised by how well the British delegation had acquitted itself. The Foreign Office, too. Our trip had begun with a huge opening ceremony at Havana's main stadium. As we entered I was asked to hold our large Union Jack banner while its bearer blew his nose. At that very moment an official appeared and led me away to a designated area where I was obliged to hold it aloft for an agonising three and a half hours while Fidel Castro delivered one of his shorter addresses. The visit ended with a reception at the British Embassy in Havana.

When I got back home, I was jobless. But not idle. Not only was I still national chair of the BYC, but once again Alan Bullock came to my rescue, fixing me up with a research project at the Aspen Institute in Berlin, on youth unemployment across Europe. I also moved house, swapping the lodger's room I had taken in Hackney after university for a tiny flat in Kennington, in south London, from where I watched the unhappy unravelling of the Callaghan government as the May 1979 general election approached.

I loved my little studio apartment. It also turned out to be life-changing politically. Occupying a much larger flat in the same block was Roger Liddle, whom I met through the local Labour Party branch. We not only struck up an instant rapport – his knowledge of, and commitment to, Labour equalled my own – but began a lifelong collaboration in politics. Roger held out the added fascination of being a political adviser to a real-life cabinet member, the Transport Secretary William Rodgers. As the election drew nearer, the question was how long Roger, or his boss, or any Labour minister, would still have a job. The omens were dire. The IMF bailout, and then the union chaos that I had watched at first-hand in the run-up to the crippling strikes of the Winter of Discontent, had left Labour stumbling towards the finishing line.

I was at the Aspen Institute in the week of the election, and arrived back at Heathrow on the morning after. Labour's defeat, however unsurprising, was depressing enough for me on its own. But on the tube from the airport I saw a story in the Stop Press of the late edition of the *Evening Standard* that hit me even harder. Shirley Williams, a kind of political pin-up in my eyes since I had first met her, had lost her seat. For me, Shirley represented everything in the Labour Party that I admired, and wanted to follow. I was so shocked by her defeat that I dropped my duty-free bag, and the bottle of wine inside it shattered on the carriage floor.

After the defeat, Roger and I commiserated with each other about the advent of a right-wing Tory government under Margaret Thatcher. We also talked, often long into the night, about the prospect of Labour finding a way back to national power. In Lambeth, where we lived, Labour appeared headed in the opposite direction. 'Red' Ted Knight had become council leader the year before. He was very much part of the hard-left vanguard about which Hans Janitschek had warned, and Harold Wilson had dithered, in the early 1970s. Ted favoured ever-higher council rates for an ever-growing series of spending commitments, as the Tory government steadily drained resources from local services.

The council ward where Roger and I lived, Princes, was dominated by Trotskyites. If Lambeth was to become a model for the future of the Labour Party, we would surely be settling in for a long, perhaps permanent, spell out of power. I remember being warned by a local Labour activist as we canvassed in a local estate one Sunday morning that the party must at all costs avoid 'compromising with the electorate'. My local comrades had absolutely clear views. Criminals were victims of the capitalist system. The police were agents of repression. Riots were popular uprisings against capitalist injustice.

Often Roger and I would go out to the local pub with members of the beleaguered Labour mainstream to lick our political wounds. When a council seat suddenly became vacant at the end of 1979 in Stockwell, one of the few wards where moderates still had a wafer-thin majority, I was narrowly selected to stand for Labour. For the next two and a half years, along with my fellow Stockwell moderate Paul Ormerod, I was part of Ted Knight's increasingly Soviet-style Labour group on the council. I suppose on some level I saw this as a first, small step towards a more grown-up role in Labour. My grandfather had been born in Lambeth, and began his political life as a councillor. There was still a Herbert Morrison primary school in Stockwell, and the rather down-at-heel Lord Morrison of Lambeth pub. However complex my views about my grandfather as a person, given the effects of his political life on my mother, I had grown up aware of his opinions and achievements, and admiring them. The defining battle in the Labour Party during the late 1920s and 1930s had pitted him against Ernest Bevin. While Bevin was a down-the-middle trade union man, my grandfather argued robustly – too robustly for Bevin – that to become a party of government, Labour had to represent more than just the unions, more indeed than just the working class. It had to be national, not sectional, and appeal to the growing middle class.

That fight was clearly still not won, certainly not in Lambeth. Mostly, my time as a councillor was an education. I was not a terribly effective brake on the Labour group's march to the drumbeat of revolution, although I did rise briefly to the dizzying office of chairman of the Town Planning Applications Subcommittee. That was only for a year, and only because one of Ted's lieutenants was in the lavatory as the Labour group was balloting on that minor post.

I rarely broke ranks on council votes, if only because I recognised that our divisions would be the Tories' gain. In our internal caucuses, however, I was much more forthright. I argued that our far-left rhetorical indulgence would do little to improve the lot of the residents who had voted for us, but would slowly, surely convince most of them that we didn't care about, or understand, their lives. Ted would almost invariably open the next meeting by glaring in turn at me and the other recalcitrants, and saying: 'Certain comrades are misperceiving the situation. . .' The atmosphere was very intimidating. The hard left was not only hard in its politics, it was even harder on those who didn't toe the line.

After the 1981 Brixton riots, I could hold my tongue no longer. Ted called for the police to withdraw from the streets, accusing them of 'concentration camp' tactics of surveillance. Asked for a comment by a local reporter, I replied: 'Given the choice between having the Labour Party and Ted Knight in the borough, or the police, 99 per cent of the population would vote for the police.' I joined my two fellow Stockwell Labour councillors in a broader attack a few months later. 'The Labour group has conspicuously failed to convince its electorate that maintaining its high level of expenditure is desirable or practical,' we said. 'The publicity-seeking statements of the council's leader have come to symbolise the waywardness and irrelevance of the Labour Party for working-class people.'

Part of the reason for my more open frustration over the excesses of the far left was that, for the first time, I had become involved in national Labour politics. In the autumn of 1980 I was hired as a researcher by the Shadow Transport Secretary Albert Booth. I was followed into the opposition offices only weeks later by Charles Clarke, who went to work for Neil Kinnock, then Shadow Education Secretary. The idea of working at this level of Labour politics, even as a lowly researcher, was exciting in itself. But before I took up my role, a generous gift from Roger elevated it to an entirely different level. When the Tories won the election, he had taken with him several boxloads of the policy papers he had accumulated at the Department of Transport. This wasn't strictly legal, and I only hope the statute of limitations on whatever crime he committed has long since lapsed. The effect on me, as I read folder after folder, was electrifying. I still remember the thrill I felt at being able to see how policy was made, the way in which different options were evaluated, advanced or abandoned. It was the first time I had seen the raw material of government. It not only fascinated me, it made me want to be a part of it, and all the more upset at those in the party who were making the likelihood of a future Labour administration ever more remote.

I enjoyed my eighteen months in the shadow cabinet corridor at the Commons. Albert Booth was an engineering draughtsman who had entered Labour politics as a Tynemouth councillor, and had become MP for Barrow-in-Furness in north-west England. He was also a favoured protégé of Michael Foot, who succeeded Jim Callaghan as Labour leader a few weeks after I started in my job. On the day of Michael's victory, I remember Frank Dobson, later Tony Blair's Health Secretary, standing in the doorway of the modest office Albert and I shared and punching the air with excitement. 'Michael's done it!' he shouted with joy. 'We're on our way!' Where to, exactly, remained to be seen.

I worked hard in my role, both for Albert and with his slightly rambunctious number two on the front bench, the Hull MP John Prescott. Albert and John, like Michael Foot, were on the moderate, Tribunite left of Labour. They were also disinclined, and by this time probably unable, to take on the rising influence of Tony Benn and the more assertive far left. At party conference just days before I began my job, Benn had brought delegates surging to their feet with his vision of what a Labour government would do, within days, once it got rid of Thatcher and the Tories: nationalise industries, pull out of Europe, abandon the nuclear deterrent and shut down the House of Lords. I wanted to get Thatcher and the Tories out no less than Tony Benn did, but I couldn't imagine that was the way to do it.

I gravitated towards a much more experienced researcher down the hallway from our office named David Hill, and his boss, the Shadow Environment Secretary Roy Hattersley, as well as to Shadow Foreign Secretary Peter Shore and his researcher David Cowling. Together, we helped to organise the Labour Solidarity Campaign, run by the indefatigable Mary Goudie, which was intended as a counterweight to the Bennites, to give heart to the moderates and keep them in the party. With David Cowling and an intelligent, iconoclastic and occasionally irritatingly self-possessed Labour MP named Frank Field,

I also joined efforts to press for a change in the Labour rulebook. Well before it became a *cause célèbre* for New Labour modernisers, we pressed for the introduction of one-member-one-vote democracy in the party.

There was also a familiar re-education in the power of the unions. Albert's portfolio meant dealing with endless disputes involving the railway workers, and I vividly recall a slightly surreal morning when Albert and I were called in to see Michael Foot. He suggested we all go off to Rail House in Euston and try to get the chairman of British Rail, Peter Parker, to compromise with the rail drivers' union in their dispute over 'flexible rostering', a fancy term for more time off for the same pay. The three of us piled into a taxi at the Commons with Michael's dog, for some reason, yapping at his ankles. We drew up at Rail House to the surprise and bemusement of all, went in to see Peter Parker, and spectacularly failed to get him to agree to the train drivers' demands.

By this time, some at the top of the party had had enough of Labour's drift into the vote-losing wilderness, and were especially alarmed at the growing prospect of the Bennites driving Labour ever further out of the mainstream. Six months after I started working for Albert, four leading Labour lights broke away to form the new Social Democratic Party. Former Foreign Secretary David Owen was one of the 'Gang of Four', as were Roy Jenkins, the former Home Secretary who had just completed his term as President of the European Commission, and Roger Liddle's former boss, Bill Rodgers. The cabinet minister whom I had most admired, Shirley Williams, was the fourth.

Years later, when I was fighting my campaign for selection as a Labour parliamentary candidate, supporters of my main rival would spread the rumour that I too had come close to joining the SDP. That was not quite true, but I did share much of their vision of what a modern left-of-centre party should be, that it should fight for fairness and opportunity, appeal to the centre ground and stand up for national rather than sectional interests. These would become New Labour principles, too. I fully understood the reasons Roger joined Bill Rodgers in the SDP, not just because of their personal friendship, but because both were acting from the values that had brought them into a different Labour Party in the first place. But the 'religion' of Labour had come to me too early in life, and was too much a part of me, for me to go with him. The SDP breakaway did have a major impact on me. The decision I faced, however, was not whether to abandon Labour, but how best to continue fighting for a modern, moderate Labour Party against the challenge of the infantile but hard-nosed left.

In fact, there was one point at which I did feel very close to having to leave Labour. It came six months after the SDP had formed, when Tony Benn contested the deputy leadership against Denis Healey, the former Chancellor who was carrying the hopes of the moderates. I still remember arriving in Brighton for the party conference on a Sunday evening at the end of September, when the result would be announced. Many of my Labour friends, and many Labour MPs, were collectively holding their breath. I got the sense that they had not unpacked their bags, and that if Benn won they would simply leave for London, and very probably leave the party as well. I believe that a Benn victory would have led to a kind of tectonic political shift. The moderate, sensible centre of Labour, including many trade unionists, who like my grandfather saw us as a party of government, could very well have left *en masse* for the Social Democrats, and re-formed the Labour Party in that shell. Frankly, I suspect that I would have joined them. A Benn victory would have sealed the ascendancy of the left, and set us on a path towards extremism, unelectability and irrelevance. Denis Healey won, but by less than 1 per cent of the vote. That meant the Labour Party I loved was not dead. But it was still on life support.

The immediate political decision I had to take was really no decision at all. An election for my Lambeth council seat was approaching, but I no longer had the stomach for my role as designated class enemy in Ted Knight's political fiefdom. Both of my parents had taken pride in my first step on the political ladder, my father in particular, although he was maddeningly prone to telling me I was being too hard on 'Red' Ted when I brought back stories of the latest council excesses. They had also taken pride in my work with Albert Booth, but even my father recognised that Labour, in its current state, did not offer much cause for optimism. My mother, in her common-sensical way, pointed out that the party probably wouldn't be able to offer her son a stable source of income in the foreseeable future. Perhaps, she suggested gently, it might be time for me to find a 'real' job.

I did. I finally left my job with Albert Booth in early 1982 – not for another party, but for what Charles Clarke described, rather disparagingly, as the 'media route'. The most serious current affairs department in British commercial TV, at London Weekend Television, was advertising for additional staff. Trevor Phillips was already working there, and my other old BYC friend David Aaronovitch and I both applied. David got the plum job, at Brian Walden's flagship *Weekend World*. One need only look at David's later career as a political writer on national newspapers to see that it was the right call. I was hired too, beginning as a researcher on *The London Programme*, but following David some months later into *Weekend World*.

In between, I was assigned to the team covering the London battlegrounds in the 1983 general election. Much as I wanted to see Labour back in Downing Street, it was obvious that we were going to lose. The country was finally coming out of a brutal recession, and Mrs Thatcher was riding on the crest of victory in the Falklands War. Our manifesto was essentially an expanded version of Tony Benn's battle cry to the 1980 party conference, with the additional promise of sky-high taxes for good measure. 'The longest suicide note in history,' it was called by Gerald Kaufman, the witty, waspish and wise Manchester MP who would become an ally in efforts to move Labour back towards the mainstream. In fact, the manifesto wasn't all that long. But it *was* suicidal. We were not merely defeated, we were routed. In Labour's worst result since the First World War, we haemorrhaged three million votes, and gifted the Tories a Commons majority of 144 seats.

Working for television turned out to be a – arguably *the* – major turning point in my political career. The knowledge I picked up of politics from the other side of the camera demystified the whole process for me. In covering the election, I got a close-up look at the

Labour campaign machine, if you could call it that. It was fascinating, if hugely disheartening, and would soon prove indispensable in framing my own efforts to head off a similar débâcle for Labour next time round. I also made good and lasting friends, including John Birt, then LWT's Director of Programmes, and Robin Paxton, a senior *Weekend World* editor who would play a critical role when I went to work for Labour again.

Two of the final programmes I produced drew me steadily in that direction. The first came in the wake of the 1983 election collapse. It was about Neil Kinnock, the Welsh MP I had got to know when I was working for Albert, and Neil was Shadow Education Secretary. After the election he had replaced Michael Foot as Labour leader, and he had begun the work of trying to rescue and rebuild the defeated and dejected party. The second was more broadly about the changing political landscape, exploring signs of disillusionment with Mrs Thatcher, the emergence of the SDP, and the prospects for a Labour revival. Watching tapes of these programmes now, I am struck by my underlying optimism. Naïvety, perhaps, would be a better word. I truly believed that Neil's leadership could mark at least the start of Labour's comeback. I felt a growing desire to come back myself as well.

My return began in a restaurant in Pimlico, shortly after *Weekend World* went off the air for its summer break. During my three years at LWT, I had remained in touch with Charles Clarke, and every six months or so we had lunch together. He was still with Neil. When we met in the summer of 1985, I told him how much I missed full-time politics. He suggested I help out in a forthcoming parliamentary by-election in the Welsh constituency of Brecon and Radnor. 'It's in the neighbourhood,' he added, referring to a little two-up, two-down cottage I had purchased the year before near the Welsh border. If nothing else, television paid better than politics. My salary had risen to the princely sum of £31,000, and a return to Labour, no matter what role I played, would pay nothing like that amount. That I never gave this much thought was a measure of the eagerness I felt to be part of the party's recovery and reconstruction.

I had already planned to be at the cottage for the summer, and I leapt at the opportunity to help out in the campaign. When I arrived, however, it was not really a campaign. There were lots of people at the local HQ, but no single person in charge, no strategy, no plan of action. I was deputised to accompany our candidate, Richard Willey. A writer and educationist, he was the son of the long-serving Sunderland MP and future Labour chairman Fred Willey – also a distinguished resident of Hampstead Garden Suburb. Richard and I immediately took to each other. I helped plan his appearances and speeches, advised him on how to handle himself with the local press, and kept his spirits up as we travelled around the large constituency. All of this was good experience that would come in handy in my later political life.

It was a solid, professional campaign, eventually. It also ended in defeat. The Tories lost the seat, but by a narrow margin we were outpolled by the Liberal candidate. The turning point came a few days before the election, and probably should have served as a warning as I embarked on my return to active Labour politics. With the miners' strike only recently over, Arthur Scargill publicly demanded that a future Labour government release all those who had been detained during the strike, and reimburse the union for all the money it had cost.

I was not to be deterred, however. Charles told me during a campaign visit that the Publicity Director at national party headquarters had left, and was to be replaced by an overall Director of Campaigns and Communications. It seemed like the perfect job for me. When I told him I wanted to go for it, Charles said that by all means I should do so. He added, however, that there would be other strong candidates. I later discovered that despite this note of caution, Charles argued my case strongly with Neil. The evening before the selection meeting in front of Labour's full thirty-member National Executive Committee, Neil made it clear to colleagues that I was his preferred choice.

Roy Hattersley, now his deputy and Shadow Chancellor, also backed me to the hilt. I had remained in touch with Roy during my time at LWT. After the 1983 election I had spent most of my free hours helping David Hill organise and support Roy's campaign for the leadership. I saw him as a more experienced and more rounded figure than Neil, and a better bulwark against the Bennites. I had a further referee in John Prescott, who provided a supportive reference, although with a cryptic handwritten postscript: 'Peter will do the job fine, as long as he keeps his nose out of the politics.'

I got the job, but only just. A mere handful of votes decided it. Two NEC members in particular would go on to help not just me but the broader push for change in Labour: the Crewe MP Gwyneth Dunwoody, who was in charge of the publicity subcommittee, and a forward-looking trade union leader named Tom Sawyer, General Secretary of Labour by the time of the 1997 election.

In my presentation to the NEC, I had echoed the optimism I felt in my final months at LWT. I argued that in the two years since our general election drubbing, the popular mood had begun to change. There was a new scepticism about the Tory government. If Labour could project a more popular, relevant, united message – and modernise its communications ideas and strategies – we would have an opportunity to recover momentum, and power. I genuinely believed this. Yet nothing in my apprenticeship since leaving Oxford – my experience of the TUC, 'Red' Ted and Lambeth, my work with Albert Booth or *Weekend World* – had prepared me for how difficult it would prove, or how long it would take.

3

A Brilliant Defeat

From the outside, 150 Walworth Road, near the Elephant and Castle in south London, was a handsome, red-brick battleship of a building. On the inside, it perfectly mirrored the party for which it was the national headquarters. The cramped offices, smoky hallways and paper-strewn conference rooms were disjointed and dishevelled. So was the machinery through which Labour made and presented what passed for policy. My cubbyhole consisted of a wobbly chair, a dodgy-looking three-legged table wedged up against the filing cabinet to balance it, a World War II-vintage intercom, and a dying spider plant on the windowsill behind me.

Barely two years had passed since our collapse at the polls. Michael Foot had retreated to the backbenches. He took the blame for the rout, but it more properly belonged to the party's real masters: the Trotskyite entryists organised in Militant, and the 'softer', or at least subtler, leftists whom Tony Benn had been rallying ever since we lost power in 1979 – in fact, ever since we had lost power under Harold Wilson in 1970. The idea of Labour as a party of government, with any regard for what voters might actually feel, had been abandoned. Neil Kinnock, however, was now leader, and it was clear he saw the need for change.

A few days before I started work in October 1985, Neil had shown the flair, and the guts, that this was surely going to require. At the party conference in Bournemouth he had thundered against the hard-left Labour council in Liverpool, the epitome of how out of touch we had become. As I heard him speak, I couldn't help but think back to

Ted Knight and the Socialist Republic of Lambeth. 'I'll tell you what happens with impossible promises,' Neil had said. 'You start with far-fetched resolutions. They are then pickled into a rigid dogma, a code, and you go through the years sticking to that – outdated, misplaced, irrelevant to real needs. You end in the grotesque chaos of a Labour council – a *Labour* council – hiring taxis to scuttle round a city hand-ing out redundancy notices to its own workers. I'm telling you – and you'll listen – you can't play politics with people's jobs, and with people's services!' How long had I waited for a Labour leader to say that? The fight was on for a Labour Party that again served, and con-nected with, the interests of the people of Britain. A few weeks short of my thirty-second birthday, I was excited to become a part of it.

I arrived at Walworth Road with two all-consuming aims. The first was to do well at my new job. Despite my brave, and evidently successful, effort to sound supremely self-confident before the inter-view panel, I feared that I was supremely unqualified. Three years' experience producing cerebral political television would not nec-essarily equip me to manage all of Labour's day-to-day communi-cations with an almost universally hostile press. It certainly hadn't given me the skills or the experience to handle the other half of my brief: every aspect of the party's campaigning, from pamphlets, post-ers and policy launches to preparations for a general election that was probably less than two years away. My other goal was to play my part in ensuring that Neil Kinnock's vision of Labour, not Tony Benn's or Ted Knight's, won out. That would turn out to be harder still.

Tony Benn's Bristol South-East constituency had been abolished by boundary changes before the 1983 election, and he had failed to be selected for the replacement seat, so it had been left to Party Chairman Eric Heffer to carry the Bennite banner in the contest for leader. With Labour still in collective shock from the scale of our defeat, Neil trounced Heffer. His only serious challenger, Roy Hattersley, was from the right of the party. But Benn was back now, having been returned to the Commons in a by-election at Chesterfield in March 1984, and was *de facto* leader of a vocal leftist core on the NEC. The traumatic year-long miners' strike had also hurt Labour, and Neil. The party was again associated in the public mind with the vote-killers of 1983: ideological infighting, rhetorical excesses and trade union militancy. Neil would later say he wished he had got on top of the issue at the start, by denouncing the NUM for having failed to hold a proper national ballot. Instead, he was left twisting in the wind, feeling he couldn't support the strike, and couldn't disavow it either. The only benefit from his months of agony was that he and those around him had used the period to plan for a fightback against the far left, and a determined effort to reposition the party. Neil's assault on Militant at the party conference had been the first step.

It is difficult to convey, twenty-five years on, how enormous the obstacles were. The Bennites and their fellow travellers were not the only barrier to the huge repair job we faced. Their Old Socialist certitudes had a resonance that went beyond their core supporters. Even many who understood that a state-run economy, unquestioned support for the unions or unilateral nuclear disarmament were impractical in late-twentieth-century Britain – and that they were certainly a guarantee that we would not get back into government – felt them to be somehow authentically *Labour*. With the radical conservatism of Mrs Thatcher taking hold in Downing Street, and Ronald Reagan's in the White House, they felt almost automatically that we should be on the other side of the argument.

And it *was* an argument. Since September 1981 a group of passionately anti-nuclear women had planted themselves in a 'peace camp' at the RAF base at Greenham Common in Berkshire, in protest against the US Cruise missiles that were stationed there. The Campaign for Nuclear Disarmament was enjoying a new lease of life. Mrs Thatcher was not only standing shoulder-to-shoulder with Reagan in agreeing to base US nuclear missiles in Britain. As she embarked on large-scale privatisation of the core of the old state economy, and curbed trade union strike powers, the default position for many in Labour was that whatever the Tories were for, we must be against. I understood this impulse. From my own Labour background, I knew it was part of the glue that held the whole party together. I recalled my own childhood experience of the annual disarmament marches from the nuclear research base at Aldermaston to Trafalgar Square. My family never marched, but in our own Labour Suburb way, we would pack my father's Sunbeam with a roast-chicken picnic, drive to the outer reaches of the capital and watch as the throng made its way towards its final rallying point.

The problem was that a modern, relevant Labour Party could not operate on atavistic instinct. We could not make policy on the simple basis that everything that the Tory government – a comfortably re-elected Tory government – did was wrong. That risked not just failing to take on board policies that might be right, but could leave us opposing policies of far greater benefit to our own voters than anything we were offering. That was clearly the case with Mrs Thatcher's programme to allow millions of council tenants to buy their own homes.

The structure of the party, too, was unrecognisably different then. As leader, Neil was in charge. Up to a point. The National Executive Committee, and indeed party conference, nowadays hold only nominal sway over policy. The trade unions wield nothing like the block-vote power they did then. But when I moved into my tiny third-floor office at Labour HQ, their influence was very real. The NEC, in particular, was the final voice on everything from paperclips to policy on nuclear weapons.

My immediate boss was the party's new General Secretary, Larry Whitty. Over time, Larry and I would develop a good working relationship, but at the beginning we were on different wavelengths. A lifelong trade union man, he had a sentimental attachment to many of the policies and practices of Labour as it then was, and felt a kind of deference towards Tony Benn. I had been, at best, his second choice for the job. He had hoped for Nita Clarke, Ken Livingstone's press chief at the Greater London Council, and would almost surely also have preferred David Gow, the *Scotsman*'s labour correspondent. At least Larry did not share the hostility of many others in Labour to modern communications techniques, which were seen as somehow *Tory*, and unclean. But he did worry that the changes I might bring about in Labour's policy presentation would impact on the policies themselves, and that I would tread on the toes of those formally in charge of making them in the NEC. He was nervous that, as John Prescott had warned, I would 'put my nose in the politics'. In this, Larry got me absolutely right.

Despite my private doubts, from the moment I arrived at Walworth Road I projected a sense of confidence. Partly, this was bravado. Partly, it was because I knew that any chance of my succeeding depended on it. But in one crucial sense I *was* confident. I was absolutely secure in my conviction that as long as we were saddled with the policies, the mindset and the public image that had led to our débâcle in 1983, Labour would never again be a party of government. And I was absolutely determined to help pull us back from oblivion. I may have lacked experience, even skills, at the start. But I did know what was wrong. Most of Britain's voters, and almost all of the media, disliked us. Worse, they had simply stopped listening to what we said, or at least taking it seriously. My work in television had given me insight into and experience of modern communications. My job, which I set out to accomplish with a drive that sometimes bordered on obsession, was to make everything about Labour look and sound modern too.

I began, as I did whenever I embarked on a new job throughout my political life, by learning what I didn't know, focusing on the most pressing problems, and taking early steps to fix them. I was very fortunate to know – or at least to have met – someone who I hoped could help me with all of this. I was first brought together with Philip Gould by Robin Paxton when I was at *Weekend World*. Philip was 'in advertising', Robin told me. He was clever, and a passionate Labour supporter. We met briefly before I left LWT, at a dinner hosted by Philip's then girlfriend, an up-and-coming publisher named Gail Rebuck. In the intervening year, life had changed for all of us. The small firm Gail had co-founded, Century Press, had done so well that it took over the larger, better-known Hutchinson. She and Philip had married. Philip had set up his own communications consultancy. And I was at Walworth Road. Now, we arranged to talk again, over dinner at Robin's home in Islington.

With his mop of long hair and oversized glasses, Philip made an extraordinary impression. I don't know whether it was shyness or single-mindedness, but he barely made eye contact as he expounded for well over an hour on what was wrong with Labour's image, presentation and political strategy, and how to begin fixing them. I had no way of knowing at that point where Philip might fit into that process, but in advance of our meeting he had sent me an eleven-page letter about how he might help me overhaul Labour's presentational machinery. We discussed it at Robin's dinner, and in much greater detail in the days that followed. A few weeks later, I took my first big decision. With a cheque for £600, a sizeable chunk of my budget, I commissioned Philip to conduct a stock-take of Labour's communications and campaigning. Larry, to my relief, signed off on the idea. It would prove to be the best investment I ever made.

The party already had a contract with a public opinion agency, MORI. Our pollster-in-chief was its American-born chairman, Bob Worcester. His role was essentially to poll, crunch the numbers, deliver and explain the results. Philip was different. He reached beyond traditional opinion polls, assembling 'focus groups' to explain *why* people felt as they did about a policy issue or a political party, how this fitted into what they valued or wanted in their lives, and what it might take to change their minds. He gave Labour, and British politics, its first taste of rigorous, American-style political consultancy. By the time he delivered his sixty-four-page report in December, I knew what its main thrust would be, as I had been among the three dozen people – including Larry and senior colleagues at Walworth Road, and other figures in politics, the media and marketing – to whom he spoke in preparing it. He and I were meeting regularly. The core challenge was obvious to both of us. Labour had to stop seeing communications as something we did with, or to, ourselves. We could no longer, as my canvassing colleague in that council estate in Lambeth had put it, 'refuse to compromise with the electorate'.

Looking back on the notes of my early conversations with Philip, I am struck not only by my concern about the obvious policy vulnerabilities that had hurt us in 1983. I felt there was a deeper problem: our inability to meet people's concerns on basic issues affecting their daily lives: health, social services, housing benefits, the economy – and crime, or as I put it to Philip, 'making people secure in their homes and on the streets'. We could produce policy reports, or catchy ideological prescriptions, but even our traditional supporters were no longer listening. Significant numbers of the 'working class' had turned away from Labour and backed the SDP in 1983. Many more had supported Mrs Thatcher. Faced with a choice between a dogmatic, ideologically pure socialism or a Prime Minister, even a Tory Prime Minister, who had allowed them to buy their council houses, it was no choice at all. 'It's not just a question of having a neat little formulation extracted from some document placed before the Home Policy Committee of the NEC, or some neat way of saying "You're number one with Labour",' I wrote to Philip. 'We can't just get an NHS ambulance with a sticker saying "I Love the Welfare State" and launch a charter. People are not idiots.'

The stock-take report was blunt in its diagnosis and unflinching in its prescription. Knowing I would have to get it through the NEC, I made the language a bit more diplomatic in parts. But I left the core message unaltered. We were so bad at communicating with voters, so seemingly uncaring about what they thought or wanted, that we had become unelectable. No longer could the NEC, the leader's office and the shadow cabinet haphazardly combine to produce press releases and policy documents, schedule press conferences and public meetings, and await Bob Worcester's monthly reports in the preposterous expectation that we were on our way back. My office would become the central focus for all party communications. I would be supported by a new organisation we called the Shadow Communications Agency. Run by Philip and me, it would draw on the expertise of outside advertising and marketing professionals who volunteered their services. Also involved would be Labour's advertising partner, the BMP agency of Chris Powell, older brother of Tony Blair's future chief of staff, Jonathan. The SCA's first task would be another stock-take, this time examining 'every aspect of Labour's corporate appearance'. Instead of relying on grassroots leaflet and sticker campaigns to get our message across, everything we said from now on would be decided and measured against one, revolutionary, objective: to win votes.

By the time I started at Walworth Road, Labour had ceded this kind of political marketing to the Tories. Larry's predecessor as General Secretary, Jim Mortimer, had been scathing about the Conservatives' 1983 campaign, vowing that we would never prostitute ourselves to the idea of presenting politicians and policies 'as if they were breakfast food or baked beans'. It was a view that resonated with most of the party when I arrived. Not only was it naïve about modern politics, it was wrong about what motivated me. I did believe that there were parallels between political parties and the business and consumer world. Both had 'products': in our case, they were called policies, rooted in values. Both competed in the marketplace: in our case, the ultimate test of consumer judgement was a general election. For political parties as much as businesses, if you forgot your customers, if you were unaware of how they were changing and failed to communicate with them properly, they would soon forget you.

Still, our 'product' was different, and the difference mattered. I was driven by the conviction that a more modern, in-touch Labour Party would not just be more likely to win an election, but would lead to a fairer, more broadly based, more socially engaged and economically successful government than the Tories. It would be better for Britain. I have no doubt that I would have been good at marketing breakfast food or baked beans – or even the Tories – but I could never have contemplated doing so. The tools of communication might be the same; the aim, the 'product', and the driving political purpose were wholly different.

Making a start on getting Labour's message heard, and making it worth hearing, was exhilarating. But the early months were sometimes brutally difficult. Politically, my position was delicate, to say the least. Neil and Roy had backed me for the job of Director of Campaigns and Communications, but I had been parachuted in, at what must have seemed an obscenely young age, to head one of the three key departments, and I felt that the veteran party operators heading the other two – Geoff Bish for policy, and Joyce Gould for organisation – although outwardly welcoming, viewed me with a mixture of suspicion and envy.

I did have some allies. Before I'd been hired, Neil had installed Robin Cook, the young Scottish MP who had run his leadership campaign, in the new post of 'Campaign Coordinator', reporting to the shadow cabinet. Robin had set up something called the Breakfast Group, which brought together pro-Labour figures from the advertising and marketing world to advise on modernising our approach. I saw the party's situation as even more dire than Robin did, and with Philip and the SCA, I wanted to go further and faster. That produced tension, at least on Robin's side. I vividly recall an early weekend brainstorming session. Robin was there, countryside-dapper in a silk waistcoat, florid shirt and corduroy trousers. He was not hostile to what I was proposing, but there was an unmistakable frisson in his comments. A sense of 'Who's in charge here? *I'm* the elected politician. I'm the shadow cabinet's Campaign Coordinator. I'm Neil's mate. Here's this ex-television kid, who has come in and started auditing, stock-taking, questioning things, challenging them.' It was understandable. Robin had put the foundation stones in place. Now, I seemed to be taking over the construction.

There was tension of a different sort with the other key member of Neil's team who was already involved in remaking Labour's communications and image. Patricia Hewitt, who had narrowly failed to be elected as an MP, was Neil's press secretary. She was only five years older than me, but she had been involved in campaign work since her early twenties, having begun as press officer for Age Concern before moving on to head the National Council for Civil Liberties. I was a bit in awe of her. She had had two years of battlefield experience in trying to get the media to take a kinder, or at least less unkind, view of Neil and of Labour, and had drawn up a range of campaigning plans, including a project to target key seats at the next election. If I wanted to go further and faster than Robin, Patricia seemed to want to go further and faster yet. With the best of intentions, she not only encouraged me but actively drove me on.

By early 1986 I was working flat out. There were two parts to my job, and two parts to my day. I would spend the mornings at Walworth Road, and was always at my precariously balanced desk by 7.30. There, my focus was campaigning, specifically a major social policy launch that had been agreed – but not planned out, designed or organised – before I arrived. Neil had set the tone. Rather than settle for the familiar NEC emphasis on 'fairness', he had insisted that it bring in the theme of 'freedom' as well. He recognised that Mrs Thatcher had succeeded in making freedom, a classic liberal value, an asset for the Conservatives. We had to start reclaiming it. But what policies would we actually be promoting? How would we present them? What would the posters and the pamphlets look like? How, and where, would we organise the launch event?

I had been at my job long enough to know what the NEC would expect. We would invite the media to one of our down-at-heel conference rooms in Walworth Road, hand out a dense tome on Labour's policies, display the leaflets and stickers we were distributing to party cadres around the country – and assail the heartless Tories. The assumption, or the hope, would be that if only we could drive home the fact that we cared more than the Conservatives, the voters would care more about us.

I was absolutely determined that the campaign, the first test of the new approach and new structure I was trying to put in place, would be unrecognisably different. The problem was that I had done nothing remotely similar before. I did not fear that I'd end up with something worse than our normal fare. Leafing through sheafs of our recent policy material, with its tired and predictable slogans and uninspiring artwork, I did not believe that was possible. I did fear that whatever I attempted might be neutered by the NEC. Or that it might disappoint Neil, and even more so, Patricia. Working at an increasingly fevered pace with Philip, the SCA, the designers and printers, I sometimes felt overwhelmed by the need to get every one of hundreds of details right, and by anxiety over how much could go wrong.

The second part of my day was spent on the other side of the Thames. After a late, quick lunch, often at a very lively but now defunct pizzeria in the Elephant and Castle called the Castello, I would drive to the House of Commons and base myself in Neil's office. My job there was to patrol the top-floor offices of the parliamentary press gallery. It seems amazing to me now, but along with Patricia I was wholly responsible for making Labour's case to the media, and through them to the country. It was the start of my career as a spin doctor. Yet 'spinning' does not begin to capture the difficulty, bordering on impossibility, I found in securing anything more than the most occasional word of praise for Labour. Virtually all the newspapers looked upon 1980s Labour as hopelessly extreme in its policies, out of touch with the country, and hobbled by internal bickering. Since that was largely true, there were limits to what I could do to convince the reporters otherwise. I tried, but mostly my job was damage control. It was frustrating, and it was exhausting.

My refuge was the cottage in Foy on the River Wye in Herefordshire that I had bought while I was at LWT. Set in a lovely, secluded spot on a horseshoe-shaped bend in the river, it was what you might call 'compact'. There was a small sitting room and an even smaller dining room on the ground floor, and three tiny bedrooms upstairs. A bathroom had been built off the back. It was also the most wonderful home I have ever owned. I bought a slightly battered, blue-velvet suite of furniture for downstairs, and within a couple of months I had the wall between the two downstairs rooms knocked through to make a living-and-dining area, and installed a big brick hearth. There was an antique-looking dial phone whose cord stretched just far enough for me to sit with it on the step outside the front door. I also acquired a – barely – portable phone, one of those contraptions with a huge battery pack you had to sling over your shoulder wherever you went.

I drove up to Foy every weekend, often with friends, sometimes alone. I would read, listen to music, watch TV, cut the grass, dig the garden, build bonfires. I would also work, often trying somehow to get a positive story about Labour, or much more frequently to soften a damaging one, in the all-important Sunday papers. Every Saturday I would wake up and steel myself for the task of spending half the morning phoning round all the Sunday papers' political journalists. Then I would go into the nearby town of Ross, where I would do a supermarket shop before taking my regular seat at a wonderful Hungarian restaurant called Meaders, for my favourite dish of layered meat and cabbage. Back at the cottage, I would try to watch whatever classic movie the BBC had on in the afternoon, then fall into a deep sleep before working in the garden or going for a walk while I prepared myself mentally for the first editions of the Sunday papers.

Usually I knew what disturbing bit of Labour news was coming, because a reporter would have phoned for a comment earlier in the day. It was often an assault on Neil's moves to expel Militant members from the party, or an alleged split on some policy or another. Occasionally I would be asked what the party thought about the latest far-left pronouncement by Ken Livingstone, or even Ted Knight. Every week, for hours on end, I had to hose down stories or stop the forest fires spreading to other papers or broadcasters. It was relentless, lonely and dispiriting work, and almost always involved arguing hard with whoever was on the line. I constantly had to make snap judgements, in an unremittingly hostile environment.

I was on the way back from Foy in a driving rainstorm one Sunday afternoon, six weeks before our 'Freedom and Fairness' launch, when all the pressures of the job – working out what to do, the antagonism of the press, the sheer scale of the task of somehow making Labour credible again, the expectations of Neil and Patricia, and myself – finally came to a head. As the rain beat against the windscreen, I was alarmed to feel tears starting to roll down my cheeks. For weeks, I had been finding it hard to sleep through the night. I would get off to sleep all right, but always awoke long before dawn, feeling very anxious. Unable to get back to sleep, I would arrive very early at the office. By nine o'clock I would feel completely worn out, and my head would be aching; I seemed to live on paracetamol. I would somehow force myself through the day, trying to focus on meetings, campaign planning, dealing with the press, just to get through to the evening. I would reach home late, and go to bed feeling simultaneously washed out and tightly wound up.

I believed passionately in what I was doing in my new job, but as the weeks passed, I just could not see how I would handle all the obstacles, anticipate everything that might go wrong. I could not see light at the end of the tunnel. As I drove towards London that Sunday afternoon through heavy traffic, anticipating another week of struggle and sleeplessness, I suddenly felt unable to cope. I was just not sure I could stay the course. I was due to attend a concert that evening at the Royal Festival Hall with an old London Labour friend, Illtyd Harrington, deputy head of the GLC before he and the rest of the sane tendency were pushed out by Ken Livingstone. When I arrived, visibly stressed and out of breath, on the terrace outside the Festival Hall, Illtyd took one look at me and said, 'Peter, what's wrong?' All the pent-up worries came rushing out. Illtyd told me that if I wanted to see my efforts at Walworth Road succeed, the first thing I had to do was take care of myself. He made me promise to see his doctor, Denis Cowan, the following day.

Dr Cowan was reassuring. There was nothing seriously wrong with me, he said. It was just the inevitable result of steadily build-ing pressure, the demands of the job and the demands I was putting on myself. He prescribed three weeks of self-discipline, and sleep. I must arrive at Walworth Road no earlier than 9.30 a.m., leave at 5 p.m. sharp, take no work home with me, and be in bed by ten. He also prescribed sleeping pills for several weeks. I was very reluctant to take them. When I was growing up, medicine was rather frowned upon at Bigwood Road: getting my mother to dispense as much as an aspirin took some persuasion. But I followed Dr Cowan's advice to the letter. Within a few weeks I dispensed with the tablets, and the crisis passed.

My recovery, and Labour's too, really began ten days before the grand policy launch, with a campaign of another sort. It was the first by-election on my watch, in Fulham, caused by the death of the sitting Conservative MP. At least in this battle I had some hands-on experience, from Brecon and Radnor. But I knew it would be the first test of the kind of modern campaigning machinery I had put in place with Philip and the SCA, and that sceptics and critics on the NEC would be keenly eyeing both the campaign and the result. There seemed to be little realistic prospect that we would win. Worse, with the Tory government growing increasingly unpopular, many pundits seemed to think the likeliest winner was the SDP, whose candidate was none other than my old south London friend Roger Liddle.

I think that only a few weeks earlier I could not have faced the challenge. But I knew we had to make every effort to at least make the election close. With Philip's constant encouragement, we organised a campaign for our candidate, Nick Raynsford, that was eye-catching, simple and, it turned out, extraordinarily effective. Both the Conservative, Matthew Carrington, and Roger lived outside the constituency – to be fair, in Roger's case this was only by a matter of a few miles – but all our campaign literature was dominated by an engaging photograph of our prospective MP framed by one, strikingly presented slogan: 'Nick Raynsford Lives Here'. The fact that local Labour supporters throughout the constituency began taping the image to their front windows made the effect especially powerful and amusing.

On the night of the election, 10 April 1986, Labour took the seat from the Tories. Roger finished a fairly distant third. This personal embarrassment for me was made even more difficult by the fact that Roger's wife, Caroline, was also a good friend from my days in youth politics. When she spotted me at the election count, she gave me what my mother would have called 'an old-fashioned look'. I could hardly blame her. I was sad that Roger had lost, and resigned to the likelihood that it would be some time before my friendship with him and Caroline could be repaired. At the same time, I was elated that our revamped campaigning team had met its first obstacle, and convincingly and unexpectedly cleared it.

Then came the 'Freedom and Fairness' launch. We had been working for months to make it unmistakably new, and it was. The result was a campaign document that not only included the kind of policy pledges expected of Labour, like increased child benefit, educational subsidies for young people and new housing opportunities, but was also about making individuals freer in their day-to-day lives. We promised a greater say for patients in the NHS, and set out measures against vandalism and crime. The design, too, was sleeker, friendlier on the eye. The SCA had given the brief to Trevor Beattie, whose talent for finding eye-catching, if sometimes controversial, ways to grab the public's attention would later produce Wonderbra's 'Hello Boys' ads. Instead of our old-style Labour stickers, we minted metal badges in edgy black, grey and silver.

In what would become a pattern for many of the changes we went on to make, I had a brief moment of drama with Neil as the posters and media packs were going to the printers. Three days before the launch, he called me in and exclaimed, 'Where does it say "Labour's Freedom and Fairness Campaign"? What's this "Putting People First"? Where's the title?' Feeling much better, more confident – and more rested – than I had for some time, I assured him that both freedom and fairness were still at the centre of the campaign. What we had done was to bring together real policy ideas to put those values into practice. Just like the imagery and artwork, the point was to move beyond talking in a political language that would pass most people by, and, yes, to say directly that we were 'putting people first'. As delicately as I could, I reminded Neil that he had signed off on every creative stage of the campaign along the way. Besides, I said, not quite truthfully, it was almost surely too late to change. But Neil was adamant. In the end, literally almost as the presses were beginning to roll, I arranged for the printers to include the words 'Labour's Freedom and Fairness Campaign', in small letters, along the side of each poster and pamphlet.

The most striking change was the site of the launch. It was not in a scruffy room at Walworth Road, but in the International Press Centre near Fleet Street. By the time we got there, Neil had been won over to the idea, and the design, of the campaign. He was typically fluent and forceful in tying together the policy prospectus with the themes of freedom and fairness. A small girl whose parents had agreed for her to be featured as the main image in our publicity material had come to the launch, and Neil – wonderfully, spontaneously – lifted her aloft. The photographers loved it.

Less enthusiastic was Eric Heffer, who had turned up unexpectedly and stood scowling at me from the back of the room. 'It's disgraceful,' he muttered. When I failed to reply, he continued: 'It's more than disgraceful. It's disgusting! The NEC never approved this. Where's the Red Flag? What is "Putting People First"?' Stalking out, he delivered a parting shot. This was *not* the Labour Party he had joined, he fumed. It was just one of a series of heartening reviews. From the other end of the political horizon Norman Tebbit, the Tory Chairman, issued a blistering condemnation of our 'slickness'. The press, too, sat up and took notice. Not only were there warm responses from our own camp, the *Guardian* and *Tribune*; the *Economist* saw the choice of venue as a sign that Labour was determined 'never again to look dowdy or old-fashioned'. Even the *FT* nodded approvingly.

Heffer was right about one thing: I had never sought detailed NEC approval for the new approach and the new look. I knew I would never have got it. At the very minimum, there would have been endless debate over every dot and comma. The most that would have come out of it was a hugely scaled-down version that would not have had anything like the same impact. I did, of course, have the NEC's endorsement for the central themes of freedom and fairness. I reassured Larry Whitty, as I had told Neil, that our job had simply been to find a new and effective way to get people to listen to that message.

This would set the pattern for much of my future dealings with Larry and the NEC. I recognised that they were my bosses, and was careful to follow the letter of their directives. But I hoped, and became increasingly confident, that by pushing the limits of the spirit of their decisions we could make a major impact on how the party and its policies were seen. I discovered one important tactic early on. When I received an especially heavy-handed policy pronouncement – on the economy, on trade unions, on defence – for our latest party publicity, I would have the text squeezed onto the right-hand side of the page. I would then sit down with the increasingly enthusiastic and hard-working team around me at Walworth Road, people like Jim Parish, Anna Healy and Jackie Stacey, and go through every vote-losing word, picking out the most attractive-sounding phrases – about growth and prosperity rather than state control, or support for a strongly defended Britain rather than unilateral disarmament – and highlighting them in big, attractive type in the wide margin.

Over time, I would find myself applying similar methods to almost every aspect of our presentation and communications. I remember one major policy pronouncement, otherwise fairly forward-looking, in which the NEC instructed us to insert the text of our socialist credo, Clause IV. It did go in, but not in the document that I initially released to the media, only on the inside cover when it was printed. I could do little about the rousing rendition of 'The Red Flag' that closed the Labour conference, but I could try to ensure that it was not the lasting image voters kept in their minds. In this, I usually failed, but sometimes I would be able to choreograph the final speeches so that the concluding hymn would come after live TV coverage had ended. If we couldn't change the policy, at least we could change the way we were seen.

The reporters I dealt with every day were less easily finessed. They knew it was policies that ultimately mattered, and that ours hadn't changed. My daily, and often nightly, dealings with the press did become less wearing, however. Their copy was still almost unremittingly hostile, but personal relationships were being built up. I was their one-man, one-stop source for what Labour was doing, thinking and saying. In that sense, they needed me. It went without saying that I needed them if our public image was ever going to change. Some of the journalists were simply cynical hacks with a settled, utterly negative, view of Labour dictated by their news desks. It was a narrative they knew by heart, and could write up almost automatically before heading off for a drink at the Press Bar or in Strangers, the meeting place for MPs and others on the Thames side of the Houses of Parliament. The facts, and what I or anyone else at Labour said, didn't really matter to them.

My reputation for toughness, or worse, with the press began with journalists like that in these early days. But many of the more serious, and more influential, writers and broadcasters were at least open-minded. I think they also had a bit of sympathy for my plight as I struggled to find ways to give Labour a new, more reasonable face. Most weeks I would have lunch with one or another of these reporters – sometimes, at their invitation and on their expenses, at one of the fancier restaurants around Westminster, but more often in the Commons press cafeteria. I kept telling myself that over time, if and when Labour had a better story to tell, they would help us tell it.

Even in this part of my job, I sometimes had to look over my shoulder. The first problem involved Rupert Murdoch's stable of British newspapers – *The Times* and *Sunday Times*, the *News of the World* and the *Sun*. After prolonged and fruitless negotiation, Murdoch had forced through the introduction of new technology, over the protests of striking print union workers, and opened up a new plant in Wapping. His titles continued to publish, with most journalists crossing increasingly violent and heavily policed picket lines. The NEC voted in a ban on any contact with reporters from the Murdoch papers. It was the classic 1980s Labour response. Not only was it on the wrong side of where most voters thought we should be, but in theory it would keep me from talking to the very journalists I needed if I was to have any hope of improving the party's image. At the news conference at which I announced the NEC boycott, I duly asked the *Times* and *Sun* reporters to leave the room. I felt ridiculous. I also realised that to do otherwise would have been the equivalent of handing in my notice.

However, I made it a point privately to continue briefing, and talking to, the Murdoch journalists. In the Fulham by-election, that was obviously not going to be sufficient. Once the campaign got under way, reporters would build their day around each of the three parties' main news conferences. They were not going to have the time – or presumably the desire – to oblige me by sharing a private Castello pizza to receive my daily spin on the campaign. If we wanted our side of the story to appear in Murdoch's papers, we would have to include their journalists in our news conferences. Making common cause with Patricia Hewitt, and with the support and understanding of Larry Whitty, I persuaded the NEC to suspend its boycott for the duration of the campaign. As I had hoped, it was then quietly forgotten.

The 'Freedom and Fairness' launch was never going to be enough fundamentally to change Labour's look or its image. The next step was more audacious, and had a more far-reaching effect. In Philip's stock-take, we had told the NEC that we planned to review 'every aspect of Labour's corporate appearance'. Though I imagine most members glossed over this bit of advertising-speak, there was never any doubt in my mind where the remake had to begin. The defining core of our image was our fluttering red flag. Eric Heffer, as an NEC member, had seen the report when it came up for approval, but neither he nor the other sceptics would have imagined that we would actually go ahead and fold up the red flag. Had he realised this at the 'Freedom and Fairness' launch, he might literally have combusted. For months, we worked at finding a new logo. It was Neil who first suggested borrowing a symbol from the Scandinavian social democrats: a red rose. We all liked the idea, and I consulted the design expert Michael Wolff, of Wolff-Olins fame, who recruited the artist Philip Sutton. The rose evoked England's gardens. It suggested growth in fresh soil. Sunlight. Optimism. The challenge was to ensure that it would pass muster – with Neil, but above all with the NEC – in time for party conference at the end of September.

In July, Patricia, Philip, Michael Wolff and I went to see Philip Sutton in his studio in south London. Hanging up on clothes pegs on a washing line running along the studio walls were scores of images of different roses. Over a stretch of two hours, we went around the room, gradually narrowing down our search for the perfect rose and agreeing a shortlist of half a dozen prototypes. Three weeks later the artwork had been refined on each of them, and we had to decide from a final batch of three. I picked what I thought was the best, and it went to Neil for his approval. He loved it – or almost: he wanted the stem shortened.

On the eve of conference, however, came a familiar last-minute hesitation. I had already got the design through the NEC publicity subcommittee. It was chaired by my early Walworth Road ally Gwyneth

Dunwoody, who deftly and deliberately underplayed the significance of the party's new symbol. It was just a 'campaign logo', she said. We had also designed a conference wallet to contain every delegate's papers. It was salmon pink, emblazoned with the red rose and the word 'Labour' in big, bold letters. Now I was summoned to see Neil in his Commons office. His wife Glenys was there too, looking upset and worried. Neil was holding up one of our salmon-pink wallets. 'Do you really think the mineworkers' delegation are going to prance around conference holding *this*? They're not going to be caught dead with these things,' he said. 'You can't do it. There'll be a riot.' This time, it really was too late to change. I persuaded him it would be all right on the night.

It was. The entire backcloth of the conference platform in Blackpool was adorned with the new logo in all its glory. The red rose was printed on everything capable of taking its imprint. For Labour to pack away the red flag, as the fury of Eric Heffer and others soon made clear, was like Nike dumping its swish, or McDonald's chopping down the golden arches. The red flag symbolised everything Labour represented in the public mind: socialism, nationalisation, state control. Everything, that is, that voters now liked least and mistrusted most about us. The red rose wasn't just a design change: it represented a transformation in how the party would present itself. It had real impact, reinforced by our now ubiquitous new strapline, recognising the need to put *people*, not the party, first.

The change did generate comment and controversy in our ranks, though not in anything like the way Neil and Glenys had feared. Delegates eagerly collected their conference folders, taking two or three at a time, briefly raising the spectre that we might run out. If they were left on seats, they were stolen. In some cases, money changed hands amongst ardent collectors. That the media were excited – and through them the country – was not only important in itself, it had an immediate effect on the morale of party members. Here was Labour doing something well and eye-catching, beating the Tories at their own game.

On the final day of conference I brought a huge box of fresh red roses, minus their thorns, onto the stage for Neil and Glenys to throw to the delegates. There was a roar of delight. Catching sight of my broadcasting officer Tony Beeton, who would tragically die in the Paddington rail disaster in October 1999, I suggested that he and his tiny son Piers join Neil on the platform. Spotting the young child, Neil's instinctive response was as it had been at the 'Freedom and Fairness' launch: he clutched Piers in one arm and held up one of the – long-stemmed – roses in the other, to shouts and cheers from the hall. It was an extraordinarily uplifting moment. At least briefly, I even allowed myself to indulge in the fantasy that it might provide a springboard for the general election, due in eighteen months but likely to come earlier.

We had had a good year. With Philip's research suggesting that many voters saw Mrs Thatcher as polarising and divisive, we had actually arrived at conference with a small lead in the opinion polls. I knew Labour's problems went much deeper, however. Branding, image, marketing, could do only so much. It was the *product* that ultimately mattered – especially if the product was a set of policies on which voters would decide what kind of future they wanted, and what kind of government they trusted to deliver it. The main reason we had lost in 1983 wasn't that our campaign was amateurish and outdated – that had merely helped turn a defeat into a drubbing. It was our policies. We were in favour of nationalised industries, strike-prone trade unions and unilateral disarmament. We were against the free market, privatisation and widened share ownership, and even allowing council tenants to buy their properties. When it came time to choose, millions fewer opted for us than for the Tories, and we had only just edged out the SDP.

Our image and packaging were finally changing. Our product – as resolution after resolution at the party conference made clear – was not. Nor, much beyond Neil and his shadow cabinet allies, did there seem to be a huge appetite for change. Modernising Labour's appearance and image was difficult enough. Getting any fundamental policy change through the morass of ideological bickering in the NEC, not to mention the trade unions or leftist local parties, was not just a matter of changing Labour's landscape. It was more like draining a swamp.

After our conference our polling numbers lifted, but they fell off as attention turned to the Tories, who were busy getting into their pre-election stride with an array of new policies entitled 'The Next Steps Forward'. Still, I entered 1987 feeling relatively upbeat. It was far too late for us to perform major surgery on our policies, but I was confident that we now had assets which could at least make this battle different from 1983. With our new communications operation, my hope was to emphasise what had changed in Labour. I hoped to build on our new image by promoting Neil as a different kind of Labour leader.

I had no doubt about the strengths of the people working most closely around him – Patricia Hewitt, and his chief of staff Charles Clarke, who I had known well since our days in student politics in the 1970s. As we geared up for election year, there was a real sense of shared purpose: to build a professional campaign around Neil as a leader who was showing vision and courage in modernising Labour, and could bring similar qualities to Downing Street. I believed this to be true. Although I had never managed anything remotely on this scale, I felt a new level of confidence about my grasp of modern campaigning methods, and in the team we had in the SCA and at Walworth Road. Within days of returning from our 'red rose' conference, we began planning for the general election campaign. Ultimately, dozens of people would be involved. Some of them – Charles, Patricia, David Hill, Chris Powell at BMP and of course Philip Gould – would go on to play important roles with New Labour a decade later. But the main connecting line was in the mechanics of the campaign we devised.

When we began mapping things out in the autumn of 1986, Patricia was not officially at work: she had just had her first child and was on maternity leave. Philip and I would gather around her kitchen table, with Patricia holding her baby daughter in her arms. Some of the features of the 1987 campaign looked new only in the hide-bound context of the Labour Party. They were basic, common-sense changes in image, advertising and presentation. That alone would make a difference, but what was really new was the degree of detail, coordination and control we wired in from the start. We began with our 'warbook', although we didn't give it that name until the process became political orthodoxy in the 1990s: an outline of our own and other parties' strengths and weaknesses, and a point-by-point plan of how to make the most of each of them. Then came what was probably the most lastingly important innovation. We began setting out a 'grid' – a day-by-day map of the entire campaign, with a single policy issue and related narrative as well as a pre-planned visual context, to provide a compelling image for TV news and the following day's papers. It was all bound together by Philip's input – the most sustained, detailed and nuanced research and analysis the Labour Party had ever seen.

In February, however, things began to go wrong. On the surface, all was still to play for. Though we no longer led in the polls, we were trailing the Tories by only a point or two, and were comfortably clear of the SDP in third place. With the economy recovering, however, a Tory policy prospectus promising growth, reduced taxes and low inflation would be a tough case to answer. While Neil's identity as a new kind of leader was gaining traction, so were escalating Tory assaults on Labour's 'loony left'. Worse, voters were about to be reminded of it all over again. The occasion was a by-election in Greenwich, prompted by the death of the veteran Labour MP Guy Barnett. Labour had held the seat for four decades – even, with a reduced majority, in 1983. If we had tapped into Philip's bank of research in picking Guy Barnett's prospective successor, we surely would have won. But under NEC selection rules, with a strong boost from her National Union of Public Employees sponsors, the nod went to Deirdre Wood, Greenwich's representative on the London Education Authority.

Deirdre had history in Ken Livingstone's GLC. She was realistic enough to recognise the difficulties her candidacy presented us with in the run-up to a general election. When she met Neil after she'd been selected, she told him, 'Don't worry, I won't drop you in it.' She didn't. She didn't propose nationalising Greenwich, or declaring London a nuclear-free zone. But with the *Daily Mail* taking the lead, there was an orgy of 'exposés', with spurious allegations about her private life and even mockery of her looks. It was a sustained assault which on more than one occasion reduced Deirdre to tears.

In 1983, Guy Barnett had a 1,200-vote edge over the Conservatives, with the SDP in third place. This time, the Tories concluded early on that they were unlikely to win. The SDP ran the candidate they had recently picked for the general election: an attractive, softly-spoken market researcher named Rosie Barnes, whose husband was a local councillor who organised her campaign. The SDP's Liberal allies sensed that Deirdre's selection made us vulnerable, and flooded the constituency with canvassers. As the campaign neared its end, our polling suggested that the Tories were encouraging tactical voting as well. Days before the vote on 26 February, we still held a lead. But it was tiny. The night before the election, journalists phoned me with advance word on the next morning's coverage. The Tories had essentially conceded defeat, and the SDP were making a late surge. As the polls opened, I phoned Charles. 'We're going to lose,' I said. 'Heavily.' When we did, by almost 7,000 votes, it was as if everything we had so painstakingly built up had crumbled away on that by-election dawn.

Before long there was a string of further setbacks, unlucky events and own-goals. The most serious involved our most difficult policy problem: defence. In 1986, Neil had gone to Washington, where he managed to deflect the embarrassment of failing to meet President Reagan by saying he'd be back before the election. Since our disarmament policy would commit a Labour government to breaking ranks with America and NATO, the last thing we needed was a tête-à-tête at the White House. I and others, including Shadow Foreign Secretary Denis Healey, tried to talk Neil out of going. He was insistent. He had said he would visit before the election. Not to do so would look weak. I was left to record in my diary the vain hope that Reagan would either fall ill, or for some reason be unable to find time for a meeting before the trip took place. The President was in robust health. When Neil arrived in the Oval Office the meeting was bad enough, with a series of predictably chilly exchanges. Then Reagan's spokesman emerged with a politically damning account for reporters. He said the President had not even needed the allotted half-hour to tell Britain's Labour leader that his policies would undermine the Western alliance. Even a friendly feature by one of our few supporters in the travelling press, the *Mirror*'s Alastair Campbell, could not curb the damage. A Gallup poll at the end of the month had us not only trailing the Tories, by nearly ten percentage points, but in third place, behind the Liberal-SDP Alliance.

I did my best to put a positive spin on it. I phoned the Press Association's man in the Commons, Chris Moncrieff, and portrayed Neil's surprisingly resilient remarks after the White House snub as stage one in a carefully planned 'April fightback' ahead of the election campaign. There was no such plan, much less any sign of a fightback. But it was one of those phrases that somehow take on a life of their own. By mid-month, although the polls gave the Tories a widening lead, we were at least back in second place. I knew we could still fall back. Although I told reporters that the polls showed that we were 'back on course, and contending for power', I truly believed only the first of these claims. 'What I really feel,' I wrote in my diary one evening in April, 'is that we are back on course to remain in existence.'

When the election was announced on the second Monday of May, with polling day set for 11 June 1987, I felt more confident than I had a few weeks earlier. From command central in Walworth Road, I found myself working eighteen-hour days to keep on top of every facet of the campaign: speeches and appearances by Neil and others; decisions on advertising, posters and party TV messages; how and what we were briefing to the media. Philip's daily cull and analysis of the opinion data was indispensable. As the campaign hit the road, I was in constant contact by primitive mobile phone with Patricia and, at key moments, with Neil.

Our frontman at news conferences and briefings was Bryan Gould, who had succeeded Robin as the shadow cabinet's campaign chief. Born in New Zealand, Bryan had studied at Oxford as a Rhodes scholar, become a television presenter, and had gone into the Commons in 1974. We hit it off immediately. He was articulate, self-assured, quick-witted and very good company, and I soon became good friends with both him and his wife Gill. He was also a huge asset to the campaign. His encounters with the media were amazing to behold. Entering the room with a few hastily scribbled talking points, he seemed capable of answering even the least anticipated question with fluency and lucidity.

Our first few days were steady rather than spectacular. Though even that represented a huge advance over 1983, it did nothing to cushion the blow of the first opinion polls. In two of them, we were back in third place. But soon, our carefully primed campaign engine got up to speed. Neil did too. His breakthrough moment came at the Welsh Labour conference in Llandudno in mid-May. He had been up much of the night fine-tuning a speech on a theme he had often promoted: freedom and opportunity. The words were strong, the argument deftly made. But the speech did not really take flight until he launched into a passionate, personal broadside against unfairness in Britain. 'Why am I the first Kinnock in a thousand generations to be able to get to university?' he began. 'Why is Glenys the first woman in her family in a thousand generations to be able to get to university? Was it because our predecessors were thick? Did they lack talent? Those people who could sing, and play, and recite and write poetry; those people who could make wonderful, beautiful things with their hands? Those people who could dream dreams, and see visions? Was it because they were *weak* – those people who could work eight hours underground, and then come up and play football? Does anybody really think that they didn't get what we had because they didn't have the talent, or the strength, or the endurance, or the commitment?' Of course not, he said. 'It was because there was no platform upon which they could stand!' There were not the conditions that allowed people who were free under British law truly to *live* that freedom.

Even watching on the TV at Walworth Road, I felt the power of his words. I knew that Neil on this form – genuine, spine-tinglingly eloquent, and speaking on the kind of social issues where the Tories were most vulnerable – would be key to the campaign. The imperative was to improve his connection with voters. We had already decided that our first broadcast of the campaign would focus on him. We had put it in the hands of a remarkable film-maker, the *Chariots of Fire* director Hugh Hudson. I'd first met Hugh the previous summer. He was one of a number of talented figures who wanted to do what they could personally to help revive and modernise Labour. Through the first part of the 1980s, such approaches had been routinely rebuffed or ignored. Eager to get Hugh involved, I asked him to produce a video of the autumn party conference. It was powerful, subtle, engaging, and perfectly captured the new 'red rose' image we were trying to bring to the party.

Before the campaign started, Patricia and I asked him to turn his artistry to Neil, in a party political broadcast. The aim was to confront his media image as weak, woolly and indecisive, and to project his personal and political strengths. When I first saw what Hugh had come up with, at a late-evening screening two days before it aired, I knew it had done the job. The media dubbed it 'Kinnock: the Movie'. It opened with a fighter jet morphing into a seagull above the bluffs of south Wales. Using footage from interviews we had Alastair Campbell do with Neil, his family and leading party figures, Hugh created a portrait of a leader whose bedrock beliefs drove him to help others, and who had the determination and strength to turn his beliefs into action. The film segued into his assault on Militant at the 1985 conference. The climax was built around the Llandudno speech. The final scene showed Neil and Glenys walking hand-in-hand along the seacoast. It was breathtaking. The only question was what words we would put up at the end. Usually, it would be the campaign slogan or the Labour logo. When the screening was over I turned to Betty Boothroyd, a sympathetic NEC member and future Speaker of the Commons, who had wandered in to watch. She said, gratifyingly, that she had loved it. 'What about ending the film with something besides the word "Labour"?' I asked her. 'Would it work to just put "Kinnock"?' She agreed. Later, I would be criticised by some of her NEC colleagues for 'personalising' the campaign. I was guilty as charged. Amid all our policy 'negatives', Neil was one of our few potential positives.

The aims of our campaign had been to build up his stock as a new kind of leader, and in effect to camouflage most of the policy prospectus on which we were asking voters to put him into Downing Street. To a remarkable degree, we succeeded. In vision and planning, management and mechanics, our campaign made the vaunted Tory machine look staid, slow, stodgy. The day before the election, the *New York Times* wrote of how dramatically things had changed. Struck by the contrast between the Thatcher rallies staged by the Tories' presentation supremo, Harvey Thomas, and our Hugh Hudson broadcasts, it concluded: 'In 1979 and 1983, Mr Thomas's rallies were the splashiest events around, yielding strong television images that helped establish the Conservatives' primacy as the party with the most polished communications operation. But this year, the slickness of Mr Hudson's films demonstrated Labour's ability to beat the Conservatives at their own game.' The article quoted a top London advertising executive as saying that we had 'rattled the Conservative campaign, forcing them to spend valuable time repudiating Labour claims instead of concentrating on Tory successes'. It also praised the way in which we had managed to use the rallies we staged for Neil to 'divert attention from defence to issues like health care, pensions and education – on which Mrs Thatcher, despite her lead in the polls, has been on the defensive'.

Realistically, however, our main rival was not Mrs Thatcher or the Tories. We were battling for second place, against the Liberal-SDP Alliance. In 1983 we had beaten them by only two percentage points, and well under a million votes. Even after our 'April fightback', the polls had intermittently shown us as neck-and-neck with the Alliance, or at times behind them. We faced the real prospect of finishing in third place. By polling day, I knew we had at least faced down that threat. From early in the campaign, especially since the Kinnock movie, we had drawn ahead. As I sat in Walworth Road on election night, the only question in my mind was by how much. I was exhausted. In one sense, it was lucky we had never really had a chance of defeating the Conservatives. By the end of the campaign I was so spent, emotionally and physically, that I had literally nothing left for the final sprint.

Bizarrely, there was a brief moment on election day when there was a suggestion that we might even win. Vincent Hanna, the BBC political correspondent, phoned me early in the evening. In a conspiratorial whisper, he said: 'Peter, it's Vincent. I have some very interesting information seeping out about the exit polls. You might just be in for a pleasant surprise.' Swearing me to secrecy, and saying he could not go into detail, he continued: 'You may want to get your "plan B" ready.' I was intrigued, or more nearly astonished. I thanked him, but said: 'For God's sake, don't tell Neil. It'll get him all wound up.'

As Vincent had hinted, the first *Newsnight* prediction was for a hung Parliament. I still frankly didn't believe it – I remember turning to Philip and saying, 'If *only*. . .' The exit poll corrected itself, and the Conservatives won, as we'd both known they would. Mrs Thatcher got a Commons majority of 102. Still, that was down by forty-two seats on 1983. We had gained twenty seats, and cantered home well ahead of the SDP-Liberal Alliance, by eight percentage points and nearly three million votes. We had survived. We had won the battle of the opposition. If the Greenwich trend had continued, we might well not have done.

I retreated to Foy that weekend. I was a tangle of emotions. The campaign had been more wearing than anything I had ever done in my life. I had never directed anything like it before, and had no benchmark against which to judge what I was doing. Every day was virgin territory. If it had not been for the two Goulds, Bryan and Philip, I am sure I would not have been able to carry it off. Never did I have more reason to be grateful for their support than on the first Saturday of the campaign, when I was suddenly confronted with the personal cost of my more prominent political role. The *News of the World*, Britain's highest-circulation Sunday paper, was planning to use its front page next day to tell the country about my private life. I had never cloaked this in secrecy: I simply regarded my life outside politics as having no relevance to my public role. It didn't preoccupy me, and I did not see why it should concern anyone else. The *News of the World* chose not only to target me, but to make personal allegations about Roy Hattersley and the Liberal Party leader, David Steel, as well.

I had been with my partner at the time for nearly ten years. He had also briefly been involved with a woman friend, with whom he had fathered a wonderful son – to whom not only his mother, but the two of us were devoted. What angered me was that the newspaper had decided to publicise this as well: identities, details, photographs and all. On Alastair Campbell's advice, I telephoned the editor, David Montgomery, and told him that if he really wanted to 'reveal all' about me, he could go ahead, but including the name of the three-year-old boy involved, or his mother, would be an utterly unjustified violation of their rights to privacy. Montgomery was cold, monosyllabic, and seemingly could not have cared less. He shrugged off my request, and went ahead. Alastair, who was by my side throughout, shared my disgust.

I was told later that the *News of the World* 'bombshell' had been discussed with the Conservative Party's high command. The Tories apparently saw this as a legitimate way of taking me out of the campaign. If so, it failed. I was fortunate that the pace and demands of the election left me little time to brood on what had happened. The rest of the media, in any case, ignored the *News of the World*'s prurience. But it couldn't help but affect the way I felt about and responded to other media intrusions into my private life. It made me more determined than ever not to make concessions to those who are interested in the irrelevances of the bedroom over the Cabinet Room. This was nearly twenty-five years ago. Thankfully, the world has moved on, and with it, journalistic standards.

With the election over, I took comfort from knowing how much ground we had reclaimed since the chaos and crisis of the spring. The campaign had been a watershed for Labour. It had shown to the party, and the numerous sceptics in the media, that we could compete with the Tories in using the tools of modern political communications to get our voice through to voters. We were at least back in the game. It had been transformational for me as well. As the central figure in the Walworth Road operation, I was always going to receive more media attention than before. If it had all gone haywire, I would have got the blame.

In the final days, the young political editor of the *Observer* wrote the first major profile of me to appear in the national press. I knew Robert Harris only professionally then, though he would later become one of my closest friends. His piece highlighted the differences in Labour's campaigning and communications since 1983. In explaining the role I had played, the obstacles I had had to overcome and the artifice I had occasionally had to use to get our changes through, he also unwittingly coined a label – sometimes useful politically, often uncomfortable personally – that would stick with me for the rest of my public life: the 'Machiavelli' of Walworth Road. Coming from him, this was not meant as an insult, and the rest of the profile was very generous, both about the campaign and my part in it.

After election day, there was far more praise than criticism, some of it from unexpected quarters. Tony Benn said we had run Labour's best campaign since 1959, the one in which he had pioneered ground-breaking TV messages of his own. The review that most touched me, however, was a note Larry Whitty left on my desk the morning after the election. 'Just in case it may on occasion have seemed I felt differently,' he said, 'can I record that I believe your efforts, political judgement and imagination have made this the most effective campaign the party has ever waged. Well done – and thanks.'

Still, in the end, as *Private Eye* put it, we had achieved a 'brilliantly successful election defeat'. The feeling that weighed most heavily on me was that when the votes were counted, we had lost. Again. The sense of frustration and failure gnawed at me in the days, weeks and months that followed as I contemplated what Labour's third straight defeat meant for the party's, and my, future. The reasons we had lost were clear. I singled out 'the three Ds: Deirdre, defence and disarray'. However alluringly alliterative, that told only part of the story. To have any hope of getting back into government, we would have to completely revisit the range of policies where we were simply, fatally, out of touch with the electorate: unemployment and health, education, crime, and of course economics, finance and taxation.

The election result also taught me something else. It was about people's feelings and beliefs, and how they projected these onto those who stood for the highest office. The electorate intensely disliked many aspects of the Labour Party. As for Neil Kinnock, while people felt that he was right to stand up to the hard left, to reform Labour and make its policies more centrist, they also had a feeling that he was not very prime ministerial, that he was uncertain what he believed in, and that his wordiness masked a lack of knowledge. While many voters had a visceral dislike of Mrs Thatcher, and believed that her policies were divi-sive, were destroying industry, generating unacceptable social costs and harming public services, they nevertheless felt that she was strong, was probably what the country needed, that they should continue taking the medicine, and anyway, that there was no real alternative. For voters, feelings prevail over beliefs. People may be torn between their head and their heart, but ultimately it is their gut feeling that is decisive: they vote for the candidate who elicits the right feelings, not necessarily the one who presents the right arguments. Ideally, of course, that should be the same person. This lesson would shape what I thought and did over the next two decades, because it ingrained in me just how subtle political communications are – and how complicated elections are to run.

In the eighteen months or so after the election, I gradually lost heart that this would happen with the necessary urgency. Intellectually, Neil understood the need for change. The trouble was that his heart, and more so his soul, weren't in the scale of change needed. Labour had to find ways of appealing to voters far beyond our old, loyal-ist core. We had to have something to say not only to the have-nots in society, but to the haves – a group of which Thatcherite Britain's 'new working class' either already had, or aspired to, membership. At times, Neil talked the talk. 'But,' I reflected in a diary note after the election, 'he is too much of a socialist, and he hates the idea of being seen by the party as anything different. That is where he gets the power and the passion of his performance.' I knew Neil could inspire. The question, especially on the tough policy decisions we had to confront, was whether he could lead the profound change that was clearly needed.

Hoping to prod him and others into action, I commissioned Philip and the SCA to begin a thorough examination of the state of mind of Britain's voters: what they valued in their lives and in their government; why they supported Labour or the Tories or the Alliance; what had convinced them, or might convince them, to switch sides. We had never done anything on this scale before. Nor had any other British political party. Patricia, as usual, jumped into the driving seat of a process that would end up taking four months to complete, drawing not only on polling and focus groups, but the work of experts in charting political, economic and social trends. That was step one. Step two would be to apply the lessons to policy. We needed an issue-by-issue policy review. This would not have happened without Tom Sawyer, the deputy leader of the public service union NUPE, whose position on the NEC had earlier contributed to the two-vote majority that got me my job. He went to Neil with the idea of a policy review immediately after the election, and convinced him to support it. What shape it would take, how far it would go, remained to be seen. But at least a mechanism would be in place.

The landmark public attitudes report was called 'Labour and Britain in the 1990s', and when I got the draft after the party conference in the autumn, it was even more sobering than I had expected. Its findings were presented to a joint session of the NEC and the shadow cabinet in November. Over two decades, our share of the vote had fallen by nearly 20 per cent, while Tory support had remained steady. Even more disturbing were the findings about why people voted as they did. In the case of the Conservatives, it was their tougher, more aspirational appeal. But more than a quarter of Labour's shrinking base said they remained with us only out of residual loyalty. Among those who had abandoned us, there was a remarkable consistency in the reasons they said had driven them away. 'Extremism' came top, followed by the dominance of the trade unions, our defence policy, and finally 'weak leadership'. It was not just the well-off who didn't like us, but in an increasingly mobile economy, the role of manual work was decreasing. Share ownership and home ownership were rising, and more voters had the kind of aspirations which they said made them reluctant to elect a Labour government. We were becoming less and less popular, less and less relevant. In its X-ray of the British electorate, the SCA report had now told us why. Our image unsettled and alienated voters, our organisation and leadership dented their trust. Our policies clashed with their hopes not only for the country, but for themselves.

I still have my notes of the presentation meeting. Tony Benn called the report 'useful', but said the voters had simply been duped by right-wing 'media propaganda', and that Labour's job now was 'to change their attitudes through our campaigning'. In other words, 'don't compromise with the electorate'. Ken Livingstone said we had been too busy 'reassuring international bankers so they'll now vote for us' to develop and present a strong, socialist alternative to Mrs Thatcher's running of the economy. He also said we had shamelessly gone along with media attacks on the hard left, instead of defending them. Still, by far most of those in the room clearly understood the seriousness of the message in the research report, and the need for us to reconnect as a party with what voters actually wanted in their lives and from their government. What mattered was what they would do about it.

The short answer turned out to be not much. The policy review, which would not finally be published until two years after the election, had all the trappings of a serious exercise. I certainly spun it in the press gallery as the start of a real change, saying that nothing would be off limits. Seven committees, each chaired by the relevant shadow minister and an NEC member, were tasked to look at every major policy area. But while Neil set out a general vision of change, he made surprisingly little personal input to the process. He didn't meet the chairs or want to float ideas. Neither arguing for nor rejecting anything, he seemed to be leaving the outcome up to the individual groups and shadow ministers. With no pressure to be radical, almost all of the review groups played it safe. There was one significant exception: Gerald Kaufman, who was now Shadow Foreign Secretary. He knew what he wanted, knew what Labour needed, and showed every sign of being determined to get it: a jettisoning of unilateral nuclear disarmament. As for the rest, they largely tinkered: except for Shadow Chancellor John Smith's group, which committed Labour to *higher* taxes, by including a whole raft of new benefits pledges.

My confidence that we would rise to the challenge had been eroding for many months. In the aftershock of the election, there was a lot of talk about 'change'. But not only was there a lack of real action, Neil's position with senior shadow cabinet colleagues appeared to have weakened. I had a startling insight into the depth of the discontent in an uncomfortable midnight encounter with Neil's two most influential colleagues. I was in Edinburgh for the international television festival two months after the election, and John Smith and his wife Elizabeth had very kindly invited me to stay with them. When I arrived after dinner on the first night, Elizabeth had gone to bed. I was greeted not only by John, but by the party's deputy leader, Roy Hattersley, and their shadow cabinet colleague, the Glasgow MP Donald Dewar. With the three of them seated in a kind of horseshoe formation around me, it felt like a courtroom drama.

John and Roy did most of the talking. They were scathing about Neil, blaming my 'image-making' for propping up a leader who they were convinced was not up to the job. John conceded that Neil had proven a formidable party manager, and 'infighter', in dismembering Militant. But that was pretty much it. He was aloof, abstract, and a nightmare to deal with on any issue of substance. John's view was that Neil didn't have an 'intellectual interest' in policy. No matter how glowing the reviews he'd received during the campaign, he was 'all froth'. Roy piled in, saying that Neil suffered from 'a lack of assurance, a feeling of being beleaguered and being out of his depth'. That, Roy believed, was because he was.

It was deeply unpleasant, and I did not know how to respond. Neil was party leader. I felt admiration for him because of what he had been put through, and loyalty to him as someone who had at least begun to revive the party. I thought John, Roy and Donald were being harsh and unfair, and I told them so. I also pointed out that while Neil's speeches may have been 'froth', without that froth we would not only have lost the election, we would have been left for dead.

The main senior figure advocating real, if undefined, change was Bryan Gould. At my urging, he had publicly said that Labour had to develop 'policies for the 1990s'. But he was paying a price, in the shape of a whispering campaign against him. He was naïve, it was said. An upstart. The more he pressed for greater influence, the more difficult his position became. It culminated in his proposal to challenge Roy for the deputy leadership at the beginning of 1988. I knew how much Bryan wanted the job, but I could not support him. Neil was dead against the distraction of a contest, and I shared that view. The party was divided enough without another full-scale power struggle, in which it was certain that Eric Heffer would also join the fray. Besides, I was a Labour Party official. Both the leader, and of course the current deputy, wanted Bryan to reconsider. I did the only thing I reasonably could: I talked him out of standing, averting political bloodshed but introducing a lasting strain in our relationship.

I began to wonder whether I should shift my focus outside the party. At one point, I even applied for a job as Director of Communications at the BBC. But I wasn't offered it, and I very much doubt that I would have accepted it if I had been. Having returned to Labour at a time that the party had begun to change, I could not see myself baling out before the process was over, one way or the other. Still, I found myself trying to work around Neil to present a public image of a party ready for fundamental change. I retained a real respect for him, and a warmth that had nothing to do with politics. Neil could be awkward in his relationships, but he had an enormous capacity for kindness, and one instance in particular touched me in a way I have never forgotten.

It was in the spring of 1988, nearly a year after the election. I was called out of an NEC meeting to take an urgent call from my brother in my office. My father had been under the weather for a couple of weeks with a chest infection. Neither of us had been unduly worried, but I spoke daily either to my mother or Miles about how he was getting on. When it became apparent that he was not improving, our family GP had referred him to the Royal Free Hospital in Hampstead. My father and I had found a new closeness over the past year or so. The grating of our unacknowledged similarities had receded, and I was much more able to recognise and appreciate the flair, the assurance, the sense of caring about politics and people which

I had got from him, while he was able to show the pride he felt in what I had accomplished, and the work I was doing. The previous summer, he had come down to spend a day in Foy. He arrived with a lovely blue ceramic ashtray, decorated with a red rose, which I still have. I cooked him trout and salad and new boiled potatoes. We walked and talked, and then he slept before I drove him back to the station. I had every expectation that we would have further time to look back, and forward, together.

But now, Miles was phoning with bad news. The 'chest infection' was being treated, but the hospital had done tests. My father had cancer, and the prognosis was not good. I could not help the tears coming as I sat, holding the phone, before I replaced the receiver. Whether it was by means of telepathy I don't know, but Neil appeared at my side, put his arm round my shoulder and cradled my head in his arms. It would be difficult, he said, but love for a father is a source of strength. 'You'll get through. We'll make sure you get through.' My father died without warning two weeks later, from a heart attack. It was months before I was over the first, terrible sense of loss – thinking of the things my father had said, the clothes he wore, the jokes we had shared, his pipe, the conversations we had or that I wished we had had. The deeper, duller throb went on for much longer.

At work, I looked for whatever examples and agents of real change I could find. I still dutifully briefed the media about Neil's speeches and over-egged the odd policy document, but I was spending much more of my time trying to boost the image of the few Labour MPs who seemed to understand that we had to reform radically or face terminal decline. In my search for articulate, forward-looking Labour spokesmen to deliver a message that would at least sound new on radio and television, I was increasingly drawn to two bright young MPs who had been elected in 1983, and had been inseparable allies ever since. They shared a remote rabbit-warren of a parliamentary office. Both were forceful, effective communicators, and both believed that Labour had to do more – much more – if it was ever again going to get a chance to govern. The senior member of the partnership, a couple of years older and with the longer political

CV, was a thirty-six-year-old Scottish MP named Gordon Brown. His ally and protégé was an Oxford-educated barrister, representing Sedgefield in northern England, called Tony Blair.

I had first got to know them before the election. We were all in our thirties, and were excited to be part of the post-1983 rebuilding project. We were young enough to hope still to be in command of our senses by the time Labour finally got back into government. The initial attraction for me was that here were two MPs who possessed a quality all too rare on the Labour benches: they had an understanding of, and a facility for, modern communications. It was natural that I should want to use their talents to help get Labour's message across, and that they should see a re-energised Walworth Road as an asset.

After the election defeat, this coincidence of interests gradually became something much more than that: a partnership, a trio, a team. In contrast to the detachment and drift of Neil's office, Gordon and Tony conveyed focus, and exuded energy. Constantly batting ideas off each other, positioning and planning, they were like a pair of very close, if unidentical, twins. Tony had the sunnier disposition. He had an easiness about him, a facility for engaging in serious politics without appearing to take the stakes, or himself, too seriously. He had a gift for putting others at their ease, even other politicians. People liked him, and wanted to be liked by him. In a different way, Gordon had that quality too. For me, he certainly did. We had much in common. Like me, he had resolved at a young age to entwine his life with Labour. Like me, he was the political equivalent of a football anorak. An intricate map of Prime Ministers and pretenders past, of alliances and feuds, triumphs and failures, speeches and manifestos, was implanted in both of us like a memory chip.

Although all three of us sensed by early in 1988 that Labour was not going to win the next election without something dramatic happening, I think that the realisation affected Gordon and me a bit differently than it did Tony. While he was frustrated, and sometimes angry, about the party's failure to put itself back in the running for government, for us, there was a deeper, more personal, almost existential, feeling of despair.

There was another bond with Gordon as well. I was spending almost all my waking hours trying to find ways of getting Labour's message into the newspapers or onto the radio or television, and through them to voters. That was not just my job, it was a fixation. For Gordon, it was nearer an obsession. It needed not be about some grand policy announcement – it rarely was. It was not done in any expectation of our winning the major arguments, much less an election, against Mrs Thatcher. But Gordon plotted a ceaseless campaign of guerrilla strikes against the Tories. He was constantly reading ministerial statements, dissecting policy proposals, culling potentially damaging leaks of internal documents. Then, sometimes acting by himself, sometimes through Tony, and increasingly often in league with me, he would zero in on just the right newspaper or broadcaster, just the right news cycle, to strike the blow. For Gordon, this was deadly serious. He viewed the Tories not only as political opponents, but as a battlefield enemy. We might not be able to kill them, but he hoped, wound by wound, to bring them to their knees. His eye for tactical opportunities was extraordinary, and he showed a master craftsman's delight and eagerness in trying to initiate Tony and me into the secrets of the trade.

For the first time I heard him expound on his core principle of political battle, and it would resurface many times, in many contexts, later on. Essentially, his argument was that our own policies weren't necessarily key to scoring a communications or campaigning success – which was fortunate, because our own policies were hardly putting us in a strong position. The key, Gordon said, was to identify, magnify and exploit 'dividing lines' with the Tories. I became an eager co-conspirator. Given the challenge of finding a way to market the pabulum of the policy review, I began to see Gordon's endless schemes to annoy the Tories as invaluable in my efforts to keep Labour in the public eye. His relentless urge to attack also gave me a sense that Labour had not given up the fight.

I saw Tony, too, as a huge asset, especially in conveying a sense of newness in Labour on television. Even before I arrived at Walworth Road, I remember having been bowled over by an appearance he made on the BBC's *Question Time*. He was accusing the Conservatives of undermining civil liberties, but it wasn't the substance of his message that most struck me, timely and apt though it was. I was impressed by his freshness, his fluency, his ability to talk politics in words that connected in a way so many of our frontbenchers seemed to find it difficult to do. I was keen to find ways of turning this to Labour's wider benefit, by steering high-profile TV invitations his way.

My increasing promotion of Tony's and Gordon's media profiles did not escape the notice of some of their more senior colleagues. The first time I put Tony on breakfast TV, to rebut Tory economic policy before the 1987 election, I felt almost as if I'd taken my life in my hands. He was at that time a junior spokesman in Roy's Shadow Treasury team. That afternoon, a redoubtable and undeniably more senior member, the Thurrock MP Oonagh McDonald, pinned me up against a wall behind the Speaker's chair in the Commons. When Roy wasn't available for an interview, she thundered, she was next in line. Did I understand? What on earth had I been playing at by putting Tony up instead? I assured her that there would be plenty of future opportunities for everyone, but I couldn't help adding, 'Tony was very good, wasn't he?' It was not what Oonagh wanted to hear.

Gordon's first real chance to shine came a year and a half after the 1987 defeat, and it happened by accident. Both he and Tony had risen up the ranks since the election. Still too junior to be perceived as a threat to those at the top, and too bright and effective to be ignored, they were voted into the shadow cabinet. Tony was Shadow Energy Secretary, while Gordon was Shadow Chief Secretary to the Treasury, under John Smith. By the time we arrived in Brighton for the party conference at the end of September 1988, I was not alone in having marked them out as faces for the future. For Gordon, the time frame was about to shorten dramatically. Two days after conference, John suffered a serious heart attack which meant that he would need several months' rest before returning to work. On paper, Bryan Gould should have been in line to fill in for him. With his responsibility for Trade and Industry, he held the second-top economic brief in the shadow cabinet. But Gordon made it instantly clear that he was able, and ready, to fill the breech. Since no one with influence went to bat for Bryan, the arrangement was nodded through. I am sure that they, like me, felt that while Gordon lacked John's political weight and dispatch-box experience, he had the intellect and policy grasp to be capable of holding the fort. Within weeks, however, he faced a first major test: replying for Labour to the government's autumn financial statement.

It had all the marks of a distinctly unequal fight. In the Conservative corner, Nigel Lawson had been Chancellor since 1983. He was two decades older than Gordon, and had been in the Commons a decade longer. He had steadily lowered income tax, and since 1986 had built an economic recovery into an income and consumer boom. There were signs of trouble, however. Inflation was rising, and interest rates, which stood at 14 per cent, even more worryingly. Though this was Gordon's first big set-piece parliamentary encounter, he at least had a strong argument to make, 'dividing lines' to exploit, a target to attack. That he would make his points effectively was something I never doubted: he, and Tony and I, had worked on rehearsing and refining them.

When he rose to face Lawson, he did much more than that. He spoke with confidence, vigour and verve. Lawson's great economic expansion, he said, was mere sleight of hand, based on irresponsible levels of borrowing. 'It is a boom based on credit,' he said. Warning of trouble ahead, he ridiculed the Conservatives' efforts to insist that all would be well despite their failure to live up even to their own economic forecasts. Then came the killer line, as Lawson sat grimacing, like an elephant improbably brought down by a mosquito: 'The proper answer is to keep the forecasts and discard the Chancellor!' When he had finished, to shouts of support from the Labour benches, I went up to the press gallery to gauge the reaction. I didn't need to tell them Gordon had done well; they had seen it for themselves. But I felt we had witnessed something of real significance to Labour in this David and Goliath drama. 'Today,' I told them, 'a star was born.' The reason the *Guardian*'s Ian Aitken and others echoed the phrase the following morning was because all of us recognised that it rang true.

Part of what drew me to Gordon and Tony, and drew us together, was simply the way they did politics. So much of the Labour Party seemed weighted down by torpor and an acceptance of defeat. Morale reached a new low the week after Gordon's Commons breakthrough, with a particularly painful by-election defeat in the ostensibly safe seat of Glasgow Govan. We lost it, with a swing of 33 per cent, to the Scottish Nationalists. Neil was feeling so despondent that for a brief period he even began speaking of stepping aside the following summer. I was feeling equally down. A fortnight later, I boarded a train north with Tony to join him at a meeting with his constituents. The contrast could hardly have been greater. Watching him use his mixture of intellect, humour and charm to communicate – with voters was like getting a blood transfusion.

The growing bond between Tony, Gordon and me was not only about politics. On policy, we also found much common ground. The specifics of the new Labour platform we envisaged would not take shape until much later. But we knew absolutely what had to go: the statist, unilateralist and class-defined prospectus that had lost us three straight elections and was surely going to lose us a fourth.

Two late-night entries in my diary, six months apart in 1988, chart the depth of my frustration and my growing certainty about what needed to be done. The first followed the NEC's approval of the initial policy review reports. It reflected my relief at the vote, and my admiration for Neil's role in arguing for and mobilising the support needed to secure it. But I worried about what *hadn't* been accomplished, the risks we had failed to take, and where we might go from here. 'The problem is that for all Neil's courage and strength of leadership, he is let down by his lack of self-confidence and his seeming lack of interest in the detail of policy,' I wrote. 'It shows not so much in what he says and does, but in what he fails to articulate and to achieve.' There was an 'awful' implication in this. I had begun to suspect that the country might never view Neil as prime ministerial material. He would end up being both 'the hero and the fall-guy of history. The likelihood at the moment is that he will be the leader who restored and rebuilt the Labour Party but who could not clinch victory.'

The second snapshot is from a few days after my trip to Tony's constituency in Sedgefield. 'Increasingly,' I wrote, 'my role is revolving around the strong future leaders – Gordon Brown and Tony Blair – and the political nourishment and companionship I get from this group. They have such political gifts, and they know that on the present course we shall remain out of office for a generation. I have now become determined to be part of that successor generation. All my political ambition has returned with the challenge that they hold out.'

While I had not yet shared this with Neil, or even Charles Clarke, I knew something else as well. If I wanted to be part of creating a truly revived Labour Party, I could not do it from where I was – as a headquarters man, whatever the range of my influence. Like Gordon and Tony, I needed to be on the front line. I needed to resume a course I had abandoned, in disgust at the shambolic extremism of London Labour politics. I would seek election as a Labour Member of Parliament.

4

The Three Musketeers

My search for a seat in the Commons need not have ended my role in organising Neil Kinnock's last realistic chance to become Prime Minister. But it did. By the time of the next election, my relations with Neil would be much more distant, while with Charles Clarke they were badly strained. With Gordon Brown and Tony Blair, however, they were not only closer: the three of us had become a political partnership, convinced that the party had to transform itself if it was to have any hope of returning to government. We were also fairly sure that neither Neil nor his likely successor, John Smith, could deliver that change.

I first broached the subject of looking for a parliamentary seat with Patricia Hewitt at the start of 1989. She smiled, an increasingly rare occurrence. Far from trying to argue me into staying the course with Team Kinnock, she had given up trying to convince herself. Working in the leader's office, she was even more frustrated than I was about the prospects for the policy changes needed for renewal. With criticism of his leadership rising, Neil was in brooding, bunker mode. A change had come over Charles as well. His ebullient, can-do confidence was less in evidence, as was the banter with which he had always entertained, and sustained, the Kinnock operation – 'Why, it's Jolly Pierre!' he would invariably greet me in my first years at Walworth Road. While I had undoubtedly become a bit less jolly myself, Charles's morale had clearly suffered from the strain of projecting and promoting, protecting and preserving, Neil's leadership against critics within Labour, and the media without.

Neil mistrusted, feared, and often despised the press, and would be upset by every unfriendly headline. He was using Patricia less and less, but blamed her when things went wrong – with sometimes distressing results that Charles did little or nothing to alleviate. She had begun helping Clive Hollick, a business supporter of Labour who headed the Mills & Allen billboard giant, in his efforts to equip the party for government over the longer term. Mrs Thatcher had entered Downing Street in 1979 with the core of a programme and a political identity – built, with Keith Joseph, largely on the work of a US-style think tank called the Centre for Policy Studies. There was no left-of-centre equivalent. With Clive's backing, that was remedied, with the establishment of the Institute for Public Policy Research. Shortly after we spoke, Patricia left to become Deputy Director of the IPPR.

I mentioned my plans to Charles a few days later. He asked me to take Patricia's place as Neil's press secretary, an offer he repeated several times in the weeks ahead. No doubt naïvely, I did believe I might succeed in using day-to-day contact with Neil to engage him more deeply in the plans we needed to put in place to win the next election. But I had a caveat. I told Charles that if I made the move, I would want to keep open the option of going for a seat in the Commons. He insisted that that wouldn't work, and he was right. Patricia's place eventually went to Julie Hall – a bright, charming ITN reporter who became a close friend, and later the wife, of my most gifted protégé at Walworth Road, Colin Byrne.

I turned my attention to securing real change through the policy review, which was due to be published in the spring. At the end of January, I accompanied Gerald Kaufman on a trip to Moscow for the overseas equivalent of the 'Freedom and Fairness' launch. It was an intricately choreographed event, designed to pave the way for us to abandon one of our most entrenched, and electorally perverse, policies: unilateral nuclear disarmament. Gerald and I took with us the trade union leader Ron Todd, a long-time supporter of unilateralism whose presence would be important in making the shift credible.

As we had anticipated, Gerald was told in his meetings with Soviet officials that even the Kremlin saw Labour's unilateral disarmament policy as an unhelpful distraction. They were also dismissive of the idea of bilateral arms talks, the halfway house favoured by some on the left. The Soviets wanted Britain involved in a multilateral disarmament process, alongside their talks with the Americans, a position they helpfully made clear to the travelling British press. Gerald held a press briefing in front of Lenin's tomb in Red Square at which he took the first step towards abandoning unilateralism, by steering the reporters away from expecting separate arms talks between Moscow and a future Labour government. Gerald then left, for personal rather than political reasons: one of his more endearing quirks as Shadow Foreign Secretary was his ambition to sample the finest local ice cream on all his travels. For reasons that were never entirely clear, he had decided that Moscow's best was to be found in the GUM department store, across Red Square. I followed up his remarks with further, off-the-record briefing that delivered the message more directly. Unilateralism, I said, was dead. When we finally released the policy review in May, it was. Labour would remain committed to disarmament, but 'in concert with action taken by the superpowers'.

The policy review was called 'Meet the Challenge, Make the Change'. With the exception of Gerald's bold move on defence, it might more accurately have been entitled 'Skirt the Challenge, Hint at Change'. There were a few significant changes, notably a retreat from the Bennite dream of reversing all Mrs Thatcher's privatisations. But on finance, John Smith's domain, we did not manage to jettison our high-tax, high-spending reputation. The booklet was glossy enough, the presentation sufficiently polished, to make some impact: for the first time since the run-up to the 1987 election, one of our internal polls even showed us leading the Tories. It also provided a platform for organising our campaign for the June European elections.

In the wake of the Chernobyl nuclear disaster in April 1986, environmental issues would play a major role, leading to predictions that the Green Party might have a singificant effect on the outcome. Many in Labour were arguing for us to adopt a raft of new environmental policies, looking to the possibility of a longer-term 'red–green' alliance against the Tories if the Greens' impact continued to grow. Though I was open to this, I came to believe that it should not be at the expense of a realistic energy policy, including a commitment to nuclear power. I was especially influenced in this by Jack Cunningham, a shadow cabinet minister whose constituency included the nuclear plant at Sellafield. He quite rightly feared that if we came out against nuclear energy he would lose his seat. In the event, I used my campaign briefings to make it clear that we would not close Sellafield, and left others, especially Robin Cook, to court the green vote by implying that we might well do so. With Colin Byrne and Philip Gould helping me plot the overall strategy of the campaign, I also played the policy review for all it was worth, which is to say I trumpeted the changes on defence and nationalisation, and skirted over the rest. I worked as hard as I had since 1987, coordinating campaign events, orchestrating media appearances and briefings.

Against resistance from most of the shadow cabinet, Neil and I insisted on retaining Bryan Gould as the main face of the campaign. Not only was he a proven performer, he was broadly Eurosceptic, and thus perfectly placed to play on the Tories' internal divisions over the EU. As Bryan's partner in presentation I chose Mo Mowlam, a young MP from the 1987 intake, a Political Science PhD with a sharp sense of humour and an in-your-face frankness about her. Mo was excited at being given her chance to shine. Afterwards, quite unnecessarily, she even went out and bought me a gift, a combination radio and television that would have pride of place in my constituency home throughout my period as an MP. Mo and I became good friends, and she and Bryan formed an effective team. Surpassing all expectations, Labour picked up fourteen seats in the European elections, while the Tories lost fourteen. It was the first election of any kind since 1974 in which we had defeated them. The Greens took about 15 per cent of the vote, though the first-past-the-post system meant they got no seats.

Despite media talk of a Labour revival, however, I suspected it was a false dawn. Judging by Neil's mood, and Charles's, so did they. In many ways, however, I was now enjoying my work at Walworth Road.

The early fears that I wouldn't be up to it were gone. I had assembled a talented, and committed, team, and the changes we had made to Labour's public face – how our literature and launches looked, how we organised election campaigns – were now embedded. Our party and its policies may not yet have been modern in any real sense, but our communications were. I was even enjoying my role as the spokesman – or more often the stage manager, interpreter and spinner – for Labour in the media. Not everybody in the media enjoyed me quite so much, but I did build working relationships, even very friendly relations, with many journalists.

Ultimately, however, I saw my role as using any tool at my disposal to ensure that Labour, and Neil, were presented in the best possible light. I paid special attention to television coverage, because of its importance and immediacy, and because my time at LWT had given me first-hand experience of the mechanics of the medium. If that sometimes meant cold-shouldering those who made Labour look bad, I saw that too as part of my job. This stored up bad blood that would do me damage in the future.

I did sometimes have to use more direct measures. Before finalising the policy review, we had launched a nationwide publicity tour called 'Labour Listens'. The idea was for a rotating cast of shadow cabinet ministers to hold meetings in which the audience would tell us what they wanted to see reflected in a future Labour manifesto. My touchingly naïve hope was that thousands of voters would take the opportunity to do so, and that their common-sense messages would prod the party towards changes in policy. In fact, it was a disaster. It began in Brighton, with Roy Hattersley chairing the panel. A Steve Bell cartoon in the *Guardian* captured the atmosphere perfectly: politicians rabbiting on in front of an audience that was snoring, or in some cases dying of boredom.

The nadir came in Birmingham, where, in front of a grand total of twenty people and a local television crew, the shadow ministers made their opening pitch and then asked for questions. A few hands went up. One belonged to an odd-looking woman who was wearing a very tall hat made of newspapers. I sent a note up to Ann Taylor, the senior shadow cabinet member on the platform, saying under no circumstances should she be called on. But before long, our lady of the newspapers was the only one with her hand up. As she began her incomprehensible question, I deliberately tripped over the wire linked to the TV crew's sound system, apologising profusely to the cameraman as I regained my balance. 'Labour Listens' was not seen or heard from again. Still, despite the occasional rows and setbacks, and my frustration that we did not have a more attractive message to convey, I liked what I was doing. I felt it was important, and that I was good at it.

I did not, however, think that over the longer term I could best help promote a changed Labour Party from Walworth Road. I did not intend to leave soon. And not completely, since I still held out some hope of applying the experiences and lessons of 1987 to organising a 'brilliantly successful', yet victorious, campaign next time round. But I believed victory would be a tall order. Though my role had given me an increasingly prominent public profile, my ability to influence the change that mattered most – in Labour's policies – was limited. I was certain that I would feel more fulfilled personally in the Commons, and that I could make a more useful contribution to turning the party round from there. My aim was, alongside Gordon and Tony, to become part of a new generation of MPs who would complete the work Neil had begun and bring a genuinely modernised Labour Party back into government.

The three of us were already working together. I began turning increasingly to Gordon and Tony as front-rank Labour spokesmen. Oonagh McDonald was no longer around, having lost her seat in the 1987 election, but other senior, or rising, MPs and shadow cabinet colleagues resented the profile they were getting. The fact is that they were the most effective and convincing means of getting Labour's message across. They helped me as well, encouraging me in my efforts to gain selection as a Labour parliamentary candidate. Gordon's role was largely tactical. Having come from the tough school of Scottish Labour politics, he was an endless source of advice on navigating the eddies of local party, and trade union, influence. Tony provided the critical, on-the-ground, support. He was convinced I would make an ideal candidate for Hartlepool, a north-east seat adjacent to his own, and when he learned that the sitting MP, Ted Leadbitter, had decided to step down, he took me to meet him. Our talk was warm and engaging, but inconclusive. It turned out that a key group of local party leaders had decided to sound out another, undeniably high-profile, aspirant: Glenda Jackson. I spoke to Glenda. Though no one had yet contacted her about Hartlepool, she was aware of the interest, and I told her that if she wanted to go for the seat, I'd defer to her. I meant it. I also sensed she would be happier with a London seat, as soon turned out to be the case.

Once that became clear, I threw my energies into trying to win support, both in the constituency and with the critically important trade unions. Masterminding my campaign was an astute and talented local party member, Bernard Carr, whose political skills were exceeded only by his ability to conjure up delicious meals. It was not easy at first. Although the national exposure I had got at Walworth Road was in one sense a big advantage, it was not without its downsides. My rivals for the nomination were understandably keen to paint me as an outsider, out of touch both politically and socially with the largely working-class constituency I wanted to represent. They especially delighted in dragging up, and embellishing, a media myth about me from a by-election campaign a few years earlier. In its final form it had me strutting into a Hartlepool fish-and-chip shop and mistaking mushy peas for guacamole. For the record, I have never mixed up the two. And I quite like mushy peas. In fact it was an American intern working for Jack Straw who had made the error.

While the invented version of this story didn't help, as I began spending more and more time in Hartlepool, I found it to be the exact opposite of its parochial media stereotype. The scores of people I met during my bid to become the prospective parliamentary candidate in 1989, and the many thousands more I would meet as their MP, were almost without exception outward-looking and open-minded. And much too canny to be taken in by the guacamole story. The choice of candidate was to be made in mid-December, and I still have the outline speech that Gordon hammered out for me on his office typewriter as the basis of my presentation to the selection meeting. The theme was hardly revolutionary, but it was modernising in the sense that it championed social justice without linking it to higher taxes, 'matching unused resources with unmet needs'. I think that what most won the day was my genuine enthusiasm both for serving the future interests of Labour nationally, and Tony-style, for engaging with and listening to my constituents.

During the run-up to the vote I had said that the first thing I would do if I were selected was to buy a home in Hartlepool, and I soon found a comfortable four-bedroom house on Hutton Avenue, near the civic centre in the heart of the town. It cost a little under £90,000. My mother helped with the deposit, and I took out a mortgage for much of the balance. The only sadness was that, to make ends meet, I would have to sell my wonderful little cottage in Foy.

In London, my living arrangements were also in flux. I was lodging in the Islington home of one of my closest political friends and her family. Sue Nye had worked as a 'garden girl', one of the Downing Street secretaries, for Jim Callaghan, moving with him into opposition, and had gone on to play a steadily more senior role with Michael Foot and now Neil. Her husband, the Goldman Sachs chief economist Gavyn Davies, was high-powered and wealthy. He was also informed and astute about politics, warm and generous and utterly without pretension. They offered me a room in their home until I could find a more permanent base, which I did when I bought a small flat in neighbouring Wilmington Square the following year. But my focus had begun to shift away from the capital, towards Hartlepool and the north-east.

On the day of my selection, Tony was in Sedgefield giving a speech. It would mark the beginning of his emergence as a politician whose weight and prominence in the party were equal to, and eventually greater than, Gordon's. None of us realised this at the time. Weeks earlier, Gordon had finished first in the elections for the shadow cabinet, and was rewarded with a departmental role of his own, as Trade and Industry spokesman. The increasingly settled view was that he was future leadership material. Tony's shadow cabinet brief had changed as well: he was now Employment spokesman. He spotted early on that the party's support for the European 'social chapter' meant that a Labour government would have to abandon its backing for arrangements under which employees could be required to be members of a designated trade union. He also had the modernising instinct to make a virtue out of necessity. As I was addressing the selection meeting, Tony was telling his constituency party that Labour would no longer back the so-called 'closed shop'. He spoke, almost literally, to three people and a dog. But by pre-arrangement with Colin, I made sure the media were primed to give Labour's most serious policy shift since Gerald's move on defence the prominence it deserved. The TV bulletins and newspaper headlines unsettled the unions and the Labour left, but gave encouragement to the growing band of 'modernisers' in the party. They also raised Tony's profile in much the same way Gordon's showdown with Nigel Lawson had done for his a year earlier. Before long he too would find himself being talked about as a future leader.

I was hugely excited by my selection as a candidate, and even more so at the prospect, in a solid Labour seat, of becoming an MP. But while I knew I would now be spending at least a couple of days each week in Hartlepool, I assumed that I would continue my work at Walworth Road. Within days, however, I realised that Neil, and particularly Charles, wanted me out. Neil was relaxed when I told him I intended to apply for the seat, because he assumed I wouldn't get it. 'I should not be hopeful, kid,' he told me. 'I wish you well, because I want you to have what you've set your heart on. But Hartlepool won't have you. I know what sort of party it is.' At first, neither he nor Charles seemed bothered by my increasingly frequent trips to the north-east to drum up support for my candidacy. I was still in London for any major media or campaign event, and in touch with journalists by phone when I was away, and Colin was doing an excellent job anchoring the operation during my absences. But when I won the selection, Neil was shocked, and Charles's attitude hardened. 'Betrayal' was the first word to cross Neil's lips, I was later told. 'I should have known Peter would have conducted this like a military operation, every door knocked on, no stone left unturned, the charm turned on,' he apparently said when he had calmed down a bit. 'He deserves it, but it's left us in the shit.' On the Monday after my selection, Charles called me into the Shadow Cabinet Room in the opposition leader's suite in the Commons. 'I have never known Neil so angry over anything,' he said. 'You cannot stay. You'll have to leave, and we'll find someone to replace you.' He added that if it were up to him, I would be clearing out my desk that day.

For four years, I had worked side by side with Charles. We could not have been closer politically. I had always viewed the challenge of overhauling Labour's image as inseparable from promoting Neil as leader, often at the cost of friction with the NEC. I recognised that in fighting for my own seat, I was going to be less directly involved in the next election campaign, but I knew I could still help, and had assumed that, in some capacity, I would do so. To be told to clear my desk, without a successor or any continuity in place, struck me as rash and irresponsible. When I told Julie about my talk with Charles, she was alarmed at the idea of my packing up and going. So were Sue and others in the office. Philip was even more upset.

When they made their views known to Neil, he decided I should stay on until party conference the following autumn. Charles acquiesced. He recognised the advantages of my staying put for now, but was resolutely opposed to my having any role in the general election. He vetoed fresh appeals from Philip as the campaign drew nearer. I am sure that he understood my desire to stand as an MP. It was a desire he shared, and would later fulfil, and I suspect this may explain why he reacted so strongly to my doing so now. He also saw my decision as an act of flight, undermining Neil's last realistic shot at power.

For a while, it looked very realistic indeed. Mrs Thatcher was being battered by protests against her Community Charge, or 'poll tax'. She was in lethal cabinet combat with her Chancellor Nigel Lawson over whether Britain should join the Exchange Rate Mechanism, a system whereby currencies' exchange rates were fixed within a series of narrow bands, linked to the German mark, intended to stabilise currency swings in preparation for a single European currency. Lawson wanted Britain to join. Mrs Thatcher did not, and had put him in his place by bringing in his rival Alan Walters as her economic adviser, a move that eventually provoked his resignation. In March 1990 I helped mount a by-election campaign against the Tories in Mid-Staffordshire, which we won with a 21 per cent swing, essentially by making it a referendum on the poll tax. In May, we made further gains in the local elections. By the end of the party conference season in the autumn – and the end of my five years at Labour headquarters – two separate polls showed us with a double-digit lead over the Tories.

I left Walworth Road in October 1990. Neil had the good grace to join me at a farewell reception for journalists, and he and Julie Hall presented me with my farewell gift: a huge portion of fish and chips, and mushy peas, all wrapped in a copy of that morning's *Daily Mirror*. A few days later, Philip and Julie drove down with me to Foy for one of my final weekends before the cottage was sold. As Charles must have suspected, I continued to speak with Philip, and received summaries of his polling and focus group data, his analysis and strategy memos.

I had hoped that my job at Walworth Road would go to David Hill, Roy's chief lieutenant. I felt his experience, seriousness and good relations with the media would mesh with Colin's youthful energy and flair. That idea foundered on Neil's unwillingness to have a 'Hattersley man' running the show. When I then lobbied for Colin to be promoted, Neil was supportive, and voted for him on the NEC. But his own staff spread the word that Colin was too close to me, encouraging NEC members to go for John Underwood, a former TV reporter who they thought would be a safer, and more easily manageable, pair of hands. Underwood saw the job very much in traditional Labour terms. Instead of acting as a change-maker, or in fact personally promoting Neil, he worked in concert with other shadow cabinet and NEC members, whatever shade of opinion they held. He and I overlapped for my final months. He lasted in the job for about a year, and when he decided to leave, in mid-1991, David was finally brought in.

I had been gone only a few weeks when the entire political landscape suddenly changed. After another test of wills over European monetary union – this time with her Deputy Prime Minister, Geoffrey Howe – Mrs Thatcher was challenged for the leadership by Michael Heseltine. She won the first ballot, but not convincingly enough to ward off a second vote. Initially, she said she would contest it, and win. Yet when one minister after another told her the game was up, she accepted the inevitable. On 22 November she announced that she was resigning as Prime Minister. Heseltine, having wielded the knife but failed to finish the job, could not strike again, and by the end of the month John Major – with just three months as Foreign Secretary, and a year as Chancellor – became leader of the Conservative Party and Prime Minister.

Neil was ecstatic. 'It's fantastic, kid,' he beamed when I saw him a few days later. He had always felt rather intimidated by Mrs Thatcher, and had feared that Heseltine – rather than the untested, unpolished and uncharismatic Major – would follow her. I believed that Heseltine would have suited us in the long run. I thought he was too mercurial, too impulsive, too flawed a politician to unite his party behind him. Whatever John Major's weaknesses, I felt he was sure to benefit simply from not being Mrs Thatcher, a leader the country had always respected more than liked. I also thought that we had made Major's job easier: by focusing so much of our political fire on Mrs Thatcher, we had made her the issue with voters, rather than developing the policies necessary to defeat the Tories. I did not, however anticipate how strong Major's political position would become in his early months in office. Domestically, he was the un-Thatcher; abroad, like Mrs Thatcher in the Falklands, he had a good war: the joint US and British operation in January 1991 to force Saddam Hussein's Iraqi troops out of Kuwait.

Far from being at the centre of Labour's response, I was now out of a job. My time at Walworth Road had transformed my political life. When I arrived, I was a junior producer of high-brow political television. Though it had not always been easy, I had acquired the tools of modern political communications and campaigning, and applied them in a way that had transformed Labour's approach and image. At first, leaving was a shock. It was as if I'd run a marathon, or stepped out of the ring after a fifteen-round fight, to find that once the adrenalin rush subsided I was left with the aches and pains, and no new challenge to work for.

But the period before the general election would broaden and invigorate me in other ways. My first bit of good fortune was to have Dennis Stevenson as a friend. Though he was nearly a decade older than me, I had got to know him when I was chairman of the British Youth Council and he was head of one of its member organisations, the National Association of Youth Clubs. He became something of a mentor, first in my youth activity and then on every step of my political and professional life. Bright, cultured, generous with his time, he gave unfailingly wise advice on how Labour might modernise its economic policy and detoxify its image with the business community. Now he offered me a four-day-a-week position at the business consultancy he had created, SRU. As in my early days at LWT, I probably learned more than I contributed. I did work hard on a number of projects that were certainly a change from Walworth Road. For one client, I travelled to Denmark and the Netherlands to explore the market for chilled desserts. I was determined to pull my weight, especially since Dennis had agreed to let me build my schedule around my commitments in Hartlepool. Dennis, his high-octane partners like the London style guru Peter York, and their clients opened up a window on the business world. I got additional work with the help of another friend, the founding *Weekend World* editor John Birt, who was now Deputy Director-General of the BBC. I took on a part-time consultancy advising the corporation on how the different parties' policies might affect it after the election.

My most important new connection with an old friend was political. Roger Liddle and I had drifted apart since the mid-1980s, first because I had moved away from Kennington, and then because we found ourselves on different sides of the Labour–SDP schism. The Fulham by-election had been painful for both of us, and especially for his wife Caroline. While we had had almost no contact since then, it was typical of him that when I came under attack during my selection campaign in Hartlepool, he leapt to my defence. I was accused of having come close to abandoning Labour and joining the SDP at its birth in 1981, but Roger, who had been part of the many hours of late-night discussions I had had with close friends at the time, refuted the suggestion.

When I was selected he sent me a note of congratulations, and we began to see more of each other. He was still in the SDP, or more accurately in the now merged Liberal Democrats, but he was starting to drift back towards Labour, or at least to see the possibility of accomplishing within a new kind of Labour Party the social democratic project that had inspired his original breakaway. He had set up a consultancy firm called Prima Europe, specialising in advising businesses on the implications of British and European regulation, and he now offered me a small, part-time role which I gratefully accepted. Roger would become a constant presence in my political life. Over the two decades that followed, I can honestly say that between them, he and Philip Gould informed every political, strategic or policy judgement I made. Early on in politics I had developed an ability to make decisions and stick with them. I also knew the importance of getting the decisions right. I invariably relied on Philip and Roger to reach a settled point of view.

By late 1991, I was concentrating on winning my own seat in Hartlepool. My direct involvement in preparations for Labour's general election campaign was limited to a detailed note, at David Hill's request, on the lessons to be learned from 1987 – ranging from the need to keep a tight day-to-day hold on events, messages and media coverage, to the imperative of avoiding burn-out in the final stages by setting aside time simply to sleep, as well as having a final-week campaign plan. I continued to talk to Philip regularly, and, if much less often, to Neil. I desperately wanted him to be successful. He had worked and driven himself hard, and taken political risks, to make Labour electable. But at Walworth Road, the unsettled aftermath of the Underwood interregnum had left Colin both exhausted and sceptical about whether there was any real will to win. Before long, he resigned too.

In October, I went to see Neil and Glenys at their home in Ealing. I could see a new desperation in Neil. He was very nervous about the coming election, and said he felt an inability to 'find words' for his speeches – an especially painful anxiety for a leader who relied so much on his oratory. He felt he was losing the battle against his poor image, and was upset at the favourable press Major was getting. As we talked, Glenys suddenly interjected: 'Why don't you have Peter back to organise things and get a better press?' If there was any doubt of how low Neil's self-confidence had sunk, it was clear in his reply. He couldn't bring me back, he said, 'because of the Mandelson myth, and what everyone will say about him pulling the strings and controlling me'. I left disappointed not so much by my own inability to help Neil, as by the growing feeling that no one could do so. He seemed isolated, down. It was as if the fight had gone out of him.

For a while, there were murmurings among Labour MPs, shadow cabinet ministers and the unions about replacing Neil. Some union leaders began quietly to canvass the option of John Smith becoming leader before the election. Gordon and Tony even went to see John to gauge his intentions. He replied that he was not interested. He said he did not think we had any chance of winning with Neil, but that he was not going to take the risk of taking aim at him and missing. So Neil survived the talk of rebellion.

My view was that even under a new leader, we would have a hard time winning. With the exception of our abandonment of unilateralism and a partial retreat on nationalisation, our policies simply hadn't changed enough since 1983. With John's commitments to £3 billion in increased pension and child benefits in the policy review, we would also be going into the election on a platform of higher taxes. And since he had pledged to unveil a fully-fledged 'shadow budget' before voting day, tax was sure to become a major issue. As the campaign approached, John finalised a package that would increase National Insurance contributions for anyone earning more than £21,500 a year. It was a formula for alienating voters of almost every class and background.

Neil knew this was trouble. He tried, but failed, to get John to scale down his proposals, and at least to phase in the NI increase. I am sure even John recognised the danger, but he felt it was outweighed by the loss of trust he would risk by a last-minute change to his tax or spending plans. Gordon, Tony and I also felt the tax issue would greatly hurt our chances in the election. But although it didn't really register with me at the time, there was a nuance of difference in the reasons each of them objected. Gordon favoured John's plans for increases in state help for pensioners and struggling parents. His problem was practical and tactical: how to pay for them, and how and when to announce and implement them. While Tony saw welfare increases as a commendable long-term goal, he felt that Labour's priority must be to demonstrate to middle-class voters, and to our traditional working-class supporters who *aspired* to be middle-class, that we would not raise their taxes. We had to show we were on their side. That outweighed all other considerations for him. To the extent that I thought about the discrepancy, I put it down to the fact that Gordon's political position was more delicate than Tony's. His roots, like John's, lay in Scottish Labour. Now that he was Shadow Trade and Industry Secretary, he held the senior economic portfolio next to John, making any appearance of disagreement with him out of the question.

There were growing strains in his relationship with John. Gordon's rise through the party's ranks had caused suspicions in the Smith camp that he might become a rival for the succession if we lost the election. These were being fed by Gordon's oldest and bitterest Scottish Labour rival, Robin Cook. John got the head of the GMB union, John Edmonds, to phone me in Hartlepool late one Friday night with the aim of putting Gordon in his place. 'I gather the mice are playing,' he began. When I replied that I had no idea what he was on about, he said: 'I hear you and others are trying to push Gordon. This isn't helpful.' I wasn't, and I told him so. In fact, Gordon, Tony and I were all sceptical about whether John could deliver the change Labour needed. We had been talking, if only in speculative terms, about the merits of a 'modernisers' challenge', with Gordon going for the leadership and Tony as deputy. The Edmonds phone call was obviously intended to pre-empt any such move.

It was followed, days later, by a more explicit signal. On the shuttle flight down from Edinburgh to London, John turned to Gordon and asked point-blank whether he would try for the leadership. Feeling cornered, Gordon answered in the only way he felt he could: 'No, absolutely not.' 'Good,' said John, 'because it would not help our friendship if you did.' Gordon was so worried about the veiled threat that he asked me to ensure that his undertaking to John appeared in print. I obliged, and later in the week a columnist duly reported that should Labour lose the coming election, Gordon would not be a candidate for the leadership against John. Nobody assumed that Neil would stay.

This did not keep Gordon from making his misgivings about the shadow budget plans clear to John. Short of going public, though, he was never going to be able to force a change. The Tories had no need for such scruples. On 10 March, the day before Major called the election, the Tories' final budget took aim at our obvious vulnerability on taxes. Lawson's successor as Chancellor, Norman Lamont, announced a new 20p income tax band.

To many in Labour, and to at least some in the media, we still had every chance of winning the election. We had a small lead in the opinion polls, even after the budget. The Tories had been in power for thirteen years. The economy was in the deepest recession for decades. Our manifesto was more voter-friendly than in 1987. But not by much. When the NEC met to sign off on it, Neil mustered a majority against a series of motions from Tony Benn, Dennis Skinner and their allies: a call for an explicit reference to socialism, a vow not to impose pay restraint, and a demand to phase out private beds in NHS hospitals.

Our campaign strategy was to play things safe, not to screw up, and to cling on to our poll lead until the finish line. David Hill did a highly professional job at Walworth Road, while Philip was an even more important mainstay than in 1987. We had a few mishaps, but none of them fatal. After the campaign was over, the media and many inside Labour singled out Neil's final, prematurely triumphal rally in Sheffield as crucial to the result. I never believed that. Nor did Philip's later research bear it out. It was our tax and spending plans, made starkly clear in John's shadow budget a few days before the election – and the way that message played into a wider image of Labour as too extreme, too much of a risk, to be trusted in Downing Street – that sealed our fate.

My own campaign involved making my case to the voters of Hartlepool. Just because I was standing in a safe Labour seat didn't mean it was fail-safe. I highlighted local issues, above all the need for investment and economic growth in a town still feeling the effects of the post-war decline of its staple industries. I also raised what would soon become a distinctly *New* Labour priority: the need for even a left-of-centre party to get serious about crime, and tougher on criminals. The personal high point for me was when my mother, always reluctant to venture into the political limelight, joined me on the campaign. The political high point was my result. The Tories added 1,000 votes, or 1 per cent of the electorate, to their 1987 tally. Our vote rose by more than 3 per cent, to nearly 52 per cent.

Still, I had no doubt by election day that Britain as a whole was going to vote in a fourth-term Tory government, and the national results were indeed the worst of all worlds for us. We had lost. But we had picked up forty seats, bringing our total to 229. The Tories, on 376 seats, had lost forty-two. The Lib Dems, with twenty-two, were two seats down on 1987. Though John Major would still have a comfortable Commons majority, the election had been close enough for many in Labour to feel we were *almost* back, that just one more heave, under a new leader, would be enough to see us into Number 10.

There was no way Neil would or could hang on as leader. The party wouldn't have it. John Smith wouldn't have it. I couldn't help feeling sad for Neil. Working with him had its frustrations, but he had shown courage in driving out the hard left. He was a good man, kind to me personally when I most needed it, and caring about the country and the people he had hoped to lead. At his podium best, he was the most inspiring speaker I had ever heard. No matter where change and modernisation went from here, one thing was for sure: there would have been no Labour Party to reform without Neil's leadership after 1983. Who would now succeed him?

A year before the election, I had met the giant of *Guardian* political commentary, Hugo Young, for lunch at Villa Bianca, a lovely, airy Italian restaurant tucked into an alleyway just off Hampstead High Street. Though we often spoke, this was the first of what would become dozens of long private conversations between us on politics and politicians that would be meticulously chronicled by Hugo in diary notes which were sent to me after his death in 2003. Looking at his record of that first conversation, I am relieved to see that I was still dutifully trying to convince him we could win the general election. I doubt if he believed me. Mostly, we talked about the aftermath of possible defeat. I took it as a given that if we lost, Neil would step aside. In that case, I said, there were three options.

The least likely, and least appetising, seemed to me to be Robin Cook, who had no obvious bedrock of party support, but an obvious desire for the crown. I described him, more glibly than I should have done, as 'the thinking man's Tony Benn'. Robin was less dogmatically of the left, and less off-putting for voters, but his natural allies, ultimately, were the Bennites. His main interest was in pushing for an end to Britain's first-past-the-post electoral system. Proportional representation would reduce the size of the hurdle we would have to clear to get back into government, if not on our own then in coalition with the Liberal Democrats. It was also an alternative to real reform of the party, dodging any serious debate not only on changing our policies but on structural questions like the trade union block vote. For soft-left party members who wanted to vote for an intelligent new leader but did not want to confront any awkward issues of policy, Robin was the man.

I felt equally unenthusiastic about option two: John Smith. He was essentially conservative, reluctant to embark on fundamental reform. He was 'Kinnock with a different face', I told Hugo. 'He is a clever man, a very good politician, but someone who would not try to change the party further.' I said that what Labour really needed was a third, radical option. I did not mention Tony. At this point, neither I nor anyone else seriously saw him as the next Labour leader. Instead, I proposed Gordon. He had all Kinnock's strengths, I said, but with 'a philosopher's brain, a thinker's qualities'. When Hugo pressed me as to why Gordon had yet to show these qualities on the public stage, I replied that he was holding back, and assured him that Gordon had a forensic ability, in private, to 'point to every loophole in Labour's policy, everything that is weak, especially our economic policy'. Hugo's summary of my eulogy was unequivocal: 'I gather that Brown is the man to deliver the last revolution in the party – the one that Kinnock, for all sorts of tribal and historic reasons, shrinks from undertaking.'

Now, the choice was not just theoretical. After the election, Tony continued briefly to press Gordon for a Brown-Blair 'modernisers' ticket to challenge John. Gordon refused, both because he had given his word not to stand, and because he doubted they could win. Any serious prospect of its happening was ended by a *Sunday Times* survey of Labour MPs, faxed to me by a journalist friend on the Saturday evening after election day. Only sixty of the 142 contacted were willing to state a preference for leader. But of those who did, 77 per cent backed John. Gordon, the only other candidate who registered double figures, got 14 per cent. Bryan Gould was in third place, on 6 per cent.

On the Monday, Neil announced that he was stepping down, followed by Roy's confirmation that he would also be retiring as deputy. There was still the question of whether Gordon, or Tony, should stand for deputy leader. Bryan was entering both contests. Also vying for deputy would be John Prescott and Margaret Beckett, Shadow Chief Secretary under John since 1989. Both Tony and I urged Gordon to go for the deputy leadership. Particularly given John's caution, it seemed critical to us that he have a genuine moderniser at his side. Gordon was hesitant, however, and not because any of us doubted he could win.

Before the nomination process got under way, I drafted a note of the arguments for a Smith–Brown ticket. Gordon, I said, would be 'the candidate of the younger generation, true to Labour's traditional values but determined to address the changed conditions and aspirations of the modern electorate'. He was 'tough, able and eloquent'. He would not only carry the torch for Kinnock-era reformers. He could 'speak with a sharp, cutting edge and offer a clear vision of what Labour must stand for and do in the 1990s'. He knew the Labour Party inside out. He could offer a unique blend of party manager, strategist and communicator. He had a political project: to make the party's programme, its organisation and its campaign 'unstoppable' at the next election. I argued that together John and Gordon would present a combination of experienced authority and lively, imaginative ideas to carry Labour forward. My hope, and Tony's, was that this would mean that John's authority in the party could be used to drive forward a modernising agenda.

Gordon accepted our view that by standing he would help answer the need for real change. But he didn't have the stomach for a fight. Besides, he said, having two Scots in the top positions wouldn't work, which was probably right. When we then discussed Tony's standing instead – arguing the advantages of a steady Scottish leader complemented by a modernising English deputy – Gordon was, if anything, more strongly opposed. Now was not the time, he said. If they held fire, John would have to give both him and Tony top jobs in his shadow cabinet. They could press for reform from there. Tony was not convinced, but Gordon got his two main parliamentary supporters, Nick Brown and Doug Henderson, to demonstrate that the numbers were not there for him to win the deputy's job. Tony was still unpersuaded. Without reaching a conclusion, we all agreed to talk further the following day. But by then Margaret Beckett, with John's tacit but clear support, had been nominated by Tony's union, the transport workers. 'That decides it,' Gordon announced. 'There is no space for Tony to run.' Tony was not happy. It was to prove a fateful decision, for Gordon, for Tony, and for me as well.

In some ways, when I took up my seat in the Commons, I was like any other new MP. At the beginning, everything about the place gave me a slightly unreal sense of delight. The building itself was not new

Left My maternal grandfather, Herbert Morrison, at the May Day parade in Hyde Park, 1939.

Below My father and mother with my paternal grandfather, Norman Mandelson.

Left The budding young spin-doctor? On the phone, next to my father.

Below At Hendon County Grammar school.

Below With my mother and brother Miles at the Aldermaston anti-nuclear march in the 1960s. I am on the left of the picture, wearing a duffel coat. Our family car, with the boot raised, is on the right.

Left With Gershom Nyaranga, Rural Dean of Musoma, Tanzania, 1972.

Below In my bedroom study in Princes Street, Oxford, 1976.

Below The *Weekend World* team at LWT: *left to right* – Charlie Leadbeater, Brian Walden, Hugh Pile, Robin Paxton, Mary Beale, Sarah Powell, me.

Admiring the red roses with Tony Blair at the Labour Party conference in Blackpool, 1990.

Keeping a watchful eye on the platform at the same conference. Julie Hall and Philip Gould are on the left of the picture.

Above The Labour candidate for Hartlepool in the 1992 general election.

Left With Neil Kinnock in Clapham, south London, July 1990. Behind Neil is Colin Byrne, my senior press officer at the time.

Above At the dedication of a bench to the memory of my father, Hampstead Garden Suburb, 1991. *Seated left to right* – my brother Miles, his wife Valerie, my mother and me.

Above Key members of the shadow cabinet economic team, 1992: *left to right* – Gordon Brown, John Smith, party leader Neil Kinnock, Margaret Beckett, Tony Blair. They all led the Labour Party at some point (Margaret Beckett was leader for a brief period after John Smith's death).

Left With a group of school children in Hartlepool.

Opposite Fielding calls from the press on an early portable phone in my beloved home at Foy, Herefordshire.

With guest speaker Mo Mowlam at a constituency summer barbeque. Looking on are, *left to right*, my close Hartlepool friends Rhoda and Leo Gillen, their daughter-in-law Kathryn, their son Leo junior, and my constituency organiser Bernard Carr.

With Prince Charles at a reception in St James's Palace.

to me, of course: I'd spent part of every working day there for much
of my time at Walworth Road. Yet I felt a shudder of real excitement
as I walked into the Chamber as a Member for the first time. There
was a sense of being part of an extraordinary history: of Parliament
itself, of MPs past, and of *Labour* MPs past, including my grandfather. In a way that was quite different from all I had been a part
of at Labour HQ, I felt that I was finally doing *real* politics: making
speeches that ended up in Hansard, asking questions, trooping into
the *aye* or the *nay* lobby to cast my vote. It was also, of course, the
first small yet indispensable step towards the wider role I had always
hoped to play not just within Labour, but at some stage, in its future
and mine, in a Labour government.

I did all the things new MPs do. I got my first small Commons office,
a narrow and rather dark room in the Norman Shaw South building across the street from Parliament which I shared with another
Labour newcomer, John Denham. I would often read and answer
my correspondence from constituents at a big table just off the central lobby, no doubt to the bemusement of colleagues and visitors.
I made my maiden speech in mid-May, with a call for investment to
help the economic revival of my new constituency and the northern
region. In the traditional tribute to my predecessor, I told a story
from the mid-1960s involving the then newly elected Ted Leadbitter
and the Postmaster General, Tony Benn. The Labour government had
a majority of only three, and one of Ted's constituents was incensed
over the planting of a telephone pole in front of his home. Ted was
doubly irate on his behalf when the protest was brushed off with
a bureaucratic reply, and left a detailed message with Benn's office:
'Mr Leadbitter regards the Postmaster-General's reply as so rude and
evasive that he does not propose to come to the House or accept the
Labour whip until the answer is withdrawn and the pole is removed.'
The pole was duly taken down.

In my own early months in Parliament, I was not so feisty or rebel-
lious, and pleased the Labour whips by playing my part in important,
if sometimes sparsely attended, debates on the Maastricht Treaty.
Politically, we saw the issue as an important opportunity to play on

growing Tory divisions over Europe, and by seizing on issues where less Eurosceptic Conservatives agreed with us, to weaken Major's position. I was a willing accomplice. I joined other debates as well, on issues ranging from disability benefit to vehicle excise duty. And above all, on investment and employment issues of direct relevance to Hartlepool.

I indulged in the novice backbencher's usual sport of speaking in the House on issues that would bring me to the notice of the party whips and my constituents. I took up the cause of fair competition between Virgin and British Airways, siding with Virgin, which led to a private meeting with the BA managing director Bob Ayling, who put me right on some of the key facts. Backbenchers, like journalists, can occasionally resist letting the facts get in the way of a good story. And I attacked the head of Carlton Television, Michael Green, for having donated £15,000 to the Tory Party, which I called inappropriate for the head of a TV station that professed political neutrality. Again, a meeting was brokered, and I went to lunch with Michael. Sitting alongside him was a fresh-faced young PR director at Carlton whose job was to ensure the encounter was cordial and didn't end in fisticuffs, which of course it didn't. His name was David Cameron.

I formed bonds with a core of other newly elected Labour MPs, including Alan Milburn, Stephen Byers, Tessa Jowell and Geoff Hoon. We became a modernising brigade, hard-working and ambitious, with a shared experience of the dysfunctional party of the 1980s that made us determined to make Labour electable and fit for government once again.

But in ways that would have a major impact on my political future, and on my relations with colleagues, I was not the typical new boy at all. Because I knew the journalists who wrote and broadcast about the Commons, and they knew me, I had the national prominence of a much mor senior MP. Above all, I was a particular friend and ally of the party's rising, modernising stars, Gordon and Tony. In fact, although I saw and spoke to both of them daily, at the beginning I tried to avoid an overly obvious public association. I was keenly conscious that the combination of my Walworth Road profile and my friendship with them risked creating the impression among colleagues that I was too big for my Commons boots before I had even tried them on for size. I was determined to make my own way up the conventional parliamentary ladder.

If I had succeeded in doing that, I have no doubt that my political career would have been less frustrating at times, and certainly less fraught. But, especially with Neil about to step aside, there was a first real opportunity for Labour's young modernising duo to make their mark. I wanted to be a part of that. And no matter how discreet I tried to be about that side of my life as an MP, the fact was that Gordon, Tony, and I were simply too close for it to be otherwise. More to the point, both of them were relying on me to provide help and support.

'The Three Musketeers', one lobby journalist dubbed us. During my early months in the Commons both Gordon and Tony would routinely encourage me to focus on my own priorities, to get stuck into the details of government legislation, speak in the House, ask questions of ministers. But almost invariably, one or the other would phone me a few hours later to say he urgently needed to discuss a theme for an interview or a speech, a tricky policy judgement, or often a response to what John Smith, as leader-in-waiting, had said or done.

The three of us had a single view on the immediate priority areas for changing Labour: completely recasting our economic and social policy, and moving decision-making power in the party away from the unions to individual members. We feared that John would move hesitantly in both of these areas. Gordon was still the senior partner among the three of us, but there were signs that Tony was establishing a political identity, personality and style of his own. His move to ditch the closed shop had not only shown that he was willing to slay sacred cows, it demonstrated that he had the nous to realise this was an essential means to a larger goal: convincing voters that the Labour Party was changing.

On the Friday after the general election, Tony went back to Sedgefield to address his constituency party. The question after our fourth straight election defeat, he said, was not 'change or no change, but what *type* of change?' He called for fundamental reform, with no issue off the table. Gordon, of course, agreed. As with every speech any of us made, all three of us had shared in its preparation. As I recall, it was Gordon who contributed a particularly mischievous bit of praise for John, noting that he had 'rightly said that ordinary party members must be given the power of decision-making'. The aim was to lock him in to doing something about 'one-member-one vote', or 'OMOV', and the union block vote when he became leader. But generally, Gordon was becoming a bit more cautious than Tony. While Gordon tended to shy away from explicit, public calls for change, Tony projected a sense of impatience and urgency. He believed that only by keeping the pressure on would change happen at all.

In one obvious sense, I was the junior member of the trio. Gordon and Tony had been in the Commons for nearly a decade. I was settling into my cramped office, building relationships with colleagues, getting to know the rules of Parliament and finding my feet in the Chamber. But my years at Walworth Road, my experience of Labour politics on a national level, my network of media contacts – and the fact that in some sense I had 'discovered' Gordon and Tony and promoted them – made us more like equal partners. As we planned how to maximise the media impact of our modernising agenda, I often found myself in the central role. The *Mirror*'s Westminster-watcher, David Bradshaw, would jokingly refer to Gordon as 'Peter's son number one' and Tony as 'son number two'. Overall, I think we had become more like a band of brothers.

The main frustration for all of us was John. I had described him to Hugo Young as 'Kinnock with a different face', but that told only part of the story. I had first met John in the early 1980s when I worked on Roy Hattersley's leadership campaign, of which he was a prominent supporter. When I was at Walworth Road I had found him to be genial, responsive to our requests for him to do media engagements, and a very safe pair of hands. I knew that on issues of policy, John was more engaged, and simply more interested, than Neil. But he had never said anything to me that suggested he would embrace, or risk, fundamental change. We had come much closer to victory in 1992 than in any election since 1979, and many in Labour had concluded that a steady ship, under a new captain able to steer the party clear of rocks and rough waters, would surely make port next time. I was sure John was among those who felt that way. Gordon's, Tony's and my aim was to help him in any way we could, but also to provide a modernising counterweight to his resistance to reform.

We knew that once the leadership contest was over, John would have to give both Gordon and Tony senior seats at the shadow cabinet table, and we traded on my Walworth Road experience, Tony's growing stature as a media-friendly voice and Gordon's base of support in the PLP for influence on framing John's campaign prospectus. Robin Cook was John's campaign manager, and he asked me to lunch at the Red Lion pub, the old haunt for politicians and journalists across from Downing Street, to solicit 'honest advice' on how John should proceed. I was certainly honest. I said that John had undeniable strengths. He had cabinet experience, as Trade Secretary in the Callaghan government. He projected authority and knowledge. He would be a stable and unifying force for Labour. But I said he had problems to address as well. He might well be seen as the right man for the last election, not the next one. He had yet to develop distinctive policy ideas. He was not dynamic.

Both Robin and I knew that John was likely to face only one challenger in the leadership contest: my old friend and campaign ally Bryan Gould. Since his feint at challenging Roy for the deputy leadership, however, Bryan's political stock in the party had fallen dramatically. John, in other words, was sure to win. Still, I argued that in order to bring the whole party behind him, and more importantly to take Labour forward, it was essential to use John's campaign to sketch out a coherent political project. Yes, he must be forceful in defending Labour's traditional commitment to helping the less well-off, but he must be credible on tax, and champion a modern, productive, mixed economy. I also urged him to address concerns of law and order, and to engage more with Europe and the wider world. Finally, I raised one-member-one-vote. I said John would have a real opportunity to 'decouple' Labour to some extent from the unions and create a much broader, membership-based party. I hoped, in short, that he would take the side of the modernisers.

I continued to advise Robin, particularly on media strategy, throughout the leadership campaign. The statement with which John entered the race reflected some of my suggestions. Gordon and Tony also had a considerable influence on it, as did Patricia Hewitt and one of her most promising young researchers at the IPPR, David Miliband, a son of the famous Marxist political thinker Ralph Miliband. In its broad aim, it was a modernising charter. 'Two words sum up what we must achieve: trust and transformation,' it said. 'Labour must become a party whom the British people can trust. To earn that trust, we must develop a pluralistic politics, building a consensus beyond our present ranks.' On policy, the direction of travel was also forward: on OMOV, on shifting from pure socialism to a social-democratic 'European model of capitalism', on moving from higher income taxes to targeting tax revenue on investment in health and education, and from a primary focus on redistribution to investment in jobs. There was not much detail, but John felt the specifics didn't matter for now. It was simply about setting out his stall, and winning.

When the results of the ballot among local parties, trade unions and MPs were announced on 18 July, John polled 91 per cent to Bryan's 9. I was sad for Bryan. I felt that he had become too focused on narrow economic issues, rather than the broader, more ambitious reform agenda that Gordon, Tony and I favoured. But I still respected him, still liked both him and his wife Gill very much, and believed that he had been an essential part of the changes we made at Walworth Road. Bryan's defeat was a humiliation, however, and would lead to his departure from national politics. For John, the result was a comprehensive triumph.

The next morning, however, it was not John's smiling face that adorned the cover of the *Sunday Times Magazine*. It was Tony's, above the headline 'The Leader Labour Missed'. Given my image as a master media manipulator, John's office assumed that this was a deliberately timed taunt. None too subtle, either, since the article ended with a fairly direct challenge: 'Will the new leader have the wisdom to put a man like Tony Blair into the job of Shadow Home Secretary? Or will he think that the Labour Party's woes can be cured by a change of leadership, a bit of platform fixing, and a quick saw through the branch on which reformers like Blair are now precariously perched?' Fortunately, John was sufficiently self-confident, in the flush of his almost Soviet-scale victory, to take this in his stride. He did make Tony Shadow Home Secretary, and Gordon Shadow Chancellor.

The suspicion that I had set up the *Sunday Times* piece was correct: I had suggested it to the interviewer and columnist Barbara Amiel. To me, it was part of promoting the modernising project through an MP who was critical to its success. I had done the same thing for Gordon before the election, through an *Express* writer whom I knew much better – Fiona Millar, daughter of two old London Labour friends and now the partner of Alastair Campbell. The timing of the *Sunday Times* piece, however, was not my call. Knowing its likely impact, I had tried to get it pushed back by a few weeks. Barbara and her bosses, however, wanted it to run right after John's victory.

She was clearly smitten by this most un-Labour-like of rising stars. She had accompanied Tony on a trip across England for an appearance on BBC radio's *Any Questions*, and when a minor car accident occurred in which he proved utterly unflappable, her admiration for him only increased. She spent time with him, Cherie and the children at Myrobella, their home in Sedgefield. Rereading the transcript of the taped interview, I can't help but marvel at the unformed, oddly uncomfortable voice of this early-vintage Blair. Barbara pressed him repeatedly to explain how his early years, his family and his university experiences had brought him into politics and into Labour. Tony was all ums and ahs and cul-de-sacs in trying to reply. He said at one point: 'This won't be very helpful to you. I mean, ask me some questions and I'll see if I can dig, dig back into it. It's quite difficult to analyse yourself sometimes.' Barbara reassured him. Don't worry, she said. Just talk. She would mould it into a 'narrative'. Her portrait of a new kind of Labour politician, with a provincial background and a core sense of right and wrong that rebelled against dogma and old-style party politics, practising a new kind of politics would become the template for how Labour and the country came to see Tony.

Gordon may have been unsettled by the sudden new prominence of his junior partner in reform, and the portrayal of Tony, and not him, as a future leader. If so, he didn't show it. His preoccupation with his own profile, and his occasional explosions of temper when a Tory or Labour rival beat him to a newspaper or broadcast slot, exempted Tony. Besides, the individual roles, and the pecking order, didn't matter in practical terms. John Smith was leader. He would remain so at least until the next election, and if we found a way to win it, for considerably longer. Whatever changes the three of us hoped to make would have to come through, or if necessary around, him.

A few days after returning from the summer recess, I organised a joint Brown-Blair news conference calling for a reduced-fee scheme to encourage trade union members to affiliate as individual members of Labour. It was part of our effort to keep the pressure on for action on OMOV and create a more modern, responsive, membership-based party. John's focus at this point was not root-and-branch change in Labour, but to avoid embarrassing errors and internal squabbles. It was a view that was understandably reinforced a fortnight later, on 16 September, when John Major and the Tories faced a truly cataclysmic political and economic setback. So profoundly did it shake them that it became known as 'Black Wednesday'.

The roots of the crisis went back to Mrs Thatcher's grudging entry into the European Exchange Rate Mechanism. Beyond any of the political arguments, the economics were horribly mismanaged. We entered at a rate of £1 to 2.95 deutschmarks. This grossly overvalued sterling. With the ERM setting a narrow limit on fluctuations between currencies, economists warned that the pound's value was sure to crash through the allowed floor rate of roughly 2.8 deutschmarks. From the late summer of 1992, sterling slipped downwards, and speculators began betting against the pound. By September, pressure was mounting. The Major government feared the effects on inflation, and its own political standing, if it took the most obvious counter-measure: devaluing the pound. By Black Wednesday, billions of pounds were being wagered against its ability to hold the line. Major and Chancellor Norman Lamont scrambled from one desperate decision to the next in their frantic efforts to stop the run. Billions of pounds of Treasury funds were used to prop up the pound. In a single day, interest rates were raised from 10 per cent to 12 per cent, then to 15. By evening, the battle was lost. Lamont announced that Britain was leaving the ERM.

It was the only time in my political life that I felt grateful to be in opposition. No government could emerge from such a political and economic wreck without lasting injury. For us, it had been the Winter of Discontent in 1978–79. For the Tories, it would now be Black Wednesday. In both the 1987 and 1992 election campaigns, Philip's depressingly consistent reports had singled out 'economic competence' as a core Conservative advantage and an enduring Labour weakness. Now, the issue would again be up for grabs. Yet I also knew that on the specific question of ERM membership, we too were on delicate ground. In Labour, there had been a range of opinions on whether or not to join. Gordon, Tony and I had been in favour. Not only did it chime with our broadly pro-European views, but in domestic political terms, we felt that supporting a regime of financial control would help to expunge Labour's past economic embarrassments – not just the heaps of rotting garbage during the Winter of Discontent, but Denis Healey's need in 1976 to go cap in hand for a bailout from the International Monetary Fund. Gordon, along with John, had played a critical part in the decision to back entry into the ERM, by throwing his weight behind it in the shadow cabinet. Very little thought was given to the level of sterling's entry. It was the politics that mattered, the need for Labour to demonstrate financial discipline.

Largely for the same reason, John and Gordon had opposed devaluing the pound in the run-up to Black Wednesday. After the currency crashed, both of them scored telling political hits on the government for getting Britain into the crisis. They could hardly have failed to do so. The Tories were in collective shock, and pretty much defenceless. But Gordon, in particular, was shaken. Repeatedly in the days that followed, he would agonise to me over the damage he feared his position on ERM might do to his political future. 'It will hurt me badly,' he kept saying. 'How can I repair this?' I said I was fairly certain that the real political victims would be Major and Lamont, and that he would be a footnote at most to the calamity. That turned out to be true, but one aspect of the ERM débâcle did have a lasting effect on him. His horror at how quickly the pound had collapsed, and how powerless the government was to do anything about it, stayed with him for years afterwards. I am sure it affected his view on joining the ERM's successor, the single European currency.

The dozens of conversations I had with Gordon over the fallout from Black Wednesday were typical. With Tony as well, there was hardly an issue on which the two of us – often the three of us – did not speak, consult, brainstorm and agree a way forward. I was also increasingly involved in their political operations. I devoted more of my efforts to Gordon. He was the more demanding, and frankly the more needy. He had risen higher, and generated more resentment and rivalry, than Tony. He also had the more difficult shadow brief.

Home Affairs was in every way a perfect fit for Tony. Barbara Amiel's profile may have woven a 'narrative' around his life story, but it was an accurate reflection of where he had come from and who he was. His instincts led him to believe that individuals mattered more than vested interests, including central government, and that judgements of right and wrong mattered more than party dogma. His political acumen led him to realise that repositioning Labour on law and order was an important way of reconnecting with voters. Facing a fellow barrister, Home Secretary Michael Howard, across the dispatch box in the Commons, Tony was in his element: self-confident in his argument, easy-going and effective in his presentation.

His office was also perfectly geared to provide the advice, support and teamwork needed to maximise his strengths. The fulcrum was Anji Hunter. A friend from his teenage years, she was as close to him, as instinctively on the same wavelength, as anyone except his wife – a constant, and ultimately unsustainable, source of friction with Cherie from the moment Tony entered Downing Street. Anji could gauge Tony's mood, anticipate problems, sense his best interests, and ensure that he performed at the height of his abilities. Though not a political professional, she had a natural sense for how politics was done. She was unfailingly discreet, and almost impossible for even the most hard-boiled party veteran or lobby reporter to dislike. Most important was what she was not: a lifelong Labour tribalist. A Sussex girl from a Tory background, she was a window onto the concerns and aspirations of the 'middle England' voter whom Labour appeared to have lost for ever. From the moment I met Anji in the 1980s, she and I had become close allies. Tony was also immensely fortunate in a pair of younger, rawer aides. The first was James Purnell, a bright Balliol PPE student who did research for him on a volunteer basis until leaving for the IPPR after the 1992 election. The second, a friend of James's whom he persuaded Tony to hire as his replacement, was Tim Allan.

Gordon had a more difficult challenge in overhauling Labour's economic policy, especially with criticism and resistance from the left as he tried to move us away from simply taxing and spending. He clearly needed as formidable a team as Tony if he was to succeed. To the extent that he had any fixed political support beyond me and Tony, he had come to rely on Nick Brown, the Newcastle MP who had also entered the Commons in 1983. Nick was a fiercely loyal protégé, but he was not, and could not be, a mainstay of Gordon's office.

The first, crucial, step in filling that need came the day after Neil announced his resignation. Sue Nye came to see me. She was depressed about Neil leaving, and disheartened about Labour's future prospects. She was determined to find a way to rescue something for his legacy as leader, but unable to see a way forward under John. 'I can't – I won't – go to work for him!' she said. It was not just that John had often disrespected or undermined Neil in his final years as leader; she didn't trust him to build on the changes Neil had begun. 'Why don't you work for Gordon?' I suggested. Though she did not know him well, I told her she would find him – in every way that John was not – committed to modernisation. For her part, she could provide the experience and the ballast Gordon would need as the most senior counterweight to John in the shadow cabinet.

When I went to Gordon with the idea, he was delighted – with one caveat. He didn't have the money. Fortunately, with Gavyn's income, that wasn't an obstacle, and Sue went to work for him four days a week, unpaid. She became as indispensable to Gordon as Anji was to Tony. In some ways, more so. No matter how many aides came and went in the years ahead, Sue was the constant, the rock on which everything rested. She made things work. She built relationships with a changing cast of strong, and not always easy, personalities.

There were two in particular whom I also had a role in bringing in after the 1992 election, vetting them for Gordon before they were hired. The first was a full-time press aide. I urged Gordon that he needed someone not only to handle, but to ration and calibrate, his appetite for media opportunities. I settled on an almost aggressively self-assured, tough-talking operator named Charlie Whelan. He had been policy and media aide to Jimmy Airlie, the Scottish Communist who was one of the leading figures in the Amalgamated Engineering and Electrical Union. Charlie impressed me as the only trade union press officer who supported one-member-one-vote. When I invited him for tea in the Commons, his wide-boy manner put me off a bit. I thought, however, that the chalk-and-cheese combination of him and Gordon might work. No less self-assured was a young *Financial Times* writer I interviewed as Gordon's economic policy adviser. Bright, and keenly aware of it, Ed Balls was a Harvard postgraduate protégé of Bill Clinton's top economic advisers. He was an obvious admirer of Gordon, anxious to help him change and eventually lead Labour. Both of these choices would come back to haunt me – and Tony too – in later years. At the time, they seemed to me precisely the kind of back-up Gordon needed.

All of us needed Philip Gould. He had been shattered by the 1992 election defeat. He was especially upset when John proceeded to wind down the SCA and downgrade the importance of focus groups, research and analysis. John's view was that while the operation Philip and I had set up may have benefited Neil, it was now surplus to requirements. In September, at the invitation of Bill Clinton's campaign team, Philip spent a month in the States. He went back again for the final days before the presidential election in November, and had a ringside seat for Clinton's victory over George Bush, putting an end to a quarter-century of nearly unbroken Republican Party rule. He returned home re-energised, having witnessed not only a state-of-the-art campaign, but the policy choices the Democrats had made to regain the trust of the electorate. Clinton was a 'new' Democrat. He had moved to the centre ground, reconnecting with middle-class and middle-American voters. This was precisely the kind of 'new Labour' shift Philip and I had been urging under Neil. Philip duly made his pitch to John. He hoped that his plea for similar change would be especially compelling in the light of obvious lessons from our own latest defeat.

The Fabian Society had just published a damning post-election report, by the Labour MP and writer Giles Radice, on our prospects of winning over upwardly-mobile voters in the south and south-east of England next time round. The pamphlet became seminal. It identified a stubborn 'southern discomfort' about Labour. Voters were becoming increasingly uneasy about Tory rule, and signs of economic trouble, even before the ERM disaster. But they had done well under the Conservatives. 'Labour, whilst thought to be caring and "fair", is seen as the party that is most likely to "take things away", the report said. We were viewed as the party that 'looked after losers, not the ordinary man'. We did not 'respect, nurture, reward or even understand' ambition. Philip sensed little enthusiasm from Labour's new leader for a Clinton-style project, but he did continue to offer research and analysis for John's office when asked. I too was ready to contribute. At one point, I wrote to John with suggestions on sprucing up his media image and raising his public profile. In reply, I received a polite note showing little interest and even less urgency.

Almost by default, by the end of 1992 Philip, Gordon, Tony and I began laying the foundations for a new Labour Party on our own. It was exhilarating. We had a sense of mission. But that mission involved somehow shifting others in the party, and ultimately John, to a recognition that Labour needed to change radically, and visibly. John was solid and sober-looking, in a way that Neil was not. He was articulate, self-assured. He was not John Major, but he was not Bill Clinton either.

We were not the only ones with misgivings about how far, and how fast, John could take Labour. His satisfaction rating, peaking at plus 16 per cent in October, had fallen by year's end to plus 4. It was still way above Major's, at *minus* 30 per cent, but the trend was hardly cause for New Year optimism. Philip's focus groups found that John did have strong assets. He was seen as decent, honest, truthful. He was unblemished by scandal. But voters also viewed him as austere and dour. In a strategy memo for John's office, Philip cautioned that however great the Tory government's travails, our support was under pressure from demographic and ideological changes in Britain. If Labour was to win a future election, it would have to 'move forward just to stand still'.

Tony *was* moving forward. He was not just making a name for himself through performances on BBC's *Question Time*, but was making an impact in the Commons. He was winning the policy argument against Michael Howard. In Labour's internal debate, he was gaining new prominence. The main immediate issue at the beginning of 1993 was one-member-one-vote. John had now committed himself to the principle, and to putting a new system to the party conference in the autumn. He was getting cold feet, however. He did not relish a fight with the unions. The details were being thrashed out in a 'review committee'. Tony was its most prominent shadow cabinet member. In the committee and then in public, he became an unflinching advocate for OMOV.

He also became the lightning rod for opposition to the wider modernising message. Clare Short, another member of the Commons class of 1983, was especially colourful in her scaremongering, speaking darkly of 'infiltration' by modernisers in the upper reaches of the party, and warning that if it wasn't stopped, Labour would be turned into some glitzy, policy-light shadow of its former self. John Prescott, a weightier figure than Clare, echoed her call to arms, saying it was essential to guard the 'tradition' and 'values' of Labour. The more such criticism mounted, the more determined and self-confident Tony seemed to become. In one TV appearance, he was challenged to answer accusations of a modernising 'conspiracy' to sacrifice the soul of the party. He responded that there *was* a conspiracy: to make the Labour Party capable of winning the next general election. He stood firm on the need to end the block vote, saying that Labour did not just need a 'process of adjustment', but a wholesale project for renewal, moving beyond the 'old battle of public versus private sector' and embracing economic opportunity, redefining the welfare system with the aim of getting people off benefits and into work, and shifting power from Westminster into the hands of individual citizens.

A major accusation against the modernisers was that we had fallen under the spell of Bill Clinton. This was true. Tony, Gordon and I all visited Washington early in 1993. They went first, just after the New Year, while I went on a separate parliamentary visit. The day before Gordon and Tony left for Washington, I was working late in my office when John called, furious. He had heard about the trip. 'I know what their game is!' he shouted at me down the phone. 'Well, I can tell you we don't need any of this fucking Clinton stuff over here. They're just drawing attention to themselves, and rocking the boat.' In fact, all three of us came back from meeting members of the Clinton team convinced, as Philip had been, that their experience had something to teach us. From memory, it was Gordon who first seized on one Clinton campaign message, on law and order, although Tony would soon make it his own. It encapsulated the Democrats' success in achieving something we had yet to do: convincing voters that a left-wing emphasis on the social roots of crime did not mean downplaying its impact, or excusing criminals. 'Tough on crime, tough on the causes of crime' became Tony's refrain.

But the moment he really broke though as the leading advocate of change in Labour came in February 1993. It was not a catchy slogan that made the impact, but a considered response to a horrible tragedy: the murder on Merseyside of a two-year-old toddler named James Bulger. The little boy had wandered off from his mother in a shopping centre and was led away by a pair of ten-year-olds who killed him and left his mutilated corpse by a railway track. Tony, like everyone in Britain, was shocked by the crime. He agonised over what he could, or should, say as a politician. In fact he was still on the phone to me, adjusting the words, when he arrived at Wellingborough station to deliver a speech there a week later. He was not sure it was quite right. We made further small changes, but I told him that what really mattered was the theme and the tone of his remarks. They had to show the horror he felt, while also drawing lessons from it. I thought his speech did both. It was as powerful for what it did not say as for what it did. There was no traditional Labour talk about how deprivation fed crime, no calls for government to fix the environment which bred it. He used words rooted not so much in policy as morality – words to which non-politicians could relate, because they felt the same way. 'We hear of crimes so horrific they provoke anger and disbelief in equal proportions,' he said. 'These are the ugly manifestations of a society that is becoming unworthy of that name.'

Gordon, meanwhile, was struggling. Since I had first begun working with him at Walworth Road, he had become a master of the television and radio interview. But 'master' was the right word. He initially won praise as a refreshingly well-briefed, disciplined and commanding voice. But by the time of the 1992 election, he had begun drawing criticism for his relentless repetition of the soundbite *du jour*. Part of the problem had to do with the constraints that came with his job. He could not at this stage credibly set out a Labour alternative to Tory policy. Not only was the economic climate too uncertain, but political support within the party was too fragile for radical new moves on how we would tax or spend. He was left to emphasise a broader, long-term change in priorities – a shift towards training and education to create a more modern, competitive economy. It was a serious, distinctive message, but it was never going to be sexy, and it became less so with each reiteration. When media criticism began to stray into ridicule, I knew it was time for Gordon to pull back.

One major reason I recruited Charlie Whelan was to organise a new media strategy, designed to maximise opportunities for Gordon to say something new to an audience primed to listen. We limited Gordon's appearances on his favourite platform, Radio 4's *Today* programme. His media currency was still high, but we had to make sure it wasn't devalued. I was worried that this alone would not reburnish his image. The challenge was to find a way of making sure his real strengths came through. I began briefing the lobby reporters to try to begin turning around the perception of him. I explained the economic and political reasons Gordon could not announce major changes in policy at this stage. The last time we had done that, when John Smith was Shadow Chancellor, we had locked ourselves into spending and tax commitments that helped lose us the election. The briefing helped a bit, but the real problem was that, unlike Tony, Gordon was at his best in Commons combat with the Conservatives, having made his name by landing blows on Nigel Lawson. Tony's particular strength was in communicating with voters. I shared my concern with Roger Liddle, who put his finger on the contrast. Gordon's aggressive style, he said, grated on the public: 'In Labour, the way to the top has always been through brilliant attacks on the Tories. But there comes a point when it is necessary to speak to the country as well as the party. Tony has done this brilliantly on crime.'

The media were beginning to come to a similar conclusion about Tony's and Gordon's respective strengths. After the Commons broke for its summer recess in 1993, the BBC political correspondent Nick Jones used a *Guardian* piece to contrast Labour's two leading modernisers. Anticipating that some future Labour leadership contest might become a straight fight between Gordon and Tony, he said that while the pair were cigarette-paper close on policy, they were strikingly different in how they communicated. Both were high-profile. Both had been 'star pupils of the Peter Mandelson finishing school' in media presentation, and had been 'ruthlessly promoted' by me. But while he portrayed Gordon as an obsessive seeker of the next media opportunity, the next news peg on which to hang a soundbite, he had noticed that Tony was resisting the quick media hit in favour of the longer, more considered interview. He saw the Mandelson 'influence' in this, and he was right. In fact, I was pressing Gordon to move in that direction as well, but as Nick was right to point out, his appetite for seizing the opportunity for any media hit on the Tories risked masking his strengths and magnifying his weaknesses: 'All too often, Brown's delivery looks wooden and unsympathetic.'

None of this needed matter in the long run. As I explained repeatedly to an increasingly unsettled Gordon, there would be time to recalibrate. The nearer we got to the next election – 1996 at the earliest, more likely 1997 if Major was hanging on for his political life – the more Gordon would be able to move on to hard policy, and a more thoughtful, engaging message on how a Labour government would revitalise the economy. I said he must accept that there would be short-term setbacks.

That much became clear at the 1993 party conference. John did go ahead with a proposal to change the party's voting system, setting up a tricameral system under which individually polled union members would account for one-third of the vote in elections for party office, with MPs and local constituency parties and affiliated political organisations making up the rest. With Gordon, and more openly Tony, having been making most of the running on OMOV, both of them fell down the order in the next elections for the shadow cabinet. Gordon had become used to winning the top spot: now he finished in fourth place. Tony was sixth. Still, sooner or later, I told myself and both of them, the need for Labour genuinely to change would win out.

Gordon's and Tony's adjacent offices on Parliament Street were a short walk away from mine in Norman Shaw South, and it was a walk I made at least once or twice each day. When I arrived, Gordon would almost always be tapping away furiously at his computer, usually getting out a fresh press release and driving his staff to provide whatever bit of research or writing he needed to polish off his handiwork. Tony was quite literally more laid-back. He would lean back in his chair with his feet on the desk, not a computer in sight, and eagerly try out on me his latest idea about Labour's policies or political positioning. Whether with his staff or talking to me alone, he always seemed to see the lighter side of politics. He was quick to poke fun: at the Tories, at Labour 'dinosaurs', and at himself. I was equally close to both of them, and believed that each of them had enormous strengths.

Both were committed to a thoroughly new kind of Labour Party, and to getting it into government. While they shared a sense of urgency about this, however, Gordon was not so sure that the rest of the party would get on board. He always told me that we would have to find a way to bring them along, no matter how difficult that was, and no matter how long it took. Tony was much more unruffled. He never explicitly mentioned leaving politics, but it was apparent to me from the many hours I spent with him in the Commons, and at his home in Islington or in Sedgefield, that if Labour didn't modernise it would at some point have to do without the services of Anthony Charles Lynton Blair. In Barbara Amiel's gushing profile, she had quoted Cherie as telling her that while Tony was ambitious, he had often said that politics was not his whole life. He was a qualified lawyer. He and Cherie had three children. He knew there was something else in life, Cherie said. 'If he wanted to, he could walk away tomorrow.' I never got a similar sense from Gordon. Partly, perhaps, this was because he was not yet married. He did not have children. It would not be fair to say, as his detractors would later suggest, that this meant he had no interests outside politics. He did love football, or at least Raith Rovers. He hoovered up books – by far the majority of them political and economic tomes, but not all. Still, it was true that while I could imagine Tony as something other than a Labour MP, it was impossible to say the same of Gordon.

Tony was not going to walk away soon, however. He was enjoying politics, and he knew he was good at it. In his view, the very difficulties we were encountering in pressing for reform validated the task.

He sensed that by challenging Labour articles of faith, we would have a better chance of convincing the people who really mattered – the voters – that the party was changing. In a speech after the conference, he launched his latest initiative to redefine Labour's identity, on an issue that had been almost forever Tory. Ostensibly talking about crime and social issues, he focused on family. 'The right lays claim to being the guardians of family values,' he said. 'The left, in the past, was sometimes perceived as treating the issue as irrelevant or even, in extreme cases, as politically incorrect.' But, he continued: 'The truth is that families matter, and family breakdown is an important underlying cause of delinquent behaviour. Parental guidance is vital.'

Driving home the theme at an IPPR conference a few weeks later, he said that rather than just take potshots at Tory morality initiatives, the left should join the argument. 'The success of the right's strategy depends on the left living up to its caricature.' Families did matter. So did proper behaviour. Society and community, in Tony's view, had the role of promoting a balance between individual rights and responsibilities.

By the end of the year, the impact of such ventures onto unfamiliar ground was becoming clear. A *New Statesman* piece observed that Tony was 'no longer regarded as the enthusiastic young pretender of the Kinnock era, who bounced his way on to Labour's front bench and Britain's television studios in the 1980s. He is now by far and away the man most likely to be the next leader of the Labour Party.'

Tony took the plaudits in his stride. When he, Gordon and I met in our huddle at the end of a day's business in the Commons the feeling was still very much all for one and one for all. Gordon and Tony had not shared an office for some time: Gordon had by now moved to 7 Millbank, where I followed him, while Tony remained at 1 Parliament Street. We felt that any rising tide around Tony would lift all modernising boats. It might change the political weather in the party, gradually pushing John and the rest of the shadow cabinet towards an openly reformist manifesto in time for the next election. To the extent that any of us thought about what might come after that, Gordon and I certainly still assumed he would succeed John as leader. At that stage, I think Tony did as well. And other MPs seemed to share this view.

But I suppose it was inevitable that Tony's greater ability to connect with the public could not fail to have an effect – not only on media commentators, but on Tony too. From early in 1993, I got the first sense that he was beginning to wonder whether Gordon's difficulties with this kind of engagement might hamper him as leader. I was chatting with Tony one Sunday in the park behind his Islington home when he suddenly mentioned that he'd been talking to Derry Irvine, his old law-chambers patron and future Lord Chancellor, who had made an 'interesting point', observing that despite all Gordon's strengths, he lacked something. There was an element missing. Perhaps it was his all-consuming appetite for politics, the fact that he was unmarried, his inability to relax or to encourage others to relax around him. Tony said he had been struck by the comment, and that, thinking it over, he was 'just not sure that Gordon has got quite what it takes to be leader'.

I was startled. It had never occurred to me that Gordon wasn't up to leading Labour, nor that he would not at some stage do so. Tony's remarks left me unsettled and confused as I turned them over in my head on the way home, and for days afterwards. Yet, oddly, not with any lasting effect. In the year or so that followed, Tony never came back to our conversation. I didn't either. I think I assumed that when the succession did finally become an issue, it might, or might not, matter. Gordon would be in a different place. So would Tony. So would I. For now, it was not really relevant.

But then, quite suddenly, all of that changed.

5

An Impossible Choice

The first sign that 12 May 1994 would be different from any other Thursday came shortly before nine in the morning, when the phone rang in my flat in central London. It was Fiona Millar, Alastair Campbell's partner. She asked if I knew where Alastair was; his news-desk wanted to pass on an urgent message about a 'big story'. Fiona's assumption that I would be able to find him was hardly surprising, given how close I was to both of them and their young children. When Neil was leader, I was at Walworth Road and Alastair at the *Mirror*, no three-way media relationship could have been closer. Neil had stepped down now, I was in the Commons, and after the death of Alastair's *Mirror* proprietor Robert Maxwell he had joined the colour tabloid *Today*. But we still spoke often. Nor was I surprised by Fiona's coyness over the 'big story' that was about to break. I had known her for two decades. She was smart. She could be charming. But I don't think I have known a non-politician so self-disciplined, or so tough. Though I was curious, I knew that if the story was really as big as she said, it would not be long before I heard about it.

Ten minutes later, I did. Tony rang from Aberdeen. He was on a campaign visit to Scotland for the June European elections. I had never heard him so sombre, or so shocked. He said John Smith had had a second heart attack. Tony was no less reticent than Fiona about the details, having been sworn to secrecy by John's office. But that John's condition was serious was clear, both from Tony's voice, and from the question he asked me next. 'What should I do?' he said. I told him

I thought he should get on the next plane to London, which he did.

I drove to the Commons. It was bucketing down with rain. By the time I arrived, I had heard the news confirmed on the radio: John had been pronounced dead at Bart's hospital in central London. I was in shock. I had known and worked with John for nearly ten years, and I considered him a friend. Despite his earlier heart attack, he had not been visibly unwell. Now he was gone.

With Tony heading back to London, my first impulse was to phone Gordon, who asked me to join him at his second-floor flat in nearby Great Peter Street. When I got there, he seemed badly shaken. He had a bond with John that neither Tony nor I had. He had heard the news from Murray Elder, John's chief of staff and a friend of Gordon's from their Fife schooldays. John's death was especially crushing for Gordon, who had been with him the night before, at a party fund-raising dinner.

Gordon's grief was real, but Gordon the politician kicked into action as soon as I arrived. To be fair, the same was true of Tony. And of me. We were distressed by the death of a colleague whom we had known well and worked with closely. The suddenness of it made it worse. But both personally and politically, all three of us had been having difficulty in our relations with John. We had become convinced that he would never deliver radical change to the party, and that the best we could do was to try to nudge him step by step in that direction. Since party conference the previous autumn, there had been some degree of coming together between the leader and us. He was wary of the modernisers. He saw us as an annoyance, always 'rocking the boat'. Yet he shared our concern that Labour was failing to break through in the south of England, and did now seem reluctantly prepared to accept, or co-opt, some of the changes we were advocating. When Philip Gould had carried out his latest research among Tory waverers at the end of 1993, the results had been bleak. 'Not one of those interviewed said that they would now vote Labour,' he said. 'Little in terms of the electorate's perception of the party has changed since before 1987.'

I arrived at Gordon's flat at around 10.30 a.m. His then girlfriend, the television presenter Sheena McDonald, was clearing away the usual piles of newspapers and policy documents. She left to get sandwiches. By the time she returned, Gordon was in full flow about what the party would, and should, do next. Instantly focusing on the succession, he calculated that both Robin Cook and John Prescott would be tempted to go for the leadership. He was sure neither had a chance. It was striking that he did not mention the possibility of Tony's name entering the frame.

On several occasions, with no obvious effect, I told him that once Tony got to London the three of us must meet. This was not because I assumed Tony would stand, but because the three of us *always* met. On any issue of importance, we always agreed a common strategy, and it was unthinkable that with the prospect of finally making a modernising breakthrough, we would not do so now. I do not think Gordon consciously wanted to exclude Tony. He felt that Labour's opportunity for real change, the modernisers' time to lead, had arrived. He assumed that, with Tony and me at his side, he would stand for the leadership. And that he would win. They were assumptions I shared at first. It was going to take time for the party to come to terms with John's death, and to decide what, and who, came next. Yet I expected Gordon to succeed him, with Tony as Shadow Chancellor. Gordon and I agreed to talk later in the day.

In the afternoon, I joined a crowded Commons to hear moving tributes from MPs of all parties. Partly, this was due to the transformation that a politician's passing so often exerts even on those who had opposed or criticised him in life. It was a process that would be felt far beyond Westminster in the days ahead. A voting public with whom John had never really connected as leader took him to their hearts. The outpouring of goodwill and grief reflected genuine strengths in John: his sense of decency, his reassuringly avuncular presence, his seriousness. For MPs, there was special appreciation of the fact that he had been an extraordinarily gifted Commons speaker.

160

His barrister's talent for argument was leavened – at least if you were not John Major – by a delightfully incisive wit.

After the tributes, there was an unusually muted tone among the lobby journalists I met on my way out of the Chamber. Inevitably, however, they began pressing me on the succession – on 'what Gordon and Tony will do'. This planted the first doubt in my mind about Gordon's assumptions, and mine, that he would become Labour's next leader. I had expected him to be the default modernising choice, yet there was an even-handedness about the media's questions. Several journalists asked me to comment on the Tories' concern that if Tony stood, he would be a more formidable opponent. I replied with uncharacteristic reluctance, but was soon confronted by a more serious signal that Gordon's succession could not be taken for granted.

As I was leaving the House I ran into Derry Irvine. Derry was extremely close to Tony, and to Cherie as well. Both had started their legal careers in his chambers. But he got on well with Gordon. Through Tony, I had become very friendly with Derry as well. 'What do you think about the leadership?' he asked. When I mumbled something non-committal, he said, repeatedly, 'It has to be Tony.' I replied that it would be wrong for us to assume that. 'Tony and Gordon have to talk,' I said. But it was clear that if Derry was pressing Tony's case with me, he must have done the same with Tony – and that Tony, in all likelihood, was at least considering running for the leadership.

Given my response, Derry assumed that I was backing Gordon, and that message quickly got back to Tony. He phoned me, and said he wanted to talk urgently, but that the last thing either of us needed was to be seen chatting by journalists. At Anji Hunter's suggestion, we arranged to meet in one of the Commons division lobbies, which were sure to be empty now that the House had adjourned. At around five o'clock, Tony strode in from one end of the corridor, and I from the other. He was still wearing the cream-coloured suit in which he had been filmed at Aberdeen airport before returning to London. We spoke for only a few minutes, but there was little doubt the political wind had changed, significantly since my talk with Gordon. Tony said a number of shadow cabinet colleagues had approached him with pledges of support if he stood. In an echo of our conversation a year earlier in the park near his home, he said that he sensed 'strong hostility' to Gordon. 'What do you think?' he asked. I was distraught at the prospect of a contest between the two of them. Obviously, Tony had every right to consider himself as a leadership candidate, and I told him so. But when he indicated that he had pretty much decided to stand, and that he was not going to bow out in Gordon's favour, I could not bring myself to say I would support him. I did agree, unhesitatingly, to his request that I do nothing, in talking up Gordon to reporters, to damage his own prospects.

That evening, Gordon and Tony met. Tony told me afterwards that Gordon began by saying he intended to run for the leadership. Tony replied that while he understood, he was not going to rule himself out. Since I was not there, I cannot say whether voices were raised. I imagine the tone was more funereal than furious, as Labour's two closest allies and friends came to terms with the fact that, at least for now, they were rivals. Whatever frustration or anger Gordon felt – and it would not be long before both burst to the surface – his initial feeling would have been shock. There had never been any formal agreement about a future leadership contest: we had all assumed that John would be leader at least until the next election. But Gordon had been the senior member of our trio for so long that it simply didn't occur to him that his claim would not take precedence, or that Tony would be anything but supportive.

Worse for Gordon, he had not registered how dramatically Tony's profile, in both the party and the country, had risen. Nor did he understand the effect that events the last time the succession issue had come up, after Neil resigned in 1992, had had on Tony. It was not so much Gordon's decision not to stand for leader against John Smith, though Tony did come to feel that was a mistake, as Gordon's effectively pressurising him out of entering the race for deputy leader. I am sure that was one reason Tony was determined not to be dissuaded this time. In any case, by the time I arrived in Gordon's office early on Friday morning, there could be little doubt that he not only faced a battle if he ran for the leadership, but that it was a battle he might well not win. An early danger signal had come from Alastair, on *Newsnight* the previous evening. Much of the interview had been about John, but when he was asked who he thought should be Labour's next leader, Alastair had replied, without hesitation, 'Tony Blair.'

The Friday papers were no more encouraging for Gordon. Most were leaning towards Tony. The *Independent* ran a front-page leader saying he was the man to take Labour forward. Gordon was furious at Alastair, and seething about the press. He wanted action. He said he could not understand how on earth this was happening. Very calmly, I told him we needed to work out a strategy to put him back on track. Regaining his focus, Gordon agreed that we had to accept Tony was now a candidate. But he was still confident that he would emerge as the winner, and suggested we put out the line that while there were two modernising 'contenders', they would not stand against each other. One would emerge as the candidate, with the other's support.

As soon as I left, I phoned Alastair. When I took him to task for having openly backed Tony, he said that while he hadn't expected to be asked about the succession, he had simply been stating the obvious. He did agree to help me brief lobby colleagues that only one modernising candidate would stand, and I phoned Tony to tell him what we were doing. He was entirely comfortable with it. I added that besides delivering my message for the weekend papers, I planned to 'even things up' by pressing Gordon's case with the media. Tony said he understood, and merely repeated his request that I do nothing to talk him down, to which I again readily agreed.

A number of the Saturday papers picked up the line that only one moderniser would stand. The *Sunday Times* went further, splashing on a 'secret pact' between Gordon and Tony about how they would handle the succession. In my TV appearances over the weekend, I tried to level the playing field. Careful to endorse neither Gordon nor Tony, I pressed the case for a 'modernisers' candidate' who would ensure we appealed to a broader, countrywide base.

When I spoke to Gordon by phone after reviewing the newspapers on *Frost on Sunday*, he was fuming over the *Sunday Times* splash. At this stage, he did not blame me, as he knew that it was he himself who had suggested the 'agreed candidate' strategy. But there were rumblings of discontent from those around him, especially Charlie Whelan and Nick Brown. They were upset that in my TV interviews I had pointed out that one of Labour's challenges would be to increase its support in the south of England. This was hardly news, but Gordon's aides took it as a clever, coded effort to drum up support for Tony. In fact, although I talked to Tony by phone regularly in the days that followed, I was very much on the outside of his fast-growing campaign, looking in. In any case, it was becoming clear that the real problem for Gordon was something beyond my power, or the media's, to influence. A series of polls in the Sunday press showed swelling support for Tony: among voters, party members, even trade unionists.

From first thing on Monday morning, I began shuttling between Gordon's office and the lobby journalists in the Commons, trying to do what I could to turn things around. That afternoon I wrote Gordon a note summarising where I thought things were headed. I began by reassuring him that there was sympathy among the journalists for his predicament: 'You are seen as the biggest intellectual force and strategic thinker the party has. Most people say there is no one to rival your political capacity.' But I did not hide from him the obstacles his candidacy would face: 'Nobody is saying you are not capable, or appropriate, as leader; merely that the timing is bad for you and that you have vocal enemies or that you have presentational difficulties.'

The main problem for Gordon was that he was not seen as the front-runner. One of Tony's obvious advantages – his 'southern appeal' – was something he would find difficult to neutralise or deny. The situation might be recoverable, but I was blunt about what I thought it would take: 'The only way to overcome the media resistance is to mount a massive and sustained briefing which concentrates on your political skills, ability to unite and manage all sides of the party, dominance in the House, a blend of party transition and modernising agenda.' I told him I had encountered little difficulty in getting that message across so far, but in order to have real impact, it would 'have to be greatly escalated, begun immediately and, I'm afraid, only done by explicitly weakening Tony's position'. I could not guarantee that it would work. There was a chance that it might, but he now had to make a choice: either 'escalate rapidly', or 'implement a strategy to exit with enhanced position, strength and respect'.

It was hugely frustrating. Gordon believed I could 'fix' anything in the press, but as I had learned at Walworth Road, there comes a point when your product, or lack of it, outweighs even the most deft presentation. I talked up Gordon's strengths, especially on the economy, the issue that had most undermined Labour at the polls and that most often decided elections, and I extolled his seriousness as a politician. I believed what I was saying. I also felt enormous pain for Gordon. He had spent his entire adult life involved, enmeshed, in politics. The leadership was the prize he had most coveted. Now I sensed it was slipping away from him.

Others had been pushing me almost from the start towards that conclusion. On the afternoon of John's death, I spoke with Gerald Kaufman in his Commons office. Gerald could be prickly with colleagues, but I liked and respected him, especially for the way he had driven through our new defence policy. 'Look, Peter, I think highly of both Gordon and Tony,' he said. 'But Tony has the stronger appeal. He's the game-changer.' Later, I got a call on my mobile that had even greater impact. It was from Paul McKinney, a fellow Scot of Gordon's who had worked for him as a researcher and executive assistant. He clearly felt uncomfortable about what he was about to say. He said that he knew Gordon expected to succeed John: 'But you've got to understand that Tony is better equipped. Gordon just isn't right for it.'

My own assistant, Derek Draper, whose political judgement I respected, was even more convinced. He had Brown connections of his own, having begun his political career, after Manchester University, as constituency assistant for Nick Brown. I took an immediate liking to Derek. He was self-confident, garrulous, desperate to see Labour succeed, and sure that unless the party changed, it would never do so. He had an ability to get straight to the point on any political question, with great clarity of argument. The first thing I did on entering the Commons was to hire him. Now, he told me he understood my determination to help Gordon, but he said Tony was the obvious leader, and Gordon had no chance of winning. Derek had seen the impact Tony was making on his own friends. They admired him; they liked him; they wanted to follow him. Gordon simply didn't sway people in the same way. 'You've got to face reality,' he said.

Derek did loyally help me in my efforts to keep Gordon's name in play, at least at the beginning. At one stage, however, Gordon asked him to phone a couple of dozen key young Labour people in constituencies around the country to gauge whom they wanted for leader, him or Tony. Derek made the calls, and then took the results in to Gordon. Every single one of those asked had plumped for Tony. 'This is not what people are telling me!' Gordon shouted. He slammed his fist down on his desk, causing a pencil to shoot up into Derek's face, narrowly missing his eye. Derek was a slightly less enthusiastic campaigner after that.

On Monday morning came a final signal that the fight was almost certainly hopeless. It was from Gordon's close friend and loyal supporter, the Glasgow MP Donald Dewar. We met in the cafeteria in 1 Parliament Street, across the street from the Commons. Donald would have liked more than anything to be able to help Gordon become Labour leader. 'But it can't be done,' he said. 'Tony has got a commanding lead. It's not going to evaporate. There's strong support for him in the PLP. Gordon's simply not going to catch up.'

By mid-week, I had received much the same message from the two fixed points on my own political radar, Philip Gould and Roger

Liddle. Both of them knew I was agonising over how to help Gordon, and both had concluded it was a lost cause. For Roger, had John not died, and the succession come later, maybe things would have been different. But the timing was wrong. Philip's reading of the polls, and his commitment to seeing real change in the party, told him the same thing. 'Post-John Smith there is only one viable strategic opportunity for Labour,' he wrote to me. 'That is to become a party of change, momentum and dynamism. This is most certainly the mood of the country, and probably of a majority of the party. At this time, through luck and circumstances, Tony exemplifies this mood more completely than any Labour leader since Wilson. Gordon has prodigious strengths, but will be seen as an interim leader, halfway between John Smith and Tony Blair.' If Tony ended up standing aside in favour of Gordon, Philip predicted three consequences: 'Enormous disappointment in the country and the party; a backlash against Labour and a belief that it is prepared to take only half a step forward; and a backlash against Gordon as the candidate who stopped Tony, which would harm Gordon immensely.'

Gordon was growing more and more frustrated. He kept saying there had to be a way to turn the situation around. I tried to get him to realise how steep a climb he faced. We needed more than briefings: we needed to be able to demonstrate support. Stung, he replied, 'I've got plenty of support.' When I asked him to help me draw up a list, it did not go much beyond a few trade union general secretaries and party officials. The only firm backers he could name in the shadow cabinet were the Shadow Agriculture spokesman, Ron Davies, and Donald Dewar.

By early the next week, after another disheartening set of newspaper stories, I concluded that there was no way Gordon could win. I felt that the best I could now do for him was to find the least damaging way out, and I set out his options. He could stay in the race, and I would help him if he decided to do so, although I added that he must accept that there was no way he could win without damaging Tony in the process. The alternative was to withdraw, with the maximum of political credit and gain. If that was his choice, I would work hard to see that he emerged with both.

My thinking at the time was that if Gordon did decide to get into a bare-knuckle fight with Tony, the only result would be damage to his own image, by making him seem more interested in his own ambitions than in the modernising cause. I also thought it might leave the path open for a credible run by Robin or John Prescott, who were as cautious about change as John had been. I am sure Gordon recognised this, but that did not make it any easier for him to come to terms with it. His initial response was to rely less and less on me for his media briefings, and to turn instead to Charlie.

When reporters began to tell me Charlie was feeding them a litany of reasons why Tony wasn't fit to lead the party, I began to despair. Some way had to be found to airlift Gordon out of the contest with his image, dignity and political capital intact. But until he himself reached that conclusion, the best thing I could do was to keep my head down: keep briefing a message of unity to the media, keep talking to both Gordon and Tony, but not involve myself in Tony's operation or drum up support for him. Not only would that be unfair, and hurtful to Gordon, it would delay the endgame, the inevitable exit which the three of us would at some point have to agree and manage.

Late on Wednesday morning, however, my restraint was tested to breaking point when I learned that Nigel Griffiths, the Edinburgh MP who was canvassing support for Gordon in the PLP, had given a briefing accusing me of having leapt into organising support for Tony from the moment of John's death, while Gordon was mourning. Since he must have known that was not true, I can only assume it was intended to frighten me off from Tony, and keep me on-side. Furious at being subjected to the same treatment Gordon's briefers appeared to be meting out to Tony, I phoned Charlie and told him that unless he issued a denial, cleared by Gordon, in fifteen minutes, I would issue an on-the-record statement denouncing their tactics.

Minutes later, Gordon phoned me. He apologised, denied all knowledge of the briefing, and promised to make sure the press knew it. The disgust I came to feel for Gordon's operation deepened when I discovered that the briefing against me had been agreed in his office the evening before. I still felt real sympathy for his predicament, however, and a determination to find a way out that would protect his and the modernisers' interests.

With the approach of John's funeral on Friday, I spoke with Donald Dewar again. My hope was that he could use his relationship with Gordon to talk him back from the brink. 'You must save him from a terrible, knockdown fight with Tony,' I said. 'We both know it won't just hurt Tony. It will hurt Gordon, and all of us.' Donald knew that Gordon would have to withdraw, but he limited himself to saying he shared my concern. By now, I was talking regularly to Tony, and Tony was talking to Gordon. But by the evening before the funeral, there was no sign of a resolution. The only real progress was that both Tony and I agreed on the need for 'sensitivity' to Gordon's situation. If Gordon did abandon the fight, he must be able to do so without humiliation, to act from at least the appearance of strength.

John's funeral was held in Edinburgh. Hundreds of people crowded into the parish church, and hundreds more filled the streets around it. I was not there, partly because I had a prior speaking commitment at a Foreign Office-sponsored conference at Wilton Park in Sussex, but mostly because I felt it was an occasion for shadow cabinet members like Gordon and Tony. I regretted my decision almost immediately. I felt I should have gone to the funeral, out of friendship and respect for John.

The difficulty of achieving an amicable resolution of the stand-off became clearer over the weekend. Tony and Gordon had both been invited to address the Welsh Labour conference. Tony decided to defer to Gordon and give him the platform. Gordon used the occasion to make a powerful appeal to the core party and trade union base which he presumably still hoped might revive his campaign. Tony was irritated and worried, so much so that he let it be known to journalists that he would not sacrifice his modernising agenda in order to win support as Labour's next leader.

With the party having agreed that formal campaigning would begin after the European elections on 9 June, time was running short. Neither Tony nor I was sure what Gordon would do. We assumed that allies like Nick Brown, Nigel Griffiths and above all Ed Balls and Charlie Whelan were encouraging him to stay in the race. But simple political realities were weakening that argument. On the final Friday of the month, a survey found that Gordon could rely on the firm support of only about one-third of Labour MPs even in Scotland. On Sunday, a poll for the BBC showed Tony with a strong lead in all three sections of the electoral college that would choose a leader: Labour MPs and MEPs, the party membership, and the trade unions.

Later that day, Tony and Gordon spoke at length. For the first time, Gordon gave Tony a strong indication that he was ready to step aside, although he did not say it outright. They agreed to meet for dinner on the following Tuesday at a restaurant called Granita, near Tony's house in Islington, to finalise things. Meanwhile, I was deputed by them to brief the media aggressively that Gordon's support was greater than the polls suggested. Not everyone bought the line, although some, to my relief, did so.

With the final act approaching, I did not underestimate the sense of loss Gordon was feeling. I did what I could to convey my support and let him know that in standing aside he was doing the right thing. Roger wrote him an honest and sensitive note before the Granita meeting. He said he didn't see how Gordon could win. Tony's momentum was too strong. Gordon's disadvantages were too great. He said he was confident Gordon knew that going on the attack against Tony would not be true to himself, or good for either of them. He was forthright in his praise of Gordon's strengths, which he said he had always seen as above even Tony's, and concluded by urging him to see that the future might not be so terrible. Gordon had every prospect of being 'the dominant figure in the next government, shaping the entire domestic agenda…the Bevin of the next government'. Besides, Roger added: 'It is not the case that an older person never succeeds the younger. The world is still rich in possibilities.'

Nailing down that future, and staking his claim to those rich possibilities, were what preoccupied Gordon ahead of the Granita meeting. From their conversation on Sunday, Tony knew broadly what Gordon wanted: assurances that he would be Chancellor, and the domestic policy heavyweight, in a future government. Tony's inclination was to go as far as he could in meeting Gordon's wishes without undermining his own position as future leader. He knew how hard this was for Gordon. He respected and admired him, and valued his judgement. Tony also believed his leadership would be incalculably weaker if their friendship were damaged.

The devil was in the detail, which was where I now had to play a critical role. As the two of them were dining in Islington, I was in Hartlepool drafting an agreed line, based on my conversations with Tony and Gordon before the dinner, that we would give to the media the following day. The understanding was that the three of us would refine it after they had talked. Throughout Wednesday morning, I went back and forth between them by phone and fax. Despite the later mythology that grew up around that night in Granita, there was never any question of an assurance that Tony would step aside in Gordon's favour at an agreed future date. I know from Tony that Gordon did raise the issue, and Ed and Charlie were convinced that Tony had agreed. But Tony told me on more than one occasion afterwards that he had not done so. He did say more generally that when his time in office ended he could think of no one he would more like to succeed him. The reason I am confident that Tony's version of events is the true one was his deep reluctance, as we worked out the briefing note, to make any firm commitments before he was leader, let alone Prime Minister.

The final, six-paragraph note was devoted mostly to describing Gordon's decision to pull out of the race as an act of strength. It was the kind of airlifting I'd hoped for. It portrayed him and Tony as having virtually equal support across the party, the shadow cabinet and the unions, noting only that Tony appeared to have an 'edge' in polls. Gordon was withdrawing not because he had to, but because he was putting party unity and teamwork above personal ambition. The key paragraph was about domestic policy. Citing Gordon's Welsh party speech, it said that he had 'spelled out the fairness agenda – social justice, employment opportunities and skills – which he believes should be the centrepiece of Labour's programme, and Tony is in full agreement with this and that the party's economic and social policies should be further developed on this basis'.

Gordon wanted more, and pressed for stronger wording throughout the morning after the Granita dinner. When the final draft was faxed to his office, Sue sent it back to me with an amendment in Gordon's unmistakable scrawl, stating that Tony has 'guaranteed' this agenda will be pursued. I ran it by Tony, who said no to the word 'guaranteed'. Gordon finally acquiesced.

Despite the tension in some of our exchanges as he finally came to terms with the fact that Tony would be leader, I think Gordon recognised the difficulty of my position. The same, unfortunately, could not be said for his aides and acolytes. My friendship with Sue was too old and close to be affected. She knew me well enough to be aware that I was as distraught as she was at Gordon's predicament. But for Nick, Charlie and Ed, the leadership issue had become a battle for Gordon's, and their own, political supremacy. When it was lost, they could not bring themselves to accept that it had simply not been there for Gordon. The first sign came within days of Granita, in their efforts to rewrite the terms of what had been agreed. Peter Riddell of *The Times* exhumed the excised 'guarantee' from the briefing note, insisting that Gordon had been promised both the chancellorship and control of Labour's wider economic policy, including issues such as business competitiveness and social justice. Gordon's camp were careful not to pick a fight with Tony; but, determined to find someone to blame for the defeat, they settled on me as a surrogate. The idea that I had 'betrayed' Gordon, and somehow denied him the crown that would otherwise have been his, was born.

Looking back on it, I now believe I should have done more to encourage Gordon to stand, rather than to have worked so hard with both him and Tony to organise a dignified exit. It is true that the contest might have been much messier. Robin Cook might also conceivably have entered the race, attracting those in the party who were nervous of, or opposed to, the modernisers. But despite the inflated picture of Gordon's support that I created for the media, all the evidence was that he would have lost to Tony, in all probability heavily. For a while, that would have been difficult for him, and possibly bruising for our relations. But an open contest with a clear result would have removed the temptation for him to agonise about what might have been, and brood over the sense that he had somehow been unfairly pushed aside. Most of all, a decisive outcome would have opened up the possibility that he and Tony – all three of us – would have come together again and worked closely in government. If the founding troika had survived, I believe that the story of Tony's government, and of Gordon's too, would have been very different.

By the time I became involved in Tony's campaign after Granita, a core of shadow cabinet and PLP supporters, led by Mo Mowlam and Jack Straw, had already formed around him. I began working with Philip not only on planning Tony's campaign, but on a broader strategy for his leadership. The political climate could not have been more different from the first national campaign on which we had collaborated. In 1987, Labour was riven by disunity and distrusted by the country. Now it was the Tories who were reeling. Especially since Black Wednesday, the government was seen as unfocused and incompetent. John Major looked weak and out of his depth. Labour was on the brink of a potentially redefining leadership election. The outpouring of goodwill towards John Smith had led to a surge in support for the party as well.

Philip and I saw the campaign as an opportunity to catch the public mood. People were taking a fresh look at our party. In Tony, we had a chance to present them with a leader who could embody a new kind of Labour. Although Philip, typically, warned that we could not take Tony's victory for granted, none of us seriously believed that he would lose to either of the other declared candidates, John Prescott and Margaret Beckett, who as John Smith's deputy had become interim leader. Still, the stakes were high. If Tony was going to succeed as leader, and bring Labour back into government, he had to start in the right way. The public would be getting its first close-up view of him, and we had to get across what kind of a politician and person he was, what kind of party he intended to lead, and what kind of vision he had for Britain.

While being the early front-runner had been important in crowding out Gordon, his only serious competition, it also made Tony a target in some of the media. Philip was especially worried by pieces in the *Mail* and the *Express* suggesting he was attractive but essentially a lightweight – a mix, in Philip's memorable phrase, of 'Bambi and bimbo'. We had to find a way to convey that Tony had steel. I was not worried on that score. Any doubts I may have had about his toughness had vanished with his swift and resolute decision to go for the top job even in the knowledge that it would mean eliminating Gordon. I believed that Tony had to deliver a clear, self-confident, policy-rich vision of a reformed party and a renewed Britain – not just a prospectus for the leadership campaign, but the start of a political project we would build upon until election day. There was never any doubt in my mind what its thrust must be: *new* Labour, and a new Britain.

Nominally, Jack Straw was made co-chair of the leadership campaign, alongside Mo. Tony liked Mo. He admired her spunkiness, earthiness and people skills. He also knew she had a tendency to say exactly what was on her mind, with sometimes embarrassing consequences. He felt it was important that her role was balanced by Jack, whom he viewed as less imaginative but a safer pair of hands. In fact, Jack's role in deciding, organising and running the campaign was limited: he focused mostly on encouraging and liaising with the growing number of supporters in the PLP. To the extent that there was a strategic 'manager', that role fell to me. Yet I had to coordinate the campaign under cover, so as not to unsettle Jack or Mo, or indeed Gordon. Tony was also keen to appeal to the widest possible range of opinion in the party, and was worried that with me openly organising the campaign it might be seen as driven by the modernisers' faction.

I understood these concerns. I had spent the past decade working, and hoping, for Labour's modernising moment. My only thought was to make the moment happen, so when Tony said I would have to keep my head down, I went along. I even ended up with a secret codename. It came from the office staff, who joked that Tony and I were like the Kennedy brothers mapping out JFK's bid for the US presidential nomination: Tony was 'Jack' to my 'Bobby'. In fact, I operated as a classic campaign manager, exactly as I would do in the general election campaign three years later. Sadly, however, one effect of the secrecy was to reinforce my image as a backroom manipulator, complicating my progress as an elected politician in my own right. It also set a template for my relationship with Tony throughout much of the time both of us were to spend in public life.

Besides, it fooled no one who mattered. Mo certainly knew I was involved, and Jack seemed to as well. So did Gordon. I was in constant communication with the key campaign figures in Tony's office: Anji was directing operations. The press team were Tim Allan and Peter Hyman, a former researcher for both Donald Dewar and John Smith who would soon make his mark as a gifted policy strategist and speechwriter for Tony, and a young aide, Tom Restrick. David Miliband headed up the policy team of James Purnell and Liz Lloyd, who later went into Number 10 for the duration of Tony's premiership. I held daily meetings with key members of the campaign team in a Commons meeting room, to map out the main message for the day. At Tony's direction, it fell to me to give the final sign-off on this and all other aspects of the campaign day: speeches and covering notes, policy documents and media briefings. In addition, I regularly briefed a small circle of trusted political reporters.

It was during the campaign that I first came across Carole Caplin, though it would not be the last time. An increasingly frequent visitor to the Blair home, Carole had a champagne-like effervescence about her. She had become a friend and confidante of Cherie. Not only was she a source of comfort and support, but as a health and lifestyle guru she came to provide Cherie with endless advice on how to dress, how to eat, how to exercise, and generally how to live well and feel good. As Carole watched me and the rest of the campaign team fuel up with our caffeine fix, she was aghast. For a few days, her descriptions of how industrial quantities of coffee meant certain death frightened us out of risking so much as a single cup. The others all slipped back soon, but I was more impressionable. I am certainly stubborn once I have taken a decision, and not just in politics. To this day, I have stayed off coffee. I don't proselytise; I'll leave that to Carole. But I began drinking hot water and lemon from that moment, and subsequently graduated to green tea.

As the campaign moved into high gear, any tensions from the Blair–Brown stand-off were overshadowed by a common goal: victory for Tony as the modernisers' candidate. Gordon, to his credit, became strongly supportive. While it would be some months before it became public, at least three of us – Tony, Philip and I – were already referring in conversation to the party Tony hoped to lead as New Labour. This was not just a matter of semantics. It signified the scale of transformation we knew was necessary, even if that meant taking on those in the party or the unions who were nervous, uncertain, or opposed to it.

Our strategy in the campaign and beyond owed much to our insistence that the party must champion both social justice and individual aspiration, rebuilding public services and supporting business. We had to be trusted to improve the quality of life for Britons of all classes and incomes. Others contributed significantly to the message. David helped craft a campaign address on education, and worked with Peter on a speech on reforming the welfare system. Gordon and Ed Balls were central to the economic message.

The driving force, however, was Tony. Well before John's death, he had been building an increasingly coherent vision of the kind of Labour Party, the kind of politics and the kind of country he meant to champion. Within Labour, he was determined to move to mass membership and end the block vote. He wanted to open up both the party, through broadening its appeal, and politics in general, by making common cause with others on the social-democratic left. His vision for Britain was rooted in the Christian socialism he had embraced while at Oxford. It extolled community and family above an all-knowing, interventionist state. It favoured fair and progressive, not punitive, taxation. It held that individual rights must be balanced by social responsibilities. While others, including Alastair, helped craft some of the words, there was not a single part of it that didn't bear Tony's imprint.

There were hitches during the campaign, moments when one or another of us lost our confidence, or our temper. But in my experience before and since, it was remarkably smooth. When the result was announced in late July 1994, it was everything we had hoped and worked for. Tony won a commanding majority from all three elements of the electoral college – 57 per cent overall, against 24 per cent for John Prescott and 19 for Margaret Beckett. The deputy leader's contest also turned out as we had wanted. John Prescott, with 56 per cent, comfortably defeated Margaret, giving Tony a political foil with deep ties to our northern, trade union-friendly constituencies. When it was over, Tony followed his formal acceptance speech with some words of celebration and gratitude to the few dozen allies at the heart of the campaign. Grinning broadly, he included a special note of thanks for 'Bobby'.

I joined in the laughter, not least out of relief that my temporary immersion in undercover politics was presumably coming to an end. Once the campaign was over, I would be an open member of the team planning to make the new leader of the opposition successful, and Labour electable. The work started immediately. Tony used a string of interviews and speeches to slay a series of Labour sacred cows. He spoke about the advantages to children of a stable, two-parent family. On education, he rewrote Labour's policy on the spot, promising more autonomy for schools.

Before leaving on holiday at the end of July, he raised with me a way of dramatically signalling his determination to create a new Labour Party by taking on a totem last addressed, with humiliating consequences, by Hugh Gaitskell thirty-five years earlier. 'What do you think,' he asked, 'about our rewriting Clause IV?' I was momentarily shocked. While the party's constitutional commitment to 'common ownership of the means of production' was so obviously outmoded that few took it seriously as a guide for policy, I questioned whether Tony should instigate a fight with the left so early on his watch. The more I thought about it, however, the more it seemed worth doing. And worth doing early. It would define Tony as a leader of conviction, and Labour as a party ready to recast itself for the modern age. I phoned him the next morning and told him that, absolutely, he should go for it.

There was another issue we both knew had to be addressed. Tony had assembled a formidably effective office team, built around Anji, Tim and Peter. Now that he was party leader, with the need to prepare for a general election, he would have to strengthen his operation in two key areas. The first was overall management and gatekeeping, political coordination and implementation. He would need a top-flight chief of staff. The second was an experienced media manager and spokesman. We discussed a number of names for each of these positions. For chief of staff, my first choice, and Tony's, was Julian Priestley. A Balliol PPE graduate whom I had got to know during my time at Oxford, he had worked since the 1970s in senior policy roles at the European Parliament, finally becoming Secretary General of the socialist group of MEPs in 1989. He was politically astute, good with people, and a gifted organiser and manager who had helped Tony on his Europe speech in the leadership campaign. After Tony's victory, I spent a weekend trying to persuade Julian to take the job. Tony also talked to him several times. Julian was tempted, but felt he could not uproot himself after decades on the Continent.

We settled on an alternative who, though he had no previous experience in the political bearpit, would turn out to be a mainstay in all that Tony did in his time in power. Tony and Gordon had met Jonathan Powell on their visit in January 1993 to Washington, where he was First Secretary at the British Embassy. They were impressed. When I went on my parliamentary visit a few weeks later, it was evident that Jonathan too had been impressed by the Labour modernisers. I liked him immediately. I had worked closely at Walworth Road with his older brother Chris, the founder of our ad agency partner BMP. In a taxi ride to one of our meetings in Washington, Jonathan had mentioned to me that he was thinking of a political career. As I usually did when I met would-be politicians during what then looked like a slow, frustrating march towards creating an electable Labour Party, I replied, 'Are you sure?' He said he was. The diplomatic service had become limiting, and he wanted to play a part in politics and policy closer to home. When Tony now phoned to offer him the opportunity to do so, he eagerly accepted.

Our first choice for press secretary also said no. Andy Grice, a first-rate journalist whom Tony and I both respected and liked, had a background in regional and local journalism, and was now the political editor of the *Sunday Times*. Although he was tempted, he decided he would rather write about Tony than turn gamekeeper. More than a decade later, I would try to lure Andy to Downing Street again, this time to take over press and media for Gordon. He took decidedly less time before saying, politely, firmly and with an engaging laugh: 'No thanks.'

Again, the man Tony soon settled on instead turned out to be a critically important member of his team. Tony had got to know Alastair Campbell shortly after arriving in the Commons, when Alastair was a dominant, and supportive, lobby presence as political editor of the *Mirror*. I had known him longer. I had first met him in the 1970s, during one of the evenings I spent with Fiona Millar's parents. Bob and Audrey were Marylebone Labour stalwarts. Bob was a gentle, gifted journalist who began at *Tribune* and was then hired by the *Express*. That night, Fiona arrived with a new boyfriend, whom she had met while they were on a *Mirror* training scheme in the West Country. We heard him before we were properly introduced: Alastair came in playing the bagpipes.

He was engaging, funny, and obviously smitten not only by Fiona but by the warmth, commitment and intellectual buzz of the wider Labour family of which she was a part. He had some rough times before we became professionally close, including a bout with alcoholism which ultimately led to a breakdown. But by the mid-1980s, when I arrived at Walworth Road, he was the senior political voice at the *Mirror* and an immense help as I wrestled with bringing Labour's communications into the modern age. He became especially close to Neil Kinnock, which may have been one reason Tony initially preferred Andy instead. But we both liked Alastair, and had no doubt that he would be good at the job. Tony phoned him, as did I, to sound him out. Tony then went to see him when they were both on holiday in France. Neil tried to talk Alastair out of it, raising understandable concerns about the personal and family pressures the job would involve, but to Tony's relief he agreed to come on board.

By the time I left for my holiday, joining my Channel 4 friend Jon Snow and his family on Cape Cod, I was feeling pretty exhausted, emotionally and physically. But I felt more hopeful about Labour's future, and Britain's, than at any time since I had left university. Over-optimistically, I had also assumed that 'The Three Musketeers' around whom the party's modernising agenda had been built, would revive and re-form after the summer. I did not underestimate the difficulty Gordon would have in coming to terms with his role as number two to Tony. Watching the hope of victory drain from him in the days after John's death, powerless to do anything to turn things round, I had felt enormously sad. Gordon, no doubt, was feeling even worse. In the conversations we had had since Tony's victory, however, he had seemed more disappointed than bitter. While I knew privately from journalists that Charlie Whelan was encouraging the belief that Gordon and I were at loggerheads, nothing Gordon said to me directly suggested he held me responsible for the political realities that had denied him the leadership.

On our return after the summer we held our first serious planning and strategy meeting under Tony's leadership. Through Dennis Stevenson's managing director at SRU, Colin Fisher, a strong Labour supporter, I arranged for us to meet at the Chewton Glen hotel, on the edge of the New Forest. Those present included Tony, Gordon, me, the newly hired Alastair, Philip, Roger Liddle, Ed Balls and Michael Wills, a friend and former LWT colleague I had brought in to help Gordon in the run-up to the 1992 election.

Tony, Gordon and I went down ahead of the others for a discussion over dinner the evening before. We chatted easily, three friends just back from holiday, as I drove them out of London. The only brief dampener was Tony's impassioned insistence that anyone he promoted to the front bench would have to do a spell in the whips' office. 'You're bloody kidding!' I said. I was pretty sure the whips would enjoy my presence no more than I would theirs. Tony replied, 'I'm serious,' and it turned out that he was. Still, the atmosphere seemed almost like old times, with Tony and Gordon excited and expansive.

Dinner began pleasantly, too. Gordon, however, had arrived with a sheaf of notes, and proceeded to press Tony for agreement on a whole range of decisions, from policy to personnel. He was especially keen to see Michael Wills installed as Labour's Deputy General Secretary at Walworth Road, in charge of 'strategy'. Tony was not persuaded. I too thought it was a strange proposal, and did not feel comfortable seeing Gordon trying to bounce Tony into agreeing to it. I suggested that these kinds of decisions needed to be thought through further, to which Tony quickly agreed, and after an hour's further discussion the dinner broke up. When Tony went off to bed, Gordon and I walked together towards our rooms. Suddenly angry, he turned to me and said, 'Why didn't you support me?' I didn't know what to say, but I explained that it wasn't a matter of supporting or opposing him; I genuinely thought further discussion made sense. 'Look, Peter,' he said, 'if you and I agree a position, Tony will always take our advice.

He can't stand out against us.' By now I was becoming uneasy about what Gordon seemed to be suggesting. 'My friendship and loyalty to you is not in question,' I said, 'but Tony is now leader. I can't be part of attempts to outmanoeuvre him.' Gordon glared at me. After a few moments' silence, he said, 'Then choose for yourself.' He turned, went into his room and shut the door in my face. I felt hurt and stunned by what he said, and feared immediately that something between us was broken that night.

When we got back to London, I made it a point to meet or at least talk to Gordon every few days. I was determined to repair the breach, but he was cold and unreceptive. Over time, our communication came to consist largely of brief phone calls, and messages and letters sent but not acknowledged. Before John's death, the modernising project had been defined by the relationship that bound Tony, Gordon and me. During our final period in opposition, and throughout Tony's time in Downing Street, it would be defined, and damaged, by the multiple tensions that plagued that relationship.

Maybe if I had just agreed to Gordon's suggestion, assured him I would make common cause with him in all our dealings with Tony, things would have been different. After all, Tony was leader: he would take the final decisions. When I told Tony about the conversation at Chewton Glen some time later, he smiled and said, 'For God's sake, why didn't you just play along?' I always suspected that it would not have made much difference, and by the end of his first term in office, Tony had reached that view as well. I may have been the focus of Gordon's anger and frustration at Chewton Glen, but the real problem was that he could not bring himself to accept that Tony was leader. The closer we got to Number 10, the more painful it became for him to imagine Tony, and not himself, as Prime Minister. He felt this to be not only intolerable, but wrong. Against all the evidence that by the time Gordon pulled out of the contest Tony had built up an unstoppable momentum, he latched on to the conciliatory fiction I had spun, at Tony's urging, around Granita: that they were in fact neck and neck. He convinced himself that if only he had held his nerve, he would have won, and that he was the victim of a terrible injustice. He came to feel that it – and he – would not be made right until it was overturned.

Tony's first challenge was replacing Clause IV, and that was the main focus of our preparations for his maiden conference speech as leader. We viewed the conference, held in an unseasonably warm Blackpool at the beginning of October 1994, as an opportunity to dramatise Tony's boldness and Labour's change of direction. The most visible sign for arriving delegates, and the media, would be the presentation. In a natural endpoint of the process I'd begun with the 'Freedom and Fairness' launch in 1986, Labour would not only be rebranded, but effectively renamed: as New Labour. On delegate packs, on banners, on the podium, our conference slogan, 'New Labour, New Britain', made explicit our modernising insistence that Labour had to look outwards and address the people whose votes we needed. This would not just be about packaging: the product was changing too. Central to that would be the leader's speech. On a range of issues on which the Tories traditionally led Labour – law and order, welfare reform, small businesses, the burden of taxation – it would place New Labour on the side of Britain's aspirational majority. By signalling our intention to replace Clause IV, we would redefine for ourselves and the country the principles on which we proposed to govern.

There was another Carole Caplin interlude as the conference got under way, and it was not about caffeine. A tabloid newspaper had unearthed some old topless photos of Cherie's friend and lifestyle adviser, who had joined her at the conference. The first I knew of the repercussions was a panicked phone call from Anji, who said I must come immediately to join her, Tony, Cherie and Carole in Tony's suite in the conference hotel. When I got there, Alastair was laying into Carole, like a bank security guard who had caught an armed intruder red-handed. He left little doubt that he felt Carole was on the make, and had herself been responsible for the photo spread and for delib-erately ruining the start of the conference. Carole looked crumpled,

Cherie appalled, and Tony taken aback by Alastair's onslaught. I did what I could to calm him down, which was not much. I did say there was no justification for speaking to anyone like that, which sparked an enduring suspicion on Alastair's part that I was somehow 'on Carole's side'. It was not a question of taking sides, but as all of us would discover, Alastair had a tendency to boil over when anyone stood up to him, and I felt that both he and Fiona, who was working as an adviser to Cherie, took an overly judgemental attitude towards anyone of whom they disapproved. The immediate 'Carole crisis' was resolved by arranging to have her spirited out of sight, back to London. But there would be others.

While Tony was full of energy and confidence as conference began, he agonised over his speech, asking himself, and the few of us who knew about his Clause IV plans, whether he should go ahead, whether he had got it right. It was a process he would go through before almost every major speech he made. But there was always a point when those who knew him best could see that he had made up his mind. This time, I sensed, it was from the moment we had first discussed Clause IV. The only questions were how to manage it politically, and how to word the replacement for our nationalising creed, which had to convey not only what ideological baggage we were shedding, but what we stood for. On the tactics and presentation, Alastair played the key role. Tony never actually mentioned Clause IV in his speech. He said it was time the party had a 'clear, up-to-date statement' of its aims and objectives. Alastair, briefing afterwards, explained what that meant.

On the politics, John Prescott was critical. This had the unfortunate effect of unsettling Gordon, partly I think because he did not want to be outflanked on the left of the party, but also because he had hoped that Margaret Beckett would be deputy leader. He saw her as more malleable, less forceful and less ambitious than John. When I had first talked to Gordon on returning from summer holiday, he blamed Tony for John's election. He was worried that John would insist at every opportunity on being Tony's number two in influence, not just in title. Realistically, as I tried to reassure Godon, that was never going to happen. Tony's relationship with him was too close. Tony wanted John as deputy mostly because he was sure it offered the best hope of bringing the whole party behind the changes he was determined to make.

That was the role John now fulfilled, first by coming round to Tony's view on Clause IV, and then by campaigning for support in constituency parties, the unions and the PLP. Deciding on what would replace it proved more difficult and drawn-out. Peter Hyman and Alastair, Tony's most gifted wordsmiths, were major contributors to the battery of early drafts. The ideological underpinning was never in doubt. The new clause would be rooted in Tony's belief that a fair society rested on a sense of community, on individuals working with and for one another. Yet the more it was drafted, the more unwieldy it became. Tony at last accepted that for it to have a single author's coherence and thrust, he would have to distil the final version himself. My concern was that it had lost its explicit, New Labour focus, and as Tony began the final draft, I suggested a number of changes. A couple of them – adding an explicit reference to crime, and deleting one to working with the trade unions, as opposed to all groups who shared our values – he decided were steps too far. He did agree that a boiler-plate paean to 'solidarity, liberty and equality' should go, in favour of an emphasis on equality of opportunity and phrases like 'duty to others' and 'the many rather than the few', which had more real-life resonance.

At my urging, he also rewrote the foreign-policy passage. The late drafts had said that Labour favoured the 'peaceful resolution' of international disputes. That was unarguably right as far as it went, but it was hardly a convincing summary of foreign-policy princi-ples for the real world. 'Won't a Blair government ever go to war?' I asked, a bit more prophetically than I would have liked, given the problems with Iraq that would later bedevil his premiership. I pro-posed an alternative, which Tony adopted almost verbatim: 'We are committed to the defence and security of the British people and to cooperating in European and international institutions to secure peace, freedom, democracy, economic security and environmental protection for all.'

By year's end, we appeared to be on a roll. We were nearing the end of the internal debate over the new Clause IV, paving the way for Tony and John to take it to the NEC and to a special conference in April 1995 to seek party-wide approval. At a mid-December by-election in the Midlands constituency of Dudley West, we romped to victory on a swing to Labour of more than 29 per cent, our largest since the 1930s. The only hiccup was a political furore that erupted around the *Daily Mail*'s revelation that Tony and Cherie had decided to send their son Euan to the London Oratory, a grant-maintained Catholic state school, rather than to a comprehensive. Tony was edgy, and Alastair, and especially Fiona, were fearful of the political ramifications. They were also personally outraged. For them, comprehensives – even what Alastair himself would later call 'bog-standard comprehensives' – were an ineradicable part of what it meant to be Labour. I happened to think it would all blow over. I also thought the *Mail* headline, though no doubt intended to injure, got it about right: 'Labour Leader Ignores Party Policy and Puts Family First'. I was confident that most people in Britain, certainly most parents, would understand this, however much Alastair and Fiona disapproved, and however openly they showed it.

Our concern as the year ended was that the excitement and momentum surrounding Tony's leadership were waning. Our upward flight in the opinion polls had stalled, and there were the first rumblings of uneasiness among some backbenchers, and the unions, over Clause IV and the pace of change. When Alastair, Philip and I began working with Tony on a 'winter strategy', Philip felt we had yet to embed what New Labour meant with voters. We had to get across the broad themes that separated us from the increasingly tired and unpopular Conservative government. We had other problems, too, if we hoped to win our first general election in two decades. The most worrying was our failure to put in place the kind of planning, strategy and policy machinery necessary to organise a successful campaign. Tony had begun to reposition Labour on tax and spending, education, the unions and family issues, and was outperforming John Major at Prime Minister's Questions. He was also forming an effective leadership team with John Prescott. Tony's approach to what would prove a critically important relationship was formed partly out of political instinct, but also on advice he had been given in a series of lengthy conversations with Roy Jenkins, the former Labour Chancellor and Home Secretary, and SDP founder. Both Tony and I were becoming increasingly close to Roy. 'Keep Prescott close to you,' he said. 'You need a loyal deputy, if only to counter the moves of others in the party against you.' The result was that John, who had deeper roots in the pre-New Labour party than Tony, sometimes had a major influence on what he decided. The balance, however, always rested with Tony, in part because John loved his job and the status that went with it, and was generally careful to avoid doing anything to put it at risk.

Still, as I wrote to Jonathan Powell a few days before he took up his post as chief of staff in January 1995, we had not yet 'created a New Labour which is supported by genuine new thinking, accepted by both the party and the public'. We were not yet ready for the election, and certainly not for government. The immediate priority was to ensure the party united around the new Clause IV. After that battle was won, we would have to get up to speed. On policy, David Miliband, who Tony had retained to head up his policy staff, had drawn up a summary of key areas that required work: industry, unemployment, school standards, welfare and crime. He had narrowed down the issues on which we had yet to settle internal discussions and debates: levels of tax and spending, and what to do about Tory creations like NHS hospital trusts and grant-maintained schools. On election planning, we were not even at that preliminary stage. Tony had mapped out a plan, under which Gordon would chair an overall election strategy committee and I would act as the campaign's 'executive officer'. For months it stayed on the drawing board.

The initial problem was that John Prescott, whom Tony had named as 'campaign coordinator' for Clause IV, clearly expected to carry on in that role for the general election. As a stopgap, strategy meetings were convened in Gordon's office with me, Alastair, Jonathan, Charlie, and Gordon's policy aide, David Miliband's younger brother Ed. They were useful, but not in planning any detailed work for the election. Jonathan suggested a new approach: Gordon, he and I would meet twice a month to deal with issues of campaign strategy, while I would chair a separate group to get the planning details under way. That didn't get off the ground either.

The main reason, though it would be more than a year before this began to seep into the media, was Gordon's increasingly corrosive relationship not only with me, but with Tony. I was certainly not blameless. I felt hurt, then shocked, and finally angry as Gordon either talked over me or ignored me in meetings. There were times when I could not restrain myself from showing my exasperation. More often, I tried to mollify him. In the first of many notes I would send him over a period of years, I wrote: 'I am very sorry we have not been getting along. You are – totally understandably – pissed off and I realise I haven't helped you at all.' I concluded: 'Let's be friends. I cannot do what I am meant to be doing – whatever that is – without you.' He never answered. Nor was there any discernible thaw early in 1995, when I went out of my way to back Gordon's candidate for my old job as Labour's Director of Communications. Tony was sceptical about Joy Johnson. She was an experienced television producer, and a linchpin of the BBC's political coverage. She was bright, well-informed, and above all tough. But she was decidedly old Labour, and an admirer of Gordon's who clearly believed that he should have succeeded John Smith. When Tony asked me to 'vet' Joy, I met her briefly, and said we should hire her, which we did. If I was nice to Gordon, I thought, he might be nice to me back.

By mid-1995, Tony too was feeling the effects of Gordon's bitterness. At the end of June, he emerged from a private talk with him literally shaking his head in anger. 'You can't go on just sulking!' Tony had said. 'I would never have treated you like this if you'd become leader.' When Tony and I were travelling back to London together from our constituencies a few days later, he was still upset. 'The only question Gordon asks of himself and his own behaviour is what went wrong,' he said, 'and what was the mistake that stopped him becoming leader? He'll never come right until he reconciles himself to it.' That, in Tony's view, would require 'massive therapy'. He did not mean that Gordon belonged on Dr Freud's couch, but that we had to coddle and cosset him. He wanted me to play a role, to which I readily agreed, by 'heavily briefing' the media about Gordon's strengths as the New Labour thinker, the driving force behind our economic strategy. Tony hoped this would enthuse Gordon to put that thinking to work, which was not happening yet. He complained that Gordon's engagement with developing new economic policies had been skindeep: 'He's been too preoccupied with all his personal and political baggage. He simply hates the world.' In reality, while not divorcing from Tony, Gordon was beginning to lead a separate life.

Frustrated though Tony was by his relationship with Gordon, he was convinced that he could not do without him. He still saw Gordon as having the best mind in the shadow cabinet, and knew that we needed him if we were going to get an election campaign in place. But Tony felt Gordon was sabotaging our election planning by blocking our attempts to get a structure up and running. Joy Johnson's role was particularly important at this time, because we were beginning to close down Walworth Road in preparation for a move to new, high-rise party headquarters in Millbank. But her closeness to Gordon was turning out to be the least of our problems: Tony felt that in her first six months in the job she had failed to improve our campaign operation.

Much less seriously, though annoyingly, Roy Hattersley was emerging as cheerleader for an assortment of left-wing Labour backbenchers who began sniping about Tony's leadership. Gerald Kaufman best described the transformation of the former darling of the Labour right: 'In his old age, Roy has discovered socialism – and it is not a pretty sight.' He had also discovered a great skill in journalism, having decided that this would be his final term in the Commons, and keen to have an alternative profession in place.

Whatever natural inclination Roy might have had to support Tony – and he was an early and enthusiastic backer – I was certain that injured pride had something to do with his turnaround, as well as any policy differences he had. With a modernising leader finally installed, he had undoubtedly expected to play at least a grandfatherly role in the new regime. Neil was being treated as a linear ancestor of New Labour, but Tony's main interest in the earlier generation of Labour change-makers was another Roy – Roy Jenkins. Tony was only mildly ruffled by Hattersley, but he was concerned that his grandstanding would encourage wider grumbling. There were three streams in Labour, Tony felt. The first was what both of us were now calling 'Old Labour', on the backbenches and in the trade union movement. The second was the 'ex-1960s radicals', who were jealous of the newcomers. The third, and we assumed the largest, was the 'governing group', MPs and party members who recognised that the only way a left-of-centre party could make a difference was by winning power. 'To lead Labour, you need at least two of the three groups on your side,' said Tony. As the summer wore on, he recognised that we risked finding ourselves 'dangerously off-side with the first two'.

I knew Roy Hattersley, of course, and liked him – he could be engaging and funny. That helps explain why I agreed when he asked to do a *Mail on Sunday* interview with me that would run before Tony's second party conference as leader in the autumn. I was stay-ing with my friends Robert and Gill Harris at their home in the west Berkshire village of Kintbury. When Roy arrived, we began by chat-ting about my family, my schooldays, and my time in Tanzania and then Oxford. After we joined Robert in the garden for lunch, the heavy-duty part of the interview began. In fact, it was not really an interview. Roy spoke much more than I did, and what passed for questions were actually a series of accusations: that I had played media favourites at Walworth Road; that my 'Bobby' role suggested

I wanted to be a shadowy, all-powerful operator rather than a back-bench MP; and that I 'controlled' Tony's office.

When Roy had finished, I gently asked what was behind his recent newspaper criticisms of Tony. He launched into a tirade, at one point exclaiming: 'I have it on good authority that Tony has targeted middle-class votes for the last year. Well, I say *fuck* the middle class. Their votes aren't anything when set against the 10 per cent who are living in poverty, or the rights of the black and Asian community.' I did what I could to explain that appealing to middle-class voters did not mean we wouldn't also do everything we could to help the underprivileged and minorities, and tried to turn things towards the New Labour principle of opening up opportunity for the many, by creating a fair and 'meritocratic society'. Mistake number two. Roy said Tony had never read any of the great socialist texts, and that he – and all of us around him – were both fundamentally anti-egalitarian and ignorant.

Whatever fairly glancing discouragement we felt from Roy, the Conservatives were proving generously helpful to the New Labour cause. John Major's government was in the doldrums, hobbled by dissent over Europe and trailing us by roughly 20 per cent in the polls. Our main concern was that they would dump Major. In late June 1995 he resigned as party leader, saying he would stand for re-election and calling on his Tory critics and rivals to put up or shut up. The right-wing and deeply Eurosceptic John Redwood, nick-named 'the Vulcan' by the journalist Matthew Parris, took up the challenge, flanked by a coterie of other eccentrics as he announced his candidacy. Sadly for us, he was never going to win. But if Major didn't secure outright victory in the first round, Michael Heseltine was waiting in the wings.

The night before the result of the Tory leadership contest was announced in early July, I joined Tony at Richmond Crescent to watch a Kevin Costner video and, as usual, talk politics intermittently. Tony was relaxed, saying he thought we would be fine even if Heseltine became leader. But he knew that by far the best result for us would be a further two years of Major. The next afternoon, Tony, Gordon, Alastair and I awaited the result in Tony's Commons office. When it came, Major was victorious, with 218 votes against Redwood's healthy eighty-nine – sufficient for Major to win on the first ballot, but close enough to make him look even weaker than before. None of us could help cheering. A smiling Gordon said, 'That's it.' Alastair added, 'We've got him.'

We didn't, yet. But the tide continued to flow away from the Tories in a by-election a few weeks later, in the Manchester constituency of Littleborough and Saddleworth. Tony asked me to manage the campaign. The election was caused by the death of Geoffrey Dickens, the well-liked Conservative MP who had held the seat since it was created in 1983. He had had a majority of 4,500 in 1992, with the Liberal Democrats in second place and Labour third. With Roy Hattersley and others, evidently including Charlie Whelan, feeding the media mill about my shadowy role in Tony's inner circle, I was relieved to get back to open operations on the front line.

Our candidate was a bright former NUS president named Phil Woolas. John Prescott was my comrade-in-arms during the campaign, along with Ian McCartney, the delightful Makerfield MP who became a friend and ally. For their company alone, I enjoyed the campaign. John and I had been through a rough patch since the start of the year. As almost always with John, the trigger was his feeling that he was being excluded from his true deputy leader's status – a sense Tony was always keen to allay, and Gordon to exacerbate. My sin was that John suspected me, rightly, of being opposed to him taking the leading role in preparing and running the general election campaign.

Now that we were both fighting for votes on the ground, the animosity evaporated. John was becoming aware of the scale of the tension between Tony and Gordon, and was determined to do all he could to soothe rather than add to it. On our missions to Lancashire, he was enormously good fun. He had an endless store of clever witticisms, whether about Major, Michael Heseltine or me, whom he would address as 'Bobby' or 'His Master's Voice'. He was a natural campaigner, who loved the cut-and-thrust of political battle, especially when he was on the attack.

In Littleborough and Saddleworth – 'Little and Sad', as we inevitably dubbed it – we *were* on the attack. After the campaign was over, not only our opponents but some in Labour would denounce our 'negative' tactics in highlighting Lib Dem front-runner Chris Davies's support for higher taxes and a Royal Commission to liberalise drugs laws. For tactical reasons, I felt we had had little choice. Labour was starting from third place, and especially in a by-election, the bulk of Tory tactical voting was always going to flow to the Lib Dems. If we were to win, we would have to make that option as distasteful as possible. In the end, it didn't work – or not quite enough. Davies won and Phil Woolas came second, though by a margin of only 2,000 votes. Our share of the vote was up by 15 per cent, while the Tories were down by more than 20 per cent. When Phil spoke at our almost victory party, he singled me out for thanks, memorably proclaiming, 'Peter may be a bastard, but he's *our* bastard.'

In other ways, too, the political weather was with us. In the 1992 campaign, Rupert Murdoch's *Sun* had typified the vitriol against Neil. Its election-day front page had a huge lightbulb with a headline exhorting 'the last person to leave Britain' in the event of a Kinnock victory to 'turn out the lights'. Now, Murdoch invited Tony to speak at a gala conference retreat for his News International Corporation, on Hayman Island off the coast of Australia. There was a brief period of classic Tony humming and hawing: 'How should we play this? What are the downsides?' We all knew that any downsides – chiefly, the likelihood of sniping from the left, who liked Murdoch even less than they liked Tony – were outweighed by what we had to gain. Within days of John Major's 're-election', Tony was off to Australia.

I was soon off as well, to Robert and Gill's home in Kintbury, to embark on a political project of my own. In one sense, I was at the centre of power in New Labour, or very near to it. I was involved in every significant political discussion, and every major decision. I was, with Gordon, the oldest and closest political friend of the man who very likely would be Prime Minister after the next election. As any politician in my place would, I sometimes found this intoxicating. But it had come at a price, which I found increasingly worrying. From my earliest days as an MP, I had largely abandoned attempting to build a political base of my own in order to support Tony and Gordon. I did not regret this. Our close political partnership had been central to the creation of New Labour, and I still liked and admired both of them. But the relationship with Gordon had fractured since the leadership election. His hostility to me, and Tony's understandable determination to keep him on side at all costs, had left me caught uncomfortably in the middle. No matter how great my influence with Tony, in the parliamentary hierarchy I was fairly near the bottom of the ladder. I was doing my obligatory stint in the whips' office, en route to a first, junior role on the front bench. But the reason I had first entered politics was that I hoped one day to be a fully fledged minister in a Labour government. The role Tony wanted me to play – as all-purpose and ever-present adviser, strategist, supporter and friend – was hindering, rather than helping, my chances of building a conventional party career. Worse, it was creating jealousy and resentment among many fellow MPs, shadow ministers, and of course Gordon. Especially after my clandestine role in Tony's leadership campaign, which by now had become public knowledge, it was also feeding my image as a shadowy power behind the throne.

In what I hoped would be a first step towards changing this, I decided to write a book. I wrote it with Roger over the summer in the Harrises' lovely house, overlooking the Kennet and Avon Canal. *The Blair Revolution* was not a guide to how New Labour could win the election, but an explanation of what we stood for, and how we would govern. Roger and I buried ourselves in writing our individual chapters, passing what we'd done to each other for suggestions and redrafting. As we were nearing the end, the *Observer* got hold of an early synopsis and splashed a number of audacious policy suggestions, all of which we had since left on the cutting-room floor: a no-strike arrangement for public service unions, an end to local council control over state schools, and, most explosively, a governing coalition with the Liberal Democrats, even if we won an outright majority at the election. All of these were extremely edgy for the mid-1990s, and we had cut them at the urging of either Tony or David Miliband. Gordon also read the manuscript. His main objection was to our including an idea, originating with him and Ed Balls, that we had been discussing with Tony for some time: giving the Bank of England independent control over setting interest rates. We took that out too. A final idea that Tony wanted to be removed concerned party funding. We favoured curbing the influence on politics of money, whether from the trade unions or individual donors, and proposed state funding for parties. Tony said he was sure he could never win the cross-party support needed to get this through the Commons. It was a failure of nerve we would all later have cause to regret.

Writing the book was a welcome retreat from the pressures of the all-purpose role I was playing for Tony. In it Roger and I sought to answer the charge that New Labour was no more than a rebranding job, an issue about which I felt particularly strongly because I had helped to bring about that rebranding. We defined the values that would guide us in government – fairness, social justice, equality – and the policy choices these implied in a modern Britain. We set out the need for left-of-centre governments to recognise that they could not mandate equality of outcomes for citizens. What they could do was work towards greater equality of opportunity, clearing away obstacles that prevented people from making the most of their lives: poor education and job training, inadequate health care, the scourge of crime.

In fundamentally recasting the old terms of debate between left and right in British politics, *The Blair Revolution* anticipated what came to be known as the 'third way' once we were in power. This was caricatured by our critics as a fancy term for a kind of value-free electoral expediency, checking what the polls and focus groups were telling us, particularly about Middle England, and picking and choosing policies to match. To a certain extent, this criticism was inevitable. The very phrase 'third way' risked being seen as a kind of mathematical exercise in which we took an Old Labour and an Old Tory manifesto, and split the difference. In fact, what we were saying was that the philosophical starting point for a modern, progressive party was to recognise that many of the old choices were false, even fatuous: the notion that you had to favour either economic efficiency or social justice; reward economic enterprise and aspiration or care for the disadvantaged; crack down on thugs and criminals or support programmes aimed at tackling the social and economic conditions that could lead to crime; stand up for Britain and its national interests or engage productively with Europe. In each case, it was not an either-or proposition. You had to do both. The book set this out clearly for the first time.

The Blair Revolution, while it sold reasonably well, did not, however, produce a revolution in my image, or my political career. It provoked resentment, even in Tony's inner circle. Alastair thought I was overstepping the mark and trying to draw attention to myself, while Gordon felt it was presumptuous to anticipate, and encroach upon, policy decisions that we would make in government. For Gordon, I am sure it did not help that Tony's name had sole billing in the title – which was, on reflection, a bit thoughtless of me. Most importantly, the book did not alter the core of my political identity. Once we were all back in London ahead of party conference in the autumn, I resumed my role in advising, brainstorming, strategising, planning, and helping Tony in a myriad other ways – the job he always called 'being Peter'. I knew that until that changed, nothing much else would either, book or no book.

Our overall campaign message, if not yet the policy or the planning, began to take shape in the autumn. It was summed up in Tony's conference speech. Deliberately looking outwards, and saying he had come into politics not to change Labour but to change the country, he stole the saner Tories' one-nation mantle, pledging to build 'One Britain' and make the country young, vibrant and hopeful again.

The speech was perfectly timed and perfectly pitched, and was all the more powerful because it came from the heart of everything Tony believed.

On campaign planning, Tony decided there was no time to waste. After conference he leaned on Gordon to accept his original plan, with Gordon in overall charge of campaign strategy and me getting started on making sure the necessary opinion research, policy work and personnel were in place. He even persuaded Gordon to agree that his representative on the planning committee would not be Charlie, but Sue Nye.

I moved into our new headquarters in Millbank early in 1996. The first thing I did was to make sure Philip was by my side. He wrote one of his confidential strategy memos, which, to his embarrassment – and mine as well, since somehow the media contrived to suggest that I was behind it – leaked to the *Guardian*. Headlined 'The Unfinished Revolution', it said we shouldn't be fooled by our poll lead. We had been in this position often before, only to lose when it counted. The Tories were resilient, and we had a host of problems to fix. New Labour was 'not yet a cohesive, integrated political party', as opposed to a modernising vanguard. It did not have a coherent project for government. It did not even have a campaign operation in place, with a clear structure and hierarchy leading through Gordon and me to Tony. On policy, Philip raised a comparison with Mrs Thatcher. She had had an outline project prepared, especially on the economy, three years before her victory in 1979. On campaigning, he cited Bill Clinton. The Democrats' operation had been marked by talent, discipline, clarity on policy and quickness on rebuttal, and most of all by clear lines of authority.

Tony was even more distraught than I was over the delays in getting the campaign operation up and running. When he sent me an especially jittery note a few months after the party conference, I tried to reassure him. Calm down, I told him. We were not fighting an election tomorrow. As I knew from my exhaustion in the final week of the 1987 election, we did not want to be burned out by the time the campaign began. My priority was to get the structure right, and make up for lost time. Tony had taken an important first step, and raised morale in Millbank, by agreeing an amicable separation with Joy Johnson. But much remained to be done if we were to assemble a functional campaign machine.

When I formally took hold of the operation, it was nowhere near as dishevelled as mid-1980s Walworth Road had been. A series of 'task forces' was already in place, though they were too numerous, unfocused and unwieldy. Nominally, it was all under the supervision of the party's General Secretary, the Kinnock-era moderniser Tom Sawyer, and Fraser Kemp, who had been given the title of General Election Co-ordinator in 1994. Fraser was a tough and effective political operative who had played a key role for Labour in a number of by-elections. But he was selected to fight the Sunderland seat of Houghton and Washington East, and would go on to be an effective MP.

I had no intention of sidelining either Tom or Fraser. My aim was to work with them. Though not exactly operating as 'Bobby', I took no title, no formal leadership role. I began to go through what was already in place, keeping the parts that worked, reshaping those that did not, creating a leaner machine that was ultimately answerable to Tony. Bit by bit, I assembled what would prove to be the most effective election team in the party's history. In addition to Philip, it would bring together old colleagues like David Hill and an array of future stars. Roger, too, was now firmly back in the Labour fold. Interestingly, one reason he had not returned even sooner was due to Tony, who viewed his continued association with the Liberal Democrats as a way of helping us build bridges with them in future. By the start of the campaign proper in 1997, there would be a cast of hundreds. But the core included my own young advisers: Derek Draper, who was still helping out despite having left for a PR and lobbying firm in mid-1995, and his quieter yet no less astute successor, Benjamin Wegg-Prosser, whom I had recruited from Sheffield after I had met him at a speaking engagement at the university's Labour

Club. Despite Tony's initial reluctance to part with him, I also spirited Tim Allan away to Millbank. Peter Hyman moved over as the key policy and presentation manager. A thirty-six-year-old former student political leader named Matthew Taylor – occasionally hot-tempered, self-possessed, but with a sharp mind, keen instincts and a hilarious sense of humour – joined us as well. He was important in pulling together our Clinton-style 'rapid rebuttal' unit.

The final major piece in the jigsaw was already at Millbank when I arrived, and took on the role of election coordinator when Fraser left. She was the kind of party professional I at first feared might be keener to answer to party committees rather than our tightly disciplined team. I could not have been more wrong. Margaret McDonagh, I soon told Tony, was excellent. She was tough, focused and organised. Like Tom Sawyer, whom she would go on to succeed as General Secretary, she was absolutely dedicated both to winning the election and to the New Labour project.

For any of this to work, we needed to operate as a wider team with key members of Tony's office. In addition to Tim Allan and Peter Hyman, David Miliband was critical, as head of Tony's policy unit. In coordination with Tony, I arranged for Roger to provide advice on building David's unit into something closer to a 'think tank'. It focused on a range of issues, from giving schools access to the internet, to empowering local communities to crack down on anti-social behaviour, and generally added grit and detail to New Labour's message.

Jonathan Powell was turning into everything we had hoped he would be. He brought order to Tony's sometimes maddeningly laid-back approach to policy discussion and decision-making, framing his conclusions into action points and ensuring that most of the time they happened. He was also important in focusing minds on what we would do in government if we won the election. As early as the spring of 1995 he had alerted Tony to four key priorities: the transition to government, through deciding how to structure Number 10 and the Cabinet Office; training the shadow cabinet and front bench;

establishing trust with the civil service; and preparing policy for government. On the first three at least, he got results. I was particularly involved in the Downing Street and cabinet preparations. On policy, Jonathan warned that we needed to 'avoid the mess Clinton got into when he came to power with no clear idea of what he wanted to do'. With a number of decisions and announcements ready for implementation, for a while we would appear to have escaped that trap. The longer we were in power, though, the more evident I think it became that we did not altogether succeed in doing so.

There was a recurring obstacle to getting the campaign on track. Gordon had ostensibly agreed to the management structure, but for months he almost ostentatiously refused to engage with the operation in Millbank. We did see each other often, at policy and strategy meetings, in his office or Tony's. I sent him notes to keep him aware of progress and to raise issues that had to be resolved. He would respond intermittently. When matters of urgency arose, I began working through Ed Miliband. There was one particularly chaotic exchange early in 1996. At issue was a £500,000 poster campaign, building on a suggestion from Peter Hyman, accusing the Tories of planning to put VAT on food. I knew from both Tony and Ed that Gordon was broadly in agreement, but he himself would not answer my requests for a formal sign-off. At the last moment, Ed told me Gordon was insisting on more cautious wording. I wrote back with an alternative version, though adding that if it was weakened any further I would be in favour of pulling the campaign and spending the money elsewhere. Gordon never answered, and the posters went up. This, however, was no way to prepare for an election, much less for government.

The 'Gordon effect' had policy implications as well. As Gordon himself knew from the unhappy experience of John Smith's shadow budget in 1992, no issue was more important, more delicate or more potentially toxic than tax. Economic strategy often dominated discussion with Tony and the inner circle. Gordon, assisted by the indisputable brainpower of Ed Balls, developed a number of astute, and politically imaginative, ideas – notably the suggestion to make the

Bank of England independent. But on tax, he was less tough, and more equivocal. He was considering a new 50p top rate for those who earned above £100,000. I was alarmed at the political implications. Tony was too. On his trip to the Murdoch conference in Australia, he had met the Australian Labor Prime Minister Paul Keating. Pinning Tony up against an aircraft door, Keating had given him a bracing bit of campaign advice: 'Under no circumstances ever go into an election saying you will put up income taxes!' Still, there was no sign that Gordon was ready to rule out the tax increase – or that he was ready to reach a final decision on it at all.

Tony's overriding concern was to keep Gordon on board, and he was careful to seek his input and involvement in every major political judgement. In meetings, he humoured Gordon. When things threatened to turn tense, he deferred to him. It was all part of his prescription for 'massive therapy'. My position with Gordon, however, was becoming ever more difficult. He alternately blanked or bullied me, in a way he could not afford to do with Tony. At Tony's urging, I went to Roger for the kind of no-nonsense advice I had sought from him on Gordon's image problems after the 1992 election – this time, on sorting out the problem of 'Gordon and Peter'. Roger was not only close to me, but at the time Gordon also trusted him, and valued his counsel.

The suggestions Roger produced were thoughtful, although looking back on them now, they seem faintly ridiculous. Getting Gordon to agree to them was not going to be easy. Roger mapped out a series of ground rules that I hoped might work. They were not that different from what Gordon had tried to get me to agree at Chewton Glen. Gordon would retain 'the final say on putting recommendations to Tony on strategy', and I would undertake to go along with them as long as I was fully involved beforehand. While I would have the final say on detailed general election planning, I would consult with Gordon. Finally, there were wider proposals for the relationship between the three of us: 'Gordon acknowledges that Tony is bound to want Peter's advice as a trusted friend. But Tony will never act on that advice without consulting Gordon on matters that are clearly within his responsibility. Peter acknowledges the centrality of the Blair–Brown relationship to the success of the government and that it must flourish.' It all made sense, in an almost comically prescriptive sort of way. But Gordon was not interested. However fruitless Roger's suggestions turned out to be, they did reflect the depth of frustration both Tony and I felt in trying to re-establish a stable relationship with an indispensable political partner whom we had also counted as a friend.

Tony managed to keep things on a remarkably even keel. But there was a point in the late spring of 1996 when, for me, the situation became unbearable. The incident, minor in itself, came at one of our Thursday-morning meetings in Tony's office, with Gordon, Alastair, Jonathan Powell and a handful of advisers. I was not in the best of moods. Despite my constant efforts to involve Gordon in our economic campaign strategy, it remained frustratingly unformed. At issue now was one bit of the economic picture, however, on which Gordon was genuinely engaged. Knitting together his interest in training with ideas on tackling inadequate education, unemployment and crime among young people, it was his 'New Deal for a Lost Generation'. For weeks, I had been working hard, as had Alastair, to ensure maximum impact for the launch on the following Monday. But no sooner had the meeting begun than Gordon said he didn't think it would be ready by then. Frankly, I lost it. I pointed out that it had been his idea, and that I and others had been trying to make sure it went off smoothly despite having had virtually no communication from him or his office. Gordon shouted at me that that was my problem. When I answered in kind, Tony turned to me and said, 'For God's sake, calm down.' I stood up and walked out. Inadvertently letting the office door slam behind me, I made my exit more dramatic than I had intended. But I was in no mood to explain or apologise.

Later that afternoon I took a flight to Prague to attend an Atlantic policy conference. On the plane, I wrote a note to Tony. It began with an apology 'for the way your meeting ended', but it was mostly a cry of frustration, and not entirely about Gordon's behaviour, which I had all but given up trying to change. It was also about my relationship with Tony. Roger's note had been right. Next to Gordon, he relied on no one more than me for advice and help. From the trivial to the critical, there were few issues on which he did not call on me to help. But Tony was leader now, probably about to become Prime Minister. Gordon was a cantankerous Chancellor-in-waiting. I was caught in between. Tony may have had his reasons for coddling, humouring, deferring to Gordon, no matter how sulky he became, and no matter how hostile towards me or others, but I felt that unless he was willing to draw the line somewhere, and to show support for me in the role he wanted me to play alongside the two of them, the psychodrama would end in tears. It was already damaging our preparations for the election, and if we won, I shuddered to think what it would mean for my hopes of playing a more formal role in the government. 'I think we have to recognise that you and I have reached the end of this road,' I said. 'I am more than willing to carry on the general election planning if you wish – although we'll reach the same brick wall on that, too, eventually.' Then I got to what was bothering me most: 'I felt greatly let down by you this morning. I do not want to be in that position again. Needless to say, I will always be available to you in any circumstance to help and advise. Operationally, however, I think we have reached the glass ceiling.' I concluded by saying that I wished Tony's situation was simpler. I hardly needed to add, so I didn't, that I wished mine was simpler too.

When I returned to London, what was left of the three-way relationship that had united Tony, Gordon and me showed every sign of heading for a final collapse. On the Saturday, Philip Webster had written a *Times* splash publicly suggesting for the first time that Gordon and I were quarrelling, and that Tony was struggling to contain the damage. Not surprisingly, given my walkout, I was suspected of having planted the story. In fact, I had had a routine chat with Philip the week before. He had put it to me that he understood things were pretty 'dire' between me and Gordon. I hadn't confirmed or elaborated on the suggestion, but I hadn't denied it either. Since it was true, and Philip was hardly a cub reporter, he had presumably built up the full, grisly picture from others.

When Tony got my note, he wrote back saying essentially that Gordon and I had to get a handle on what was 'indeed a serious situation'. He said my walkout, and stories like Philip's, were part of the problem. Carefully removing himself from sharing any responsibility, he said that both Gordon and I were 'more desirous of victory over each other than of trying to make it work'. He added: 'We have one overriding responsibility: to deliver an election victory. Though it may seem pious, it is just not fair to all those people who really want such a victory and are working for it, to be casualties of some titanic but ultimately irrelevant personality feud. . .Have you any idea of how despairing it is for me when the two people who have been closest to me for over a decade, and who in their different ways are the most brilliant political minds of their generation, will not lay aside personal animosity and help me win?'

Tony's note was, like mine, a record of the frustrations that were eating away at both of us. It was telling that he did not, so far as I was aware, send a similar note to Gordon. His view was that each of us was as responsible for the tension as the other, and in this he was being unhelpfully encouraged by Alastair, who for some reason seemed to regard me as a rival and who took the opportunity to see my wings clipped. In reality, however much Tony relied on me, he simply could not afford a break with Gordon. If Gordon decided to walk away, he could, and surely would, cause real trouble in the party. Tony knew that, out of loyalty to him, I would never do the same. He also knew that I could not. I now had my junior front bench post, as Civil Service spokesman. What I did not have, and was no nearer to achieving, was a political path separate from Tony, or any realistic hope of dealing with the resentment and suspicions it was sure to cause.

The immediate crisis passed. Tony and I spoke at length. Gordon and I spoke too, briefly but at least fairly politely. I think all three of us realised that a split in the founding triumvirate might prevent, or at least greatly complicate, New Labour's getting into government. All the more so because we were still some way from making the modernising agenda felt or accepted across the whole party. Clare Short used a *New Statesman* interview at the beginning of August to attack Tony's media and strategy circle, clearly meaning me, Alastair and Philip. Basically, she said we were trying to win the trust of the voters on a false prospectus. Tony and the 'dark men' around him were obsessed with the media and focus groups, and were making Labour look 'as if we wanted power at any price': 'They think Labour is unelectable, so they want to get something else elected, even though really it's still the Labour Party. This is a dangerous game, which assumes people are stupid...They are saying: "Vote for Tony Blair's New Labour. We all agree that the old one was absolutely appalling and you all know that most of the people in Labour are really the old ones, but we've got some who are nothing to do with that, vote for us!" ' Roy Hattersley piled in. 'Miss Short's attack, rightly or wrongly, reflected what a lot of rank and file members are thinking,' he wrote in the *Observer*, no doubt straining to avoid adding that what a lot of members ought to be thinking was 'Bring back Roy!'

The real problem was not Clare's self-indulgence, or Roy's: it was what they had said. They were wrong about New Labour. It was not just about presentation. The focus groups, polling analysis and strategy sessions were not a value-free exercise in finding out what the political market wanted and gift-wrapping the appropriate product. They were right, however, to say that by no means all of the party yet understood, or was actively part of, this process. At least two of Tony's 'dark men', Philip and I, had been highlighting that challenge for months, stressing the importance of Tony's reaching out, explaining and broadening the base of New Labour.

Now the Tories had been extended an open invitation to make political capital from this, to attack us where we were still most vulnerable, on trust. Exactly as I would have done in their shoes, they seized the opportunity. Within days, posters went up showing a grinning Tony with black-masked, blood-red demon eyes. Their campaign slogan read 'New Labour, New Danger'. There was an explanatory caption underneath, quoting one of 'Labour's leaders', Clare, as denouncing our dark forces and calling New Labour a dangerous lie. Tony was on summer holiday, as were Alastair and Philip. But I knew this was trouble if it hit home. Armed with an indignant quote procured by Peter Hyman, in which the Bishop of Oxford criticised the Tories for their Satanic imagery, I branded the posters as not just offensive, but as proof that the Conservatives were so bereft of policy, direction or a positive message for the British people that they had been reduced to demonology. I seized the opportunity of an *Evening Standard* platform to turn the fire back on the Tories. 'Demon eyes' was a mistake, I said. But then, the Conservatives were desperate, 'and desperate people make mistakes'.

This succeeded in largely blunting the Tory message. But while some in Conservative Central Office might indeed have been feeling desperate over our opinion poll lead, I did not for a moment think that victory was assured. Nor did I really believe the demon eyes poster was born of desperation. 'New Labour, New Danger' was precisely the right message for the Tories to try to get across. It tapped into concerns that could still deny us victory: the residual distrust of old Labour, and a feeling that despite our slick new leader and polished presentation, we hadn't really changed. It allowed them to define us, and Tony, in the most damaging way.

There was only one antidote: we had to get better, quickly, at defining ourselves. We were making some strides in the right direction. In a break from political orthodoxy, we had published a draft election manifesto, 'New Labour – New Life for Britain', and put it out for endorsement by the whole party. It included an innovation: six 'early pledges' that amounted to a formal contract with voters. We would cut primary class sizes, institute 'fast-track punishment' for persistent young offenders, slash NHS waiting lists, get 250,000 young people off benefit and into work, and legislate for devolved Scottish and Welsh assemblies. The pledges were short and catchy, and they addressed problems affecting millions of Britons. Tony's 'tough on crime, tough on the causes of crime' had made voters sit up and take notice. It had got Labour a hearing. But fast-track punishment, or training and jobs for a quarter of a million young unemployed, were a real-life translation that connected in a different way. The one slightly disappointing pledge was on the issue that was likely to loom largest once the campaign got under way: the economy. It was good as far as it went. Written by Gordon and Ed Balls, it pledged that we would 'set tough rules for government spending and borrowing; ensure low inflation; and strengthen the economy so that interest rates are as low as possible'. What was missing was specifics, especially on tax.

I had been pressing for a tougher, clearer economic message. Of the two specific ideas Gordon had put out so far, one of them, a limit on eligibility for child benefit designed to demonstrate our readiness to take tough decisions, was unclear, and was now being reconsidered; the other, Gordon's hope to establish a new 10p income tax band for the least well-off, was commendable, but opened us up to the obvious question of what we were going to do with other tax bands, thus playing into voters' concerns about 'old' Labour's record of overspending. This was one reason that the 10p commitment, originally pencilled in as part of the early pledges, was replaced with the more general economic policy statement. My view was that we should commit ourselves to tight spending rules for at least our first years in government, and should make it clear that we did not plan to increase the current 40p top band of income tax. Tony agreed, but Gordon was not convinced, or at least was not prepared to say so. He was still opposed to making major policy announcements until nearer the election.

By party conference in 1996, our polling showed that Labour's lead was slipping. This was in part because the economy was showing renewed signs of life, but also because Clare Short had revived the spectre of a divided Labour Party. As I informed Tony before conference, focus groups we had commissioned suggested voter concerns about him on 'trust, sincerity, convictions', and a sense that he would 'do anything to win votes'. That was fixable: I knew Tony had deep and utterly sincere convictions. But we needed greater policy definition, and to sort out the election campaign, especially in respect of our economic and tax policies.

Conference went smoothly. In his speech, Tony set out a broad programme for government, stressing fiscal responsibility as well as dramatically changed priorities in the way money would be spent. The most forceful, and detailed, passage concerned the priority closest to his heart, and on which we had made the most progress in formulating a detailed strategy. 'Ask me my three priorities for government,' he said, 'and I will tell you: education, education and education.' He pledged to reduce primary class sizes, set up literacy summer schools, modernise comprehensives to take account of children's varying abilities – all with 'continual assessment, targets set, and action where they were not met'. He highlighted our plan to bring computers into schools and train teachers to use them, with Dennis Stevenson drafted in to head an independent group on how best to make this work.

After conference, things even began to progress on the campaign. The arrangement we finally agreed had Gordon as overall coordinator, with me as deputy coordinator and 'executive head' of the campaign. At Jonathan Powell's insistence, decision-making would include 'TB, GB and PM on a continuous basis'. The Musketeers were back, at least on paper. But there were still tensions. Until the campaign began, Gordon remained often unwilling to engage with, sometimes even to communicate with, me or key players at Millbank. Almost every decision was a struggle. At some points this left me feeling literally ill – not, thankfully, with anything like the seriousness of my early months at Walworth Road, but with what my GP diagnosed as cluster headaches. The pain was all the more difficult to deal with because I suspected the cure I needed was not so much medical as political.

By the turn of the year, Gordon was at least intermittently more involved. Crucially, he also came round to the need for specifics on spending and tax, and finally to bury the idea of a new top rate of 50p. Guarding his decision with almost conspiratorial closeness, he got Charlie to set up a *Today* programme interview in January, in the course of which he made the announcement that we would not raise the top rate during the next Parliament.

We were far better prepared to win an election in 1997 than we had been in 1987 or 1992. We had a lead in the polls that had never fallen much below twenty percentage points. We had a leader who looked, sounded, and would campaign like a credible Prime Minister. While in the last two elections our manifestos had pretty much been written by Charles Clarke over the space of a weekend, this time we had produced, published and won endorsement for the first draft already, and David Miliband and his team were on their way to producing the finished article. The Tories were looking and acting tired. They were divided over Europe and bedevilled by accusations of sleaze, highlighted by a libel battle waged and then dropped by Tatton MP Neil Hamilton, over *Guardian* accusations that he had taken cash in return for asking Commons questions. Despite the confusion and delay surrounding our campaign preparations, we had every chance of winning.

Taking a step back from the day-to-day organisation, I wrote Tony a note on the overall shape of the campaign we needed – and of his, and John Prescott's, complementary roles in making it work. John would be perfect as our point man against the Tories. He was a very good campaigner, a 'rumbustious, tell-it-like-it-is politician' who would 'reassure our core vote'. Not realising how prophetic this would turn out to be several years later, I said that voters expected John 'to hit out' at opponents. Tony's role would be to 'make it safe for newcomers to support us'. Overall, the message had to be 'optimistic, upbeat and inspirational'. It had to enthuse voters to turn a page, make a new start.

That was pretty much the campaign we would run once the election was called. It had taken us a while to get there: we were much further along in our plans to attack the Conservatives and warn of a fifth-term Major government than we were in finalising our own message. Until we did, I feared that we would be vulnerable to the Tories' one possible line of attack: to encourage mistrust, and fear, of old Labour. The danger began to pass with Gordon's tax announcement, which we included in a revised list of final 'pledges' that we had printed on cards and distributed to voters. Our advertising strategy began to take shape. I addressed a shadow cabinet away-day, explaining the strategy and core message of the campaign. Our message was 'the future not the past, the many not the few, leadership not drift', I told them. 'We are saying Britain doesn't have to be like this. Britain can be better.' These themes had to be tied to values: 'one nation, fairness, opportunity for all'. I went through the chronology of the campaign, and finished by saying that with the plans in place, if we all played our parts, not only could we bring Labour back into Downing Street, I was confident we would. We were now down to detail. I signed off, with Alastair, on the ad agency's latest creative work for the campaign: arrestingly bright colours, simple and powerful design, all around the four words that summed up the message we most wished to convey: 'New Labour, New Britain'.

The start of the campaign galvanised, energised, exhausted, and refocused all of us. By calling the election in mid-March and setting polling day for 1 May, the Tories gave themselves an uncommonly long campaign – forty-four days – in which to attempt to claw back a poll deficit that stood at more than twenty-five percentage points. I felt we were ready for anything. I had a gifted core at Millbank, including the Clinton-style 'rebuttal unit' to nail inaccuracies in anything Tory Central Office threw our way. We had a grid in place for Tony, John and key shadow ministers. We had the pace and narrative of a campaign geared to fight hard while building towards a hopeful, positive message in the home stretch, in which we would transform the whole look in the final week, including changing our campaign colour from red to purple. We had Tony, the kind of campaigner any campaign manager would pay to work for. We had Philip, constantly engaged, focus-grouping every evening, and indispensable in helping fine-tune each day's message as required. Philip played another crucial, unseen, role: drawing up a summary at the end of each campaign day, he added a brief personal note for Tony, telling him the truth, good or bad, but always looking ahead, always reflecting the confidence we all felt that when it was all over we would be back in government.

Tony was unconvinced, to put it mildly. He was endlessly skittish throughout the campaign. None of us was taking victory for granted, but despite our commanding lead in the polls, he more often acted as if we were certain to lose. He deluged me with phone calls after every campaign appearance, every fresh poll, every slightly worrying newspaper headline. Even when I managed to get away from the Millbank 'war room' for a quick dinner or to see friends, Tony would almost invariably call. Was our message right? Was his latest speech right? Were the polls right? All this had the virtue of warding off what for Tony was the cardinal political sin: complacency. But it also added to the pressures of the campaign. It was wearing for all of us, and by the end of the campaign I had begun to dread yet another worried call from 'moany Tony'.

The campaign could hardly have started better. On day one the *Sun*, having packed away its lightbulbs, came out in support of New Labour. The next day, sleaze resurfaced to haunt the Tories, when the Liberal Democrat leader Paddy Ashdown accused Major of having started the campaign early to prevent publication of a preliminary Commons report into cash-for-questions allegations. The newspapers had a field day.

The problem for us was that by the end of the week, many voters seemed to be turning off and tuning out. The good news was that Philip's focus groups suggested that the only thing giving the campaign any real interest was Tony. The Tories fought back slightly in week two, and there was a brief period when we were concerned, and Tony was alarmed. The only real hope the Conservatives had, however, was the economy. It was out of recession, and voters had a sense that things were looking up. As I had repeatedly told Tony before the campaign, this meant that we always had to keep in mind the issue of trust. We had to get across to people that New Labour was not a risk to their well-being, or a brake on their aspirations. The difference between now and 1987 or 1992 was that I was fairly sure we could succeed in this. It wasn't just a matter of campaign messaging, but of the hard work, the battles fought, in the long modernising crusade ever since the 1980s. New Labour did embrace aspiration. It was not going to tax people till the pips squeaked. We had pledged not to raise income tax.

Astonishingly, in the first part of the campaign Gordon still refused to work properly with Millbank. Ed Balls, Ed Miliband and Charlie Whelan were in effect running a parallel campaign centred around Gordon. Only when Tony laid down the law did the operation come together. From that point on, shared fatigue, shared adrenalin, a shared sense that eighteen years in opposition might finally be ending, took over. A particularly effective counter-strike at the Tories came in mid-April. Over a period of days, an assortment of Eurosceptic Conservative MPs had begun to break with party policy, saying that EU integration had gone far enough. Edwina Currie, sent onto the *Today* programme to fight back, lamented imprudently that the backbenchers seemed to be 'making policy'. By the time of our morning news conference, we had Gordon armed with the transcript of her interview. He performed at his combative best.

Our only nagging concern was the Lib Dems, who made a mark with their deliberately off-piste announcement of a 1p rise in tax to fund school improvements. This inevitably raised the question in some voters' minds of how we would pay for our education plans. But even a late attempt by John Major to portray Tony as slavishly pro-European, German Chancellor Helmut Kohl's puppet, made only a glancing impact. To my own frustration, although I understood the political logic, Tony had moved to neutralise the Europe issue by downplaying our Euro-enthusiasm and promising a referendum on any decision to join the single currency. Now he was able to shrug off the Conservative attack.

In late April, barely ten days before the election, a poll had our lead down to 16 per cent. But it bounded back, and we were perfectly set for the final week – a week, as I had hoped and planned, in which we would seek a national consensus around a positive vision for a renewed Britain under a new Labour Party and a new Prime Minister. The themes had been mapped out weeks earlier: education, health, crime. So had the artwork and the message for our final posters: a photo of Tony urging the country to vote, 'because Britain deserves better'. The question now was not whether we would win, but whether we would win by enough to be able to govern with energy and confidence. We imposed a self-denying ordinance on Millbank: no talk of taking victory for granted, no talk of winning big, certainly no use of the 'l' word, no talk of a landslide. In truth, I expected a comfortable but not overwhelming victory. Philip felt the same way. In his final note to Tony, on the morning of polling day, he wrote: 'You will win today by a good margin. You have been magnificent in this campaign and you deserve your success.'

I spent the last day of the campaign in Hartlepool. Before leaving Millbank for the train journey north, I wrote Tony a final campaign note of my own. It was the media 'line to take' for his first day as Prime Minister of Britain. 'We were elected as New Labour and will govern as New Labour,' it said. 'We will keep the promises we made to the British electorate.'

In longhand below, I added: 'Well done. Bobby.'

6

Being Peter

I awoke early on election day, made a cup of tea in my cluttered kitchen in Hartlepool, and went out to vote. I was lucky to be there. The night before, as Ben and I were driving around the constituency doing some eve-of-poll campaigning, a large wheel flew off a flat-bed truck in front of us and clipped the roof of our car. Had it been a few inches lower it would have gone straight through the windscreen and into the passenger seat where I was writing. When I turned in that night, I felt that perhaps my lucky escape boded well. After eighteen years, I knew Labour was going to return to government. By the next day, Tony would be Prime Minister. I felt relief that the long wait was over, pride in my part in making it possible, joy that it was finally happening. I could not help thinking back to my early infatuation with Labour under Harold Wilson. To the realisation, from my time in the TUC in the 1970s and my experience of Labour lunacy in 1980s Lambeth, that our party had to change or die. The feeling that we might never secure, or deserve, power again. I recalled the hard slog of modernisation, first at Walworth Road with Neil, then with Gordon and Tony.

I also felt a kind of wonderment, a sense of unreality – and a momentary shudder. I feared that this new Labour dawn, like others before it, would prove an illusion. We would somehow foul up in Downing Street. We would miss the opportunity to establish ourselves as the natural party of government, the default Tory dominance of twentieth-century British politics would return, and our climb would start all over again. This was not just the superstitious caution that all politicians feel before an election result; it went deeper. The fact that Tony felt it too would have a major effect on the way we governed in our first term: not so much in our considerable achievements as in the things we did not do, the risks we did not take.

Tony had admitted to no one that he was sure we would win. The more he harassed me during the campaign, the more I sensed that he really believed we might lose. At Jonathan Powell's insistence, however, we had set aside time in the months before the election to work on 'transition'. On the afternoon of polling day, Ben drove me over to Sedgefield. Tony was asleep on a garden chair in the sunshine when I arrived. Jonathan and I were running through a list of junior ministerial appointments when he stirred, and joined us to discuss cabinet posts. Caution was the watchword from the start. Tony had decided that he could not buck party convention, and PLP rules, by denying elected shadow cabinet members their seats around the cabinet table. At most, he could shuffle a few around. Even that he did with reluctance. Top posts were left unchanged: Gordon as Chancellor, Jack Straw as Home Secretary, Robin Cook as Foreign Secretary. When we discussed some tinkering around the edges, like moving Chris Smith from Health to National Heritage, a new set of problems arose. Who would be Health Secretary? The only suitably senior candidate, Frank Dobson, did not seem right. At most, he would be a very reluctant moderniser. We hovered and hesitated, but finally Tony decided to give Frank the job. 'I don't exactly have a choice,' he said.

Next, we turned to a portfolio that would turn out to have even more serious implications: the Department of Social Security, with responsibility for welfare reform. Tony was tempted to vault my old 1980s campaign partner for one-member-one-vote, Frank Field, into the top spot. Unlike the other Frank, he *was* a reformer. He would not only promote change, he might attempt to steamroller it through. As I knew from personal experience, however, Frank was a lone ranger. He would work out in every detail the immutable blueprint that he felt to be acceptable. He was then entirely capable of flouncing out if others – junior ministers, civil servants, Gordon, even Tony – raised questions or objections. Tony's fallback choice, Harriet Harman, seemed safer to me. Tony was unsure, but in the end he made Harriet Secretary of State, with Frank her minister for welfare reform.

That left two other issues. The first was my job. Tony had told me weeks earlier that he wanted me to play a ministerial-rank role on issues reaching across government. He knew I would prefer something better defined, if less grand-sounding. I was eager finally to embark on a conventional political path, beginning with a junior post and working up to become a member of cabinet. Now I suggested a specific starting point, as Minister for Europe in the Foreign Office. While I was a bit more instinctively Euro-enthusiastic than Tony, we shared broadly the same vision on engaging with, yet helping reform, the EU. Briefly, Tony seemed to see attractions in giving me the Europe job.

The more we discussed it, however, the more he worried that I would be 'caught in between' him and Robin Cook. Besides, he said, Europe was not what he needed me to do during his early months in Downing Street. His first priority was to make sure we got a handle on government, and did not become just another one-term Labour interlude. 'I need you to *be Peter*,' he said. 'I need you around me to help make sure things run smoothly.' The job he settled on was Minister without Portfolio in the Cabinet Office. I was sceptical about how, or whether, this would work. 'I'll end up like a cork bobbing around on the surface of the government,' I told him. He replied that it would only be for six months or so. In his first reshuffle, I would be made a full departmental cabinet minister. I was still doubtful, but Tony's mind was made up. We agreed that I would nail down the details of the job with Jonathan over the weekend.

The final issue concerned a policy option we had been discussing for months, and which offered an opportunity to set an early stamp on government: giving the Bank of England independent authority to set interest rates. This was the idea Gordon had first raised two years before the election, and which Roger and I had left out of *The Blair*

Revolution. The question was when to announce it. Gordon apparently favoured doing so within days. Tony was enthusiastic about the policy, but seemed uncharacteristically hesitant about the timing of the announcement. I felt that the sooner, the better. It would reassure the markets, and show that New Labour was not just a project for party reform, or for winning elections, but for decisive government.

I returned to Hartlepool late in the afternoon. Shortly before 10 p.m., as the polls were closing, I set out for the civic centre to await the declaration of my result. As soon as I arrived, my pager buzzed with a message from Anji: 'Call TB, ASAP.' The first exit poll was pointing to a Labour victory by a commanding margin. 'It's unbelievable,' Tony said. 'What do you think? What should we say?' I advised caution, not because I doubted the poll, but because I felt that if we reacted too ebulliently, too soon, we risked making the actual result seem almost an anti-climax. 'We should say the exit poll is encouraging, but we must wait and see,' I told him. The problem was that as the constituency counts began to come in, 'waiting and seeing' looked increasingly perverse. After my result was announced – I had doubled my majority to 17,500, with a swing to Labour of 11 per cent – I saw little point in pretending that I wasn't moved by the scale of our gains across the country. 'In every generation, there is a change of a truly historic kind,' I said in my acceptance speech. 'I believe we are seeing just such a small political earthquake occurring today.' It felt extraordinary to be a part of it.

After the count, Ben and I drove to Teesside airport to link up with Robert Harris and return to London, where a victory rally had been organised at the Festival Hall. Robert had been in Sedgefield all day for a major *Sunday Times* feature he was doing on the election, and he had persuaded the newspaper to charter a small plane. Tony and Cherie, Alastair and Anji and the rest of Tony's key staff would be taking off half an hour or so behind us. When we were airborne, I turned on my portable radio and listened to the election coverage through my earpiece. As seat after seat fell to Labour, I announced the results to Robert and Ben with a growing sense of astonishment.

I drove Robert almost to distraction by repeatedly asking, 'Will this majority be bigger than 1945, bigger than Grandpa's?' When we landed at Stansted, the full import of the victory – and the idea that Labour was going into government – truly sank in. A prime ministerial limousine and half a dozen other official cars were lined up on the tarmac awaiting Tony's arrival. Police and protection officers were everywhere, and there were banks of television cameras and lights. As we stepped off the plane, TV reporters crowded round. I did several brief interviews, as coherently as I could in the grip of my excitement and fatigue, then we set off for the Royal Festival Hall.

Thousands of people were already there celebrating. We were heading for a Commons majority of nearly 180 seats – yes, more even than the majority of 145 that had brought Clement Attlee, and my grandfather, into government after the war. The venue also had a Morrisonian resonance for me. The Festival Hall was the enduring legacy of the Festival of Britain, in which my grandfather had played the central role. What most struck me, however, was the sheer elation the landslide had produced in everyone. As we waited for Tony and Cherie to arrive shortly before sunrise, even Gordon smiled at me. This was surely the only time I would ever dance with John Prescott – to the strains of our campaign theme, 'Things Can Only Get Better'.

When Tony arrived he grasped the outstretched hands and took in the extraordinary atmosphere as he made his way through the crowd. He smiled at me, as if words were unnecessary, and maybe inadequate, to express the emotions we both felt. I winked. His message, as he stepped before the cheering throng, was spot on. We had been elected – resoundingly – as New Labour. We would govern as New Labour. His opening words caught the spirit of the moment. 'A new dawn has broken, has it not?'

It had, and I was caught up in it as much as anyone. From the Festival Hall, I went to Millbank to thank the members of the campaign team who remained there. There was also a practical matter to deal with. We were getting calls from journalists asking for information on some of the new Labour MPs. I called the press office staff together and said we had better find out who they were. Even though I had been confident of a comfortable victory, nothing had prepared me for something on this scale. The reason we knew nothing about many of the newcomers is that it had never occurred to us that they would actually win. As the meeting broke up, a huge bouquet of flowers arrived from Robert's wife Gill. I don't know whether it was the kindness of her gesture, or the sheer relief and wonderment that the campaign, and eighteen years in opposition, were over, but I burst into tears.

Shortly afterwards, a batch of security passes was delivered so that the campaign team could join in the welcome for Tony outside Number 10. The entire staff hurried off towards Downing Street. I sat at my desk, surveying the war room that had been my home for the last year. I felt overwhelmed by the feelings of the past few hours, and overwhelmingly tired too. Also a bit at sea. It seemed to me that I did not belong in the flag-waving crowd to whom Tony would address his first words as Prime Minister. I suppose I could have joined the party inside Number 10, but unlike Jonathan or Anji or Alastair, I did not feel I belonged there either. Nor was I a member of cabinet. My new job might well turn out to be important, but I couldn't help feeling I would still be operating in an all-too-familiar grey area. I would have influence, but my real authority would depend on the fact that I was close to Tony. Much of what I would do would be out of the public eye. At least some of what I might be asked to do by Tony would spill beyond any single policy area, and beyond the generally accepted definition of a minister – even a Minister without Portfolio. That would risk resentment among the owners of political toes on which I might be required to tread. It would reinforce my image as an interpreter of Tony's wishes and an enforcer of his will, rather than as an emerging front-rank minister in my own right. It was exactly the territory I had been trying to vacate.

My formal job as Minister without Portfolio was to 'coordinate the presentation of policy' across government. On paper, once Jonathan and I had worked out the details of other related responsibilities, it appeared quite august. I would sit on a majority of cabinet committees. I would join Tony, Gordon, Alastair and Jonathan for a weekly meeting to discuss overall government strategy. I would be copied in on key memos and policy documents flowing in and out of Number 10. I would chair a daily meeting of special advisers from key departments to decide the media strategy for the day. Like Tony and everyone else, I was simply excited to be in government. The idea of being in Number 10 – or in my case, in the Cabinet Office, one swipecard away – was exhilarating.

The same could be said of my new job, at least to begin with. Within days of the election, I was part of a meeting to map out the contents of our first Queen's Speech. At Tony's instigation, I also took hold of ensuring we made rapid progress on our pledge-card promises. Yet mostly, as I had anticipated, the job turned out to be a movable feast. It would expand or contract according to what Tony wanted, or felt was needed. At some times, in some areas, I felt that I was making a real difference. At others, I did slightly bob like a cork. While that was frustrating, it at least allowed Alastair to delight in his own rendition of my title, as 'Minister without a Job'. The fact was that most of my influence, which at times was very considerable, flowed from the familiar informal, unofficial part of my role: as all-purpose adviser, strategist, ally and friend to Tony Blair. That was especially true when things went wrong. Then I became Minister for Bad News.

There was only good news, however, in the early months. Or at least that is how it seemed at the time. On our first Tuesday in government, Gordon sprang his surprise announcement about the Bank of England, to the glee of the markets and almost universal acclaim from the media. Then he moved ahead with our plan for a windfall tax on the privatised utilities. He used the cash for a new scheme to tackle youth unemployment, one of our campaign pledges. In another move worked out with Ed Balls before the election, he drew on Treasury reserves to add more than £1 billion to the health budget. While keeping to our promised Tory levels of taxing and spending,

Gordon conveyed a dazzling mix of fiscal prudence, political imagination and raw energy.

Tony got off to a good start too. His extraordinary gift for communication, his ability to connect, his sheer political presence lifted both the government and the country. We made early progress on keeping campaign commitments: smaller class sizes, fast-track punishment of young offenders, a national minimum wage, preparing for referenda on devolved government in Scotland and Wales, signing up to the European Social Chapter. We seized other bits of low-hanging policy fruit, banning handguns, restoring trade union rights at the GCHQ intelligence facility, and announcing free entry to museums. Building on our move towards smaller primary classes, we set up a unit to monitor targets for literacy and numeracy. Tony's poll ratings were not only high, they were like something out of the Soviet Union or North Korea. So were Gordon's. So were the government's. After the final years of tired, sometimes sordid, Tory rule, the country had voted for change. They had got it, and clearly they liked it.

Despite all our early achievements, however, literally within days of Tony's arrival in Number 10 I saw signs of trouble ahead. Signs, also, of the central tension that would define Tony's entire time in power: between him and Gordon, and the policy and political teams around each of them. I suppose my relationship with them both meant that I was always going to be aware of the first, fairly minor, strains. But the main reason I knew that all was not well was my job. Since the Cabinet Office was a coordinating centre for government, I worked closely with a range of senior civil servants – especially Robin Butler, the Cabinet Secretary, and Terry Burns, the Permanent Secretary at the Treasury. I already knew Terry socially, through John Birt and his then wife Jane, and I liked and respected him.

A fortnight after the Bank of England announcement, Gordon pulled off another *coup de théâtre*, this time summarily stripping the Bank of much of its financial regulatory authority. Since its governor, Eddie George, had been led to believe by Gordon that he would be consulted before any such move, he was furious. So was Terry:

not so much because of the decision, as the way it was handled. 'This is simply not the way to do things,' he said. 'All Eddie needed was to be talked to properly.' In fact, from the moment Gordon arrived at the Treasury, he paid only perfunctory attention to Terry and other officials. He was operating – with considerable panache, it had to be said – through a tough and trusted political team, chiefly Ed Balls and Charlie Whelan. Now Eddie George was talking of quitting. When I spoke to Tony, he was alarmed. Losing the Governor of the Bank of England two weeks into government, in what was sure to become a very public spat, would hardly promote an image of economic and political sure-footedness. Tony talked to Gordon, and insisted that he find some way to restore a semblance of dialogue with the Bank, then he phoned Eddie George, and talked him back from the brink.

Number 10 had early civil service problems of its own. Tony had decided to give the key members of his team, Jonathan and Alastair, executive authority, empowering them to give instructions to civil servants. The Cabinet Secretary Robin Butler believed that this might blur the traditional line between political appointees and the civil service, but in government, as in the formative years of New Labour, Tony didn't think that way. It wasn't that he was out to humble or humiliate the civil service; he simply felt that the structure was not right. What counted was what worked. He believed that in order to govern most effectively, he needed Jonathan and Alastair to be unquestionably in control at Number 10.

I would go on to work closely, and well, with Robin Butler. Though he could be a bit difficult at times, he had huge experience in government, and his intelligence and insight should have been used better. But his initial clash with Tony meant there was an uneasiness, on both sides, in his relationship with Tony's core political team. I think Robin should have been less insistent in opposing what the new Prime Minister wanted, and I believe he came to feel that way too, at least about the change in status for Jonathan. He thought extending it to Alastair was a step too far, however.

I had a considerable hand in assembling the Downing Street Policy Unit, and especially in persuading Tony to leave David Miliband in charge. Tony had thought of looking beyond politics for somebody to run it. He had sounded out Bob Ayling, the chief executive of British Airways, as he felt that Bob's combination of intellect, sympathy for the New Labour cause and business experience would bring an originality and energy to the role which a policy specialist simply could not offer. Even Tony's charm failed to win Bob over, however, and he said no.

Tony viewed David as a bit too inflexible, and possibly not New Labour enough. I argued that he was right for the job. He was very bright. He could grasp complex policy issues. He had a sense of how decisions would play in the real world. He didn't get rattled. He inspired confidence in those around him. In the end Tony agreed, and came to value, trust and rely on him. Alongside David was an extraordinarily gifted team. Roger dealt with European issues and defence policy. Peter Hyman straddled policy and communications. James Purnell joined, fresh from a stint at the IPPR and as a planning executive at the BBC. As I saw in my regular dealings with them, they were assiduous in developing ideas, anticipating problems, presenting options and suggesting ways forward.

The real problem was a lack of hard policy preparation before we got into Number 10, and now a lack of structure and rigour in the way we, and Tony, set priorities, reached decisions and took them forward. Just two weeks after the election, I wrote Tony a note: 'Government is bigger, more complex, than opposition. We used to rely on speedy, informal ways of working – including daily knowledge of your thinking and demands.' That would no longer work. What I failed to say, because none of us would fully recognise it until many months later, was that Gordon's operation was altogether different. It is true that being Chancellor was easier than being Prime Minister – a point I would try to impress on Gordon, not too successfully, years later. But Gordon and Ed had arrived at the Treasury with a carefully prepared set of policy plans. They were rigorously disciplined in carrying them out and, with Charlie as spinner-in-chief, in building an image of a Chancellor in control of his brief and setting the pace and tone for the new government. It was an operation run entirely separately from Number 10. It was also more efficient and effective.

Even at this early stage I was aware of personal tensions. Not so much between me and Gordon, although he kept a watchful eye on what I was doing at the Cabinet Office. He obviously bristled at my closeness to Tony, aware that in the unwritten part of my job I was involved in the key issues of policy strategy and political judgement. Any direct conflict between us was limited by the fact that I was not in charge of a spending department with a claim on Treasury funds. But in my formal 'policy presentation' role, difficulties with Gordon's team became inevitable. My morning meeting with political and media advisers obviously had to include Charlie, and also Nick Brown, who was now Chief Whip. Charlie generally attended in the early period, but he was awkward, sometimes truculent, and clearly uninterested in cross-government coordination. He saw his job as image-making for the Treasury, above all for Gordon. What the rest of us did – including Alastair as the spokesman for the Prime Minister – was our affair. Before long, both Charlie and Nick attended only sporadically.

At the time, these were fairly minor aggravations – a bit of annoying turbulence in the serene passage of our first months in government. I was working long hours, and was often on the phone to Tony or others in Number 10 after I left the office in the evening. I was also happy in my personal life. I finally had a real home, a lovely Georgian house in Notting Hill which I had managed to buy in the run-up to the election campaign. Most important, in Reinaldo I had found my long-term partner. I had a core of close friendships: 'work' mates like Roger and Philip, and others as well. Robert and Gill Harris and their children were like family; Dennis and Charlotte Stevenson and their four boys; Robin and Linda Paxton and their sons, Conrad, my godson, and Caspar; the Birts. I had a lively, and when I chose a decidedly A-list, social life. New Labour was not only electorally popular, it was chic, and people wanted a bit of that chic at their parties and receptions.

Tony, of course, was the most sought-after, as he had started to discover before the election when Mick Jagger decided he wanted to meet him. I had always been more Beatles than Stones as a boy, but Mick was engaging, intelligent, politically astute, a lively conversationalist and simply good fun. Earlier in the year, Tony, Cherie and I had joined Robert and Gill, Tom Stoppard, and Mick and Jerry Hall for dinner at the English Garden in Chelsea. Tony and Jerry hit it off at once, and chatted non-stop. Afterwards, Tony summoned up his courage and went up to Mick. Looking him straight in the eye, he said: 'I just want to say how much you've always meant to me.' He looked wistful, perhaps remembering his frustrated rock-star ambitions from his student days. For a moment, I thought he might ask for an autograph. In the flush of our early popularity in government, I was invited to spend an evening with Mick, this time in the company of Kate Moss, at the home of mutual friends outside London. At one point, Mick was singing, Kate was dancing, and I felt an urge to join in. Fortunately for all concerned, I lost my nerve.

Mostly, however, my engagements were more sedate. In London's political social circles, Charles and Carla Powell adopted me, much to my enjoyment. I had first met Charles, the elder brother of Chris and Jonathan, in the early 1990s, after he ceased being Margaret Thatcher's foreign policy adviser. Not only were Carla's pasta suppers a magnet for an array of interesting people, from politics and business, literature and the arts, but she was wonderful company, with an ability to get those around her to take life, and themselves, a bit less seriously.

The change in our first term began, at least for me, as early as the summer of 1997. On the surface, we were enjoying an extended political honeymoon. Our poll lead over the Tories was enormous. In June, the Conservatives chose William Hague as their new leader. Though he was bright, and a good Commons speaker, it was clear from the start that he was no match for Tony in his ability to communicate with the public.

I was already beginning to feel concerned, however, by the lack of direction and drive in key areas of government policy. Our early achievements were important. The reason Tony decided to make a priority of fulfilling our pledge-card promises was because we knew that in order to retain the country's trust, we had to show we were keeping our bargain with the voters. Like Tony, I was haunted by the history of one-term Labour administrations. Even so, I felt that the overriding goal of securing a second term was causing us to shy away from major policy changes. I thought that was wrong. Philip's final election campaign note had urged Tony to do the difficult or potentially unpopular things early on, when he would be at the height of his power. Instead, we were doing the easy things. I feared that this might come back to haunt us. This was not just because we might lack the support to do them later on, but because the huge scale of our victory had produced equally huge expectations about what we would deliver. Even with the smoothest of policy operations and the most single-minded determination, we might not be able to meet them. In all probability, no government could. But we had to try.

In July, I joined Tony and his team at Chequers for a discussion of our first months in office. Beforehand, I had a long talk with Roger, and suggested he draft one of his memos for me to use to ward off early complacency. 'We are still in our honeymoon phase, where people think changes in style and tone amount to real changes of substance,' it began. 'But how many big decisions have we pushed through? What are we going to be judged by in five years' time?' I was equally forthright with Tony. Of course we were right to focus on our pledge-card, but 'box-ticking' was not enough. Nor could that narrow prospectus explain the scale of our landslide. Roger's memo boiled down the voters' message to a single sentence: 'The New Labour victory was a vote for better education and health without a return to tax and spend.' He was right, although I would have added 'and a better, fairer welfare system' to the mix. We had yet to pave the way for real progress on any of this.

Our promise to keep to the Tories' financial strictures for our first two years in office had been essential to establishing our credentials as stewards of the economy. But it was also slowing down the pace of change, and delaying serious thought about what we would do when the moratorium ended. On education, at least, thinking was under way. Tony had made the issue a priority: he felt the urgency of change not only as a politician, but as a parent. Whenever I visited the Department for Education and Employment, I was struck by the energy of David Blunkett, who was far and away the most dynamic member of the first cabinet. His top adviser, Michael Barber, was a zealously reformist academic who had advised Tony on education before the election. David was engaged in designing a new structure for education that put parents' and pupils' interests first, and, crucially, sought to make local education authorities responsible for helping schools, not running them. Andrew Adonis, who would soon be drafted into the policy unit to focus on education, was even braver in his thinking, and more impatient for change.

The contrast with health policy could hardly have been greater. There, we had not focused on where we wanted to be in five years' time. Frank Dobson was not thinking through reform, other than unpicking Tory changes and a laudable attempt to 'localise' health provision. Our internal feedback predicted that no matter what we did, NHS waiting lists would begin to fall only in 1998. Even that would turn out to be optimistic. Our immediate challenge was to head off 'winter crisis' pressures on the health service. We knew that our brave talk about clearing away bureaucracy would play well in the press, but there were limits to how much of it could be eliminated: the NHS had to be managed. Health professionals would also welcome our commitment to end the Tories' 'internal market', but we had no clear idea what we would put in its place.

Tony did want to move further and more quickly. But neither he, nor the rest of us, were quite sure how to achieve this. Later, he would be accused of running a 'presidency' rather than a premiership. In fact he was caught between the two. He was more like Bill Clinton, or Barack Obama, than past British Prime Ministers in his use of speeches, news conferences and set-piece appearances to establish policy tone and momentum. He did much of his work in our own, smaller, version of the Oval Office: the 'den', with its sofa and armchairs and desk, next to the Cabinet Room, which I remembered from my childhood visit to Number 10 as Marcia Williams's office. Tony lacked the machinery and the mindset, however, to exert presidential power over government. He liked to receive presentations. He was stimulated by them, and was good at responding for the duration of the discussion in hand. But he did not have the time – or always the inclination – to read papers in advance and get a grip on the broader debate and planning needed to drive hard policy decisions. 'I know Tony does not look forward to ministerial meetings,' David Miliband wrote in a plaintive memo to me at one point. 'But often things are not done and dusted without his input, and they can affect decisions. Thatcher chaired 24 meetings on her last NHS White Paper. Tony says he is interested in endgame, not process. But without influencing the process, the endgame is never satisfactory.'

I pressed Tony to create a more rigorous structure for policy development, oversight and implementation. In the months that followed, I would work on the details of an alternative with David, Jonathan, Robin Butler and, when Robin retired in 1998, his successor as Cabinet Secretary, Richard Wilson. I had by now abandoned an idea Roger and I proposed in *The Blair Revolution*, the establishment of a 'Prime Minister's Department'. I feared that would demotivate front-line departments and unsettle the cabinet. It would also imply that Tony and his office could somehow run the entire government, which was frankly impossible. What was needed was a mechanism for Tony to set the agenda, and ensure that all departments were on the same page and moving forward with the decisions required. This 'strengthened centre' would have the aim of allowing him to exert the kind of leadership, influence and control that a CEO had over any successful business. It would have to be coordinated by a senior politician, trusted by Tony and carrying political weight in Whitehall. That person, I made it clear from the start, should not be Peter Mandelson. More than ever, I wanted a role as a departmental head.

Still, it seemed to me that the job had to be done. I could, and perhaps should, have filled the role when I was at the Cabinet Office, but Tony never settled on exactly what the job should be. In all but a very few instances, when I had to sort out specific policy difficulties at Tony's request, I deliberately avoided intervening on policy issues with individual departments. I was anxious to escape my image as Tony's all-purpose confidant and alter ego, and I feared being accused of meddling on other ministers' turf. Perhaps I shouldn't have worried – I was accused of that anyway.

I did try, and abjectly failed, during that first summer in government to reinvent myself as a more independent presence. With Tony's approval, I decided to stand for one of the places on Labour's National Executive. The NEC had nowhere near the hold over policy it had when I was at Walworth Road, but being elected to it was still an indication of support within the broad range of the party. I did not expect to romp home to victory: rarely did candidates make the grade on the first run. In an early campaign blueprint that I worked out with Ben, we accepted that we were never going to be a match for shoo-in choices like Robin Cook, David Blunkett or Dennis Skinner when the votes were tallied ahead of party conference in the autumn. Our best hope was to secure one of the last of the seven slots available – effectively putting me in competition with Ken Livingstone. I hoped to make my case on the basis of my lifetime commitment to Labour, my work at Walworth Road, the 1997 election campaign victory, and my current role alongside not just Tony but the ever-popular Labour traditionalist John Prescott. It proved to be a chastening experience. I was not helped by a truly terrible August, in which the confused nature of being a minister and 'being Peter' made me a magnet for criticism.

Tony and other senior ministers were away on their summer holidays, so John was formally in charge. I was Tony's and Alastair's primary long-distance contact, however, and was their obvious surrogate of choice in dealing with political, and especially media, problems. From their very first days away, in early August, I was charged with managing the repercussions of the *News of the World*'s discovery that Robin Cook was romantically involved with his diary secretary, Gaynor Regan, and his decision to split from Margaret, his wife of twenty-eight years. As so often, my role turned out to be informal and unofficial. In this case, it was also intensely personal. Tony had written a note of sympathy to Margaret, saying that he felt upset at the pressures she was having to endure and hoped she would be able to rebuild her life. She wrote back that it was odd he had not expressed sadness over the fact her marriage was over.

She phoned me a few days later. I did not know Margaret then, but said I could understand why she was distressed, and that I was sure Tony was genuinely upset at the break-up of her marriage to Robin. With Tony's encouragement, I went to see her in Edinburgh. I found her enormously impressive – a successful haematologist, she was obviously both bright and strong. She was distraught as we talked in the sitting room of her home, with reminders of Robin all around us. Over a period of a couple of hours she told me of their life together, starting with their marriage and honeymoon. Her pain was heart-rending. This was the first of a number of meetings and phone calls in the months that followed. I found myself acting as a go-between with Robin and Margaret over aspects of the divorce settlement. On the day the divorce became final, Margaret wrote me a kind note thanking me for mediating between them during the settlement, and added: 'I really do feel a great sense of relief.' Robin married Gaynor in April 1998. When he died of a heart attack in the Scottish Highlands in August 2005, I was impressed by Margaret's tribute to him. Calling the news 'a terrible shock and a terrible tragedy', she praised him as a politician who still had 'so much to offer', and as an exemplary father to their children.

I handled a variety of other media issues in the weeks that followed. Always sensitive to any encroachment on his own role as Deputy Prime Minister, John resented this, seeing it as undermining the impression that he was in charge. I am afraid I made things worse. In addition to my need to deal with genuine issues in the press, I actively welcomed media exposure as a way of lifting my profile ahead of the NEC election. I should have remembered from my time working for John and Albert Booth in the 1980s how important media exposure was to John. The moment Albert left on his summer holiday, John would come straight through the door, prodding me to help produce press releases or arrange media appearances on every conceivable transport issue. Even a cow stranded on a level crossing somewhere was enough, as long as he could find someone in government to blame it on. Now, at the height of the silly season, the papers delighted in creating an impression of the two of us scrambling like schoolboys to see who could be in charge while the teacher was out of the room. On a visit to the Millennium Dome site in Greenwich, John picked up a jar containing a small crab, and memorably dubbed it 'Peter'. That would have been fuel enough for headlines. He went on to conduct a mock conversation with the crustacean that the broadcasters loved. 'Me and my mate Peter,' he chortled. 'Do you think you will get on the executive, Peter?'

I didn't. I wasn't all that far off, but I wasn't that close either. Ken got around 83,000 votes, to my 68,000. If ever there was a signal of the need to build a more open, traditional political identity in the party, this was it. So was the tortuous time I had in August. Tony, and especially Alastair, returned from holiday not only angry over the media coverage in their absence, but blaming me for having allowed it to happen. Alastair's criticism was, as usual, the more pointed, and in my view the more unfair. It was true that I had sought more headlines than I should have done, but that wasn't what was aggravating him. Ever since the election, the presentational responsibilities of my Minister without Portfolio role had grated with the alpha male in him. He saw me as a rival, not a minister, let alone a friend, and clearly felt that I aspired to displace, or at least compete with, him as Tony's media chief. He missed the obvious point that I did not see my political future as a media spokesman, but as a successful minister.

The first thing I did in response to Alastair's criticism was to say that I would stop briefing journalists. I would stick to the 'strategic implementation' part of my job, happily leaving the media to others. But the problem was that whatever I did or said was bound to be filtered through an image that had been years in the making, first at Walworth Road and then reinforced by my role in Tony's leadership campaign. 'When I became "Bobby", it was a bad setback for me,' I said to Tony towards the end of August. 'I understood the reasons for having to do it, but let's be honest, I've never really recovered.'

A few days later I left for holiday myself. I was staying with friends in the States when the news broke that Diana, Princess of Wales, had been killed in a high-speed car accident in Paris. I had met Diana on a number of occasions through our shared involvement in the English National Ballet – she was patron, and I was on the board. About a year earlier, we met at a reception at the Ballet's headquarters on the day of her divorce from Prince Charles. I always found her enjoyable company, and felt that her ability to touch a chord with the public had modernised the image of the royal family in much the same way that New Labour had reconnected us with the lives of British voters. But we were acquaintances rather than friends – my feelings certainly never approached the near-teenage infatuation that seemed to envelop Alastair whenever he returned from meeting her. I got the sense at our final meeting that although she felt liberated from all the pain she and Charles had endured, she was not prepared simply to let go of that stage of her life. When I saw Tony's televised comments on her death, however, I knew they would touch a nerve in the British people. They certainly touched me. 'How difficult things were for her from time to time, surely we can only guess at,' he said. 'But the people everywhere. . .they kept faith with Princess Diana. They liked her. They loved her. They regarded her as one of the people. She was the people's princess.'

In the days that followed, public grief would at times border on hysteria, in equal parts celebrating Diana's memory and targeting the royal family, especially Prince Charles, for the supposed lack of respect they had shown her in life and now in death. I do not think that was fair. I was not in any real sense a personal friend of Charles either, but only three weeks before Diana's death, I had unexpectedly got to know him better. We had met only on the odd public occasion since a reception to which I had been invited in the early 1990s, when Charles had greeted me warmly: 'Ah,' he had said, 'the red rose man!' Now I was telephoned by a royal aide who asked me to a private lunch at Highgrove. All I was told was that Charles and I would be joined by Camilla Parker Bowles. When I was ushered into the entry hall, Charles's then press adviser, Mark Bolland, was chatting to Camilla. He introduced us, and seconds later Charles came bounding down the stairway. As he showed me around the garden, it began to drizzle. He rushed inside to fetch umbrellas. On his return, he started to unburden himself about the media pressures he was feeling in the wake of his divorce from Diana.

I could see that he wanted to talk about his and Camilla's situation. I asked how he had felt about remarks by George Carey, the Archbishop of Canterbury, suggesting that a remarriage would create a difficult situation for the Church of England. He replied that they hadn't said anything about marriage, and wondered why people felt the need to presume things about their intentions.

Given the excruciatingly public collapse of his marriage with Diana, I said that the new openness of his relationship with Camilla struck many as coming too quickly. He again insisted that they had no plans to marry, and said they just wanted to lead a more normal life. That could happen, I said. But he had to recognise that public acceptance would have to evolve: 'You will need to be patient, let things find their own level and not force the pace.' He seemed to accept this, but was obviously concerned about his image in the media. How did I think he was seen? 'I think you command more affection, or sympathy, and respect than you realise,' I said. After all, his work for the country extended well beyond what was expected of him. His range of interests and involvements clearly trumped the 'good causes' normally associated with someone in his position. But, I added, some people had 'gained the impression you feel sorry for yourself, that you're rather glum and dispirited. This has a dampening effect on how you are regarded.'

I feared I had gone too far. Camilla turned towards him with obvious concern about how he might react, while Charles himself seemed momentarily stunned by my remarks. He said that he couldn't comprehend why this was so. I said perhaps it was because he often had reason to feel down, given how he was treated in the press, and the unhappiness of his marriage to Diana. Before I left he made a point of thanking me for my frankness. It was a message he repeated in a handwritten note barely a week before Diana's death.

The day after Diana's accident, Charles's office phoned and asked me to call him. I could tell from his voice that he was shaken. He was especially worried about the children. I said that however difficult his relationship with Diana may have been, he would feel utterly bereaved – and not only because she was the mother of his young sons, whom the loss would hit even harder. In an effort to reassure him I said that over time, and out of the tragedy might come the possibility to move on with his life.

Like so many millions of others, I felt a deep sense of sadness about Diana, and when I returned to London I went to Kensington Palace to see for myself the sea of flowers, cards, candles and other tributes that members of the public had left in front of her home. The whole nation was in mourning, and their feelings were immortalised in the public remarks that Tony made in Sedgefield.

The more I came to know Charles over the next few years, the more I was convinced that the coldness and distance attributed to him and his mother after Diana's death were not due to a lack of genuine grief, but were a reflection of the life they were required to lead.

The royals are simply different from the rest of us – even from other subcultures, equally strange and strained in their own way, like the Westminster village. I had had reason to fret over media intrusion into parts of my life that had nothing to do with my public work. At least for me and other politicians, however, there was a dividing line to defend. For Charles and the Queen, their lives were quite literally their job. Every move they made, every smile or raised eyebrow, every relationship made or severed, was seen as part of their defining function: simply to be the royal family.

Still, as I and others at Downing Street liaised with the royals over the mourning and funeral arrangements, I could tell that Charles was both saddened by Diana's death and deeply hurt by the public criticism of him and his family. A fortnight later, when he visited Manchester, Alastair and I helped him draft a statement to encapsulate his and his mother's feelings. 'As so many of you will know from the experience of family loss in your own lives, it is very difficult to cope with grief at any time,' he said. 'It is even harder when the whole world is watching. The public support and warmth helped greatly.' He spoke of his pride in his sons, and praised the way the funeral had been organised, in an attempt to answer media suggestions that he and his mother had been unsettled by the service, which included pointed pulpit remarks from Diana's brother and a moving musical performance by her friend Elton John. As it happened, I had been asked by Number 10 before the funeral for my opinion on the idea of Elton participating. I said I was a huge admirer not only of his music, but of his work for charities, and that I was sure he would perform with dignity and sensitivity. Finally, he made a plea for a change in media attitudes as a result of the tragedy. 'I am not worried for myself so much as for my sons,' he said. 'They need their privacy, and I really hope this will be respected.'

Interested as he was in issues from architecture to agriculture, after Diana's death Charles would write me notes about areas of public policy which he believed to be misguided. I would always answer, and of course pass on his views to Tony. At times I would be the carrier of messages in the other direction, for example when Charles began publicly to speak out against genetically modified crops. I was on a visit to New York when Number 10 phoned to ask me to urge caution on him, and I spoke to Charles from a traffic jam in the middle of Manhattan. Like Tony, I felt that his remarks were becoming unhelpful. I thought they were anti-scientific, and irresponsible in the light of food shortages in the developing world. I am sure Charles did not change his mind as a result of our conversation, but he did tone down his public interventions on the subject.

On a personal level, I grew to like and respect him. I argued privately within government that when the public was ready to accept the idea of his marrying Camilla, we should support him in his desire to do so. Camilla seemed to me warm, stable, intelligent and a perfect match for him. She was cheerful company, without a trace of pomposity or arrogance. After my NEC defeat, Charles wrote me a sympathetic note: 'It only goes to show, I suppose, what a ghastly, cut-throat business politics is. The throwing of knives into other people's backs seems to be a pretty prevalent blood sport and it is not a pretty sight. But then, you would perhaps expect the representative of an "outmoded" hereditary organisation to make such an observation!' He said he was writing to let me know that he felt for my predicament 'as a *person*, who despite the inevitable outer carapace which has to be worn to confront the world, nevertheless has a rather vulnerable and sensitive inner core'. I reflected on how unthinkable it would have been for a fellow politician to have paused to reflect on, or try to understand, what might lie beneath my outer shell, or to grasp my 'predicament'. Ben Wegg-Prosser provided a less gentle, though no less accurate, assessment of where August and the NEC defeat had left me. He began with a masterstroke of understatement. 'Your current position is highly unsatisfactory,' he said. 'The public wonders what you do. The party views you with suspicion. Your colleagues find you an irritation. The Prime Minister expects you to be omnipresent.'

In the autumn of 1997, the tension between the Prime Minister and the Chancellor finally burst into the open. It was not, as I had anticipated, over domestic policy-making, but over Europe. In the formative years of New Labour, Gordon, Tony and I had seen eye to eye on European policy. Through the 1970s, Labour had been sceptical of engagement with the then European Economic Community. It was an article of faith for the modernisers that we must be more deeply, self-confidently, involved in European affairs. I remember when the French referendum on the Maastricht Treaty was taking place in September 1992. We were so alarmed that it might be lost that the three of us and Derry Irvine – who picked up the bill for the rather expensive breakfast we enjoyed at the Savoy Hotel – met to consider how to avoid such an outcome encouraging the Eurosceptics within Labour. In the event, the French vote was narrowly won. By the time we got into government, we were agreed on the need to reverse the truculent attitude with which the Tories, and especially Mrs Thatcher, had approached Europe. But Gordon's attitude had become more cautious, largely I think because of the trauma of Black Wednesday and Britain's forced withdrawal from the Exchange Rate Mechanism. The main issue now was whether to join the follow-up to the ERM, the single European currency. It was inevitable that Gordon was going to tread carefully.

That alone need not have caused problems. Tony and I also recognised the need for caution. Given the disastrous rate at which we had gone into the ERM, we knew it was essential to ensure that the circumstances were right for joining the single currency. Almost since election day, Gordon had been taking a much more sceptical line. At a speech at Chatham House two months into government, he invited a national debate on the single currency, but also set out a series of economic tests for our joining. Now, a succession of stories, briefed to the *Financial Times* and the *Independent*, were alluding to divisions between Gordon and Number 10 on the issue. The markets were in danger of being spooked. Sooner or later, something had to give. In mid-October, Gordon got Tony's go-ahead to issue a public 'clarification' to stop the speculation. Tony assumed that its aim would be to show a unified face on the broad areas where the three of us agreed: that Britain was determined to be engaged in Europe, that the decision to join the single currency would depend on economic circumstances, but that we were ruling nothing out or in regarding the timing.

Charlie sent a fax setting out the position to Philip Webster of *The Times*. The intention was to create the impression of a considered interview by the Chancellor. This had been agreed by Alastair on the Prime Minister's behalf. The literal meaning of Gordon's words was not earth-shattering. They were more cautious than those Tony would have used, but not startlingly so. Recalling that we had said before the election that it was 'highly unlikely Britain can join [the single currency] in the first wave', he said: 'If we do not join in 1999, our task will be to deliver a period of sustainable growth, tackle the long-term weaknesses of the UK economy, and press for reform in Europe.' What mattered was the headline put over the story: 'Brown Rules Out Single Currency for Lifetime of this Parliament'. What mattered even more was that Charlie, without consulting Alastair, briefed a similarly explicit message for *Newsnight*, ITN and the following day's *Sun*.

The first I knew of the apparent abandonment of our prepare-and-decide approach was around ten o'clock that evening. I was in Hartlepool for the weekend when I was called by a political editor who had just seen the next day's *Times* front page, which he faxed to me. I phoned Tony at Chequers to find out if he had known Gordon was going to 'rule out' entry. Clearly surprised, he said all he had known was that Gordon was going to clarify the policy muddle of the past few weeks. He hadn't expected a major policy shift. I suggested he do whatever it took to *un*-clarify Gordon's *démarche*. Otherwise, we were going to cause further confusion, and not a little frustration and anger among Britain's businesses, which were broadly Euro-enthusiastic. We would also look amateurish. Even if the change of policy did make sense, surely it was the kind of shift that should be announced in the Commons, not planted in the press.

Tony said he would get on to Gordon. Unable to raise him, he was reduced to calling Charlie. Had he spoken to Gordon, I have no doubt his tone would have been more enquiring than inquisitional. Charlie was a different matter. Tony had never liked or trusted him. He knew Alastair and I had been driven to distraction by his separate, and often deliberately malevolent, briefings before the election, and had asked Gordon to replace him when we moved into government. Now he was in no mood for social niceties. He demanded that Charlie tell him what was going on. When Charlie replied that all Gordon had done was convey government policy, Tony said that ruling out joining the single currency for the entirety of this Parliament was not a policy of which he, as Prime Minister, was aware. He told Charlie he must at least soften the message in the *Times* headline, and brief reporters that it was over the top. Charlie responded that he couldn't. It was too late.

By the time we got into work on Monday, Tony's hope was that it would not be too late to recreate at least a figleaf of unity, and leave a sliver of a suggestion that we were not shutting the door on EMU membership altogether. He summoned Gordon, Charlie, Alastair, Jonathan Powell and me for a meeting. He was resolute and stern. He steered clear of going into exactly who had said or done what in the course of the weekend's embarrassment, but he insisted that Gordon deliver a further statement, this time in Parliament, on terms to be agreed between Downing Street and the Treasury.

Gordon delivered his statement a week later. It softened the *Times* message, if only slightly. He said we would not join the single currency in this Parliament, 'barring some fundamental and unforeseen change in economic circumstances'. As a measure for determining this, he rehearsed his economic tests. Alastair did try to get Gordon to show at least some contrition in the Chamber for having chosen a newspaper, rather than MPs, as the audience for his new 'clarity' on the EMU, faxing him a shopping list of five possible phrases of 'regret'. The briefest and easiest was: 'Madam Speaker, I wish to make a statement on the EMU. May I say that this is the place to make such a statement, and that all important statements for which I am responsible will be made here, and nowhere else.' Gordon binned the suggestions. There would be no 'regret'.

Nor would it be long before the divide over domestic policy-making became clear as well. Any Chancellor wields major influence on all aspects of government, through control of tax and spending. Our administration was not the first to have to deal with the tensions inherent in having bright, strong-willed tenants in Numbers 10 and 11 Downing Street. But Gordon's influence would be of an entirely different order. He believed that his own acumen, and the talents of his inner circle, served the government's policy-making far better than anything in Number 10.

Reporters were being briefed by Charlie to expect a powerful demonstration of the Chancellor's intellectual and political strength as he embarked on a Comprehensive Spending Review that would set out each department's funding for the next three years – up to the next election. Especially after the EMU dispute, I pressed Tony to be aware of the implications of this. He might well decide that he was happy with the CSR as a road map for future spending, but it was important to recognise that any exercise that set spending priorities for the balance of our first term would also define our policy priorities. If Tony wanted to ensure that his and Gordon's plans coincided, we would have to establish a better working relationship between them.

The CSR would not be finalised and announced until the summer of 1998, but the Treasury was already negotiating with individual government departments. Tony's early efforts to insert himself into the process provided little cause for optimism. His meetings with Gordon were like a game of hide-and-seek, with Tony trying to tease out Treasury intentions and Gordon keeping him at bay. I told Tony it was essential to find a way to make their future discussions more serious and less aggressive. I also urged him to see the EMU experience as reinforcing the importance of our getting a better handle on policy in Number 10. I said we had to create working methods that would allow him to focus on priorities and provide a detailed lead in the most important policy areas. Tony agreed. He also believed that as time passed, the mere fact that he was Prime Minister would allow him to find a way of exerting his will without confronting the Treasury head-on. That was a last resort, to be avoided at all costs.

It was not the tug-of-war between Tony and Gordon that finally ended our government's uncommonly long honeymoon. Even our first sex scandal, Robin's relationship with Gaynor, had made little political impact, to Tony's immense relief. Instead, it was our first encounter with 'sleaze'. It boiled down to money and politics. It always does. The money came from the Formula One racing boss Bernie Ecclestone. As I would come to recognise in my later role in trade and industry policy, Bernie was an energetic entrepreneur whose business activities had added huge value – and valuable jobs – to the UK economy. He was a supporter of New Labour who had donated £1 million to our 1997 election campaign chest, and was now prepared to give a further million. The politics involved a manifesto commitment to ban tobacco advertising, and our subsequent decision to seek to exempt Formula One sponsorship from an EU-wide ban. Especially when it emerged that Tony had met Ecclestone shortly before that decision was confirmed, the media drew the inevitable conclusion: we were trading influence. That wasn't true. Tony had been persuaded by what he saw as the common-sense case against a Formula One ban. It would have a minimal anti-smoking effect, as TV audiences in Britain and worldwide would still see omnipresent cigarette logos, but it would risk thousands of jobs that depended on the motor-racing business, and could put an end to our home grand prix at Silverstone. None of this, however, mattered to the politics of the issue. It looked like cash for favours. It had the whiff of sleaze.

Our handling of the crisis made things worse. For a government reputed for its expertise in media management, I suppose we at least had the satisfaction of proving that wrong. Nobody –

not Alastair, Jonathan or Tony himself – had had the good sense to spot trouble when a seven-figure donor with a personal interest in tobacco sponsorship was ushered in for a private meeting with the Prime Minister. As the first newspaper enquiries about Ecclestone were coming in, we dithered. No one said the obvious: when you're in a hole, stop digging. Go public before the stories appear, explain the reasons for the policy change, and announce for any avoidance of doubt that you're paying back Ecclestone's million and refusing any further donations from him. The strategy adopted by Tony, at Derry's and Gordon's urging, was to write to Sir Patrick Neill, the head of the Committee on Standards in Public Life, in the hope that he would clear us and say we could keep the money. He wrote back, a mere three days later, with the opposite advice. 'The conduct of those in public positions must be judged not only by the reality but also the appearance,' he said, rightly. He suggested that we announce the amount of Ecclestone's donation, and give it back.

This episode was my first experience of being Minister for Bad News. An array of spokesmen and ministers who usually leapt at the opportunity to see their names in print or their faces on camera were suddenly indisposed. Given the mood in the media, and the experience of the few ministers prepared to venture forth, this was hardly surprising. When *Newsnight* addressed the issue, Jeremy Paxman pointed to an empty chair and quipped that there was 'no ministerial bottom to fill it'. This was vintage Jeremy. In our on-screen encounters over the years I would come to see him as a bully, making up for his occasional lack of knowledge by deploying his undeniably large and effective personality. I found that the trick was not to get riled, to answer his questions at my own pace, and if he started interrupting with another question, to insist on first answering the question he had already asked. But he had a fine sense of humour, which as long as he was not too far up on his high horse, he would share in an interview. When he now shared it with an empty chair, I suppose we could hardly complain.

When ministers did take to the airwaves, myself and Gordon included, to try to deal with the Ecclestone affair, we got into trouble over the chain of events. By the time I made my final attempt to counter the growing tide of media suspicion, in a Channel 4 News interview from a studio in Cambridge, I knew it was futile. As soon as I'd taken my earpiece out, I called Number 10. The only way to draw a line under the controversy, I said, was for Tony himself to address it. John Humphrys had asked the Prime Minister to appear on the Sunday political TV programme *On the Record*, and I urged him to accept. It might be risky, but nowhere near as risky as letting the episode and the innuendo surrounding it drag on. There was obvious hurt and passion in Tony's voice when he assured Humphrys that he 'would never do anything improper', and that most people who dealt with him would accept that he was 'a pretty straight sort of guy'. And because he was, the message finally, just about, got through.

How did we allow the Ecclestone affair to happen? Honeymoon hubris, partly. We knew that our policy change had been based on rational arguments against a Formula One ban, and I think we assumed that the millions of voters who had put us into office would recognise and accept this. But we had a specifically New Labour problem of money and politics that ran deeper, and went back further. It began when John Smith was party leader, and Gordon, Tony and I jointly launched what the media dubbed a 'charm offensive' with the City of London and the business community. Our aim was to convince them that a modernised Labour Party could be trusted. We would tax out of necessity and with prudence, not out of spite or dogma. We would regulate, not nationalise. We believed in social justice and a system of progressive taxation. Within this framework, we would work with business and the financial sector, not try to undermine them. But we also saw a role for business supporters in helping us break free of our funding dependence on the trade unions.

This inevitably led to contact with wealthy individuals. Among them was Michael Levy. Tony had been introduced to this eager and experienced fund-raiser shortly before John's death. Michael had struck it rich by selling his successful music business. He was a long-time Labour voter, and had already been in touch with a fairly unenthusiastic Smith office about helping with fund-raising. Tony took an instant liking to Michael, and settled into a pattern of weekend visits to the Levy residence for tennis and swimming. I was more hesitant. Michael had been a fund-raiser for a range of Jewish community charities, testimony to his genuine sense of social responsibility. But the very qualities that had allowed him to excel in that role – his hand-grabbing, cheek-kissing genius for corralling one person after another and working a room – left me with a feeling that he was far too self-promoting for his own, and our, good. He obviously revelled in his increasingly close ties with Britain's probable future Prime Minister, and in letting everyone know about them. It did help him bring in unheard-of levels of private donations for Labour, and as the beneficiary of a war chest of £15 million for our 1997 election campaign, I was hardly in a position to ignore or belittle that. When Tony stressed the importance of this new support for loosening our reliance on the trade unions, I agreed with him. But he, and most of us around him, were far too slow in recognising the dangers of trading one form of reliance for another.

To say Michael Levy was 'self-promoting' is a bit ungenerous. Yet not only he, but the donors he brought in, were obviously on some level 'investing' in a New Labour government. This did not mean they wanted a specific trade-off, whether in policy or, as later damaging accusations would suggest, peerages. We never dangled, much less delivered on, any such deal. But it would be ridiculous to suggest that most of them did not hope for something in return. At a minimum, they hoped to enjoy a degree of personal association with Number 10. I am sure that Michael, for all his genuine commitment to helping New Labour, also felt that way. When we were drawing up our first honours list, he made it clear that he expected to go into the Lords. Tony was uneasy about how this would look. I was sent to ask Michael to hold off, to try to persuade him that the time was not yet right, and to warn him that he risked stigmatising himself if he collected a peerage so quickly. Michael held his ground with some tenacity, and duly became Lord Levy of Mill Hill.

Except for the timing, there was nothing new in this. The Tories had made it established practice to put fund-raisers and donors into the Upper House. Perhaps with them, as with us, there was no explicit trade-off. It would also be odd to bar someone from a working peerage just because he had given help to the party he believed in. I felt this about Michael as well. Still, as long as political parties had to find money to fund increasingly expensive campaigns, the appearance of corruption was unavoidable.

After the Ecclestone fiasco, Tony asked the Neill Committee to look at the future of party political funding. I took the opportunity to revive the argument I had wanted to make in *The Blair Revolution* for a system of state funding. After several conversations in which Tony again insisted that this could not be done except on an all-party basis, I tried to get him at least to consider the option, telling him that we were out of step with practice in Europe, and that independence from vested or financial interests was a good argument in favour of the principle. I suggested having a cabinet minister write a newspaper opinion piece putting forward the case, as a means of nudging Neill in that direction. If he was persuaded, surely the public would be too, especially after the Ecclestone affair. Finally I tried an approach I knew would resonate with Tony: if we didn't get state funding like every other modern left-of-centre European party, we would never be able to do anything about the trade-union link. When we next spoke, Tony simply said that Labour couldn't do it alone, and he didn't think the other parties would wear it. He would later regret this. In his final years in Downing Street he would attempt a barely less significant change: a cap on party donations, whether from private or trade union sources. By then, however, he was too weak to push it through, while Gordon was too strong, and too impatient to see him out. Gordon derailed it, presumably in part to increase his support amongst the trade unions.

Gordon's strength, and the rest of the government's policy weaknesses, came to a head at the end of the year, over an issue Tony and I had always considered central to our first term in government. Welfare reform had the potential to be a defining cause for New Labour, in much the same way that it had helped to reposition the Democrats in America under Bill Clinton. Critics on the Labour left saw it as a sop to the middle classes, and to Middle England. In fact it was nothing of the sort. Our aim was to combine social justice – help for those who needed it – with the individual responsibility expected by people of all classes in all parts of the country. In appointing Harriet Harman and Frank Field, Tony had urged them to come up with a plan that would radically reshape the welfare state. Almost from the moment they got down to work, however, they were at each other's throats. I wondered whether I had been mistaken in arguing for putting Harriet in charge, but in truth, that wasn't the problem. No matter which of the two had got the top job, it was obvious that they could not work together. By December, with a welfare Green Paper already two months behind schedule, they could barely tolerate being in the same room.

I had known both Harriet and Frank for years. Now, each of them would call me to say that the other was impossible to work with. 'What are we going to do about them?' Tony repeatedly asked me. Except for telling them that they had to find a way to work together, there was not much we could do. Besides their personality clashes and turf wars, Harriet and Frank had very different views about welfare reform. Frank wanted a system of compulsory private insurance, with tax breaks to encourage the better-off to buy in and subsidies for those who lacked the means to do so. It was broadly similar to what President Obama would introduce for health care in the US more than a decade later. It re-established the original Beveridge thinking in setting up the welfare state: help for those in need, balanced by a responsibility for those who could work to do so. It also had the advantage of being universal, based on the idea that every citizen should pay into the system, and everyone should be entitled to benefits in times of need. Harriet took a more traditional view, favouring a means-tested system targeted on helping the least well-off. Although a member of the Number 10 policy unit, Sharon White, was doing an excellent job of trying to distil their conflicting views into a workable compromise, we could not realistically draw up a welfare policy on our own and simply impose it on a government department.

Gordon was much better placed to make his voice heard. Since the Treasury controls the government's purse strings, it can, and routinely does, deal with individual ministries and their Secretaries of State. It was doing so now on the Comprehensive Spending Review. Moreover, Gordon and Ed had a fully formed idea, much nearer Harriet's than Frank's, on welfare. It combined support and training to get people back into work with a complex system of means-tested tax credits to help the poor. It wasn't the radical reform that Tony had wanted, but it looked to be the inevitable outcome unless he himself intervened.

In late December I joined Tony and the Downing Street policy unit at Chequers for a day-long brainstorming session on the welfare stand-off. We began behind schedule, because Tony, and then I, had to take telephone calls from Harriet in which she made it clear that she wanted Frank hung, drawn and quartered. Tony was by now convinced that Frank was too impetuous and politically clumsy to get his ideas accepted by Harriet, even if she had been sympathetic to them, which she clearly was not. Yet he was instinctively more drawn to Frank's radicalism than to Harriet's and Gordon's more conventional approach. 'We can only help the poor through real welfare reform, not taxing and spending,' he said. He understood the need to put a stop to the policy chaos, and agreed to my suggestion that he chair a ministerial committee to decide on a welfare reform package and then embark on a 'Clause IV-style' effort to explain and sell it to the party and the country. But neither he, nor anyone else, had worked out a final vision of the kind or extent of the reform we wanted. To get the Green Paper published at all, David Miliband and I had to chair a series of painfully tense meetings in the new year with Harriet, Frank and their officials at Social Security. Inevitably, the paper turned out to consist of the bare minimum they could agree on, long on guiding principles but short on specifics. It was certainly not radical reform, and the sorry episode ended with the departure of both Harriet and Frank in the next reshuffle.

The antidote to our inability to deliver fundamental change on issues like welfare, and to the tension between Numbers 10 and 11, seemed straightfoward to me: it was the 'strengthened centre' I had been pressing on Tony. This would have to involve Downing Street, the Cabinet Office and the Treasury – and, ideally, the old trium-virate, Tony, Gordon and me – pulling together rather than apart. I am not sure I ever believed that was possible. But during the early part of 1998 there were occasional glimpses of hope alongside the more familiar signs of Gordon's bitterness and anger towards me. At the start of the year Paul Routledge, a journalist so close to Gordon's tribe that he sometimes seemed almost a wholly-owned subsidiary, published a biography of Gordon with which he had cooperated. It accused me of having betrayed Gordon and of having plotted, from the moment of John's death, to anoint Tony as leader. When it appeared, Gordon sent word that he wanted to see me. Clearly embarrassed by the claims, he said we must put our enmity behind us: 'Why should both of us go on not enjoying our work? We need to work together or we'll bring the whole government down.' I told him I was hurt by the Routledge allegations, and that he knew they were not true. But I agreed we needed to turn a new page. The rapproche-ment lasted only a few days. Without rhyme, reason or warning, a new spate of Treasury-inspired criticism of me began to appear in the press.

Gordon and I did, however, talk at length shortly before Easter. He invited me to his office in Number 11 to discuss the overall policy direction of government. He said he felt we were not making progress 'fast or deep enough' on major issues like health and education. I could hardly disagree with that. His prescription for fixing it, however, was to put the Treasury in control. Only it had the 'tools', meaning the financial and political clout with individual departments, to push through policy changes. That was the idea behind the CSR, he told me. What was blocking the process was Number 10, and Tony. Gordon and his team were 'piling on the pressure' with government departments. Number 10 was trying to intervene, and was 'siding with the departments'. Gordon was convinced that this was part of a deliberate campaign to challenge and undermine him. He said that the proper role of the Prime Minister should be to step back, and act only as a court of final appeal in the case of disagreements. I told him that the last thing Tony wanted or needed was to be at odds with the Treasury. Ultimately, the only way to move forward on the big policy challenges was for the Prime Minister, the Chancellor and the Cabinet Office to pull in a single direction. At present, there was no proper coordination. He accepted that, but insisted that he and the Treasury had to be the leading force.

Gordon clearly intended me to convey our conversation to Tony, and I did, along with my own view that as Prime Minister he could not simply remain a spectator while the Treasury put in place its direction for government over the next three years. I told Tony it was not a question of going into battle with Gordon. There needed to be real communication and cooperation between the two of them, most immediately on the policy side of the CSR. Number 10 was beginning to develop far-reaching ideas about how the education and health systems should be reformed. Despite the considerable work Gordon and Ed had done on developing fiscal and financial policy, there was no sign that they had worked out a coherent view of reform in other areas.

Neither of us, however, saw much hope that Gordon would accept Tony's involvement in setting the policy framework for the CSR. And very soon it became clear that he was certainly not ready to repair the relationship with me. Ten days after our meeting in Number 11, a Sunday newspaper piece was full of the familiar sniping against me. Alastair's partner, Fiona, wrote me a card after she read it: 'I wanted to let you know how appalled I was by Gordon's latest onslaught. If that is his idea of a peace pact, God help you when he goes to war. I'd be disgusted if my children behaved the way he does.'

Gordon was right to say that the Treasury's capacity to peer into the nuts and bolts of every department was unique in Whitehall. Allied to a creative policy function, and Gordon's toughness, the results could have been extraordinarily positive. But it was impossible to ignore the effects of the unresolved rivalry between the Chancellor and the Prime Minister. Tony did keep trying to involve himself in the CSR decisions, but one of the reasons why he failed was practical. Much as he and Number 10 struggled to change this, they were denied timely access to key information and paperwork. On each of the crucial policy areas, Tony would make a final attempt to make his views count, but it would always be too late.

Nothing better dramatised the predicament than the Strategic Defence Review, timed to coincide with the announcement of the CSR in July 1998. The SDR was a serious, rigorously developed piece of work. It was chaired for government by the Defence Secretary, George Robertson, and for the military by the Chief of the Defence Staff, General Sir Charles Guthrie. The exercise was 'foreign policy-led'. The aim was to start with the role Britain expected to play in international politics and security, and to create a forward path for the armed forces that would allow them to deliver on it. At the preparatory meetings the Treasury was represented, and it raised no serious objections when the final proposals were drawn up. Tony was impressed when they were delivered to him. They not only envisaged a military that would be more fit for the purpose we asked of it, but General Guthrie, recognising the need for economies beyond funding cuts already made under the Tories, was pledging further net savings.

But with only weeks to go before the review was published, Gordon stepped in, demanding a sizeable further annual reduction in military spending. General Guthrie was astonished. He phoned me, and implored me to get Tony to find a way out. He also sent me a note on the effects of further reductions. 'Our proposals do not contain fat waiting for easy efficiency gains,' he said. The additional cuts would 'go to the meat' of what the armed forces were being asked to do, and would limit the degree to which British forces were able to operate alongside our US and NATO allies. I had no way independently to test his claims, but by the time General Guthrie went to see Tony, I had relayed them to him. Even that didn't prepare him for the depth of the General's concerns, or the anger he felt about Gordon's eleventh-hour demands. Tony said that he was sympathetic, but that the politics were difficult. He offered a suggestion which at first shocked, then alarmed, the Chief of the Defence Staff: that he should go and try to convince Gordon himself.

Charles replied, 'With respect, you are Prime Minister and First Lord of the Treasury. I think it only right that *you* speak with the Chancellor.'

Tony replied, 'Frankly, I think he's more likely to listen to you.'

Charles saw Gordon, and according to his account, Gordon was emollient in manner and tone, but firm in his demands. He did give slightly on the further economies he wanted, but insisted there would still have to be considerable savings. This scaling-back helped to explain, if not to excuse or justify, General Guthrie's public attacks on Gordon after his insistence to the Iraq War inquiry in 2010 that he had always given Britain's military what it had asked for.

The CSR in July 1998 cemented Gordon's image as a central force in government. Its main focus was on domestic policy. Ostensibly, he was implementing the blueprint Tony favoured: increased expenditure on education, health and other public services alongside reform in the way they were managed, delivered and held to account. The problem was in the balance of funding for the various departments, and the kind and scale of the reforms envisaged. This was exacerbated by inflated claims about how much new money was actually involved. Gordon announced that a total of £40 billion in new investment was going into health and education, £21 billion into the NHS alone.

I was not in the Commons for his statement, but was driving to a long-scheduled event at an east London school. When I heard Gordon on the radio reeling off the figures, however, my first thought was that they seemed too good to be true. In fact, the totals did turn out to have been exaggerated. Significant further money was also earmarked for Gordon's complex apparatus of means-tested tax credits and benefits, as well as for undeniably worthy, but less politically urgent, tasks like an increase in overseas aid. As for the 'modernisation' and 'reform' demanded in return, Gordon said this would involve tackling 'inefficiencies in hospitals and cost overruns', simplifying management, emphasising long-term planning, and publishing league tables and an array of new 'performance targets'.

Even Tony was seduced by the idea of targets, of quantifying what we were setting out to achieve. We all were. They seemed a way of being able to tell voters that they had been right to put us in power. The CSR did not, however, amount to a fundamental reform of the way hospitals or schools were run. As I had expected, the Treasury team lacked the resources, and the inclination, to move beyond the surface issues of efficiency and structure. They did not address what would later become our key goal: to re-orient the culture and operation of the public services away from central control and towards the interests of the people they were meant to serve.

By the time of the CSR, morale was flagging in Number 10. There was a sense that despite all the things we had achieved in our first year, we were less effective, and less loved, than we had hoped to be. We had failed to create the more powerful centre needed to maximise Tony's effectiveness across government. Astonishing though it now seems, given his importance to Tony throughout his years in power, even Jonathan Powell's head was at least briefly on the chopping block. Alastair, Anji and Tony's political aide, Sally Morgan, were all arguing that he had to go. They recognised that he had a good mind, and they liked him, most of the time. But they felt he lacked the political background, and the personal skills, to bring together and work with the team in Downing Street. The manner he adopted with Tony annoyed them, and Tony too. It was as if Jonathan felt that in order to establish his authority, he had to adopt a rather high-handed attitude towards the Prime Minister. With a gaucheness that sometimes stopped just short of being rude, he would burst into Tony's office, interrupt him, and insist he give him decisions on a list of items on his ever-present 'to do' pad.

I was virtually alone in insisting that Tony resist plans to redeploy Jonathan to Northern Ireland or the Middle East. It was true that he had shortcomings as a personnel manager, but that resulted mainly from his reluctance to interfere with the baronies that jostled each other in Downing Street. He had huge strengths. He worked fantastically quickly and precisely. He was good at conveying others' views to the Prime Minister and getting an efficient and effective response. He could articulate and follow up on Tony's opinions and wishes – as time went on, sometimes without actually asking him. I strongly opposed moving him. In the end, Tony agreed. He never regretted it.

After the CSR, Philip Gould wrote a sobering summary of his opinion findings. The good news was that Tony's poll ratings remained high. But the impression was gaining that New Labour was running low on ideas and policy. The CSR had brought some of the reasons for this into sharper focus. Gordon's high-profile unveiling of his spending plans had left Tony looking like a marginalised chief executive. The content of the CSR had failed to establish a coherent order of policy priorities. Almost everyone in Number 10 knew what our major long-term goals should be: investment, improvement, modernisation and real reform for the two key public services, health and education. Tony wasn't getting that message across effectively enough, to the rest of government, to the media or to the country.

Two other projects with which Tony had hoped to make an early impact were also running into difficulty. He had made real progress in rehabilitating our role in Europe. EU leaders were more at ease with Tony than they had been with John Major. He was more European in outlook. He spoke French. He holidayed on the Continent. He acted like a Prime Minister who wanted Britain involved in the EU and in helping to shape its future. But once the single currency, the euro, was up and running in 1999, we knew that exerting influence was going to be trickier. It was not so much that we hadn't joined it – even I recognised that the time wasn't right, and our European partners understood this as well. The problem was that, with Gordon's 'tests' ruling out any change for the foreseeable future, we weakened our claim to a major voice on wider economic issues. The immediate question for Tony was when, and whether, to pave the way for eventually joining the single currency by holding the referendum we had promised. He toyed with the idea, but always set it aside. Since we weren't going to join the euro in the immediate future, he felt it would risk political pain for no obvious gain. My view was that there was much to recommend holding a referendum on the principle of joining, and that we should hold it as soon as possible, while Tony's standing was at its highest. He was worried about the reluctance of a good part of the cabinet, and of course Gordon, to agree. He also feared a backlash from the Murdoch papers, especially the *Sun*. A referendum now was a step too far.

The same proved true of a more daring, and at the time secret, attempt to redraw the landscape of British politics by negotiating a policy agreement with the Liberal Democrats and bringing some Lib Dems into the cabinet. I was involved from the outset. We had begun exploring the idea shortly after Tony became leader. It was incubated in a series of talks each of us had with friends from the original SDP. For both Tony and me, the intellectual and political influence of Roy Jenkins mattered greatly. Over lunch in the garden of Roy and Jennifer's home at East Hendred, or in his book-filled study with a glass of his favourite claret, Roy was impassioned in his argument that New Labour and the Lib Dems had a rare opportunity to 'correct' a historic error in British politics, when the split between Labour and the Liberals in the early 1900s had ushered in a century of Conservative dominance. It helped that Tony and the Lib Dem leader Paddy Ashdown not only shared this view, but liked and respected each other.

On paper, some sort of partnership made sense for both sides, at least before the election. While all signs were pointing to our winning, we could not be sure that we were on course for an outright majority, much less a landslide. With Lib Dem support, we would be able to form a stable government. There was an additional attraction for Tony – much as there would be for David Cameron when he allied himself in government with the Lib Dems more than a decade later. He saw a governing arrangement with them as a way of diluting the power of the old-left Labour MPs and the trade unions, just as Cameron's alliance would trim the wings of the Tory right. For the Liberal Democrats, the main attraction was the prospect of finally having a direct say in government. There was considerable policy overlap between our two parties. Some senior Labour figures, above all Robin Cook, were long-time supporters of the Lib Dem view on an issue likely to be key to any agreement: changing the first-past-the-post system of electing MPs, in favour of proportional representation.

The serious work on seeing whether a deal was possible began about a year before the election. At Derry's home in West Hampstead, Tony, Robin, Donald Dewar and I met Paddy and his three trusted allies, the Lib Dem peer Richard Holme and the MPs Bob Maclennan and Archie Kirkwood. The upshot was a working group chaired by Robin and Bob on constitutional reform. Tony and Paddy spoke often about the broader terms of cooperation, while Richard and I held regular talks to try to chart a detailed plan that would work for both sides. I liked Richard. In a way we were natural partners. Not only for Paddy, but for David Steel before him, Richard had been a trusted ally, adviser and all-purpose help for the party leader on an array of delicate political issues – in a sense, 'being Richard'. We made progress. For the 1997 campaign, we worked out ground rules to minimise clashes between our candidates in constituencies where only one of us had a realistic prospect of beating the Tories. We discussed a framework for partnership after the election, and specifically for making two Lib Dem MPs, Alan Beith and Menzies Campbell, members of Tony's first cabinet. It was not quite the formal 'coalition' Roger and I had proposed in our early, leaked version of *The Blair Revolution*. We knew, however, that it would still be controversial for many in both of our parties.

Until election day, Tony was inclined to go ahead with the deal. What killed it, or at least was sure to delay it, was the result. It was not just our landslide. The Lib Dems had reached a historic high, up from twenty seats to forty-six. For many in the Labour Party, especially those who still seethed over the SDP split, the idea of offering the rebels' successors a place in government was unpalatable, to say the least. The same would have been true for Lib Dems had Paddy made any early attempt to convince his reinvigorated party to risk its separate identity by playing a bit part in the new cabinet. The day after the election, when I was doing a series of interviews on College Green in front of Parliament, I ran into Ming Campbell. 'What's happening with bringing Lib Dems into the cabinet?' he asked. It was clearly a question of more than passing interest, since he was to have been one of the ministers. 'I don't know,' I replied. 'But the idea seems to have gone away.'

Two months after the election, Tony, Paddy, Roy and I met for dinner at Number 10 to see how and whether we could bring it back again. Tony and Paddy were still enthusiastic in principle. Paddy's view was that the Lib Dems should chart a course of 'constructive opposition', emphasising areas on which we agreed. We could begin looking at a new voting system, giving impetus to the effort by introducing proportional representation for elections to the European Parliament. Lib Dems could be included in a cabinet committee on constitutional reform, and a cross-party commission could pave the way for reforming the system for domestic elections. Paddy was not only still eager to have Lib Dem colleagues in Tony's cabinet; he now hoped that there could be as many as four of them.

Tony was fine with introducing PR for European elections, and shared Paddy's enthusiasm for forming a joint cabinet committee as a preliminary move to constitutional reform. He was much more cautious on the domestic voting system. I knew from our conversations that the most he was likely to countenance was the so-called 'alternative vote' – not a proportional system, although fairer than first-past-the-post as it allowed voters to cast second and third preferences. He was never going to agree to four Lib Dem cabinet members, which would invite an outcry from Labour MPs who naturally felt that they should be at the top table.

When Richard and I met two weeks later, I managed to persuade him that four Lib Dem ministers was a non-starter. He also seemed to accept that AV was the likely limit to any electoral reform. In the autumn, the two of us met Tony and Paddy for dinner at Number 10. I wrote a note to Tony beforehand saying I still felt 'the prize is worth the pain', but that for it to work, both sides needed to begin serious preparatory work in selling any deal. For us, this meant explaining the long-term benefits and emphasising that we would remain a New Labour government. Paddy would have to start dampening expectations over how many places the Lib Dems were likely to get in cabinet or on government committees.

The high-water mark would turn out to be the creation of the cabinet committee on constitutional change in the summer of 1997. Until the latter part of 1998, our talks continued. As Paddy and Richard pressed for more and speedier progress, the obstacles on our side became more difficult. Roy Jenkins was named to head the electoral reform commission. When it reported, it proposed 'AV-plus', an arrangement whereby MPs would still be elected for single constituencies by AV, complemented with a regional top-up of additional Members determined by each party's voting strength. Tony was non-committal in his response. He praised the report, but said the issue needed wide debate. Richard and I continued to hold back-channel talks on defining areas of policy agreement, and even on the timetable he and Paddy wanted for formal coalition government. But after our referenda on Scottish and Welsh devolution, both of which had been won, but by an extremely narrow margin in Wales, Tony's appetite for a further public vote was waning. If he was worried about the obstacles to holding and winning a referendum on the single currency, he knew that those to remaking Britain's voting system were likely to prove even more difficult, especially within the cabinet and the PLP. Among ministers, only Robin was unswervingly enthusiastic. The others, only generally aware of the talks, were puzzled about why we should be talking with the Lib Dems at all. John Prescott thought the whole idea was crazy. We had been elected with a huge majority after years in the wilderness. It was incomprehensible that we should contemplate dealing away cabinet seats on the hypothesis that it might help keep the Tories from returning to power ten years down the road.

Tony's ardour waned. He never wavered from his broad historical view of the need for some new form of left-of-centre partnership in British politics, but the urgency had gone. My view was that a deal was possible. I saw the attraction of a grand political realignment, but my reasoning was more mundane than Paddy's or Tony's. I still feared that our government was not immune to some unanticipated mishap, or a reverse in political fortunes, before the next election. Broadening our base seemed a useful insurance policy if we needed to ward off a Tory revival. I didn't anticipate that it would become relevant more than a decade later, when David Cameron's Tories finally defeated us at the polls – after which I, along with Andrew Adonis, would lead an ultimately futile effort to convince the Lib

Dems to form a left-of-centre coalition.

What ultimately killed the prospect in the late 1990s was that nei-ther side was ready to sign up to the only workable deal: a baseline of two Lib Dem cabinet members and a gradual move towards a simple AV voting system. At the end of the day I think Tony might have signed up to this, but Paddy insisted on a larger number of cabinet seats, a governing 'coalition', and a proportional voting system, not just AV.

My powers were insufficient to convert every doubter to the vir-tues of another project that would occupy a considerable portion of my time during our first years in government. At the beginning of our first summer I was given an additional role alongside my Cabinet Office job when Tony put me in charge of the Millennium Dome project, on a long-contaminated site on Greenwich Peninsula on the south bank of the Thames. The project had been initiated by Michael Heseltine, and he had signed Tony up to it before the elec-tion. One reason Tony gave me the task was that I had been among the fairly small minority who thought we should keep going with the Dome; the majority of the cabinet were sceptical or opposed. I saw echoes in the planned Richard Rogers structure of my grandfather's 1951 Festival of Britain. Echoes, too, of the scepticism and criticism that had greeted the Festival as well. The main reason, however, was that it was a properly defined job. I felt that it would provide an opportunity for me to show the skills and mettle I would need as a departmental minister.

Under the plans devised before the election by the Tories, millions of pounds had been poured into the proposed Dome. Hundreds of millions more of National Lottery money was earmarked for it, and for the millennium celebrations of which it was to be the centrepiece. Now, we had to make it work. It didn't take long to realise the mag-nitude of the challenge. The Tories had left us with a building site, contracts with a few major companies, and a Millennium Experience Company of which I was the sole ministerial shareholder. We had to get the dome built, and fully fitted out, on schedule. We had to attract about £150 million in private sponsorship to make the numbers add up.

We also had to decide what would go inside Richard Rogers's dramatic design. The overall framework was set early on: a series of 'zones' reflecting different aspects of life in turn-of-the-millennium Britain, and the country's place in the world. We settled on the theme of 'bringing the country together'. But there was no central creative vision. One plan that I liked was to anchor the zones around a theatrical extravaganza produced by the West End impresario Cameron Mackintosh, starring a rotating cast of 2,000 children from around Britain. When I think back, I believe this would have injected a sense of humanity into the whole experience. But I allowed myself to be talked out of the idea by Jennie Page, the chief executive of the Dome project, because of concerns over cost, technology – and possibly health and safety. Cameron was naturally put out by this, and I was sorry for him after all the work he put into developing the concept, but there was nothing I could do. Later Mark Fisher, known for designing sets for bands like U2 and the Rolling Stones, became the main creative force, but I always felt it was a shame we couldn't bring Cameron's original concept to life.

By the time the Dome opened, I had moved on. On a personal level, that may have been fortunate. I attended the Dome's grand opening on Millennium Eve. The event had been built up for months, not least by Tony, but it was blighted by transport bottlenecks and lengthy delays at the security screening for VIPs, who included the editors of most of Britain's newspapers. I couldn't help but think back to a letter I had received from Jim Callaghan early in 1998. 'I like the Dome,' he said. 'I am sure it will be a great success – if there are good transport facilities.' The media savaged the Dome, and revelled in reporting that visitor numbers, though running into many millions, were lower than some had predicted. In fact, the visitor surveys showed that almost everyone who went to the Dome enjoyed the experience. Even though the year before its opening was under the watch of my successor, Charlie Falconer, I played my part in the Dome's successes and its failures. I believe we were right to take it on. The Dome allowed us to mark the millennium as a nation, and also helped regenerate a deprived part of London. As a privately run venue for music and other events, it has since become an increasingly appreciated part of the capital's cultural life and landscape, as friends attending events at the O_2 Arena sometimes text me to point out.

When Tony gave me responsibility for the Dome, I hoped that it would pave the way for the cabinet position he had promised in his first reshuffle. That reshuffle finally came not in six months, as he had initially hoped, but after the CSR in July 1998. I did not know until the weekend beforehand what job I would be getting. Gordon had told me a few months earlier that his only concern in the reshuffle was what would be best for me. In his view, this would be taking charge at the – ill-defined and slightly peripheral – Department of Culture, Media and Sport. My old role model, and now friend, Shirley Williams had counselled me to go for the Department of the Environment. She also suggested a second option, the Department of Trade and Industry, but cautioned that this was likely to be overshadowed by the Treasury.

Tony had decided that I should go to the DTI, which needed to address the challenge of reinvigorating the UK economy. He felt that Margaret Beckett, whom he was moving to become Leader of the Commons, hadn't made this the priority he thought it should be. He was aware of the danger of appearing to encroach on territory that Gordon saw as his own, but especially since the CSR, Tony's attitude towards his next-door neighbour had acquired a new edge. A few days before the reshuffle, I suggested to Tony that moving me might help clear the air, reasoning that it would be better for both of us if I was in a cabinet role where Gordon could not make out that I was a threat to him all the time, but where there was a chance I could cooperate with him.

I still felt, however, that at some stage Tony would have to deal with the more fundamental issue of his relationship with Gordon.

At stake was not simply their respective political power bases in the government, but the matter of who had practical control over the broad swathe of economic and domestic policy, a question that had remained unresolved when Gordon stood aside for Tony in 1994. Whatever my own role, Tony had to meet that challenge: 'You have to tackle this head-on,' I told him, 'without destroying Gordon. Or it will destroy you – not now, but in years to come.'

He intended the reshuffle to be a first, small step towards doing so. Not just through my appointment, but by demoting a number of Brown protégés, Tony wanted to convey the message that he was in charge. The most painful casualty for Gordon was Nick Brown, sacked as Chief Whip and moved to a cabinet post which few, and certainly not Nick himself, wanted: Agriculture Secretary. Tony parachuted a loyal Blairite, Stephen Byers, into Gordon's back yard as Chief Secretary to the Treasury. However, in my case neither Tony nor I wanted my appointment to be seen as a deliberate provocation or a slight to Gordon. Both of us hoped that he would let me get on with the job at the DTI, and that where our policy remits did overlap, we could work together. Tony even contrived an audacious bit of choreography. Informing Gordon of my appointment, and pretending I was still in the dark, he suggested that Gordon be the one to give me the news.

The night before the announcement, Gordon invited me to his Westminster flat, where we had last met after John Smith's death. He greeted me warmly. Opening a bottle of wine, he said, 'Congratulations. You've got one of the top jobs.' He told me that the DTI post was a promotion I merited, and that whatever differences we might have, the importance of a coherent and united government approach on business issues made it imperative that we work together. This was music to my ears. It was made slightly less melodious by Charlie's deftly spun briefing for the following day's *Mirror*. It was Gordon who had told me about the DTI appointment, the paper splashed, with an unnamed source adding that I had 'listened carefully' to every word he had said to me. 'Peter knows that Gordon is boss, and he will defer to him,' the story said. 'He wants to learn from him.'

Even that could not detract from the sense of liberation, and the sheer energy and excitement, I felt upon arriving at the DTI. For the first week I barely slept, and barely noticed the effects. I immersed myself in my red boxes, reading up on the issues I would have to deal with, focusing mostly on the three that would require the most attention. The first was to review, revise as necessary, and bring into law a 'Fairness at Work' White Paper on industrial relations and trade union law which had been published by Margaret in the spring. The second was to decide what to do with the Royal Mail, a great national institution we had pledged in our manifesto not to privatise, but which clearly needed transforming if it was to survive in the modern telecommunications market. Finally, there was a major Competitiveness White Paper that was due on my watch, framing policy to ensure that British businesses could prosper in a changing world economy.

I inherited a team of civil servants who were gifted and dedicated, but also demoralised. This was not Margaret's fault. She was just the latest of a succession of briefly incumbent Trade Secretaries from both parties, under whom the DTI had failed to carry much weight in government. The root of the problem lay in the department's history. Created in the wake of Harold Wilson's embrace of the 'white heat of technology', it had evolved since the late 1970s to take a narrower role as sponsor of the interests of individual business sectors. It had a range of satellite responsibilities, including a network of regional offices whose role overlapped with other ministries.

In a sense, I was arriving at the DTI at a fortunate time, with the opportunity to champion a clearer and more contemporary role for the department, as the voice of business across government, taking the lead in creating a knowledge-driven economy for Britain. Since before the election, I had been urging Tony to give me a proper job. This certainly qualified. I also hoped that it would allow me to move on from my image as a back-room plotter. Broadly speaking, then as later, I rather modelled myself on a predecessor at the department, Michael Heseltine, and his famous pledge to 'intervene before breakfast, lunch and dinner' on the side of British industry.

Almost as soon as I arrived at the DTI, I felt that I was able to start redefining what 'being Peter' meant. Instead of giving advice to others and enabling them to take decisions, I was taking my own, and setting an agenda for the department. Instead of being a member of someone else's team, I was picking one of my own. Instead of living with someone else's judgements, I was able to exercise my own. Seeing how my officials and other ministers in the department responded to this gave me a genuine thrill. I loved receiving advice from others, and then providing leadership and taking responsibility for policy decisions, justifying them to Parliament and the press. The union legislation was my first challenge. I did not want my approach to be parodied as anti-union Thatcherism with a red rose. But nor did I want to turn the clock back on Mrs Thatcher's basic reforms. I left in place a number of the union-friendly provisions in the 'Fairness at Work' Bill, notably a clause allowing for automatic recognition in workplaces where a union could claim a sizeable membership. I did, however, insert an extra audit into the process, to make sure such claims were credible. I added constraints on secondary strikes and picketing. In a speech in September to my old employer, the TUC, I put the case that with falling membership among younger workers, the unions faced the kind of modernising challenge Labour had confronted before 1997. They had to provide a more relevant service to their members. They had to be seen as responsible by the public. They had to engage flexibly with employers in the face of rapid economic change. New Labour didn't want to pick fights with the unions, I said. What we wanted was for 'modernised trade unions to be our active and committed partners'.

The Royal Mail was trickier. There too, I managed to produce a White Paper that took account of a changing market that was increasingly threatening to make Post Office services uncompetitive. The

Planning the 1997 general election campaign: *left to right* – me, Margaret Beckett, Alastair Campbell, Tony Blair and Gordon Brown.

New Labour's kings of spin: standing between Alastair and David Hill prior to our 1997 election manifesto launch.

Above A new dawn: the election victory party at the Royal Festival Hall on the morning of 2 May 1997. I am standing behind Pauline Prescott.

Right Minister without Portfolio: outside the Cabinet Office on my first day at work.

At the Millennium Dome site: *left to right* – Chris Smith, Michael Heseltine, Tony Blair, John Prescott, me.

John in conversation with his mate 'Peter'.

Relaxing in the company of Sabrina Guinness and Mick Jagger.

Left With Bobby *(left)* and Jack on the steps of Hillsborough Castle.

Above At Stormont with Tony and Bill Clinton, on his third and final visit to Northern Ireland as President, December 2000.

Right As usual, Bobby is the centre of attention when the Queen visits Hillsborough. The housekeeper, Olywn McCarthy, keeps hold of him.

Above With Tony in Hartlepool, September 2001. This was the first time we had been photographed together since my second resignation.

Left Making my resignation statement outside Number 10 after leaving the government for the second time, January 2001.

Below Supporting the campaign for justice for the families of the victims of the Omagh bombing. My special adviser, Patrick Diamond, is on the far right.

Above With my constituency agent, Steve Wallace, outside a pub in Hartlepool.

Right Anxiously awaiting the result at the Hartlepool count on the night of the 2001 general election.

Above Jubilation with my supporters after my victory is announced.

document we eventually published stopped short of privatisation – a non-starter given our manifesto commitment – although it did leave the option open for the longer term. In the shorter term, I proposed giving the company latitude to borrow and invest in order to find ways of remaining competitive, and leaving open the possibility of its becoming a PLC at some later stage. Competitiveness was also the central theme of the White Paper I published in mid-December. Alongside the rest of the team at the DTI, I worked hard on what I saw as a major change in Labour's definition of what government could and should do with regard to business. In the digital age, the premium would be on fleetness of foot, innovation, entrepreneurship, and above all knowledge and the ability to apply and profit from it.

I was especially impressed by a ministerial trip to the United States, on which I saw at close range an array of business success stories. During a visit to Silicon Valley the boss of Hewlett-Packard, Lew Platt, threw a question to me about the Labour government being anti-success, and opposed to rewarding entrepreneurs who took risks and grew rich. 'We are intensely relaxed about people becoming filthy rich,' I replied, 'as long as they pay their taxes.' It was an off-the-cuff riposte, but for ever after it would be partially quoted, omitting its crucial second half, as evidence of New Labour's alleged love affair with wealth and greed. The broader message I intended was that we had to encourage business success, rather than demonise the people who made businesses work and grow. The real beneficiary, if Britain could move towards a US-style entrepreneurial culture and equip and educate young people to be part of it, would be the country as a whole.

That was the vision set out in the White Paper. It pointed us away from the interventionist policies of the past. In the 1960s and 1970s, 'modern' industrial policy had meant a belief in state planning, and the encouragement of forced marriages between companies. I did not think government should, or could, play that role any longer. Instead, meeting the demands of the knowledge-driven economy meant making markets work better, through collaboration between companies as well as competition. It meant investment in education and training. The Competitiveness White Paper included a provision for a public–private venture capital fund to encourage entrepreneurship. It advocated allocating millions of pounds to forge ties between business on the one hand, and schools and universities on the other. It proposed subsidies to put small enterprises online, and included looser planning and immigration rules to help high-tech businesses get established and, where necessary, draw on overseas expertise. It was a wholly different approach to the new economic realities that Britain had to face if it was to thrive.

I was beginning to earn a reputation, not least among my team of junior ministers and civil servants, as a capable Secretary of State. In common with others in our first-term government, I arrived with no ministerial experience. But with my early education in policy-making from Roger's purloined Transport Department files, and my more recent experience at the Cabinet Office, I had a head start. I began with the need to create an overall vision of what we wanted to accomplish, and a set of clear policy priorities to achieve it. I listened to my civil servants' advice, gave them their fair share of credit for everything we accomplished, and took personal responsibility for anything we did not. Most importantly, I took decisions. Having read all the relevant papers and taken on board all the relevant views, in briskly conducted meetings or in discussion with informed outsiders, I would come to a judgement, communicate it, and not retreat from it.

My first five months at the DTI were in many ways the most fulfilling I had spent in politics. I had managed to lead and enthuse a large department, producing legislative and policy results. As the end of the year approached, I had every reason to believe I would remain there at least until the next election. Tony certainly wanted and expected that. But whatever the next steps I would take in my political career, one thing was sure: I had proved to myself, and demonstrated to my doubters, that I was as capable of being a minister as I was of 'being Peter'. This gave me confidence and, I have to say, a lot of satisfaction too.

Just days after the publication of the Competitiveness White Paper, however, a political firestorm broke out around me which would ensure that my first five months as Secretary of State for Trade and Industry would be my last.

7

Being Fired

It was my own mistakes that caused my downfall. It was my image, only partially repaired in the short time I had spent at the DTI, that ensured that it was greeted with glee by so many. But the engine of my destruction was Gordon Brown.

On the afternoon of 16 December 1998 I presented the Competitiveness White Paper to the Commons. That evening, Ben Wegg-Prosser came to see me, with news that he had held off telling me ahead of the launch, confiding instead in my Principal Private Secretary, Anthony Phillipson. It was about a new book by Gordon's biographer Paul Routledge. This latest volume was a poisonous polemic against me. We had known for months that it was in the works, although we did not know what would be in it. Now, Ben had been tipped off about its contents. 'He has included your loan from Geoffrey for the house,' he told me very quietly. 'I think this could be trouble for you.'

For five years before the 1997 election, I had lived in the small flat I had bought after my year living with Sue Nye and Gavyn Davies. If you believed the estate agents, it was on the edge of Islington. In fact it was in not-yet-up-and-coming Clerkenwell, or more nearly Lower King's Cross. I had been thinking for some time about finding somewhere larger, with the sort of private space I had had in Foy. It was Robert Harris who introduced me, inadvertently, to the attractions of Notting Hill. Early in 1996, after I had spent the previous summer writing *The Blair Revolution* in Kintbury, he and Gill began talking of buying a *pied à terre* in London. Neither of them wanted to live wanted to live in the capital, but they liked going up for weekends. Robert thought they could let it to me during the week, leaving my weekends free for my constituency home in Hartlepool. When we began looking, he was drawn to west London, where both he and Gill had lived before. The houses were elegant, quiet but close to restaurants and cafés, small shops and the famous Portobello Road Market.

In the end, Robert decided not to buy, but when I began thinking of moving from Clerkenwell in the spring, the idea of Notting Hill remained in my mind. I obviously could not afford a house, and given the prices of the flats I looked at, it was pretty clear I could not really afford to live there at all. As summer approached, however, I was doing back-of-the-envelope calculations in the hope that I would be able to find some way to scrape the money together. On balance, I wondered if it might be wiser to forget the posher post-codes and settle for something a little cheaper. Barely two years later, with my political life in tatters, I would ask myself why on earth I hadn't done just that. I would have done, had it not been for a dinner invitation from Geoffrey Robinson, the Labour MP for Coventry North-West and now Treasury Minister.

Geoffrey was a wealthy businessman, although he hadn't been when I'd first got to know him almost twenty years earlier. The venue for our dinner was his apartment in the Grosvenor House hotel. He wanted to discuss how he might help repair my relation-ship with Gordon, who wasn't talking to me at this point, before the election. I had known Geoffrey before either of us had even heard of Gordon or Tony. When I went to work for Albert Booth, it was Geoffrey – fifteen years my senior, an MP for five years and a transport whip – who had helped get the trade unions to fund the post. He and I had remained on friendly terms, and he always took an avuncular interest in my career. Especially since the modern-isers' advance after 1994, he had been generous in different ways to both Gordon and Tony. He had helped fund office salaries and expenses, and had offered them the use of his home in Italy, and his flats in Cannes and London: Tony spent his first summer holiday as

Prime Minister at the Robinson villa in San Gimignano. Geoffrey was especially close to Gordon, never having wavered in supporting him as the leadership crown slipped away. Not only Gordon, but Ed Balls and Charlie Whelan, had free run of Geoffrey's London apartment. They met there to chat, strategise, or simply to watch football on TV.

I had never benefited from Geoffrey's financial generosity, nor had I ever asked or expected to. As we sat down to dinner, it did not occur to me to do so now. We began by talking about Gordon. It was paramount, Geoffrey said, that we find a way to repair our friendship. I didn't need convincing. When he urged me to 'reach out' and let Gordon know that I still wanted the best for him, I mentioned the multiple occasions on which I had done precisely that. I would keep trying, I said.

It was when Geoffrey asked how things were going in my life, as he always did, that I mentioned the frustrations I was experiencing alongside the excitement at helping New Labour get into government. I spoke about the rootlessness I was feeling, the desire to find a home I would be comfortable in. Geoffrey sympathised. He said that I needed somewhere I could feel 'settled' and where I could entertain. A base. We were likely to win the election. I would be part of the government. 'You shouldn't have to worry about these things,' he said. When I told him I was hoping to pay for a move through a combination of help from my mother and a mortgage, he said I should try to buy something that would be a good investment, and assured me that I would be able to pay for it over time. It was at this point that he suggested he could tide me over if my mother couldn't. He said he had the resources, it was nothing to him, and he was confident that I'd be able to repay him.

It all took off from there. Over the next few weeks, the two of us had a lot of fun flat-hunting. Some of the flats were lovely, but they were not much bigger than what I had, nor were they any more secluded or peaceful – but they were much more costly. It was Geoffrey who suggested an option that was barely more expensive: a small house. The one I settled on was a narrow, three-storey Georgian property in

Northumberland Place, near Westbourne Grove. It was comfortable, it was peaceful, it was in every sense a home, and I instantly fell in love with it.

I certainly didn't think then that there was anything wrong, or politically perilous, about accepting a loan from Geoffrey. Perhaps, I would reflect later, I didn't allow myself to think through the implications. But I was caught up in preparing for the election, and entranced by the prospect of having a real home of my own, a place I could be proud of, with a desk on which to spread out my papers, shelves filled with my books, and the kind of dining and living space I could share with friends.

Without realising it, or at least admitting it, I was getting in a bit over my head. In my brother's profession, this would be called 'denial'. I was certainly in denial about the political ramifications. I saw nothing odd in Geoffrey's having helped me to buy the house rather than my mother, who although she had the funds, left to her by my father, I did not want to pressure into helping me out financially if I could help it. Geoffrey had always been supportive towards me, someone I could trust and open up to. There was no conflict of interest I could see that put me under any obligation to him. It never occurred to me – or I believe to Geoffrey either – that his closeness to Gordon presented a danger that Gordon, or those around him, might at some point use the loan against me. After the conveyancing had been completed, I faxed to Geoffrey at his apartment a draft of the formal agreement between us for a loan of £373,000.

Even now that Ben had warned me the loan would soon become public, it took me some time to understand what that might mean. Like Geoffrey, I regarded the loan as private rather than secret, something that was between us, and had nothing to do with our political or public lives. It had been made because we were friends, and at a time when neither of us was a minister. I was supposed to be Tony Blair's big, strategic thinker. Asked a few weeks after the election to describe what I did as Minister without Portfolio, I had described myself as 'Minister for Looking Ahead'. I was clearly not particularly good at doing that for myself.

If there was one 'psychological flaw' that I shared with Gordon, it was tunnel vision. It separated both of us from the less obsessive, inherently more self-confident Tony, and it was one reason I did not focus immediately on what was about to unfold. I was so upset by what the Routledge home-loan disclosure implied about my relationship with Gordon – the assumption that the information had come from his camp was never doubted – that I failed to grasp what its effects were bound to be on me. I kept telling myself I had never misled, undermined or betrayed Gordon in 1994. Ever since then, all I had wanted was to put those painful few days behind us. Gordon could not accept this, however. He was convinced that he had been wronged, and was determined to get even. I never found out whether it was Gordon himself who told Routledge about the loan. I suspect not. But Geoffrey's flat, to which the agreement had been faxed, was home from home for Gordon, Charlie Whelan, Ed Balls, Nick Brown and the rest of his team. The media's suspicion, and Downing Street's, soon fell on Charlie, or on Nick, who had had his nose put out of joint by his removal as Chief Whip earlier in the year. Both denied it. Whether it was one of them, or another of Gordon's acolytes, didn't matter. Gordon had always wanted to get even, or at least cut me down to size, and now he had.

The first thing I did on the morning after Ben told me about the Routledge book was to call my Permanent Secretary, Sir Michael Scholar, to my office and tell him the full details. Whenever a politician takes up a ministerial post, he discloses potential conflicts of interests to his senior civil servant as a matter of course. When I entered the Cabinet Office after the election, I asked my then Principal Private Secretary, Rupert Huxter, for guidance on a range of my outside activities. On speaking engagements, I was told that if I accepted them, I could under no circumstances get a fee, even if I passed it on to charity. I was advised to give up my unpaid roles as trustee for the English National Ballet and the Whitechapel Art Gallery, and with regret I did so. Rupert said that the rule of thumb had to be to avoid any risk of a conflict of interest, or any perception of such a risk. He concluded with a question for me, in writing: 'Are there any other outside positions we should be considering, and (very important) any major financial interests we should be aware of?' In that context, it genuinely didn't occur to me to mention the loan. I assumed that a 'financial interest' meant a shareholding or a stake in some company or other organisation which might come across my radar in government, not a loan from a fellow Labour MP.

My conversations with Sir Michael at the DTI had been different. There, the question of my relationship with Geoffrey Robinson did arise, the previous September. I was the one who raised it, after Sir Michael told me the department was beginning an investigation into allegations of impropriety in Geoffrey's business dealings with the late *Mirror* tycoon Robert Maxwell. I replied that since I had known Geoffrey for many years, I could have no role at all in the inquiry. I should see no papers about it, nor would I discuss it with Geoffrey.

When I now told Sir Michael about the loan, he didn't shout. He was the consummate civil servant. But his initial silence indicated concern. We were fine, he said, on the DTI inquiry into Geoffrey: 'You acted properly. You completely insulated yourself from it.' But he added: 'You should have taken the precaution of telling me about the loan.'

I shuddered at the prospect of confronting the implications with Alastair or Tony, though I knew the time would come soon enough. Ben phoned Number 10 and told them about the loan, about Routledge's book, and the fact that the story would soon be public knowledge. Alastair and Fiona had been disapproving of my move to Notting Hill in the first place, regarding it as a sign that I was adopting a swanky lifestyle, leaving my old friends behind and replacing them with people higher up the social scale. In fact I was nesting, rather than socialising, but newspaper gossip suggested otherwise, and that became the received wisdom. Now, Alastair said he was astonished that I had taken a loan of this size, and that I had not declared it after we came into government. This view was transmitted to Tony, who echoed the theme. 'How could you *do* this?' he kept asking me. 'What were you *thinking*?'

In our conversations and meetings over the next week, I tried to explain how it had happened. I pointed out that on the central issue of principle – whether Geoffrey's loan had won him favours or potentially preferential treatment – my behaviour had been entirely proper. The issue for the Ministerial Code, however, was not just the reality of a conflict of interest; as Rupert had warned me from the start, it was the perception of a conflict. During my time at the DTI I had ensured that I took no part in discussions or decisions affecting Geoffrey. But that did not alter the perception that I might have been influenced by the loan.

My instinct was to come clean, to try to explain my failure to inform my officials of the loan, but also to fight against suggestions that I had ever acted improperly in my ministerial work. Tony and Alastair broadly backed me in this at first, hoping that any media controversy would soon pass. So did others, like Charlie Falconer, whom they consulted about how to handle the issue. Charlie, I was later told, had in fact heard about the loan very early on. But from the first newspaper reports, I could sense that Alastair, in particular, feared a long-running media frenzy that would damage not just me, but the whole government. The loan story was bad enough; the personal and political narratives swirling around it made it worse. There was the size of the sum involved. The fashionable character of the neighbourhood where I had chosen to live. The people I hadn't told: not just Tony or the civil service, but the Commons and the Britannia Building Society, from whom I'd got my mortgage. It did not matter whether or not I was under an obligation to inform these bodies. It was what the media would make of it that mattered.

There was also the issue of Geoffrey himself. Working alongside Gordon at the Treasury, he had shown a knack for attracting criticism and controversy that sometimes made me seem like Teflon. The Maxwell allegations were his latest difficulty. Months earlier, it had been revealed that he was managing – quite legally – to avoid paying large amounts of UK tax, and only Gordon's intercession had stopped Tony from sacking him in the reshuffle. Finally there was

Gordon himself, or the painful saga of Gordon's relations with me. Neither Alastair nor Tony doubted that someone in Gordon's camp had been behind making the loan public.

My final few days in office passed by in a blur. The *Guardian* had got hold of the story, and published details of the loan. At times, it felt almost as if I was watching someone else's march to the ministerial gallows. I spoke on many occasions to Tony, to Alastair, and to Gordon as well. Alastair would later tell me how astonished he had been that I was reaching out to the author – or at least the co-author – of my demise. He saw this as an extraordinary sign of a closeness that somehow survived between Gordon and me. It was more complicated than that. Yes, there was still a bond, of sorts. Given the strength of our early alliance, that was inevitable. But I think Gordon and I also recognised the destructive power, for each of us, in what had happened. My sense then, and now, was that Gordon wanted to damage rather than destroy me, perhaps to make me more dependent on him and less on Tony. But that is a subtlety that would have been lost on his lieutenants, who would have seen no reason to hold back from the kill. On Gordon's part, I think there was at least a tinge of guilt as well. I am sure we both felt that my hopes for a future as a cabinet minister, and his as Prime Minister, might not survive a further battle between us. When I first phoned him, he seemed sympathetic and supportive. He recommended that I apologise for the lack of disclosure, but was firm that I need not, and should not, resign.

The media criticism, though not uniformly harsh, or headline news, was showing no sign of going away. When I spoke to Tony on the evening of 22 December, six days after I learned of the leak, I sensed for the first time that he thought I might have to go, especially when we finished our conversation with an agreement to 'sleep on it' and talk again. The next morning, Alastair and Jonathan came to see me at the DTI, arriving like a couple of undertakers. We arranged for me to have a further, private call with Tony. I rehearsed the areas on which I knew I had been wrong, and the key issue on which I had been right: the avoidance of any conflict of interest either at the Cabinet Office or the DTI. Tony listened, but his response was firm. It was best for all of us, he said, that I go. The media atmosphere was too ugly, the potential damage to the government too great if it carried on.

For one of the very few times in my public life, I felt my eyes welling up. Less than half a year into my first real job in government, I was suddenly, summarily out. The only consolation, one that I would hold on to like a life raft in the months ahead, was that Tony made it clear to me that there might be a way back. 'If you resign,' he said, 'you, and we, can start over. It makes it easier for you to come back sooner.' In his formal, published reply to my resignation, he wrote: 'It is no exaggeration to say that without your support and advice, we would never have built New Labour. . .In future, you will achieve much, much more with us.'

That afternoon I had a call from Cherie at Chequers, where the Blairs had retreated for the Christmas holiday. 'We want you to be with us tonight,' she said. I drove with Reinaldo into the Buckinghamshire sunset to spend the first night of my cabinet exile with Tony and his family. Cherie wrote me a personal note after we had left the following day. She, Tony and the children wanted me to know their door was always open. She invited me to return, with my mother, for Christmas. Her note made me realise for the first time the toll Gordon's behaviour since the election was exerting on Tony, and the fury towards Gordon that was building up in Cherie. 'I have no doubt you have been the victim of a vicious and selfish campaign,' she wrote. 'My only consolation is that I believe that a person who causes evil to another will in the end suffer his returns. That he is prepared to risk the whole Labour government and to plot against a vital part of it means that to me he has lost any claim to the moral high ground he affects to inhabit.' She was, she said, 'angry and upset by what has happened, and worried for Tony'. Another victim of the episode was Geoffrey Robinson himself, who was removed as Paymaster General, making me feel guilty that I had been the trigger for his ejection as well as my own.

The next few months were hard. Tony's generosity in the days after my resignation, and his assurance that there might be a way back, were a comfort. Over time, I also benefited from a reassessment of my resignation. The media, and my fellow MPs, recognised that I had gone quickly, and had acknowledged the mistakes I had made. The building society vindicated my insistence that I had done nothing wrong in omitting to mention Geoffrey's loan on my mortgage application, not least because I had not yet even agreed it with him at the time. The Parliamentary Standards Commissioner acknowledged that the rules of reporting such benefits were too vague to suggest unequivocally that I needed to register the loan, although she did conclude that it would have been better if I had done so. Not least, Tony and Alastair had finally insisted that Charlie Whelan had to go. This probably did more than anything to lead people to the conclusion that my resignation had at least as much to do with the ongoing tug-of-war between Gordon and Tony as with any failings of my own.

Still, I felt adrift and alone. Adrift because, at least for the foreseeable future, I could play no formal part in the party and the government I had worked to bring into power. Alone, because there were limits to what even friends could do to help me come to terms with what had happened. Reinaldo was soon gone, too. He was in Tokyo for the academic year, and had to fly back to Japan after Christmas. Friends did help: Roger Liddle, Robert Harris, Dennis Stevenson and his family, and Ben. Roy Jenkins was among those who let it be known that he did not see any grounds for my resignation. John Major caught my arm in the Commons Members' Lobby and said he was sure I would soon be back, a kindness that was not expected from a political opponent, and was therefore all the more important to me.

For Easter, Jacob and Serena Rothschild, old and good friends, invited me to join them at their home on Corfu, no doubt confirming Alastair's worst fears about the circles I was moving in. On a succession of balmy evenings, I began to write in my diary. I tried to take stock of where I was: possibly taking a detour in my political life, or conceivably at 'the nadir, from which I never make a full recovery'. I tried to reconstruct for myself what had happened, how I had finally got into the cabinet, and then blown it. My expulsion was all the more difficult to face because I had had a good run at the DTI.

I had got things done. For the first time since my earliest days at Walworth Road, I had attracted intelligent reviews rather than hostile headlines. Even writing for an audience of only myself, I could not bring myself to exonerate other actors in the drama: Gordon, and even more so his cronies, whose obsession with getting even for his loss of the leadership I had underestimated; the media, whose eagerness to turn an error of judgement into a scandal on a grand scale that I had not anticipated.

But why had I not seen the problems in borrowing such a large sum? The fact was that I hadn't even thought about them at the time: I just wanted to settle into a nice home without waiting any longer. I could see now that I must have been aware of some potential danger or embarrassment. 'Had I become so detached from reality that I simply failed to think how it would look for an impecunious politician to be moving into such a smart neighbourhood?' I asked myself. The answer, as best as I could work it out, was that I felt I had suffered enough intrusion in my life. 'I wanted my privacy. I wanted a slice of life to enjoy, something of my own to have and to hold.' And, yes, 'a bit of high living had definitely crept into my soul. I saw what others enjoyed and I wanted to share it. Not glamour, or luxury, or swank. Just comfort and smartness. I had absolutely no desire to show off. Social life was always secondary. Work always came first. But I cared about money because I didn't have it. I wanted my own savings, my own ability to spend on myself and others. I have never been greedy for riches. And yet it was my eyes getting too big for my stomach that brought me down.'

One evening on Corfu, after everyone else had gone to bed, Serena lingered on the terrace and asked, suddenly: 'Peter, why do you have so many enemies?' I tried to explain the world of politics as I had come to see it: jealous, competitive, resentful, back-stabbing. I added that my particular role in the birth of New Labour had earned me a special hatred, from those on both the Labour left and the Tory right who had wanted the party to stay as it was. My own excesses had made things worse. I had forged ahead like a zealot, but too often I had behaved as if I was indifferent to other people's feelings, to the dismay and anger of those who were being defeated. The fact that

I was acting for the good of the party meant nothing to those who were caught up in their personal war of resistance. For some who believed in change, I was a hero. To others, I was the anti-Christ. To the public I was someone whose toughness and determination they could admire, but also a dark figure, 'the sinister minister', as my witty friend Nicholas Ward-Jackson had dubbed me. Not warm. Not human. Some of this was far too ingrained to be easily or speedily changed. But I knew I had to try.

On my return to London, I attended the Commons regularly and unobtrusively. I spent more time in Hartlepool, in an attempt to repay the enormous generosity that my constituents and the local party had shown after my resignation. I spoke at fellow MPs' constituency dinners. I tried not to make news, and to stay out of the papers. With real regret, I put the house in Northumberland Place on the market, because it was the only way to pay off the balance of my debt to Geoffrey, which I knew I had to do if I were to have any hope of returning to a front-line political role. I arranged to buy a small flat in a less upmarket road. Without an official car and driver, I bought a decidedly unministerial car for myself, a Fiat Punto. I concentrated on my duties as a constituency MP. After arriving in Hartlepool from London I would go shopping in my local Tesco, then go back to Hutton Avenue and prepare something like my mother's old recipe for roast pork, red cabbage and roast potatoes. Sometimes my constituency agent, the jolly and amusing Stephen Wallace, would join me. Often I would welcome neighbours who had become close friends: Leo Gillen, a local businessman and Labour stalwart, his wife Kathryn and their two children, Alexia and Leo junior. In London, I spent more time going to contemporary art shows and exhibitions with friends like Janice and David Blackburn.

While I began to live a more normal life, I also tried to repair my two most important political relationships: with Tony and Gordon. Gordon was the more difficult. Relations between us had been fraying even before my resignation. Despite the wine and the collegial words he had offered me when I was appointed to the DTI, Treasury sniping had accompanied almost everything I did there. A series of sneering stories had appeared in the press about my 'knowledge economy' agenda, even though I knew that Gordon supported it: he would later appropriate it as his own, first at the Treasury and then as Prime Minister. My plans to promote the modernisation of the Royal Mail had proved even more difficult. Gordon knew as well as I did that if it stayed as it was, the organisation could not remain competitive. But he raised last-minute objections to the borrowing and investment powers I wanted to include in the White Paper, and conveyed a series of demands through Ed Balls that greatly weakened the amounts that could be borrowed without Treasury agreement. With the publication date for the proposals fast approaching, I was at one point reduced to insisting that if they were gutted I would drop them altogether. In the end, Tony had to intervene, and we worked out a compromise. Charlie then proceeded to brief the more Labour-supporting newspapers that I had gone too far in my Royal Mail changes, while telling the Conservative-leaning ones that Gordon felt I had 'bottled it'. In retrospect, as all this was going on, I probably should have seen the Routledge leak coming.

If anything, since my resignation, relations with Gordon had become easier. Back in January 1999, Sue Nye had invited us for tea, hoping that the two politicians to whom she was closest could find a more civil way forward. When we met, Gordon seemed genuinely chastened by the events before Christmas. 'There has been huge damage, to all of us,' he said. 'We have to find a way to get things back on track.' He spoke nostalgically of the relationship the he, Tony and I had had before 1994: 'The people who know us don't understand what we were like before.' He urged me to rebuild myself as a politician, and said he had no doubt that at some stage I would be back in government. I reciprocated, as I always did in these moments of détente. I told him again that I had never acted to betray him in 1994, but had operated in what I, and those who truly cared about him, felt were his best interests. The main thing for us both was to move on, and to work together.

With Tony, my work never really stopped. As January wore on, I began getting regular phone calls from Number 10 or Chequers: on policy, strategy, presentation, or the 'message' for a speech or interview he was about to give. By the spring, the focus of our conversations had shifted from politics at home to the remote and mountainous Balkan territory of Kosovo. This mostly ethnic Albanian part of the former Yugoslavia had first come to Downing Street's attention shortly after the election. I vividly recalled one of the top officials at the Cabinet Office pressing for it to be included in the Prime Minister's weekly round-up of political issues. Tony had replied: 'Fine. You'd better give me a full note on it. Starting with: where is it?'

Now he knew. Kosovo's struggle for independence had run up against Serbia's determination not only to retain but to strengthen its hold over it, and to expel ethnic Albanians from Serbian border areas. In January 1999 a massacre by Serbian forces in the tiny village of Račak left forty-five civilians dead and sent the thousand or so remaining inhabitants fleeing for their lives. NATO had responded by threatening air strikes to force compliance with demands for the Serbian leader Slobodan Milošević to engage in talks for a peaceful settlement of Kosovo's future. At the end of March, NATO bombing began, in the hope of pushing Milošević to accept a NATO peace-keeping force. He had no intention of backing down. Serbian attacks on towns and villages in Kosovo intensified. Within the space of a week, a new campaign of ethnic cleansing pushed some 300,000 frightened, freezing, hungry civilians over the border into Albania and Macedonia.

Tony was certain that NATO, and Britain, were right to intervene. As in his first experience of military action – a joint US–British bombing campaign against Saddam Hussein in mid-December 1998, at the time my ministerial career was unravelling – I was struck by his quiet focus. He seemed 'a natural battle commander', I noted in my diary during the Kosovo campaign. I meant it as a comment on his temperament, but by the time the campaign was over, I would begin to sense that it ran deeper. To say that Tony enjoyed military conflict would be wrong. He felt, and spoke to me about, the weight of responsibility involved in ordering British troops into war. But he was coming to the view that combat was sometimes essential, and that one measure of leadership was a readiness to fight the necessary battles and win them. In late April 1999, on a visit to the United States for talks with Bill Clinton, Tony delivered a speech in Chicago that amounted to something very near to a 'Blair Doctrine'. In the past, war had been a last-resort response to direct threats to a nation's security or sovereignty. Tony said that would no longer work at a time when democracies faced the challenge of confronting 'two dangerous and ruthless men – Saddam Hussein and Slobodan Milošević'. The world had not only the right, but a duty, to act.

As the crisis intensified, with wavering certainty in the media and even in Number 10 about whether we were right to ratchet up the pressure, Tony, if anything, was determined to push further. Bill Clinton was proving very hard to bring along, but with the eventual threat of a ground invasion, Milošević backed down in early June. Tony's initial reaction was relief. Publicly, he was restrained rather than triumphant. Privately, he felt vindicated in his judgement that military action had been right, in his evolving world view, in his determination to overcome scepticism at home and challenges on the battlefield. Most importantly, he felt reinforced in his belief that military intervention would succeed. For weeks after it was over, I sensed a whole new level of self-confidence in him. It was a feeling I would recall, and recognise, four years later, in the run-up to a larger and more difficult war, in Iraq.

By now, I was again discreetly being asked to see Tony in his office in Number 10, or the family flat above Number 11. I was back where I had been before the 1997 election: involved, influential, but only, I felt, as an appendage, and a valued friend, of the Prime Minister. There was an irony in this, which those around me seemed to see more clearly than I did. Gordon and Tony were both urging me to rebuild myself politically, as a way back into the cabinet. But the more my political life was defined in terms of my relationship with Tony, the more difficult any real reconstruction became. I did have flashes of understanding about this. In a diary note, I reflected, 'The trouble with writing a journal is that every time I think of anything interesting it revolves around Tony Blair.' Even when I was at the DTI, 'the days would be punctuated by TB phone calls and summonses'.

I liked and admired Tony, and I am sure I enjoyed the need he felt for me, and the access he extended. More than anything, I wanted him to succeed as Prime Minister, and our New Labour government to make the mark we had hoped it would. I knew that my contribution mattered. Breaking free of this, or at least branching out from it, would not be easy. But it was essential.

I began thinking seriously about writing a book, as well as working with a producer on plans for a parallel television project. Robert Harris, clear-headed as usual, was supportive, but sceptical about how Downing Street would feel about this. He felt I should be focusing on my 'single biggest area of weakness' as a politician: 'Don't hang around waiting for Tony's calls. Don't let him give you "tasks" to perform. Your interests and theirs are not identical.'

Philip Gould also thought that writing a book would allow me to 'develop political ideas'. But he saw it as only part of remaking myself as a politician, and as a person. 'I start from a position of unqualified support for you,' he wrote to me. 'I believe the New Labour Party exists only because of you; that Labour was saved through you; that this government with its majority of 179 is a testament to your work. I also believed that you need not have resigned, and I counselled against letting you go.' That was the good news. 'You are the architect of New Labour, but you are also the architect of your own recent difficulties,' he added. 'It is true you did not need to resign, but it is even more true that you should never have got into the position that led to your resignation. At any time in the last two years if you had spoken to me, or Alastair, or Tony, or Anji about the loan, you would have been helped and supported and the need to resign would never have occurred.'

The rebuilding project Tony had in mind for me – appearing in the Commons, reaching out to colleagues, getting along with Gordon – was child's play compared to what Philip felt was required. In his view, I needed nothing less than a personality transplant. 'You've always said in the past that for you to change was neither possible nor desirable – that you are who you are, with your positive bits and negative bits.' But these two Peters – the 'warm, generous, outward, loving side' and the 'darker, more defensive, closed and sometimes more menacing one' – could no longer co-exist. My strengths had helped to save Labour and propel me in politics. 'Your vulnerabilities undid you, and they will undo you again unless you change.' He said that this would require being open and honest with friends. I would have to learn not only to advise others, but to *take* advice. Real recovery would also mean being more open in every way.

Philip was expecting a lot, but I knew he was right. If only a personality were like some Lego toy, to be disassembled and refashioned at will. If only the make-up of my personality, or anybody's, were as clear-cut as Philip's tough, but well-intentioned words suggested. If only I had been anything, anywhere, except a politician in Westminster. I did work at dispensing with my 'menace', a change made easier by my absence from front-line politics. It had almost always been a weapon deployed in zealous defence of Tony's and New Labour's interests, and against those who seemed to threaten them. That was no longer part of my job description. But opening up did not come easily, or quickly. In the bearpit of politics, there is often a feeling that you have to kill or be killed. There is always someone, somewhere with an interest in playing on and redoubling any pain you are feeling. When I had tried to describe the stage on which I lived my life to Serena on Corfu, I had used words like 'jealous', 'competitive', 'resentful' and 'back-stabbing'. Still feeling raw from my resignation, I may have exaggerated. But only slightly. Gordon's campaign against me, and less openly against Tony, since 1994 may have been an extreme case. But friendships, true friendships, are rare in politics, and there are times when even they come under strain.

Within a matter of weeks, I was reminded of this all over again. Mo Mowlam and I had known, worked with, and liked each other since the 1980s. She was brash and gutsy, not least in the way she had quietly got on with her life and her work as Northern Ireland Secretary despite being diagnosed with a brain tumour before the election. She was also generous. A few days after my resignation she took me out to breakfast at the Savoy. It was a huge tonic. She offered sympathy and support, and said that it was not just her expectation but her wish that I would be back in the cabinet. Neither of us, however, could have anticipated the circumstances, difficult for both of us, in which that was to happen.

One of the most significant and far-reaching achievements of our first year in office had been the Good Friday Agreement in April 1998, committing unionists, loyalists, republicans and nationalists in Northern Ireland to a future course of devolved government, disarmament and reconciliation. We had inherited a peace process from John Major. An energetic and endlessly patient American legislator, Senator George Mitchell of Maine, had been drafted in to help the process. But talks had been sporadic, and ceasefires announced in 1994 had been jettisoned. Crucially for the hopes of any meaningful agreement, Sinn Féin had effectively been excluded from the talks because of IRA violence. Tony, Ireland's new Taoiseach Bertie Ahern, Bill Clinton and Senator Mitchell had played the key parts in the negotiating process. But Mo's no-nonsense style, the courage with which she devoted herself to the task while undergoing radiotherapy, and the personal ties she developed with Sinn Féin's Gerry Adams and Martin McGuinness were important in getting talks under way and keeping them going. She also kept the hard-liners on the other side on board at a crucial juncture, going into Belfast's Maze prison to persuade jailed loyalist paramilitaries to withdraw their opposition to the negotiations.

But by the summer of 1999 the process was stuck, the peace agreement made but not implemented, and there had been no progress on actually setting up a devolved government or getting the IRA to decommission its weapons. Tony was convinced that Mo's role had reached a natural endpoint. The forthright style and salty language that had initially endeared her to Sinn Féin had alienated her from the Ulster Unionist Party and its leader, David Trimble, whom she clearly didn't much like. Even Sinn Féin seemed to have concluded that she was past her sell-by date, and Adams and McGuinness increasingly insisted on dealing directly with Tony and Jonathan Powell in Number 10.

Mo, always popular with the media and the party, had been elevated to almost saintlike status as she had shrugged off her illness and helped deliver the Good Friday breakthrough, and Tony knew he had to tread carefully if he was to replace her in a job she had grown to love. Many in the media would go on to suggest that Tony wanted her moved because of her popularity – evidenced by the standing ovation a mention of her name received in the middle of Tony's speech at the 1998 party conference. I never believed that. He was simply certain he needed a fresh start under a new Northern Ireland Secretary. He had an equally challenging assignment in mind for Mo: standing as Labour's candidate to become London's first elected mayor. Tony's worst political nightmare, Ken Livingstone, had made it clear that he intended to go for the nomination, and there was every chance he would succeed, feeding on sentiment on the backbenches and in the grassroots that New Labour somehow wasn't *Labour* at all, and Tony wasn't either. Mo was the one cabinet member with the style, drive and broad appeal to scare Ken off. If he didn't scare, she could beat him to the nomination.

But Mo didn't want to move. She resisted suggestions that she would be the ideal mayoral candidate, and that she would enjoy the job. At first I was only peripherally involved. I agreed with Tony that the peace process needed new impetus, and accepted his view that with the unionists seeing Mo as boorish and hostile, and the republicans increasingly treating her as irrelevant, her usefulness was undermined.

As Tony began planning for a second reshuffle, my own, very cautious, hopes for an early re-entry into cabinet lay elsewhere: in Europe. This was the area where he and I had agreed that I could work in the months after my resignation. I had been representing him in efforts to secure what, for both of us, was the flipside of our commitment to European engagement: fundamental reform of the EU's economic model. We wanted a more modern, decentralised approach, with an emphasis on equipping member states and their citizens to benefit from the open markets and open borders that increasingly defined the world economy. In talks with EU allies, above all the Germans,

I acted as Tony's unofficial envoy. More openly, I continued to speak out on European issues, balancing support for the single currency with calls for EU reform.

After a speech to a UK-sponsored political conference in Brussels at the end of June, I even received a handwritten letter of praise from Neil Kinnock. Now an EU Commissioner, he had been civil but distant since my departure from Walworth Road for the Commons. In a p.s., he said he was glad to see I was on the way to recovery from the 'house episode'. He urged me to 'stay as clear as possible from an Organiser Peter, Spinner Peter Role'. I should leave that to others, he said, in favour of a 'chance to run some policy again, whenever the right opportunity comes'. As I pointed out in my reply, though I 'hoped to God' to avoid reverting to fixing and spinning, I was not exactly in a strong bargaining position to determine what I would be offered next. Neil did reflect a sense that my stock was rising, and my luck might be about to turn. While I kept it to myself, I did hold out hope of persuading Tony to do what he'd balked at in 1997, and make me a junior minister for Europe. What I wasn't prepared for was what he did offer me: Northern Ireland. Mo's job.

In the spring I had had a long talk with Mo in the Smoking Room at the House of Commons, during which she asked me to intervene on her behalf with Tony. She wanted me to get across to him that if she did leave Belfast, it would have to be for a bigger cabinet post. She said she wanted to be Foreign Secretary. I couldn't bring myself to respond in the way I knew Tony would: that this would be hard to imagine. The reason the Foreign Secretary is known as Britain's senior diplomat is that one of the prerequisites for the job is a talent for being diplomatic. Mo had many gifts, but that was not one of them. Still, I promised to pass on the message. When I did, Tony simply looked astonished. He remained determined to move her – into the coordinator and 'enforcer' role at the Cabinet Office which I had been meant to play in 1997, and which Jack Cunningham had been filling, with some frustration, for the past year.

Tony then delivered his bolt from the blue: he wanted me to take Mo's place in Northern Ireland. His reasoning was that he needed someone in Belfast who would start with a clean slate, especially with the unionists, and who could understand not just the negotiating issues but the politics that often overshadowed them. Of course I was flattered, intrigued and tempted. Six months earlier, I had wondered when, even if, I would return to government. I certainly never expected Tony to invite me back so soon. I also knew that Mo would be furious when she found out that Tony had definitively decided to move her.

She was. She phoned me and accused me of trying to steal her job, a message she promptly began sharing with colleagues and reporters. She then went further, saying that if the Prime Minister wanted to move her, he obviously had the right to do so, but that she wanted to stay and see out the peace process she had helped make possible. I was shaken by the idea of finding myself cast as the agent of Mo's removal, even though I realised the principal target of her anger was Tony. In mid-July, with the reshuffle only a fortnight away, I wrote to him that whatever other ministerial moves he might be contemplating, I had concluded that it would not be right for me to come back into the government at this stage. I said he should leave Mo where she was. Tony had told me that one reason he had wanted to move her was that he was having increasingly to do her job himself. It was not an ideal arrangement, but it meant there was no urgent need to replace her.

Tony decided to delay the reshuffle until Mo's rebellion had died down. It came in October, occasioned by Frank Dobson's agreement to leave the Department of Health and run against Ken for the mayoral nomination. At the Ministry of Defence, Geoff Hoon replaced George Robertson, who was nominated as NATO's Secretary General. The other big promotion, to Health Secretary, went to Alan Milburn. He had been made a junior minister in the Department of Health after 1997, and in the mini-reshuffle prompted by my resignation at the end of 1998, Tony had moved him to Chief Secretary of the Treasury, Gordon's number two, a role previously occupied by another of his favourite young reformers, Stephen Byers, who replaced me at the DTI. The rationale had been to put a pair of Blairite eyes inside Number 11. The effect was only to heighten suspicion, and to make for an especially tense relationship between Gordon and both Stephen and Alan in their later cabinet roles. With Alan, who was now designated to take hold of health, the top policy priority next to education on our domestic reform agenda, this would prove particularly significant.

The third major change in the reshuffle involved me. Tony stuck to his decision, moving Mo to the Cabinet Office, and me to Belfast. Mo was upset, but she was typically big-hearted in easing my arrival as her successor. 'The past is the past. I want to help you be a success,' she said That evening I went to discuss the post with her at her north London home, and got an early education in how different my life would now be. There was a pillbox in the front garden, staffed by policemen armed with machine guns. From that moment on, for the next four years I had an armed protection team attached to me. They did not leave my side from the moment I walked out of my front door each morning, and I became good friends with my succession of protection officers. The next day, Mo went with me to Belfast to introduce me to my team at the Northern Ireland Office and the local media. With real delight, she showed me around Hillsborough Castle, the eighteenth-century mansion that was now my official residence. I couldn't help laughing at Mo's observation as we arrived in the grand entry hall: 'Makes Notting Hill seem a bit scruffy, doesn't it?'

I did fear that living in Hillsborough would be a bit like living in a National Trust property. It was also the official residence of the Queen in Northern Ireland, full of imposing antiques and set in wonderfully manicured grounds, with an enormous park surrounding it. Mo assured me that it was a great place for having parties, and that on many weekends she had brought friends and acquaintances over from London to enjoy the house and its gardens. I later learned that in the course of the partygoers' boozy fun and games, even bouncing up and down on the Queen's imposing bed had not been unheard of. My subsequent use of the house would be decidedly sober in contrast.

I quickly found that one of the nicest things about being Northern Ireland Secretary was being able to spend time in the Province. I did so as much as possible, and was frequently reluctant to leave, especially at weekends. I would recuperate from the week's trials and tribulations at Hillsborough, thinking and working things out in my head as I relaxed, walked or ran in the grounds. I visited the many friends I made – people like Bill and Daphne Montgomery at Grey Abbey, Neil McClure and his family, and the wonderful Lindy Dufferin at Clandiboye. I would spend two Christmases at Hillsborough, with my family and Reinaldo's enjoying the open space and the freedom to roam around the house.

It soon became not just a house, but a home, with two additional residents. The first was a golden retriever puppy, whom I named Bobby, at Tony's suggestion. Then, as a friend for Bobby, a parson's terrier. Of course I called it Jack. Bobby in particular was to become quite the star in dog-loving Northern Ireland. My office started to receive requests for photographs – not of me, but of my trusty retriever. I remember visiting a girls' school and being greeted by an excited group of pupils. 'Where is he? Where is he?' they shouted. 'I'm here!' I replied. They meant Bobby.

After an initial weekend reading reports on the state of the peace negotiations and talking with my civil service team, I spent the bulk of my time not at Hillsborough but in the less prepossessing Castle Buildings, headquarters of the Northern Ireland Office, in the shadow of Stormont Castle. George Mitchell had agreed to return for a final attempt to turn the Good Friday principles into reality. The aim was to get a devolved Northern Ireland Executive up and running. The main, apparently immovable, obstacle was decommissioning. Gerry Adams and Martin McGuinness were insisting that under the original peace plan, the Northern Ireland Executive, including Sinn Féin ministers, had to start work before any disarmament process got under way. David Trimble, facing pressure not just from within his own party but from Ian Paisley's Democratic Unionists, said that he could not join the executive without evidence that the IRA really was going to turn in its arms and explosives.

Any doubt about the seriousness with which each side was determined to hold to its position vanished in a series of private meetings I had with the three main players. Gerry Adams was the most intriguing. I could sense that he was used to playing on his reputation for toughness and guile to get what he wanted. As we both recognised going into our first encounter, so was I. With Adams, as with Martin McGuinness and David Trimble, I was less keen to establish personal chemistry – that would come, or not, over the course of the negotiations – than to build a bedrock of trust, without which any hope of breaking the deadlock would be futile. The key was to be straight with each side, and to deliver a consistent message to both of them.

To Adams and McGuinness, I made it clear from the start that I valued the Union. A majority of the inhabitants of Northern Ireland wanted it to continue, but it was not my role to block the emergence of a united Ireland if that became the majority's wish. My job was to facilitate the establishment of devolved institutions through which the people of Northern Ireland would, over time, decide whether that happened. I told them that I would try to persuade the unionists to accept Sinn Féin's view that the executive should begin work. Even if I could do so, however, I told them it would not lessen the urgency of visible movement towards decommissioning. If that didn't happen, I would have no hesitation in turning to my nuclear option as a last resort: I would have to reinstate direct rule from London, and would lay the responsibility for it on the IRA and Sinn Féin.

I was equally forthright with David Trimble. He projected none of Adams's steel, or bravado, when we first met. He had become vulnerable as a result of having championed political engagement with Sinn Féin and, as yet, got no movement on decommissioning. I understood his predicament, and shared his view that without a credible sign that the IRA was going to disarm, the peace process would sooner or later hit a dead end. I stressed that this would represent a defeat not only for the citizens of Northern Ireland, not only for the governments in London and Dublin, but for David himself. If this opportunity was missed, another was unlikely to arise for many, very possibly murderous, years.

For fourteen months I worked with the rival Northern Ireland leaders, including John Hume and Seamus Mallon of the nationalist SDLP, with George Mitchell, and with Tony and Jonathan in Number 10 to put a devolved executive in place and then, amid pressures from all sides, to keep it there. Given the circumstances in which I arrived, my first job was to rebuild bridges with David and his Ulster Unionist Party. But I also had to forge ties with Sinn Féin, and with Gerry and Martin. In the main, I did so successfully. It was not easy to maintain the proper balance all the time, and both sides were eagle-eyed for anything they could interpret as bias. I had to learn to rely on a skill which, to my detriment and perhaps New Labour's, I had deployed all too infrequently in my political career: quiet diplomacy. In Belfast I had to listen as much as talk, understand the goals and motivations of all sides, identify areas where they, and I, could give ground. I also had to keep an eye on the prize: securing a deal which, however difficult, would serve the interests of everyone. There were also times when I had to be tough, even at the risk of upsetting David or Gerry – or, in one stretch of especially tough bargaining on Britain's security presence in the Province, Tony too.

Our first imperative was to end direct rule from London and get a devolved executive in place. In an intensive round of talks, in which I was guided by two excellent officials, the political directors Bill Jeffrey and Jonathan Stephens, we reached the outline of a deal. It hinged on agreed wording for statements each side would deliver. The unionists would recognise the republicans' right to pursue their campaign for a united Ireland by peaceful means, and to join an 'inclusive' executive, with David as First Minister, Seamus Mallon as Deputy First Minister, and Sinn Féin getting two portfolios. Sinn Féin would endorse the political process, commit the IRA to discussing decommissioning, and declare their opposition to violence.

But when David met the twenty-seven UUP members of the devolved assembly, they were lukewarm, and insisted on a clear-cut commitment on decommissioning arms. He returned to Castle Buildings and told us he could not go ahead. I did little to hide my view that both sides would regret having come so close to a compromise only to see it unravel.

Gerry, not with overt hostility but with steel in his voice, turned to David and said he had one question for him. Had he tried to persuade his colleagues to back the deal? David was indignant. He had made a concession with real, practical implications, agreeing to join an executive alongside representatives of a republican party tied at the waist to the IRA. In return, he had so far got only words on decommissioning from Sinn Féin. Still, I felt that Gerry had a point, and I pressed it further.

It became clear that David had not in fact argued the case, or called for a formal vote. He had simply read the mood in the room. Very possibly, he had read it accurately, but I said he would regret it if he did not make a concerted effort to put the case for the agreement and change the minds of the doubters. We retired to a room along the hallway, where I tried to persuade him to do so. I reminded him of an offer he had extended to me to address his UUP representatives directly, and asked him to let me do so now. If he, or I, lost the argument, we would have to accept the deal would not work. But walking away without a real drive to win acceptance would leave him with the worst of all worlds. The Good Friday process, in which he had invested so much, might be over. He would come out looking not only rebuffed, but too weak to have fought his corner. I did not underestimate the pressure he was under, but I had come to know him well enough to recognise him as a politician with conviction, dedication, and considerable guts. After leaving for further consultations, he returned an hour and a half later with an invitation for me to accompany him and address the group.

I spoke for barely twenty minutes. I felt passionate about the need to keep the process on track, and I have no doubt that feeling was evident. But my tone was calm, my words deliberately businesslike. I said that I had not come to cajole or threaten. If they rejected the deal, London neither could nor would try to impose its views. Any successful peace process had to be decided and agreed by the parties themselves. I was not trying to tell them that the deal on the table was perfect. No deal was. But I believed it was the best, and probably the only, option in the present circumstances. Another opportunity might not come for a generation. Then I played the sole card I had at my disposal. I made a personal promise: 'If the IRA *don't* follow through with decommissioning, I will stand by you. I will not allow you to take the burden or the blame for failure. I will do it myself.' In the question-and-answer session that followed, a number of the delegates pressed me to tell them how I could 'guarantee' decommissioning. I couldn't. Some of them also wanted the disarmament process to be completed well before the following May, the deadline set in the Good Friday Agreement. Privately, my worry was whether it would even have begun by then. But I told them, as I had told Gerry, that decommissioning was essential once the executive began its work, and that I was committed to seeing it happen.

I returned to my office to await the outcome of David's final pitch. When he arrived, I could see from his face and his stride that he had won. Not by much, but it was a start. In the days that followed, he and I worked to build on the momentum. A crucial meeting of the full Ulster Unionist Council was called for the final Saturday of November, and in the run-up I accompanied David on visits to constituency branches. In Portadown, we had to run a gauntlet of baying protesters from Paisley's DUP, calling David a traitor and me worse. Inside the hall, the UUP audience was barely less hostile. For David to tell me about the pressure mounting against him was one thing; to see it and feel it at first hand was another. On the way out, as my protection officers led me through the crowd, a man grabbed my forearm and hissed: 'There are only two models of Northern Ireland Secretary: Mo Mowlam and Roy Mason' – a reference to the hard-line Labour minister in the 1970s. 'If you know what's good for you, you'd better be Mason, not Mowlam. Got the message?' I said nothing, and walked on. In the end, the council vote went better than either David or I had expected. Nearly 60 per cent were in favour of going into the devolved executive. The deal would go through. Maybe, I dared hope, we were in for a period of smooth sailing, with decommissioning next, and a formal, final peace not long after.

But Northern Ireland rarely does smooth sailing. The executive officially took power on 2 December 1999, with David Trimble as

First Minister, Seamus Mallon as his deputy and Martin McGuinness as Education Minister. It was a historic moment; but it emerged that in order to get the deal through, David had told his council that if decommissioning did not begin by early February 2000, he would resign, in effect collapsing devolved government. This meant trouble. John de Chastelain, the Canadian general who was in charge of the international group monitoring decommissioning, had concluded that for the IRA to meet the original May deadline, the process would have to get under way months before. I believed that I had an unwritten understanding from Gerry and Martin that a token act of decommissioning would take place by the end of January, as a confidence-building measure to keep the new executive in place. David Trimble now formalised this timetable. By making it public, he had made it harder politically for Sinn Féin, and the IRA, to deliver. I understood why he had felt the need to act as he had, and conveyed that message when I was interviewed on the BBC's *Frost on Sunday* after the council vote. I was also careful to make it clear that I understood Sinn Féin's situation, characterising disarmament as a 'voluntary act' in the hope of providing them with cover to move. I was walking a tightrope. I hoped that when the executive got to work, the desire to keep shared government from imploding would focus everyone's minds on the need for an early act or gesture on decommissioning. If not, as Martin and Gerry both knew, true to my word to David's unionist colleagues, I retained the last-resort option of reinstating direct rule.

Though they knew this, I am not sure they believed it. To the extent that they had any real deadline for decommissioning in mind, it was May. They would often remind me that, like David, they had internal pressures to deal with. It was clear that they had done little to prepare the IRA for the reality of laying aside their arms, and as the end of January approached, there was no sign that they felt any particular urgency about doing so.

When Gerry told Tony that he might be able to get a strengthened, though still long-term, IRA commitment to decommissioning, I did manage to get David to defer his resignation for a week.

The next meeting of his party council was not until 11 February anyway. The initial IRA wording passed on to us by Sinn Féin, however, was so watery that both Tony and I agreed it was useless. On 3 February I took a step that was necessary in practical terms, and which I also hoped would bring home the gravity of the approaching deadline. I told the Commons that if there was no visible move towards disarmament – at the very least, a clear IRA signal it was going to happen – I would have no alternative but to suspend devolved government.

Until that point, the government in Dublin, our Good Friday co-sponsors, had clearly shared Sinn Féin's belief that I would not make good on my threat. Now Irish ministers began a series of meetings with republican leaders to try to find a way forward. On the morning of 10 February, the day on which the suspension was to come into force, Bertie Ahern's office faxed through to Downing Street a 'draft statement' from the IRA. We were told it was to be read only by Tony and me. It was four paragraphs long. The first was a delicately hedged endorsement of the Good Friday Agreement. Then it got on to decommissioning: 'In the context of a process that will progressively and irreversibly remove the causes of conflict, the leadership of *Óglaigh na hÉireann* [the IRA] will initiate an internal process subject to our constitution that will finally and completely put IRA arms beyond use. This process will be designed to avoid risk to the public and misappropriation by others. The leadership of *Óglaigh na hÉireann* will facilitate verification of this.' It concluded: 'This will be done in such a way to ensure public confidence and to resolve the issue of arms in a complete and acceptable way.'

It was undeniably a step forward for a group among which there were inevitably different views about when and how decommissioning should take place. The statement committed the IRA to putting its arsenal finally and completely beyond use. But it was frustratingly vague on how, and utterly silent on when. Even if I felt I could go along with it, I could not see the unionists doing so. Yet more difficult, with the scheduled suspension of the executive only hours away, Gerry was insisting that the text be withheld from both David and

General de Chastelain. In the first of many conversations I had with all parties over the six hours that followed, I made it clear to Gerry that the statement would at least have to be given to de Chastelain, and summarised for David – which I am sure he must have realised from the outset. But he remained firm that it could not be made public, as the IRA had not yet briefed its rank and file.

Tony and I did not think, even if the whole text could be published, that it would be enough to prevent David's resignation. It was too hedged, and crucially, it lacked even the hint of a time frame. Throughout the afternoon we tried to cobble together a way to win some breathing space. Gerry's bottom line was that he would be willing publicly to confirm a commitment in principle to put the IRA's arms 'beyond use', but that in return David would have to withdraw his resignation and I would have to cancel the suspension of devolved government.

David did recognise that the IRA statement was a move forward, but he said it was too little and too late. When I tried to get him to put off his resignation for a fortnight to allow time for further talks, he – and Gerry too – turned this down. Twice, I delayed announcing the suspension. Tony was coming under enormous pressure from Bertie Ahern and then, at Ahern's behest, in a phone call from Bill Clinton, not to suspend the devolved government. Both of us concluded, however, that there was no alternative to suspension if I was to retain the trust of unionists and keep my word that I would act unless there was at least some early move towards decommissioning. Shortly after 5 p.m. I signed the order to suspend devolved government. I said we had come 'much closer' to resolving the disarmament issue, 'But until commitments are clear, they simply cannot command confidence.'

The immediate effect was a campaign by Sinn Féin and Irish government ministers – some of it in public, some through whispering and briefing – accusing me of having acted precipitately and irresponsibly in folding up the devolved institutions. In a phone call between Tony and Bertie Ahern that evening, Bertie had passed the phone to his Cabinet Secretary Paddy Teahon, who let rip at me in furious personal terms, calling me every name under the sun, not realising that the Number 10 switchboard had silently patched me in to the call. I knew what I was being lined up for. Gerry made a point of warning me before the attacks began. 'Don't take it personally,' he said, 'but you're going to become public enemy number one.' I did my best to heed his advice, but it was hard. A ferocious campaign was unleashed in the media. Posters and graffiti in republican areas portrayed me as the man who had killed the peace process. There was nervousness about my safety, and my personal security was stepped up. I knew, however, that I had had no option but to act as I did if both sides were going to be kept in tow. My main aim now was to find a way to ensure that the suspension did not become permanent. It was obvious that the original May 2000 target for disarmament would not be met. Even had the IRA's vague draft been enough to save devolved government, it was hard to see how it would have led to actual decommissioning in the short term. But if May came and went without some progress, and without the executive being revived, the whole Good Friday framework could collapse.

As I began to map out a new way forward, I could not ignore the obvious political aim of the republicans' propaganda campaign. By directing their fire on me, and implying that I had made my decision without Tony's involvement and support, they were trying to drive a wedge between me and London. By suggesting that I had sided with the unionists, they were trying to get Tony to step into the process and 'right the balance' in favour of Sinn Féin. The premise was wrong, the tactics transparent, and none of it fooled Tony. But it didn't make it any easier for me in taking the first step towards any revival of the peace process: frank, open, talks with both Sinn Féin and the UUP on where we were, how we had got there, and how to find a way out.

I had no doubt that both Gerry and David wanted devolved government to succeed. I did doubt that the negotiating path we were on would get us there. In December, David had taken a leap in the dark, agreeing a deal and getting down to work as First Minister, on the expectation of at least a first step on decommissioning. There was no way he was going to take that risk again without a firm commitment by the republicans to start setting aside their weapons, especially with the tide of opinion in the unionist community moving against him. For his part, Gerry was clearly not going to deliver decommissioning on anything like the scale or timetable envisaged in the Good Friday Agreement, especially if it seemed he was doing so under unionist duress. Unless we could find a way around this, we were stuck.

It seemed to me that the only option was to get both men to look at the issue in an entirely different way. I began with Gerry, inviting him to a Saturday-afternoon talk at Hillsborough in the beginning of March. We began by taking a long walk around the grounds with Bobby. It was Gerry, in one of our very first meetings, who had prompted me to get a pet. He had told me how much easier he found it to think difficult issues through when he was on a long walk with his own dog. He even offered to get one for me. That was vetoed by my security officials, no doubt because they feared a listening device would be embedded into one of the dog's paws. But it had prompted me to find Bobby, whom Gerry seemed to dote on almost as much as I did.

Once we were back inside, I told him that I wanted informally, with no commitment on either side, to suggest a way that we might get devolved government going again without risking another stand-off. 'Look, you don't want this linkage between the devolved institutions and decommissioning,' I said. 'Why don't we link it instead to the overall implementation of the Good Friday Agreement, including the other issues you care about, like policing and a new justice system?' I emphasised that I wasn't taking decommissioning off the table: without it, no matter what kind of deal we might be able to fashion, the peace process would fail. We still needed a clear public commitment from the republicans to end violence as part of the Good Friday process. There would have to be an early decommissioning gesture – not a full disarmament move, but something that would at least build confidence that it was going to happen. Gerry listened carefully, nodding as I explained. 'Interesting,' he said finally. 'It's worth thinking about.' In the circumstances, it was the equivalent of a round of applause.

David was more sceptical. Having insisted so long and so publicly on early decommissioning, he felt that backing off and putting the emphasis on other parts of the agreement would embolden his critics. As we talked further, however, he began to accept my argument that the current approach presented greater problems. 'By making this trade-off between devolved government and decommissioning,' I said, 'you're giving the IRA a veto over the peace process. The longer the disarmament stalemate goes on, the higher the price you'll have to pay in other areas of the agreement to get it, the less likely it becomes that we'll ever restart the executive, and the weaker your position becomes.' I understood that he needed something in return for going back into government with Sinn Féin: 'All that I'm saying is, let's change what you're pressing for. Let's focus on getting something that will be significant, but also possible.'

'Possible' did not mean easy. But from March through to the original Good Friday target date at the end of May, a series of meetings with both sides moved us fitfully towards a deal on the redefined terms I'd suggested. The benefit of the new approach was that there was something in it for everyone. The unionists would get an IRA commitment that went beyond the wording offered in February, as well as a 'confidence-building measure' to demonstrate that decommissioning had started. For Sinn Féin and the IRA, we were now linking disarmament to the broader implementation of the entire Good Friday Agreement, rather than making it a price for participation in a devolved government. As Secretary of State, I had the job of navigating our way through the details. Tony was again called on to intervene at key stages, and Jonathan Powell was even more deeply involved, in London and on regular visits to Belfast.

The key hurdle for the unionist side was selling the deal. David often needed encouragement, and I did everything I could to provide it. But there were moments when he also needed to recognise the need for decisiveness. At one point near the end of the talks, he pressed for me to get further amendments to the draft of republican commitments. This was simply not going to happen, I told him. For the first time, the IRA would publicly be committed to 'a process that will completely and verifiably put arms beyond use'. They would be undertaking to deliver a confidence-building measure, opening a number of arms dumps to inspection by a pair of international monitors, the former Finnish President Martti Ahtisaari and South Africa's Cyril Ramaphosa. This was a real advance, and it was the most he was going to get at this stage. He had to embrace it, and sell it. At a tense council meeting at the end of May, David did both. It was the clearing of this final obstacle that allowed me, the following day, to sign another order, this time restoring the devolved institutions of government.

The Sinn Féin leadership had been no less prone to last-minute wobbles, and last-minute demands. In their case, the main issue was 'demilitarisation', or 'normalisation', as we called it. In essence, Gerry wanted a link between any move towards decommissioning and a visible reduction of the British military and security presence in Northern Ireland. On a number of occasions Tony, and especially Jonathan, were so frustrated by the negotiations and so eager for a deal that they were inclined simply to say: 'Yes. Now sign on the dotted line.' In political terms I too understood the need to deliver on security 'normalisation'. Though peace had not fully broken out, as continued threats and punishment killings made clear, the full-scale war was obviously over. The IRA ceasefire had been reinstituted in 1997, when the negotiations began for the Good Friday Agreement, and showed every sign of holding. That our military presence would be reduced was not only inevitable, but desirable.

I felt, however, that the appearance of a straight trade-off might be presented as the British government being prepared to take risks with security for the sake of a deal. Our military and intelligence chiefs had understandable objections, both because of the IRA's failure to disarm and, more importantly, because terrorist activity had shifted to a pair of splinter groups, the Real IRA and the Continuity IRA. Barely eighteen months earlier, in August 1998, a Real IRA car bombing in Omagh had left twenty-nine people dead and more than two hundred injured. I insisted, to the obvious frustration of Number 10, that major early demilitarisation would be irresponsible. To my relief, we undertook in the May agreement only to deliver 'as early a return as possible to normal security arrangements in Northern Ireland consistent with the level of threat'.

For a brief while, it appeared that we had got the Good Friday process on track again. The executive was back at work, and we were no longer involved in the day-to-day business of Northern Ireland government, although we retained responsibility for justice and policing. At the end of June, earlier than we had dared hope, the IRA opened some of their weapons bunkers to the international monitors. This was a hugely important step forward, and confidence grew as a result.

Still, the core issues had not gone away. Without decommissioning proper, David Trimble felt vulnerable. When the most strident of the leading UUP sceptics, Jeffrey Donaldson, put down a council motion in the autumn demanding withdrawal from the executive if there was no substantial decommissioning by Christmas, David chose to acquiesce rather than fight. Sinn Féin, though obviously reluctant to see devolved government collapse yet again, were in no mood to oblige. More than ever, they were pressing for clear 'normalisation' moves by the British government. The non-violent face of nationalism, the SDLP, was pressing its own, broader demands: decommissioning, a scaling back of our security presence and radical reform of Northern Ireland's police force, the Royal Ulster Constabulary. This overhaul was a very sensitive issue for all sides, and arriving at a consensus was hard. I had managed it, just, on the basis of a report delivered by the former Conservative minister Chris Patten, who proposed the setting up of a new Police Service of Northern Ireland. But certain aspects of the reform still rankled, chiefly but not only with the SDLP and Sinn Féin, and they were pressing me hard to rewrite some of what I had implemented.

The stage was set, as we entered the winter of 2000, for yet another high-stakes round of diplomacy. My own view, sadly borne out within a matter of weeks, was that no matter how far we might be willing to go on security normalisation, the IRA was unready or unwilling at this stage to deliver the major move towards disarmament that the unionists were demanding. But in the final weeks of the year, as pressure built on Tony for concessions on demilitarisation, including the scaling down of electronic border surveillance to monitor movements of arms and bomb-making equipment by the IRA splinter groups, differences between me and Number 10 grew. They were not over issues of principle, but security judgements and negotiating tactics. We differed on whether it was right, or responsible, to play the 'normalisation' card without clear evidence that it was merited by the behaviour of the IRA or the threat posed by its splinter groups. Tony understood my caution over security, but was unsettled about the situation as Christmas and New Year approached. He was anxious to find some way – at times, it appeared, *any* way – to avoid another collapse in the talks and another interruption of devolved rule.

He was also increasingly fixated on another date: the general election, pencilled in for the beginning of May 2001. Since spring 2000, whenever Northern Ireland pressures allowed me, I had begun attending twice-weekly meetings on election strategy and planning. On Monday mornings, if I was in London I joined Tony and his inner staff at Number 10 for a 'look-ahead' to determine our strategic objectives for the week. On Thursdays, following cabinet meetings, I participated in what Jonathan called the weekly 'strategic powerhouse' to consider longer-term issues. This group included Tony, Gordon, Alastair and Philip, as well as Douglas Alexander, the young Brown protégé deputised to deal with campaign issues.

By mid-June 2000, amid signs that the party, and particularly the campaign operation at Millbank, were nowhere near up to speed, I was placed in charge of putting a key missing piece in place. Tony, with Gordon and Alastair, would be the crucial figures in dealing with daily and weekly planning issues for the campaign. Along with Philip, they would start looking further ahead, towards the manifesto, and early versions of a campaign grid. I would be tasked with shoring up operations at Millbank and ensuring a pre-election coherence in our policies and presentation over the next several months.

The early indications were not encouraging. When Lance Price, Alastair's deputy, was moved over to the election headquarters, I asked him to write down his first impressions. The individuals in place were gifted and dedicated, he said, but added: 'Millbank does not have the feel of a place geared up and ready to fight a general election.' As for the response and organisation needed to do day-to-day battle with the Tories, 'If it is true that speed kills, then we're dead in the water.' Though my influence was being felt, he said that I was in danger of becoming like a firm but fair headmaster, who was respected and got his way when he was around, but was too often out of sight and bogged down by paperwork. I heeded the message, and by the autumn I was able to tell Tony with confidence that if he went ahead with plans to call a spring election, the machinery was in place.

The machinery was the least of our worries. A series of crises during the summer of 2000 fed a perception that we were more spin than substance, out of touch with the people who had elected us. In May, despite our best efforts to prevent him, Ken Livingstone, standing as an independent, defeated the official Labour candidate Frank Dobson to become the first popularly elected mayor of London. This was followed in early June by Tony's disastrous speech to the Women's Institute at Wembley Arena, where delegates slow-handclapped and heckled him. In September came the most serious incident of all, when the country was brought to a standstill as road hauliers blocked oil refineries in protest at what they saw as punitive fuel duties. For the first time since Tony became leader, we fell behind the Tories in the polls. Philip's findings reflected this, with Tony perceived as either 'pandering' or 'out of touch', and our failure to understand the gravity of the initial fuel protests put down to arrogance.

Gordon did not help things at the party conference in Bournemouth in September. Not only were we facing demands from our own rank and file to do something about petrol prices, but the unions were up in arms about his budget provision for a mere 75p weekly increase in the state pension. He was determined not to give ground on either of these at conference, although he knew that at some stage he would need to do so. On petrol prices, he said that an early concession would embolden other pressure groups to take to the streets whenever they wanted something from the government. This was not an unreasonable view, but politically it was tone-deaf. Tony's position, and mine as well, was that without making an outright U-turn, Gordon could offer sufficient mood music to make it clear that we were listening, especially on pensions. The problem was that Gordon, as was so often the case, personalised things. His main concern was not to lose his hard-earned reputation as a tough, resolute steward of the economy. The pre-budget report was coming in November, and we suspected, rightly, that he would come up with a formula to ease petrol prices and boost pensions then. But there were an agonising few weeks to endure until he did so.

After conference, Tony felt that he had to put the real campaign structure in place. When we met in his flat a few days later, he seemed haunted by the prospect of frittering away the fruits of our landslide and ending up as another one-term Labour Prime Minister. He wanted the time, and the mandate, that would enable him genuinely to shift Britain's electoral geography away from the Tories. He wanted the chance to leave a real policy imprint on the country. 'We have to get cracking,' he told me. 'And we have to run this campaign the way we did in 1997.'

'Meaning?' I asked.

'Meaning you and Gordon jointly in charge.'

He knew I could not say no, but I was open about my misgivings. The 1997 campaign, however successful, had been nightmarish until the final weeks, with Gordon largely shunning me and the operation I had put together at Millbank. After my resignation from the DTI, things had got easier between us, and on the infrequent occasions when we met, Gordon had been friendly enough. After the Northern Ireland deal in May, he had even phoned to congratulate me. 'I don't know how you did it,' he said, 'but you boxed in the IRA and made a statesman of Trimble.' But the truce had been made easier because I was no longer in a front-line domestic policy role. While Gordon knew that Tony and I still spoke often on issues far beyond Northern Ireland, I was safely parked in Hillsborough.

Even so, to Tony's alarm, there had been flashpoints. In a trade union speech I made in Belfast early in the summer, I had included a comment that it was hard to see how we could protect ourselves against destabilising swings on European currency markets as long as we were outside the single currency. This seemed to me a statement of economic common sense. I was not agitating for an early entry into the euro zone, which I knew was not going to happen. Gordon, however, went ballistic. So did Tony. I said my fear was that Gordon would be even more unsettled if I took on a central role in the election: he wanted to keep that territory for himself. I was right. In the early weeks, Gordon essentially worked around me. When he did engage, he was grumpy and often monosyllabic.

In November, Tony summoned both of us to a strategy session at Number 10. He began by outlining the organisational and policy challenges for the campaign, and emphasised how important it was for his 'two best people' to work together. Gordon interrupted. The whole approach to the election was nonsense, he said. Not just the idea of my involvement, though he made it clear he was not keen on that, but the fact that Tony just didn't 'get it'. He was focusing on 'side issues', like law and order or asylum or immigration, and didn't have the faintest idea of what the campaign should really be about. Gordon said the only thing that had distinguished our first-term government was the economy: 'It's about time you realised that the economy is what we should run on.' The key 'dividing line' was his plan for the economy versus the Tories'. 'The Tories screwed up the economy, and we've given people stability and growth,' he said. 'It's about time you fucking realised that's all the election is about.' I was shocked. Not by Gordon's Treasury-centric view of the universe, nor of course by his resistance to my involvement in the campaign, but by the venom he was directing at the man who was, after all, Prime Minister, and by the language he used. It was embarrassing. Without a word, I left the room. Jonathan was in the office outside. 'I can't believe the way Gordon is talking,' I said. Jonathan smiled, and replied, 'This is what we put up with every week.'

By the time Tony stayed overnight at Hillsborough a few weeks later, amid the quickening pace of diplomacy in Northern Ireland, I had decided it was best to leave the election planning to Gordon.

I suspected that the campaign would be difficult enough due to the tension between the two of them. If I took a front-line role, the likely effect seemed to be weeks of 1997-vintage cluster headaches for me, and political headaches for Tony. I knocked on his door shortly before retiring for the night. Tony was installed in the Queen's Bedroom, with his Bible as always on the bedside table, when I entered. 'You know, it is really awful with Gordon at the moment on the election planning,' I said. 'I have a real sense of foreboding. I feel very insecure about it all. It's just not going to work.' Tony said I was making too much of it: 'Gordon is Gordon.' He insisted that he wanted me – and needed me – to organise things as I had in 1997. 'Don't worry,' he said. 'I'm going to protect you from Gordon. Nothing is going to happen to you.' Little did I know then that it was not Gordon I would need protecting from.

By January 2001, with David Trimble reviving the spectre of resigning as First Minister, Northern Ireland totally dominated my mind, not the election. Once again, we were scrambling to keep devolved government in place. In the familiar balancing act this required, Tony and Jonathan were pressing for early 'normalisation' concessions to keep Sinn Féin on board and encourage them to speed up decommissioning. I remained reluctant to go too far. With military, police and intelligence chiefs all concerned about the possible effects of a major reduction in our security apparatus, I still felt that a more gradual and measured shift was preferable. From my year of dealing with intermittent threats and crises, I was convinced that rather than rash, makeshift concessions, a more steady, balanced approach was crucial to getting an agreement that might actually last. On the third weekend of January, before a critical round of meetings on the issue in Downing Street, I flew to Paris for what I hoped would be a politics-free break. Instead, there were constant calls from officials in the Northern Ireland Office and from Downing Street.

Then, on Saturday afternoon, my special adviser Patrick Diamond rang me. The next day's *Observer*, he said, was running a story alleging that I had had a role in obtaining British citizenship for Srichand Hinduja, a wealthy Indian businessman who had financially underwritten the Faith Zone in the Millennium Dome. I had suspected that this might be coming. In December, Jack Straw had sent me a message that a Liberal Democrat question had been put to the Home Office asking about my involvement and that of the Labour MP and Europe minister Keith Vaz in making any representations on behalf of Mr Hinduja. I told Jack that while I was still in the Cabinet Office in 1998, dealing with the Dome, I had received an enquiry from Mr Hinduja. It was not about an existing passport application, but about whether the changes to immigration and naturalisation law that the government was undertaking would affect any future application. I had passed the enquiry on to the Home Office, through my private office. Jack said that Mike O'Brien, the immigration minister at the time, recalled that I had phoned him directly about it. I replied that I had absolutely no memory of having done so, and was sure that my office had handled it, but that in any case, I was only trying to elicit information from the Home Office about general policy. Now I told Patrick the same thing, and said he should pass it on in reply to the *Observer*'s request for a comment: 'To the limited extent I was involved in this matter, I was always very sensitive to the proprieties. The matter was dealt with by my private secretary.' And, crucially: 'At no time did I support or endorse an application for citizenship.'

I did not see the Sunday papers until I was at Heathrow early the next afternoon, on my way back to Belfast. I glanced fairly quickly at the *Observer* piece. The headline on the story was predictably blunt: 'Mandelson Helped Dome Backer's Bid for Passport'. The part of the story itself that suggested impropriety, or conflict of interest, was untrue. It said that my office's enquiry to the Home Office had been about whether Mr Hinduja's passport application 'would be welcomed'. In fact it had been nothing of the sort. We had simply conveyed an enquiry about the effects of the new regulations. Neither I nor anyone else had offered the slightest suggestion that we were supporting an application for citizenship. The *Observer* ran the story at the bottom of the front page, making me wonder if the paper itself realised that its scoop was a bit threadbare.

When Alastair phoned me at the airport, I was much more preoccupied with another story in that day's *Sunday Times*. It was an attack by Gordon on my involvement in the election campaign. 'How should we deal with this?' Alastair asked. I thought he meant the campaign story. 'Why should Gordon and his people attack me?' I replied. 'I'm no threat or competition. It's not like I'm out to undermine them, or say they shouldn't have a major role.' He brushed this aside. 'Yeah, yeah, yeah. But what about the *Observer* story?' I told him, with an assurance I absolutely felt, that it was no problem. I said I had got Patrick to put out a statement to the reporter, making it clear that my only involvement had been to ask my private secretary to pass on Mr Hinduja's enquiry on naturalisation policy and to relay any – publicly available – information back to him.

I gave the matter no more thought for the rest of the day. On Monday morning, I was closeted in meetings with Northern Ireland Office political directors and security officials about Number 10's mounting pressure for me to agree to offer Sinn Féin the dismantling of security watchtowers and border surveillance as the price of their continuing engagement. In the evening, I asked the Chief Constable, Sir Ronnie Flanagan, and the army commander, Lieutenant General Sir Hew Pike, to meet me at Hillsborough. I explained the pressure I was coming under to oil the wheels of the talks by dispensing with some of the infrastructure that I knew they regarded as key to Northern Ireland's security. They were receptive politically, but were firm about how far they could go. As we spread detailed maps over the dining table, I was called to the telephone to speak to Alastair.

What I didn't know was that Alastair, in his morning lobby briefing, had gone well beyond what I had told him, or the *Observer*, about the Hinduja story. He said I had 'refused' to get involved in the matter. That was obviously untrue, since my private office had passed on the enquiry to the Home Office. The Home Office had been on to Alastair to correct his briefing. They not only pointed out, rightly, that I had been involved, but passed on Mike O'Brien's recollection that I had phoned him personally, rather than asked my staff to do so, thus investing this aspect with an importance it did not merit.

Alastair now wanted me on a conference call to thrash out what had happened. With Mike on the line as well, he said to me, 'You told me you weren't involved, but Mike says you rang him.' I replied that I had not said I wasn't involved. What I had told him was that I had relayed an information enquiry to the Home Office, and had never raised the specific issue of granting Mr Hinduja a British passport. As for my having phoned Mike, I told both of them – as I had told Jack – that I had no recollection of having made such a call. I was certain that I would have remembered it if it had happened. 'I think, I believe, we spoke,' said Mike. 'Well, I'm afraid I don't believe that we did,' I replied. 'I think we will just have to accept there's a difference of recollections. But this does not affect the central point: which is that I never used my position to help anyone get a passport.'

Alastair appeared satisfied with this. But when he briefed the lobby the next day, he again made things worse. He said – wrongly – that now I had had a chance to look at my files, I had discovered that I did phone Mike. 'Although Mr Mandelson had no recollection of the call, clearly it had taken place,' he said. He apologised to the reporters for having misled them in his initial remarks. He had indeed misled them, twice. On Monday he had done so by telling them something I had never suggested. Now he had delivered a version of events that was the opposite of what I had told him in our conference call.

Our talks with the Northern Ireland parties now came to a head. Early on Tuesday, I flew to London for a day-long series of bilateral meetings in Number 10 with Tony, Jonathan, Gerry Adams, David Trimble, John Hume and the leaders of the other parties. I had been speaking with Tony by phone from Sunday evening onwards – not about the Hindujas, or even Gordon's salvo in the *Sunday Times*, but about demilitarisation and decommissioning. The talks lasted until late Tuesday afternoon. When I stumbled out after the final session, I felt fairly confident that we had identified a way of handling not only the 'normalisation' issue for Sinn Féin, but the policing and devolution issues troubling the other parties.

Almost in passing, I asked Alastair how 'the other story' was going. At that point I was still unaware of his latest press briefing. Alastair replied, 'You know, this phone call definitely took place. The Home

Office have a tape of it.' I said I found that astonishing, because I was still certain it hadn't happened. 'What should I do?' I asked him. 'Would it be helpful for me to do some TV interviews, clearing up the claim once and for all that I had been asking for a passport for anyone?' On balance, he said, yes.

I did a series of interviews. It turned out to be a huge mistake. Inevitably, I was pressed on the side issue of the phone call rather than the central issue. Not only Mike, but Alastair, had now said that it occurred. In fact, he had said that I now remembered it too. Why the sudden memory flash, I was asked. Why had I 'changed my story'? All I could think of in reply was the truth. I hadn't changed my view of what had happened, and I hadn't changed my story. As I spoke, I was feeling wound up by the Northern Ireland negotiations. I had been thrown off-balance by Alastair's insistence that there was a tape in the Home Office of the phantom phone call – though it would turn out, much later, that, far from a tape existing, there was merely a post-it note referring to the conversation with my private secretary. So when I was asked why Number 10 was suggesting that I had 'forgotten' and then recalled my conversation with the Home Office, I replied, 'You'll have to ask them that.'

On Wednesday morning, I made my way to my London office ahead of Northern Ireland questions in the Commons, but was diverted to Downing Street to see Tony. The morning papers had been grim. None was calling for my head, but some seemed to be gearing up to do so, and, based on Alastair's briefing, heavily suggesting that I had 'lied'. As I entered Tony's office, Jonathan was leaving, looking very upset. Tony said things looked bad, and it would be 'a hell of a job' to clear up the mess. He upbraided me for having given the TV interviews: 'If you'd asked me, I'd have said don't do them – just as I told Alastair he should stop briefing on all this stuff until he knows what the facts are.' But the phone call was now a 'big problem'. He accepted that I was sure I hadn't made it, and he understood my explanation of my TV remarks about Downing Street: 'I was being faced with the suggestion that I had deliberately decided to remember the phone call, that I had lied.' But he didn't like it. Any of it.

Turning to 'barrister Blair' mode, and choosing to dwell on the existence or not of the phone call, he said, 'If we find that no phone call took place, how would we explain Jack and Mike O'Brien saying that there had been a phone call? We would then have a situation where they became "liars", and then we'd have real trouble.' At this point Alastair entered the room, and sat at a table near the door.

The longer the conversation went on, the clearer it became that in Tony's view, I should fall on my sword. Alastair had started to grow impatient. He said he needed to 'get the story out' for the morning lobby briefing. At first I was disbelieving. Apart from the furore over a phone call I was still certain I had never made, the key fact remained that the worst I might have done was to pass on an enquiry on naturalisation law from S.P. Hinduja to the Home Office. With no comment. No nudge or wink. Not so much as a word to suggest that they should give him a passport. Later, I would discover that the Cabinet Secretary, Richard Wilson, far from backing up the Number 10 line as the press were later led to think, had made essentially that point in a memo to Tony the previous night. Richard's advice was that Downing Street should steer clear of getting too involved in the controversy, and simply insist that no one had produced a shred of evidence that anything improper had taken place. The Prime Minister should do no more than set up a quick inquiry to satisfy himself that there had been no wrongdoing in the Home Office over any passport application

Tony had agreed to an inquiry, but was now clearly intent on cutting his losses. With an election coming up, he didn't want an endless rumble of media coverage about the Hinduja matter to cloud the campaign. Srichand and his brother Gopichand – who, as it happens, had been given fast-track citizenship by Jack's Home Office in 1997 – were politically controversial. Both had been cosying up to a Who's Who of government ministers, above all Keith Vaz, but also Jack, and Tony himself, who had visited them for dinner before the 1997 election. Nor did it help that Alastair was egging Tony on. He and the Home Office had, wrongly, convinced themselves that I had misled them about what had happened. Alastair was now fuming at having misled the lobby journalists, and was behind schedule for his next briefing.

When he left the room, I could see there was no persuading Tony. 'This is absurd,' I said. 'How can you dispatch me because of a purported phone call and a bunch of inaccurate briefings and a stream of Chinese whispers? You've decided on an inquiry. Why not at least wait until the facts are established?' He mumbled that things had gone too far. We had to put an end to the story. In a final, feeble, appeal, I said, 'You're not going to end my entire ministerial career for *this*, without even knowing the full picture?'

He replied, 'I'm sorry. There's no other way. It's decided.'

Anji embraced me, crying, as Tony wrote out my resignation statement, which, in a gusting wind, I read to reporters outside Number 10. In going along with it, I did my best to resign in a way that would be least disruptive to Tony, and of course to Alastair too. The statement gave their version of the phone call, saying that I accepted 'that when my office spoke to a Sunday newspaper at the weekend, I should have been clear that it was me personally, not my official, who spoke to the Home Office minister', and regretted that as a result, information that was 'incorrect' had been given to the media by the Prime Minister's spokesman.

I felt I had no choice but to accept this language, although I was later furious with myself for going along with it. But I was not about to acknowledge that I had intervened to get Srichand Hinduja a passport. 'I do not accept in any way that I have acted improperly in respect of any application for naturalisation,' I said. The aim of everything I had said since the *Observer* story broke had been 'to emphasise that I had not sought to influence the decision on naturalisation in any way at all, merely to pass on a request for information. And the Prime Minister is entirely satisfied with this.' Still raw from reading the morning papers and from Gordon's latest *Sunday Times* attack, I added a final personal note: 'There must be more to politics than the constant media pressure and exposure that has dogged me over the last five or so years. I want to remove myself from the countless stories of controversies, feuds and divisions – and all the rest, all the other stories that have surrounded me. I want, in other words, to lead a more normal life, both in politics and, in the future, outside. That is my decision, and I hope that everyone will respect that.'

In the Commons that afternoon, I insisted on fielding my final questions as Northern Ireland Secretary. Knowing that I had acted properly throughout, I was not about to skulk away as if I had not. The MPs from Northern Ireland who questioned me were clearly amazed that the Secretary of State should be banished at such a delicate moment in the peace process. At Prime Minister's Questions, Tony did not try to clear up the multiple confusions and contradictions of the last few days. Of my resignation, he said: 'I made it clear that if people did something wrong, they would pay the penalty. And he has paid the penalty.' As William Hague milked it for all it was worth, Tony did at least offer me a shred of comfort, saying, 'I believe he is a bigger man than many of his critics.'

This time, however, there was to be no consoling phone call from Cherie. No invitation to Chequers. No assurance that I would 'always be part of the family'. More ominously for what was left of my political career, and more hurtfully, there was not the slightest sign from Tony that he saw a way back for me. Much later on, Alastair would come to acknowledge that had it not been for my first resignation, their finger of suspicion would not have come to rest on me a second time. But that small comfort was not available to me now.

Perhaps if I had been less happy at Hillsborough, I would have been better able to absorb the shock of having to leave it at a few hours' notice. As soon as I had finished Northern Ireland Questions in the House, I sped off to the RAF base at Northolt to fly back to Belfast and pack up all my accumulated belongings. I was fortunate in having become very close to David Anderson, who effectively ran Hillsborough under successive Secretaries of State, and the housekeeper Olwyn McCarthy, whose cooked breakfasts and spaghetti bolognese necessitated all the running I had to do to keep my weight in check. Through that evening we packed together, trying to keep each other as cheerful as possible. At one point Gerry Adams rang to offer his commiserations, which was kind and thoughtful of him.

Next morning came the challenge of leaving Hillsborough without providing the spectacle that the assembled media were hoping for. Because of their size, the grounds have many exits, most of them well-barred against intruders. A particularly obscure one was found for my departure, the security cameras revealing no lurking reporters or photographers, and after tearful farewells from the staff who had gathered to say goodbye to me, Bobby and Jack, I left Hillsborough for the last time, barely able to control my emotions.

As my plane flew out of Belfast, I wondered what I had done to deserve such ignominy, and how I would ever recover. In the following weeks I received hundreds of letters from people in Northern Ireland. Some, from whatever sectarian position they held, were glad to see the back of me. But most were warmly worded messages about my own role, with expressions of hope, or anxiety, about the future of the peace process. I am ashamed to say that not all of those who wrote received replies. Partly, this was because the shock of my sudden departure was too great for me to respond. But another reason was that I felt too humiliated to find the right words with which to do so.

On a personal level, I felt not only bereft, but betrayed. Politically, the weeks and months ahead would be a period of conflict and crisis for me. But they would also see the beginnings of a new and even more bitter struggle between my two fellow members of New Labour's founding triumvirate. One that would threaten the core vision of what New Labour was all about – not just a party that could win elections, but that could deliver the changed Britain we had promised on entering Downing Street.

8

Fighting, Not Quitting

I next spoke to the Prime Minister by telephone on Friday, two days after he had effectively fired me.

My shock had given way to hurt, and then to a growing anger. I felt hurt mostly by Tony. Over a period of fifteen years, we had become not only the closest of allies: we were friends, or as near to being friends as is possible in politics. Yet when I needed him most – not for blind support, but for the simple fairness and trust to establish the facts before he acted – he had cut me loose. My anger was directed more at Alastair, especially after a phone call following my sacking from Emma Scott, the number two in my private office when I was Minister without Portfolio. She confirmed what I had insisted all along – that the enquiry we made to the Home Office was entirely innocent, and that I had not made a phone call to Mike O'Brien. It was she who had telephoned his office.

Even more gallingly, I learned from my Principal Private Secretary at the time, Rupert Huxter, that he had tried to pass this information to Downing Street on the morning I was forced to resign, only to be told they were not interested. As so often in government, this could have been more cock-up than conspiracy. What I did know was that while it was Tony who had handed out my P45, the main urgency to get rid of me seemed to come from Alastair. After my departure, both of them presented my resignation statement as a signal that I was ready to 'wind down' my parliamentary career and quit politics. Taking their cue from this, others followed suit. An aside from Geoff Hoon caught the flavour of the gathering consensus: he said that my future in the Labour Party would be to 'knock on doors and hand out party leaflets'. Alastair proceeded to brief the press with a suggestion that I was mentally 'detached' – meaning, presumably, that I was ripe not only for retirement, but residential care.

Nothing could have been further from my thoughts than leaving politics when I next spoke to Tony. If there did come a time when I walked away, I wanted to go with my head held high. I was not about to retreat under a cloud of innuendo, leaving suggestions that I had been dishonest or corrupt behind me. This was not just a matter of pride. I had devoted much of my life to a political cause in which I still passionately believed. I had helped make Labour electable again. I had supported the efforts of a uniquely gifted leader to change not just the party, but the country. The task was far from complete. The election for a second term was approaching. I knew there was now no way I would play a role in running the campaign, but I was not prepared simply to disappear. I would provide what help I could to Tony. Assuming, of course, he still wanted it. I would fight my own corner too, using the inquiry he had set up on the day of my firing. I would also put my case to my constituents in Hartlepool. No matter how high I had risen in Tony's political court, I had never lost sight of the fact that it was they who had put me in the Commons. If they turned on me, I really would have to accept that my part in the political project I had helped to create was over.

The immediate aftermath of this second resignation was very different from that of the first. Then, I had felt consumed by a desire to return to cabinet, almost from the moment I was out. Now, perhaps because the circumstances were so bizarre, I just felt tired of the whole Whitehall circus. I had been the subject of too many media storms. I thought back to moments when the press pack had blown a story out of all proportion just because it involved me. I was still bewildered by the overreaction that followed a discussion on the BBC's *Newsnight* between Matthew Parris and Jeremy Paxman, during which Matthew referred to my private life before being cut off by Jeremy. In response to this supposed 'outing' – which had in fact already been accomplished by the *News of the World* more than a decade previously – the

BBC decided to ban any reference to the exchange on any of its programmes. My initial irritation at the intrusion was soon overtaken by the realisation that the BBC's heavy-handed response had made a mountain out of a molehill.

Even though my first time out of government had been unexpectedly brief, it had given me time, space and a reason to become a bit less politically driven. I stayed at home most nights. I rediscovered the joys of reading, not just policy papers or political tomes but books about the arts and business, and novels too. I could quite happily sink back into my sofa in Hartlepool, turn on the TV and watch a video. Alastair may have over-interpreted my resignation remarks to suggest that I had decided to leave politics some time soon. That was not true, but their tone did signal a real change in me: an acceptance that if it were to happen, it would not be the end of the world, or the end of my life. What transformed my mood was the news from Emma and Rupert. Not only did I know that I had done nothing to intercede on behalf of any bid by Srichand Hinduja for British citizenship, I now had evidence that the rest of my account was also correct.

That Thursday night I turned to John Birt, who had been among the first on the phone following my resignation. I talked him through the events of the previous forty-eight hours, and he suggested that we meet for breakfast the following morning at his home to discuss my response. I arrived with Ben Wegg-Prosser in tow, and also, in a demonstration of friendship that I appreciated a lot, with Tim Allan, who had offered his help. We agreed that doing nothing was not an option. Together we tabulated every relevant fact, building up a detailed picture of the sequence of events – precisely as Downing Street had failed to do. It provided the basis for everything I said and did subsequently, starting with an article I decided to write for the *Sunday Times* setting out my side of the story.

Robert Harris also came to London to be at my side. He had already started to back me up in the media, which drew phone calls from Anji and Fiona telling him to back away, and claiming, falsely, that there was documentary evidence of my guilt. Robert took control of the article. Ordinarily, he would have toned down my prose, smoothed my excesses. But as I spoke to more people in Downing Street that morning about the new evidence that confirmed my account, his blood began to boil as much as mine. When I told Alastair about the phone calls from my private secretaries he was nonplussed, and then made it clear that he felt the matter had already been put to bed. I rang Derry Irvine, reasoning that as the chief judicial figure in the land, he might be keener to see justice done. He replied: 'Peter, you have to understand that it is all water under the bridge now. You need to move on.' I was startled, and angry. I next telephoned Richard Wilson. But what could he do? He had not been in favour of firing me in the first place. In the newspaper article, these emotions would blaze through, setting the tone for my response in the weeks and months to come. At the suggestion of the barrister and Labour peer Helena Kennedy, I approached Jonathan Caplan QC, a top-flight lawyer, to ask him to help me. He became a huge source of legal, and personal, wisdom. From that moment on, he, along with John Birt, helped me prepare for every encounter connected with the subsequent inquiry.

I was keen for Tony to accept, or at least to understand, my deter-mination to fight back, and that I was doing so in order to rescue my reputation, not to damage him or the government. When we spoke, I told him there had been a rush to judgement, but he insisted that he had acted on the basis of the facts as presented by Richard Wilson. I pointed out that Richard at that point had not talked to the officials who knew what happened. 'I didn't know that,' Tony replied. Maybe I should have anticipated his reaction when I mentioned my news-paper piece for the following day, but that made it no less upset-ting. 'I don't think that's a very good idea,' he replied. I said I felt I had no option but to put my case, especially now that my civil serv-ants had confirmed my account of events. 'I've got to respond,' I told him. 'I've got to demonstrate my innocence.' He thought I should 'reflect on the wisdom of doing that'. When I asked why, he replied, 'You have to consider what's best for the long term. Just accept what happened. Let it go. Then, things will heal. You'll be able to work out a different future for yourself. If you fight it, you'll make enemies. It will be harder for you in the longer run.'

On that score, Tony turned out to be right. Hours after my article appeared, the counter-assault began. Jack Straw went on television to say that it had been right and necessary for me to go. I had – he said untruthfully – 'told an untruth'. When I persisted in putting on record what had really happened, the Downing Street machine cranked into overdrive. 'The future for Peter Mandelson,' according to 'a Downing Street source', would be 'to shut up, and then go off and have a lovely life with Reinaldo'. The briefing campaign was partly a reflection of the fact that both Alastair and I, two big players in Tony's circle, had our competence and reputation on the line. It was more than that, however. I soon realised that I was caught in a zero-sum game. If I was exonerated, questions would be asked about others: not just about Alastair, but about Mike, about Jack. And ultimately about Tony.

The immediate issues that Downing Street wanted buried related to my sacking. Why had they been so intent on dismissing my account of what had happened? Why had Tony fired me? But as I worked with my lawyer on my presentation for the official inquiry, headed by the former Home Office legal adviser Sir Anthony Hammond, I realised that the stakes were higher. When Hammond began taking evidence from me and others, I met either hostility or a wall of silence from former cabinet colleagues and Tony's team at Number 10. There were a few exceptions, principally David Blunkett and Tessa Jowell. Gordon was also briefly warmer towards me than at any time since my 'betrayal' in 1994. When I was at my lowest, as after my first resignation, or at my most remote, as during my period in Belfast, Gordon seemed to be at his most engaging. Sadly, it never lasted. Alastair didn't talk to me at all. Nor, for a period, did Jonathan Powell. Much more painful was the fact that some of my oldest and closest friends in politics, even Philip Gould, kept their distance. Robert all but launched a personal crusade on my behalf. He was especially disappointed in Tony, whom he had respected since his time as political editor at the *Observer*, but who he now felt had acted callously, selfishly and wrongly in tossing me overboard. He said this not only to me, but in an article in the *Independent* which touched me deeply. Based on this, Hugo Young wrote a forensic piece supporting me. For Robert, it was not just a matter of friendship but of principle. His respect for Tony never recovered.

Hammond, as far as I could tell, seemed determined to find some means by which he could remove the unfair – and now indisputably false – stain on my character without setting the dogs on others in the government. 'Mr Mandelson,' he said to me with breathtaking frankness as we were leaving one evidence session, 'I know that you contest the account of events, and as far as the supposed phone call to Mr O'Brien is concerned, I know you want me to make a finding that it didn't take place. But I think you will have to understand that having lost one minister is unfortunate. To lose another would be doubly unfortunate.'

When he released his report in March, he concluded, inevitably, that neither I nor anyone else had acted improperly with regard to passport applications. I was glad to be cleared of any wrongdoing. Where the phone call to O'Brien was concerned, however, he came to an extraordinarily acrobatic and almost comic conclusion. He said that he could not 'reach a view with any certainty'. He accepted that my account was sincerely held, and that I had been 'frank and honest' in all my testimony. But he shied away from challenging Mike's or Jack's contention that the call had taken place. He decided that the 'best conclusion' – by which I can only assume he meant the most convenient – was that the call had occurred. Later, when I asked him to justify this, he said that as I had been such a high-profile member of the government at the time, Mike was more likely to have remembered receiving a call from me than the other way round. The implication was that as Mike was supposedly so unimportant, it was understandable that I did not recall having phoned him. For me, this was beyond parody. Many in the media branded the report a whitewash. I agreed, if not for the same reasons as them. Hammond was explicit in the finding that mattered most: neither I nor my office had leaned on anyone to grant Mr Hinduja citizenship.

I was in Hartlepool when the report was published. Asked for my reaction, I said that I was grateful for the clean bill of health. 'Sir

Anthony's report makes it clear that I did not lie, I did not mislead, and I did not deceive,' I said. For people like Shirley Williams, who later wrote to me, the findings were decisive: 'It's clear now you should not have had to resign, and it's marvellous you've been so resilient about it.' Tony's immediate response was more equivocal. He welcomed my exoneration: 'I said I believed Peter would be cleared from any impropriety,' he told reporters, 'and I am very pleased for his sake he has been.' But he had warned me, when my fightback began, that I risked making enemies along the way. Now I began to understand the full implications of his words. 'Peter has made it clear, and I have also made it clear,' Tony said, 'that there is no question of him coming back into government...I hope he will be able to get on with rebuilding his life.'

I was not so naïve as to expect an early return to the cabinet. I accepted the possibility – the 'near-certainty', as friends kept telling me, for my own good – that there was no way back at all. Yet for Tony publicly to rule out the prospect seemed gratuitous, and unfair. All the more so because when we spoke by phone the following day, at the personal level there was no doubting that our friendship survived. He did not directly raise the question of when, or whether, I might return in some formal role. Nor did I. In increasingly frequent conversations over the days ahead, he urged me to take a step back, 'reposition' myself politically. The time to talk about the next political move would come when all of us – me, Tony, the government, the rest of the party, the media – were in a 'different place'. But he did say that he counted on our relationship personally and politically. He said that he needed my support and my input, especially as he looked ahead to the election. At first, I took this to mean that he envisaged something like the broad, ill-defined role I had played immediately before and after the 1997 election. 'I guess it's back to "being Peter",' I joked. That, I would soon discover, was not the case. What Tony really wanted was an undercover partnership. He wanted me to go back to 'being Bobby'. Or perhaps he was just stringing me along.

While he had said that I should get on with 'rebuilding my life', Tony was facing a rebuilding project of his own. For months he had been working towards the election campaign. The first aim, obviously, was victory. Demonstrating that we could win successive elections would be a litmus test of New Labour's success. Neither of us feared actually losing. The economy was too buoyant. The Tories were too divided, and too strongly identified with the serial calamities of their final years in power. William Hague was still performing well in the Commons, but he was not making an impact with voters. The question was not so much whether we would win, but by how much. Would the margin be too narrow, the turnout too low, to constitute a convincing endorsement? Crucially, what would we be asking voters to endorse?

With the campaign just months away, Tony knew that the initial wave of enthusiasm for New Labour, and for him, had gone. He was desperate to find a way of enthusing voters again. He kept telling me he wanted his second-term government to be 'more radical, more ambitious'. He had formed a broad idea of what that would mean. More far-reaching changes in health and education. More visible results on 'quality of life' issues, not least curbing the corrosive effects of thuggery, anti-social behaviour and crime. He wanted to assemble a more cohesive and energetic cabinet. To hold the euro referendum. Everything he had come to wish he had done in the first four years. His fear was that too many in the party would be tempted to take the easy way out. They would believe that we could beat the Tories simply by reminding voters of their sleaze and Black Wednesday, by pointing to the growth and stability we had delivered, and by trumpeting the billions of pounds we were now committed to pouring into the public services. 'Radical, ambitious' reform would seem frightening to some, superfluous to others. What most frustrated Tony was that he felt he had not yet come up with a sufficiently compelling vision of a second-term government to engage the electorate. Rather provocatively, I told him that the New Labour project was in danger of running out of steam, and that if he didn't find a new way of defining it and re-energising it, its support would drain away. I advised him to campaign strongly on public service reform if that was going to be his priority in the second term.

As if Tony's election campaign doubts were not disheartening enough, he soon found himself mired in a crisis with haunting echoes of the fuel protests. In February, an inspection at an abattoir in Essex found signs in some pigs of foot-and-mouth, a disease that had last struck British livestock at the end of the 1960s. A trickle of cases became dozens, topping the hundred mark by the time Tony raised the issue with me in one of our conversations after Hammond. He was worried, but not overly. His preoccupation was the election, which he was gearing up to announce for the first Thursday in May, ten weeks away. The groundwork was more or less in place: Philip was polling, Millbank had a 'warbook', Michael Levy had raised nearly as much cash as in 1997, around £15 million. But what mattered most was still missing: the message.

The foot-and-mouth crisis got much worse before it got better. There was every prospect of major damage to tourism, which in economic terms is far more important to the countryside than farming. The man in charge of dealing with the outbreak was Nick Brown, who had been given his job at the Ministry of Agriculture, Fisheries and Food mostly because Tony saw it as the best place to park one of Gordon's protégés. I would later wonder whether one reason Tony was reluctant to look too closely over Nick's shoulder at the start of the epidemic was to avoid upsetting Gordon, especially with the election drawing closer. Whatever the reason, as he followed the daily bustle of activity and announcements from MAFF, he chose for a long time to assume that the measures being taken were the right ones. But with the number of cases growing, with predictions of a £13 billion price-tag for tourism – and, most of all, media rumblings that the election might have to be postponed – Tony's mood changed. On Easter Sunday, he and I spoke. With encouragement from Anji and me in particular, he had decided to push back the general election until early June as a result of the crisis.

He was also overwhelmed with other problems in his in-tray: law and order, health reform, transport in London. All needed new direction and energy, he said, but almost none of his ministers – he mentioned David Blunkett at Education as the exception – seemed on top of the challenges they faced. Struggling to map out the policies and the ministerial team he would need for an effective second term, he said that he was feeling increasingly on his own. Europe, too, was frustrating him. He said he wanted to bring Britain into the single currency, and he still hoped Gordon could be won round to agreeing to a referendum. But he felt that the Foreign Office, and Robin Cook, were failing to advance the argument effectively.

He told me he had finally settled on the campaign's central focus: a 'post-Thatcher Britain – beyond Thatcher, not just anti-Thatcher. A meritocratic, aspirational Britain where anyone is able to share in opportunity.' I agreed that it was a starting point, but I was unclear where it would lead in policy terms. It lacked detail, a sense of the choices he would make and the changes he hoped to drive through. 'Flesh out the idea,' I urged him. 'Go away and write down the whole thing. Develop it.' He said that he would, and would fax it to me in a day or two.

But he seemed distracted, unsure of what exactly he thought the message should be. I doubted that he would get around to narrowing and nailing it down, and he didn't. Every aspect of campaign planning seemed to be lagging. We were well behind where we had been in the run-up to 1997. I wanted to do what I could to help, but there were limits to how directly or openly involved I could be – although Tony in his frustration sometimes seemed to forget this. When I told him I had run into a friend on the campaign advertising team, Tony's response was 'Good! You should be involved.' I laughed. 'Are you kidding? Think about it for a minute. If I did, Gordon would go bonkers, Alastair would get upset, and you'd get nervy.'

I knew that would distract both of us, and everyone involved, from the real aim of running a coherent campaign, and getting a convincing mandate. There was clearly unfinished business between Tony and me: why he had fired me; why I had been cleared by Hammond but not rehabilitated; what role, if any, I might have in a future government. But to the surprise, and in some cases the dismay, of my friends, I settled back into 'being Bobby'. My ties to Tony, and my commitment to New Labour, were too strong for me to do otherwise. Resentment at my sacking, and frustration about my uncertain future, did churn inside, but rarely did they come out into the open.

At the end of one of our talks Tony asked, all of a sudden, how Robert was feeling about him. It was his way of gauging how I was feeling. When I tried to steer us off the subject by mumbling something non-committal, he said, 'It's not so black-and-white, you know.'

'It's pretty black-and-white to me,' I said, more abruptly than I had intended. 'You absorbed all the stuff you were being fed by Jack and the Home Office and Alastair, didn't question any of it, pronounced me guilty, and pushed me out the window.'

'That's not what happened,' Tony said quietly. 'I know you think there was some deeper meaning or reason for what I did. But there wasn't.'

The truth was that I didn't suspect there was some 'deeper reason'. What bothered me was the lack of *any* reason. It was my sense that Tony had decided, amid the comedy of errors that had ended my ministerial career, that I was simply not worth the trouble, and was dispensable. Maybe that just illustrated something about the nature of government. It may have been especially true of us after 1997: too often ruled by the next news cycle, and how to react to it and shape it, rather than focusing on issues of longer-term judgement. In this occasionally brutal environment, everyone – except the man at the top – was ultimately dispensable. But there was a paradox, too, which would be brought home to me once I was back in government under Gordon, and Tony was gone. A Prime Minister cannot make it on his own. Success depends on a huge web of factors. Some are beyond his control. But without the ability to assemble and inspire an effective team, and to work with them – without a talent for making them feel indispensable and totally committed – he will fail.

By late April, the early-morning calls from Downing Street were coming with increasing frequency, a time-tested barometer of Tony's level of anxiety. Foot-and-mouth was one worry. Having delayed the election, he had raised expectations of progress in bringing the epidemic under control. Progress was being made, but slowly. There were other political concerns as well. A plan for a private-public partnership to bring funds into the London Underground had degenerated into a political free-for-all, with the Tube management and Ken Livingstone drumming up opposition. Tony was also fretful about his own office. He had decided to promote Anji as his Director of Government Relations in a second term, but was not sure that she was relishing the prospect. 'Who can blame her?' I could not help saying. We both knew that she feared trouble from Cherie, who had never reconciled herself to Anji's role. But I had known Tony long enough to recognise that all these worries were compounded by his larger frustration about the coming campaign. At one point he remarked that what he really needed was someone he could trust to help him get a grip, and focus. 'I need a you,' he said. 'I need a Mandelson.'

As I was driving back from a day with friends in Oxfordshire in late April, Cherie phoned. Why, was not immediately clear. We chatted amicably enough, until the mobile signal cut out on the M40. I planned to phone back when I got to my office in the Commons, but she reached me first, as soon as I had arrived. Though she did not raise the question directly – that was not her way, especially on territory that was difficult for both of us – she wanted to know how I saw my political future. In part, I think she was asking because she felt that the issue of my future would inevitably affect Tony's, but I don't doubt that she spoke out of concern for me as well.

I saw little point in hiding my feelings. I was talking to Cherie, after all, not to a newspaper editor or the cabinet. I had come to feel that there was no one around Tony who was cleverer and better able to untangle a complex situation than she was. I said that I had no way of knowing what my future held; it was not in my hands. But I had done nothing wrong in connection with the Hindujas. I had been cleared by Hammond. I saw no reason why I should not, at some point, return to government. The timing, and what role I might play, were obviously delicate issues that would take time to work through. All I felt for the moment was a need for clarity. That could come only from Tony telling me what he was planning: openly, honestly, and face-to-face. Cherie said that she agreed, and would tell Tony so. In one sense, that was a relief. But the conversation also left me feeling sullen, and sullied. 'I feel embarrassed by all this,' I wrote in my diary. 'I find the whole subject humiliating.'

On the last Friday of April, Tony and I met for the first time since he had fired me in January. I felt odd setting off in the early morning for Chequers. Though we had been speaking often by phone, I was afraid that our meeting would be difficult. As we settled down in his study, Tony broke the ice. He began strumming on an electric guitar that Cherie had given him, and joking – at least, I hoped he was joking – about plans to join an amateur rock band on holiday in the summer. Then he asked, 'How are you?' I said I was OK, but frustrated.

Tony, no doubt having been nudged by Cherie, got right to the point. 'Let's leave the past alone,' he said. 'Let's talk about the future.' He wanted me back. As a first step, he wanted me to take a political role, outside cabinet, after the election. That would accustom people to my being involved again. But he said there were problems in moving beyond that, at least for now. The main one was the media. 'They won't leave you alone,' he said, 'and everything that appears in the press gets blamed on you. It's destabilising.' He gave examples, pointing in particular to a recent *Times* piece predicting that in the light of Nick Brown's uncertain response to foot-and-mouth, not only the minister but his ministry would be axed after the election. That would turn out to be true, but I had heard nothing of any such plan. Tony knew that he hadn't mentioned it to me, and that I was still estranged from the few people he may have told. 'What matters,' he said, 'is that Nick was convinced you were behind planting the leak. Or at least, that's what he was led to believe, by Gordon and his people.'

'Isn't that the real problem with bringing me back?' I asked. 'Isn't it Gordon, when all's said and done?'

'Yes,' he said. 'That's the gist of it. Gordon wants you buried. That's what he wanted from Hammond. He was very angry with the outcome.'

I was not especially surprised by Gordon's attitude, nor by his power over whatever came next for me. What unsettled me was the degree to which Tony now seemed cowed by him. From our first months in Downing Street, I had become used to Tony humouring Gordon, deferring to his moods. As recently as six months ago, when Gordon had verbally assaulted him during our campaign planning meeting, Tony had seemed supremely unruffled. Partly, no doubt, this had been because he still felt a residual fondness and respect for our old friend and ally. If ever a truly make-or-break moment arrived, he had also felt that he could exert his authority. Now, however, I had the sense that he wasn't quite so confident about his own position, or quite so sure how to deal with Gordon. 'He's out of control,' Tony said, reading the concern on my face. 'He's been out of control for weeks.' He said that Gordon had been contributing next to nothing to the campaign planning, except to launch assaults on Tony's lack of 'vision' and the government's lack of purpose. 'I have no illusions any more,' he said. 'He could come for me – and he would do, probably, if he got the chance.'

Tony said that he was tempted to strike back. 'What I should really do,' he said, 'is move him after the election. I should put him in the Foreign Office.' But no sooner did he raise the possibility – a possibility he would return to more seriously a few years later, when he was much weaker politically – than he dismissed it. 'I'm sure he'd just resign, make trouble, and bide his time.' That was possible, I said, but Gordon would have to be careful not to overplay things. He would risk just looking like a big sulk. 'The party wouldn't like such tactics,' I told Tony. 'They'd see him as a splitter. They wouldn't forgive him.' Tony said that I was wrong. 'They would blame me,' he replied, 'for sacking a successful Chancellor and provoking the split. I said to him the other day, when things got really bad, that if it weren't for the economy I would have cut him off at the knees, given the way he has treated me.'

If nothing else, our conversation helped me understand why Tony was finding it so difficult to settle on the message he wanted to take into the election. Developing a strategy against William Hague was the easy part. The Tory leader had made a fool of himself in the public's mind with his baseball cap, his ride on a water chute and his fourteen-pints-a-day boast, all intended to make him appear 'normal' and one of the lads, but having the opposite effect. More importantly, he had made little or no effort to change his party from its previous Thatcherite incarnation. Yet Tony still needed Gordon on-side, not only because he was to chair the campaign, but because without a unified approach it was hard to see how we could make a coherent pitch to the voters, and win a clear mandate from them for our second term.

Tony and I met at Chequers again the following weekend. The campaign launch was now only days away. My hope was to help him set aside the distractions and get a better idea of what he wanted the election to be about. The choice was clear. We would almost certainly win if we simply highlighted Tory weaknesses and ran on Gordon's mantra of 'Labour investment versus Tory cuts'. Or we could be more ambitious and radical. Tony obviously favoured the second option, but in all the conversations we had had over the past few weeks, he hadn't got much closer to defining what his post-Thatcher Britain would look like. I told him he needed more than a soundbite, a head-line. If he didn't provide a clear vision for voters, he would have little chance of converting an arithmetical victory into a mandate. The stronger he could make the message, the better-placed he would be after the election to make the changes he wanted.

We spoke well into the evening. The message began to take on a sharper focus. Tony's starting point remained a post-Thatcher Britain, but with a better sense of what that meant. He admired Thatcher's depth of conviction, her decisiveness, her leadership qualities. But in seeking to bring necessary change to the economy, she had over-looked the social consequences of her actions. He said she had been wrong in promoting a rampant individualism that too often ignored citizens' responsibility for, and interest in, promoting the wider health of society. She had done untold damage by denying adequate funds for our public services, and she had been wrong on Europe. Tony wanted a social-democratic Britain in which individual opportunity was encouraged. Government's job was to make sure that all citizens enjoyed an equal chance to reap the rewards of their talents and efforts. It obviously had an obligation to help those who couldn't help themselves, but not to coddle the criminal or subsidise people who deliberately chose welfare over work. He wanted rebuilt and reinvigorated public services, better tailored to how individuals wanted to organise their lives. He wanted Britain to engage with Europe, and to join the euro.

As he spoke, the energy seemed to flood back into him. I also had a sense that he had a much broader idea of what he wanted to accomplish, and how to achieve it, than when he had first entered Number 10. He knew how government worked now, and understood that in order to leave a mark not only on the Labour Party but on Britain, he would have to prioritise a core of major areas in which we could deliver real change. Education and health were obviously paramount: 'Schools and hospitals first' would become the campaign slogan.

But as we got into the detail, both of us recognised that there were too many political obstacles, and too little time, for all of it to be weaved into a fundamentally redesigned campaign. On none of the issues that Tony wanted to address was there a settled government policy, much less agreement with his neighbour in Number 11. Our manifesto was written. It was slightly more adventurous than that of 1997, but ambitious or radical it wasn't. Very few people in the party except Tony seemed to want it that way.

I was one of them. In some areas, I wanted to go further than Tony. For instance, I thought that if we were going to re-engage with voters, we had to have something to say on an issue that was becoming increasingly difficult and controversial: immigration and asylum. In our early campaign meetings, Gordon had been adamant that we should do everything possible to avoid any mention of it. He felt the same about law and order. Raising such issues would fuel rather then calm public anxiety, he argued, and given that we could not trump the Conservatives' tough posture, risked putting us on the wrong side of our campaign 'dividing line' with the Tories. I thought that pretending the issues did not exist would not make them go away. Immigration and asylum were generating debate, and sometimes anger, in pubs and on shop floors as much as in gentlemen's clubs or leafy suburbs. I was hearing that concern on the doorstep in Hartlepool, and I knew that other MPs were getting a similar message in their constituencies. I tried to convince Tony that we needed to inject a credible Labour voice into the debate. Drawing on the example of Roy Jenkins and Jim Callaghan, I advocated coupling an impassioned condemnation of racism or xenophobia with support for firm and balanced rules. It was a case Tony would soon accept – and Gordon would too, in his final year as Prime Minister. Yet at this point, for both of them, it was uncertain territory.

Still, Tony was determined to find a way to push beyond the limitations of the manifesto, and Gordon's core campaign message of 'investment versus cuts', even if it meant adding to the tensions between them. He delivered half a dozen major speeches during the campaign. He spoke of the need for individual rights to be balanced by social responsibility as part of our approach to both crime and welfare. He made clear his hope to hold and win a referendum on joining the single currency. His most significant intervention came on public services. Compared to the reforms he would go on to champion a few years later, it was pretty tame. But the response to his mere mention of involving private and charitable groups in helping to improve schools and hospitals was an early sign of the obstacles ahead. There was discontent on the left, and warnings from trade union leaders, who interpreted Alastair's rather clumsy briefings after the manifesto launch as suggesting that Tony wanted to 'privatise' the public services. The seed was sown for later, louder opposition to the reforms.

Gordon believed – or at least argued – that Tony was being deliberately provocative. That he was only interested in defining himself politically by the opposition his proposals aroused, enabling him to look strong and to demonstrate the left of the party who was in control. For years afterwards, this would be an article of faith for Gordon's followers, taking the place of any serious engagement with the substance of what Tony was proposing to do. The accusation was absurd: Tony wanted to change the country for the better, not confront the party for its own sake.

Our campaign as a whole turned out to be flat. The media, and the public, seemed to take only a perfunctory interest in the election. The emotional high point came in an incident which I watched repeatedly on television at home in Hartlepool, mesmerised by its comic nature. John Prescott, confronted by an egg-throwing protester in Wales, responded by throwing a punch and getting into a brawl. For a brief moment I thought, like many in Downing Street, that John might have to step down. That would have been a loss not only for him, but for Tony and the government. In fact, John's pugilistic instinct turned out to be more a help than a hindrance, and he became something of a radio talk-show hero. Also, the scrap conveniently overshadowed an incident in which Tony was confronted at a Birmingham hospital over failures in the NHS.

My focus was on Hartlepool. It is no exaggeration to say that not just my job, but my credibility and my future in public life, were on the line. If I lost, or just squeaked through, it would be curtains. Our early canvass returns indicated that the fact that I had had to resign from the cabinet twice in two years had taken its toll on my support. Rather than make me feel like throwing in the towel, this spurred me on. It also galvanised my local party and my London-based friends, all of whom, it seemed, flocked north to lend a hand. Roger Liddle took on the role of field marshal, deploying our forces across the town, Patrick Diamond was his able deputy, and Steve Wallace, my long-standing and unflappable agent, provided logistics and humour.

Even at the peak of my now blighted career in Whitehall, I had prided myself on being a good constituency MP. I looked forward to arriving at the house on Hutton Avenue on a Friday morning, and to the Saturdays spent meeting, talking and listening to the people who had elected me. Although I had little prior interest in the sport, I even enjoyed supporting my adopted football club, Hartlepool United, of which I became honorary president. The team thrived during my time in the town, although I suspect this had little to do with my support. Like all MPs, I had often said that my real job was to serve my constituents, and in my case I believed it. But the reality of Westminster, especially if you are close to the centre of power, is that it can dazzle and distance you. Since my second firing, the fact was that representing Hartlepool had become not just my real job, but my only job.

When Geoff Hoon had said that my future would be to knock on doors and hand out leaflets, he had meant it to sound like a death sentence. But every week until the election, that was exactly what I did, and I don't think I have ever found anything in politics more invigorating. Door by door, school gate by school gate and leaflet by leaflet, I wanted to convey to my constituents the gratitude I felt for their support, my pride in representing them, and my determination to meet their concerns and fulfil their hopes. Listening to them also informed my vision of what Tony's next government had to do: help people who needed it, but get tough on those who were milking the welfare system rather than working; address the causes of crime through social programmes, but crack down on the yobbishness on estates; put more money into schools and hospitals, but make sure it was used to make them better, and more responsive to the people they were meant to serve.

I knew that some of my colleagues in the party, and former colleagues in government, would not exactly go into mourning if I got a kicking. The former NUM leader Arthur Scargill had even entered the race in Hartlepool, representing his newly formed Socialist Labour Party. Like Tony, I felt that I not only had to win, but win convincingly. For him, the issue was to secure a governing mandate. For me, the election was a personal referendum. Every Fleet Street sketchwriter made the trip to Hartlepool, presumably expecting to record my final humiliation, this time at the hands of the voters. They were disappointed by the town's response, and returned to London with more sympathetic copy than I am sure they, or I, expected. The energy and warmth of the campaign had rubbed off on them, as my favourite cartoonist, Posy Simmonds, showed in her pictorial record of her visit. I have the original hanging on my wall thanks to her, and Robert's, generosity.

Election day in 2001 could not have been more different from 1997. Then, my preoccupation with my own contest had been over-shadowed by my euphoria over New Labour's entry into government. This time, I was riveted by the local count. As the declaration drew nearer, I became more and more nervous. By the time the announce-ment came, well after midnight, I was close to fingernail-chomping point. Scargill, the Returning Officer announced, had won 912 votes, about 2.4 per cent of the total. My Tory opponent, Gus Robinson, despite a well-run campaign, polled 7,935 votes, a little under 21 per cent. I received 22,506. Nearly 60 per cent.

As I stepped forward to speak, it was as if all the pressures since January had suddenly evaporated. 'Before this campaign started, it was said I was facing political oblivion,' I said. 'My career was in tat-ters, never to be part of the political living again. Well, they under-estimated the people of Hartlepool, and they underestimated me,' I went on, my voice rising in a surge of emotion. 'Because I am a fighter. . .a fighter, not a quitter!'

I had won, and won well. In keeping with the trend nationwide, my margin of victory was down from 1997, but only by a whisker, and by less than the national swing. Shortly after I had finished speaking, my mobile rang. It was Tony. He was relieved that the campaign was over, happy that we were on course for a large Commons majority, and gracious about my result. 'Well done,' he said. 'Your swing was better than mine!' Alastair phoned afterwards. 'Good speech,' he said, with a trace of the trademark irony in his voice. 'But a bit shouty.' I smiled. Perhaps I should have found a way to whisper about being a fighter. But I was too exhausted, and too happy, to take Alastair's comment to heart. To the extent that it caused me any concern, it was because I knew that, for both of our sakes and for Tony's, Alastair and I would have to find a way to heal the tensions between us and re-establish an ability to work together.

That would take many months. Far more discouraging was a bat-tery of disappointments for me – and Tony too – after the election. We had won a less enthusiastic endorsement than in 1997. Voter turnout had slumped from an impressive 71 per cent four years earlier to 59 per cent, lower than in any election since 1918. But not only had Labour won a historic second successive term, we had lost only five seats. The Tories had gained just one, with the Lib Dems up by a handful. It may have been a grudging landslide, but it was another landslide all the same. As Tony planned his post-election reshuffle, I contemplated my own next steps. With a fresh start as a comfortably re-elected Prime Minister, Tony was again at a peak of power and influence. I wanted to be a part of his new start. I had been cleared by Hammond, and revalidated by the voters. In retrospect, I realise that I should have been more patient, and more realistic about the pressures around Tony. But despite wise words of caution from those closest to me, I found myself sitting by the phone, waiting for a call from Number 10.

I was at the tiniest of victory parties in London on the afternoon after the election, with just Patrick, Roger and Ben, when the call came. It was not about my place in a new government, but someone else's. Tony sounded tired as he went through the details of his reshuffle. He had had a 'bloody difficult' day, he said. Then he came to it. 'I know you're not going to like this. Jack is going to the Foreign Office to replace Robin.' I could hardly deny that I thought it was a mistake. Jack Straw seemed to me an inappropriate choice, because he had Euroscepticism in his DNA. As it happened, that turned out to have been an attraction for Tony. He reasoned that once Jack was 'locked in' to his new job, he would toe the line on Europe and the euro. Due to the very fact he was a known sceptic, Tony said, his support would count for more with voters, MPs and the Murdoch press. 'That remains to be seen,' I replied. In fact, it seemed to me that even Tony had his doubts. He sounded as if he was trying to convince himself.

On one level, of course, I was disappointed not to be part of Tony's new beginning. On another, I realised he was right not to bring me back. My return would have provoked controversy, and would have risked distracting him from making a start on governing with more effectiveness and ambition than in his first term. He now set himself two major benchmarks. One was Europe, and the referendum on the single currency. More urgent was his domestic agenda, which revolved around using the new investment in the public services to modernise and reform them.

He began his second term well enough, setting up a new delivery unit inside Number 10, with the aim of finally giving him the tools to drive through his policy changes. He ensured that he had ministers he rated in key departments: keeping Alan Milburn at Health, and promoting the promising if untested Estelle Morris at Education. David Blunkett took over from Jack at the Home Office, and Charles Clarke became Party Chairman.

Almost immediately, however, there were signs of trouble. The main target was Tony's fervent, although still vaguely defined, desire to revamp the way the public services were organised and run. He wanted to give the best-performing schools and hospitals more freedom, and had made it clear that this meant loosening the government's monopoly control and possibly bringing in other providers to offer added expertise and money. After the election, the opposition to this grew. Much of it came from familiar quarters on the left. But there was also a deeper problem. With the campaign over and the second victory in the bag, many in the broad swathe of the PLP that was neither passionately Old Labour nor New seemed simply to lack the appetite for the kind of changes Tony had in mind. He first sensed this when he addressed Labour MPs after the election, and at a discussion with the NEC shortly afterwards. 'I feel my persuasiveness is slipping,' he told me. 'For the first time, I felt they were not buying in to what I was saying. They were listening, and rejecting. And at the NEC, there were more voices saying "We don't want more New Labour. We've been there, done that." They want more authentic Labour.' Tony was not worried about objections of substance. In an argument about the merits of reform, he was confident that he could make his case and win it. The thing that concerned him was the overall mood, the lassitude and the grumbling, at precisely the time when the party and the government most required renewed purpose.

What he found hardest was that the ally he most needed was clearly not disposed to help. Relations between Tony and Gordon had grown worse before the election. The campaign had not been easy, but with the election won, Tony had expected – or hoped for – a period of détente. He had believed that a degree of collegiality and partnership would reassert itself. A successful second term was not only in Tony's interest; it was in Gordon's too, if Labour hoped to win a third election and he was to become Prime Minister. In New Labour-speak, vintage 1997, Tony had reckoned that things could only get better.

They got worse. The first flashpoint was Tony's Downing Street reorganisation. The 'delivery' machinery was essential if he was going to push through his programme for the public services. Gordon pressed for, and won, a commitment that it would operate within the Treasury's mesh of some two hundred Public Service Agreement targets. He was also working to encourage the new mood of scepticism towards Tony in the PLP, the NEC and the unions. Sometimes behind the scenes, sometimes more openly through Ed Balls and other allies, he gave credence to the canard that any role for the private sector in the public services amounted to 'Thatcherite privatisation'. A media consensus formed of a second-term government that had hit the ground stumbling, and of a Prime Minister losing his touch. Publicly, Tony tried to project confidence, and to avoid any suggestion of tension with Gordon. Privately, he was frustrated, resentful and increasingly angry. He told me he felt he had been misled by Gordon's first CSR, and that the result had been lost time in prioritising investment and reform in the public services. 'I asked all the right questions,' he said, 'but I was lied to.' Bracing himself for similar resistance on his reform agenda, he said, 'I'm ready this time.'

Tony's real distress about Gordon – and Gordon's real agenda – went beyond spending details or policy priorities. Within days of the election, Gordon began a campaign to secure what he had failed to secure at Granita seven years earlier: a commitment not only that he would be Labour's next Prime Minister, but that the second term would be Tony's last. In fact, he began to lobby for a handover that would clear the way for him, rather than Tony, to lead Labour into the next election. It was not a 'coup'. Not yet. But to Tony, and especially to an even angrier Cherie, it began to feel like one. In their frequent conversations, Tony found Gordon sullen and aggressive. Far from helping to marshal support for Tony's reforms in the PLP, he was encouraging the doubters. He was refusing to engage, much less work, with Tony on his key domestic priorities. On the euro, he was holding firm to his insistence that only he would decide when the time to join was right. 'It's intimidation,' Tony said. 'He is eclipsing me in order to dislodge me.'

I knew that Tony was always depleted as the summer Commons recess drew near. But he would return from holiday recharged at the start of September, having written a long note on future plans as we looked towards the autumn party conference. Now, however, the fatigue went deeper. It was reinforced by a mood of distraction and, at times, something that seemed very much like despair. He feared that all his plans for the second term would be buried in a battle to stave off a war of attrition with Gordon.

The media were not the only ones who noticed. In mid-July I had a long lunch with Robert Harris and Roy Jenkins at the Royal Oak, at Yattendon in Berkshire, one of their favourite haunts. Roy had drifted away a bit since the collapse of the project to bring the Lib Dems into government and reform the voting system. He still liked Tony, however, wanted him to succeed, and hoped in particular that he would lead us into the single currency and a closer relationship with Europe. He was alarmed at signs since the election that a euro referendum was once more being kicked into the long grass, and would stay there unless and until Gordon relented. 'Tony is Prime Minister,' Roy said. 'He needs to show some vision, and some backbone.' Coming from such an experienced and broadly supportive elder statesman, whom both Tony and I respected, his remarks brought home to me how rapidly our second-term expectations had faltered.

I wrote to Roy the next day. I said I would tell Tony about our talk, and added that I had made much the same points to him since the election. I also tried to get him to understand the difficulties Tony was facing: 'He is his own best analyst and critic. Nobody knows better the very fraught situation he finds himself in with Gordon. But anyone who thinks that a crude exercise of prime ministerial

power would resolve it is deluding themselves.' I held out hope that
the narrow issue of the euro referendum would resolve itself: 'When
the economics move, so will Tony.' Maybe Gordon would move as
well. I told Roy that I was convinced his opposition was not to the
principle of joining the single currency. Nor was it merely about getting the economic circumstances right. I suspected that what Gordon
was really against was Tony, rather than him, deciding when to go in.
'In the meantime, Tony has to fight a mighty battle over public sector
reform and financing. It would not be wise to fight a simultaneous
war on both fronts with Gordon.'

In early August, Tony asked me to Chequers. We spoke for hours,
first in his study, then, joined by Cherie, in the garden. The Commons
had risen for the summer, and I could see that Tony's focus was
already trained on the party conference, and the chance to make a
real start on his second term. As we took stock of the dissension and
drift since the election, it seemed to me that he was facing the toughest challenge since he had won the Labour leadership. The lie of the
political land had changed since 1997. We had done well enough as
a government in the first term, and his two landslide election victories had validated New Labour, and his leadership. But if the second
term was going to be more ambitious than the first, he would have to
return from holiday with a sufficiently compelling vision to enthuse
the country and win over the party. It had to be bigger than any of
the individual policies that we wanted to get through.

I did not even mention Europe. That was obviously off the agenda
for now. But I said that we needed a new focus, and a new momentum, if our domestic policy ambitions were not to go the same way.
I had come to feel much greater clarity in Hartlepool about what our
government should do, and why. I said we had to go back to a message that united Old Labour and New, and tied together the reforms
we hoped to bring about in the second term: 'a strong, revived social
justice narrative' to help bring the party along with Tony in what he
was setting out to do. I am sure his instincts told him much the same
thing. What was missing was his usual drive and self-assurance. The
chill he had felt in his meetings with the PLP and the NEC after the

election had dented his confidence. Roy's criticism had stung too. 'I feel a lack of allies,' he said. 'I feel isolated – in government, from the Lib Dems, from individual supporters who were with me in 1997.'

Most of all, he felt isolated from Gordon. Since the election, all restraint had gone. He was now certain that Gordon not only wanted to defeat his reform plans, but to force him out. Alastair and others had been telling him for weeks that he was too relaxed about the threat Gordon posed. They were wrong, he said: 'You know, his behaviour is having the opposite effect on me. I used to feel guilty about him. I felt a sense of obligation to him. I've said that he can, and he should, take over from me. But I've told him that it won't happen on any condition. Only if he supports me. It's hard for me to understand. It's incredible. But he's thinking of only one thing. Only of removing me. But I am not going to be pushed out.' Tony said he had always felt eight years was enough for any Prime Minister. He had no desire to serve a third term; he didn't want to 'go on and on', like Margaret Thatcher. But he now had renewed doubts about whether Gordon would make a good Prime Minister – 'certainly not if he behaves like this'. Finally, with the nearest he ever got to a scowl, he said, 'I will *not* go on these terms.'

When I got back to London, I wrote a note in my diary: 'TB has GB in his sights.' It was a reflection of the steel I had heard in Tony's voice. It would also prove to be wrong. Partly, I think, I underestimated the complexity of the relationship between Tony and Gordon, on both sides: the intensity of Gordon's concern that Tony would go on and on; and the mixture of dependency and intimidation he triggered in Tony. I failed to take account of the practical constraints on Tony's ability to move against a successful Chancellor, and his very real fear of risking civil war in the PLP if he did so. Most of all, I did not – could not – anticipate how dramatically Tony's political strength would drain away over the course of our second term in government. Some of this was because of wilful action by Gordon and his allies to encourage opposition to his public service reforms. But it was mostly because of a train of extraordinary events overseas that began on a Tuesday in September that would become universally known as 9/11.

When I awoke on the morning of 11 September, my focus was on a lunch appointment at the bright Thames-side restaurant of the Savoy Hotel. After a painful political divorce, provoked first by him and then by me, I was due to meet Philip Gould. He had taken the first step towards mending fences, sending me a very moving note in the summer. Until he had joined Alastair and others in Downing Street in freezing me out after my resignation, Philip and I had not only been political partners, but the closest of friends, for more than fifteen years. I was so upset by our falling-out that even after I had begun 'being Bobby' again for Tony, I had not been able to face trying to rebuild my ties – closer, in some ways – with Philip.

Rereading his letter nearly a decade later, I realise I had forgotten how deeply the hurt ran on both sides. 'I have tried many times to contact you, but have failed,' Philip began. He wrote that he had especially missed my presence during the election campaign. He accepted I was angry, and that my anger might be justified. But now that the election campaign was over, he felt I owed it to him to sit down and talk through what had happened.

We met shortly before one o'clock. 'You have to understand how difficult things were after you left,' he said. 'The whole atmosphere, the whole tide, in the office was against you. It was impossible to stand up for you. Alastair was determined. Everyone had to take sides. You were either with him – which meant with Tony – or with you, which meant being against them.' I later learned that, as in my first resignation, Philip had been one of the few people who had urged Tony not to let me go. But like Tony, he now insisted that if only I had not fought my firing, things could have been different. I explained to him, as I had tried to do with Tony, that there would also have been no prospect of me ever returning to front-line politics. He understood this, but said that Alastair, in his own way, accepted that mistakes had been made on all sides. Still, Philip and I both now realised that these were matters for the past, or perhaps the future. It was time to rebuild our friendship. We had just agreed to make a start on doing so when his mobile rang with the first of a succession of increasingly urgent messages from Number 10. The World Trade

Center in New York and the Pentagon in Washington had been targeted by terror attacks, and it was quickly established that Osama bin Laden's al-Qaeda network was responsible.

Philip rushed back to Downing Street. I returned to my office in the Commons, more out of instinct than anything, as the House was still in recess. But I was not alone among MPs in feeling drawn to digest the full significance of what was happening in the place where our personal and political lives intersected. As we huddled around television sets, the scale of the carnage, and the immediacy of the horrific images from the most powerful nation on earth, were almost physically jolting.

I spoke to Tony that evening. He had just emerged from COBRA, Cabinet Office Briefing Room 'A', a heavily secured, high-tech basement retreat behind Downing Street. When he came on the line, I expected to hear uncertainty, perhaps apprehension, in his voice. Certainly fatigue. I was struck instead by his resolute sense of calm. He did feel raw fury over the murder of thousands of innocent Americans, and dozens of Britons too. The religious believer in him felt assailed. For him, the killings were not just a tragedy, they were sinful, evil. Yet while his judgement was powered by these emotions, it was not overwhelmed by them. He was focused on the political significance of these terrible events. He was clear in his mind about what needed to be done, and the dangers of getting it wrong.

The aftershock of 9/11 so dominated British politics that there was briefly some talk of cancelling our party conference, and when it did go ahead, it was in truncated form. It was less about Labour than about the altered world. The tone was a lot less shrill than we had feared, leading some in Number 10 to assume that opposition to Tony's domestic policy reforms might be overcome more easily than had been anticipated. I was unconvinced. Nor was I much encouraged by the lack of visible tension between Tony and the man most likely to determine the outcome of that struggle. Gordon was, by instinct and experience, every bit as pro-American as Tony. He recognised the scale of the challenge posed by 9/11, and broadly shared Tony's views on what had to be done. But I was certain that his determination to complete the unfinished work of Granita had not gone away.

Between the attacks on the Twin Towers and the Labour Party conference at the end of month Tony embarked on a whistle-stop tour of global capitals to sign up world leaders to plans to root out al-Qaeda terrorists and topple the Taliban in Afghanistan. He also needed to build a consensus at home, and told delegates at the Brighton conference that 'the kaleidoscope has been shaken. . .the pieces are in flux. Soon they will settle again. Before they do, let us re-order this world around us.' By the beginning of the following month these plans were well under way, with American and British troops invading Afghanistan and taking control of Kabul by mid-November. The rest of the year was dedicated to improving the security situation in the war-torn country.

Through the early part of 2002, my own future role became no clearer. I still thought about it, but not so much in the expectation of an early return to government, as in the context of how I would get on with my life if that didn't happen. Before the election, Tony had told me he wanted to appoint me to a non-cabinet role, to accustom the party and the media to my being back in circulation. At the end of June, he appeared to have settled on a suitable post. Belgium's Prime Minister Guy Verhofstadt had set up a working group to chart the future of the EU after its projected expansion from fifteen to twenty-five member states, and Tony told me he planned to name me as Britain's delegate. It was a job he knew I'd do well. It was in a policy area – Europe and Britain's vision of the EU – that was important to both of us. Anji phoned me later that night to say the decision had been made. 'It's all been cleared,' she said. 'Congratulations.' But when I went to see Tony the following day, the clarity was gone, muddied by last-minute fears that my Euro-enthusiasm would unsettle Tony's relations with Gordon. Jack was against it too. 'I just can't do it,' Tony said. 'I'm very sorry. I can't.' He decided to give the post to David Miliband – a good choice, though I was left pretty much where I had been since he had fired me.

My friends were all telling me the same thing. None of them suggested that I abandon hope of a political recovery, probably because they felt it was unlikely that I would do so. I remember talking at this time to John Sawers, Tony's former foreign affairs private secretary and the Ambassador in Cairo, who I was visiting. He was very plugged in: 'Nothing is going to happen soon, if at all,' he told me, displaying the insight befitting a future head of MI6. 'Focus on Brussels, not London. That's where you're more likely to come back. In the meantime, he said, 'Get a life.'

The first step I took was to get a house. My flat in Pembroke Villas had been home since I had sold Northumberland Place. It was perfectly adequate, if a bit cramped. I decided to move somewhere more modest and low-key, in Archel Road, off the North End Road in Fulham.

The second step was to help create a new advertising agency, CHI, with a key player in Labour's 2001 election campaign, Johnny Hornby, who also happened to be Robert Harris's brother-in-law. It became a huge success – with little thanks to my creative genius – and when it was later partly sold off, I made enough from my small share to buy my current home near Regent's Park

I also extended my wingspan to Asia, and China in particular. I visited its main cities, in the interior as well as on the fast-developing coast. My familiarity with the country also grew from talking over many years to a living legend, the founder of Singapore, Lee Kuan Yew. I had originally met 'Harry Lee', as he is always called, through Charles Powell, and he taught me not only about China but about Asia as a whole, and why the world will continue to tilt east for a long time to come.

Of all the friends who helped clarify my thinking in those days, none was more important than my former election aide and DTI adviser, Ben Wegg-Prosser. He knew that I still hoped eventually to return to the cabinet, and was honest enough to tell me that it would not come easily, if at all. He did not go so far as to cite Tony's famous test of the success of New Labour: the need for the party to learn to 'love Peter Mandelson'. That did not appear imminent. What he did say was that any prospect of re-establishing my political career depended on colleagues and the media coming to what seemed an equally unlikely conclusion: 'It's about time we had Peter back; he's done some interesting things out of office, and now it's right that he should be back in the government.'

He urged me to find a platform outside government, outside Number 10, outside Tony. He said that I had to reconnect with like-minded colleagues, not least because some of them might feel that I 'could have been closer to them in the past'. This was a delicate way of telling me that I had not always been the best at reaching out, or down, when I was flying high. Much as I enjoyed the working side of the Commons, it is true that I was never a natural tea-room politician. I am sure that my relations also suffered early on from the fact that I had given too little time to the more conventional concerns of a new MP while I worked so closely with Tony and Gordon. He told me to normalise my life. Get out, dine and talk with friends, stop worrying about the media, relax, read more books – even if it meant 'spending less time supporting Number 10 and making it clear that you are not always available'.

He concluded with a message that could only have come from a friend as attuned to me politically and personally as Ben. It was difficult to read. It was also right. 'Being seen to constantly apologise and serve your penance following the Hinduja affair may not be very attractive, but it is what TB and others will want to see you do again and again before they move in your direction.' Ben knew, of course, how difficult I would find it to prostrate myself for a sin I – and Hammond – knew I had not committed. 'None of this will be easy,' he said. 'But some of it will be fun, and you can get something from it in the long run. And we will all help you get there.'

I did broadly take his advice – with one exception. Though I managed to restrain myself from picking new fights over my firing, I could not bring myself to apologise for things I hadn't done. In fact, I sent Tony some papers I had come across in my office which further bore out my own account. This led to a second inquiry. I predicted that Hammond was never going to drop his bizarre reasoning regarding the phone call to the Home Office, and I was right. But his second report did reinforce the conclusion that I had not acted improperly. The media coverage of 'Hammond Two' interpreted

Downing Street's response as the closest thing to an apology it could have given. That helped clear away any barrier to my looking forward rather than backwards from now on.

Without the pressures of government, I had more time on my hands, and this was a welcome opportunity to get back in touch with old friends. I even found I had the time to enjoy simple pleasures such as going to the theatre and the cinema. My film tastes are eclectic, but for sheer relaxation you can't beat an old James Bond. Perhaps the most difficult aspect of this period of adjustment involved my extended family. Bobby and Jack adapted well at first to the move from Hillsborough, a canine wonderland, to London. But before long Bobby found that big-city life was not for him, especially being shut indoors all day. My wonderfully supportive government driver, Harry Small, finally suggested that he might be happier with a willing family he had helped to find in Kent. One weekend we took him to meet his new would-be owners, a couple and their three children. Bobby barely looked back. I, however, was heartbroken, and was already in tears as we began the drive back to London.

I started engaging more with my PLP colleagues, from old friends such as Party Chairman Charles Clarke to recent New Labour entrants from the previous election. I spoke more often in the Commons, both on matters affecting Hartlepool and on wider issues, especially Europe. I assumed the chairmanship of an organisation called Policy Network. Set up as an international think tank, it was more a mechanism for allowing politicians and thinkers to explore how progressive ideas in Britain, Europe and the US could inform policy responses to the problems all governments faced. In a series of conferences over the next few years, we would bring together not only prominent European politicians, but other leaders ranging from Bill Clinton to Brazil's President Lula da Silva and South Africa's Thabo Mbeki. I travelled for speaking engagements in Europe, the Middle East, Africa and America. I even started writing a regular column for *GQ* magazine. I was careful to say nothing of great political controversy. As a result, I said nothing of great consequence.

I became the chair of a political, academic and business partnership called the UK–Japan Twenty-First Century Group. I worked with the cross-party Britain in Europe group, which I had helped organise with the Liberal Democrat leader Charles Kennedy and Tory Euro-enthusiasts Ken Clarke and Michael Heseltine after my first resignation. Its executive director was a young Scottish Lib Dem, Danny Alexander, whom I came to know well and to like.

But Tony was uncomfortable with my taking on any domestic political role that might prove controversial in the party and the media, or unsettling for Gordon. At one point, we exchanged faxes on how I might best deal with the 'big personality' problem he saw in my formally coming back. 'Do you have any other suggestions I might pursue in order to shrink my persona?' I asked. His answer, with an exclamation mark presumably intended to take the place of a hand on the shoulder and an ironic chuckle, was 'Genuine "in the soul" humility!' That took little effort. It is not hard to be humble when you have been humiliated twice.

I have kept copies of other notes Tony and I exchanged after my second resignation. In one of them, I reflected that understanding one's position was the first step to doing something about it. 'I am not a natural politician in certain respects,' I wrote. 'I do not always mix easily. There are reasons for this, but when you have been on the receiving end of so much personal nastiness, you develop a shell and an insularity as a means of protection.' But I felt that I was a happier, more relaxed and less imperious person than I had been before my first experience of forced humility. I was also learning another lesson. It was a much more difficult one for any politician, and was probably not fully absorbed until I left Westminster for Brussels a few years later – the need to separate my ambitions from the reasons I had entered politics in the first place: developing policy, solving problems, helping to effect change.

The hopes for change with which we had entered our second term seemed to be fading. Yes, we had a big majority. Moreover, the Tories had replaced William Hague as leader with Iain Duncan Smith, who not only lacked his parliamentary skills and rhetorical flair, but owed his leadership victory over Ken Clarke to the Tories' comfort zone: Euroscepticism, or perhaps more accurately, Europhobia. The source of our electoral strength lay in the centre ground of British politics, and there seemed little prospect of him challenging us there. But there appeared to be limited enthusiasm in the PLP for Tony's reform agenda, and no sign that Gordon was inclined to help. There was even ferment within Number 10 itself. Alastair's role had been evolving. So had his mood, and his relationship with Tony. They were still close, but by the final year of the first term, with the government being accused of favouring spin over substance, Tony had begun to feel that Alastair's high profile and volatility were creating problems. His role had now shifted to focusing on overall political and media strategy, rather than briefings to the press. He was still at Tony's side, but he seemed frustrated and disillusioned, and attracted by the idea of leaving.

There were two other familiar faces in unfamiliar places. One of them was me. I was in no way a major player at Number 10, but by the summer of 2002 I was again in regular touch not only with Tony, but with Philip and even with Alastair. The other personnel change included Anji Hunter. Tony had gone ahead with his plan to give her an enhanced role after the election, but it did not go smoothly. Anji's new job, and new status, overshadowed the part Sally Morgan had played as his main political liaison, and Sally left to become a minister in the Lords. The real problem with the arrangement, as both Tony and I had known it would be, was Cherie. She, and most of Downing Street, had been told months earlier that Anji did not plan to stay on. When Tony revealed that he had decided to promote Anji and get her to stay, Cherie was furious. Tony was torn. He felt that he needed Anji, but he knew it would be impossible to keep her unless Cherie relented. He asked me to speak to Cherie. I found her even angrier than I had expected, and she launched into an attack on Anji's character and political skills.

It did not take long for everyone to realise the new arrangement wasn't going to work, and towards the end of 2001 Anji left for a high-flying job at BP. Like me, she continued to talk often to Tony, who relied on the unique mix of friendship, support and Middle England political antennae she had always provided. But things were not the same. Sally later returned as Tony's political aide, and he would come to rely on her even more during his final years in Number 10.

I had always liked Cherie, and what I liked most about her were the qualities that could sometimes make her difficult. She was opinionated, strong-willed, and never hid her emotions. She was capable of extreme acts of kindness, as I had been reminded after my first resignation, but she could also be brusque to those around her and Tony. She could throw her arms around you one day, and ignore you the next. Once, during a Policy Network conference I organised involving Tony and Bill Clinton, she walked up to me, looked me straight in the eye, and actually accused me of trying to kill her husband. I thought at first that she was joking, but she said quite seriously that the conference demands I had put on him at the weekend would give him a heart attack. 'Back off,' she said protectively. She was at her fiercest when she thought Tony was being threatened, which was why she came to distrust and then despise Gordon. Tony would later tell me often that without Cherie's sheer strength and willpower, he could never have got through his toughest periods as Prime Minister. I am also sure he would have found life boring if he had shared it with someone less spirited than Cherie.

For Cherie, life with Tony was also hard. The successful young barrister I had first met at his side in the 1980s found it understandably difficult when, following his election as party leader in 1994, he was suddenly at the centre of the political stage, and she felt left behind. Entering Downing Street was even more testing. With little help from anyone, she was expected to transform her and her family's life and change their home, while Tony was catapulted into a world where his slightest wish would send aides and officials scurrying to do his bidding. He would try to defuse the occasional tension with humour. I remember visiting them on the Sunday evening after the 1997 election as they settled in to their flat above Number 11 Downing Street. As Cherie showed me around, with Tony trailing behind, I could see that it would take work to make it a real home for them and the children. It would obviously take a bit of money, too. But it would be fine, Tony joked, as long as she 'kept her Imelda Marcos instincts in check'. Still, the burdens and pressures of office were real for both of them, with Cherie less shielded from them.

The most urgent issue now among Tony's core aides and advisers was the emergence of a faultline over key items of his policy agenda. A reformist core believed in the need for a radical overhaul, and an opening up, of public services. This group included me, Jonathan, Andrew Adonis and Anji. Some had misgivings, most of all Alastair. He accepted the broad case for reform, but more as a communications concept than an act of policy. He was uncomfortable with anything that smacked too much of market competition where state schools or the NHS were concerned. In his view, the first-term accomplishments which had most galvanised the party were 'cutting-edge from the left' – things like the minimum wage, and fairness-at-work legislation. That, rather than politically risky reforms, was the kind of policy he felt Tony ought to be pursuing now.

Then there was Gordon. His reasons for resistance were different. One of them was open and explicit: he wanted the Treasury to retain overall control of all domestic reform. He was dismissive and disparaging towards the ministers Tony had placed in charge. But while he was careful never fully to abandon the New Labour ship, he also understood the potency of an unsettled PLP as a means of weakening Tony, and encouraging a sense that he was losing the 'trust' of the party.

Given all the pressures and uncertainty around him, I was not surprised when Tony took me aside and for the first time raised the prospect of quitting. He would not leave immediately; he would serve out his full second term. But he was beginning to sense that unless he did something dramatic to reclaim the political initiative, the prospect of accomplishing the central goals of his government was slipping away. He was intrigued by the example of another European Prime Minister for whom he felt a personal fondness and political respect. Spain's José María Aznar had won re-election in 2000, and shortly afterwards had declared that his second term would be his last. 'It seems to be working for Aznar,' Tony said. 'Why not me?' I am sure he expected me to try to argue him out of it. I did point out the obvious potential dangers. It might weaken him, or even make him a lame duck. But I understood the attraction. 'What you have to judge is the effects of doing it,' I told him. 'If you really conclude that it will free you to govern with greater confidence, and with freedom from all these distractions, then it has to be worth considering.' He asked others as well. Alastair was broadly neutral. Like me, he said Tony would have to weigh the likely impact on his own position and his government's. Sally was against, convinced it would weaken him. Cherie was even more so, and not only because of the political implications. Long suspicious of Gordon, she was by now furious with him. She believed he was not suited to become Prime Minister, and that given the way he was behaving towards Tony, he did not deserve to be.

For a brief period in the early summer of 2002, Tony was drawing closer to taking the 'Aznar option'. In the end, two things swayed him against it. The first was familiar, and seasonal. While he and Cherie were on a short holiday in Cumbria, Tony found the renewed energy and determination that always seemed to come with a summer break, and the prospect of addressing party conference in the autumn. The second factor had nothing to do with the policy concerns that had dominated our discussions before the summer. Like the terror attacks of 9/11, it had not even been on the policy agenda at the beginning of Tony's second term as Prime Minister, but it would go on to overshadow it. It was the American government's determination to force Iraq's President Saddam Hussein to give up his programmes for weapons of mass destruction, and Tony's view that this was both necessary and right.

When Tony returned from holiday I was on a visit to Indonesia, Malaysia, Thailand and Singapore, delivering a series of speeches on behalf of the London-based Asia House on relations between the Western world and Islam. My message was straightforward. The challenge of the post-9/11 world was to defeat terror, not to embark on a 'clash of civilisations'. Osama bin Laden was not an embodiment, but a perversion, of Islam. All the Abrahamic faiths shared a commitment to certain values, and we needed to use this common ground to find a common language, and to make common cause. My words were well received, but in the question-and-answer sessions the focus turned towards the growing signs that America, and quite possibly Britain, might be ready to consider military action against Iraq. For some in the audience, this seemed to belie my message of consensus and conciliation. President Bush, and Tony, saw disarming Saddam as a necessary part of defeating terror. For many Muslims I met in Asia, it looked more like a crusade of convenience against an Arab state whose political culture – antipathy towards Israel, and distrust of America – they themselves shared. This worried me.

When I got home, I went to see Tony in the back garden at Number 10. I had been heartened by his recent visit to Camp David, where he had persuaded President Bush to work through the United Nations, rather than take precipitate military action against Iraq. I was reassured by Tony's determination to build up diplomatic pressure that might, just, succeed in disarming Saddam. But if that failed, I said that the argument for war would be much harder to make than had been the case with Afghanistan after the terrorist attacks on America. 'There are a lot of Muslims out there who will not understand this,' I told him. 'They feel this has nothing to do with 9/11. It's not an open-and-shut case for many people around the world.' He smiled and rolled his eyes. 'For God's sake,' he said, 'have you been spending all your time with George Galloway?'

His response said less about my views, or George Galloway's, than about his own. One of Tony's strengths was that he was a big-issue leader. That is not to say that he did not do policy detail. But he worked from first principles. Where Iraq was concerned, these soon overwhelmed everything else. They led to a kind of tunnel vision, which got in the way of his dealing thoroughly with some of the political nuances, and practical implications, of the campaign against Saddam. As military preperations intensified, those who had reservations of the sort I had raised were lumped together in his mind with anyone who he felt wasn't 100 per cent on board. The distinctions between them became blurred in Tony's mind.

In some ways, Tony had rarely been stronger than during the weeks leading up to our party conference in the autumn of 2002, but even then, there were intimations of the fights that lay ahead. The most difficult and debilitating – the fall out from the Iraq war – was still to come. Without it, the other policy battles might well have been less bitter. Yet it was already clear that there would be opposition to much of his agenda. The more forceful, the more prime ministerial, Tony became, the more he had to reckon on trouble from the increasingly impatient Prime Minister-in-waiting in Number 11. Tony phoned me shortly before midnight a few days before his speech. He was in a foul mood. He had just had a meeting with Gordon, who had ridiculed his drive for public service reform, and pressed for shared control over the policy agenda ahead of what he really wanted: a move into Number 10 before the end of the second term. 'He's behaving outrageously,' Tony fumed. 'This time, he's gone too far.' When I asked him how he had replied, Tony said, 'I told Gordon he will have my answer next week – at conference.' Yet when conference came, he stepped back from confronting him. Anji, who said she had never heard Tony so angry at Gordon as he was at the time of their pre-conference bust-up, told me, 'This time, it really is a parting of the ways.' But it never came to that.

In the months after conference, as political pressure built over Iraq, Tony did again sometimes come close to breaking point. In late November, an Andrew Rawnsley column in the *Observer* claimed that relations between him and Gordon had never been worse. It portrayed Gordon as a social-democratic knight in armour defending party and country against Tony's 'Tory' approach to public service reform. Tony phoned me, furious. 'I'm totally fed up with Gordon and his game-playing,' he said. 'He'll find he's gone too far this time.' Of course, it turned out again that he hadn't.

When we spoke a few days later, Tony was no less frustrated. 'The government is being held back by Gordon in so many ways,' he said. He was tempted, again, to move the Chancellor – particularly with new economic figures showing that growth was down on Treasury forecasts, and public borrowing was sharply up. For the first time, he even dropped his mantra about Gordon's achievements on the economy. 'He's a good macro Chancellor,' Tony said, 'but he's a terrible micro Chancellor. He interferes all over the place. He messes things up. He's created huge costs in administration with things like tax credits. The pensions credits are costing us £2.5 billion to administer. It would be cheaper just to restore the earnings link for pensioners.' But he feared replacing Gordon would risk all-out insurgency. 'There are three groups in the Labour Party,' he said, returning to one of his favourite refrains. 'There's Old Labour. There are people who are not Old Labour, and will follow New Labour, but who aren't really New Labour. And there are those who are genuinely New Labour.' 'Who are they?' I asked. He replied, 'Me. You. And that's about it.'

While Tony felt he could not fire the Chancellor, he seemed determined not to bow to him either. 'There's no point in being Prime Minister and not getting your way,' he said. He had genuinely been minded to take the Aznar option, and not fight for a third term, but now he was no longer sure about leaving. He was certainly not going to do so unless he got through what he wanted during the second term. He felt he had spent his first four years as Prime Minister 'clearing the ground', and getting an understanding of the changes necessary in the economy, social policy and public services. 'Now I've got only eighteen months or so before everything starts moving towards the next election campaign,' he said. 'I've got eighteen months to do what needs to be done. If I don't – or if I fail – that is my record. I cannot let anything stand in my way.'

I had come to an Aznar decision of my own. Before the party conference, I told Tony I had decided to stand down as an MP at the next election. I was simply not doing enough in national politics to make my life fulfilling and challenging. I would still be available to consult, advise, support – like Anji. But from outside Westminster. Tony responded by urging me to hold off on a final decision for a year or so. I was non-committal. But in my own mind, I saw little prospect of a sufficient change in my situation, or in Tony's, to alter my thinking.

As Tony dealt with the twin pressures of Gordon and Saddam Hussein, however, we not only spoke much more often in the final months of 2002, he also began involving me more directly in a variety of issues with the team in Downing Street. My formal return was probably accelerated by a personal crisis that, for a brief period in early December, hit Tony very hard. It was dubbed 'Cheriegate' by the *Mail on Sunday*, which started it all, and involved Cherie's purchase of a pair of flats in Bristol, where Euan, their eldest son, was beginning university. She had relied on the help of Peter Foster, a dodgy former boyfriend of Carole Caplin's. I was in New York at the time of the initial Downing Street denials that Foster, a convicted fraudster, had acted as Cherie's 'business adviser' in buying the flats. I got a call from Michael White, political editor of the *Guardian*, asking me what I made of the controversy. I did what I could, with what little I knew, to explain it away. As the week went on, I was aware that media pressure was building. I had heard that Alastair – and Fiona, as Cherie's media adviser – were not best pleased about this latest example of what they had long seen as the pernicious influence of Ms Caplin. Still, I thought little more of the matter until I arrived at Heathrow on the following Sunday. When I switched on my mobile, I saw a series of messages, all from Number 10. Moments later, the switchboard called again and said Tony wanted to be put through urgently.

I had rarely heard him so upset. Revelations in Thursday's *Daily Mail* of email exchanges between Cherie and Foster made it clear that he had indeed played a role in helping with the purchase of the flats. But what distressed Tony even more was an attack on Cherie from Alastair in that morning's *Sunday Telegraph*. Quoting 'friends of Mr Campbell', the article said that he and Fiona were furious at Cherie for 'allowing a convicted conman to get close to the Prime Minister'. Tony said that he, Cherie and Alastair had been at loggerheads all weekend, and asked if I could help find a way forward.

I arrived at the Downing Street flat shortly before noon. Tony was on one of the sofas in the sitting room, looking pale. He ran through the allegations swirling around Cherie, and the facts as he understood them. She had been naïve. She had fallen into using Foster as an intermediary through Carole. She had not known about his background. Tony said her reluctance to submit to Alastair's questions about the affair had not been an act of dishonesty: unaware of Foster's past, she had felt protective of Carole, especially given Alastair's record of hostility to her. She was also embarrassed by the media furore the affair had unleashed: 'But Alastair's going around claiming Cherie and I misled him. He's saying Cherie's a liar, and that she's embarrassed him with the media.' Tony added a postscript that had struck me as well: 'He's doing to Cherie exactly what he did to you on the Hinduja stuff. He takes a grain of truth about what you've said, he turns it around into something it isn't, and then he takes a position. It becomes about Alastair as much as it's about the facts, and then he turns against you. I am not going to allow him to do the same to Cherie.' Even without Alastair personalising things, however, the situation was difficult, and it was getting worse with each day's headlines. It was painful for both of them.

After Tony and I had been speaking for nearly an hour, Cherie walked in. She was in her dressing gown, and looked more exhausted than Tony. He said nothing to her. 'Tony,' I suggested, 'why doesn't Cherie sit down, and we'll talk the whole thing through?' Cherie took her place on the other sofa. I was in an armchair in between them. Before Cherie had arrived, Tony had been broadly defending her, but as I asked Cherie to explain what had happened, and how Foster had become involved, he interrupted. 'Oh, Cherie, why on *earth* did you do that? Why would you write emails like that? The whole thing is so ridiculous!' Finally I said to Tony that I didn't think his reaction was helping things, and tried to get Cherie to unburden herself about the entire series of events, misunderstandings and mis-steps of the previous few weeks. All told, it was a long, uncomfortable ninety minutes or more. It left me – and both of them – clear that we had to provide convincing answers to the growing tide of questions in the media.

From Monday, amid a cold war between the Blairs and Alastair and Fiona, I became point man and arbitrator in working out the response. It was hardly helped by a fresh *Mail* allegation that Cherie had phoned Foster's solicitor, at Carole's urging, when he was fighting deportation to his native Australia. Nor by Alastair's unabated rage. The two of us had by now gone some way to repairing our relationship, but it was still only two years since he had helped to force my resignation from cabinet in what seemed like similar circumstances. I had sympathy with Cherie's plight. I could see that Alastair would have forced *her* to resign, if only he could have worked out what she would be resigning from. He did at one point demand that Tony extract an undertaking from her to withdraw completely from public life. Tony refused. In the end, the price of Alastair's staying at Tony's side was an agreement – accepted as sensible by all of us – that the Blairs cut all ties with Carole.

We all recognised that the only way we could draw a line under the affair was for Cherie to provide a full account of what had happened, and an apology. On Tuesday, she had an early-evening public engagement in central London. That afternoon I joined Alastair, Fiona and Sally Morgan to begin drafting the main points of the statement she would make. Tony was at first reluctant to have her speak, fearing that any acknowledgement of error would be seized on as an admission of guilt. But in the end he, and Cherie, agreed. Fortunately, she never saw the original editorial suggestions made by Alastair and Fiona, which would essentially have had her admitting to being the worst person in the world. I steered us towards wording that Cherie might actually be willing to use.

After making her own minor amendments, she delivered a frank, honest, at times almost tearful explanation of her actions. She said her initial instincts had been those of a mother with a son leaving home for the first time to start university: to protect his and the family's privacy. She said she was an ordinary woman acting under extraordinary circumstances. 'I am sorry if I have embarrassed anyone. But the people who know me well, know that I would never want to harm anyone, least of all Tony or the children or the Labour government.' Her speech lanced the boil, and the controversy faded away. So did Tony's fury with Alastair, who would remain a key player as the far more serious challenge of Iraq came to a head in the new year.

I was now meeting Alastair and Philip in Downing Street each Wednesday afternoon to talk political strategy, after which we would join Tony in his office. Of all the domestic and international policy issues that came up, inevitably Iraq worried me the most. Tony still wanted to press the UN route. He hoped it would succeed. But what if it didn't? I felt that he was right to believe that if the threat of force did not work, force itself would become the only realistic option. Of course, I would have been much, much more cautious had I known that Saddam did not have weapons of mass destruction, but not even Tony's most strident PLP critics doubted at the time that Iraq's WMD programmes existed. I had other concerns, however, even if we did attack and defeat Saddam. 'What happens after you've won?' I asked Tony in January 2003. 'You can go in there, you can take out Saddam, but what do you do with Iraq? You're going to have a country on your hands. I don't know what your plan is. I don't know how you're going to do it. Who is going to run the place?' Tony replied: 'That's the Americans' responsibility. It's down to the Americans.' I said I certainly hoped they knew what they were doing.

As the invasion drew nearer, I had another worry. In a series of phone calls with Tony, and finally in a long discussion at Number 10, I told him I feared he was losing the political argument at home. 'Nobody knows exactly why you're doing this,' I said. 'There has to be a compelling reason. Is it weapons of mass destruction? Saddam's killing of the Kurds? Using chemical weapons? Is it just that he's a bad guy? A regional threat? A totalitarian? I mean, what is the compelling reason?' At first Tony brushed me off, no doubt bracketing me with hard-line anti-war protesters. He felt these people did not want to hear the reasons, and when they did, they would oppose him anyway. I replied that the protesters weren't the problem. It was many, many others. 'You've got to write down what the core argument is, what the central justification is. If you're not clear, nobody else is clear, and if you go on like this you're losing the argument.' He did write it out. The argument turned out to be a combination of reasons, but three above all: Saddam had WMDs; he had played games with and defied the international community in the past; and crucially, after 9/11, with a new brand of terror limited only by the targets it could hit and the weaponry it could acquire, the world could not afford inaction.

This would form the core of the message Tony delivered in the early part of March 2003, as efforts faltered to secure a diplomatic solution. Despite my misgivings, I agreed with him in the end, although he never asked me directly whether I did. Shortly before the invasion, Alastair and I were talking when he suddenly asked me, 'Do you think we're right to be doing this?' I couldn't help but laugh. 'Gosh,' I said, 'it's a bit late to ask that, isn't it? I thought you've made up your minds.'

He said, 'Well, we have.'

'And?' I replied.

'And we're going to do it,' said Alastair.

The US-led invasion began on 20 March. Despite the early military successes and the rapid toppling of Saddam, the political price was enormous. Most of the British public, and most MPs, had backed the invasion. A significant minority had been sceptical, or opposed. The same was true of the Labour backbenches. Once the euphoria over Saddam's fall had passed, the political mood darkened. At the end of May, the criticism gathered new force with a report on Radio 4's *Today* programme. At issue was the intelligence dossier released by Number 10 to make the WMD case in the run-up to the war. *Today* reporter Andrew Gilligan quoted an unnamed intelligence source as saying that the government had 'sexed up' the document to strengthen the argument for war. The story was offensive, and false. It might have faded within a few days, however, if Gilligan had not gone on to name Alastair as the alleged sexer-up of the dossier. That was also false, but it became the catalyst for a counter-attack by Alastair on Gilligan, and on the BBC. He wrote to the BBC's head of news, Richard Sambrook, who replied that the BBC would apologise if the story turned out to be false, but broadly defended *Today*'s report, not on the grounds that the BBC was certain it was true, but that it reflected reasonable and accurate reporting of what Gilligan's source had told him. Even that would turn out to be wrong.

Alastair was furious. When Channel 4 asked if he would rebut the letter on air, he rashly made his way across town to do so. First he cleared it with Tony, who added a caveat, although since he knew Alastair at least as well as I did, he must have known it was pointless. 'Be calm. Be careful,' he said. 'Don't go over the top.' Alastair did the opposite. Prodded with questions, did say that if the BBC apologised, 'we can move on'. But he attacked the 'weasel words' of Sambrook, and said the BBC was defending a travesty of journalistic values. Then he raised the stakes. This was not just an assault on him, it was 'a fundamental attack upon the integrity of the government, the Prime Minister, the intelligence agencies. . .' Given the letter of Gilligan's report, he was not wrong, but turning this into a battle over Tony's fitness to govern was the last thing anyone needed. I did not blame Alastair. Given the circumstances, there was no way he was going to keep his cool. But I did wish that Tony had just said no when the Channel 4 invitation came. I told him so as soon as the interview was over, and he agreed.

We tried to de-escalate the situation. I told Alastair that I understood his anger, and his determination to get the BBC to acknowledge Gilligan's errors. But things were in danger of getting out of control. Alastair did make an effort to rein in his anger, and I talked to a number of senior BBC figures to explore a basis for both sides stepping back. But then a whole new tragic dimension emerged. Dr David Kelly, an internationally respected British expert on biological warfare and a former UN inspector in Iraq, came forward and told his employer, the Ministry of Defence, that it was he who had spoken to Gilligan. This was an act of honesty, under no doubt insufferable pressure. If Kelly was indeed the source for the *Today* report, it was also evidence of laziness or dishonesty on Gilligan's part. Kelly was an expert on biological warfare, but he was not an intelligence source, and had had no part in drawing up the dossier. After the MoD revealed that a source had come forward, journalists began zeroing in on the name. When asked if it was David Kelly, the

MoD confirmed it. Eight days later, having testified to one Commons committee and with the prospect of appearing before another, Kelly disappeared after going for a walk near his home in Oxfordshire. His wife raised the alarm, and a a few hours later his body was found. He had committed suicide.

On hearing the news, I felt sickened. I felt a kind of shame, too, at the human stakes when political arguments got out of hand. And I felt anger: at the rush to suggest that the government was somehow complicit, but with not a shred of contrition from Gilligan, *Today* or the BBC. If I felt all these things, I knew Alastair was feeling them more painfully. I phoned him, and told him to try to take a step back. Kelly's death was a tragedy, but Alastair had not caused it. He said he felt devastated, and he now knew for certain that he had had enough of Downing Street, of the pressure cooker of politics.

I was pretty sure he was right. For too long he had been operating on low batteries. His relations with the media had become increasingly difficult, his animosity towards them more pointed. Invaluable as Alastair was as one of the last surviving members of the original inner circle in Number 10, I sensed that even Tony was now reconciled to his going. I said none of this to Alastair. I spoke to him not as a strategist, something he clearly didn't need, but as a friend. I deliberately built him up, believing that he would only come to the right decision through strength, not weakness. 'Don't cave in. That's what they want you to do,' I told him. 'We know who you are. Just hang in.'

Tony was flying to Tokyo for summit talks when he was told about the death of Dr Kelly. In a statement issued before they landed, his spokesman said that Tony was 'obviously very distressed for the family', and that an inquiry would be set up to investigate the circumstances leading to the scientist's death. As he emerged for a news conference at the end of the day, however, I doubt that anything could have prepared him for the question shouted out by Jonathan Oliver, then the number-two political man for the *Mail on Sunday*. I imagine he saw himself as the star in some made-for-TV American docudrama. He may still see this as his finest hour. For me, it showed what is most distressing about our contemporary political journalism. It was not the issue he raised: whether the government was somehow responsible for Kelly's suicide. I was certain that the answer was no, and that only Kelly himself would ever fully know why he took his own life. Still, that would not in itself have been an unfair question. What angered me was the preening theatricality with which he shouted his challenge: 'Have you got blood on your hands, Prime Minister?'

Tony called from Tokyo. 'This is the lowest point,' he said, very quietly. He knew that David Kelly's blood was not on his hands. His own involvement in the battle over Gilligan's report had consisted largely of trying to find a way to de-escalate it. As Alastair's private diaries would later confirm, once Kelly had come forward to reveal that he had talked to Gilligan, Tony was hesitant about moves to make his name public. Still, he was weighed down by sadness that the train of events should have ended with a fifty-nine-year-old scientist losing his life. He knew that Alastair would face public questioning from Lord Hutton, the senior judge heading the inquiry he established, but he was confident that he would be shown to have acted in good faith throughout. He also knew that Alastair's departure from Number 10 was now inevitable: 'He can't stay on. He's a marked man.'

Tony spoke about Alastair as he only did about the few people around him who had become not just aides or colleagues, but political family: with an affection tempered by insight into both his strengths and his weaknesses. 'I don't know what we'll do without Alastair. He's irreplaceable,' he said. But he added, 'It's gone too far. I've had to begin to order him not to do things. He's totally headstrong. In the end, I think, he's just got too big for his boots. I think I've always had a sense of humility, despite what people sometimes say. At times in government, maybe too much.' But not Alastair, he said, at least not recently. Without that core humility, he felt, politics almost always ended badly, reminding me of earlier advice he had offered to me.

What most worried Tony was not Alastair. Nor was it Hutton, at least not yet. It was not even Iraq, at least directly. It was the cumulative effect, the grinding erosion of trust, and the fact that this was being fed and encouraged by Gordon. 'We're disabled from fighting back by the black cloud next door,' Tony said to me after his Tokyo news conference. 'I could handle any of this, if it wasn't for the constant undermining.'

The undermining had come to a head the previous month, with a major test for the public service reforms in the Commons. The issue was the creation of new 'foundation hospitals'. The idea had been conceived by Alan Milburn, and its aim was to give the most successful hospitals more independence within the NHS. Gordon had fought the plan from the start. At first it was a simple turf war, and he used much the same argument he had made against my plan to allow the Royal Mail to borrow, invest and expand. But ultimately it was a clash between Chancellor and Prime Minister, and a proxy war between Gordon and Alan Milburn.

Alan would not allow his reforms to be picked apart without a struggle, and many of his original provisions did make their way into the Bill that went before Parliament in May 2003. Crucial aspects were either shelved or pared back, however. Although the Bill was passed, dozens of Labour MPs rebelled. For weeks, Gordon and his team had tacitly, in some cases openly, given succour to its critics. When I spoke to Tony a few days later, he was in no doubt that the pattern had been set for a full-scale battle over all his reforms. 'What I want to do is being blocked by Gordon,' he said. He feared that if he fought back, he would risk splitting the party: he was sure that at least a quarter, and maybe as many as two-thirds, of Labour MPs would line up against him if he took on the Chancellor.

Tony warned me not to underestimate Gordon. He was one of the two big figures in the government, and had political, strategic and intellectual depth – and deviousness. Tony said that he was no longer sure what Gordon believed in policy terms. 'Perhaps he's another version of New Labour. Perhaps not New Labour at all.' But he was sure that the policies mattered less than the politics. Gordon was giving that part of the Labour Party that wanted to delude itself about policy the grounds on which to delude itself. He could inflict huge political damage on Tony.

He had certainly damaged Alan, who resigned in June 2003, the month after the Commons vote. The official explanation was that he felt front-line politics was giving him too little time to spend with his wife and children. That was true, but it was not the only reason. Alan was incensed by the whittling away of the health reform package. Tony had repeatedly told him to forge ahead with the changes needed to deliver genuine competition and choice in the NHS, but when the crunch had come, he had compromised in the face of Gordon's objections. Alan not only felt bitterly disappointed, he felt betrayed.

When I had first told Tony of my decision to leave Parliament, he had told me to be patient. Alan's departure from the cabinet reinforced my view that it was time to go, and I told Tony that my mind was now made up not to stand at the next election. I had decided that my future lay, if not outside politics, certainly outside government. But if not much had changed for me in the intervening months, Tony's situation had changed dramatically. Iraq was unravelling, and the political fallout was getting worse. Opposition to his public service reforms was mounting among Labour backbenchers. Gordon was increasingly determined to push him out. Alastair would soon be gone. Tony felt cornered.

He told me that he needed me actively involved again in Number 10. He needed me to help him fight back.

9

Back in the Shadows

Over the year that followed, I would not only work more closely with Tony than at any time since 1997, aiding the effort to rescue his premiership; I would also reconnect in a different way with Gordon, my former friend who was now determined to drive him out. By the time it was over, Tony would survive, and emerge strengthened, at least for a while. Gordon would be badly damaged. And I would leave Westminster altogether.

I slipped into Downing Street a few days after Tony got back from Tokyo in July 2003. He felt too weak to fend off Gordon's challenge, much less defeat it. He was weighed down by Iraq – 'an albatross around my neck,' he said – and saw his hopes for making a success of the second term draining away. Especially if the Hutton inquiry went badly, he feared that before long he might not be Prime Minister at all. The role I took was kept secret from all but the key political staff inside Number 10, and certainly from Gordon, for as long as possible. Tony also kept his own fears well hidden from Gordon, and his intentions too. Those, it would later turn out, he sometimes kept secret even from me.

My feelings about Tony's predicament were complex. I absolutely wanted to help him, and felt it essential that he be given the space to govern. I felt this even more strongly because, in policy terms, I believed that we were far better placed than at any time after 1997 to make advances in the reforms needed. The key public service departments, Education and Health, were much better positioned to take the steps necessary to make state schools and the NHS more efficient and more responsive to the needs of pupils, parents and patients. The Number 10 policy unit, headed by Andrew Adonis, since David Miliband was now an MP, had done equally serious work.

Even allowing for the fact that, as Tony's favoured safety valve for his anger and frustration, I was getting an especially dramatic view of Gordon's machinations, I had no doubt that he did not share Tony's vision about the changes required. This was partly because he viewed public services as any Chancellor would, wishing to keep control over spending and borrowing. It was also because Gordon believed that Tony's ideas were not thought through, and that there just wasn't the depth of knowledge available to him in Number 10 to enable him to make sound judgements.

This, of course, was all quite convenient for Gordon, because there was another reason for his opposition: he saw a political opportunity to wrong-foot Tony in the party. In this, I believed that Gordon was harming his own cause as much as Tony's by positioning himself as an opponent of New Labour reform. At the beginning of the summer, he had actually replied to one of the occasional, conciliatory notes I still sent him, and we had talked. I tried to convince him that he was badly misjudging the situation if he thought political pressure would force Tony out. 'He's tougher than you think,' I said. I told him that if he cooperated with Tony, it would not just help Tony and the government, it would help Gordon himself when the time did come for the succession. But in Gordon's view, Tony was the problem, and a lack of 'trust' in him was damaging the whole government, and the whole party.

My first task was to try to strengthen Tony by bolstering the operation around him. From my earliest days in the Cabinet Office after 1997, I had tried to persuade him that he needed a more structured and politically effective way of working. That still hadn't really happened. It mattered more now, because Tony was so much weaker. The political 'faultline' in his team had grown more serious as well. There was still the core of out-and-out enthusiasts for his reform agenda: Andrew Adonis, Jonathan Powell, and me. Most of the rest were now more sceptical, or at least more cautious, as a result of Tony's weakened position. Sally Morgan, his key liaison with the party, certainly was. It was not that she objected to the principle of Tony's reforms, on the contrary. But rather, in surveying the political landscape she saw threats on every side. Iraq. A hostile media. Restive MPs. Angry unions. Gordon. She told Tony that if he persisted with his evangelical passion for reform, he would not only lose the party, he might lose his job. In the months after my return, Sally's warnings echoed in much of what Tony said and did. His heart told him to reform, but his head told him Sally was right. His first decision was to replace Andrew Adonis with Matthew Taylor as head of the Number 10 policy unit. Matthew was by instinct a reformer and moderniser, but was more sensitive to the compromises needed to ensure Tony's survival.

Tony had brought John Birt into Number 10 after the 2001 election, in the hope that he could use his experience in revamping the BBC to inject 'blue skies' thinking into the way policy priorities were identified and carried through. John, who was a close friend, became my main partner in the reorganisation project. To his critics, he seemed dry, cerebral, managerial. He was all of those things, but he was kind as well, as I had rediscovered in the days after my firing. He was also very bright, with a gift for breaking big problems into their component parts, and working on each with unflagging determination. Together with Tony's Principal Private Secretary, Jeremy Heywood, we now set out to reshape the way Tony worked.

At the centre of the new arrangement was a new 'Political Strategy Team'. Led by me, it would closely coordinate the work of the policy, strategy, and communications units in Number 10 under Tony's authority, and would report to him with proposals each week. We also outlined steps to improve the way Tony himself operated. We wanted to complement his so-called 'sofa government' with more formal meetings, a greater involvement of cabinet ministers, and better liaison with the PLP. We proposed weekly meetings between Tony and Gordon, accompanied by senior aides from Number 10 and the Treasury. We believed that all of this would help. The problem, which was obvious not only to us but to Tony, was that the effect would be limited if Gordon did not buy into it. As Tony left for his summer holiday, he told us to think radically, and to find some way to ensure that the Treasury came on board.

The result was the most closely held secret of my return to Downing Street. It was code-named 'Teddy Bear', and was known only to Tony and the handful of people involved in drawing it up, including John, Jonathan Powell and me. The name 'Teddy Bear' was chosen so as not to give away the slightest hint of its true meaning. It began with the premise that we had to face up to the fact that Gordon wanted Tony out. Barring the prospect of the two of them coming to a co-existence pact, things would surely get worse. There was certainly no reason to expect that Gordon would encourage us in our efforts to make Tony more effective. 'Teddy Bear' proposed major surgery. On the model of the United States, we suggested dividing the Treasury in two. A new Ministry of Finance would handle the macro-economics: taxation, international markets, financial services. A separate US-style Office of the Budget and Delivery (OBD) would be split off from the Treasury and placed either in the Cabinet Office or made a stand-alone department. It would deal with all government funding and spending. The idea was to leave Gordon with the Finance Ministry, but to put a different person, trusted by Tony, in charge of the departmental purse strings, so that the way was opened up for the reforms to advance.

When Tony got back from holiday at the end of August, he was sorely tempted by 'Teddy Bear', but he was hesitant about whether he should, or dared to, go ahead with it. He asked us to break down all the options, saying that he would make a final decision after party conference at the end of September. He seemed slightly more confident than he had been before his holiday, but the usual annual recharging was less marked than in earlier years. Except for me and the ever-steady Jonathan Powell, most of the fixed points on his political horizon were gone. Though Alastair had been talking about leaving for months before his battle with the BBC, his formal announcement at the end of August was not easy for any of us. It was not just that he had been with us from the start – there was tension over the timing of his departure. He felt that he should stay at least until party conference, and ideally until the Hutton inquiry reported in the new year. But Tony had decided that he should go almost immediately, and asked me to help him convince Alastair of this, which we had done at a meeting with him in Tony's flat in Downing Street. In an effort to bring a new, low-key stability to our relations with the media, Tony settled on David Hill, an old hand and an old friend, as Alastair's successor.

It was the last Monday of September when Gordon addressed the party conference in Bournemouth. Tony was not there – he was attending the funeral of Gareth Williams, Labour's leader in the Lords, who had died a few days earlier. Gordon had the stage to himself, and he used it audaciously. After a nod in the opening sentence of his speech to a 'Labour government led by Tony Blair', he proceeded to deliver a *cri de coeur* directed at all those in the party who were unsettled by Tony's policies, and by Iraq. His refrain was the need for the party to be truly Labour: 'I believe that at every point in our history, Labour needs not just a programme – but a soul.' It may have been unsubtle, but it was effective, setting out a clear, campaigning contrast between a zealously reformist Prime Minister and the true Labour alternative.

Tony spoke on the following day. He did not hit back at Gordon personally. That would come, if at all, with 'Teddy Bear'. Instead, he answered the political argument Gordon seemed to be making. Government was tough, he said. Opposition was easy, until you actually got there. Borrowing one of Gordon's favourite catchwords, he said that 'values' mattered – but only if you could put them into action. Far from retreating from reform, he said that he was determined to keep going: 'The reason I bang the drum for change is I get so angry that it takes so long, restless at how much there is to do. I want us to go faster, further.' He left the conference rattled, but somehow revived. Still, he knew that Gordon's speech would be a rallying point for opposition to his reforms.

By the third week of October, we had further refined 'Teddy Bear'. We would move competition policy and some of the functions of the DTI to the new scaled-down Finance Ministry to make it potentially more attractive to Gordon. Later still, it was envisaged as a further way of reconciling him to the proposals that the OBD should operate as a separate entity but within the Treasury.

We then drew up a summary of all Tony's options. Option one was to do nothing. That would keep a 'talented and proven' Chancellor in place. It would also be 'less disruptive', a phrase that would surely qualify for the Nobel Prize in understatement. Yet it would leave us with a continued stalemate.

The second option was what we called the 'enhanced status quo'. It would leave Gordon in charge of an unchanged Treasury, but with a new cabinet committee including Tony, Gordon and their top aides. Downing Street would also 'assert the Prime Minister's right to a more open dialogue' on tax and spending. We felt it was highly unlikely that the Treasury would go along with such a plan, which was much like what I had originally suggested to Tony, and to Gordon as well, when I was at the Cabinet Office and their tug-of-war was nowhere near as serious as it was now.

Option three proposed a more direct solution: leave the Treasury's structure unchanged, but move Gordon to the Foreign Office. The problem, and the reason Tony had resisted doing this before, was that he believed Gordon would almost surely resign.

All of which left 'Teddy Bear'. Gordon would remain as Finance Minister. That might reduce the prospect of his resigning, especially with the new department's added trade and industry portfolio. It might not. But what was clear was that it would strengthen Tony, and allow him to govern.

Tony agonised over 'Teddy Bear' for several weeks. With barely a year left until we would again be in election campaign mode, he knew that his decision might determine the fate of his second term, and very possibly his record as Prime Minister. He outlined the plan to Gordon, who responded with a flat 'no'. Tony decided his position was just too weak for him to impose it. It was a fateful moment.

He knew he had to do something, however. Beginning in November, I found myself drawn into an extraordinary series of manoeuvres to keep Gordon at bay until Tony was in a position to dictate the terms of the succession. I was also drawn in, by Gordon, to try to bring that succession closer. John Prescott was the other key player. Having been alarmed from the start by the tensions between Tony and Gordon, he believed that he was well placed to mediate a 'transition' arrangement, and invited the two of them to a private dinner at his official flat in Admiralty House, overlooking Horseguards. Gordon set out his stall: Tony must agree to leave before the next election.

Over the months that followed, as reports began seeping out from Gordon's team suggesting that there was now a deal, Tony denied to me that he had said he would go before the election. But the more I listened to his accounts of the discussion, the clearer it became that he had in fact left Gordon with precisely that impression. Much later, he admitted to me that a deal had actually been done, and that he had in fact agreed to Gordon's demand that he do just that. So there *was* a deal between Tony and Gordon, but it was in 2003, not 1994. For this deal to hold, Tony and John were always clear that the agreement had come with a proviso: that Gordon would support Tony in the meantime, and help him to deliver his domestic policy agenda. Of course, it would not have been worked out what this agenda was, or what Gordon believed he was signing up to. The wriggle room for Gordon was that he was not giving Tony a blank cheque: the reforms had to be sensible and achievable, and affordable.

I found out about this dinner, indirectly, the next day. I had gone north for a speaking engagement at the Chamber of Commerce in St Helens, and was staying at the home of the local MP Shaun Woodward, who had defected from the Tories before the last election. He and his wife Camilla had been kind to me during my early months in the ministerial wilderness, and I enjoyed their company. Shortly before my speech, I got a message from John. He was on his way to Chester, but said he wanted to see me urgently, and could stop in at St Helens. Rosie Winterton, John's right-hand woman from way back when we were working together under Albert Booth, and now an MP, was with John when we met in the living room of the Woodwards' stylish home. It was the type of setting from which John would ordinarily have run a mile.

'You will know,' he began, 'about the discussions Tony has had with Gordon and me about his plans to step down.' I had no idea, in fact, but I said yes, and let him get on with saying his piece. 'We're all agreed that this can't happen unless you are part of making it happen,' he said. 'When Tony is ready to move on, sooner rather than later, we've all got to help him. We've got to create the right circumstances. Gordon thinks unless you're signed up, there's a possibility that Tony won't see it through.' I replied in the only way I felt I could – in a vague fashion: 'Yes, I agree, we really need to nail it down. But we've got to pace ourselves, and get it right.' I had no idea what Tony had said to them. Days earlier, he had been pondering the equivalent of a nuclear strike against the Chancellor. Now it appeared he was talking terms of surrender.

I phoned Downing Street as soon as I had finished my speech. 'What on earth is going on?' I asked Tony. 'I had the weirdest meeting with Prescott.' Tony told me to calm down. 'Just play along,' he said. 'Just keep talking to them.' Feeling no less confused, I told him that I was not keen on getting involved in his game-playing with Gordon. It wasn't game-playing, he insisted: 'What I've told him and John, and I really mean it, is that if Gordon really backs me and helps me and implements my policy, I'll be happy to step down.'

'Really?' I asked.

He paused a moment before replying. 'Well, I don't think he'll help me. So the situation won't arise. It won't happen. But I've got to do this – so play along.'

He said he was certain Gordon was planning a final assault, in the expectation that the Hutton Report would deliver the *coup de grâce*. In mid-December – with not only Hutton but a difficult vote on university tuition top-up fees a few weeks away – I received an invitation from John to meet him and Gordon in John's office in the Commons. I arrived determined to avoid slipping into the role I had told Tony I did not want to accept: as an accessory in a political game of snakes and ladders. At that point I was unaware how far Tony had gone at the dinner at Admiralty House. But the main elements of the battle with Gordon had not really changed. Gordon wanted to become Prime Minister. Tony *was* Prime Minister, and wanted the space and the political support necessary to deliver on the reforms he had promised the voters for his second term. I felt that needed to happen, and that if Gordon's insurgency didn't relent we would find it very difficult to win a third term in any case. 'It's about unity, you're saying,' Gordon replied after I had made my pitch.

'Yes, mainly,' I said, 'but really it's about overcoming the dysfunction at the heart of government.' Gordon scowled. 'That's your favourite word, isn't it?' he shot back. He said that he didn't agree with me at all. Ideologically, there was no divide between him and Tony. Though I knew Tony was no longer sure that was true, I conceded that Gordon might well be right. The two of them may have represented different versions of New Labour, but they were still broadly modernisers who wanted to take the party and the country in the same direction. But in every other way, the relationship at the heart of government *was* dysfunctional.

'I agree,' John interjected. 'Gordon, that's right.'

'OK,' he said. 'I'll accept that.' But he accused Tony, and above all me, of having tried to create the impression that he was somehow 'old' Labour. With John as an obviously worried, mostly silent, referee, we proceeded to rehearse all the points of contention on both sides of the 'TB–GB' divide. On Tony's side there was Gordon's conference speech overture to the left, his past opposition to foundation hospitals, and his likely future opposition to top-up fees. And for Gordon, pretty much everything about Tony. The policies he opposed were simply wrong, he insisted. They were not properly thought through. 'You think – your people think – that you can brief the *Sun* here, *The Times* there, as Milburn did, and then start working out policies to fit the briefing.' Tony and Alan and the policy advisers at Number 10 were, in Gordon's view, reforming dilettantes who lacked the Treasury's interest or competence in detail: 'I've told Tony all this. But he didn't want to know. Number 10 is all over the place.' Ironically, Gordon was to face identical accusations when he eventually took office.

I thought that while that might have been true, or more nearly true, after 1997, Tony and Downing Street did now have a more rigorously developed sense of the policy changes they were attempting to make, especially in promoting a less centralised education and health system, where rather than the state, it was the requirements of pupils, parents and patients that would drive performance. The problem was that Gordon either disagreed with the policies, or had decided against supporting them for fear of strengthening Tony and making an early handover of power less likely. I also knew, more than ever, that the longer the struggle between them went on, and the more bitter it became, the worse it would be for all of us.

'Look,' I said, 'you're never going to get anywhere with Tony by simply opposing everything he wants to do. You give him no chance of a legacy. And I tell you, he won't leave Number 10 in those circumstances. Public services. Europe – at least a target or a track leading towards joining the euro. Something on development – like Bob Geldof's idea to make 2005 a "year for Africa". If you just continue fighting him all along the way, not only will he have no legacy, but you'll have no inheritance either – apart from one that is divided and poisoned, with the party looking like a fragmented rabble.'

'I am *not* fighting him,' Gordon replied. 'Yes, you are,' I said. 'You've never stopped doing so.' 'That's what *you* say,' he snapped, at which point John jumped in. 'Come on, Gordon,' he said, 'it hasn't exactly been brilliant, has it? The way you and Tony have got along.'

I tried to get some movement on tuition fees, which was obviously going to be the next Commons battle. Gordon insisted that he had told Tony he would support him on the vote, and that he meant it. He also made it clear that he, and the PLP, felt the policy was both wrong and unnecessary. 'I've talked to people, told them to support him. But it's not easy.' One thing was clear from Gordon's remarks. Whatever his private efforts to help Tony stave off a Commons defeat – and they would remain to be seen – there was no prospect at all for open, explicit support. 'Don't kid yourself,' I urged Gordon. 'Tony will not go if he loses. You're not going to get his job by watching him being carried out on a stretcher. You think he's weak. You think you can push away at this prop – Alastair – or that prop – me – and he'll collapse. He's stronger, and more stubborn, than you think. The strategy you've been trying has got you nowhere. Keep up with it, and all it will do is weaken all of us.'

But I ended with a personal assurance that was honestly meant. I told Gordon that while I was determined not to see Tony bundled out, or the core policies of his premiership wilfully blocked, that did not mean I would try to prevent Gordon from following him into Number 10. Despite all that had happened between us, I still felt a residual sense of closeness to him. 'My position,' I said, 'is that I support Tony. I believe in him, and in what he is doing. I also accept that you are a version of New Labour, which is why I will support you in succeeding. I will support it happening, as long as it's at a time of Tony's choosing, not yours.'

We met alone the next morning. Gordon was keen for me to get involved more directly, and had clearly prepared what he would say. He wanted certain things, he told me, starting with tuition fees. 'The proposals won't go through in their present form,' he said. Tony would have to incorporate some points being made by the policy's opponents if he was to get the votes he needed. This was another way of saying that Gordon wasn't going to offer Tony his unconditional support. If he had done so, even then things could have ended differently. There could have been the kind of true partnership that might have persuaded Tony to cooperate in an early handover of power. But I think Gordon had ceased to believe that would happen. The combined weight of Tony and Gordon would surely have quelled any Commons revolt, but what Gordon really wanted now were new rules of combat. He said the briefing and comments to the media by 'anti-Brown *poseurs*' – he mentioned the now-departed Alan Milburn, as well as Stephen Byers – had to stop.

The mere mention of Alan's name seemed to cause the bile to rise in his throat: 'He's a lightweight. He picked a fight with me, and he couldn't win it.' He seemed to have even less time for what he called the party's 'Kinnock rump', whom he also held to be complicit in delaying Tony's departure. Patricia Hewitt, who had followed Stephen Byers as Trade Secretary in 2001, when he moved to Transport, had 'no practical judgement'. John Reid, who had also had a role in Neil's office before becoming an MP and who had now taken over from Alan at Health, was 'clever, but not an innovator'. He said that he totally disagreed with Neil Kinnock's view that we should emphasise Europe more in the campaign. As for Charles Clarke, now at Education, Gordon said he was 'out of control, poisonous'. So much for my hopes to persuade him of the need for greater collegiality to ease things forward.

Then he turned to Tony. His half-baked policies. His inability to attract broad party and trade union support. His insistence on new reforms, new coalitions, as if his government were 'some sort of year zero'.

'Isn't that the kind of brave new start you lot are planning?' I asked him. 'Like Pol Pot?'

'I don't want these last years to come to nothing, to be wiped out,' he said. 'That doesn't help me, or serve my interests. We have a shared interest in continuity. But we have to crack the intellectual issues first.'

Then came an extraordinary final comment, clearly meant as an incentive for me to help him, but no less shocking for that. Gordon said that he knew I still hoped to return to the cabinet one day, but that Tony could never bring me back for a third time. Omitting the fact that his own opposition was one major reason for that, he said the reason was because the 'political establishment' would never allow it. 'But,' he said, 'I can.'

Tony simply laughed when I briefed him on our talk. After their first major feud in 1998, which was beginning to look like a mere schoolyard scuffle in retrospect, the *Observer* had quoted a source at Downing Street as calling Gordon 'psychologically flawed'. The media had assumed that Alastair was the culprit, something he always denied. Later, it would be suggested that it was Tony who had made the remark, but he too denied it. He certainly made it to me now, or near enough. Gordon was 'flawed', Tony said. 'He thinks he can do no wrong. He has a lack of perspective, and a paranoia, about him.' The question for Tony was whether this was a disqualifying handicap to Gordon's becoming Prime Minister. He said he was not sure. He did wonder whether Gordon was politically fit to lead, and called the suggestion – which he had heard from Gordon almost constantly since the 2001 election – that his policy lacked intellectual depth 'claptrap'.

He said he had now decided to try to ignore the invective, and engage in reasoned discussion, in the hope that Gordon would listen.

Tony felt that there was a genuine difference in the way he and Gordon saw modern Britain. University policy was a classic example. Our universities, even Oxford and Cambridge, were increasingly living on their reputation. They were still world-class institutions, but even with large and growing government support, there needed to be some supplementary funding mechanism. Otherwise they could not keep pace in future with leading universities in America, and perhaps also in new economic powers like India. Gordon's only real engagement on university issues before tuition fees had been an intervention in May 2002 – factually wrong, it turned out – to berate Oxford for having turned down a teenage applicant for a place to study medicine because she had attended a comprehensive school. Tony felt that was telling. It had been born of class-war Labour instinct, and reflected Gordon's belief that the way to fix our public institutions was to attack those at the top, rather than to take steps to ensure fair access for all.

Tony had no illusions about the corner in which he now found himself. 'People have been licensed by Gordon to rebel,' he said. He reflected that most in the PLP had always seen him as a 'winner, albeit with a fair amount of pain to digest'. That had changed. 'Now Gordon is viewed by many as a winner without any pain. That's the alternative he offers. He always thinks that when you're confronted with a policy problem, you can simply change the issue in argument, or the presentation, and avoid the row. But if the party goes down the path of always avoiding the hard changes, they'll lose.' Tony felt that the short-term challenge from Gordon, which he knew would flare all over again before the tuition vote in January 2004, obscured the deeper divisions over the direction in which the party and the government should go: 'I have to have this out with Gordon. I have to weaken his belief in his own position, intellectually. It's the only way.'

For a brief while, it appeared that their feud was subsiding. John Prescott had separately told both of them, after our meetings, that it was a huge waste for the three of us – Tony, Gordon and me – not to be working together as a team. At one point Tony told me: 'Gordon and I are talking properly. He's listening to me. Or at least I think he is.' But the nearer we got to the vote on tuition fees, the more difficult things became. Gordon still let it be known that he thought the policy was a mistake, and that in any case universities should get no new funding until they could show they had opened up their doors to more underprivileged applicants. At times it seemed he would even be happy to see Tony lose the vote, which could leave him so weakened he might be forced to quit. Gordon must have been all the more tempted by the fact that on the day after the tuition fees test, the Hutton Report was due for publication. If Tony lost the education vote, even a whiff of opprobrium over David Kelly's death would surely be enough to finish him off.

But then suddenly there were signs that Gordon had changed tack. Privately, he still made it clear that he opposed tuition fees. But I think he finally recognised the risk of being seen as complicit in a possibly fatal Commons defeat for Tony. For all his bravado during our meetings in December, he had left me in little doubt that he understood the danger of inheriting a party in chaos, especially if he emerged looking like an 'Old Labour' successor. As the vote drew nearer, he did not go so far as to align himself publicly with Tony, but he did call in allies like Nick Brown and get them to drop their opposition, and his aides let it be known that he was talking to dozens of other backbenchers to urge them not to defeat the government. The result was to achieve the next-best thing from Gordon's point of view: emerging as the agent of rescue without whom Tony could not survive. The Bill got through, but with a margin of just five votes. For Tony, however, it was still a victory. And it was part of a double triumph: hours before the vote, he had been given an advance copy of the Hutton Report.

Despite a public show of confidence that Hutton would vindicate him, Tony had been worried, especially after the top civil servant at the Ministry of Defence, Sir Kevin Tebbit, told the inquiry that he understood at the time that the Prime Minister 'wanted something done' about Kelly coming forward. Tony feared that this would be used to suggest that he had encouraged the leaking of Dr Kelly's name. He was on the record, accurately, as denying this. But while he had not been involved in any of the meetings that led to the decision, he had not actually blocked the MoD or Number 10 from confirming the name to reporters. In 'barrister Blair' mode, he convinced himself that this distinction mattered. 'Leaking is improper. Confirming isn't,' he said. He was keen to narrow down the argument, for both Hutton and the media, to a core issue of principle: did he lie, either in the weapons dossier or over Kelly? He knew that he had not, as long as the question over Kelly remained only about deliberately leaking his name.

Not only did Hutton's report clear Tony of wrongdoing or dishonesty, it was sharply critical of Andrew Gilligan and the BBC. My worry was about what came next. Despite media criticism of the report as a whitewash, I saw it as an opportunity finally to draw a line under the whole issue. The worst thing we could do would be to stir things up all over again by crowing over the outcome, or going after the BBC. I feared that Alastair would do both. When I told Tony the evening before the report's publication that he should make sure this didn't happen, he agreed that Alastair must be 'kept in his box'. Whether Tony communicated this to Alastair is unclear. In any case, Alastair called a press conference at the Foreign Press Association's premises in Carlton House Terrace. After descending a rather regal staircase to the microphones awaiting him, he unleashed an unnecessarily sharp attack on the BBC. If the government had received the kind of criticism Hutton had directed towards it, he said, heads would have rolled. When BBC heads did roll, with the resignations of both the Director General, Greg Dyke, and the Chairman, my friend Gavyn Davis, if anything this evoked sympathy for the BBC. What should have been a moment of closure after a terrible tragedy simply reopened old wounds. In one ill-judged press conference, Alastair had managed to throw away the shield of Hutton and replace it with the worst side of New Labour hubris. The whole mess – not just our feud with the BBC and its media supporters, but the questions about the so-called 'dodgy dossier' and all the rest – was back.

The tuition-fee victory also began to feel uncannily like a defeat. It wasn't just the knife-edge margin of the vote; it was that Gordon's team were soon whispering to the PLP, and the media, that he had come to Tony's aid out of duty rather than conviction. In fact, nobody came out of it well. 'He has been left doing a bit of a Grand Old Duke of York with the rebels,' Tony said of Gordon. But he knew he himself was growing ever weaker too. He also knew that he could not strike back.

Tony felt safe from assault for the moment, but he was apprehensive about how the related issues of Iraq and trust in his leadership would play in the local and European elections in June. We knew we were going to do badly. The situation on the ground in Iraq was violent and chaotic, and practically no one, not even Tony, still held out hope that stores of WMDs might be uncovered. The impression had taken hold that even if Gilligan had been wrong in his facts, in some way Tony had manipulated the nation into a war it shouldn't, or needn't, have fought. Domestically, after the battles on health and education, Tony looked like a wounded general barely able to command his own troops, with Gordon poised to arrive on his white charger. In November 2003 the Tories had finally ditched their hapless leader Iain Duncan Smith for the steadier, older hand of Michael Howard, the former Home Secretary whose colleague Ann Widdecombe had described as having 'something of the night about him'. It was a choice that Tony and I both felt, over time, would do us more good than harm. We were confident that, despite the usual 'pull together' noises of the new leader and his assured performances in the Commons, Howard would drift back to the Tories' right-wing comfort zone. That would turn out to be true. But in the run-up to the June elections, the polls put Tony's leadership rating at a paltry 29 per cent. Howard was drawing neck and neck, the first Tory leader to come near him since 1997.

There was another, unexpected problem: Europe. For months, a new constitutional treaty to deal with the expanding membership of the EU had been in limbo. With a change of government in Spain, a target for wrapping up an agreement was suddenly set for the end of June. The draft treaty was a great, unwieldy document, largely the creation of a man seen by his admirers as a great, elegant thinker: the former French President Valéry Giscard d'Estaing. Much of it involved common-sense fixes to accommodate the growing number of member states, but the tone was, in British political terms at least, rather federalist. Some provisions, whose inclusion in the final draft Tony had already pledged to reject, would encroach on prerogatives that obviously belonged to national governments: defence and foreign policy, the judiciary and taxation.

None of this needed to become an election issue, but the Tories, much of the media, and a core of Labour ministers including Jack Straw, John Prescott and, latterly, Gordon, were pressing Tony to commit to a referendum before Britain signed up to the treaty. Tony was opposed to this: he felt that the proper route was to seek Parliament's approval. Not only would a referendum be an invitation for Howard to rally the forces of Euroscepticism; we might lose it. Besides, the issue was a needless distraction before an already tough election campaign.

But Jack was adamant. Partly, as I had warned Tony when he was made Foreign Secretary, this was down to his instinctive Euroscepticism. Jack had written Tony a long personal letter at the beginning of the year setting out how and why the treaty should be junked. Instead, Tony junked the letter. But now Jack added a cogent political argument: by being the one party leader opposing a referendum, Tony would look like a lone voice against giving the British people a direct say in the EU's future. Gordon and John echoed that message. In late April, someone – Jack himself, Tony assumed – briefed reporters that the Prime Minister had changed his mind, and was now in favour of a referendum. That was not quite true, but Tony had let it be known that he was open to the proposition, so when David Hill, his press secretary, was asked about the story he did not knock it down. 'The argument of principle in favour of a referendum is wrong,' Tony had told me a few days earlier, 'but politically it's irrefutable.' Still, Jack's briefings created the impression that he had been bounced into a U-turn. 'I intended to take the whole thing at a different pace,' Tony said. 'I've screwed myself on this.' He suddenly seemed not in control of events, and I told him so in no uncertain terms.

But Tony took some heart from the fact that Gordon was facing an unanticipated problem of his own: from Michael Howard. The Tories had tapped into the unease in the Labour Party, and the fevered comment in the media, caused by Gordon's increasingly overt desire to see Tony out. The Tories had sensed that this would scare many people, and had begun to warn loudly and continuously of the danger of 'voting Tony, and getting Gordon'. Combined with his alarm that he was being portrayed as 'Old Labour', this badly rattled Gordon. 'He phoned *me*, at Chequers, which shows how worried he is,' Tony told me one Sunday evening after returning to Downing Street. 'The Howard stuff has woken him up.' It had shaken Gordon's view of the political landscape, and of his own place in it. 'He's surrounded by people who tell him how wonderful he is, and how hopeless I am. He gets fed all this Jackie Ashley nonsense,' Tony said, in a reference to one of the *Guardian's* more reliably Brownite columnists, 'after they feed it to her. It's just bollocks from bollocks the whole time.'

By now I was being inveigled by Tony into playing a more open part in preparing for the June elections. After our initial strategy meeting, Gordon asked to see me privately. At first, he was disarmingly warm. 'My boy John is always singing "Imagine" because of that singing bear you got him. It's the only song he knows,' he said with a smile. Then his mood changed. 'Do you think Tony knows how bad these elections are going to be?' he asked. I said I thought he probably did. It was clear that we were being hit by two big problems at once. The first was 'delivery frustration', exasperation that things had not changed more quickly. The second was Iraq. 'Iraq is a disaster,' Gordon agreed. 'It's doing us all, but Tony in particular, real damage.' At which point, as I had suspected he would, he launched into how Iraq was contributing to Tony's central vulnerability: the issue of trust. 'He said we would do too much, too early on. He over-promised, shouting about what we would do. People feel let down.'

Even Gordon must have recognised that the let-down had much to do with the genuine sense of elation that had greeted our arrival in Downing Street. I knew this conversation would lead nowhere. I also knew better than to argue when Gordon proceeded to rehearse his view that Tony's lack of 'intellectual rigour' was at the heart of our delivery woes. Then he moved on to an extraordinary dressing-down of the abilities of pretty much the entire cabinet, in an echo of our earlier discussion. At Education, Charles Clarke lacked 'strategy or direction'. David Blunkett as Home Secretary was 'all image', stirring up a media storm around issues, demanding money to solve them, and then failing to work out what needed to be done. John Reid was at least 'better than Milburn' at Health, but Gordon added: 'Everyone thinks he's suddenly so marvellous. I've known him for over thirty years.' When I asked him who, if everyone was so hopeless, he would put in his government when the time came, he said nothing. He went on about how bad the elections would be – locally, because John Prescott had messed up the previous year's council tax settlement, and on Europe because Tony was 'in the wrong place'. Then, abruptly, he asked: 'What should I be doing?'

It was the start of an extraordinary shift in our relations leading up to the elections. No doubt this was partly because the Tory attacks had given Gordon a shared interest in trying at least to avoid handing Howard an early victory. But the two of us began working together to make sure the mechanics of the campaign were in place, and to sharpen our message on Europe to maximise chronic Tory divisions on that subject. Gordon's entire demeanour seemed to change: his tone of voice, his body language, his readiness to engage. At one of our discussions he asked me, with none of the raw hostility towards Tony I had come to expect, 'When do you think he'll go?' I tried to be as honest as I could. I replied that I genuinely didn't know, and that I was pretty sure Tony himself didn't know. I did say that unless Gordon stopped obstructing him on every policy, he would definitely seek a third term. 'The working assumption,' I said, 'is that Tony will fight the next election, and stand down a year or so later.'

Given the blistering report card he had delivered on most of the government's senior members, I offered him a bit of advice: 'You need, for your own good, to become more inclusive towards your colleagues. They all think that if you take over, there will be a firing squad and they'll be taken out and shot at dawn.' He chuckled. 'The real thing that matters,' he replied, 'is for your lot to stop portraying me as Old Labour.' The truth is that Tony did regard him as Old Labour, or at least as not convincingly New Labour. He also sensed that cabinet ministers were, for reasons of both politics and personality, increasingly uneasy about the prospect of Gordon taking over. They seemed worried that he *wouldn't* go on, not that he would.

Yet all of us – Tony too – were feeling as drained and disheartened as I could remember. I was working long hours and wanted to be located within walking distance of Westminster. So I sold Archel Road and bought a flat overlooking Trafalgar Square. I still yearned for a Foy-like home in the countryside, possibly in Sussex, where I had stayed with my mother during two recent summer holidays. The London flat would be my base during the week. But when I did find the cottage of my dreams, I couldn't afford it. This time, I just accepted that I would have to do without. Anyway, my life was dominated by my efforts to rescue, and shore up, Tony. That was enough to think about.

Our reorganisation plan in Number 10 had made some difference. Tony's working style had become a lot more effective, but the change was not as transformative as we had hoped. 'The bewildering problem with Tony,' John Birt remarked at one point, 'is that while he knows what he wants, and he has the focus and direction of a good CEO, he doesn't give clear, direct orders. He doesn't do anything when people fail to carry out his wishes. They can keep coming back, knowingly not doing what the Prime Minister requires. Tony simply doesn't confront them or have it out with them. He'll discuss and interrogate, and try to move individuals along, but he doesn't do a Thatcher on them.' We were doing little to attempt to fix that problem. Perhaps it was unfixable. Any renewed push on policy was being largely nullified by Tony's lack of confidence about his position, and the understandable warnings from Sally, Matthew and others around him of the risks Gordon still posed to his position in the party.

Despite later media speculation about the famous 'wobble' Tony experienced at the time, brought on by the failure to find WMDs, the total breakdown in security in Iraq and the appalling depravities in Abu Ghraib, I do not believe he was ever really ready to quit. He cared too much about seeing out Iraq, and ensuring that if and when he handed over to Gordon it would be on his own, New Labour, terms. But it is true that he was increasingly disheartened. I was feeling that way myself. I remained angry, too, at the way he had handled the issue of the referendum on the European treaty. Beyond the merits of the argument for and against a referendum, I felt that he had got the politics utterly wrong. A vote that potentially threatened both the treaty and his own position was not something he should invite, however keen Jack and the Murdoch press were about promoting one. If he believed in his case, he could and should have stood his ground.

Barely a week before the June elections, Cherie phoned me. 'What are you saying to Tony?' she demanded angrily. 'You're demoralising him. You should be backing him up and bolstering him!' I admitted that I had been feeling less supportive since the referendum fiasco. With all that was going on, I had been pressing him to take a firmer hold of Downing Street and government. I told her, as I had told him, that he was looking tired, and that some people were beginning to wonder if his heart was still in it. 'It most certainly is!' Cherie replied, if only because of Gordon. 'I am not seeing Tony give way to that man. I will stop him moving in here with everything I've got.' I allowed that that was probably in my interest as well, to which she replied, 'Well, you should be encouraging him.'

I took the message to heart. So did Tony. He told me not to take offence at Cherie's call. 'She's OK. She's very robust,' he said. 'She'll not give up.' He also recognised that she was right. And that I was, too, on at least one subject. He had allowed himself to appear worn down. 'I absolutely have to avoid giving any word or signal supporting any talk about the timing of my departure,' he said. He accepted that there were long-term issues that might force him to go. Iraq could collapse into chaos. He could lose a European treaty referendum. He could win a third election, but with a 'seriously bad result'. But he did not think that even a catastrophic result in the local and European elections would force him out. He even forgave John Prescott for an offhand remark ahead of polling day that the 'tectonic plates' in British politics appeared to be shifting. John had phoned to say he didn't mean it to be taken in the way it was.

Tony's view was that the problem wasn't John, but Gordon. He said he was no longer in any mood to have an endless back-and-forth battle over the succession. The condition he had put down in November still stood. If Gordon was genuinely on side, Tony would back his taking over. Not otherwise. He had increasingly little expectation that Gordon would accept this. He did now admit that the previous December he had told both Gordon and John Prescott that he would 'probably' not fight a third election – *assuming* Gordon supported him and his programme. At that time he had pretty much decided to step down after two terms, but it was the only way of managing Gordon, he said, of getting through until he was stronger. That no longer mattered. As the situation in Iraq continued to deteriorate, he felt it would be difficult to walk away; and with Gordon increasingly restive, there was every sign that the party actually wanted him to stay on. He suspected that even Gordon wouldn't want him to go immediately. That would give the media, not to mention any succession rivals, too much time to 'do him in' before the election. As for John Prescott, Tony said he was 'not stupid about Gordon. He's scared by him. He knows there's something wrong with him.' Crucially, Tony added that if he did fight the next general election, he was now determined to do more than just stay for a few months and then pass the baton to his successor, as I had told Gordon in our campaign discussions. 'People need to realise that if I stand for a third term, I stay for a third term,' he said. 'I am not staying for a year and then going.'

The June results were dire. We finished in third place, behind the Tories and the Lib Dems, in the local elections. We also lost MEP seats, ending up with barely 22 per cent of the vote. But to the relief of all of us, Gordon included I am sure, the Tories fared little better. They did not reach their hoped-for 40 per cent threshold in the local council vote, while on Europe their share suffered even more than ours, with many Conservative voters defecting to the Eurosceptic United Kingdom Independence Party.

But for Gordon, no less than for Tony, the politics of their power struggle now dominated everything. Gordon painted the election results as a damning verdict on Tony, and he and Ed Balls stormed into Number 10 to press him to get on with handing over power. Short of being pushed out, however, it was now clear that Tony was going nowhere. He told me the lesson he had taken from the past few months was that until he made it absolutely clear that he was staying, discipline within the party would not return.

We persisted with efforts within Number 10 to try to ease the pressure from Gordon, and to establish better relations between Tony and him. A new set of 'rules of engagement' was even drawn up in the early summer of 2004. It was never implemented, or even shown to Gordon and his team, as far as I am aware. But it provided a telling summary of the many points of friction, and the depth of mutual suspicion. The blueprint stipulated that Tony would 'always act on the basis that GB is his natural successor', while Gordon would 'never seek to set himself up in opposition to TB'. They and their allies would 'stress their common commitment as reformers and modernisers', and personal attacks or criticisms would be reined in. Tony and Gordon would 'work as one' on the general election campaign.

But no peace pact could hide the difficulties of making the relationship work. While it debarred Number 10 from promoting any alternative to Gordon as successor, it said that other cabinet members would 'remain at liberty to point out that the succession will be an election, not a coronation – and that a wide range of candidates might feel they wish to put themselves forward'. That would, of course, have been anathema to Gordon. The scale of the difficulties was brought home best by the final clause, which sounded more like an arms pact than a political entente. It proposed setting up a 'hotline system to operate between Number 10 and Number 11 in case of flare-ups'.

I had no doubt that the flare-ups would come. Maybe not for a while, but certainly before the general election, which was pencilled in for the following year, in May 2005. But however the struggle ultimately played out, the immediate rescue mission I had been called in to lead was over. Tony had survived and was feeling stronger. He, and the team around him, were ready for the fight, not just with Gordon but over the policy reforms they still had to navigate through the Commons. I was ready to do everything I could to help Tony lead New Labour into a third-term election and win it, but I was now resolved to do so at a distance. When I returned to active duty in the summer of 2003, I had still not given up my hope eventually to return to cabinet. If nothing else, my resumed relations with Gordon during the year had made it clear that that was not going to happen. It was a bit like joining the euro: it wasn't that Gordon was necessarily opposed, it was just that there was no way he was going to allow it to happen on Tony's watch.

At various times Tony had dangled a series of more open political roles before me: a return to the DTI; making me Deputy Chairman of the party and in charge of the general election campaign; and most recently, Defence Secretary after the election. But both of us knew that none of these appointments would pass muster with Gordon. It was immensely wearing. It was also sad, not just because it meant a definitive end to my ministerial career, but because, as John Prescott had remarked, it seemed so wasteful of the combined strengths that the three of us might have deployed to make our government much more effective.

The only definite job offer Tony had made to me in the year I had been working away for him behind the scenes at Number 10 was to go to Brussels as an EU Commissioner. When I now told him that I had decided that I would accept, he tried hard to convince me to stay at Westminster. I have no doubt that he was genuine when he told me I would be making the wrong decision for my own future. He was sure I would miss British politics, and at least the prospect of returning to government. 'You'll be a super civil servant in Brussels,' he said, 'with a lot of detail and drudge. You won't enjoy it.' But he was honest enough to recognise that he had other concerns too: 'It worries me to lose my shield against Gordon. If you go, Gordon will celebrate. He'll believe I've lost my shield. And he'll be right.'

In fact, when I told Gordon that I had decided to go to the Commission, he seemed more rueful than triumphant. He recognised the terrible damage, to all of us, that had been caused by the continuing political warfare of the past year. 'We've lost further trust in each other, and now the public doesn't trust us,' he said. 'We've killed each other.' I told him that I feared he was right. He also made a parting effort to keep me on side for the final battle: the succession to Number 10. He told me that he knew why I was leaving: I had felt 'deceived' by Tony bringing me back into the shadows. 'Well,' he said, 'we've both been deceived. Your mistake is that you should never have gone back. I tried to tell you when you left Northern Ireland to go away, remake yourself, and I would bring you back.' That was 'a deal', he said. He just couldn't be explicit, 'because I thought you would tell Tony'.

Gordon had not been completely right to say that I felt 'deceived' by Tony. But it was true that on some level I did feel let down. Not so much during the past year, but certainly over the longer period since he had fired me, without good reason or proper judgement, from my second job in cabinet. He knew that when he had asked me to come to his aid, I would not, and could not refuse. He also knew that sooner or later, if I was to have a real political life, I would have to move to an open, independent role of my own.

Nevertheless, Tony continued to try to get me to change my mind. Or at least he appeared to do so. The slightly bizarre final act came towards the end of the third week of July. As I was driving up Constitution Hill towards Hyde Park Corner, I was speaking to Tony by mobile phone, when suddenly his motorcade with its police motorcycle outriders overtook me. When I told him, definitively, that I had decided to go to Brussels just as his convoy drove straight through the Wellington Arch rather than around Hyde Park Corner as mere mortals have to, I couldn't help adding: 'You know, you've played me like a fiddle.'

We talked often over the summer, as I disengaged from Downing Street, began taking French lessons, and prepared to leave for Brussels after the party conference. When Tony got back from holiday, we spoke at length in Number 10. It was difficult for both of us.

'I'm feeling distinctly queasy and creaky,' he said. 'I wonder what I've done in appointing you to this.' He said it felt almost like a divorce. Then he said that it was not quite like that in our case: we would still talk, consult, plan, and support one another. 'You can still play a role. I'll need you, perhaps more now than ever. I've got lots of ideas that I'll want to talk through with you.' I assured him I would be ready to help. He knew that was true. He added, with real feeling: 'You will be a great success in Europe. I know you will. There's no doubt...It's me I worry about.'

'It was ever thus,' I said, laughing.

'That's not fair,' he replied. 'I'm not sure how I'll do, with you going. But I have done the right thing for you.'

He had. In fact it seemed as if he had done the right thing for both of us. In the weeks before I left for Brussels in October, and even afterwards, there were few major challenges or decisions on which we did not speak, question each other and debate. It was not so much a divorce as a kind of modern marriage, in which the fact that we were less often together, that we each had a space of our own, gave our relationship a more relaxed feeling. My new job would soon turn out to be not only a challenge, but a source of invigoration, accomplishment and real fulfilment – not at all the senior civil servant's post Tony had warned me about.

10

Trading Places

When I opted for my new life in Brussels, whatever pleasure I may have felt was balanced by a concern among some of my Labour colleagues that we would lose the resulting by-election in Hartlepool. I assured them, with slightly more confidence than I actually felt, that we would hold on to the seat. Gordon, in particular, had told me he was certain that the effect of Iraq made defeat inevitable, especially since our main local rivals, the Liberal Democrats, had been against the war. He had a point. But I knew the town and its people better, and I felt sure that issues closer to home than Iraq would weigh more heavily with them. If I had been running the Lib Dem campaign, I knew what I would have campaigned on. Three years earlier, after all, Peter Mandelson of Hartlepool had been 'a fighter, not a quitter'. Now, as they would no doubt point out, the only thing he was fighting for was a seat on the Eurostar to Brussels. As the votes were being counted after our party conference in September I still felt fairly confident, but I was relieved nonetheless when the Labour candidate, Iain Wright, won with a majority of 2,000 votes. I also felt for the first time that I could now focus fully on my move to Europe.

It is hard to capture the sense of liberation I felt when I left the Westminster village for Brussels. Every aspect of my new job, and my new life, was exciting: I was right at the heart of the world's largest economic and trading bloc, with a chance to shape its future direction. But before I got started I had to find a place to live, and to recruit my new team. Two people helped me organise all this.

The super-energetic Beverley Tempest – never was anyone more aptly named – had looked after Neil Kinnock during his time as Commissioner, and now became my executive assistant and office manager. And Simon Fraser, whom I hand-picked from the Foreign Office as my chief of staff, selected the other members of my policy team, my 'cabinet'. He led them with a mixture of iron rod and sardonic humour, supporting and indulging me unless I seemed intent on doing something he thought unwise or untimely, in which case he would deftly steer me in another direction. I was sad when the time came for Simon to return to London near the end of my time in Brussels, but he was replaced by another Foreign Office rising star, Julian King, who with his French deputy Denis Redonnet led a first-rate team.

The three-room flat I found to rent was in a seventeenth-century building bang in the centre of Brussels, on the Petit Sablon, an area teeming with cafés, delicatessens, art galleries and antique shops – a mini-heaven. My flat had a set of tall windows around the sitting room, and I looked out on a delightful little park, complete with a fountain and statues of Brussels artisans encircling it. I would have been lost without a friend of Beverley's, Ruth Ringer. With her original and expert eye for twentieth-century furniture, she made my flat and office special places to live and work in.

My work was entirely new to me, and completely engrossing. The allocation of Commission portfolios was decided by the new President, José Manuel Barroso. As a centre-right leader, he had been Portugal's Prime Minister for two years before coming to Brussels. He and Tony had become quite close, and Tony had been a key voice in the bargaining that got him the top Commission job. I was given an important and much sought-after policy portfolio, in charge of trade. Along with competition policy, it was one of only two among the more than two dozen Commission posts with responsibilities and powers transferred from individual member states. In other portfolios, nothing much was agreed unless the majority of member states came to a joint position. This led to uneven influence across the Commission's members, and I was relieved not to find myself in that position.

It was a complex and hugely technical area, especially since I was taking over at a crucial period in efforts to secure a new world trade agreement. I did have some general background knowledge in this field from my time at the DTI, but as in my first days at Walworth Road, I was keenly aware of the huge amount that I didn't know. Now, as then, I set out to educate myself. by reading incessantly and seeking out experts to guide me: business people and academics, economists and politicians. In late October and early November the European Parliament held American-style confirmation hearings for each candidate on the new Commission, and I was determined that when my turn came, I would be in command of my brief. I was prudent to have done so: the MEPs judged that two of my fellow nominees were unprepared for their posts. As I entered the hearing room, I felt the mix of andrenalin and apprehension I had last had when sitting exams at Oxford. This time, I was better prepared, and I got the equivalent of my First. I also got a foretaste of how intellectually fascinating and politically compelling my new responsibilities would become.

I not only had a new job, I had been thrust into a world totally different from Westminster. Especially near the centre of power, British politics is something of a high-wire act: exhilarating as long as you are able to keep your balance amid the political, public and media pressures, but also leaving you vulnerable to sudden gusts that can knock you over. As an EU Commissioner, I found myself insulated from anything up to a force-ten gale. Commissioners were appointed for a fixed term, so unless they committed some gross error of judgement – and not necessarily even then – they could plan and work on the basis that their job was secure. They would not be reshuffled at the whim of member states or the Commission President. This gave them the opportunity to think long-term – and as the European Union was basically in the business of setting the right framework for the long term, that made a lot of sense.

Another huge difference was that the Commission was an executive which began its term without anything resembling a proper political platform. The overall direction of travel would emerge only gradually, as all twenty-seven of the Commissioners, with their different national and political backgrounds, got down to work. There was a fair amount of stop-and-go. Internally, I argued that growth and jobs needed to be our priority, and I helped José Manuel develop a programme that reflected this priority rather than social and environmental policy areas. In time he redressed this imbalance, partly because he became worried about falling foul of the powerful socialist group in the European Parliament, which wanted more labour- and trade union-friendly legislation, and partly because climate change emerged as a major challenge, and the Commission led the EU's response.

My trade role gave me a far greater degree of autonomy than most of my Commission colleagues, but since the glory days of Jean Monnet and Jacques Delors, the Commission as a whole had steadily lost power both to the Council of Ministers, representing the member states, and the European Parliament, and this was accentuated with the passing of the Lisbon Treaty. This was leading to a weakening of the EU as a whole, in my opinion, because it was the Commission's job to see and protect the European dimension in every policy area, and it did so in a more consistent and dedicated way than either the Parliament or the individual member states. Instead, the Council was trying to claim more power back for itself, and the Parliament was far from being merely a talking shop: it had acquired real legislative teeth.

It took me time to learn the ropes, and to adjust to the weekly Commissioners' meeting, known as the college. There was a warmth and camaraderie among us, although I occasionally missed the cut and thrust I was used to back home. I was lucky to sit next to Charlie McCreevy, the dry-humoured former Irish Finance Minister who later had to grapple with the brunt of the banking crisis, and later next to Neelie Kroes, the Dutch Competition Policy Commissioner, whose combination of political intelligence and *haute couture* distinguished her.In the British system, collective responsibility is a mechanism for making all ministers stick loyally to decisions taken by other ministers in which they themselves had played no part and had no real say. In the Commission, technically every decision is taken by the college. So, at every step of the way I had to learn to carry key colleagues with me, starting with José Manuel. He backed my free trade instincts most of the time, but he always had a sharp eye for political pressures, and more than once I had to fight very hard to get my way. Thankfully, our relationship survived.

Once I had settled into the routine, the most important obstacle I had to overcome was to be master of my own house. In Brussels, unlike Whitehall, a Commissioner is not the head of his or her administration: there are two heads. The Commissioners are the political guides, while the Director Generals, the last real mandarins in Europe, are the heads of the administration. As a British minister I had grown used to having levers of executive power in my hands. If I pulled on them, I knew what the outcome would be. In Brussels I was surrounded by professional staff who were highly expert in the minutiae of trade issues, and the Director General I inherited, Peter Carl, was not only extremely knowledgeable about all the issues that crossed my desk, he had strong, fixed judgements about each one. He was interested in my view as well, of course, but I sometimes had the impression that he felt, unlike in the British system, that it was not binding on him. I felt he did not like me getting a sense of what the other officials under him thought, since I knew that his was not the only view. I was not prepared, however, to leave my Whitehall model and instincts behind me and accept that my job was to act merely as the mouthpiece of a highly technocratic bureaucracy. When he was moved to another directorate within a year after I came to the Commission, I was pleased that the more subtle and effective David O'Sullivan, who had been Secretary General of the Commission, took over his job. We got on well together, and I valued his advice, while he respected my judgement, once all the arguments had been aired and the decision taken. I preferred this approach.

The key to my effectiveness was my 'cabinet'. I was the first British Commissioner to have a majority of non-Brits working for me, and I was proud of the fact that they were seen as possibly the best cabinet team in the Commission. Most of them were experienced Commission insiders who knew where the bodies were buried on every issue, and had an impressive range of contacts with people working in other Commissioners' cabinets and in the 'services', as the directorates were known. The misfortune of the Commission was that while it contained some of the most impressive public servants I had ever met, and it did a first-rate job integrating the interests of twenty-seven member states, somehow the total added up to less than the sum of its parts. I put this down not only to a risk-averse political culture, but to the desire of leading member states to keep us in check. I could understand this, on purely democratic grounds. But the Commission brought hugely important legitimacy and expertise to the EU's policies and legislation. It needed to show strong, strategic leadership, and I became ever more convinced that an effective and respected Commission was key to strengthening the EU as a whole, both internally and in projecting its influence in the world – a particular focus of my work as Trade Commissioner.

I spoke to Chris Patten, my predecessor as the UK member of the Commission, before I arrived. He had told me that I might find myself spending much more time in far-flung capitals than in my flat on the Petit Sablon. He was right: my time in Brussels might more accurately be described as my time *away* from Brussels. Most weeks, I was on the road. I travelled to every continent, promoting EU commerce and, through the trade talks, trying to achieve a deal that would spread the fruits of globalisation more effectively among the poor as well as the rich nations. From the outset, I saw my role as achieving these larger goals, not just as a technocratic negotiator's brief.

I had to make the case for economic openness against an undercurrent of resistance to global integration, which still makes many people nervous. My first challenge – the so-called 'bra wars' – involved dealing with a surge in textile imports from China when a long-standing international agreement expired shortly after I had taken up my post. Rather than respond by trying to impose new tariffs, I made the argument that cheap Chinese competition was not inherently unfair, but could in fact act as a spur to innovation and lower prices over the longer term. I insisted on agreeing with China a temporary, voluntary arrangement to ease the transition. This was my introduction to the hard-nosed school of Chinese negotiation on the one hand, and the equally tough school of European protectionism on the other. Many Europeans intuitively believed that China and India achieving export superpower status had to mean that Europe's prosperity would be reduced proportionally. That was clearly not true. Europe had created many millions more jobs during China's dramatic rise in the second half of the 1990s than it lost due to competition with China.

However, I avoided glib, abstract arguments about the need for workers battered by globalisation simply to adapt and move on. I felt that such arguments, often made by politicians in the more liberal northern European states, including Britain, were dismissive of the real, and understandable, anxieties that globalisation was causing. I felt that these concerns had to be addressed if the benefits of globalisation were to be preserved. Not just through parroting arguments for trade liberalisation, but by policy solutions that made it easier for European workers to live with expanding world trade, easier to create jobs and move between them, easier to retrain. Basically, a reformed European social model.

In Europe, I realised that we faced a huge external challenge. The global economy of which we were a part was changing rapidly and fundamentally. Where globalisation had been driven at first primarily by Western capital and Western preferences, it was now increasingly being shaped by Asia and Latin America, with the emergence of China, India, Brazil and other advanced developing economies. These countries were not just trading across borders, they were producing across borders. They offered growing markets for European exports, which was why we needed them to succeed and raise their wealth levels, and of course to make these markets open to our goods and services, as our own are to others. But they were also making many traditional European industries increasingly unviable in the face of lower-cost competition. To survive, I argued at conferences and in speaking engagements across Europe, we had to prioritise the kinds of higher-value specialised goods – and increasingly services – that Europe was good at, or at least had the potential to be good at. This would involve difficult, even painful changes, as I never shied away from acknowledging. My job gave me an important political platform to address issues of globalisation, and I made it a rule to give a carefully prepared speech, lecture or interview in almost every country I visited. Fortunately one of my staff members, Stephen Adams, had a razor-sharp brain and a brilliant writing ability, and he helped me maintain an impressive rate of speech-making.

My decision on dealing with Chinese textiles was an early sign of my determination to avoid knee-jerk protectionism. At best, I felt that this would only slow down inevitable economic change. At worst, it would make it harder to adjust later on. Still, I genuinely sympathised with European producers and exporters who stood to lose out. It was hard not to feel an intense identification with the producers of shoes, clothing or furniture whose industries – at least at the cheaper, mass-market end – were struggling with competition from a booming China. Especially in countries like Italy, where industries like these were clustered together in particular towns or regions, adjusting to the new economic reality could have dramatic social costs. I met textile manufacturers from the Vosges in France and shoemakers from Milan with proud histories that went back centuries. Even as I recognised the economically inevitable, it was impossible not to regret the potential human costs of rapid change. But I also felt anger with both company managers and politicians who refused to see the need for Europe to adapt, to move up the value chain or invest in new skills, and had put their faith in protectionism instead.

The balance between protectionism and free trade was at the centre of almost everything I did as Trade Commissioner. An area where I tried to make a particular personal impact was in re-negotiating the long-standing trade agreements between Europe, and the African, Caribbean and Pacific (ACP) nations. In my view, these countries, which included the poorest in the world, were trapped by their dependency on European agricultural trade concessions and our generous development aid handouts. I wanted a new agreement to encourage them to produce more diverse exports and make their aid work better for them. Economic reformers in many of the ACP countries knew this was highly desirable, but others remained locked into old modes of production and exporting. I was strongly supported by the pipe-smoking Belgian Development Commissioner, Louis Michel, but I was frustrated that many European parliamentarians and non-governmental organisations, including those at home in Britain, sided with the anti-reformers and frequently opposed my negotiating efforts. Few appreciated my point of view, though Bob Geldof was an exception, in that he understood better what I was trying to achieve. I regarded my lack of progress, apart from in the Caribbean, as a significant setback for the ACP nations' economic development.

During my time as Trade Commissioner I also spent many days negotiating with Russia on the terms of its entry to the World Trade Organisation. The arguments boiled down to how much Russia would open its markets to free trade in competition with home agriculture and manufacturing industries. The Russian negotiator for most of this time was the charming and intelligent pro-market German Gref, the Economics Minister. We shared many hours over long Russian dinners, even resorting to a Russian *banya* on one occasion with our respective teams in an effort to find agreement. But without his President's support Gref could not compromise enough, and Mr Putin never felt that Russia was receiving a fair enough deal for him to accept.

The tension between protecting markets and opening them to free trade lay at the heart of the most important aspect of my new

role, the trade talks being held under the auspices of the WTO
in Geneva. They were known as the 'Doha Development Round',
because they had begun in 2001 with a ministerial meeting in the
Qatari capital. In the scale of their ambitions, the complexity of the
issues involved and the controversy surrounding them, the world
trade talks made seeking peaceful co-existence between Tony and
Gordon seem almost simple. At the root of most of the outstanding
disputes was a clash of interests between the developed and developing nations: the rich, the soon-to-be-rich, and the poor. The
wealthier countries wanted to bring down barriers to selling their
manufactured goods and services in the developing world. The
poorer states, depending on their stage of development, wanted
the mirror-image: better access to markets like the EU, the United
States or Japan for their agricultural, processed or primary goods.
Both were reluctant to end tariffs, subsidies and other mechanisms
that helped their own producers and exporters. Agriculture was
a huge problem area. For less well-off countries in Africa, Asia
or Latin America, farming was both an economic mainstay and a
potential source of export earnings. In the EU, with our Common
Agricultural Policy, or the United States, with its farm payouts, politicians had grown used to subsidising a sophisticated but shrinking
farming sector. In America's case, they were also funding agricultural exports to developing countries.

The United States and the EU had been widely blamed for the collapse of the first stage of the negotiations, at Cancún in 2003, when
we were accused of pressing too hard for the developing countries to
open up their markets, while offering too little in return, especially
in reducing agricultural subsidies and other protectionist measures.
Despite the efforts of my predecessor as Trade Commissioner, the
Frenchman Pascal Lamy, who had gone on to head the World Trade
Organisation, the impasse remained when I arrived in Brussels.
A meeting in Geneva a few months before my arrival had at least
produced a 'framework agreement' providing a road map for our
efforts to reach a compromise, but hundreds of issues, technical and

political, would have to be worked out if we were to have any prospect of a deal.

The more I immersed myself in the talks, the more certain I became of the need to do whatever I could to help achieve an agreement. The benefits of freed-up trade and the stimulus to growth and jobs would be too great, for both the developed and the developing world, for us to fail, but every party would have to compromise if it was to work. I decided early on that the EU needed to get on the front foot and remove the frequent temptation among the other negotiating parties to use Europe's Common Agricultural Policy as an excuse to avoid the tough bargaining necessary. Step by step during my years in Brussels, I joined the reformist Danish Agriculture Commissioner, Mariann Fischer Boel, in expanding our offer to cut farm subsidies and tariffs to the very limits of the mandate we had been given by the member states. I always believed that success in the world trade talks was possible. No other issue during my time at the Commission seemed more important. None took up more of my time or energy, whether in discussions among member states or as the EU's negotiator across the globe. Barely a week passed when I was not involved on some level with trying to nudge agreement forward: with African states, with China or India, Brazil or America. And, at key junctures, with Tony and then Gordon, and other European heads of government.

The Doha negotiation was a microcosm of the wider change in the world economy. It was the first major forum in which, for example, China, India, Brazil and South Africa found themselves sitting opposite the EU and the US in an attempt to agree global rules. In that sense it was a dry run for the G20 and Copenhagen climate-change negotiations in 2009, which finally pushed this new balance of power into mainstream diplomacy. It was an object lesson in how complex this new world and the trade-offs it involved were becoming, and it also began to break down the prevailing assumption, often fuelled by NGOs, that the developing world had a single set of interests. It didn't. The large emerging economies often saw their own interests as diverging. South American producers were as worried by cheap Chinese exports as many Europeans were. India's small farmers had diametrically different views on the value of open farm trade to those of the agribusinesses of Brazil. Doha also emphasised the fact that a small group of exporters from the developing world, especially China, Brazil and India, were often closer in their interests to the developed countries than to those at the bottom of the development ladder.

The complexity of these issues was enlivened by a cast of fascinating characters. The Japanese were, without fail, represented at all meetings by both the Industry and the Agriculture Minister, each, it seemed, not trusting the other to negotiate on his own, accompanied by dual teams of many officials and interpreters. For a long time they said that at some stage they would table an enticing new negotiating offer they had in their back pockets. If it existed, it remained in their pockets. Chinese Commerce Minister Bo Xilai – my tough, urbane and effective opposite number during the textiles negotiations – became a good and respected colleague. He was replaced by the equally impressive Chen Deming when he graduated in 2007 to the Chinese Politburo and became party boss in Chongqing, where he embarked on high-profile efforts to stamp out corruption. Brazilian Foreign Minister Celso Amorim lived up to his international reputation for having a tough, and at times emotional, negotiating style, coupled with a forensic grasp of his brief. India was represented by Commerce Minister Kamal Nath, who combined the grandstanding populist style of the Subcontinent's regional politics with an uncanny ability to negotiate while simultaneously sending emails and text messages on his multiple BlackBerries. He also had a wonderfully dry sense of humour: when he noticed that I had a habit of singling out the 'emerging economies' as candidates to pay more in tariff reduction, he took to describing Europe and the US as the 'submerging economies'. All of us spent hundreds of hours locked in often intensely technical negotiation. The talks were presided over by Pascal, who seemed to sustain himself on a diet of bananas and brown bread as he banged heads together, and used the spells between group sessions to hold individual meetings with the negotiators.

It was all a world away from Westminster, and I found it utterly fulfilling in almost every way. I still cared, of course, about what was happening to New Labour, and to Tony, and about the pressures he was facing from Gordon and the PLP. But when I woke up in Brussels or Beijing, Delhi or Johannesburg, São Paulo or Washington, not easily contactable by phone, I felt not so much political homesickness as relief at the distance from Downing Street. There were moments of sadness, especially when I sold my home on Hutton Avenue in Hartlepool, finally cutting my constituency cord. This was a wrench, because in addition to the good friends I had made, Hartlepool grounded me and gave me a sense of identity which I valued. It also enabled me to frame my political ideas through the real experiences of those whose lives I was aspiring to improve. But I was involved in new and complex challenges, with responsibilities and a political identity that were no longer defined by my estranged fellow-founders of New Labour.

I was still in regular, if less frequent, contact with Tony, and I could not help but be aware that pressure was once again building on him. I felt that I had left him on a high. He had recovered from his immediate post-Iraq trough, his April wobble and the renunciation of his arrangement with Gordon to quit before the next general election. His domestic agenda was back on track too, as was evidenced by the fact that Gordon was clearly displeased by much of it. Tony had successfully launched a series of five-year plans on the public services, and had a distinctly New Labour agenda on which to base his manifesto for the next election. But the more assertive he became, the more he risked open rebellion by Gordon. In the run-up to the party conference, Tony had tried to get Gordon to cooperate on an agreed election campaign strategy. The result was a hardening of attitudes on both sides. 'Basically, Gordon is on strike,' Tony told me. 'He goes on about my obligation to him, but I don't feel it any more.' Clearly losing patience, he responded to Gordon's work-to-rule with an act of political daring – or self-harm, depending on your outlook – naming Alan Milburn as coordinator for the general election campaign. He told me about the decision, rather than asking me whether I thought he should do it. In fact, I was ambivalent. I rated Alan highly, and had been very disappointed when he left government in the wake of his bruising battle over foundation hospitals. I also had no doubt that the appointment would enrage Gordon.

I felt the same about a second *démarche* he had told me he was planning shortly before I left for Brussels: the 'Aznar option'. He would announce that the next election would be his last. This was undeniably good news for Gordon, but he also intended to make it clear that if we won, he would serve out his full final term in office. I could see the attraction of this plan. Tony wanted to put the constant manoeuvring and speculation over the succession to one side, and finally get on with his 'radical New Labour' agenda. But I warned him that the announcement, which he made at the end of party conference in September, should not appear to be a petulant, short-term response to Gordon. Of course, Gordon was always going to see it that way, but fortunately he was travelling to an IMF meeting in Washington when Tony used a succession of TV interviews to make the news public. This did not dampen Gordon's rage, and on his behalf Tony's announcement was likened to an 'African coup'. The real problem, I now saw, was that the two of them were locked in a fatal political embrace. Tony could not, or at least would not, sever his dependence on his Chancellor completely. As for Gordon, any faint prospect that he would support Tony as long as he remained Prime Minister vanished now that Tony had retreated from his side of the Admiralty House deal – a deal which Tony insisted, rightly, that Gordon had not honoured either. Gordon must have felt that the succession date was always being pushed off. It was always *mañana, mañana*; but tomorrow never came.

Within a few weeks of the party conference, however, Tony's rediscovered drive, determination and confidence seemed again to be waning. 'Gordon definitely wants me out before the election,' he told me in a long phone call at the end of October. I said the likelihood of that happening struck me as so remote that it was not worth worrying about. Now that Tony had publicly said he would contest the next election, Gordon's only option would be to force Tony out. But there wasn't the time, or the mechanism, for him to do that before election day in May 2005. Nevertheless, Tony remained concerned about how he could fight the election, and govern as a radical New Labour leader, without finding some way of dealing with Gordon. He told me that Gordon was now engaged in a no-holds-barred war of subversion.

In the months leading up to the campaign, it was as if there were two Tony Blairs. The first was steeling himself for the election. He knew that defeating the Tories a third time would be tough. Michael Howard was a more formidable opponent than William Hague, and the Conservatives were promising tax cuts while also fighting on red-button populist issues like crime, asylum and immigration. Tony thought that their campaign captured a certain public mood by playing on grievance, anger and fear, but that it completely lacked a vision and hope for the future. Philip's focus groups suggested that while voters wanted to give us a much narrower majority, they didn't want the Tories back. His sense was that if the Conservatives really looked like winning, people would run a mile. They just hadn't changed enough. The implication, in Tony's mind, was clear: he had to go out and show he was still at the top of his game. He had to convey that he and the government had 'got the message' of voter discontent. He had to persuade voters that he was the real agent of the change.

But there was the other Tony, too, the one who felt vulnerable and feared the effects of not having Gordon on board. At the beginning of January 2005, he had another attempt at re-establishing some semblance of a working relationship. When he phoned me that evening, he was shaken. He had tried to get Gordon's response to the first of his election strategy memos, and to get him talking about how to organise the campaign and win the election. 'He started shouting at me,'

Tony told me. 'He said, "What's your proposal, then?" ' When Tony replied that he proposed they 'work together', Gordon had exploded. ' "That's not a proposal!" he said. He meant that it wasn't a date for my exit.' Nothing else mattered to him, Tony complained. 'He's like something out of the mafiosi. He's aggressive, brutal, in order to get what he wants.' Until the very eve of the campaign, things worsened. 'There is no one to match Gordon,' Tony said in one late-night phone call, 'for someone who articulates high principles while practising the lowest skullduggery.' He did understand the sense of grievance Gordon felt, but he no longer felt any shred of empathy, obligation or guilt. At one stage he even said that if Gordon's behaviour didn't change, he would have no option but to challenge him publicly before the election. I had long ceased believing that that would happen, and even Tony must have done so too.

I saw my role throughout this time as keeping Tony upright and sustaining his appetite and stamina for the fight. I felt it was not for me to second-guess him or put myself above the battle. If Tony wanted to remain in his job, I would do what I could to help him. The phone conversations we had as I continued my global travels were sometimes heart-rending. He variously believed, and told me, that Gordon was mad, bad, dangerous and beyond hope of redemption. Of course, many of the things he said were merely offloading the anger and pressure he felt. I was happy to serve as his relief valve, but what concerned me – and increasingly infuriated me – was the response of some, not all, of those in his inner circle in Number 10. I came to feel that they were sucking energy out of him by constantly telling him he was politically weak, that he was trusted less by the public, and badly isolated in the party. They may have been right about all these things, but I believed that their responsibility was to help him regain his confidence. Their chosen remedy was to force him to make up with Gordon, on whatever terms. They did not seem to understand, as I did, that both of them were well past the stage where genuine cooperation was possible. Gordon wanted to depose, not rescue, Tony. Sueing for peace in these circumstances would be an invitation for Gordon to demand, and quite possibly win, Tony's surrender. No doubt, if they had heard my views they would have said it was much more complicated than that, and that the situation had to be managed, hence their appeasment. Of course it was complicated, but ultimately Tony had two options: fight, or go. He ended up half-fighting and half-going.

Philip and Alastair had returned to Labour HQ to work their magic on the election campaign in the new year. But the paralysis that had been brought about by Gordon's team going on strike alarmed them, and they quickly came to the conclusion that unless the two wings of Downing Street – the official and the provisional – came together, there would not be an election campaign worthy of the name. They embarked on a private mission to bring Gordon round. Within days, their efforts were being reported in the press and used to embarrass Tony. As Philip explained to me later, the problem with Gordon was that if you gave him an inch, he took a mile.

By late March, only days before the campaign launch, Tony was close to panic. Gordon had the PLP clamouring for him to ride to the rescue. With time running short, there was no alternative but to beg him to join forces with Tony. Gordon's terms were simple: the humiliating exclusion of Alan Milburn. Tony felt that he had no choice but to agree. He could not run the risk of not embracing Gordon. If he did so, and won only a small majority – and even more so if we lost – the party would not forgive him. After the deal was done, a joint party political broadcast was filmed, and grid dates were set for them to campaign together. These included one especially memorable outing during which Tony bought two ice-cream cones and shared in a televised moment of sweet harmony with his campaign partner.

I had a conversation with Philip shortly afterwards. He told me to accept that Tony's weakness had left him with no alternative but to sue for peace with Gordon. I argued back that nobody saw the senselessness of this conflict more than me, but the British people would not re-elect a Prime Minister who sounded defeated and appeared to be in hock to his Chancellor. Whether by accident or by design, Philip did not call me again for the rest of the campaign – probably, knowing his all-consuming drive at campaign time, it was because he was far too busy. Nor did I speak to Alastair. But I talked to Tony from time to time during the campaign, including as the polls were closing on the night of 5 May. I was briefly back in Britain, watching the results coming in at Robert Harris's house in Kintbury. Tony sounded spent, like someone who had just lost an election and was being evicted from office. I tried to fire him up, and told him to 'get up off his knees', and look and sound like a leader with a substantial renewed majority, but it was hard going. I reminded him that this was not 1997; it was two terms later. Time had inevitably taken its toll, but he was heading for a good, if reduced, majority of sixty-six seats. He had been bound to lose a lot of votes, especially as he had the aftermath of the Iraq war to contend with, but the country had decided to stick with him. He had his mandate, and Labour had won a historic third term.

But the circumstances of the campaign, and the understandable media emphasis on the fact that this election victory, unlike the previous two, was far from a landslide, left Tony half-doubting whether he'd actually won. No doubt Gordon's words were ringing in his ears, the constant refrain that he had forfeited the trust of the British people. He began to believe it. In the end, Gordon had campaigned effectively. He probably felt that he was approaching the home stretch. Whether he would be in Number 10, or out altogether if Tony refused to budge, he knew the day of reckoning could not be far off.

Tony went into the mid-summer of 2005 buoyed, then painfully jolted, and finally regaining the confidence and determination that had often flagged during his second term. The dramatic change in fortunes began over a momentous forty-eight hours in July. First, Tony played a crucial role in the final salesmanship and bargaining in Singapore that secured the 2012 Olympic Games for London. Then, amid the celebrations of that victory back home, he flew to Scotland to open an ambitious G8 summit at Gleneagles. As the meeting was getting under way, a series of suicide bombs hit London's transport system. It was our 9/11.

By coincidence, I was in London that day, having invited a core group of Doha negotiating partners to meet under my chairmanship in the Foreign Secretary's official residence in Carlton Gardens. The anguish I felt at watching the images of carnage in the city where I had been born and spent most of my life was made even more painful by having to absorb the blow in the presence of my guests. Tony responded with the calm, measured outrage he had shown after the 9/11 attacks. He was no less certain of the seriousness of the threat this new form of terror posed. It was followed by a second round of bus and tube attacks two weeks later, but, thankfully the bombs malfunctioned on this occasion. Tony was at his best in these moments; he found the words to speak for the country, and most of the country stood solidly behind him.

By September, his political position looked more secure. The pressure to name a departure date had receded, the mood in the PLP had quietened, and Tony went to the party conference feeling stronger than he had done for some time. Although there was no head-on clash with Gordon this time, Tony's would-be successor's intentions were pretty clear. When Gordon spoke, he praised Tony. In future, he added, Labour – New Labour – would 'not just inhabit the centre ground, but dominate it'. What was inescapable to anyone in the hall was that this was not the speech of a Chancellor, but the pre-inaugural address of a Prime Minister. There were paeans to Britain and Britishness. There was a poetic passage about how his parents had given him a set of firm ethical and moral values. There were name-checks for virtually the entire cabinet. And then came the clincher, after praising Tony for having challenged the party to renew itself for the future: 'Because the renewal of New Labour will be as profound a challenge, as rigorous a task and as great an achievement as the creation of New Labour, I will, in the next year, visit every region and nation of our country. With you I want to listen, hear and learn, and to discuss the economic, social and constitutional changes we need to build for the future.' At least Tony's got a year, I remember thinking to myself.

Tony felt the need to fight back. Not against Gordon's taking over, which he recognised was probably inevitable. But he didn't trust Gordon's assurances about sticking to the centre ground, and was convinced that he would not embrace the 'radical New Labour' policies necessary to deal with the new challenges of twenty-first-century Britain. He was therefore determined to have a 'big debate' on policy. I said he should push ahead sooner rather than later. I was more and more sure that one of our greatest missed opportunities in 1997 had been our failure to broaden the base of New Labour, and build an expanded, membership-based party. I urged him to make sure the debate went beyond Westminster: if he really wanted to embed New Labour, he had to take one last stab at making it 'more of a movement, less of a club'. I also encouraged him to accelerate his plans for an ambitious ten-year 'forward policy review', building on the reforms he had begun to put in place.

Politically, I saw obvious dangers ahead. I warned Tony that there would be a sense among some in the PLP that he was simply living out the last remaining stage of his leadership – meaning that he would be tolerated, but not endorsed if he pushed them too far. Another danger was that Gordon would work hard to get him out by trading on the inevitability of his succession and the damage that would be done to the party if Tony hung on for too long. I did see one, rather ironic, reason to believe that might not happen – at least not yet. Michael Howard had stepped down as Tory leader, and there was a growing likelihood that he would be replaced by the youthful David Cameron. Cameron would be eager to set out new 'dividing lines' of his own, and would seek to contrast his energy and freshness with a Labour Party that looked stale, out of touch, and with a future agenda which, under Gordon, would look at best hesitatingly centrist. At least some of our MPs were beginning to sense the peril in this, and to recognise that our best response would be to promote a radical New Labour agenda that would leave us well-placed for an election battle with Cameron.

But that feeling might not last, and I urged Tony to strike while the iron was hot. He tried to do just that, beginning discussions on future policy not only within Number 10, but with Gordon. They made some halting headway, but it never led to the big debate he wanted. That was effectively blocked by Gordon and his allies, who saw it as just the latest in a series of devices by Tony to delay his departure.

While policy-making in the Commission was difficult and time-consuming, it was done in the spirit of unity. It made me thankful that I was in Brussels. Without doubt, the hardest blow I had to endure during my time there was the death of my mother. The news came early on the morning of Valentine's Day 2006, as I was driving to my office, a short distance away from the Petit Sablon flat. My brother Miles telephoned with the news that she had passed away peacefully in her sleep in the residential care home she was living in near him and his wife Valerie in St Helens, in north-west England.

She had been suffering from Alzheimer's disease, and her condition had been deteriorating steadily in the three years following her move north to live with Miles after our Bigwood Road home had been sold. After two years, Miles and I reluctantly took the decision that she could no longer be left alone during the daytime while he and Valerie were out at work. She did not want carers she did not know coming in to look after her, and introducing her to the care home we chose was a painful step. I could not imagine her, with all her dignity and independence, living with strangers, but there was no alternative. She was utterly stoical as she settled in, and we did our best to recreate a setting she was used to in her room, with furniture, pictures and other possessions that were familiar to her.

She became more and more withdrawn as the Alzheimer's steadily took hold, until she no longer recognised me when I came to visit her. Miles and Valerie were wonderful with her, as they had been throughout her illness, looking after me as well when I found it hard to cope with what was happening to her. In the end she did not recover from a bad chest infection she caught at the beginning of the year. My feeling was that she did not want to get better, preferring instead to close down and quietly leave us.

At her funeral, Miles's daughter Leonie spoke beautifully about her grandmother. Leonie's daughters, Lauren and Amelie, whom my mother loved, were there too, with their father Robin. Many other kind friends also made the journey to say goodbye, but I was most glad to see my schoolboy friend and fellow rebel Steve Howell. His presence reminded me of my teenage years, when my mother was at her finest, keeping open house for everyone of my generation who wanted to stop by and eat and drink, and above all talk to her.

I was still visiting Tony in Downing Street about once a month. Early in 2006, Alastair and Philip had persuaded him to begin a series of transition meetings with them and Gordon, who was flanked by two of his most trusted protégés, Ed Balls and Ed Miliband. I told Tony that I disagreed strongly with this move. I felt that it would weaken him, add fuel to Gordon's expectations of Tony's departure date, and quite likely hasten it. I don't know if the talks ever had a realistic prospect of succeeding. Their tone, I heard, was just as I would have expected: Alastair and Philip conciliatory, Gordon truculent and impatient. Tony always returned from them feeling worn down. The talks collapsed in mid-March, overwhelmed by a crisis that tempted Gordon to ratchet up the pressure on Tony, yet strengthened Tony's determination to cling on. Tony had been badly disconcerted by a conversation with Gordon that was supposed to be about their latest policy dispute, on pension reform, which Gordon opposed. 'It was the ugliest meeting I have ever had,' Tony told me when he phoned afterwards. 'I have never been confronted with such ugliness in my life. It was a naked, undisguised threat.' The threat was about to get worse.

It became known as 'cash for honours', and it stemmed from Tony's decision to accept millions of pounds of loans for the party's 2005 election campaign – which did not have to be publicly disclosed. Accepting loans from political supporters was a practice pioneered by the Tories. While it did not break any rules, it sat uneasily with the legislation we had brought in to make party funding more transparent. It all fed into a wider political narrative, in the media and in the country, of a Prime Minister from whom authority was draining away. Tony knew it looked terrible. 'It's ghastly,' he said. 'A nightmare.'

A few hours after the pensions row Jack Dromey, deputy head of the Transport and General Union and also the Labour Party Treasurer, announced on television that he was launching an inquiry into 'the securing of loans in secret to the Labour Party in 2005'. This further increased the political pressure on Tony, by suggesting that the campaign funding strategy had been adopted without the support, or even the knowledge, of his own party. Was that the deliberate aim? Tony was certainly convinced that it was. Jack was no ordinary union boss: his wife was Harriet Harman, a long-term ally of Gordon's.

Tony had no doubt when the next threat would come: local elections in England were seven weeks away. From early April, he phoned me more and more often. It was not just Gordon that was his immediate worry, but how their renewed friction, and his eroding position, would play in the PLP. For the first time, he accepted that his remaining time in office was going to be a lot shorter than he had hoped. He would certainly not serve a full final term. Even before this latest crisis, he had begun to scale down his expectations. But he had still assumed he would be around for the best part of another two years, and would hand over to his successor for the second half of the Parliament. Now he realised that even that was unrealistic. He settled on a new date for his departure from Number 10: the summer of 2007, barely a year away.

The question was how to communicate this. He was against a public announcement, which would risk making him not only a lame duck, but possibly a dead one. It would also remove any incentive for Gordon to support him during his final period in office. If anything, Gordon was becoming less cooperative. When Tony privately suggested agreeing on a general time-frame for his departure – a 'landing zone' around the summer of 2007 – Gordon told him that wasn't good enough. He was no more enthusiastic about the other side of the bargain: that he help Tony get his policy agenda through. In the second week of April, the two of them had another Admiralty House dinner with John Prescott. Tony emerged less, rather than more, comfortable about formally setting a departure date, although the meeting did convince him that the very most he could hope for was to stay until the summer of 2007. If he pushed for more, he suspected that he would face an open campaign to get him out.

His main fear was what would happen after the local elections on 4 May. The weeks running up to the election could hardly have been less encouraging. Most worrying was 'cash for honours'. After Jack Dromey's grandstanding appearance, other parties had pushed for probes. In response to a complaint from one SNP backbencher, the police had opened a criminal investigation. Other troubles were also brewing. Patricia Hewitt, the Health Secretary, had been heckled at a speech to the Royal College of Nurses, while Charles Clarke, at the Home Office, was hit with the revelation that a thousand foreign nationals had somehow escaped deportation after serving jail sentences in Britain. To top it all, John Prescott was revealed to have been having an affair with his civil service diary secretary. These were hardly the best circumstances in which to reconnect with voters. Tony and his team at Downing Street were convinced that Gordon was simply waiting for a 'meltdown' in the local elections to launch a push for power.

The prognosis looked dire. Yet despite all the background pressures, Tony still seemed to be governing the country well in the circumstances. He was heavily focused on his domestic policy agenda, both current and future – pushing ahead with a new programme for school and health reform, as well as on security and his 'respect' agenda on law and order. This was not without its controversial aspects, but, having learned the lessons from his first two terms, he was determined that difficult issues and decisions should be taken earlier in the Parliament. But the 'TB-GBs' – as the destructive relationship between Tony and Gordon had come to be called – were rarely out of the newspapers. Those on both the right and the left of the media, for their different reasons, clearly wanted Tony out and Gordon in. The right thought this would pave the way for the Tories, while the left wanted revenge over Iraq. As polling day approached, the frequency of Tony's phone calls increased. We both knew that if the results were as bad as the polls were predicting, Gordon's tanks would start rolling down Whitehall as soon as the results began flowing in. I agreed with Tony to reorganise my travel plans and return to London on the Thursday of the election, so I could be around if trouble broke out next door.

It was clear that there would be a cabinet reshuffle, if only because the foreign prisoners issue had stoked up unstoppable speculation that Charles Clarke would be moved. We agreed that Tony should make the cabinet changes not on the Monday, but on Friday, the morning after the election. John Reid would be made Home Secretary, while Margaret Beckett got the Foreign Office, replacing Jack Straw, who had served in the post for the whole of the previous Parliament and had stood by Tony in exceptionally tough circumstances. David Miliband was made Environment Secretary. The key members of Tony's team were lobbying Tony to appoint David as Foreign Secretary, but Tony argued that this would be too big a leap. Besides, environment was one of the main issues that the newly installed David Cameron was using in his efforts to convince voters he was a different kind of Tory leader.

I am sure that these were not the real reasons Tony balked at giving David one of the top roles in cabinet. Instead, he believed – rightly – that Gordon would have seen it as a boost for the credentials of a potential leadership challenger. Though David was a friend, and I rated his abilities very highly, I was not part of the lobbying effort on his behalf. I was focusing most of my energy on trying, without success, to convince Tony to transfer Charles to the Foreign Office. Charles was upset at being moved at all, saying that if Tony did not have confidence in him as Home Secretary, it was only right that he return to the backbenches. I thought Charles would be good at the Foreign Office; I also thought it might be the one job that would persuade him not to quit.

I later came to regret the outcomes for both David and Charles. I now wish I had added my weight to the calls for David to be named Foreign Secretary, and that we had found a way to keep Charles in cabinet in another of the major jobs. Either might have made it at least slightly more likely that when Tony did go, there would have been a contest rather than a coronation for his successor. The outcome might have been the same, although I am not entirely sure of that. But even had Gordon still become Prime Minister, he, the party and his government would have been strengthened by a contest. Still, the cabinet changes were much better handled than Tony's earlier reshuffles. He was seen as a Prime Minister decisively getting on with the job.

The election results were bad, but not quite as awful as had been forecast, and the reporting of them was more upbeat than might have been expected. Gordon still went on television to argue that they had been a wake-up call, and that Labour had to embark on 'renewal' – his favoured code-word for a change in Number 10. But the results had left him awkwardly placed. The expected meltdown had turned into a mere disaster; a calamity rather than a catastrophe. Even so, two of Gordon's close political allies, Nick Brown and the Oxford MP Andrew Smith, told TV interviewers that the results were so dire that Tony needed to set out a clear timetable for his departure.

On Saturday morning there was evidence of further rumblings from Gordon's camp, and there was a danger that the Sunday papers would be used for a major renewed push against Tony. I had cycled up to St John's Wood to have breakfast with David Alliance, a wise counsellor and a good friend who had agreed to become trustee of the modest blind trust into which I had put my savings on going to Brussels. He was later to become a Liberal Democrat peer, his non-Labour affiliation being an important reason why I had asked him to act for me in the first place. After a truncated breakfast, I found myself closeted in his sitting room, yellow pad in front of me and phone glued to my ear as I helped plan Tony's fightback. At Tony's request I had been silently listening in to the conference calls taking place among his key political staff and channelling my advice through the young man who had become Tony's strategic communications director the year before, my friend and former aide Ben Wegg-Prosser. This arrangement suited me. As a European Commissioner, it would hardly be right for it to become known that I was involved so directly in the affairs of an EU member government, even if it was my own. This was, however, neither 'being Peter' nor 'being Bobby'. It was even more clandestine, more akin to the original Third Man of Orson Welles, or Michael Rennie in his television incarnation, hidden deep in the shadows.

There were three elements to the fightback strategy I devised. First, make it an issue of policy, not personality. Second, do not do anything to provide a public timetable for Tony's departure; I said that we might as well erect a countdown clock in Parliament Square if we did that. And third, we needed quietly to expose what Gordon's team were up to, and to put Gordon's fingerprints on it. I had no doubt that Tony needed someone to go out on the airwaves and speak of a coup being mounted against the Prime Minister. This was a brutal, and risky, counter-measure, but there seemed little alternative, and in the new Home Secretary John Reid, the heavy cannon was ready to fire. John took aim, and hit his target. He described the pressure on Tony as an attempt to change leader by 'coup'. At least for the time being, the accusation probably helped to forestall one.

Still, the atmosphere was becoming so poisonous that there was a risk things would spin out of control. Tony talked to Gordon over the weekend. He came back shaking his head in frustration. He was particularly angry about the 'renewal' campaign by Gordon and his allies. 'The whole situation is like a love affair gone wrong, in which you keep doing terrible things to the other person for no rational or sensible reason,' he said. He had already told Gordon privately of his intention to leave Number 10 in July 2007, but he said Gordon now wanted a formal announcement in September, with an election for the party leadership in January. Such an arrangement would leave Tony neutered for months before he stepped down: 'I would be a total lame duck. But that would suit him. He could then come in and rescue the situation.' For now he consoled himself by concluding that things could have been even worse: 'At least we've disarmed them from making an immediate strike, and they can't make a challenge this autumn,' he said. I strongly disagreed, and told him that in my view Gordon would be back.

Tony had got through the weekend more or less intact, but on Monday evening, when he spoke to the weekly meeting of Labour MPs, he was prey again to the voices around him telling him to give ground to Gordon. He responded by announcing that he would offer 'ample time' to his successor. This may have been the right thing to say in the circumstances; perhaps he had no alternative. But it gave the impression to his followers, not least the valiant John Reid, that it was not worth sticking their necks out for Tony. John had been brave to say what he did. But how many people would rally to his side in future if they felt there was a chance he would then only retreat, leaving his supporters exposed? I began to feel Tony's position really was becoming untenable.

My focus in Brussels, a source of ample frustrations of their own, was the trade talks. There was no formal deadline, but a US law that prevented Congress from making changes to an agreement was due to expire in June 2007, and the prospect loomed of dozens of Congressmen unpicking any deal that was struck for domestic political reasons. We had been making progress. At a ministerial conference at the end of 2005 my Farm Commissioner colleague Mariann Fischer Boel and I conceded a deadline of 2013 for eliminating all Europe's agricultural export subsidies. The agreement also committed industrialised countries to opening their markets significantly to goods from the developing world. That provided momentum, and at least some hope that our latest target date, the end of 2006, might be met.

By the new year, it had become clear that that would be no easy task. There were continued divisions between the major developed countries, especially the United States, and the key developing powers, India and Brazil. The Americans, and the EU too, wanted a reduction of barriers to industries or services in the developing world, but India and Brazil were moving very little, and very slowly, on the issue, insisting that there could be no agreement without much greater movement by the richer countries in removing agricultural subsidies. I felt especially frustrated by the lack of understanding of the steps the EU had been taking to encourage compromise. We had removed all quotas and duties for imports from the world's poorest countries in 2001, and had undertaken significantly to reform the Common Agricultural Policy. Mariann and I were ready to go even further on agricultural subsidies. I was confident that I could get the EU member states to agree to doing so, if the developing world's negotiators signalled readiness to move on opening access to their markets. It sounds technical, and in its detail it was. But ultimately it came down to a political decision by all sides to reach a compromise they could live with.

In early 2006 I began a series of efforts to try to use Tony's standing on the international stage to help break the logjam. I was concerned that Britain was putting too much emphasis on its calls for reform of the Common Agricultural Policy. The effect was to encourage the Brazilians, in particular, to hold back on any serious move regarding their tariff barriers, thinking they could squeeze yet more out of me. In March, I flew to Rio with the US negotiator, Rob Portman, for talks with the Brazilian Foreign Minister Celso Amorim. We informally laid out a proposal under which the USA would make further reductions in agricultural subsidies, and the EU would move towards the developing countries' demands for tariff cuts, in return for Brazil and others opening their markets to industrial goods. Amorim's response was tantalising, but maddeningly unspecific. Nonetheless, it had been a more productive meeting than usual, perhaps because on this occasion Brazil was negotiating away from the other developing countries that were keener on putting a brake on progress.

A serious setback followed, however – not in Rio but in Washington, barely a week later. Rob was promoted to head the

Office of Management and Budget, and his position as trade negotiator went to his deputy, Susan Schwab. Her role was going to be
crucial at our next major round of talks, in Geneva in the summer.
There was a danger that the Americans' change of negotiator might
lead to a destabilising change in their negotiating position. Whatever
the reason, the approach did change dramatically. The result – a virtual collapse, at least for the immediate future, of any hopes of a deal
– was not Susan's fault alone. The Brazilians, and in particular the
Indians, were not forthcoming on the US demands for opening up
their markets. From the outset of the meeting in Geneva, however,
Susan made it clear that the Americans simply did not want to continue talking at this stage. She said she had no intention of revealing
how far they would go on cutting agricultural subsidies. Why should
she, she scoffed. 'There is no market access from anyone else on the
table.' I was not alone in being both surprised and disheartened. Was
this Washington's way of saying it had given up on a deal? Or was it
simply Susan's style and tactics?

I wrote to Tony with a detailed account of what had happened,
and asked him to see, through President Bush, if he could flush out
whether the US action was agreed by him, what it meant, and where
he thought things would go from here. I still had faith in Bush's desire
to see a deal. At a recent meeting I had put it to him directly that if
we failed, 'the wrong people would be cheering' – not only those in
the developing world whose political stance was anti-globalisation
and anti-Western, but others in our own countries who looked at
protectionism as a comfort blanket for their desire not to reform.
I offered him a list of countries and their leaders – designed to appeal
to his political prejudices – who would relish a breakdown in the
negotiations and enjoy being able to point the finger of blame at the
US and Europe.

At lunch, Bush took me aside to say that he could see the political
logic of what I was saying, and that he would do his best. In any case,
he had once remarked of the trade negotiations that 'In this game,
you can make the numbers look like you want.' In other words, if a

deal was to be had, the details could be made to suit how you wished to present them. With a modicum of goodwill on all sides, the distance separating us was not that large. The question was how long the hiatus in serious negotiations would be. All parties knew that the nearer we got to the June 2007 expiry of Bush's leeway to sign a deal without having it rewritten by Congress, the more likely it became that a deal could take years to achieve; and I was afraid that Bush had other priorities and pressures to contend with.

So did Tony. After his May scare, he did begin to regain at least some of his self-confidence. He even stood firm against Gordon on a major policy decision – on taking forward the pension reform he had set his mind to, including restoring the earnings link. But I was struck by a powerful sense of inner struggle. Part of him remained intent on driving his agenda ahead. He also had strong views about how Labour should deal with David Cameron, disagreeing with Gordon's preference for painting him as a closet right-winger and drawing the old ideological 'dividing lines'. Tony's fear was that until such a charge could be made credible, it would not work, and would hurt Labour more than Cameron. He reasoned that Cameron's strategy rested on New Labour vacating the centre ground. If we were assertively, steadfastly New Labour, that would force him to differentiate himself from our chosen territory. Then that would be the time for dividing lines. But Tony was also a leader looking over his shoulder. He insisted that in the months leading up to the autumn party conference – his last as leader, if he left the following summer – the emphasis had to be 'less on dates, than purpose'. He wanted to get things done. But he knew – we all knew – that the issue of dates was here to stay.

He might have navigated his way around it, but for an unexpected new crisis in mid-July. Tony's very measured response to the Israelis' military incursion into Lebanon following the Hizbollah attack on an Israeli border patrol upset many in the party. But Tony stood his ground, because much as he felt that Israel's response was excessive, he would not conspire in encouraging the idea that somehow Hizbollah were innocent victims.

Politically, however, his standing was hugely damaged. His position caused anger not just among the usual suspects, whose point of departure in any debate on the Middle East was that Israel was always in the wrong. A majority in the cabinet – including David Miliband and even more assertively loyal Blairites like Tessa Jowell – were uncomfortable. As he left for his summer holiday, it seemed Tony could count on fewer friends in the PLP than at any time since the invasion of Iraq.

He returned from his summer holiday with a strategy designed to win him the space to govern in his final year. Three issues would have to be confronted: Gordon, his departure date, and now Lebanon. He began with a series of meetings at Chequers with party figures to tell them why he had acted as he did. He stressed that there had never been any question of condoning Israel's excesses. He might not be able to convince the critics, but he would at least reach out to them, and make the effort to explain.

But Gordon had now lost all patience. Placated, strung along and then disappointed time and again, he was at the end of his tether. The final trigger was an interview Tony had given to *The Times* in late August, in which he had repeatedly deflected attempts to get him to name a departure date. When he had asked me about it beforehand, I had questioned the wisdom of the interview, fearing that it was unlikely to make the situation with Gordon easier, and could well make it worse.

When key members of the team gathered on Friday, 1 September, the morning the *Times* interview appeared, however, they were confident of weathering any immediate storm. There was even an interlude of black humour, over agreeing a strapline for the forthcoming party conference literature. The Treasury had objected to the word 'future' in the slogan. Ben couldn't resist forwarding me an email exchange he had had with the party's General Secretary, Peter Watt. 'GB hates "future",' Peter had messaged him. Ben had replied: 'I'm aware of that!'

Now Gordon was ready to move. The claim that he knew nothing in advance of the backbench plot over the week that followed is frankly incredible: the ringleader, Tom Watson, the Labour MP for West Bromwich East and one of Gordon's closest allies, would not in those days have blown his nose without Gordon's say-so. The fact that it recruited erstwhile, but ministerially disappointed, Blairites such as Siôn Simon and Chris Bryant, was an indication of its careful planning. The more interesting question was how far Gordon wished them to go at this stage. Did he want them merely to shake the tree, or topple it? My view was that he was determined to get a clear, unequivocal, public commitment to a date for Tony's departure, and that he was prepared to go as far as necessary in order to obtain it. In my judgement, Gordon had long given up hope of a friendly, agreed handover, and now believed that the only circumstances under which Tony would go were if he was forced out, and that no amount of cooperation with him would achieve the outcome he sought. Indeed, working well with Tony, Gordon reasoned, would simply make Tony feel that things were going well, which would ease the pressure on him.

From my office in Brussels, I followed the course of events, beginning with reports of a letter from backbench MPs calling on Tony to step aside. This would only have any real force if there was a clear signal that it was being backed by Gordon. By Tuesday morning, there were reports quoting a number of MPs criticising Tony. Some, but by no means all of them, were long-time critics or spurned former ministers. Some objected to the lack of 'clarity' over the transition. Others wanted an early timetable.

David Miliband agreed to go on the *Today* programme that morning to try to regain the initiative. He did not give an exact departure date, but with Tony's approval he did concede that the 'conventional wisdom' was that he would carry on for another year: 'It seems to me that that conventional wisdom is reasonable.' Before long, it became clear that even that would not be enough.

Though I was in Brussels, I felt as if I was living through the firestorm myself. During these days I was in constant contact by phone: with Tony, with Ben, and others in Number 10. Little by little, details

At the Progressive Governance Conference in London, 2003: *left to right* – President Lula of Brazil, Tony, President Thabo Mbeki of South Africa, me.

At the EU-China political summit in the Great Hall of the People in Beijing, with Tony applauding in the background.

Arriving at the World Trade Organisation talks in Geneva, July 2008

Irish farmers protesting in Dublin against the proposed WTO deal.

'Cashmering my way into Number 10' on my return to government for the third time, October 2008. Some thought my jumper was a little casual.

Gordon and I see the funny side during a question-and-answer session with local business people in Kent on 21 October, my birthday, shortly after I rejoined the government.

At the Cabinet table: *left to right* – Alan Johnson, David Miliband, Alistair Darling, me, Douglas Alexander, Ed Balls.

Resplendent in my robes on the occasion of my introduction to the House of Lords, with Roger Liddle.

On a return visit to Brussels, with the President of the European Commission, José Manuel Barroso.

In a military aircraft during my visit to Iraq, April 2009.

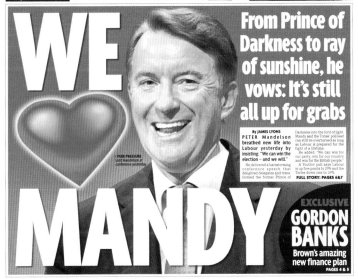

Above Comeback kid: delivering my speech to the Labour Party conference, September 2009.

Left The *Mirror* headline the next day summed up the mood of delegates in the hall.

Dancing with Hannah Rita-Mackenzie in the Blackpool Tower Ballroom during the general election campaign, April 2010.

Our final day in Downing Street: *left to right* – Douglas, Alastair, Gordon, me, Ed.

of the MPs' letter became public. Tom Watson was named as a signatory. Given that Tom was a fully-fledged member of Team Brown, who owed his promotion as junior defence minister to Gordon's lobbying, any pretence that Tony's next-door neighbour was a mere spectator was now gone. Gordon himself was no doubt weighing the moment to enter the battle. With Matthew Taylor, Tony's chief adviser on political strategy, and Tony's Parliamentary Private Secretary, Keith Hill, masterminding the fightback, the former Transport Minister Karen Buck agreed to take the lead in urging MPs to sign a counter-letter. It welcomed David Miliband's virtual confirmation that Tony would go within a year, and urged an end to actions that might undermine an orderly transition. By mid-morning, there were seventeen signatories. By shortly after noon there were thirty. By the end of the day, nearly sixty.

In the next morning's press, Gordon ramped up the pressure. His aides were quoted as saying that David's radio reassurance, and the prospect of a further twelve months for Tony, were unacceptable. Gordon wanted a firm timetable. From Tony. In public. When I spoke to Tony on the phone, he seemed determined not to surrender to these demands. We agreed that he needed to build on the Buck letter's momentum, and to convey that the broad majority of the PLP, whatever they thought of Tony, were appalled by Gordon attempting to hound him out of office. More MPs steadily signed the letter, but what ultimately turned the tide was that not only in the Commons, but across the party, there was growing anger. Most of it was directed at Tom Watson, but only slightly less at Gordon himself. The Labour Party switchboard, website and email in-boxes were full of messages voicing fury at the way Tony was being treated.

Tony and Gordon held the first of two meetings on the morning of Wednesday, 6 September, in Gordon's office. When I spoke to Tony afterwards, he said that Gordon had made four demands in return for calling off the battle. The first was that, 'for the good of the party', Tony had to leave well before next July. The second was that in the interim, he and Gordon would have to agree all major decisions – they would, after all, soon be affecting Gordon's government. The third was for Tony to 'repudiate' calls by Gordon's principal Blairite nemeses, Alan Milburn and Stephen Byers, for a debate on future policy. Finally, he wanted Tony's formal endorsement as his successor. Tony said no to all of them. He tried to explain why each was unacceptable, and that for him to attempt to shut down a policy debate would be simply unworkable. Gordon knew Tony was the prime mover in the push for such a debate, but Tony said, 'Gordon, why fight it? Why don't you make a virtue of people like Byers and Milburn and bring them into an inclusive debate, around you, about where the party and the country should go? That would mean more to the cabinet, do more to inspire trust in you, than anything else you could do.' Gordon stood firm. He could sense victory. It would soon appear, however, that he had failed to appreciate how the momentum had changed.

By the time the two of them met again, at around 2 p.m. in the garden behind Number 10, the endgame was approaching. Gordon was less aggressive, and Tony knew there would have to be some sort of compromise. After two hours of bargaining, a deal emerged. There would still be no firm date announced for Tony's departure, but he would use a visit to a London school the following day to confirm that this year's party conference would be his last as leader. Gordon would issue a statement basically accepting this.

Tony had made up his mind, once and for all. Quietly and by himself, sharing his innermost thoughts only with Cherie, he decided that he could not go on fighting any longer. He was not going to allow his government, and then the party, to fracture over his future in office. Instead, he wanted to complete the unfinished policy business he had begun. He felt fully across the agenda he was pursuing, confident in his ability to articulate it, and more at ease, finally, with both the country and the party. He had better allies in Europe, in France's President Nicolas Sarkozy and Germany's Chancellor Angela Merkel, than ever before in his premiership. That was Tony's tragedy: he came fully into his prime only in the year before his time was up.

After speaking with Cherie, he told the team in Number 10, all of whom were ready and willing to wage war on his behalf, that the price of fighting on indefinately would be too great. His announcement that the forthcoming party conference would be his last meant that by September 2007 at the latest he would be gone and a new leader would be in place, thus setting the timetable for his departure.

Tony called me on the evening of the day he made his announcement. He was calm, but he was also unforgiving. 'I'm never going to plead for my job,' he said. 'I think the public can see through Gordon. They're not deceived by him. He's turned himself into a backstabbing character. I think I may have won some public sympathy today.' He added: 'I won't endorse him. I'm relaxed. They knew last summer when I was going, because I told Gordon. They know now. They just wanted to humiliate me.'

I could not bring myself to say that he had made the right decision. I was far from convinced by then that Gordon succeeding him, though surely inevitable, would be good for the government, or the country. For all his undoubted qualities, I felt that Gordon's behaviour towards Tony had diminished him. I had no doubt now that Tony had made promises to him – not at Granita, when he was not in a position to make bankable promises in any event, but certainly at their first Admiralty House dinner at the end of 2003. Ultimately, Gordon had felt entitled to make his move because Tony had not kept to his side of that bargain. Yet Gordon had not kept his side of the deal either. I did not feel he was right to have demanded the deal in the first place, to have kept pressing Tony for a departure date after his re-election in 2005, but to have refused to cooperate or work with him in office, and finally to have forced him out, was in my view unforgivable.

By the time we arrived in Manchester for conference at the end of September, Tony was feeling less bruised. He certainly had no appetite for publicly attacking Gordon – not least because it was now clear that the coup had backfired. You only had to look at the polls. Very few people believed that the assault had been anything other than a Gordon-led attempted *putsch*, and most of them didn't like that, or what it said about Gordon.

Conference turned out to be a triumph for Tony. Searching for a phrase to describe the supreme ease with which he delivered his speech – serious on policy, good-humoured about himself, charitable towards even Gordon – and the thunderous ovation it received, I couldn't help smiling. It was all in Ben's infamous memo: Tony was leaving the conference stage as 'the star who won't even play his last encore'. I clung to the hope that something good might come of the time still remaining to Tony. Gordon was not going to risk pushing him any further. The real question was whether he would support, and participate in, what Tony hoped to accomplish before leaving.

Tony returned from conference with two ambitious priorities. The first involved his current policy agenda. Domestically, he was determined to move ahead on his public service reforms, especially in the NHS, to tackle security issues like ID cards and the deportation of foreign terror suspects. Overseas, if with considerably less optimism, he wanted to make a new push on Israel–Palestine diplomacy. He also hoped finally to get the unionists and republicans to take part in a permanent Northern Ireland government. The second priority was the *future* policy agenda. It hinged on a series of painstakingly assembled documents: a root-and-branch review of Britain's welfare system by the former banker and *Financial Times* journalist David Freud, and a series of ten-year plans on the other challenges facing twenty-first-century Britain.

He hoped Gordon would be a full partner in all of this. He saw it as a last chance for him to show he was qualified to be a New Labour leader. 'Gordon and I have an identical interest now,' he told me. 'I need to be free of continual speculation as the only political issue. He needs a suspension of judgement about him, and then, at a later point, a renewed judgement on more favourable terms.' For a while, relations between them were less fraught. But by the start of 2007, with Tony's June exit date in sight, it appeared that Gordon wanted no part of either the welfare reform initiative or the ten-year policy review. When David Freud tried to get Gordon to discuss his draft report, he was snubbed. Gordon and his aides showed equally little interest in or engagement with the policy review.

By the end of February, however, an assortment of pressures had begun to build on Gordon. He was determined to succeed Tony uncontested. Having waited so long, the last thing he wanted was to leave anything to chance. The polls suggested that voters were deeply uncomfortable at the prospect of a coronation. Not only they, but some in the PLP, still seemed unsure what kind of leader Gordon would turn out to be. Despite this, Gordon wanted Tony to help head off a contest by agreeing to back him publicly as his successor.

In early March, Gordon finally began giving Tony at least some of what he had hoped for. He unexpectedly attended the launch of the Freud review, and even heaped praise on it. The next sign of Gordon's new willingness to associate himself publicly with the New Labour agenda came a fortnight later, at the unveiling of the first and most important of the ten-year policy reviews, on public service reform. The central message of the report was the need for further, bolder Blairite reforms: greater diversity of provision, and incentives to drive innovation. Gordon's presence at Tony's side appeared to indicate his support. In fact, until days before the launch, he had been adamant that he would not attend. 'Why should I?' he challenged Tony. 'It's not *my* policy, it's yours.' Tony replied that if Gordon appeared to be separating himself from New Labour and its achievements, it would not be credible to the public. 'I would be on that platform,' he said. Gordon replied, 'I'll let you know.' In the event, he was there.

In truth, Tony did not believe that Gordon would ever really be in favour of the kind of reforms he sought in welfare, health or education, and in these circumstances he questioned whether Gordon could win an election against David Cameron. Tony knew the Tory leader had vulnerabilities: he was not, at least not yet, a substantial figure, and he was in charge of a party that had yet to change as Labour had in the 1990s. But he was seen as having attractions as a politician: he was bright, he had an easiness about him, and he had good political instincts. He would be the most difficult possible opponent for Gordon.

I agreed. Not only because of my long experience of Gordon, but because of my more fleeting encounters with Cameron. The first had come in 1992, at my lunch with the then Carlton TV boss Michael Green, after I had questioned Michael's donations to the Tories in the Commons, which Cameron, having left his post as a Tory special adviser to become Carlton's director of corporate affairs, had attended. I remembered him as affable but not especially assertive. When I met him again in Brussels at the end of 2006, he was much more self-confident, and not unimpressive. We began by talking about Europe. Though obviously no Euro-enthusiast, he seemed open to serious discussion about the EU. He said that his principal concern was not with what it was doing in the main, but to ensure a coherent, united position within his party.

I suggested that our aides and officials allow us a brief chat in private, and we talked politics. 'How are you feeling about the great clunking fist that's coming your way?' I joked, recalling Tony's warning to him during an earlier Commons exchange that he would not have things all his way. 'You'd better be ready for an opponent who's a lot more confrontational and brutal than Tony.' He laughed, and said that he and his party were 'totally prepared' for a Brown premiership. 'Look,' I said, 'you cannot be totally prepared for someone who doesn't take hostages when it comes to political street-fighting.' Cameron seemed relaxed, even eager, at the prospect of Gordon as leader. He said they had a very full reading of Gordon's personality. In their view, he would turn out to be his own worst enemy. I told him I wouldn't be so confident. Cameron sent me a Christmas card a few weeks later, with a p.s. saying he was awaiting 'the big clunking fist'.

It was not yet finally decided, of course, that Gordon would succeed Tony. But if not Gordon, who? Tony had high opinions of some of the senior ministers thought to be considering a challenge, especially Charles Clarke. But he also feared that they would be hobbled by being seen as 'part of the past'. He had come to believe that what the party should really do, if it was to keep New Labour new, was skip a generation. We had to recapture the vigour, the appetite for new ideas, and the popular enthusiasm we had had before 1997. He said he hoped Charles would stand against Gordon, but mainly because by prompting a leadership contest this would create the opportunity for David Miliband to enter the race. Ever since 1997, Tony had harboured doubts about whether David was wholly New Labour. He still did. If by that he meant that David wasn't an evangelical Blairite, he was right. But he was certainly a principled moderniser. He was also thoughtful, likeable, articulate and fearsomely bright. Tony was convinced that if David entered into a contest with Gordon, at least the critically important debate about policy would be unavoidable. He was sure that David would be a candidate of renewal and reform, and had some chance of winning.

I too felt that we needed a contest for the leadership, not a coronation, and when I talked to Tony in March I gently chastised him for not having done enough to pave the way for any other possible successors to build themselves up. If he had meant all those things he said about Gordon, admittedly often in exasperation, in the scores of conversations we had had, why had he not done more to promote other candidates? 'You are in danger of being blamed by history for saddling us with Gordon because of your own desire to keep buying him off to save yourself, and because of your failure to build up an alternative in the Cabinet,' I told him. 'I fear you may be right,' he replied.

David himself was conflicted over whether to stand. Publicly, he praised Gordon, and said he was flattered to be mentioned in the media as a potential leader and Prime Minister. He was not ruling himself out, or in. When the Commons broke for Easter, he left for a holiday in France with the intention of thinking through the implications of standing. While he was tempted, he was worried about the likely effects on his family. Politically, he was uncomfortable about the prospect of being seen as the Blairite standard-bearer in a tribal showdown with the Brownites. That was understandable. It was widely known that most of Tony's supporters, were urging him to run. But it would have been like entering a football game at half-time when your team was already 4–0 down.

Gordon did not want a contest at all, especially one against David. In early March he had tried to kill him with kindness, asking David to manage his campaign, with the prospect of becoming his right-hand man in a Brown government. The wooing went on for weeks, but David, politely but unequivocally, said no; at the end of the month Jack Straw eagerly accepted the call instead. Not being part of Gordon's team was one thing, however. Taking it on was another. In the end, David felt he couldn't. In late April – by which time Gordon's team had lined up the support of nearly half of the PLP – he used an *Observer* article to say that he would vote for Gordon Brown to lead Labour to a fourth successive election victory. He also said that in the *real* fight, against David Cameron's Tories, it was essential that Labour embarked on a 'broader and deeper' commitment to reform and renewal, and embraced a new style of politics. It was a tantalising hint of the leadership contest that wasn't. Without David, the succession issue was effectively closed. Tony felt that we now all had to support Gordon.

Tony's last month in office saw a final triumph for him, one that gave me particular pleasure. In early May, republicans and unionists at last established a comprehensive peace in Northern Ireland. The IRA had finally decommissioned its weapons. Martin McGuinness entered a devolved government not only with the unionists, but alongside his formerly implacable foe Ian Paisley. It was one of those breakthroughs that truly deserve the overused label 'historic'. Many people had worked to make it possible. I had been part of it, as had successive Secretaries of State. Jonathan Powell had played a crucially important role. So had the leaders on both sides in Northern Ireland. But no one had toiled as tirelessly, and creatively, as Tony. It was a fitting way for him to end his decade in office.

I had no involvement in the negotiations that finally brought success, but I had never stopped hoping that we would get there one day. After my resignation as Northern Ireland Secretary I had continued to take an interest in one issue in particular: ensuring at least some degree of comfort, and ultimately justice, for the families of those murdered by the Real IRA in the Omagh bombing. From the moment I had first visited the bereaved families I had taken a special interest in the attempts to bring the perpetrators to justice. It would be many years before anyone was brought to trial, and even then it was only as a result of a civil prosecution initiated by the families themselves. The proceeds of the *Sunday Times* article with which I began the fightback over my firing were put towards the fund set up for this. I also publicly supported their long civil action against the alleged bombers, persuading the government to provide £800,000 in legal aid, which ultimately led to £1.6 million being awarded in damages. It could never undo the crime, or remove the pain of bereavement, but at least it was some measure of justice, and I was proud to be actively involved with the families and other supporters, like the campaigning writer Ruth Dudley Edwards and the Conservative peer Robert Cranborne – and, I have to acknowledge, because it has never done me any favours, the *Daily Mail*.

A few weeks before Tony left office, he invited the entire 1997 inner circle for a farewell dinner at Chequers. We arrived in time to have drinks on the terrace before the light went. It was an emotional evening. For all the difficulties we had been through, all of us were approaching Tony's final days in office with a sense more of achievement than regret. Our future Prime Minister wasn't there, of course, but the resentment and bitterness of the months of insurgency were gone. When I rose to speak, I think I reflected the feelings of all us. It had been a privilege, I said, to have been part of all that Tony had accomplished. We valued his comradeship in politics. We valued his friendship. And even though we were going on to other projects, we shared some things that would never change. 'We want the Labour Party to modernise,' I said. 'And we want the Labour Party to be successful, whoever is its leader. Whoever is the Prime Minister.'

By the time of our Chequers dinner Gordon had ensured that he was the only leadership candidate to receive enough nominations, and was duly elected unopposed. With John Prescott also standing down as deputy leader there was at least one contest, which Harriet won narrowly. I followed the final days of Tony's premiership from Brussels. Having done so much to support him and his team in their efforts to get into office, I found not being there at the end slightly unsettling. On 27 June, I watched Tony's final PMQs on the televison in my office with a mixture of pride and admiration. He delivered a virtuoso performance, which was rounded off by a moving tribute from Dr Ian Paisley, who praised the impact of his powers of persuasion in Northern Ireland. Dr Paisley was not someone who had always been on the same side of the argument as Tony or me, but in the end he put an appropriate full-stop to the end of New Labour's first decade in government.

Gordon, the second man in our triumvirate, was now about to be tested. In the afternoon following Tony's last appearance in the Commons he strolled up Downing Street and into Number 10. In his remarks to the assembled media he emphasised the change that he wanted to bring to Britain. His speech was fine as far as it went, but even then I was concerned that he was planning to substitute rhetoric for action.

Meanwhile, recognition in China of my growing connection with the country came from Premier Wen Jibao at around this time when I visited during a serious nationwide health scare caused by contaminated milk. At a routine press conference before leaving Beijing I was widely photographed and shown on TV sipping from a large glass of my favourite yoghurt drink. Later that day, Wen publicly commended me for this: 'Mr Mandelson is a good and wise friend of China, and we will not forget his sensitivity to our milk producers.' He was true to his word, and gave me an hour of his time when I next returned to Beijing.

My life in Brussels was consumed by frantic efforts to conclude the Doha trade round. The package of farm subsidy and tariff cuts on the table by now was the most ambitious that the global economy had ever seen, and key players had begun to take the prospect of an agreement increasingly seriously. Gradually the outlines of a possible deal emerged, in which, in return for what Europe and North America were prepared to offer, the large emerging economies like Brazil, China and India would 'pay into' the openness of the global trading system with potentially substantial trade tariff cuts of their own. But the detail of just how much they would pay in, and what they would receive in return, became pivotal. For the first time ever, Europe was being seen not as an obstacle to a possible world trade deal, but as arguably the party working hardest to make it possible. This was not to everyone's liking. Fearful about what they claimed would be the impact on European agriculture, the French in particular professed horror at the unfolding endgame.

President Sarkozy had already publicly held me responsible for the defeat of the Irish referendum on the Lisbon Treaty. At a press conference, he had asked rhetorically: 'One child dies every thirty seconds because they are hungry, and we should negotiate within the WTO framework a 20 per cent cut in European agricultural production? There is only one person who is of that opinion – that's Mr Mandelson.' I could understand the President's anger, because Irish farmers had indeed taken to the streets of Dublin in what was a mass uprising against my negotiating stance. But I thought his argument about world hunger was misplaced in relation to the Common Agricultural Policy, and I also believed that the explanation for the Irish 'No' in the referendum was more complex.

Soon after I arrived in Geneva for what we hoped would be the breakthrough ministerial negotiation in July 2008, I was summoned to Paris to clarify my position to President Sarkozy. This was very awkward. At the time, France had just started its six-month rotating presidency of the EU, so Sarkozy was in one sense my boss. It was right that I should, at the very least, inform him of what I was doing. But as Trade Commissioner I had negotiating autonomy from the member states, including France, and I did not want to compromise this independence. I had a great deal of respect for Sarkozy, because he used his huge personality not just to lead France but to project the EU on the world stage as I believed it should be. I also liked him and enjoyed his company. Our relationship went back to before I had arrived in Brussels, and before he was President. He was fascinated by New Labour, and a great fan of Tony's. Through an intermediary, he had asked me to see him privately in his splendid offices in the French Interior Ministry. He told me that he wanted to refashion French policy in Europe to embrace Britain's ideas and approach to economic and social policy, rather than remain tied to Germany. Then he was ready for the full tutorial on the concept, creation and delivery of New Labour. '*Superbe!*' he exclaimed at the end of my two-hour presentation, punctuated by his searching questions. 'Now I have the same strategist as Tony Blair. I am going to win!'

Despite the warmth of this and subsequent contacts, we were on opposite sides of the argument as the Geneva negotiations opened. Most uncomfortably, I had to tell him that I would not come to Paris if the aim was to bend my negotiating position to his will. After discussions with Commission President Barroso, and the equally understanding Angela Merkel, I decided it would be best for me not to go and see Sarkozy. Chancellor Merkel had always given me strong support as Trade Commissioner – understandably, given Germany's huge exports. Soon after David Cameron became Conservative leader, when he was turning his back on the main right-of-centre alliance in the EU, she made it clear that she intended to have little to do with him. My advice to her was to do exactly the opposite. When I visited the Chancellery, I suggested that she should see Cameron, and make him aware of why Continental politicians and parties on the right saw European integration as vital for their national interests.

My most serious disagreements in Geneva were with the Americans. I believed that in order to get agreement, their negotiator Susan Schwab would have to show more flexibility. President Bush had let it be known again that he wanted a deal and would push for one, and I continued to take him at his word. In all the half a dozen or so times I met him while I was Trade Commissioner, I found him easier and more straightforward to talk to than any other member of the administration, mainly because of his sense of humour and his unfailing ability to call a spade a spade. He gave nicknames to people he liked: mine was 'Silver Tongue'. When we reached a stand-off in the trade talks with, say, China or India or Brazil, he would invariably say, 'OK, Silver Tongue, how are you going to talk yourself out of this one?' During one EU–US summit, when Luxembourg was in the chair, we were entering the Rose Garden at the White House for a press conference when the Luxembourg Prime Minister, Jean-Claude Juncker, asked Bush if he minded if he lit up a cigarette. 'You can do anything you like,' said Bush, 'except kiss me, because I know what you Continentals are like.' I piped up, 'You know, these days there are a lot of votes out there tied up in men kissing.' 'Perhaps,' Bush replied, 'but I don't think I'm quite ready yet.'

The other chief character of the Doha Round was President Lula da Silva of Brazil. I had got off to a wobbly start in my relations with him when I visited Brazil in 1998. He was in opposition then, largely unknown in the West, and in a speech I referred to the irrelevance of 'backward-looking' policies still held by some on the left. Inevitably this was written up as a personal attack on Lula, and when I returned to London, Tony said to me, 'What have you been doing? The office has had some guy called Lula complaining on the phone about a speech you've made.' In office, there was nothing backward-looking about Lula. Not only did he command huge popularity in his own country, but he had become a force to be reckoned with internationally. This was partly due to the size of Brazil and its fast-growing economy, but also to his leadership skills and the strength of his personality.

President Lula, like so many others, did everything he could to push the trade talks towards an agreement. But for all our efforts, that proved elusive. The final breakdown came when the US and Indian ministers refused to make any further concessions on agriculture. Without this, it was not possible to move on to other issues that might have been equally hard to resolve, but in my view not impossible. Celso Amorim and I, with the support of Pascal Lamy, tried every way we could think of to get through the impasse, but the two sides were simply unwilling to compromise any further. I warned repeatedly that if we did not get a deal then, a new administration would come into office in Washington, probably Democrat, that would make the chances of success even harder. I knew which way the Democrats were going. The Clinton free-traders were taking to the hills, and Barack Obama was hardly making the progressive case against protectionism in his campaign speeches around America. The Australian minister in the inner core of negotiators, Simon Crean, also pushed hard to keep the talks going, as did China's Commerce Minister, Chen Deming. But without further flexibility from the US and India, we could go no further.

By this time, hundreds of reporters from around the world had flocked to Geneva, and all of us gave a series of despondent press conferences. It seemed incredible that the long history of successful trade rounds, which had done so much to spread economic growth and create jobs across the world, should now be coming to a shuddering halt. Each of us said that this was a breakdown, not a collapse; but as events have shown since, it is easier to halt a trade round than to start it again. In the short term, what was at stake was the confidence that developing and emerging economies could have in the WTO and its ability to reach an agreement that benefited them. In the longer term, it was the likelihood of these fast-growing economies devising new arrangements at the expense of the richer, developed world. Either way, the world as a whole seemed bound to lose out, in the absence of a broader vision of how to manage globalisation for everyone's benefit.

I felt intensely sorry for Pascal when the negotiations stalled despite his skilful and committed leadership. After midnight on the night the talks finally collapsed, I walked down to Lake Geneva with my negotiating team. It was a beautiful summer evening, the mountains still visible across the lake, against the night sky. My team were bitterly disappointed after so many years of hard work. We were all aware that the most important goal we had set for my time as Trade Commissioner was now out of reach.

11

Comeback Kid

Following Tony's departure, I had watched the rise and fall of Gordon's fortunes during his first year in power from my Brussels base with a sense of growing apprehension. At one level I felt that, with Tony gone, I no longer had the same emotional stake in the government. But detaching myself was not as simple as that. I cared too much about the New Labour project.

Gordon made an assured start with his handling of the events of the summer of 2007 – the terrorist incidents, the foot-and-mouth scare, the floods. But I had a foreboding that his team were overplaying their hand, both in their projection of Gordon as 'protector of the nation' and in their stoking up of expectations that he would call an early election. It gave me no pleasure to be proved right in my misgivings, or to watch the calamities that befell Gordon after he had marched everyone to the top of the general election hill, only to march them down again. What I certainly did not anticipate in the first few months of Gordon's premiership was that he would ever turn to me for help.

Gordon and I had been as one in our desire to conclude the Doha trade talks successfully. He had been working hard to help find a solution, and I acknowledged and praised his support in interviews. That no doubt had helped smooth things on both sides at our first face-to-face meeting after he became leader, during his visit to the Commission headquarters in Brussels. Following a series of phone calls, and a visit to my Brussels office by the new director of political strategy in Number 10, David Muir, by the summer of 2008 I was in daily conference-call contact with Gordon, offering him advice as he sought to turn the page on a first year in office that had gone horribly wrong for him. Now, amazingly, I was back in London, back in the cabinet.

When I made my unlikely return to government in a reshuffle at the start of October, Gordon had just survived an attempt to oust him. For Labour, this seemed to be becoming habit-forming. It was not a habit I liked, and it was certainly not one that was likely to help us regain governing momentum and energy. At least it was not a fully-blown coup attempt. A few junior ministers had resigned before party conference, and a few backbenchers had asked for nomination papers to spark a leadership election. No cabinet ministers had joined the fray. Still, Gordon was convinced the 'plotters' had not given up. Though they lacked a credible leader-in-waiting, he was undoubtedly right to assume that the murmurings about his unpopularity had not gone away. Despite a strong conference performance from Gordon, Labour MPs were still restive, and pessimistic about our electoral prospects. Gordon's political predicament was dwarfed, however, by the financial contagion that had spread across the world from the US, dramatised by the collapse of Lehman Brothers bank.

My misgivings about accepting Gordon's summons when we met in Downing Street had been real. I would be giving up a fulfilling job, and a life I enjoyed, in Brussels, and I had no idea how a return to British politics would work out for me or the government. While Tony had urged me to say yes, other Blairite friends were not so encouraging. I had never hidden my feelings about Gordon's conduct in his relentless campaign to replace Tony. More than once I had told him of the danger to his reputation of pushing Tony out, and that if Tony was forced to leave without securing the legacy he wanted, Gordon's inheritance would turn very sour. I had warned him privately of the electoral risks in his taking over, and had called publicly for a contest not a coronation – as much for his sake as the party's. Now, I was not just going to work for Gordon, I was helping rescue him. Some of my political friends suspected I was driven by a desire for personal and political vindication, or by simple ambition. No doubt that was part of it. I had spent much of my life working towards one goal: being a member of a modernising Labour government. I had got there twice, for a total of only nineteen months. Of course I wanted the chance to put that right. In fact, it was not until I had been back in government for some time that I fully realised how much those two unhappy endings had distressed me – and how upset I still felt about the unravelling of the relationship that had bound Gordon, Tony and me so closely together at the beginning. I now began to understand that all this mattered much more to me than I had managed to convince myself while I was in Brussels. But I can honestly say that it was not the main reason I decided to return. Not only Gordon, but the reshaped Labour Party that I had helped to create, was in deep political trouble. Britain was in deep economic trouble. I felt a responsibility to do what I could to help. More than at any time since 1997, I felt well placed and well qualified, given my Brussels experience, to do so.

Once the mix of media mirth and astonishment over my appointment had passed, there was a brief period of sniping. How on earth could Gordon have brought back a minister who had twice been forced to resign? How would the backbenches feel? How would Ed Balls react? How could Gordon and I possibly work together? Was this a sign of Gordon's desperation? They were entirely predictable questions, and not entirely unreasonable. I had asked them myself. But few people understood the complexities of the relationship between Tony, Gordon and me. Few realised that despite all our battles, a bond had always remained. I was also coming back a different politician from the one who had left Britain four years earlier. I was more grown-up, more self-assured and self-aware, more relaxed, happier.

Brussels had been a political rebirth for me. I had no longer had to duck and weave in the crossfire between Tony and Gordon. I had felt less hunted, misrepresented and misunderstood. Instead of politicians and journalists looking for hidden meanings and motives in everything I did, I was being taken at face value. I was also valued: for the job I was doing well, but also for the warmth and humour that Brussels brought out in me. The hard outer shell I had developed over the years seemed less necessary. I never regretted what I had done on Labour's front line. To get things done, however, I had felt I could not show any sign of weakness. As a result I had made enemies. Partly because I was occasionally too rough with people; partly because I allowed myself to become caught between Tony and Gordon, and often to serve as a weapon in their battles with each other; and partly because when they finally fell out and I became aligned with Tony, I not only had my own enemies to contend with, but his too.

Now, when I returned to cabinet all this was behind me for the first time in over twenty years. Tony had left the stage, so his enemies had melted away. Gordon embraced me, so his friends became my friends. But it was more than that. In Brussels, I felt that I had finally become a front-line politician in my own right, achieving things in my own way, using my own skills and not being defined any more as 'Tony's friend' and 'Gordon's enemy'. In other words, I was no longer the third man, and I relished it. I felt free.

This feeling showed as I walked up Downing Street on the day of my return to the cabinet, in front of banks of TV cameras, and stunned reporters and photographers. Gary Gibbon of Channel 4 News described me as 'cashmering' my way into Number 10. This wasn't just a reference to the brightly coloured sweater I was wearing. It showed that I was seen as bringing new life and a bit of pizzazz to a government that had begun looking increasingly despondent and almost resigned to failure.

Something else had changed, too. I was joining a quite different, younger cabinet, that did not share the rivalries and jealousies my role as Tony's *consigliere* had provoked among ministerial peers a decade earlier. My new colleagues knew that I was not a threat. They knew I had returned to help, and for no other reason, and that they could look to me for support. I was impressed by their ability to run important departments, and by their policy grasp. Discussions around the cabinet table were longer and more substantial, and overall, the cabinet was stronger, than had been the case under Tony.

This did not always please Gordon. Still, he listened to everyone who wanted to speak, even if the impatience I sometimes detected suggested he would rather be elsewhere.

Seating arrangements around the cabinet table are always politically sensitive, and I was curious to see where I would be allocated a place. Those who are regarded as most senior or important are invariably seated opposite the Prime Minister. The further you are from the centre, especially if you are on the same side of the table as the Prime Minister, the more difficult it is to catch his attention when you want to speak. I was relieved, therefore, to find myself placed opposite Gordon, alongside the Chancellor Alistair Darling. I was equally fortunate to have Douglas Alexander on my other side. He was one of the wittiest members of the cabinet, and with Alistair's dry humour on my other flank, I knew that at least I would be kept quietly and occasionally amused.

To bring me back to the cabinet, Gordon had made me a life peer. I immediately took my seat in the Lords, becoming Baron Mandelson of Foy in the County of Herefordshire and of Hartlepool in the County of Durham. I had not intended to take both localities, and when I saw Garter King of Arms, the official responsible for agreeing the name, style and title of new peers, I had wondered aloud whether I should take Hartlepool or Foy. Both places had come to mean so much to me in my life. 'Don't worry,' he said, 'you can have them both,' and with a flourish of his pen and no further discussion I instantly became 'of Foy and Hartlepool' – in proper alphabetical order. I did not anticipate the fun the media would have at my expense over my apparent appetite for long titles.

When I first spoke in the Lords shortly afterwards, I could not help but feel the shadow of my grandfather, Herbert Morrison, who had made his own maiden speech in the Upper House more than half a century earlier. He had emphasised the importance of the American Marshall Plan in rebuilding the shattered post-war economies of Europe. I was joining the Lords at a time of almost equal economic crisis. But what I mainly thought about was my parents. I told my fellow peers that I wished both of them had lived long enough to see my entry into the Lords. In fact, my mother would probably not have attended. As the daughter of one politician and the mother of another, she had always preferred the simplicity of Bigwood Road to the pomp of the Palace of Westminster. My father, however, would have loved it. I vividly remembered, as a boy, occasionally driving with him into the centre of London. He was not above driving into the Commons itself, before post-9/11 security made that an ordeal even for people who were supposed to be there. He would rely on a cheery wave and a dog-eared copy of Hansard, left casually on the rear window shelf of the car, to get us past the policeman at the gate.

Not being in the Commons, of course, had its drawbacks. That was where the main political action took place, and I was removed from the centre of battle and the cut and thrust of debate that I so enjoyed. The Lords, although erudite and informed, was tame by comparison. But in truth I was happier there. The Commons had too many bad memories for me. I did not feel I had had long enough as a minister to build my reputation and to learn how to deploy the debating skills I needed to be thought of as a front-rank political performer.

Things began well for me on my return to cabinet. When I showed up for my first day of work at the Department of Business, Enterprise and Regulatory Reform, I was greatly moved to be greeted by hundreds of applauding civil servants. BERR was the department formerly known as the DTI, so broadly I was re-entering the same job, in the same Victoria Street office, as in 1998. I was not unaware of the fact that on two previous occasions, ministerial posts that had started well had ended in tears. I could not help smiling at a conversation between the two civil servants closest to me on the day I arrived. The Permanent Secretary at BERR, Sir Brian Bender, remarked to my Principal Private Secretary, Richard Abel, that he was retiring the following spring. 'Your job,' he said wryly, 'is to make sure I go before Peter does.'

Richard, together with Maree Glass, my former Commons executive assistant who followed me to BERR, did indeed successfully apply a policy of zero-risk in respect of any potential conflicts of interest between my ministerial and personal affairs, almost to the point of suffocation. He surveyed literally everything, even my personal emails, to ensure that no threat was lurking on the horizon, and I trusted him to do so. In policy terms, I was also picking up where I had left off. Competitiveness, innovation, the 'knowledge economy' – all these had been cast into starker relief by the economic crisis, and mattered even more now than when I had promoted them at the DTI a decade earlier. If ever there was a time for government to do all it could to encourage a diversified economy, making our GDP less reliant on the financial services, this was it. In that sense, it was both the best of times and the worst of times to get my feet under my old desk.

An early challenge came in my first cabinet meeting, on the Tuesday after the reshuffle. It was made no easier by the fact that I had had to have emergency treatment the day before for a painful kidney stone – erroneously connected by some to my showing off by drinking yoghurt in Beijing not long before. Not since my vetting in Brussels by the European Parliament had I so felt the need to be on top form. If my political resurrection was going to work, not only for me but for Gordon, it was crucial that it got off to an assured start. I opened my presentation with one of my line in kidney -stone jokes. I recalled the horror I had felt when Gordon said to me, as I writhed in pain, that all would be well, because he was sending the Minister of Health to sort me out – until I realised that the minister, Ara Darzi, was also a highly respected physician. But my main point was a serious one. In pin-dropping silence, I outlined the depth of the financial and economic crisis that I believed we were facing, how much more serious it was likely to become for businesses and jobs, and the risk of our whole economy heading over a cliff. I think we all realised that wallowing in past infighting was a distraction we could not afford.

The most extraordinary omen that my third ministerial stint would be different from the first two did not involve New Labour, or the cabinet. It was a dust-up with the Tories. The Shadow Chancellor George Osborne had evidently been regaling his friends about our summer chat on the taverna terrace on Corfu that summer. Just forty-eight hours after I had told reporters outside Number 10 that I was proud to be invited to join Gordon's government, a Sunday newspaper took understandable delight in unsheathing George's allegation that during the summer I had 'dripped pure poison in his ear' about the Prime Minister. The timing mattered more than the substance. If anyone with even the most casual knowledge of me or Gordon had been told that I had been critical of the man I was now working for, they would have thought: a bit embarrassing, but so what? My differences over the last decade with Gordon were hardly a secret. When Sky's Adam Boulton asked me about the report on his Sunday programme, I shrugged it off, and added that George had had some pretty interesting things of his own to say about his Tory colleagues over his ouzo.

Still, the story appeared to have legs. There was particular fascination with my relationship with Oleg Deripaska, a successful Russian industrialist whose interests included aluminium. There were unsettling, and totally false, suggestions that I had done special favours for him in Brussels. EU duties on aluminium had indeed been reduced on my watch, but the pressure for change had come from several EU member states, but not from Russia. Certainly not from Deripaska, with whom I had never discussed the matter. It was the result of an internal tug-of-war between Europe's aluminium-producing countries, such as Germany and France, which wanted to keep the duties, and Italy and new EU member states from the former Soviet bloc, which suddenly found themselves paying more for Russian imports. We agreed a classic EU fudge, splitting the difference between the existing rate and eliminating the surcharge altogether.

The facts were not the issue, however. It was the narrative, which soon turned spectacularly in my favour. Over the previous decade Nat Rothschild, Jacob and Serena's son and one of our hosts on Corfu, had become a good friend. He was furious at George, whom he had known since university days, because he felt that his family's hospitality had been abused. He and I spoke by phone to discuss a letter we planned to send to *The Times*. Not only did it have a go at George for gossiping, it said the media's 'obsession' with me was trivial compared to the more significant facts about Corfu and Oleg Deripaska. George, it said, had found 'the opportunity of meeting with Mr Deripaska so good that he invited the Conservatives' fund-raiser Andrew Feldman to accompany him onto Mr Deripaska's boat to solicit a donation'. This was important, because foreign donations to British political parties are illegal. Nat was usually allergic to political involvement, but now he was prepared to see a grenade lobbed onto the field of battle. 'Do you really want to let yourself in for this?' I asked. He felt the true facts should be known, and George immediately found himself in the firing line – from the media, from other parties, and from his own.

One of the side-effects was more lasting. George had been enjoying a reputation as the Tories' bright young thing since his party conference *coup de théâtre* on inheritance tax the previous year. Now, he was just a young thing. Since everyone assumed that I had been behind Nat's letter, the moral of the story became: Don't Mess with Mandelson. The whole affair left me politically stronger, not least in my own party. I happened to run into George a couple of months later at a Christmas reception, and he somewhat sheepishly approached me and made the closest thing possible to an apology. He said he had never intended our conversation to become public. I resisted the temptation to thank him for his help. Now, of course, as Chancellor he has made a political recovery, so neither of us has suffered any long-term damage from the affair.

The episode marked the turning of a corner in the media's treatment of me. For the first time I was given the benefit of the doubt, at least by most, and regarded as someone who, having come out of the shadows, was refreshingly unguarded and had a licence to be honest and occasionally to shock. This was ironic, because I was breaking out of the world of scripted soundbites that I myself had done so much to create. In a government of ministers who could often seem inhibited and constrained by the 'line to take', I looked and sounded as if I was enjoying myself, and had little to lose by speaking my mind. I had left the government nearly a decade before as a big embarrassment, and now I was back as a big beast.

The spat with George was trivial compared with the real problems facing the government, and Gordon. There were two parts to the job he had in mind for me. One was political, an ill-defined role in help-ing dig us out of the electoral hole in which we found ourselves. I felt that I would have been able to contribute more on this if I had a clear line of authority in his office, and he had clearly empowered me to act on his behalf. In time, I proposed weekly strategy meetings of his key political staff with Ed Balls and myself. It was an attempt to bring together the two political spheres that Gordon inhabited – the 'Peter sphere' and the 'Ed sphere' – and give him a single channel of advice. It worked, after a fashion, but it never succeeded in resolving the effects of the fragmented and highly personal way in which Gordon worked.

The more immediate challenge was the economy. I was involved through my day job at BERR, and my seat on the newly created National Economic Council. The economics and the politics were intertwined. No matter what any of the rest of us did, both would ultimately hinge on Gordon. If I had forgotten his extraordinary abilities during our period of estrangement, it was not long before I got a refresher course. Any leader needs to have a strength that is able to withstand pressure of quite an extraordinary kind. This is a combination of an outer strength that keeps you going physi-cally, and an inner strength that gives you the self-confidence and the determination to prevail over the obstacles in your way. I also think the best leaders have something else as well: an inner repose, an ability to project calm even when everything around them is far from stable. The reason this is important is that it gives you the abil-ity to listen to others, to reflect, and to convince people to trust and follow your leadership when you have made up your mind. I did not have this before I left for Brussels, but I did by the time I returned to Westminster. Gordon certainly had inner and outer strength, in large quantities. But he lacked that other quality, and more importantly, too often he showed this. He craved a structure and an orderly pro-cess around him, but as I once told him – and he agreed – he was the first to disrupt it, because he was so impulsive and tired so quickly of any hierarchy or system that was put in place to help him.

As I digested my first ministerial red box on the weekend of my return, talks were under way at Number 10 and the Treasury to negotiate a rescue of our banking system. We were filled in about the arrangement at our first economic council on Monday. The following day, after cabinet, Gordon asked me to join him next door, in what had been Tony's den, and was now his. For nearly five hours, with a rotating cast of half a dozen others, I helped him draft his most important statement since becoming Prime Minister, on the plan to recapitalise the banks. For Tony, writing had been an exercise in contemplation punctuated by the skating of fountain pen on paper. He had little time for computers. Gordon, by contrast, had been wedded to his keyboard ever since I had known him. Not just one, but two, computer screens now dominated the den. There was a large one on the table in front of Gordon, and an even larger one displayed his handiwork so others could join in the karaoke of drafting, editing and polishing.

The key for Gordon's statement was to get the contextual argument right. We had to make the case for unprecedented action in the face of an unprecedented challenge; all the more so because at that stage no other government, even the Americans, had grasped the need to inject emergency capital into the banks. Gordon was classically Gordon. Intellectually, he was on top of what had to be done and why. He had the courage, and his particular brand of *force majeure*, to drive ahead. He was aware of the political significance, too. Before returning to government, I had repeatedly told him he had to get across to the British people what he and his government were *for*. This was a hugely important opportunity to provide the answer. Still, it was an agonising few hours. Gordon attacked the keyboard. He cut and pasted. He edited and re-edited. Whole passages got lost, giving rise to explosions of expletives until they were recovered or recrafted. He did get there in the end. As always – and this was my neurosis – I wondered if it could have been made better, clearer and simpler. Certainly shorter.

There were some knife-edged days to follow, with Shriti Vadera, the human dynamo Gordon had brought into the Treasury in 1997 and who was now an indispensable minister with me at BERR, offering detailed technical support. Still, the £500 billion package, including up to £50 billion of direct state investment to ward off trouble in individual banks, was original in its thinking and bold in its execution. It was also timely and necessary. It would be a shot in the arm not only for the banks and the economy, but for Gordon.

In the weeks that followed, a Prime Minister and a government that had looked clueless and possibly hopeless began to be seen as coherent, in control, and doing the right things. The media gave me some of the credit. Gratifying though that was, it was an overstatement. My presence did help, if only because it seemed to give Gordon a new spring in his step, which was not lost on any of his colleagues. I certainly saw and talked to him often enough. In the weeks and months ahead, barely a day passed – sometimes, barely an hour – when we didn't speak.

To my relief and considerable surprise, I also renewed my relations with members of Team Brown who had played central roles in the insurgency against Tony. Although we never worked out any rules of engagement, from the moment Gordon brought me back, Ed Balls never crossed or criticised me in front of others. I reciprocated, and came to have a healthy regard for his toughness and intelligence, his analytical skills and strong opinions – for his strategic judgement, too, despite initial differences over our economic policy message in the months ahead. There was a similarly rapid rapprochement with people like Ian Austin and even Tom Watson, close Gordon aides who had previously worked against me and Tony, but who now welcomed me back. Even Charlie Whelan got in touch and visited me in my office. His role in my first ministerial demise never came up. What would have been the point?

But the main reason for Gordon's October recovery was Gordon. Britain faced a potentially cataclysmic financial and economic crisis; he was perfectly suited to dealing with it. His instincts – Keynesian, interventionist – led him to what were clearly the right decisions. His personality and image – clever, serious, 'not flash, just Gordon' – were, in these circumstances, not a liability but a huge asset. For the first time in many months, he seemed a round peg in a round hole. When I went abroad with him, for example to the Gulf States and South

America, foreign ministers and heads of government looked on him as a kind of Moses who was going to deliver them out of this crisis into the promised land. Later, I heard that his wife Sarah remarked that whether Gordon won the coming election or not, like Franklin D. Roosevelt, he would go down in history for saving his country from economic depression. I think she was right.

Gordon was completely re-energised, a change symbolised by his decision to set up a 'war room' in Downing Street, made up of his senior economic and political staff, to lead both the economic recovery and his political fightback. I was initially given a seat at Gordon's side. Whether because of the cheek-by-jowl discomfort, or my inability to memorise the password I was given for the computer system, I soon ceded that place to the excellent Justin Forsyth, who had previously worked for Tony and was now in charge of Gordon's strategic communications.

The layout was less like the West Wing than a newspaper office, complete with big-screen televisions tuned to twenty-four-hour news. At first the open-plan arrangement seemed to have a certain logic: a 'hub-and-spoke' operation suited to Gordon's leadership style, with him at the centre. But it also served to magnify his tendency to react to events as he had in opposition, rather than to stand back, reflect and provide the considered judgement of a Prime Minister. The result was not just a newsroom atmosphere, but often the shouts, curses and barked orders of a short-tempered editor on deadline. In time, Gordon requisitioned the large oak-panelled room in the corner of the office – Alastair Campbell's old home when he was the *maître d'* of Tony's press operation – so quieter meetings could take place there. It always amazed me that, given this was where the Prime Minister spent much of his time, the room could not be filled with more comfortable furniture, and even some nicer art. But Gordon had never been one for creature comforts. He was too busy, and genuinely too lacking in self-indulgence or vanity, to care about such things.

I was seeing Gordon's operation from close-up for the first time, and it was apparent that there was fraying within all parts of Team Brown. Gordon's loyalists and protégés had always looked like an impregnable phalanx when they were ranged against Tony, but with their common enemy gone, cracks had emerged, particularly after the fiasco of the previous year's aborted election. Gordon had allowed a briefing operation to put the blame on Douglas Alexander and Spencer Livermore, his long-standing political aide. Douglas was still angry at having been rubbished in the media, and was less close to Gordon than before. Spencer had long since left. Ed Balls and Shriti were still very much in favour, and relied upon, but they didn't seem to be on frequent speaking terms with each other. Ed Miliband clung close to Gordon, but had no time for the other Ed. He was, in any case, pursuing his own career interests, and had disappointed Gordon by not lending him more practical support when he was originally placed as a minister in the Cabinet Office. The only person who managed to be on good terms with everybody was my friend Sue Nye. Unfailingly discreet, upbeat, all-seeing, she did more than anyone to hold things together.

The more I talked to the two Eds – Balls and Milliband – and to Shriti and others in Gordon's old Treasury team, the more I understood why he was finding it so hard to get to grips with the very different demands of a very different job. Ed Miliband told me that by the time Gordon became Chancellor in 1997, he and his team had devoted months of detailed work to how they would operate and the policies they would pursue. That was why they had hit the ground running. I don't think Gordon realised how different the job of Prime Minister was. Throughout his decade in Number 11, his political aides and a few dedicated civil service officials ran day-to-day operations, keeping much of them away from him and driving the Treasury machine on his behalf. A Prime Minister could never operate in this way.

At the Treasury, Gordon never settled into the normal ministerial rhythm of following a demanding daily diary and doing his red boxes in the evening. He had not needed to. His calendar centred on the big decisions, and on set pieces like the PBR and the budget. Otherwise, his diary was kept open and flexible so that he could switch from one thing to another as he wished. Now, in Gordon's Number 10, Jeremy Heywood was playing a crucial role in oiling the wheels of government decision-making. He was a *de facto* chief of staff, but constrained by the fact he was a civil servant, and not in any sense a party political animal, in contrast to Jonathan Powell, who straddled the civil service and the political staff. Events, people, decisions flowed fast and furiously, requiring a close-working civil service and political machine to keep the Prime Minister up to date, turn his attention to each new development as it unfolded, then start all over again with work on red boxes following his final evening engagement. Although no one could ever say that Gordon did not work hard, he and those working for him never created a system to handle this disjointed, express-train flow of work. It required strong personal discipline, and concentration by the Prime Minister on many things at once, with clear decisions taken in good working time.

A particular gap was the absence of anyone to lead the political side of the operation. Gordon told me that when he moved to Number 10 he had tried to replicate his Treasury approach and re-form his old political team. He had attempted to persuade Ed Balls to accept a double-barrelled job, as his own effective chief of staff, and Alistair's Chief Secretary at the Treasury. He would have a foot in both camps. But Ed said no. He knew it couldn't have worked. Spencer Livermore had tried to play the chief-of-staff role for a time before his departure, but that hadn't worked either. Out of the blue, at the start of 2008 Gordon recruited Stephen Carter from the public relations company Brunswick to run the office. He didn't last either, because he never succeeded in winning Gordon's trust, and while he was notionally in charge, Gordon never stopped relying on what remained of his original Treasury clan. When I returned to government, Stephen was made a peer, and I was fortunate that he was assigned to my ministerial team, where he was a brilliant digital economy minister, becoming part of an energetic ministerial team which included Mervyn Davies, recruited from Standard Chartered. I have never seen anyone make such an effective transition from businessman and banker to high-flying minister as Mervyn did. Alan Sugar was also later ennobled, and came in as small business 'tsar', rather than a minister. He had an admirable capacity for ruffling feathers, even mine, although I quickly got over his habit of parking his enormous Rolls-Royce in the space at the rear of the department that was reserved for the Secretary of State.

My feet barely touched the ground in those first months, as we embarked on a task that was nothing short of preventing a severe recession from turning into a major depression. Critical to this was injecting an economic stimulus to revive demand in the economy, which would be the task of Alistair's November Pre-Budget Report. The key issues were what the size of the stimulus package would be, what form it would take, how and when it would be paid for, and how to rebalance the public finances once the crisis had passed. Gordon wanted the biggest stimulus possible. In pure economic terms, he was right. I too was arguing for a major injection to help small and medium-sized businesses. At the centre of the PBR was a £20 billion stimulus to the economy, including a temporary £12.5 billion VAT cut, from 17.5 to 15 per cent, to help stimulate demand. But to make up for collapsing tax revenues and pay for this package, we needed to borrow heavily, and to raise other taxes.

Alistair was alarmed by the possible economic and political consequences of a return to pre-New Labour tax-and-spend, even in a time of crisis. Reluctantly, he agreed to a new top-rate tax band for the highest earners, at 45p. He was still worried, however. When Gordon was out of the room, he turned to me and said, 'I don't want to get blamed for losing the next election. I don't want a repeat of the John Smith shadow budget in 1992.' I told him I thought a 5p increase in the top rate of tax was defensible. It was right that those with the broadest shoulders, who had benefited most from a decade of growth, should bear the biggest burden – with the proviso that he should keep the option to shelve it if conditions made that possible before it came into effect. I also promised to make sure that any fallout from the PBR, and from the even more important budget in the spring, would be borne not just by Alistair, but by the whole cabinet, myself included.

Inevitably, the newspapers used the decision to raise the top rate of tax to declare that this signalled the death of New Labour. But there was no alternative. The global whirlwind that had hit us required unprecedented action. The central decision of the PBR was correct and necessary: to give the economy the fiscal stimulus that was needed to fight back against the recession. On the need for such a stimulus, the government was as one. Yes, it would mean we would have to borrow more, at a time when the deficit would rise to alarming levels as tax revenues collapsed. But if we had not injected this stimulus – combined with the later monetary boost provided through the Bank of England's programme of quantitative easing – recession would indeed have turned to depression. The cost would have been colossal in human and financial terms.

It was a frightening time. The economy was on life support, and we needed to restore it to health. My department was at the centre of the resuscitation mission. We were working around the clock to get business the help it needed. I made announcement after announcement: to help free up credit from banks that had been on the verge of collapse; to provide assistance direct to small business, and to a car industry which was on its knees. We were throwing everything at the problem, and I was having to make decisions on government intervention on which I would once have showed reluctance. But despite the fact that we were in uncharted waters, we felt confidence in the actions we were taking. My ministerial team – headed in the Commons by the clever and witty Pat McFadden, Tony's long-standing political aide – were superb.

Of course, the support we were giving was not unconditional. I wanted to set my own agenda rather than allow a queue to form at my door. Only in circumstances where businesses were looking ahead and applying new research and development with a view to maintaining their share of the future market would I extend government help, and even then only after other options were exhausted. It was a model that I would soon have to apply to one of Britain's most famous brand names, when Jaguar-Land Rover ran into trouble, sparking fears it might be closed. I resisted pressure from both Jaguar and the media simply to rescue the company. That would not only have risked turning the Treasury into a giant cash machine, it would have ignored the capacity of the company's shareholders, private capital sources and owners – in Jaguar's case, its Indian parent conglomerate, Tata –

to act. I did declare a 'pragmatic' readiness, along with these other parties, to help put the company on a firm footing, saying that this might include the government acting as a 'lender of last resort'. That did not prove necessary. Tata, a substantial and important overseas investor in Britain, secured financing from its private lenders, and the crisis receded.

I also felt that we needed to learn the lessons from the crisis for the longer term. In a series of statements and speeches, I used the new economic circumstances we faced to set out a new strategy for how government should develop Britain's productive base, and rebalance the economy, during the crisis and beyond. In Brussels, I had come to feel that if we were to develop long-term industrial strength in Britain, government needed to play a more active role. I was encouraged in this view by three industrialists I particularly came to respect. The first was Sir John Rose, chief executive of Rolls-Royce engines, who was a keen proselytiser for modern manufacturing and the need to rebalance the UK economy in that direction. The second was Sir John Parker, the sage-like chairman of National Grid Transco and the mining company Anglo-American. The third was Sir Kevin Smith, the gritty chief executive of GKN engineering.

Given the crisis in the financial services, and Britain's dependence on them, it was not surprising that I should look towards strengthening manufacturing. I asked Geoffrey Norris – Tony's, then Gordon's, business adviser – to draw on his huge knowledge of every sector of the UK economy and join me in the department to work on our plans. The recession had only reinforced my view that we needed less financial engineering and more real engineering. I argued for a new kind of smart, targeted government intervention. Not the old Labour practice of 'picking winners', which had ended up more often than not with losers picking government. Not a renewed government role in owning, or running, businesses, or using protectionist tariffs to skew the rules of open international competition.

What I had in mind was a broader, strategic industrial activism. We needed interlocking policies to ensure the investment essential to building a modern economy capable of competing on a world scale.

Government would have to help in those areas where businesses and technologies would not, or could not, take the lead because market signals or incentives were not strong enough: areas like the transition to low carbon; high-calibre research; the commercialisation of inventions and innovations; training and skills programmes to create a world-class workforce; and infrastructure improvements to underpin a competitive economy. This was a stronger role for government than I had envisaged in my 1998 Competitiveness White Paper, and initially some of my old Blairite friends teased me about the bigger industrial role I was envisaging for the government. Tony himself was more persuaded when I explained that this was about making markets work better, not replacing them. I was not running against the tide of business opinion. In fact when I addressed the CBI in November, they were urging this agenda, and a stronger role for government, upon me, not the other way round.

Gordon had been thinking about the future too. He told me he had settled on a 'big plan' to reshape Whitehall. It was far more audacious than 'Teddy Bear': he wanted instead to restructure government into three major policy directorates: foreign policy, domestic policy, and the economy. He hadn't decided who would be the foreign policy supremo – possibly Alistair Darling. But he was thinking of moving David Miliband from the Foreign Office to head the domestic portfolio. He envisaged a new governing executive of the National Economic Council, made up of himself, me, the Chancellor, Shriti Vadera, Mervyn Davies and a handful of others. I was fairly sure that this grand reorganisation was not going to happen. Gordon had a fertile, intellectual mind, and tended, magpie-like, to latch on to a constant stream of ideas and proposals. But the practical complexities of planning and pushing through such a scheme were too great, and it never left the drawing board.

On 6 March 2009 I was scheduled to give a speech alongside Gordon at a low-carbon conference at the Royal Society's premises in Carlton Terrace. As I arrived, I was just getting out of my car when a young woman shouted a question to me. Assuming she was a journalist showing the usual forwardness of the profession, I turned towards her. However, it was not a question she shot at me, but a large quantity of a slimy green substance. She threw it in my face, saying as she did so, 'This is for your support for the third Heathrow runway,' then strolled off, cool as a cucumber. I walked briskly to the Royal Society gents, where I cleaned up, commandeered my private secretary Paul's tie, and went straight out again to face the media, who were by now in a state of high excitement, not to say amusement. I decided to join in the merriment, and in answer to their shouted questions, I replied, 'Was it green custard? Are you sure it wasn't guacamole or mushy peas?' recalling the apocryphal Hartlepool story. I had learned from experience that the more embarrassing such incidents are, the greater the insouciance needed to get through them. Footage of my humiliation was broadcast on news channels all over the world, and the public's mixture of enjoyment and sympathy at this latest episode did me a power of good, judging by the texts and emails I received.

In 2009 Britain took over the leadership of the G20, the nascent steering committee of the global economy which included both the leading developed countries and the main emerging economies. Gordon was determined to transform it before the world's eyes into a second Bretton Woods, an engine for restructuring the international economy. Working the phones, refusing to take no for an answer, he had secured agreement for a meeting in London at the beginning of April to plot the way out of the global crisis.

The event was seen by us as make-or-break for Gordon and the government. Mark Malloch Brown, who had been ennobled and brought into government by Gordon from the UN in New York, led the core group of ministers driving it, along with Shriti. Gordon knew that we needed to get the presentational aspects of the event right, as well as the substance. So much was riding on it. The whole thing crystallised all our arguments about the need to fight back against the crisis, and to do so internationally. Yes, this would require heavy borrowing to finance the government action needed, and that would need to be paid back over time. But the global economy would not pull through without the strongest possible stimulus over the next year or two, after which it could be steadily reduced.

The G20 was Gordon's chance to show his strength and skills on the world stage, as a former finance minister unrivalled in his knowledge of the global economy. If we succeeded, we would not only demonstrate the appeal of our policies, but also Gordon's gifts as a leader. If we failed, the pillars of our economic and political argument would have been kicked away, and it would be difficult to see a way back for Gordon. Everything about the event built up its importance. From the turn of the year, preparations crowded out almost every other policy or political issue. Gordon, in this mode, was like a giant battering ram. Once he had set himself a clear goal – in this case, a summit that would deliver agreement on the stimulus and other regulatory changes necessary to fight off the recession and re-prime the world economy – he let nothing get in his way. He was immersed in the detail, and remorseless in driving those around him to make sure every aspect of the event was planned to ensure success.

The summit, which opened on 2 April, was held in the gigantic ExCel Exhibition Centre in London's Docklands. The plush meeting room looked like the centre of world government – rather like the war room from *Dr Strangelove* – and the media facilities seemed to stretch for miles. The traffic jams created by the event did indeed stretch for miles. The sight of cavalcades sweeping across London with their VIP passengers and motorcycle escorts really gave a sense that everyone of any importance had flocked to London to save the world economy.

The weeks of planning paid off. Gordon gave a virtuoso performance. In a crucial lunchtime meeting with his fellow world leaders, he essentially locked them in until he had obtained practical agreement on a range of stimulus measures, interest-rate cuts and regulatory moves. Even those in the media who were usually hostile to him recognised the scale of his achievement.

I spent the morning doing broadcast interviews from the venue, until a lunchtime intermission to greet the arrival of the King of Saudi Arabia. We sat in an anteroom, chatting amicably, waiting for the official lunch to conclude. I had not anticipated Gordon's decision to hold everyone hostage until he got a deal. The King and I talked. Then talked further. And further. Until finally the doors were thrown open and the throng of world leaders stumbled out.

One of the day's stars was undoubtedly Barack Obama, who had been inaugurated as US President only a few months previously. His height made him stand out, and I could see people gravitating towards him. I was keen to follow, and eventually managed to introduce myself to the new leader of the free world. My old friend from Clinton days, Rahm Emmanuel, was his chief of staff, and we exchanged jokes about him. Obama excelled himself during the meeting. It was his first such high-powered summit, and the way in which he conducted himself was both understated and like an old hand, demonstrating both guts and charm. At one point he intervened to resolve a disagreement over tax havens between President Hu of China and President Sarkozy of France that was becoming heated.

But above all this was Gordon's success, and it reinforced his status as the leader of the world's fightback. As in his initial response at home to the financial collapse, the G20 was an instance where his boldness and determination matched the scale of the challenge. These were strengths which David Cameron, despite his smoothness and political acumen, had failed to show when the crisis hit. Even allowing for the fact that the Conservatives were in opposition, his knee-jerk resistance to Gordon's sure-footed response seemed to me a failure of imagination and judgement. After the summit, Gordon returned to Downing Street where we clapped him in, tired but elated. The next morning he was straight on the phone to me, wanting to capitalise on the success of the G20 to mount a wider political comeback. He was issuing instructions like the Gordon of old, and I sensed his confidence returning. The omens looked good.

On 6 April I led a twenty-member trade delegation to Iraq, in response to messages from the Iraqi government that British companies were not pushing themselves forward enough to benefit from the new business opportunities that were arising there. I attributed this engagement to the strength of the historical relations between the two countries, but also to the goodwill felt towards our armed forces, which had endured the agonies of the war's aftermath. Unfortunately, although we had good meetings with the Prime Minister and others in the Iraqi public and private sectors, I saw even less of the country than is usual on such a trip. In Baghdad we were restricted to the heavily fortified 'green zone', while anti-missile-equipped aircraft and helicopters ferried us to our destinations, including a visit to Basra. The scale of protection seemed overdone, but then, from my Northern Ireland days I had learned to leave threat-assessment to others.

Gordon's G20 triumph was matched by an immediate boost in our polling numbers. It seemed there was an opportunity to put behind him the woes of his first year as Prime Minister. But that prospect was quickly buried by one of Gordon's own inner circle. Damian McBride had worked as part of his media operation for some years, first as a civil servant and then as a special adviser in the Treasury, and had moved into Number 10 with him. He was Gordon's attack dog, and had developed a reputation for briefing against anyone who was perceived to threaten his boss's interests, not only the Tory opposition but those of the Blairite persuasion. For cabinet colleagues, his presence was a reminder of a side of Gordon that they viscerally disliked. Damian was an accident that had been waiting to happen, and it duly did, when venomous emails from his Downing Street account, containing fabricated allegations about the private lives of Tory politicians and their wives, leaked out. The story broke on Saturday, 11 April, Easter weekend. I was enjoying a short break in Marrakesh with an assortment of French, German and Dutch friends and their children. By that evening, Damian had resigned. On the day Gordon invited me back into government, I had raised the issue of Damian with him, and I thought we had a clear understanding that he would be transferred to the Cabinet Office, as a stepping stone to departing altogether. But, to his cost, it was something Gordon had not followed through. For some reason he couldn't give Damian up.

If the G20 represented all that was good about Gordon, the Damian McBride email scandal revealed the reverse. Of course Gordon had no knowledge of the emails, but he knew what my reaction would be to the breaking scandal: why the hell didn't you get rid of him when you said you would? Damian had been wise enough to keep out of my way – in fact I had not even realised he had resumed his role until the previous month, when I was flying back with Gordon on a chartered flight from Chile, where we had been attending the Progressive Governance Conference. Damian was on the flight, but I couldn't bring myself to talk to him. I asked Sue Nye what was going on. She shrugged, then defended Damian's role. 'He's clever, and good at what he does. Someone has to take the Tories on at their own game.' She did not, of course, mean writing email smears about them. Gordon's justification was that as long as the Tories used people like their communications director, the former *News of the World* editor Andy Coulson, to engage in bare-knuckle fighting in the media, he was entitled to keep Damian.

But this time Damian had gone too far. Not only had he done something totally unjustifiable, he had been caught doing it, inflicting embarrassment on the government and political agony for Gordon. My own view, although I did not share it with Gordon, was that he had concluded from his 'defeat' to Tony in 1994 that he needed to be more ruthless. This manifested itself in the tactics used by Charlie Whelan, which had persisted under Damian. It may have gained Gordon some advantage on his journey to the top, but it did immense damage to Tony's government, and now to his own.

The email scandal wiped out our G20 success, and provided the worst possible backdrop to the forthcoming budget, which was already shaping up to be the most difficult of our time in office. It had originally been set for March, but it was put back by a month for economic and political reasons – the world crisis and the G20 summit – amid escalating tension between the Prime Minister and the Chancellor. Proper discussion of the details was overshadowed by a tug-of-war over growth projections for the economy. The outcome of this battle would be vital: our assessment of the future course of public finances depended on the growth forecasts, and would determine the limits for affordable spending on the stimulus.

Gordon repeatedly, and often angrily, rejected Alistair's fore-casts, saying they were too conservative. He said the whole Treasury approach was wrong, and insisted that orthodox methods couldn't be applied to measuring the structural deficit. If we did that, we wouldn't be able to sustain the levels of spending needed for his 'invest and grow' strategy for recovery. Alistair told Gordon he was being ludicrously optimistic, not only about growth prospects but about Britain's ability to support such a large, and expanding, deficit. The foundations of the budget had to be realistic, he said. If they weren't, the markets wouldn't buy it. The pound would come under pressure, and Britain's credit status might be downrated.

The main argument was not just about projections, however. Gordon was pressing for an increased injection of finance that Alistair was insistent we could not afford. He was about to present enormous deficit figures, and needed to show that we would be taking action to get debt under control once we were through the recession. At this stage Ed Balls backed Gordon in the small group discussions that included him, me and Alistair. As budget day approached, Alistair was nearing the end of his tether. 'I know Gordon doesn't have confidence in me,' he said. 'He might as well do as he wishes and put Ed in Number 11 to do his bidding.'

I thought Alistair was right about the need for us to show that we had a long-range plan for getting spending and debt under control. I told Gordon that if we were going to make a case for investment and a growth policy to secure economic recovery, we had to demonstrate that we were prepared to tighten our belts in other areas, as everyone else was having to do. Yet he would be pushed no further. In truth, at this stage I wasn't inclined to push harder. I was reluctant to disagree with or contradict Gordon in front of others. On the economics of our response, I had an open mind about what he was saying. Politically, I thought it was essential to preserve the unity between us, not just because of our unhappy history, but because I felt it was essential to the wider recovery of the government. I had genuine sympathy, moreover, for Gordon's emphasis on 'growth' as the engine for Britain's recovery and future expansion. My intention had been for us to accompany the budget with a public preview of a paper from my department setting out the 'New Industry, New Jobs' policies at the heart of our industrial activism plans. Unfortunately the fallout from the McBride affair distracted media attention from the important, but obviously less sexy, substance of what we were trying to do. Our failure to get it up in lights certainly made Alistair's task for the budget more difficult.

One especially unfortunate effect of the long battle over the budget was that there was almost no discussion about its most politically delicate provision: a further increase in the top rate of tax. Alistair had by now come round to the view that we should announce a full 10p rise in the top rate – to 50p rather than 45p. He didn't like it, but he needed the revenue, and an increase for top earners was the fairest way. In principle, I agreed. At the time of the PBR I had re-assured Alistair over his plan for a 5p rise, and I felt I could not oppose him now, as he galloped through the main points of the budget with me on the weekend before he presented it to the Commons. I later learned that at one stage in the discussions it was contemplated that the 50p rate should be temporary, to finance a five-year 'crisis fund', which in my view would have made better sense.

The media's response to the budget was even more hostile than it had been to the PBR. Virtually all the main provisions made their way into the press before Alistair rose to announce them on 22 April. There was one exception: the 'tax bombshell'. The next day's headlines swamped any hope of our offering an explanation of the financial justification for the move. The reaction was made worse by Alistair's commendably unspun acknowledgement that our public borrowing for the year would rise to £175 billion.

Gordon was apoplectic as the media panned us and the Tories accused us of believing that the deficit and the debt would simply take care of themselves. He saw Alistair's announcement of the borrowing figure as part of a Treasury campaign to build up pressure for spending cuts. When I spoke to Tony, who was in the States, he was critical of the 50p tax announcement. I bristled slightly, feeling it was easy to lecture from afar. 'We do have quite a deficit, you know, and it needs to be plugged somehow,' I replied. He was having none of it. 'Remember the politics,' he said, 'and where we've come from on tax.' He felt that the main problem was Gordon's fixation on his 'spend-versus-cuts' dividing line, which he thought was inhibiting members of the cabinet: 'Any young one with any sense should be developing a broader narrative and policy offer than this.' During this period Tony was pretty much absent from domestic politics, but that did not stop him thinking about the future, and where New Labour should go next. I agreed with him about the need for future thinking, but I believed he overestimated the appetite for it among the 'young ones', who were consumed by the day-to-day running of their departments. In the case of people like James Purnell and David Miliband, he did not appreciate how hard it had become for them to project their own voices without it being presented as plotting against Gordon.

Gordon was unbudgeable on the subject of the deficit. In private, he accepted that it was a major issue, but he believed the important argument to get across was about the need for stimulus, to grow our way out of recession. He felt it would be counter-productive to try to follow, and explain, two strategies at the same time. In a rare moment of calm a few days before the budget, I had gone to see him at Number 10. It was early evening, and as we talked on the back terrace, Sarah joined us, the first time the three of us had sat together since my return.

Gordon was in an unusually light mood, given the intensity of our budget discussions. 'You seem very relaxed,' I said. 'Why?' He replied that it was because he had received so many blows that nothing could surprise him any more. I smiled. 'I'm not sure you should bank on that,' I said. I told him he had to learn the lessons of the McBride mess. He needed to show the party, and the country, that he was breaking out of the tiny political circle he had assembled when he was Chancellor. He needed to put a political strategy group in place at Number 10, and an organisation to look ahead to the election. He needed to trust, enthuse and empower more people around him.

With issues like Damian's smear stories, he had to resist his old urge to hunker down, say little or nothing, and hope the crisis would pass. Finally, whatever we eventually decided on our economic plans, he needed to establish a strong policy agenda up until the election. 'You have to make it clear that we're not running out of steam,' I said. 'You have to do what you did when the banking crisis hit. You have to galvanise people. That's what you do well. You have to get ahead of events.' He seemed to take in what I was saying, but I wondered how much would really change.

Gordon hated criticism, especially from his own side, and over-reacted to it. He became especially tetchy when an assortment of former Blair government ministers voiced public concerns after the budget. 'They're on a revenge mission,' he fumed, convinced they were part of a new plot to force him out. My own view was that no matter how strong their views, there was no organised move afoot. Others around Gordon were not quite so sure. Jon Trickett, his Parliamentary Private Secretary, came to see me in my room in the Lords shortly after the budget. He said a number of fellow MPs were convinced that Gordon's critics were in discussions about getting a change of leader. One of them, whom he knew well, had even been approached and told that if he wanted a 'conversation' with Harriet Harman about a post-Gordon future it could be arranged. Given the plunge in our poll ratings since the McBride affair and the budget – we were now flat-lining at around 25 per cent – I could well believe that some MPs and former ministers were thinking of a challenge. I told Jon: 'Don't say anything to Gordon. It will just wind him up and make things more difficult.'

Days later, however, the rumblings became public. The *Daily Telegraph* splashed a story, quoting 'friends' of Harriet, saying that she would go for the top job if Gordon were deposed. Within hours, she had to go on the BBC to quash the suggestion, and prevent the situation from getting any worse. She would 'definitely' not go for the leadership, she said: 'I will be a strongly supportive, loyal deputy to Gordon Brown and help him win a further term of Labour govern-ment.' I believed her. I suspected that her leadership ambitions were not being talked up by her, but by others who wanted to flush them out in order to obtain the denial.

At least the budget and its aftermath made a serious discussion about our future spending strategy unavoidable. It happened falteringly, beginning at our first cabinet meeting in May. James Purnell, the Work and Pensions Secretary, spoke calmly but deliberately, and said we should review our position on the public finances and our future spending plans. It was a point he had first raised, to no effect, at the outset of the economic crisis, when he canvassed the idea of holding a revised spending review. This time it did have an effect: Gordon took him into the den after cabinet and berated him. He told James he had no understanding of the financial situation, and accused him of disloyalty for raising the matter at all.

James was not alone in his concerns. Alistair, David and I all shared them, as, I later discovered, did quite a few other members of the cabinet. David and James came round for dinner the following Saturday. They both feared that the government was in danger of losing its economic credibility, and wondered what we could do to get out of our political tailspin. They didn't directly raise the issue of Gordon, so I did it for them. I said that in the end it would be the public who would resolve his future. If he didn't turn them round, Labour MPs, and the rest of the party, would not stay quiet for long. I also told them that I would not – could not – be part of any move to force Gordon out. I saw my role as supporting him, and putting in place the kind of 'future narrative' Tony and I had discussed after the budget.

At successive cabinet meetings, other ministers, including Yvette Cooper, raised the need to discuss future spending. Gordon was becoming more and more unsettled, especially after the cabinet debate began leaking into the press. The tension intensified with the approach of local and European elections at the beginning of June. Our prospects did not look good, not least because no initiative, apart from a committee chaired by Harriet, had been taken to put any sort of campaign in place. We were taking a beating in the polls, and the country was in the midst of an economic crisis. But things would soon get far worse.

The issue of MPs' expenses had been a ticking time bomb for years. Now it detonated with full force as the *Daily Telegraph* began leaking details of MPs' claims over the past five years. It was a massive story, and instantly created a political crisis every bit as dramatic as the economic one. The scale and nature of the revelations provoked a justifiable fury in the country, as embarrassing claim after embarrassing claim was leaked. Many were completely unjustified. It looked awful, especially in a time of painful recession. In reality, the ramshackle expenses system had been allowed to grow and to be used by MPs as an alternative to pay increases, which successive Prime Ministers, from Mrs Thatcher onwards, had rejected in deference to public opinion. Now, much greater public outrage had been triggered as a result of the system's abuse. My view, which I expressed, was that it would be better to clean up the system and put MPs' pay up, so that everything became clear and above board. By the time the daily exposés had run their course many weeks later, no political party would escape unscathed. But the *Telegraph* began its front-page splashes with Gordon – for a relatively minor oversight regarding cleaning bills – and proceeded to run through the expense claims of other Labour ministers and senior MPs.

I was in Scotland on an official visit on the day the *Telegraph* began its revelations, and I was not alone in failing to realise that this was the beginning of one of the biggest crises in Parliament's history. It particularly annoyed me that the paper had chosen to splash on Gordon's cleaning bill, and that only Labour ministers were being targeted, something that continued for the next four days. My own expenses back in 2004 were written up, to create a misleading impression of wrongdoing. As far as Gordon was concerned, I quipped that knowing how he lived in a paper-strewn state at the best of times, his cleaning bill would have been entirely justified. The *Telegraph* was right to expose an expenses system that needed clearing up, but it did so in a way that tarnished many in Parliament unfairly.

Gordon was furious, at first about the implication that his own claim reflected deliberate dishonesty, and then about the initial focus on Labour alone. To his credit, however, he also understood the bigger picture from the start. No matter what the merit of any MP's individual claims, and despite the fact almost all of them were within the arcane and elastic Commons expense rules, the damage to people's already weakened trust in politics and politicians would be immense. He had been trying to get ahead of the issue before the *Telegraph* revelations broke, using a YouTube clip on the Number 10 website to announce his intention to clean up the entire expenses system. It turned into a presentational disaster. Gordon felt hurt and humiliated by the fuss made over the broadcast, which was typical of the exaggerated criticism he was subjected to. But, not for the first time, he had only himself to blame. He did the broadcast in a tearing hurry, because he wanted to get the credit for the proposals Harriet was about to announce in the House, and spent little or no time rehearsing it. In what became a torrent of words during which he could barely draw breath, he crammed in far too much information, and smiled in the wrong places. It was not the end of the world, but for his internal critics it symbolised his attitude to communication, as too often an afterthought, rather than fundamental to what a modern politician has to do. In fact, the broadcast represented a wider failure to think the expenses issue through fully with our own side, and more damagingly, with David Cameron and the Liberal Democrat leader Nick Clegg. There had been a chance for the three main parties to develop a unified response to cleaning up expenses, with Gordon taking the lead. But his pre-emptive move, and a take-it-or-leave-it meeting with the other party leaders afterwards, ended with him being blamed for moving impetuously, rather than credited for seeing first and most clearly what needed to be done. It also did little for his personal relationship with Nick Clegg, which would have later ramifications.

With Labour MPs in growing ferment over the expenses scandal, the time was ripe for those who wanted to make another move against Gordon. The atmosphere was made more febrile by two cabinet ministers, first Jacqui Smith and then Hazel Blears, announcing in quick succession on the eve of the local and European elections that they were quitting the cabinet. I was a friend of both of them, and thought they had each done good jobs in their departments. I knew Hazel better because in 2001, following my resignation, she had made a point of coming to Hartlepool to address my local party members and demonstrate her support. My understanding was that Jacqui's decision to leave the government had been made quite a time before, and she had been awaiting the next reshuffle to announce it. But the news leaked to Sky, and she confirmed it without intending any ill will to Gordon. Hazel's case was more complicated. She had been very hurt by Gordon's description of her expense claims as 'totally unacceptable'. I thought Gordon was wrong to single out Hazel, and had told him so. Now I thought she was wrong to resign on the eve of local elections. It could only harm the party, especially in view of her responsibility as Local Government Secretary. Throughout the day I did a non-stop media round in an attempt to limit the damage, but there was no doubt that the drumbeat of questions surrounding Gordon's continued leadership was growing louder. Once again, an air of crisis was beginning to form around the government.

In the end, the local and European election results were predictably awful. Locally, it was our worst showing in nearly a century. But we had little time to digest them, as events were to take an even more dramatic turn. In the run-up to polling day, Gordon's focus had been on a cabinet reshuffle to try to regain the initiative, and we had pencilled in the announcement for the following Monday. Gordon was considering moving Alistair Darling from the chancellorship, and replacing him with Ed Balls. The potential pitfalls were obvious: media allegations of 'cronyism', and unhappiness or worse in the cabinet about replacing a Chancellor who was popular with his colleagues and had provided a steady hand on the tiller in the midst of an economic crisis. That did not even take account of possible upheaval in the markets. Gordon had first raised the idea with me in an awkward, snatched conversation. I felt in a difficult position. He was Prime Minister, and allocating portfolios in the cabinet was his prerogative. I knew from Tony's experience how critical it was for Number 10 to have the best possible working relationship with Number 11. But I also believed strongly that such a move would be unfair to Alistair, and would be universally criticised. My hope was gradually to bring this home to Gordon, but things moved faster than I anticipated.

On election day, Thursday, 4 June, I went to see Alistair. He said he knew what was coming. I asked him whether, if Ed was indeed made Chancellor, he would take another major post – like the Home Office, since Jacqui was leaving. He was polite, but resolute: 'If I'm replaced as Chancellor, my intention would be to leave the government. I'll go to the backbenches.'

That was clear enough. I remained unclear, however, about Gordon's intentions as I joined him in Downing Street that night to await the exit poll results. A few minutes before 10 p.m., the phone rang. Gordon answered it, and as I looked on he grew increasingly astonished and angry. 'You are wrong!' he barked. When I mouthed, 'Who is it?', he handed me the receiver and said, 'James. *You* speak to him.' I thought for a moment he meant James Murdoch, but I immediately recognised James Purnell's voice. When he told me he had decided to leave the government, I was as astounded as Gordon. I had spoken to James the night before, and he had given no indication of what he was thinking. I had asked him whether he wanted the schools department, because I knew Gordon was thinking about Ed Balls moving to the Treasury. However concerned I was about the Treasury move, if it was going to happen, I wanted James – a long-standing friend for whom I had the highest of hopes – to benefit from it if he wished. He said firmly that he had decided to stay at Work and Pensions.

Now I found myself at odds with him for the first time. 'That's ridiculous. You're *not* leaving,' I said. 'You are *not* going to do this.'

'I am,' he replied quietly.

'You're not.'

'Peter, I am. I can't go on television any more to defend Gordon's premiership.'

'Well, keep off the bloody television then,' I said.

But James had had enough. He put the phone down. By this time, the argument was already moot, as someone rushed in to say his resignation was on the TV news broadcasts. I watched them with Gordon. 'James is making a big mistake,' he said.

My mind turned to the political implications. The immediate question was whether any other cabinet ministers were likely to follow James out of the door. I phoned a clutch of them, but David Miliband was key. He was the only heavyweight in the cabinet who was both qualified for, and might be interested in, Gordon's job. It is a myth that I persuaded David not to follow James. When I called him at around 10.15, he confirmed straight away that he was not resigning, and he followed this with a public statement saying so. Had he resigned, it would have been very damaging, possibly fatal, for Gordon, but it would not have helped David to get the leadership – he might well have found himself in the same position as Michael Heseltine in 1990, having wielded the knife, but failed to reap the benefit.

The reason I was calling around cabinet members was because, although I shared some of the misgivings of Gordon's critics, an apparently Blairite *putsch* was not the way to go. In my view, the repercussions it would have created would have meant the end of New Labour because of the inevitable spilt blood within the party. If successful, it would also have triggered an early general election in the midst of the economic crisis, and left a poisonous legacy in the party for years to come. That was not what the party or the country needed. In any case, I felt strongly that Gordon deserved the chance to see his economic fightback work, and to be rewarded for it.

As for Ed Balls's proposed move to the Treasury, it was clear the moment James resigned that Gordon was too weakened to carry this out. The first thing I said to Gordon after hearing James's news was, 'Ed will be disappointed.' I said this to test whether he was reading the situation properly. He was. And to Ed's credit, when he arrived at Number 10 shortly afterwards, he did not try to sway Gordon. One instruction I gave very firmly to everyone in the office was that there should be no Number 10 briefing against James or any other Blairites. The unofficial briefings by Gordon's team, led by Damian, after David Miliband had written his article in the *Guardian* the previous summer had created needless bitterness and division, from which Gordon had come out worst. I did not want the mistake repeated.

This instruction was honoured by everyone except the Chief Whip, Nick Brown. The next morning, as the reshuffle was under way, I was called to the telephone on the writing desk outside the Cabinet Room. It was Alan Milburn, furious at having read in the *Northern Echo* that Nick was accusing him and Stephen Byers of being the ringleaders of a plot to overthrow Gordon. Alan told me he wanted a retraction straight away, otherwise he would put out a statement of his own, and it wouldn't be helpful. Just at that moment Nick came padding down the corridor towards me. 'What on earth are you doing, saying that about Alan?' I shouted at him. 'Do you want to start a civil war?' Nick stood his ground and shouted back at me, which brought Gordon storming out of the Cabinet Room to see what the raised voices were about. When I told him, he put his hand firmly on Nick's back and shoved him into the Cabinet Room, telling him not to be so stupid. Nick later rang Alan to apologise.

My promotion to First Secretary of State in the reshuffle was not a reward for keeping Gordon afloat. Some weeks before, the Cabinet Secretary, Gus O'Donnell, had remarked to me that Gordon needed a Deputy Prime Minister to strengthen the centre of government, and that in his view I should do the job. In the event, I became Deputy PM in everything but name, partly because of the sensitivity of my doing this from the Lords, and also because Harriet, as deputy leader of the party, was likely to object.

The cabinet reshuffle was completed by the end of the day, held up only by the question of who should go to Defence. Shaun Woodward believed he had been promised the job, but Gordon was reluctant. He gave it instead to Bob Ainsworth, who had been an able and well-liked number two there. Shaun protested, and asked to be named Minister for the Cabinet Office in addition to his role as Northern Ireland Secretary. I saw no justification for that, and argued that Tessa Jowell should be given the job instead, to enable her to come back into the cabinet. Tessa's work on the Olympics was drawing plaudits from all quarters, and although she was very close to Tony, she had always been ready to perform in the media in support of Gordon. It was a popular move with everyone but Shaun, who took a little time to forgive me.

As the day went on, it became clear that Gordon would survive. I embarked on a series of media interviews to stabilise the situation and shore up the government's position. But there was no doubt that we were weaker for James's departure, and I was personally extremely upset to see him go. What I am grateful for is that our friendship never faltered. Between interviews, I also went to see David. He reiterated that he had never seriously thought of following James out of the door. He did, however, mention his misgivings about Gordon. It was not the weaknesses that Gordon himself recognised that worried David: the lack of communications skills, or a camera-friendly face. Rather, it was his seeming lack of direction, and of a coherent policy vision for the future.

David knew I had been saying the same thing to Gordon myself. I had spent the weeks since the budget trying to start putting in place a coherent political narrative, and a strategy, to take us through to the general election. I called it 'policy-led recovery'. The first step was a document entitled 'Building Britain's Future'. It contained a range of policy announcements, some new and others timely revivals. They included the kind of new industrial activism I'd been introducing at BERR, as well as a commitment to more individually tailored and locally responsive government and public services. At Andrew Adonis's urging, it coupled a project to help the most disadvantaged with a recognition that our governing constituency also included Middle England – in his words, 'people who are in jobs and not attending chronically failing schools, and have already got broadband and an insulated loft, but who want to know what we are going to do to get them better public services in return for all the extra tax they are paying'. The document was published shortly after the local and European elections, at a time I had anticipated we would be in need of a relaunch. To the extent that it generated any media attention, it was well received. But it was overshadowed by the aftershocks of James's departure.

The first indications of the political damage this had caused were always going to come on the following Sunday. It started badly. The *Mail on Sunday* not only took aim at Gordon, but used the leak of an email from me to my old research assistant Derek Draper, sent eighteen months earlier, as its weapon of choice. The email was genuine. So were the juicier quotes extracted from it. I had said that Gordon was a 'self-conscious person, physically and emotionally', that he was not 'comfortable in his own skin', that he came over as 'angry'. The irony was that these observations had been part of a longer, fundamentally supportive message about how to improve Gordon's and the government's fortunes. I was warning Derek against attempting to glue some artificial, PR-friendly persona on the Prime Minister. Gordon's hopes for success would depend on his being himself, with both his weaknesses and his strengths. As I had also told Gordon, he needed not just better presentation, but clearer, bolder policies. If that could be fixed, I said in the email, he would have both policy definition and policy achievements: 'He will visibly relax...He will find his voice.' Still, the story was clearly going to complicate my role as Gordon's defender-in-chief when I went on the BBC's *Andrew Marr Show* that Sunday morning.

I had known Andrew for years, from when he was the BBC's political editor. He was the first person to bring a kind of theatrical panache to the job, following his more sober predecessors, a style continued by his own successor, Nick Robinson, who elevated Andrew's sense of drama into an art form. Their reporting sometimes came across as being as much about themselves as about the politicians they were reporting on, but I felt that both brought a sharpness to the screen. Andrew had also developed a tried-and-tested interview technique on his Sunday-morning programme. When he was feeling impatient, he would interrupt you before you got to the end of your second sentence – a trademark tactic for which I now prepared myself to do battle over the Draper email.

As I expected, Andrew was poised to pounce. I was poised to pounce back. I started to interview *him*, asking him what his next question was. It was an enjoyable sparring match, from which, judging by the messages I received even from old critics in the party, I did not come off badly. I did not bother denying that all of us in the cabinet, Gordon included, would rather James had not resigned. My central message was the one I had delivered to Derek all those months ago, to Gordon ever since, and to cabinet colleagues: what mattered if we were to turn our fortunes around was policy. I didn't exactly bubble with optimism, but I did convey a sense of confidence that the past few days might focus minds on the policy areas we intended to drive forward: issues like further constitutional and public service reforms, and above all dealing with a recession whose effects were likely to be of far greater concern to Andrew's viewers than a year-and-a-half-old email.

The accelerated Purnell reshuffle had placed me at the centre of that economic strategy. I was head of an expanded, and again renamed, department which now also included universities, science and skills. To Andrew's amusement when he introduced me, I now had a *seventeen-word* job title. I was also First Secretary of State and Lord President of the Council. My grandfather had been Lord President in Clement Attlee's government after the war, as I was reminded by the Queen at my first Privy Council meeting and audience at Buckingham Palace following my appointment.

What really mattered, however, was not titles but the policy challenges we were facing. Some things we were getting right. The creation of the larger ministry I now headed – Business, Innovation and Skills – reflected a properly expanded commitment to growth, enterprise and jobs as part of our strategy to get Britain out of recession. But the central argument over future economic strategy was no closer to being resolved. Gordon was resisting any talk of new cuts in spending to reduce the deficit and debt. I was sure he was right to argue that the last thing the economy needed at a time of recession was any early reduction in government stimulus. But there was also politics involved, and the inevitable impression that we were simply in denial about the scale of the financial hole we found ourselves in. The Tories and the media latched on to this and did not let go. David Cameron made it his political refrain. I can't say that I blamed him.

Even if the cuts themselves could be deferred, to avoid admitting the need to make them was not sustainable. Ed Balls now firmly allied himself with me in encouraging Gordon to change tack. Our argument was that in order to win the case for protecting current spending while private sector demand was weak, we would have to emphasise our commitment to taking firmer action later, when the recovery was locked in. Ed and I had a series of meetings with Gordon. His response was that his critics didn't get it. He believed that in the current circumstances, Keynesian stimulus was justified and essential. The costs of not pouring money into the economy would be greater over time, as businesses failed and unemployment mounted. We were not alone in our indebtedness. Other countries were far worse off than we were. And in the longer term, we could pay down our debt out of growth, once the stimulus had fully worked. He intended his message on cuts and investment to apply now. Politically, however, it left him, and us, looking as if we were not facing up to the deficit in the longer term. He created the impression that we would simply keep on spending, borrowing and taking on debt – a burden that would take an eternity to pay off, and would create a tax bill for generations to come.

The more we pressed him, the more entrenched he became. I assured him that we could maintain a strong 'dividing line' from the Tories. They wanted to cut immediately, and would always want to cut more. We would remain on the right side of the argument, as long as we were prepared to show we would cut sufficiently, in the right ways and guided by the right social priorities. Gordon replied, 'You're saying we should tell people we will make nice cuts, but the Tories will make nasty cuts.' I said we could sort out exactly what cuts we would make, and their extent, over time. What we could not do was continue to give the impression that we would make no cuts at all. 'You don't have to perform an instant U-turn,' I assured him. Other ministers could prepare the ground. The important thing was for us to end up in the right place.

Slowly, he seemed to come round. With his grudging approval I used a speech at a Press Gallery lunch in July to take the first step towards repositioning ourselves. I had worked out an agreed formula with Ed the day before, passing notes back and forth in cabinet. I echoed Gordon's view that we needed to spend to get out of recession, and that we must not lose our nerve as the economy began to show signs of recovery. Once we were out of the crisis, however, we would be operating under considerable public spending constraints. Front-line services like the police, schools and hospitals would still get sustained investment, but after the economy recovered, I said, 'There will be spending choices, and a growing need for greater efficiency across the board – and less spending in some programmes.' I deliberately didn't mention the dreaded 'c' word, but the headline-writers used 'cuts' anyway. The argument was finally out there.

From early in the year we had also been facing another delicate issue, familiar to both Gordon and me from a decade earlier: the future of the Royal Mail. Put simply, the Royal Mail needed to modernise, or else it was not going to survive. Not only was it having to vie with other postal and package handlers, but the age of email and the internet meant that its core business was shrinking fast. It had a pension fund deficit of £8 billion, seventy-five times its annual profits, and it had been plagued for years by terrible industrial relations: trust between management and the Communication Workers Union was badly fractured. Long before my return to the cabinet, the government had commissioned a report from Richard Hooper, former deputy head of the communications regulator, to examine the way forward for the Royal Mail. The final report landed on my desk in my first weeks as Business Secretary. It proposed that the Treasury bail out the pension fund deficit, but said that in return the Royal Mail should be modernised by bringing in a 'strategic partner' from the private sector, with new capital and management expertise.

Given the size of the pension hole, it was a solution that would not come cheap. But from the moment we had read the Hooper report, Gordon and I agreed that it offered the best way forward. It would keep the Post Office itself, as opposed to the Royal Mail, entirely in public hands, and would provide for the new money, new technology and new practices the Royal Mail needed if it was to compete successfully. The problem was the politics, or more specifically the CWU. No sooner had I made it clear that we would legislate along the lines of Hooper's recommendations than the union launched a furious campaign against our intention to 'privatise the Post Office'. We were not privatising anything, but we did strongly believe that a private partner was desirable for the Royal Mail. The CWU began to lean on Labour MPs to oppose the reforms, and to warn that they would withhold support from candidates in marginal seats who backed the government's plan. That was no empty threat. The CWU was one of Labour's largest union sponsors, donating hundreds of thousands of pounds to the national and local coffers. It used every political tool it could think of to try to whip up sentiment against the Hooper plan, and modernisation. Following my introduction of the legislation in the House of Lords, it became more obvious with each passing week that if we were going to proceed with the Hooper recommendations, we would have a major fight on our hands in the Commons.

Gordon was fed up with the CWU. Privately, he did not hide his anger. He was convinced that Hooper was right, but the more we talked about it, the more nervous he seemed about the prospect of a political scrap to get the Bill through. I had sensed from the beginning that this might happen, and I now left it to him to reach his own conclusion and give us the go-ahead. What I did not tell Gordon was that my ministerial team and I had been careful to leave ourselves an exit strategy. It was not difficult to devise. Given the world economic crisis, these were not exactly the ideal times in which to open bidding for a private partner for the Royal Mail. But I still felt we would be much better off if we saw the legislation through. I made the argument, not only to Gordon but to other ministers and the media, that to retreat from difficult political decisions carried the risk of suggesting that we had simply lost the appetite and the energy for government.

I had one particularly gratifying ally. John Prescott and I had long since put our former tensions behind us, a process that had begun with our shared attempts to mediate the fabled 'orderly transition' from Tony to Gordon in Number 10. John was in no doubt that the CWU had to accept change and modernisation, and he agreed that it would be bad for the government if we retreated. He volunteered to use his influence to help drum up support for the legislation among MPs. Still, I could not proceed without being sure that Gordon would stay the course. I went to see him, and told him that since it looked as if he was reluctant to force the issue with the union or the PLP, I planned to announce within the next twenty-four hours that due to current market conditions, we were withdrawing the legislation for now – unless he got back to me and said he was willing to go ahead. He did not get back to me, and I made my announcement at the beginning of July.

When I introduced the Royal Mail Bill into the Lords, I knew there would be pressure on my side of the House to oppose it. As it happened, save for about twenty or so peers, support was strong across the Lords. But I had taken the precaution of talking to my 'shadow' in the Lords, Lord Hunt of the Wirral, beforehand. I had known him well for many years, since we had been active in the British Youth Council together. I also talked to the Shadow Business Secretary, Ken Clarke, because he would be dealing with the Bill in the Commons. Both understood the urgent need for change in the Royal Mail, and were firmly behind the legislation. I enjoyed dealing with both of them, and count them as friends. When Ken had been appointed as my Tory opposite number, I took it as a compliment that David Cameron felt the need for a 'big beast' to shadow me.

Ken was a thoroughly affable and intelligent man, who I knew from our days campaigning for British engagement with Europe, and we got on well when we met to discuss political business – which we did more often than anyone realised. Later on, in the months leading up to the general election, I was careful to keep him posted on all items of major expenditure by my department, including industrial grants and loans. I gave him the opportunity to discuss anything he objected to, both because it looked likely that he would take over from me after the election, and because I thought it would make it easier for the opposition to accept and carry through the decisions I took. Ken appreciated this as a grown-up way for government to be conducted – a response that to my mind demonstrated David Cameron's good sense in bringing him back to the front line.

Despite all our efforts to project a strong, united front, I entered the summer greatly worried about our prospects. We were still bumping along at 25 per cent in the polls, while the Tories were above 40 per cent. On those numbers, we were in danger of being wiped out when the election came. Even those closest to Gordon in Downing Street were disheartened. I had been back for ten months, but I had clearly been unable to turn things around in the way I and others wanted. David Muir and Justin Forsyth were kind enough to say I had made a great difference in rallying everyone – 'You don't know what it was like before you came back,' Justin remarked. But Sue Nye told me at the start of the summer break that she had hoped I would have been able to make more of a difference. She had expected me essentially to function as Gordon's political commander-in-chief, the equivalent of Ed's role when he was at the Treasury. From a different quarter, Alistair Darling said he had assumed that I would at least take control of all general election and campaign planning. 'Isn't that what he brought you back here to do?' he asked.

The truth was that I wasn't sure. My hunch was that Gordon did want me to take charge of his political organisation; or at least part of him did. I also expected to be given responsibility for the coming general election campaign, but Gordon would not confirm that either. The more I worked with him – and apart from Ed Balls, no one worked with him more closely – the more I was struck by his reluctance to cede too much control to anyone. He seemed happiest when I was in his room talking to him with Ed. But this contentment was ultimately dependent on Ed and me agreeing with how he saw things. The consequence of this, for me, was that I sometimes too readily conceded to his point of view rather than argued back. It was not that I failed to raise questions, or that I feared putting a counter-position to his when necessary. But as time went on, I began to think I was not pressing my point of view hard enough on key policy and strategic issues. I did not want to put Gordon on his guard, and make him resistant to unwelcome advice I might have to offer in the future. Dealing with him involved a constant balancing act. It was hard to avoid being either too forceful or too conciliatory.

Whatever Gordon's intention had been in bringing me back, one effect was now unmistakable: it had shored up his defences against a cabinet rebellion. When I had returned to government, I had joked to friends in Britain and Brussels that Gordon and I were now 'joined at the hip'. That was true. There was no way I would, or could, turn against him. David Owen, who seemed delighted by my resurrection both for the weirdness of it and because he felt it would be good for the government, said to me shortly after my return to London, 'It's absolutely clear you've got to stick with Gordon now. No matter what really happened in 1994, the image stuck that you betrayed him when Tony got the leadership. You'll do a lot of harm not only to Gordon, but to yourself, if you abandon him.'

This had lodged firmly in my mind. Now, I wondered whether I was heading for an awful catch-22. I might end up being able to do just enough to save Gordon, but not enough to save the party's election hopes. Most of the Blairite fraternity – Alastair Campbell, Philip Gould and Tony himself – were beginning to warn me of the dangers of taking loyalty too far. They feared that if I helped to prop up Gordon beyond the point of no return, the result might be an even worse election drubbing than already seemed on the cards. The message from all of them, though, seemed to be that they accepted there were no circumstances under which I would participate in forcing Gordon out. But they also felt I should not stop him using the revolver if it came to that.

I went to see Tony at his home in Buckinghamshire at the end of August. 'You have a great, grave responsibility,' he told me. I was right to have helped Gordon, and right to stay on, he said. 'It's important that someone shows that Labour is still interested in governing, and you're certainly doing so in your department. But be careful. Very quickly, the credit you're getting for helping Gordon could turn into criticism that you are the only person propping him up, and are therefore responsible for the party's demise.' If the political forces gathered to sweep Gordon away, he said that I should not be the one pillar keeping him upright.

When we returned to Westminster in September, after the summer break, I was convinced that no recovery would be possible without a change in Gordon's economic narrative. Ed and I started trying to win him over again. Much as he might resist it, he had to signal publicly that he understood people's concerns about the deficit, and acknowledge that spending cuts would be necessary once growth was under way. With Alistair Darling and Ed, I had worked out a long-term plan to reposition him and the government on the issue leading into the next PBR, and to set our course towards the election. My speech to lobby journalists before the recess had been the first piece in the jigsaw. Gordon had been meant to use the same or similar language in a select committee appearance in the Commons soon afterwards, and at his final press conference before the summer. But he had not been able to bring himself to mention, or even hint at, cuts, future or otherwise. We had also agreed that both Alistair and I would make speeches in September acknowledging the need for future budget restraint.

My speech, at an event sponsored by the New Labour group Progress at the LSE, also outlined a wider policy framework, setting out the narrative I wanted to take into the election. To get through the recession, I said we needed to prioritise economic recovery before we concentrated on the deficit. We had to protect the front-line delivery of public services, but spending reductions would have to be part of the mix. I pointed out that Labour's decade-long investment in public services, health and education in particular, had transformed their delivery. That meant that there was no longer a need for additional catch-up investment in those areas. The task now was to continue with a programme of reform, increasing choice and diversity of provision. In other words, there was a substantial difference between our approach and that of the Tories. David Cameron wanted a smaller state. He would pursue spending cuts not just because he needed to, but because he and his unchanged party wanted to. What we advocated was a wiser, more cost-effective and fairer state. I reprised the New Labour maxim that we would be 'wise spenders, not big spenders'. I also explained how, while cutting back the branches of public spending, we needed to avoid severing the roots of economic growth. These should continue to be nurtured through business support, technology and enterprise policies to create new 'growth sector' jobs. Deliberately, however, I still did not use the word 'cuts'.

My hope was that Gordon would do that the following day, at the speech he was giving to the TUC. To my relief, he took the plunge. He repeated his warning of the 'across-the-board spending cuts' that would await Britain under the Tories, and said Cameron would take 'the wrong choices at the wrong time for the wrong reasons'. But he did say, finally: 'Labour will cut costs, cut inefficiencies, cut unnecessary programmes and cut lower-priority budgets.' In fact, he used the word 'cut' no fewer than eight times.

'Well, are you satisfied, all of you?' he asked testily when Ed and I met him later in the day. It was obvious that he had not been happy about using the word at all. We reassured him that he had been right, and tried to get him to focus on a new 'dividing line' with Cameron – on the speed and nature of any cuts. 'We should not be in this place!' he replied. 'We have got to move to growth! Don't give me all this about spending cuts!' He added that if only we had a fair press, he was certain that he could win the argument with the public. 'Now it's useless. The Treasury will be turning the screw. They and others have set the terms of this argument, and we've just followed them. We should not have gone down this course. It's got to be about growth, not deficit.' He said he had never wanted to make the TUC speech: 'Cuts versus cuts will just kill us.' I tried to get him to accept that we needed greater credibility on the deficit if we were to press home our wider arguments about the economy and growth, but to no avail. I had hoped that this series of speeches would be the prelude to a more credible economic platform that we could present at the forthcoming Labour conference, but Gordon was unmovable. A political faultline was growing between us.

I was also getting nervous about my own speech to the conference. It was a huge moment for me, the first time I had spoken to conference as a cabinet minister for over a decade, and I had no idea how I would be received. I wanted to use the speech to give the party hope. We had been through a tough couple of years. I wanted to give the delegates confidence that David Cameron and the Tories were not invulnerable, that they had not changed to anything like the degree they wanted voters to believe, and that a thumping Conservative victory at the next election was not a foregone conclusion.

My butterflies only increased when I arrived at the conference hall in Brighton – the same venue where I had watched Tony's triumphant first appearance as Prime Minister, and had learned of my failure to beat Ken Livingstone to a place on the NEC, in 1997. The night before my speech, I went through a rehearsal with an autocue, an experience made more nerve-racking by the fact that I had used the machine only once before. As I rehearsed the speech a final time the following morning, I was especially worried that its more personal aspects might backfire. For years I had dreamed of being able to make a big conference speech, the kind that made an impact not only on a political level, but personally too. By the time of what I thought was my final farewell to Westminster five years earlier, I had given up any hope of doing so. Now, I had an unlikely last chance. It was not just a matter of fulfilling Tony's memorable test for the success of New Labour: teaching the party to 'love Peter Mandelson'. What I wanted to get across most of all was my own love for Labour, my experience of its highs and lows over the past quarter of a century, and my genuine sense that together we might still stage a political revival in time for the general election.

My special adviser, Patrick Loughran, who had been working in Number 10 when I came back from Brussels and had joined me at the business department, was crucial in helping me to write the speech. All the more personal – and, to my mind, riskier – parts were inspired by him. Waheed Alli, one of my closest friends, who had successfully made the transition from entrepreneur to life peer at an indecently young age, also helped shape the speech, as of course did Roger Liddle too.

All I had to do now was not make a mess of delivering it, something that I was not at all confident about as I walked onto the stage. 'Conference,' I began, 'let me say after these years away – it's good to be back home.' From the first burst of applause, I knew that my genuine sense of homecoming was getting across, and that the party – my party, from the moment I had first cared about and been entranced by politics – felt it too. I spoke of my shock, and apprehension, when Gordon had asked me to return. 'I had been in this movie before –

and its sequel,' I said. 'And neither time did I like the ending.' I traced my connection with the party, the bond that had begun long before New Labour, and that had informed every step or decision I had taken along the way. 'I did not choose this party,' I said. 'I was born into it.' I had always loved working for it, 'even if, at times, perhaps not everyone in it has loved me'. I said that I knew I had made enemies, sometimes needlessly. I had been too careless of the feelings and views of others. But I had always been guided by the goal of returning Labour to where it needed to be: in government, helping the hardworking people of our country. I joked that Tony's famous remark about Labour learning to 'love Peter Mandelson' had probably set the bar a bit high. But I did feel, finally, that the anger and mistrust, on both sides, were gone. We were all in this together now. 'If *I* can come back,' I told the cheering, and more importantly cheered, delegates, '*we* can come back!'

That evening's news broadcasts reported that I had brought the conference to its feet. The next day, the newspapers were unusually kind. I especially treasured the front page of the *Mirror*, given over to a photo of me with the headline 'We Love Mandy'.

Gordon had been sitting behind me, quite a way back on the stage. Before I began speaking, I sensed that he was apprehensive, not knowing if I would pull it off. When the emotion started to flow, he must have wondered where it would all end. But by the time I finished, he was not only relieved, he was obviously pleased, for both of us. It had been his hunch to bring me back. Despite all the frustrations of the past year, that decision at least had been validated. Improbable though it seemed, Labour had, at long last, learned to love Peter Mandelson.

12

The End of New Labour?

I had barely twenty-four hours to savour my extraordinary feeling of reconnection with the party, and the political cause, to which I had devoted nearly all of my life. The real problem, of course, remained: that the country showed every sign of falling out of love with Labour.

The evening after my speech, and just hours after Gordon had delivered a powerful and well-received leader's address, the two of us were in a crowded banqueting suite in Brighton's Grand Hotel when we began getting a series of voicemail and text messages from Rebekah Brooks (formerly Wade), the ex-*Sun* editor recently promoted to chief executive of Rupert Murdoch's News International. She wanted urgently to talk to Gordon, or failing that, to me. We were attending Labour's main fund-raising dinner, and Gordon's staff asked me whether I thought he should slip away and speak to her. I said firmly that he should stay. After all, he was the star attraction at the dinner. Barring a national emergency, which this clearly was not, he should surely avoid leaving. The main reason I wanted Gordon to stay put, however, was that I had a fairly good idea what Rebekah wanted. For months it had been apparent that the *Sun* was cosying up to David Cameron. In my conference speech I had joked that I had 'been in this movie before', a reference to my earlier rises and falls as a cabinet minister. I had also been in the Murdoch movie before.

In the run-up to the 1997 election I had been the first to receive word of the *Sun*'s dramatic conversion from Kinnock-basher to supporter of New Labour, in a phone call to my office at Millbank from the then News International executive Jane Reed. As Chancellor, Gordon had gone on to develop a good relationship with Rupert Murdoch, and especially with Murdoch's favourite economic adviser and columnist, Irwin Stelzer. He had never warmed to Rebekah, in part because he saw her as a fan of Tony's. During the weeks leading up to the party conference he had become nervous about the *Sun*, and I was pretty sure that Rebekah was now going to deliver the opposite message from the one I had heard from Jane a dozen years earlier. With Gordon still feeling lifted by the way conference had gone, the last thing I felt he needed was to be on the receiving end of news that would not only deflate him, but would overshadow the otherwise positive coverage of his speech I was expecting in the following morning's papers. Frankly, I also felt it would be wrong for Gordon to dignify the *Sun*'s deliberately timed snub by answering Rebekah's messages. I told the Number 10 aides that I would phone her instead.

When I called her from my mobile in the corridor outside the banqueting hall, I was determined not to betray surprise, or even particular concern, about the news of the *Sun*'s switch, which she duly delivered. I used one of my favourite words to describe whoever at the paper, or News International, had decided on a grandstanding shift of political allegiances. They were chumps, I said. Some later media reports suggested that Rebekah misheard me, and thought I had used a far more offensive term. I did not, although I did tell her that I was certain turning the *Sun* into a Tory fanzine would not go down well with its readers.

After we spoke, I went back into the dinner and told Gordon about my conversation. I urged him not to say or do anything that indicated he was stung by the *Sun*'s move. The truth was that he *was* stung. He showed admirable restraint in not allowing this to show. In the weeks and months that followed, however, it grated on him more and more. He was convinced that a deal had been struck between Cameron's team and the Murdoch media, with political dividends for the Tories and commercial ones for the Murdoch empire, given the prospect that a Conservative government seemed unlikely to take a restrictive view on issues of media competition. At his urging, I spoke out on that issue publicly on a couple of occasions following the *Sun* switch. In fact, I suspected that the real reason for the change was simpler, and in a way even more discouraging. The *Sun* was a mass-market paper. It saw its interests as backing a winner. While I was still not convinced, or at least not ready to accept, that a Tory victory at the next election was inevitable, given the yawning gap we would have to make up in the opinion polls, it was certainly looking that way.

After conference, thoughts turned to the general election. We set ourselves the target of raising our poll ratings from their stubborn 25 per cent to 30 per cent by Christmas. David Muir and Justin Forsyth, together with Gavin Kelly and Nick Pearce on the policy side, rallied the Number 10 team behind this objective. Patrick Loughran became my point man on campaign planning while continuing his day job in the department. Philip Gould weighed in with his strategic advice. I also started courting Alastair Campbell, in an effort to bring his talents and experience on board. He was reluctant. Not only could he barely face returning to the daily grind and the campaign treadmill, he was unsure about Gordon. Wouldn't we be propping up a lost cause, he asked me. I appealed to his loyalty to the party, but it was months more before he started to engage.

Gordon was meanwhile veering back onto his original 'no cuts' track. 'We have to attack the Tories for their pessimism,' he said. 'They're ushering in a no-growth, high-unemployment decade. They're just throwing in the towel.' I don't think he had any idea how discouraging this was to many of us. It was not as if there was a gulf of policy difference between us. All of us opposed premature spending cuts, but we differed on the question of how we should frame and express our economic message. Almost everywhere I looked, and for everyone I talked to, the question was whether Gordon would – and perhaps should – throw in the towel. Douglas Alexander had concluded that his old patron and mentor lacked the 'skill-set' for Prime Minister: 'Every question we face comes back to leadership. Everything.' He also worried that Gordon was resigned to defeat. A couple of days later, Gerald Kaufman was only slightly less bleak. 'Gordon is what he is. He's not Tony and never will be. But we're stuck with him.' He added, with a smile, 'What you cannot cure, you endure.'

When I went to discuss election planning at the Saatchi agency, their research findings were not exactly encouraging either. 'As things stand at the moment,' their head of research said, 'Gordon is a walking magnetic field for everyone's negative feelings: their anger, anxiety, their broken washing machine or their kids' disappointing school results. They don't like the Tories. But given the choice, it seems they won't have Gordon.' At least there was still the odd lighter moment – if gallows humour can qualify as light – around an increasingly despondent cabinet table. At a meeting in October, I was delivering a presentation on communications strategy when Harriet suggested, quite reasonably, that we base it on the 'three Fs – future, family and fairness'. On either side of me, Alistair and Douglas could not help adding some 'F's of their own. 'How about "fucked"?' Alistair proposed. 'Futile?' said Douglas. 'Finished?' I added.

Deep down, none of us was amused, just worried. I was ready for the fight. But, not for the last time in the crucial months that followed, I could not seem to make the levers and buttons work in the way I had in previous campaigns. Gordon at least acknowledged how bad things were getting, and also seemed more focused. 'So much of the problem is me. I realise that,' he told me. He said that he recognised we needed to move up a gear. We had to make the election campaign a choice between optimism and pessimism. He felt the Tories were too gloomy with all their talk of austerity, and that he could take people by surprise by being upbeat. His instincts struck me as correct. Even in difficult times, people feel more comfortable voting on their hopes, as long as they are credible, than their fears. But I added, 'You're going to have to cheer yourself up if you're going to convince people you're optimistic.'

Or convince the cabinet. After the Cenotaph wreath-laying on Remembrance Sunday in November, I sat down with David Miliband on a leather bench in the Locarno Room at the Foreign Office. He asked me what I thought about our election chances. For the first time in all our months of conversations, I did not prevaricate. I said that I did not think we could win with Gordon as things stood. Barring a huge turnaround, I feared the scale of defeat could be colossal. 'That's quite something, coming from you,' David replied. He asked me to repeat what I'd said, as if he wasn't sure he had heard me correctly. I did so, and added that I knew the cabinet was growing disillusioned and restless about our prospects. As we were preparing to head home, Harriet walked past, and I asked her to join us. She urged me to take charge, soon, of a strategy for the general election. She said that Gordon had made it clear to her during the reshuffle that I would be asked to do so, and she wanted me to know that she was happy with that. But she said Gordon seemed incapable of making this clear to all involved, and of actually reaching or conveying a decision. 'It's getting everyone down,' she said. 'If he doesn't raise his game, and if we don't start sorting ourselves out, everyone's going to get very uneasy.'

I had known Harriet since my time at Walworth Road in the 1980s. She was already a keen campaigner back then, and I had helped her to rehearse soundbites to camera as she worked to improve and polish her performance. She was aware that she irritated some people with her style of gender politics, and I am afraid I was among those who sometimes bridled at her strictures. But although I don't always agree with Harriet, she does have guts, and I admire her for speaking her mind. She has a feeling for the public's attitudes towards politics and politicians which transcends Westminster's Punch and Judy show.

Polling day, provisionally set to coincide with the local elections on the first Thursday of May 2010, was just six months away. I had been trying to get Gordon to focus on the necessary organisation and preparations since the start of the year. In a note as long ago as February, I had warned that we were nowhere near having the machinery and personnel capable of delivering a winning campaign. As Harriet recognised, this was part of a wider series of problems. One of them was policy. We needed a credible message to take to the electorate, and not only on the vexed question of spending and budget cuts. We needed to convey energy and imagination for the future, the kind of broader policy programme we had tried to set out in 'Building Britain's Future' and my Progress lecture. Gordon was still in dividing-line mode: Tory cuts versus Labour spending. During discussions in the cabinet, at which civil servants were not present, other ministers were preoccupied with picking holes in Cameron's policy prospectus. David Miliband, Douglas Alexander and I dissented. Each of us, in different ways, argued that in order to break through with a relaunch of the party and the government – and to have any hope of winning the election – we had to bring out the policy choices *we* were making. When Gordon asked me to sum up at the end of one such discussion in November, I said, 'Dividing lines with the Conservatives are fine. They're important. But in order to succeed, to get people listening to us, we have to concentrate on the decisions we will take on different policy options and spending priorities – the message that we are making these choices, however hard.'

Intellectually, Gordon understood this. That much was obvious in his comments to me about the need to do a 'gear change' and project a new optimism to the public. But the difficulties went deeper, and he was a big part of most of them. He was surrounded by some truly excellent people in Downing Street. Heaven knows, they worked all hours, often for little thanks or reward. But they bemoaned his inability to work with them as a group. Gordon was on top of what was happening in the economic world. But he was trying to do too much. I remember challenging him after what I regarded as an ill-judged Downing Street briefing. 'Who do your political spokesmen look to for their "line to take" with the media?' I asked. 'Me,' he replied, as if the very question was absurd. 'It's pretty good to have the Prime Minister as your line manager,' I replied. But it was a bad recipe for effective government. It reinforced Gordon's short-term instincts, his urge to react rather than reflect, his tendency to personalise and obsess over the implications of a newspaper headline, a columnist's criticism, or a Cameron initiative. We needed to focus not on tactics, but strategy. Not on where we were today as a government, but where we wanted to be a few weeks or months ahead, and the decisions needed to get us there. The delay in addressing preparations for the election was only a symptom of our failing to do this.

Soon afterwards, there was another illustration of this. With a pared-down version of the new EU constitution finally ratified by member states, two new major posts had to be filled in Brussels. The first was the full-time President of the European Council, the body that brought all the EU heads of government together. The other was the grandly titled High Representative of the Union for Foreign Affairs and Security Policy, who would be Europe's voice in world diplomatic and defence forums. Over a period of months, speculation had grown that Tony might get the presidency. Tony wanted the job, but Gordon was conflicted. He was careful to avoid saying anything in public that might suggest he wasn't supportive, and he kept assuring me that he was doing his best to get him appointed. Yet from the start, he talked down Tony's chances in private, saying it was a lost cause. He even told me early on that *he* had been asked if he was interested in the job. 'If I stood, they would have me,' he said. I immediately tried to draw him on the idea. If it was true, it struck me that it would be good for Gordon, good for Britain and very possibly good for our electoral chances. 'Are you interested?' I asked him. 'It's a good job.' He quickly replied, 'No. No.' I let it drop.

Gordon turned out to be right about Tony's candidature. I believed Tony would have been perfect for the job, and the EU would have benefited from heightened stature on the international stage. For a short while, the tide appeared to be moving in his direction. Two key players, Germany's Angela Merkel and France's Nicolas Sarkozy, recognised Tony's strengths, and the benefits a Blair presidency would bring. Sarkozy was especially keen, I gathered from a source close to him, but not if Merkel was not fully committed and he risked ending up by backing a losing candidate. Soon there were counter-pressures from those who thought that Tony was too big a personality from too big a member state, and had dangerously reformist views about the EU. There was growing support for a less threatening and less well-known candidate: Herman van Rompuy, a Belgian Christian Democrat who had briefly served as Prime Minister. The decisive week came in mid-November, shortly before the meeting to decide the new posts. Tony had phoned Merkel, and told her that if it was decided that he and the job were not a good fit, there would be no hard feelings. She replied that she thought it was not going to work.

Gordon shifted into fallback mode. Britain was still clearly in line for a major role: either the High Representative's job or a weighty economic portfolio on the European Commission. I had long argued that an economic portfolio was more important for British interests. I knew the Commission, and the importance of having a heavy hitter in a core job. But again, tactics trumped strategy. David Miliband was briefly tempted by the High Representative's job if Tony was no longer in line for the presidency. Ultimately, however, he decided it was not for him, as he wanted to remain in Westminster politics. Gordon was ambivalent over what prize he wanted for Britain. The key players in Downing Street were divided. Some favoured the foreign-policy post, and still held out hope that David could be persuaded to take it, even though they made no secret of their worries about the political effect of his leaving the government. Others, like me, advocated going for a top economic job, ideally the internal market portfolio. This would ensure that Britain's voice carried weight on new regulatory initiatives, with obvious implications for the City. Three possible names were in the hat: the Financial Services Authority chief Adair Turner, the CBI's Richard Lambert, and Shriti Vadera. Until the day before the decision, Gordon had apparently not made up his mind.

It was at this point that my name suddenly entered the frame for the High Representative's post. Tony called me and said he had just spoken to Gordon, who as best he could tell, was leaning towards pressing for a Briton as High Representative. Tony had told him there were only two serious candidates, myself and David, and that since David had decided to rule himself out, he should turn to me. Gordon phoned shortly afterwards, and asked if I was interested. Although I didn't say so, I was hugely tempted. To be the EU's chief voice on the international stage was something I not only felt I would be good at, but, combining my interest in Europe with coming as close as I was ever going to get to my lifelong ambition to be Foreign Secretary, it would in many ways be the best possible culmination of my career in public life. What I did say was much more circumspect. I told him I was interested, but that I was also aware of the practical problems. I had obligations here, to the government and to him, and it would obviously be difficult for me to leave just now.

Gordon said it would not just be difficult. It would be 'terrible' for the government because of what it would signal, quite apart from the loss of my campaigning experience. The media would represent it as my walking away because I had lost confidence in our winning the next election. Later that day, he told me that if I quit the government, the party, which had just started to love me after all this time, would hate me all over again. By that evening, I had accepted that I was not going to be put forward. I was astonished, however, when I heard that Gordon was leaning towards my interim successor as Trade Commissioner, Cathy Ashton, the former leader of the Lords, as High Representative. I had no personal animus against her, I just thought she would have difficulty in projecting herself and making an impact in the job. I phoned Number 10, and asked for the Prime Minister. After a long pause, the switchboard put me through instead to Stewart Wood, Gordon's Europe adviser. When I said that I had heard Cathy's name was being considered, he replied, 'Absolutely not!'

Gordon phoned me the next morning and asked if I was still interested in the foreign-policy post. I told him that I was, but again added that I understood all the constraints and concerns, and said I would defer to his judgement. He replied that although he would do his best, he thought it would be very difficult. Despite my years in Brussels, I would be almost as controversial a choice as Tony for the socialist MEPs, who were in effect being given the key voice in the High Representative's post because the presidency had gone to a right-of-centre candidate. I telephoned some of my own friends in the socialist group, and senior government contacts in Berlin, Paris and Madrid. None was averse to my name being considered. That afternoon, Gordon rang after his talks with the socialist group. 'The only person they would accept was Cathy,' he said. 'They want a woman. I'm sorry. I did my best.' Twenty minutes later, the decision was announced. It was an extremely slapdash process by which to fill such an important job.

In the space of a fortnight, Britain's proposed representative in the new architecture of the EU had gone from Tony, to David, to me – and finally to Cathy. It was not my failure to get the EU post that upset me: I understood that. It was that Britain had gone for the wrong job, and the wrong candidate. I knew by then that a delegation of political staff in Number 10 had spoken to Gordon, and strongly opposed my going back to Brussels. They had told him I was integral to any hopes we might have of fighting back as a government, and winning the election. I was moved by their confidence, but as with Gordon's protracted unwillingness to focus on election strategy, the EU farce had brought to the fore worrying flaws in our ability to take a hard-headed view necessary for success – not just in Europe but, more worryingly, I felt, in framing our strategy for the coming election campaign.

By late November, there was at least some progress on the election. Harriet had been admirably gutsy, marching into Gordon's office and saying, 'Enough is enough. We've got to have structures. We've got to have organisation. We've got to work out our strategy.' The core structure, although Gordon had taken for ever in making it formal, had long been clear. I would be in charge of strategy. Douglas Alexander would be General Election Co-ordinator. Harriet, in the traditional role of deputy leader of the party, would be a leading face in the campaign across the country. Ed Miliband would draft the manifesto. Now an inner group of senior cabinet ministers – Douglas, Harriet, Ed Balls, David and Ed Miliband, Alistair Darling, Jack Straw, Alan Johnson and I – began meeting with Gordon to work on the direction of the campaign. Philip agreed to present to the group and work on strategy. With Douglas and my own special adviser, Patrick Loughran, he helped put together a draft for our campaign warbook. It was, finally, a start on real election planning. There was just one problem. Though our poll ratings were inching up, they hardly suggested enthusiasm for a fourth-term Labour government. 'Great strategy,' Douglas quipped after one of our meetings, 'pity about the *voters*.'

Alistair's final pre-election PBR was due to be delivered on 9 December. There was growing evidence of public recognition that he and Gordon had got the early response to the economic crisis right.

As we started to emerge from recession, public optimism was rising, and our electoral prospects seemed to be improving. We had to get crucial judgements right in the PBR, however, and to avoid the sort of presentational hits we had taken on previous set-piece occasions. I was impressed by Alistair's firmness of purpose. When we first discussed his plans, at the end of October, he told me he wanted to be bold, and to surprise the government's critics. He would maintain the stimulus throughout the current financial year, and would protect front-line budgets in three key areas: the NHS, schools and the police. But he would recognise the need for cuts elsewhere, announcing specific, symbolic savings in a number of major projects to convey our seriousness about making the longer-term reductions needed to bring down the debt. His proposed surprise announcments would reduce the bill for basic-rate taxpayers, and lower corporation tax. But – and here was the shock – to balance these moves he was minded not only to restore VAT to its previous level of 17.5 per cent, but to raise it over time, to 18 or even 19 per cent, rather than push up the only alternative, National Insurance charges. He would compensate low earners with a package of measures to negate the impact of the VAT increase on them.

I was impressed. These were exactly the sort of hard choices that would enable us to regain the initiative. Within days, however, I sensed trouble at Number 10. Gordon was on an entirely different track. He wanted to minimise the need for either tax or spending changes by delivering new, cheaper 'government for modern times'. He argued that through the internet, digital communications and other technological and organisational efficiencies, we could provide better, more cost-effective government. We would contrast this new-model administration with the prospect of withered and underfunded public services if Cameron took over, underpinned by a strong message about 'Labour optimism versus Tory pessimism'.

Gordon tried to fire up the cabinet strategy group. It was hard going. At one session, David Miliband was blunt: 'Instead of just fighting the Tories, we have to look as if we are fighting for Britain.' Alistair took this as his cue, and said we had to ask ourselves why people weren't listening to us any more. 'We have to make the weather.

We have to make ourselves the story. We have to take risks. We have nothing more to lose. To attack the Tories, we have to have our own lines clear first. The PBR has to be the game-changing moment.' I strongly supported him. Gordon did accept the need to present voters with a reason to look at what we had to offer, but his main emphasis was on confronting people with what they would lose as a result of the heavy cuts and changes he said the Tories would be sure to introduce.

When the argument over detail began, it was even more difficult than before the April budget. Gordon again insisted that we had to go for growth, not cuts, and rattled off a series of new investment priorities: rail modernisation, pharmaceuticals, the digital and low-carbon economy. In addition to protecting investment in the NHS, schools and the police, he should minimise cuts in other areas by modernising and 'restructuring' government, by which he meant releasing resources from the back office to the front line. But the credibility of our goal to halve the deficit in four years depended on addressing the issue of future tax and spending. On tax, he vetoed, point blank, Alistair's proposed VAT rise. He favoured an increase in National Insurance contributions, combined with a slice off bankers' bonuses. In this, he was strongly supported by the political staff in the office: David Muir said that his focus group research had revealed sharp antipathy to increasing VAT. Alistair, however, was worried about a National Insurance increase. Unlike VAT, it would be portrayed as a 'tax on jobs', which was hardly the signal we wanted to send at a time of rising unemployment. In any case, he insisted that the kind of growth plan Gordon wanted, without a sufficient new tax base or credible indications of future spending cuts, would not hold water. I agreed. Gordon remained unmoved, and said that by talking about future tax and spending we would be doing the Tories' job for them. The pace of economic growth was a great unknown. Therefore, he insisted, we did not have to go further in spelling out our plans at this stage.

I was not at all happy with what I regarded as a lack of realism. Yet as we drew nearer to Alistair's Commons statement, Gordon gave no ground and did not encourage further discussion. In a more receptive economic and political environment, his strategy might have worked. I supported him on growth, and welcomed the additional resources for my policies of industrial activism, which were fostering well-targeted investments and winning support from economic commentators and the business world. The problem was that we were deep in a pit of debt, and still digging. The markets and the media knew it, and the country felt it. Alistair, though ever less confident of winning the argument, insisted: 'We cannot just borrow more to pay for front-line services. If we are not credible in what we do and say, people will just assume there will be more borrowing or huge tax rises to come.' Gordon countered that growth would reduce the deficit, reeling off a by-now-familiar list of programmes for technology, infrastructure investment and support for small businesses.

'But we are already doing most of those things,' Alistair protested. 'They're in the pipeline. We have to focus now on what cuts there will be in non-front-line services.' If we kept to our promise not to cut the NHS, schools or the police, the obvious effect would be significant cuts elsewhere. Unless we increased the tax take – and he remained of the view that a rise in VAT, if done with the right compensating measures, was one way of doing this – we would not be believable. The only support for Alistair from Gordon's main PBR ally, Ed, came on taxes. He insisted that simply protecting his schools budget would not be enough: in order to take the argument to the Tories, he needed an above-inflation increase. 'I accept we cannot increase borrowing to pay for this,' he said, 'so we will need to tax more.' I asked him to at least consider the case for raising VAT, but either because he genuinely disagreed with it or because he didn't want to differ from Gordon, he did not follow up the proposal.

The key argument on tax began a week before the PBR. Gordon opened the meeting by reiterating his determination to 'go for growth', but accepting that at least something would have to give on taxation. He asked Alistair to give him the options for taking in more revenue. Repeating concerns about a National Insurance hike as a 'tax on jobs', Alistair said we were left with an increase in either income tax or VAT. Gordon held firm against VAT, while Alistair was equally against further increasing the income tax take from the highest paid: 'We are already at the boundary of what we can do there.' When Gordon suggested even more spending, Alistair simply rolled his eyes. The figures would not add up. Gordon responded that efficiency savings would trim 20 per cent across government, but the civil servants responded with a reality check, saying that they would yield only £5 billion at the very most. Alistair added that even with some additional tax we were going to have to make painful cuts in other areas to protect Ed's school spending, the NHS and the police.

The PBR, when it was announced, was not viewed as particularly bold. The bankers' bonus tax went down well: it was the equivalent of legislating for the public flogging of estate agents, or politicians. Unfortunately, it had the downside of stymieing the efforts Alistair and I were making to get the banks to contribute to a business innovation investment fund we had been discussing with them. This was a great disappointment to me, as I had been looking to it to help deliver growth capital to innovative and fast-growing small businesses. Still, commentator after commentator pointed out the obvious, elephantine flaw in the PBR: there just wasn't enough tax, or enough savings – unless we were contemplating sizeable cuts in spending after the election which we were not owning up to.

A post-PBR poll in *The Times* made dire reading. When asked who they most trusted to deal with Britain's economic future, nearly 40 per cent said the Tories. Only 27 per cent trusted us. In Gordon's first halcyon days as Prime Minister, he had led David Cameron on that measure by a margin of 61 per cent to 27. As recently as a year ago, in the wake of our action on the banks, he had still been ahead by 40 per cent to 31. Alistair had been right: our package had failed to convince. One immediate effect was a growing tide of pressure for us to come clean on the cuts we were planning for non-front-line departments. All in all, we had missed an opportunity with the PBR to recapture the initiative in framing the economic debate ahead of the election.

The unresolved issues and frayed nerves around the PBR were hardly the ideal starting-point for our discussion of campaign strategy before we parted ways for the Christmas break. I was scheduled to make a brief official visit to India, and having done breakfast interviews on the day of the PBR, I had imagined with some relief that I would not be required for further media duty in its aftermath. Soon journalists began speculating on my uncharacteristic absence from the airwaves. Certain lobby correspondents wrote that I had become 'disengaged' and 'offside'. A big effort was mounted in Number 10 to persuade me that this briefing had come from Tessa Jowell, one of my closest friends in politics. I knew that was rubbish.

In the meantime, Gordon was pushing us to go after the Conservatives' vulnerabilities. 'They have a fairness hole, a growth hole, a services hole,' he said. 'We have a plan for Britain. They haven't.' At PMQs, he took dual aim at Cameron's tax policies and at reports that one of the Tory leader's most high-profile protégés – his fellow public schoolboy, the multi-millionaire and prospective parliamentary candidate for Richmond Park, Zac Goldsmith – had been non-domiciled for tax purposes. The Conservative tax strategy, Gordon said, 'seems to have been dreamed up on the playing fields of Eton'. The media took this as the first salvo in a campaign of class warfare. I was fairly sure that it wasn't. If it was, I was determined that it should not be the centrepiece of our election strategy, if only because it would get in the way of formulating a convincing message of our own.

There was a further, ironic, danger as the Christmas holidays approached: some polls were suggesting that we were slightly narrowing the gap with Cameron. This seemed to reflect some greater public nervousness about the scale of cuts to come. Even Gordon recognised that we were still far behind, but he took the movement in the polls not as a blip but as vindication of his strategy to slam the Tories on cuts while keeping ourselves free, however implausibly, of any such charge. In my view, if we had been more convincing about our own fiscal plans, we would have been able to mount a stronger attack on what the Tories were planning.

When Douglas, Philip, Patrick and I met shortly before I left for India, Douglas was especially downbeat. He may not have known Gordon as long as I had, but he had spent virtually all his adult life at his side, beginning as a twenty-three-year-old researcher and speechwriter. As we discussed how to broaden Gordon's campaign approach, he felt it would be a hard battle. We would be fighting Gordon's oldest, deepest campaign instincts, the 'dark places' he went to when he was fighting the Tories: 'He sees the recent poll blip as substantiating his dividing-lines approach: the Conservatives are a remote elite, so let's drag them down further.' Douglas's fear was that Gordon did not understand what the public were feeling: 'We have to convince him on the numbers and the evidence that, deep down, his approach isn't working, and the blip is misleading him. He'll say it looks as if it's working, and anyway what's the alternative, what else is there to say? We have to offer him the right alternative.' Douglas also worried about Gordon's ability to adapt his leadership style to the emotional connection and language of humility needed on the campaign trail. Gordon saw himself as a political soulmate of Barack Obama, and in their joint response to the economic challenges of the past year, he could genuinely claim to have secured a working alliance with the US President. But as a campaigner, Douglas observed, 'the model of Obama versus McCain won't work. Gordon is McCain, even though he wants to be Obama.' Philip agreed: 'He's trying his best as Prime Minister, but he's failing. The public feel it.'

I decided the draft of the election warbook we had prepared was good enough to send to Gordon for his holiday reading, along with a covering note from Douglas and me setting out the polling picture, especially in the marginal constituencies. Nationally, we told him, the Tories had held a stable, double-digit lead for months. They were at roughly 40 per cent, while we were around 28 per cent, and the Lib Dems around 20 per cent. The good news was that we had rebounded from a low of 23 per cent in May. But the Conservatives held commanding leads in the marginals in the south and the Midlands, and leads in all of our own marginals in the north. As things stood, we were heading for a heavy defeat. Crucially, the lower the turnout, the worse we were likely to do.

There were three implications, we said, for how we should run the campaign. The first was that a full-on anti-Tory assault, by itself, was likely to backfire. Unless we offered hope, a positive and forward-looking message of our own, 'negative campaigning alone is likely to reinforce the public rejection of politics and politicians, drive down turnout, and increase our electoral vulnerability'. Second, while a 'core-vote' strategy might get us to 28 or 29 per cent of the vote, it would not get us higher: 'We have to balance that with an appeal to swing voters in Middle England.' Finally, Gordon himself had to change tack from his recent, highly partisan 'dividing lines' – people versus privilege, Labour street cred versus Tory entitlement This was especially important because, with televised debates between the leaders of the three main parties taking place for the first time, the campaign was bound to be personal. 'Your ratings were highest when you positioned yourself as speaking for Britain as a whole, inclusive and non-divisive,' we said. He had to rediscover that statesmanlike and broad-based voice and appeal.

Even if Gordon took our message on board, we knew that winning the election would still be a gargantuan struggle. But it was not a lost cause, especially if Cameron messed up or began to look shaky. We still weren't as directionless and unpopular as the Tories had been in the late 1990s, and Cameron was a long way from the kind of lead Tony had built up before 1997. But what if Gordon didn't shift his ground? I was not the only one worried about the implications of failing to bring him round to supporting a more positive and broadly pitched campaign strategy. The following day, I phoned Alistair. 'We're going to lose,' he said. I could hardly disagree. 'The numbers at the moment indicate that,' I replied. Alistair went on: 'You can tell, just by going into Tescos. People look away. They're embarrassed.' Then he said, 'We all know what the real problem is. It's not because of what the government is doing. It's who is leading it.' As in my talk with David on Remembrance Sunday, I saw little point in pretending that was untrue. 'A lot of our colleagues think the same thing,' Alistair said finally. 'But they don't think anything can be done about it without making things even worse. And they're probably right.'

I did some last-minute clearing up of departmental business before setting off on Christmas Eve for a week's holiday in Marrakesh. But before closing my laptop, I sent Gordon a long personal email. I tried not to make it unsettling, or hurtful. I began by agreeing with a remark he had made in a number of our recent meetings: on the need to shift the election from 'a referendum on Labour, to a choice between us and the Tories'. I was straightforward in my view that we were not yet succeeding in this, and set out what we would have to do differently – what he would have to do differently – if we were to have any hope of winning. All the signs at present, I said, were that the Tories would prevail, even in a 'choice, not referendum' election. Yes, Cameron had lost some support by being a bit too open about the scale of austerity he believed lay ahead, but that was a failure in getting the nuance of his message right, not in the message itself. Cameron was saying the country had taken an economic beating, recovery would be difficult, and at some stage this would have to mean spending less and taxing more.

On paper, the Tory lead was not insuperable. We were right to point out areas in which Cameron's supposedly 'new' Tories were the same as the old ones: instinctive public service cutters at home, right-wing fringe players in Europe. But that would not be enough. We needed a bolder, more visionary future offer of our own for the electorate. This was inevitably going to be a 'change' election, and we could not credibly offer change after thirteen years in office. But we could, and must, offer an alternative vision. Their 'change' versus our 'future'. We were in danger of courting our core vote alone, at the risk of losing the middle-class, Middle England voters who were crucial to the alliance that had won us our three election victories. Of course it made sense to emphasise our commitment to the most vulnerable in society, but as long as no one believed us about the public finances, they wouldn't believe us on anything else. To fix that problem, I told Gordon it was imperative that he accepted the need for a more forthright position on the public finances. Above all, his message had to be consistent with Alistair's.

I had made most of these points to him before, but never quite so bluntly. I had been moved to write, I told him, because the time for a recovery was short, and similar suggestions from me and others in the past had seemed to have little effect: 'It seems that once you have made up your mind, it is hard to discuss things frankly and collectively.' We needed more serious discussion, I said. Gordon replied the following morning. He began, as so often, by saying that I had made good points, and that he agreed with them. But he dealt with none of them in any detail. 'We have to launch a prosperity plan for Britain,' he concluded. Who could disagree? But that did not address the central points I was making.

In Marrakesh over Christmas and New Year, I heard nothing more from him. I welcomed the time away, unbothered by daily calls. I knew we had to take the initiative, and once I was back in London I convinced an initially reluctant Alistair to take a page from New Labour warbooks past. We totted up the Tories' tax and spending commitments, and identified a £34 billion funding gap in their plans. Alistair launched the attack in a polished press conference at party headquarters on the first Monday of January 2010. It was no substitute for the strategically focused election campaign we still lacked, but it did unsettle the Tories, and gave us a bit of momentum and a morale boost. Sadly, that lasted all of forty-eight hours. Then the focus suddenly shifted back onto us – and Gordon.

I had the first hint that something was up shortly after 11 a.m. on Wednesday, the day of the first PMQs on our return to Westminster. I was told that Tony had got wind of rumours of some kind of move against Gordon. So I telephoned him. We both agreed that if anything happened I should not be involved in encouraging it, but nor could I go into overdrive as I did when James resigned. Minutes later, Sue Nye called and said there were reports of some sort of initiative by Geoff Hoon and 'others' against Gordon. Downing Street had decided not to tell him about it before his dispatch box bout with David Cameron, a sufficiently nerve-racking enterprise as it was. By the end of PMQs, it was all over the TV news bulletins that Geoff and Patricia Hewitt had sent an email to all Labour MPs urging them to put an end to the 'grumbling…speculation and uncertainty' over Gordon's leadership by holding a secret leadership ballot.

For reasons unrelated to Geoff's and Patricia's concerns – or even to Gordon's refusal, as I saw it, to engage properly with the issues raised by the PBR or to respond to the points in my email before Christmas – I was a bit disgruntled with him by then. It was to do with a major speech I had given that morning at the Work Foundation. My theme was growth, and I was setting out precisely the case Gordon wanted made for the measures the government was putting in place to rebalance the UK economy away from finance and towards a healthier, stronger industrial future. The previous evening, however, David Muir had called to say that Gordon wanted a change in one of the paragraphs about taxation, where I planned to say we were near to reaching the limits of the tax burden on business. This intervention irritated me, because it seemed to show defensiveness rather than an ability to grasp the bigger picture I was trying to convey. It was unusual for me to be sharp with David. He and Justin – my 'Ant and Dec', as I called them – were the hardest of workers, and the last thing I wanted to do was to make their jobs more difficult. On this occasion, though, I snapped: 'If all Gordon can do is try and censor my speeches, don't rely on me to be hanging around to take much more of this.' David sounded shocked, and I instantly regretted saying it.

I had heard nothing more until an hour before I was due to speak, when there was a call from another one of Gordon's aides at Number 10. Gordon wanted me to change a further section of the speech, which concerned spending, because he felt it would be 'misinterpreted'. When I again balked, Gordon himself came on the line. I told him that the real problem wasn't a word here or a phrase there, but that we had a real policy difference, and different judgements on some fairly important things. I could tell that he was taken aback by my sudden forthrightness, and in truth so was I.

Now, my mind went back to this testy exchange. I hoped that Gordon would not be linking it to Geoff's and Patricia's move. I had known nothing about their plan, and given all the hard work that my team and I had put into writing my economic policy speech, if I had been asked beforehand, I would at least have asked them to choose another day. After news of Geoff's and Patricia's move became public, Sue phoned and asked me to take a call from Gordon. 'It would be a bad idea,' I said. 'I'm in such a bad mood with him I'm not sure what I would say.' When she then asked what Gordon should do, I felt I had to suggest something. 'Don't overreact,' I said. 'Play it calmly. If everyone thinks we're running around in a great sweat, it will build up and create a frenzy. You want to wind this *down*, not wind it up.' It was probably good advice. It was also a convenient explanation for my own silence over the Hoon–Hewitt email. I was still trying to work out its significance, and wondering where it would lead. I also had to rush out of the office to keep a lunch date with a good friend from Paris, the economic analyst, writer and Sarkozy confidant Alain Minc.

When I returned at around three in the afternoon, nothing much more had happened. Geoff and Patricia had made the rounds on TV, and Charles Clarke, Gordon's nemesis, who had been calling for him to go almost from the moment he took over as Prime Minister, had proclaimed his support for them. With the exception of a handful of ministers, principally Andy Burnham and Shaun Woodward, and, rather later, Ed Balls, the cabinet was lying low, and backbenchers even lower. My office was being besieged with requests for comment.

I phoned David Miliband to get his thoughts. He seemed none the wiser about what was happening. I decided that the whole thing was likely to blow itself out, and asked Patrick to issue a short statement saying that we should all get on with doing our work as government ministers. Shortly afterwards, David rang me back. He said that he had heard that Alistair was going in to see Gordon at Number 10, and that Harriet and Jack Straw were due to meet him shortly afterwards. I talked to Alistair after his meeting. It was pretty clear that while he remained frustrated and deeply pessimistic, he was in no mood to hand the Prime Minister a revolver. David phoned again after Harriet's and Jack's meeting. Apparently Jack had not even raised the leadership issue, and nor, in the end, did Harriet. This latest, and potentially most serious, 'coup' was over. Jack did at least provide one of the few lighter moments for Gordon before it was certain that the latest crisis had passed. With no obvious attempt at irony, he had arrived in Gordon's room in Downing Street wearing a long black coat and a big black hat: a perfect impersonation of the Grim Reaper, as Gordon laughingly described it afterwards.

On the day of the Hoon–Hewitt email I had been scheduled to do an interview with *Newsnight* on my growth speech. Originally it was to have been taped in mid-afternoon, but in the wake of the first 'coup' reports, we agreed to put it back to the evening. I was tempted to cancel altogether, but Sue phoned again and urged me to go ahead. I couldn't resist replying that she should be careful what she wished for, as I was still angry and frustrated with Gordon. The interview got under way with Jeremy Paxman asking me if I thought Gordon was the 'best leader Labour could possibly have'. Of course I answered that he was, and added that after the day's events, it was clear that the 'preponderant and settled view of the Labour Party is that they want Gordon Brown to remain as their leader…They want Gordon Brown to lead the party as Prime Minister into the general election, and they don't want to open the question of the leadership.' I rejected Jeremy's suggestion that a number of fellow ministers wanted him replaced, and even agreed with his sarcastic description of the recent PBR as 'an exercise in frankness, and a good job'. There was little else I could have said. I had come to praise Gordon, not to bury him.

The next morning, Sue rang again, and asked me to come in to see Gordon. He said that it was important we sort things out between us. I said we should start by thoroughly discussing the campaign handbook that Douglas and I had sent him before Christmas. He replied simply that it didn't have enough in it about jobs and growth. I suggested that whatever strategy we agreed, he needed to stick to it in a clear, disciplined way. 'You can't just keep veering around and making things up as you go along,' I said, in the least threatening way I knew how. He smiled. 'Peter, you are always right. Just carry on being Peter, and we'll be all right on the day.' I was not so sure about that. We had still not discussed the campaign handbook. But at least we were talking again.

One overriding political reality was now clear. Gordon was not going to be toppled before the election. None of his ministers was minded, separately or together, actively to move against him. As the elected deputy leader, Harriet was the one among them who would have carried most weight. David, as the figure most likely to benefit from a change in leadership, knew that he could not wield the knife. Alistair, who among all the top-rank politicians I have known is the most devoid of personal ego, felt a residual loyalty from his long personal association with Gordon. So did Douglas. And so in my own way – despite everything – did I.

Gordon visibly relaxed in the weeks ahead. In my focus on the recent differences between us over political strategy and our approach to the campaign, I think I had underestimated the strain that the continued questions over his political survival were causing him. I was certainly less sensitive to his personal predicament and the anxiety this had generated than I should have been. Yet with the election campaign approaching, I remained uneasy. Deep down, I knew that we were unprepared. General elections tend to expose all the flaws in a party's platform. They require you to have worked through your strategic disagreements and tensions, and to have addressed your vulnerabilities many months beforehand. This is hard and gruelling work, but if you are to withstand the unforgiving scrutiny of an election campaign, it is essential. We hadn't done any of this. Nor, I knew by this stage, were we likely to be able to do so.

I also suspected that the electorate had made up their minds about Gordon. They thought that he had been a good Chancellor, and effective in the financial crisis, but they did not feel he should be Prime Minister for five more years. Persuading them to reconsider their perceptions of him, and of Labour, was a prerequisite to any kind of campaign success, but it seemed a nearly impossible task. I also worried about how Gordon would fare as a candidate. In past Labour campaigns he had always been the strategist, pulling strings from party HQ or from government, but shielded from the full exposure that any leader has to bear. Now he would be out on his own in a completely different role, having to display new skills in the full glare of media scrutiny. With the party leaders' three televised debates agreed, we were facing the prospect of the most presidential campaign in our history, led by a candidate who freely acknowledged that he preferred the policy over the communications aspects of his job. I was anxious not just for us, but for him.

We had another problem, too: money, or more accurately the lack of it. The party was under the constant threat of bankruptcy, staved off only by the Herculean efforts of the General Secretary Ray Collins and the Finance Director Roy Kennedy. We had accrued massive debts from previous election campaigns, and our ability to attract high-value donations had dropped sharply since our New Labour heyday. It had become controversial to donate to the Labour Party, even before the 'cash for honours' allegations. In 1997 we had had something like £15 million in the campaign war chest, and we spent closer to £20 million. Now we would be lucky to have £5 million. That meant probably 150, rather than four hundred, staff working at campaign headquarters, and a handful rather than a small army organising the party leader's campaign tour and other events. It would also mean, astonishingly, no paid advertising. Even in 1987 we had been able to afford that.

But we still had a campaign to run. I had to try to submerge my doubts and work for the best result possible. I began working even longer days, dividing my time between my ministerial job and preparations for the campaign. I was flitting between my Business Department office in Victoria Street, party headquarters, Number 10 and an office I had in the Cabinet Office to carry out my duties as First Secretary. This was a bright, high-ceilinged room overlooking Horseguards Parade. I had it cheered up with a set of photographic landscapes by Julian Opie from the government art collection, and a wonderful photo of Lucian Freud, brush in hand, standing in front of the Queen, crown on head but otherwise in un-regal garb, as he painted her portrait. I also chose an oil painting by the Italian-sounding, but

Huddersfield-born, artist Arturo di Stefano, of the Hotel Splendide in Mornington Crescent. When Sue wandered across from Number 10 for the first time, she looked at this and laughed out loud. 'We used to have that when I was in the Treasury with Gordon,' she said. 'What goes around, comes around.' What really mattered about the spacious office, however, was that it had a long table and ten chairs, where I could sit with officials or the core team from Number 10.

From the start, the campaign team realised that the thing that was different about this election, and that would therefore dominate it, was the televised leaders' debates. Whenever the suggestion of debates had come up in the past, Gordon, like Tony before him, had done everything he could to avoid them. In Tony's case, in the 1997 campaign, this was just political common sense. He was the front-runner, by miles. He had much to lose, and John Major everything to gain, from televised debates. The reason for Gordon's reluctance was quite different. As he had so often told me in the months before he brought me back into government, he felt, rightly, that he wasn't a politician for the television age. Even though David Cameron was the front-runner, it was Gordon who believed that he had the most to lose. I was not so sure about this.

I was initially blamed in Number 10 for the fact that the debates were taking place at all. In an interview with Anne McElvoy of the London *Evening Standard* the previous summer, questioned repeatedly on why, with Cameron and the Liberal Democrat leader Nick Clegg enthusiastic about debates, Gordon seemed to be running away from them, I replied that, on the contrary, I didn't think they would be a problem for him. 'While Cameron is good with words, he doesn't always have the ideas or policies to back them,' I said. 'I think people will see through the smile. The more the public sees of the other two, the more they will realise that Gordon is the man with the substance.' Apart from the simple fact that I believed this to be true (and was later proved right), I thought that with broadcasters, especially Sky, pressing publicly for debates in a way they had not done before, it was inevitable that they were going to happen. I didn't see why we should feed the impression that Gordon was fighting shy of them. And, I rationalised, they would at least excite voter interest and raise the turnout, which would benefit us.

We took the decision to devote a high proportion of our meagre resources to preparing for the debates. David Muir took charge of the preparations, with Douglas Alexander providing political oversight. The first task was to negotiate the format. David and I started out doing this in secret meetings with Andy Coulson, Cameron's communications director, and Ed Llewellyn, his chief of staff. We had agreed in this preliminary discussion to exclude the Lib Dems. I found Coulson to be the sort of person I expected of a former *News of the World* editor – rather sure of himself, and used to getting his own way. In time, it would be he who found himself under more pressure over the debates, because Cameron, universally expected to perform well, had more to lose. I had come across Llewellyn before. He was able and authoritative, having worked for Chris Patten in Hong Kong and Brussels, and then with Paddy Ashdown in the Balkans. Early on, we agreed on most aspects of the format of the debates, but not on the order of their subject matter. We wanted to have the economy debate first, but lost out on this – not that it ultimately made any difference.

Despite the obvious importance of the debates, my immediate concern was to start chipping away at the Tories' opinion poll lead, and to ensure that we were not so far behind by the time they came around that they wouldn't matter. The odd thing was not that we were beginning the race from so far behind. It was that David Cameron was still in our sights at all. By all normal political logic, the campaign should by now have been a Cameron coronation. The Tories' election chest was brimming with money, and they were facing a government that had been in office for more than a decade, with the public feeling that we had had our innings and that it was time for a change at the crease. Add to that the economic beating the country had taken and the fallout from the expenses scandal, and you would have expected the Tories to be romping towards a convincing Commons majority. But it wasn't happening. The public had warmed to David Cameron, but there was something about him, and about the ill-defined yet austere 'change' he was promising, that had not quite won them over. Voters obviously retained real doubts about the Tories. Cameron had not done enough to convince them that his party had undergone a genuine transformation since it was last evicted from office in 1997. He had too often trimmed his message of change, and had been too timid about taking on vested interests in the party. Against the odds, there was still a glimmer of a chance that, for all the doubts about us, the Conservatives might not get the comfortable victory so many politicians and pundits had assumed.

One effect of the failed 'coup' against Gordon was that it focused all of Labour's key election team on the campaigning tasks at hand. I had Philip Gould back by my side, as indispensable to the cause now as he had been in 1997, and in 1987. And, finally, Alastair Campbell too. I had been trying intensively to lure him back for the last six months, and Gordon had been trying for even longer. While Alastair and I had been talking every few weeks, he had been reluctant to commit to helping us on the campaign. The thought of getting sucked into the political whirlpool made him feel ill, he told me. 'Gordon is impossible to advise,' he said. 'He listens to so many people, and you go round and round in circles and then he never wants to take a risk.' In the autumn, however, Alastair had agreed at least to come into Number 10 with Douglas on Tuesday evenings to help Gordon prepare for the gruelling weekly ritual of Prime Minister's Questions. Together they would form some good ideas, but the next morning a cacophony of voices could be heard in the Cabinet Room where the full team would be gathered, unpicking or obscuring the same ideas as Gordon prepared to go into the Chamber. I chose not to get involved in the briefing sessions, thinking that one more voice was much more likely to confuse, than improve, things. Gordon's performances definitely sharpened as a consequence of Alastair's involvement, but the sessions were hard work and, prior to the new year, Alastair had made it clear that PMQs was the limit of what he would contribute.

Now that it had become certain Gordon was going to survive, Alastair began to play a wider role. This was a great relief to me.

Time away from each other had healed the rift created by my forced resignation from the government, and if we were to have any chance of turning things round, we needed all hands on deck. I viewed Alastair's political and media experience as vital. 'Is the election winnable?' he had asked me before Christmas. I had been tempted to say yes, just to get him back, but after the PBR, and with Gordon still prevaricating over the presentation of our economic policy and election strategy, I told him the truth. No, I said, I didn't think so. Now I told him that I wasn't so sure. It depended on how much pressure we could exert on David Cameron, and whether he cracked up rather than Gordon. We had to make him, and his vision of 'change', look shaky, and flaky, and persuade voters to take a long, hard look at what the Tories were offering.

That task was not impossible so long as we could persuade enough of the media to shine a spotlight on the Tories' policies and their implications for jobs and public services. We had our election war-book to guide us in these initial months. Douglas and I were intent on implementing it, whether Gordon's interest could be engaged or not. Partly, this was because of professional pride, but mostly it was because we had real concerns about the 'core vote' strategy that seemed to be the only alternative. We felt that the approach we had mapped out was the only way of achieving the single most essential goal of the campaign: to get people to take a new look not only at the Tories, but at us as well. Encouraging doubts about the Conservatives was the easier challenge, both because it chimed with Gordon's natural attacking instincts and because I felt we had a powerful argument to make. The Tories had clearly made the wrong early calls on the recession. With the recovery still fragile, a similar lack of judgement would pose a huge risk to Britain's ability to regain its footing and prevent a lapse back into crisis. Equally, David Cameron's failure genuinely to transform his own party could be used to cast doubt on his promise to transform the country for the better.

Yet we could not succeed without promoting a reassessment of Labour too. That obviously had to begin with the economy – using the country's emergence from recession to show that we had taken the right decisions to fight back against the financial crisis, and that we were the only party that could secure the fragile recovery. We would need to bring about a reassessment of Gordon as well, to show that he was a more agile politician than the media caricature suggested. Unless we could get voters to re-open their minds and reach a different view of him we would be sunk by the time the campaign proper began.

We received some welcome help in this from our opponents. If I was uneasy about our failure to resolve the strategic differences at the heart of our campaign, I was heartened by the evidence the new year brought of the Conservatives' even bigger failure to do their necessary groundwork. For months I had been saying that the Tories' sense of entitlement was giving the impression that they were taking victory for granted. It was part of my strategy to paint ourselves as the underdogs, so that media scrutiny fell on both parties, not just us. Now the Conservatives began to create the impression that they viewed the coming months as a mere procession into Downing Street. David Cameron had returned from his Christmas holiday promising 'a policy a day' in the run-up to the election. Given the slight narrowing of the opinion polls at the end of 2009, he was right to replace his relentless message of future economic pain with something that would entice, rather than frighten, the electorate. But they had not done the policy preparation to sustain their campaign, particularly on the economy. Their position on how they would secure the economic recovery was confused, suggesting big, immediate public spending cuts at a time when the world economy was too fragile to risk them. They had also left themselves with a whole array of tax and spending promises, but could not show how they would pay for them.

These were vulnerabilities which I knew we could exploit to highlight the risk the Tories posed to the economy, and Labour's research head, Steve van Riel, and his team were frantically mining this seam. Alistair Darling's press conference on 4 January, totting up the Tories' policy promises and poking a multi-billion-pound hole in their sums, put an entirely different cast on the succession of new commitments Cameron was gearing up to announce. On one flagship policy which he had already announced, his tax break for married couples, he suddenly appeared unclear, and was forced to apologise for 'messing up' in a comment suggesting that it might not happen after all. On the same day, he launched a poster campaign with a huge image of his face staring out from billboards in key marginal constituencies across the country. It was immediately lampooned, with the blogosphere, and then the mainstream press, concluding that his features had been airbrushed. This was a gift for us, sitting perfectly with our objective of persuading people to reconsider the choice between an authentic Gordon Brown and an inauthentic David Cameron whose slick PR approach was an attempt to conceal the fact that the Tory Party hadn't changed. I had a lot of fun in TV studios contrasting the airbrushed Cameron with the unbrushed Gordon.

Our message was also reinforced by the publication of the economic growth figures at the end of January. Although they were later revised upwards, they showed that the economy had grown by 0.1 per cent in the previous quarter. We were out of recession, but only just. The Tories had expected the figures to show stronger growth, which would have allowed them to shift the focus of the election to cutting the deficit. The day before the growth report was published, David Cameron rashly boasted that he would tear up Labour's spending plans and make huge immediate cuts. But the figures suggested that the recovery was too uncertain to risk the scale of cuts that the Tories were proposing. Cameron and George Osborne were now thrown into confusion, and at the following weekend's World Economic Summit in Davos, the Tory leader tried to row back from his earlier tough rhetoric. In doing so, he only added to a sense of confusion around his economic policy. I piled on the pressure at a press conference the following Monday, 1 February. Suddenly, we had some momentum and the Tories were on the back foot. Our 'reassessment' strategy was beginning to yield early fruit.

But that still left the challenge of persuading people to rethink their views on Gordon. Convincing the public to vote for five more years of him was a hard task, and the Tories continually contrasted his tired demeanour with the fresh-faced energy of David Cameron.

One major problem for us was that Gordon *did* look tired. Given how hard he worked, that was little wonder. Ever since I had returned from Brussels, but especially over the past few months, I had been urging him to work less and sleep more, to eat more healthily, exercise, relax with Sarah and the children, and recharge his batteries at weekends. It was not just that otherwise he could not possibly operate at the peak of his powers. In any election campaign, energy, and frankly the appearance of energy, in a candidate matters. In this campaign, it would matter even more. This was not just because of the leaders' debates. More importantly, if we were to succeed in countering Cameron's 'change' message with our 'future' vision, the last thing we needed was a candidate who looked so exhausted that he might not make it to the future.

Alongside David and Justin in Number 10, my political preoccupation was with setting the stage for our fightback, first by arranging an interview for Gordon that focused more on personality than politics, then with the launch of our broad campaign themes, and finally with Alistair's last budget at the end of March. The interview was not with John Humphrys on *Today*, or Jeremy Paxman on *Newsnight*. In fact it was not really an interview at all, but more of a conversation with the former *Daily Mirror* editor Piers Morgan, which would be broadcast on St Valentine's Day. We knew it was risky, as Gordon would be totally removed from his comfort zone. He never liked talking about personal matters, but the interview presented a huge opportunity if we got it right. I pressed its importance on him, and the need for him to understand that this was not the kind of encounter in which he needed to machine-gun out statistics and policy detail. He had to relax, and open up. He took the point, but I knew that was not the same thing as getting him in the right frame of mind. The preparatory sessions consisted of Alastair bombarding Gordon with the sort of questions he thought Piers was likely to ask: about himself, his marriage, his children, his past and his relations with Tony. Alastair goaded him about why he had been so persistent in trying to drive Tony out of office. 'I did no such thing!' Gordon barked back, his voice showing the anger he felt. 'We had a deal, and he didn't keep to it!' We didn't know whether to laugh or cry. This was meant to be an opportunity for him publicly to put his angst behind him.

In the event, the interview was gentler than we had prepared him for, but it was very personal, particularly when Gordon emotionally recalled the death of his baby daughter Jennifer. Despite the predictable sneers and cynicism from some of the media, it succeeded in revealing his more reflective, engaging, human side. For us, this was encouraging, because it showed that he was willing to unlearn old habits and challenge himself to do things differently for this campaign. That is hard for any politician, but for someone as proud, and as fixed in his views, as Gordon it was the hardest thing of all, and I admired him for it.

The interview seemed to give Gordon new confidence as well. Six days later, at Warwick University in Coventry, he did an equally impressive job of launching our themes for the election campaign. This was the next stage of our 'reassessment' plan, and showcased more of the work we had done for the warbook. It was very professionally organised by the party staff. The set looked bright and modern, and reinforced the slogan we unveiled that day: 'A Future Fair for All'. But what really made the event a success was Gordon's performance. His speech was uncharacteristically short. He looked straight into the camera, and delivered our message with clarity and precision. On a personal level, he made a rare, and I thought effective, *mea culpa*. 'I know that Labour hasn't done everything right,' he said, then added with a half-smile, 'I know, I really know, I'm not perfect.' He said that Labour, not Cameron's Conservatives, were still the real change-makers. 'Take a second look at us, and take a long, hard look at them,' was the soundbite that made it onto all the news bulletins.

It was exactly the message we wanted, and needed, to get across. And it seemed to be working. Things were going to plan, and were not even derailed by a hand grenade lobbed into the pre-election campaign by the publication of *Observer* journalist Andrew Rawnsley's new account of the history of New Labour, the newspaper serialisation of which began the day after our Warwick event. The book portrayed Gordon as having a volcanic temper, which was true, of course. But it went further, making the claim that he had been given a talking-to by the Cabinet Secretary Gus O'Donnell about his bullying behaviour towards his staff.

I went on *The Andrew Marr Show* on the morning the first extracts appeared, and they dominated the interview, which was hardly a surprise. I had done my preparation thoroughly, and worked out what I wanted my message to be. This was my first appearance on Andrew's show for a while. I had been annoyed at him for asking Gordon, in an interview at our 2009 party conference, whether he took prescription drugs to cope with stress, a question based on nothing but false internet rumours. It was unworthy of the BBC, and I attacked it strongly at the time. In responding to Rawnsley's allegations, I did not want to dispute that Gordon had a temper. That would have been untrue and unconvincing. Rather, I wanted to explain that side of him as showing his commitment to the job. He was a passionate, impatient man, who was driven and who drove others around him hard to get things done. But as I said, that did not make him a bully.

These comments led a woman from a bullying helpline to come forward on the BBC and say she had received complaints about bullying from staff at Number 10. The BBC political staff could hardly contain their excitement at this 'revelation', but the woman's credibility melted away over the next twenty-four hours, as it became evident that whatever complaints she had had were not about Gordon. That did not stop the media frenzy, however, stoked not only by the BBC, but also Sky and ITN. I felt this was unfair, and let my irritation show at a press conference the next day. To my mind, the press were quite outrageously eliding together legitimate reporting of Gordon's temper with a qualitatively different and more serious allegation of bullying in the workplace. In my view, political journalists did this because they allowed their own negative experiences of Gordon to influence their reporting. Tom Bradby, the softly spoken but highly articulate political editor of ITN, who had won my respect by tripping me up in interviews a couple of times in the past, told me that interviewing Gordon was unlike interviewing any other front-rank politician. Normally such encounters would be brutal, highbrow or merely probing as circumstances required, he said, and when they were over, after a few pleasantries everyone would part as friends. With Gordon, things were more emotionally complicated. He interpreted difficult questions as frontal attacks. Contrary positions taken by the interviewer to elicit a strong response were taken personally, as if they were intended to wound or insult. As a result, he became hurt, sulky or very angry.

I knew from talking to both the BBC's Nick Robinson and Sky's Adam Boulton that they felt the same way. Like Tom, both are highly professional journalists, but somehow, when it came to interviewing Gordon, they could quite easily lose their patience and even their composure. Gary Gibbon of Channel 4 News also found Gordon provocative. Everyone came off badly from these interviews, but mainly Gordon, because the tension generated between him and the interviewer would communicate itself to viewers. They would become unsettled, and would wonder if there was something wrong with him. Unfortunately, however hard he tried, Gordon never managed fully to overcome his instinct to feel assaulted, and hurt, by the rough-and-tumble of a challenging interview, although his highly combative interview with Jeremy Paxman during the election proved to be one of his best. In the end, the Rawnsley serialisation and its media fallout did not do us any lasting harm. In fact the polls began to narrow. By reinforcing the image of Gordon as a man of toughness and passion, who cared about what he was doing, the episode helped in our aim of persuading voters to reassess him.

Things continued to go well for us. On 28 February, in a speech at his party's spring conference, David Cameron attempted to draw a line under what had been a bad couple of months for him. The following day, however, these hopes were dashed by the revelation that the Conservatives' Deputy Chairman, Lord Ashcroft, was non-domiciled, and did not pay British tax on all his earnings. A decade earlier, Ashcroft had been given a peerage by William Hague, apparently on condition that he became fully tax resident in the UK. The Tories had been dogged for years by questions about whether this condition had been met. The answers they gave had been evasive, but left the impression that the tax issue had been resolved. With the news that it had not been, our party machine swung into action, and put the Tories on the back foot for a week. It was another example of their having been insufficiently rigorous in dealing with an issue that came back to haunt them as we neared the campaign. At least for now, our small campaign team was giving the impression of running rings around the much larger and better-resourced Tory operation.

Still, I remained worried. It was almost as if the better things went for us, the more agitated I became. The vulnerability the Tories were showing served only to heighten my frustration that we had not resolved our own strategic differences, or sufficiently addressed our own vulnerabilities. I was certain that the Tories were not going to allow the current trajectory of the campaign to continue. Once they got their act together, I feared that our inherent weaknesses would be exploited. There was a damaging breach in the very concept of the election campaign we were putting in place. Gordon and I had different ideas about the message we wanted to take to the country. Along with Philip, Douglas and Patrick, I felt that we needed to project a positive vision of how we would make Britain's future different and better once the economic crisis had passed. Gordon wanted to attack the Tories, and play on the risks a Cameron government would pose to recovery and to basic services – essentially, fear of their future, not hope in ours.

As is always the case in campaign strategy, there was some overlap in these approaches. I too wanted to highlight the risk posed by the Tories' plans. That was obviously important in getting people to take a second look at Cameron. I wanted to draw contrasts between him and Gordon, and to present Gordon as the more solid, substantial and serious of the two: granite versus plastic. But there were hugely different implications in our campaign outlook. First, in tone: attacking and negative, versus forward-looking and positive. And in the intended audience: targeting our core vote, the people most likely to feel fear about a Conservative government, versus appealing to the broader national constituency who had brought New Labour to power in the first place, and whose support we needed if we were to win again.

The argument between Gordon and me had been simmering for months. It was at the heart of my messages to him before Christmas, of his dismissive response to the warbook, and of the new uneasiness between us since. It finally boiled over in a crucial election strategy meeting around my Cabinet Office table at the end of February. The whole senior team were present: Philip, Douglas and Alastair, as well as Ed Miliband, who on a separate track of his own was preparing the manifesto. Patrick and Ben were there too, and from Number 10, David Muir, Justin Forsyth, Gavin Kelly and Sue. I opened with a note of optimism. We had had a good new year, and the Tories an extremely wobbly one. The polls were narrowing slightly, and we were in a reasonable position to persuade people to reappraise the two parties and their leaders.

Then the faultline opened. Philip, typically, got to the core of why Gordon's attack strategy might pose a great risk to us. David Muir, Gordon's strategy director, was the main architect of this strategy. His single-minded focus was on protecting the economic interests of 'hard-working families', and convincing them that Cameron would not do so. He wanted to lay bare the implications of the Tories' extreme deficit reduction policies as well as what he predicted would be their plan to raise VAT. Philip argued that this should be part of our approach, of course, but that there were dangers in it. For one thing, these voters' interests were not just economic. Yes, at one level, we had a good story to tell on the economy. Gordon had handled the financial crisis well, and he still might come across as the better alternative for dealing with the repercussions as we emerged from recession. But people wanted more than that. Most of all they wanted hope, and a positive vision. 'This election is going to be about the future,' Philip said. 'Voters thought Cameron was the future. Now they're not so sure.' As for us, unless we could find a way to bring a new voice to that argument, we would be left looking exactly the way many voters now viewed us: as a rather tired old banger that was fast running out of steam.

David Muir was equally blunt in reply. He agreed that our campaign choice was essentially between hope and fear, but he clearly felt that fear was the more powerful weapon. We had to attack Cameron hard. I knew this argument would carry huge weight with Gordon. David was also his focus group manager. He now told us, as he was certainly telling Gordon, that every time he put propositions to his groups about the Tories' austerity plans, they had 'run for safety' to Labour. I had no doubt that David's views should be taken note of, but I also knew that the findings of focus groups could be skewed by all sorts of factors. Reading public opinion in politics was extraordinarily difficult, and focus groups were only a part of the picture. I also knew that our campaign had to be about more than visceral attacks on the Conservatives, more even than about presenting Gordon as a safe pair of economic hands. Both were important, but we had to tell voters what we could offer. Why we, not David Cameron, were the future.

Three or four times a week I would go through the familiar connecting door to Number 10 and try to talk election strategy with Gordon. But we never thrashed out our differences of approach. There were no raised voices. The period of tension over the new year had long passed. We had been through too much together since the founding days of the modernising *avant garde* to relapse into sulkiness or acrimony. We had come to understand each other again. We respected each other. We liked each other. There was also a fair amount about the campaign on which we agreed. We believed that the changes David Cameron had made in the Conservative Party did not amount to a fundamental, New Labour-scale shift. We felt he was electorally vulnerable: a bit too smooth and not quite convincingly a 'change' Prime Minister. Perhaps I should have pushed harder on the campaign message. I could have insisted that our overriding theme had to be about the future, about us and not just the Tories, about every aspect of how we intended to improve people's lives, instead of only how we would protect their savings, their jobs and their public services But we never properly battled it out.

In any case, I doubt that I would have been able to talk Gordon out of his approach, which seemed to be reinforced by a parallel campaign operation working somewhere in the background. Perhaps I was wrong, but I felt that too many judgements and decisions were being formed elsewhere, and I sensed that a core-vote, scorched-earth attack strategy had been agreed and was being acted upon by people unseen by me, possibly influenced by old political hands in the US with long-standing links to Gordon. He had always gravitated towards advice that supported his own instinctive view of what our message should be. I could, of course, have fallen in with running a fear-driven, negative campaign that was aimed simply at shoring up our core support. But to me that would have represented a negation of everything New Labour had originally stood for. It was not a step I was willing to take.

Some of this argument was played out on the issue of VAT. Alistair, with my backing, had floated an increase in VAT as part of a wider economic package, in which those on low incomes would be assisted, prior to the PBR. Gordon had objected; one reason he had plumped for a National Insurance increase instead was that he wanted to attack the Tories on VAT by publicly committing us not to increase it for the duration of the next Parliament. He regarded this as a significant potential vote-winner. But as a Chancellor facing a commitment to halve the deficit in four years, Alistair could not responsibly bind his own hands in this way. He repeatedly made the point that we had not made such a pledge in the last three manifestos, when Gordon was Chancellor at a time of growth. It seemed odd to do so now, when the economy was not growing and we faced the daunting task of turning around the public finances.

Gordon and his supporters did not share these qualms. In their view, we would never raise VAT, so we should publicly rule it out. I could see the attraction of hitting the Tories on the issue. Indeed, I had piloted the argument in an interview I had done on Sky's *Sunday Live with Adam Boulton*. Yet I now had a good sense of how far we could take this campaign plank, and I had my doubts. To me, it always came back to a question of credibility and responsibility. Our lack of clarity on future spending cuts had already sowed doubts about our determination to cut the deficit. Ruling out specific tax increases, for political reasons, would reinforce a view that we lacked the required fiscal responsibility. In any case, the point was moot. Alistair was not going to be shifted. He was determined that his final budget would not succumb to the temptations of a pre-election giveaway or political game-playing, however much he believed the Tories would be prepared to disguise their own policies or make promises they could not fulfil. And Gordon himself, I think, now recognised the political damage we had suffered as a result of our earlier set-piece financial statements.

My fear was that we had left it too late to set out a credible position on spending, a failure that I found especially frustrating after a late-night phone call with Tony shortly before the budget. Although I had been unaware of the details at the time, he reminded me that during his final year in office his policy aides in Number 10, with grudging engagement from the Treasury, had underaken a Fundamental Savings Review. It was not just the familiar exercise in efficiency savings, but an attempt to take a hard-nosed look at every department's budget and decide which programmes were necessary and value-for-money, and which were not. Gordon, he said, had resisted the premise of the initiative: that the era of spending increases was over, and that the whole fiscal basis of government had to be recalibrated. I could not help thinking that if only Tony had been able to drive it through to its conclusion, or convince Gordon to become a full partner in it, the situation would have been much easier for us when the economic crisis hit. Still, the final budget did offer us a chance to reclaim at least some lost ground.

Gradually, over my months back in cabinet, Alistair had come to trust and rely on me more as an ally. In thrashing out the details of the budget he insisted that I join him in all the major discussions with Gordon. Given the lower than forecast borrowing requirement as a result of unemployment rising less than feared, Gordon at first insisted on a much larger spending boost than Alistair could accept. Ed Balls wanted a new pledge to provide free school meals for all five-year-olds, paid for out of an addition to his departmental spending. 'We *are* in a recession,' I commented as delicately as I could. But in the end, common sense – and Alistair – won the day. Gordon, to his credit, fully signed off on a budget that was not only more modest than he had originally wanted in its expansion of the economic stimulus, but also scaled back our economic growth forecasts and repeated firm commitments to bring down the deficit. Delivered on 24 March, the budget was a sober occasion, except for one moment of light relief – Alistair's wonderfully understated announcement of an agreement to exchange tax information with Belize, the place Lord Ashcroft called home. Overall, it was solid, credible, responsible, and above all, honest.

With the budget agreed, we were now ready to finalise our campaign policy pledges. I was unhappy with them. They seemed to me insufficiently original or pithy, and therefore unlikely to create news or be memorable. I had a bigger problem with the draft version of Ed Miliband's manifesto, which seemed to have been road-tested more with *Guardian* columnists than Philip's groups of voters. There were lots of different policy ideas and little stories here and there, but they did not add up to a coherent or compelling vision for the future that would set pulses racing. Of course we were limited by the spending constraints the next government would have to work within, but we had operated under self-imposed spending constraints in 1997, and had still come up with modest but eye-catching proposals. These had involved months of work by Peter Hyman, who had honed and tested them to destruction. I didn't feel the same spadework had been done on this manifesto, or on the pledges. Fortunately I had a good enough relationship with Ed to talk frankly to him about it, but my problem with the manifesto was quite basic: it adopted a radical rhetoric, but when it was boiled down it was vague, and appeared to avoid any hard choices. I felt it was written so as not to offend, rather than to re-instil a sense of New Labour's vision.

With the campaign fast approaching, I went to see Gordon one evening before heading home. He still looked tired, but I had noticed over recent days that he seemed calmer and more focused. When I mentioned that his mood seemed good, he replied, 'The thing is, I'm really looking forward to the campaign.' I was glad, but for my part I felt both excited and worried. So much seemed unready, in a way that had never been the case in 1997, or even, as far as I could tell, in the campaigns of 2001 or 2005. I was supremely confident in our core team, but with our constraints of money and staff, and with Gordon and David Muir seeing the fundamental thrust of the campaign differently from us, I felt like a commander with no control over his forces in the field.

My fears were not allayed by the Tories' announcement, following the budget, that they would cancel most of the National Insurance increase we had agreed to help balance the books. It showed how concerned they were that the overall majority that had seemed a certainty only weeks before was slipping away from them. They had clearly been regrouping and rethinking, and their decision was to go for us on National Insurance, and worry about the deficit another day. I had feared they would do just that. It was our Achilles heel, and the media hardly put them under any pressure to explain how they intended to make up for the forfeited revenue, and what alternative options they were considering – or hiding. For the previous year the BBC's political editor, Nick Robinson, had continually pressed us on the deficit. Now it seemed the Tories were being given a free ride, not just by Nick but by the media in general. Still, by saying they would cancel the greater proportion of the so-called 'tax on jobs' the Tories were able to damage our message on growth and jobs, and to muddy the waters about who would be a greater risk to the recovery. A few days before the beginning of the election campaign the Tories' argument would gain further lift-off when they arranged for a letter from leading businessmen in support of their proposal to appear in the *Daily Telegraph*.

I got into trouble at a press conference later that week when I said George Osborne was peddling a deception about how the Tories' plans were going to add up. The media, and the Tories, mangled my words to suggest that I had insulted the business figures who had appended their signatures to the letter by asserting that they had been duped. That was not in fact what I had said, but many head-lines now alleged that the business world had finally fallen out of love with New Labour. Of course business was going to campaign against a National Insurance increase – any tax increase could be said to hit jobs. But I stuck to my guns in arguing that George was practising a deception by pretending that he could cancel a major tax increase, and cut the deficit, without paying for it either through deeper spending cuts or a major tax rise elsewhere, prob-ably in VAT. I knew the debates we in Labour were having behind the scenes on this issue, and it would have been as plain to George as it was to us that tax giveaways were not possible without pain being felt elsewhere. I was certain that this was a short-term politi-cal calculation that would come back to haunt him.

But it did give the Tories the momentum going into the campaign, and put us on the back foot. In previous elections we had been able to respond to Conservative tax promises by convincingly demolish-ing their figures and using them to reinforce our message on the risk they posed to the economy. This time, the media were not buying it. They did not believe our own spending figures, so they were not going to take our word on the Tories' plans. By this stage they felt that none of the main parties was being open about how the defi-cit would be cut, meaning that the economic debates between them were a phoney war. For a governing party, being able to take apart the opposition's spending plans is a major weapon in any election. For us to be deprived of it was disabling, and was an inevitable consequence of our failure to grasp the spending nettle earlier.

My biggest source of anxiety remained Gordon. Analysing the campaign with me a week before it started, he acknowledged that while voters were worried about risking the recovery with the Tories, they did not want five more years of him. If possible, he suggested, our campaign should indicate that he would remain in office for one more year to secure the recovery, followed by a fresh chance for voters to opt for change. I told him that it was an interesting sugges-tion, but I gave it little more thought, as I could see no practical or realistic way of demonstrating how this would be achieved.

But Gordon did not let it drop. On Good Friday, 2 April, I joined him in Number 10 for a campaign discussion with Douglas, Patrick, Sue, David Muir and Justin Forsyth. Gordon now unveiled an astonishing proposal. He began by saying that two big issues provided the backdrop to this election: the economic crisis, and the political crisis that had followed the expenses scandal. He said he had decided to bring these two challenges together in a statement he would make on the day the election was called. He would ask voters for a mandate both to secure the recovery over the next year, and then, separately, to 'renew our politics'. This would involve the announcement of a mega-referendum, to be held in 2011, which would include proposals on a raft of constitutional measures: changes in the voting system, House of Lords reform, state funding of political parties, and measures to recall MPs and clean up expenses. By the time the referendum was held, he said, voters would be able to judge whether he had turned the economy around, and that would inform their voting decision. If he lost the referendum, he would stand down as Prime Minister. In effect, he was proposing to ask voters to suspend judgement on him.

We all felt a bit stunned. The plan was undeniably bold. In that sense, it was typically Gordon. There was a superficial attractiveness to it. David said it gave the voters an escape clause from the dilemma he believed they were wrestling with. But to me, the scope for a proposal of this kind to unravel during the four weeks of an election campaign seemed enormous. We started gently to pepper Gordon with questions. Was he signalling that he would only stay as Prime Minister for eighteen months? If he didn't have confidence in five more years of Gordon Brown, why should anyone else? Would he stay on if he won the referendum, conceivably for the whole five-year term? How would this plan, with all its inherent uncertainty, be perceived by the markets? Would he resign if people voted no on every question in the referendum, or just on some of them? If he lost and resigned, would there be another general election? Gordon merely listened, and absorbed the questions.

There was, of course, a more central objection. We had to face reality about how this would be seen and reported. I doubted that the media would regard it as a bold and reforming gesture. It was much more likely to be viewed as a last-ditch attempt to hold on to power; an act of political calculation rather than political renewal. After the fiasco of the 'election that wasn't' in 2007, it would be seen as another manoeuvre by Gordon to avoid the verdict of the voters. By the time we came back to it later in the day, he said that he had decided not to announce it on the day the election was called, but would keep it in reserve for a speech on political reform the following day. I sensed he was becoming unsure about the idea. In the end, he delivered his reform speech minus his bombshell, but it was touch and go until the last minute, which rather destabilised those in the campaign team whose job it was to sell the speech to reporters.

On Tuesday, 6 April, the starting gun for the campaign was fired: election day would be 6 May. During the campaign I would be based at Labour Party HQ, where I had been spending more and more time. We had a good team – people of real talent, with a mix of youth and experience – and they did an incredible job with little in the way of resources, and kept the show on the road in the toughest of circumstances right up to the end. There just weren't enough of them. Each member of the team was covering work that two or three people had done in 1997. The working conditions were awful. We were crammed into an office that couldn't really fit us all in. There was no air conditioning outside office hours, so in the evenings and at weekends it was stifling. I did a fairly poor job at masking my discomfort, taking refuge in the large meeting room whenever I could.

At seven o'clock each morning I chaired a meeting at which we set out our plans for that day. I held more detailed planning discussions throughout the day, trying to figure out a workable division of responsibilities with Douglas. But the campaign felt flat from the start. We never really seemed to get into a rhythm. Apart from the day of our manifesto launch, we lacked strong policy stories to lead the news agenda. The constant train of meticulously organised appearances around the country with which Tony had driven the 1997 campaign was simply impractical this time. We didn't have the advance troops, the back-up staff, or the funds to organise such a tour for Gordon. The main reason for the dullness of the campaign, however, was the TV debates. Everyone – politicians and media alike – seemed to be in a state of suspended animation, waiting for them to begin, and then for the next one to take place. This sucked the energy out of the rest of the campaign. The old tempo of election campaigns, with each party holding a daily news conference and the media generating controversy by batting each argument or set of claims and counter-claims between the parties, wasn't happening. The press conferences, such as they were, made almost no impact. The debates certainly would.

We had been right to put them at the centre of our campaign preparations, even though this meant giving them resources that were badly needed elsewhere. The debate team, led by David Muir and Douglas Alexander, had spent a lot of time preparing Gordon prior to the campaign. Michael Sheehan, the gifted media trainer who had assisted Bill Clinton on his presidential campaign and had worked on the US debates with Barack Obama, had been helping Gordon since February. In our mock debates, Alastair Campbell played the part of David Cameron, and Theo Bertram, Gordon's adviser and PMQ specialist in Number 10, stood in for Nick Clegg. In the event, I was relieved that neither Cameron nor Clegg was as good in debate as either Alastair or Theo.

The time allocated to prep sessions for the debates sharply reduced the number of Gordon's campaign appearances. I initially favoured building his campaign around a series of hard-hitting speeches, but David, Sue and the rest of Gordon's inner team insisted this simply wasn't practical. They said that I had no idea how much time and energy they involved. I argued back that speeches were not some sort of luxury or outdated accessory in a campaign. For someone like Gordon, who was not a natural street campaigner or TV performer, they were an essential means of allowing him to find his voice, get his message and inspiration across and fire up his campaign. But they did not happen until the final week, when the debates were over.

When I spoke to Alastair about the debate preparation, he seemed confident that Gordon would do well. So did the rest of the team.

On 15 April, the day of the first debate, as Gordon was closeted in final preparation for the big event, I took a busload of the reporters attached to his campaign to Blackpool. It felt good to be out on the road campaigning, chatting and briefing the media, and most of all meeting voters. I went up Blackpool Tower. I also couldn't resist visiting the famous ballroom, where, to the strains of a Brazilian two-step I danced with a delightful pensioner called Hannah Rita-Mackenzie, who it turned out was a spiritual healer. 'Well, she certainly did a lot for me,' I told the reporters, who looked relieved to see a bit of fun being injected to what had been a rather dull campaign. Before we headed back, I couldn't help adding: 'I hope Gordon is this relaxed after tonight.'

As he prepared to walk on stage at the Granada studios in Manchester that evening, I could see that he was nervous. Who wouldn't be? But the strengths I had always admired in him – purpose, determination – were there too. My task for the evening was to brief the journalists after the event, in 'Spin Alley'. We had brought back Matthew Doyle, now Tony Blair's Political Director, to coordinate our media operation around the debates. For me it was almost like being back in the 1980s, briefing lobby journalists with gusto on Gordon's behalf. As the debate was taking place our operation at Labour HQ in Victoria Street fed us minute-by-minute rebuttal points on what Cameron and Clegg were saying.

It was apparent after the first half-hour that it was going well. Gordon looked and sounded confident. Although none of us knew quite what to expect, we had primed him to go after the main target, Cameron, and to be nicer to Clegg. In the same way that he had done during his soundbite phase in the 1980s, and as he still did occasionally in interviews and at PMQs, he probably took this too literally, saying 'I agree with Nick' a bit too often. But he was steady, serious, on top of the issues, effective and impressive. Cameron, surprisingly, seemed more nervous than Gordon, and oddly off his game. Clegg was always going to be the winner in one sense: for the first time he, and the Lib Dems, had equal exposure and equal billing to the two main parties, on a huge stage. He played things perfectly. He was fluent and relaxed, and he engaged with the studio audience. Still, when we rushed to Spin Alley as soon as it was over, we had a good message, and one that I felt was absolutely true: Gordon had won on substance, Clegg on style. Cameron was squeezed from both sides, and ended up looking shallow in the middle. He was the loser. I loved being part of it all, and the adrenalin was flowing.

The first debate utterly changed the tenor of the campaign. Clegg and the Lib Dems surged in the polls. I was not worried by this, and in fact probably contributed to it with my praise for Clegg's perform-ance in my post-debate briefing. I thought that we needed to see more than our own vote rising in order to pull support away from the Tories. And they, and especially Cameron, had taken a real psycho-logical hit. However the Lib Dem surge played out until election day, I was certain that it was a welcome development. It was disruptive to the narrative that the Tories were marching confidently to a healthy majority, and that was exactly what we needed. The first debate also gave us a morale boost. There was a belief among everyone in our team – and in Gordon too – that with Cameron losing his footing, we were back in the game. A campaign that had been flagging had received a shot in the arm. Unless all the polls had been wrong for more than a year, I accepted by now that it would take a minor mira-cle for us to win. But a hung Parliament was looking more and more possible. Originally I had been dismissive of this prospect. I thought the country would vote decisively in favour of one party or another. But Gordon had always felt it might be the outcome, and for some time his mind had been turning to whether a deal could be done with the Lib Dems if that eventuality arose. So, like me, he was on balance encouraged by the Lib Dem surge.

Others were alarmed, however, especially when a number of polls put us in third place, just as they had in 1987. It led to a certain amount of internal criticism that we were cosying up to the Lib Dems too much. Some of this came from a surprising quarter: Tony called me to say how dangerous he thought these developments were, and to urge me to step up the attacks on the Lib Dems. He felt that we would be seen to have made a mistake of historic proportions if the

Lib Dems finished above us in vote share. I didn't need that pointing out to me. Nor did I feel we had been cosying up to the Lib Dems. In one of the campaign memos I wrote to our supporters, I attacked their policy positions on child trust funds and child tax credits, and their proposal for an amnesty for illegal immigrants, as well as warning about some of the dangers of a hung Parliament. But at the same time I felt it would be a mistake suddenly to launch an all-guns-blazing attack on them. It would have sounded shrill, and would have jarred with the public mood, which clearly wanted something different to come out of this election.

Amid the rising alarm, I had no shortage of advice. Harriet and Ed Miliband each came to me to urge that we get Gordon to build every appearance around 'fairness', and relentlessly go after the unfairness with which the Tories would apply future spending cuts. I was not opposed to campaigning on this, not least because it was such familiar political territory for Gordon. But it all depended on what you meant by 'fairness'. When I raised this concern with Harriet, she said simply that we had to send up a flare to our own supporters about whose side we were on. A bit of class war was what she felt was needed, and when I pressed her for an example, she suggested more attacks on bankers. It sounded like a return to core-vote politics, and, I feared, would risk looking defeatist.

I agreed with those who said that Gordon had to move away from the daily events he was doing, which were making little impression. His organisers on the campaign trail had a thankless task. The television images of his appearances were not as attractive as they needed to be, but to reinvent his campaign at this stage would have required resources we simply did not have, whatever miracles our Presentation Director, Carol Linforth, and her team could deliver.

The second debate, which took place in Bristol on 22 April, was never going to have the same game-changing effect as the first. I didn't spin, or even attend, this time – an absence that was noted by journalists. I had been sensitive to suggestions that I was taking too large a role in the campaign, and was in danger of stealing the limelight. So I asked Harriet, who thought she and other Labour women were getting too little coverage, to go instead. As the theme of this debate was foreign policy, David Miliband also attended. I was relieved that Gordon acquitted himself well once again. Clegg did fine, but had less impact than in the first debate, as he was no longer a novelty. Cameron certainly performed better than he had done the week before, but he failed to deliver a knock-out blow. This left one more debate, with the media now paying almost no attention to anything in between, and one crucial last shot at improving our position before a final spurt to election day. Some members of our team were still edgy about the Lib Dems. We, and the Tories too, had abandoned the kid-gloves treatment of Clegg. There was no more 'I agree with Nick.' While the occasional poll still had us in third place, however, most had us back in second. The margin between us and the Lib Dems was narrow enough for me to feel confident that the normal order of things would resume as Labour voters realised what was at stake.

Then, on 28 April, disaster struck. I was getting ready for a rare couple of hours away from campaign headquarters, to address the Institute of Directors convention at the Royal Albert Hall. I was looking forward to it, especially since during my time as Secretary of State at the DTI in 1998 I had delivered a keynote speech to the same event in the same venue. I would express my hope in the speech that the two occasions did not provide bookends to my ministerial career. As I was giving my speech a final read-through and gathering up my papers to leave, one of our senior press officers, Tom Price, came up to me. Very calmly, he told me that Gordon had been filmed chatting to a woman voter on a walkabout in Rochdale. They had had a spirited debate in front of a scrum of reporters, and parted amicably. However, when Gordon returned to his car a live microphone he had forgotten he was wearing on his lapel had captured him calling her a 'bigoted woman'. The Rochdale pensioner who was about to be thrust into the media spotlight was a lifelong Labour supporter called Gillian Duffy.

It was only a matter of minutes before the news broke on the bank of television screens around us. The room fell quiet. Gordon was being interviewed by Jeremy Vine for Radio 2, and the BBC started broadcasting live pictures of the interview on its television news channel. I said we had to let him know he was being filmed, and the team with Gordon informed me that the message had been passed to him. Not that it mattered. When Jeremy Vine played the recording of Gordon's 'bigoted woman' remarks, Gordon put his head in his hand. It seemed to many who were watching to indicate that he was in the very depths of despair. To those who knew him, it was a familiar pose. He always put his head in his hand in that way when he was concentrating.

Still, the image made a distressing situation even worse. There was no disguising what a disastrous turn of events this was. Everything about it was bad: the contrast between the kind words Gordon had spoken to Gillian Duffy's face, and the sneer behind her back; the appearance of being out of touch on the issue she had raised with him, which was the source of his embarrassing remark: immigration. Not only was immigration at the top of many voters' list of concerns, it spoke directly to their sense of fairness and unfairness. There was also Gordon's rush to blame someone else, in this case Sue. I didn't really feel angry with Gordon. There was a certain inevitability to the incident, which had contributed to my unease during the past few months. He had held up well, but now he was overtired. He was in the home stretch of a very difficult campaign. The remark about Sue was, as she would know and understand, just Gordon being Gordon.

I called David Muir, Sue, Alastair, and Gordon. The first thing I told them was what not to do. Gordon wanted to hold a press conference. That sounded crazy to me. I said he should not do it under any circumstances, as it would magnify the embarrassment, not contain it. I followed up with a call to Gordon's press spokesman Iain Bundred to make sure the press conference didn't happen. He didn't need convincing. I said Gordon had to apologise, of course, and in order to make it clear that it was heartfelt, he should go and see Gillian Duffy at her home in Rochdale. Gordon followed my advice, but afterwards, when he stepped outside into the midst of the throng of waiting media, my heart sank. What he was saying was instantly undermined by the return of a classic Gordon idiosyncrasy: the appearance of a broad grin, very often in an inappropriate context, when he was nervous. In this case, he grinned as he was saying that his remarks about Mrs Duffy had left him mortified. The effect was unfortunate.

Before my speech to the IoD, I gave a series of live broadcast interviews. I tried to explain that we all let off steam occasionally, and say things we don't mean. Gordon was human. But he was wrong to say what he had, and was genuinely apologetic. It was the best I could do. Deep down everyone felt that any glimmer of hope that we would actually win the election was over. That was the view I expressed to Tony when he rang me as I was on my way back from the Albert Hall.

That night, Gordon seemed to be in a very bad way. He was upset and angry with himself. The final debate would take place the following evening, and I worried how he would get through it. He told me he was thinking of reviving his idea of offering to resign if he lost a referendum on political reform. David Muir was, again, keen on the idea, but I thought it would look desperate, although I didn't want to rub this in. I advised him to test it in his debate preparation with Alastair and Theo. Fortunately, and predictably, the idea didn't survive the test.

In the final debate, Gordon looked dog-tired, but he still performed well. I thought it was Clegg's weakest performance of the three, which was encouraging for us, since I felt that after the Gillian Duffy incident, we might now genuinely be battling the Lib Dems for second place. The feeling of the Spin Alley media was that Cameron had been the winner. George Osborne and the other designated Tory spinners certainly spoke, and acted, as if that was the case, and as if they were now very confident of gaining an outright Commons majority on election day.

Oddly, the final days of the campaign were in many ways Gordon's finest. Once again he showed his extraordinary resilience and reserves of stamina, as his inner strength took over. With the debates behind him, and perhaps also because he felt the result was now simply beyond his control, he sounded liberated. His message never really changed, but he started to make the big speeches that allowed his passion to come through. The star out on the road with him was undoubtedly his wife Sarah. I agreed with those journalists who argued that if she had been with him in Rochdale, as she was on many of his other public walkabouts and visits, it might well not have ended as it did. On a practical level, he simply felt better, and therefore looked better, with Sarah at his side. I always believed that one reason Gordon married so late was that, as with every single decision he took, he wanted to make sure it was absolutely the right one. In this case it was. Sarah, who was running a PR company when they met, was a source of sound, common-sense political advice, and was a tremendous support in every other way. There always seemed to me to be a real depth of feeling between them; and, on her part, a recognition that his foibles were just a part of the person she loved.

She had been in Scotland for the day when Gordon was in Rochdale, but managed to get to Manchester by train that evening. Gordon wanted to meet her at the station, and asked me what I thought. I said that he shouldn't. The camera crews would follow him there, and he had had quite enough exposure for one day. He needed rest now, a bit of calm, and Sarah would be at the hotel soon enough anyway. Gordon ignored my advice, met her off the train, and led her through the crowds at the station. The genuine warmth people showed the two of them, and Sarah's presence at the end of a hellish day, lifted his mood, and helped get him through the final debate and the last days of the campaign.

The polls finally opened on 6 May. As a peer I was barred from casting a vote in the general election. It seemed very strange not to be putting my cross next to the name of a Labour parliamentary candidate, but at least I got to vote in the local elections before making my way to Victoria Street. There was the usual polling-day mixture of excitement, reports on the efforts to get out our vote, and an awful lot of waiting around. I kept going back and forth to Alicia Kennedy, the party's field director, and Greg Cook, our polling number-cruncher, to see what they were forecasting the final tally of seats would be.

They confirmed what the final opinion polls had indicated – we were on course to finish second, pulling away from the Lib Dems and a bit closer to the Tories, with every likelihood of a hung Parliament. Gillian Duffy had decided to put her Labour postal ballot in the bin, and I can't say I blamed her, but Gordon's remarks about her had seemed in the end to have a greater effect on the media than on the electorate. He and Sarah were voting in Scotland, and I phoned him to tell him I thought he had done well in the campaign.

I did not feel the same about my own performance. We had had some successes in the opening months of the year in halting the apparently unstoppable march by Cameron to a large overall majority. But I had struggled in the weeks leading up to the election, and had never felt able to get a grip on the campaign. Philip was a wise head, and Alastair had brought great spirit to our efforts, but we had never really seemed to be able to set the campaign agenda. My frustrations showed. The debates had altered the rhythm of the campaign, and I felt the media's view of the parties' lack of candour on the deficit had closed off any meaningful policy debate on the economy. What we could have done to change this, I didn't know. In my first campaign in charge, in 1987, we had lost badly, but the campaign itself was seen as a triumph: a 'brilliant defeat'. I did not feel that way about this campaign. I was now certain it would end in defeat, but brilliant it wasn't.

That night I was in the BBC studios when their extraordinary exit poll came in. It showed that, with just over three hundred seats, the Tories were going to be the largest party by some distance. However, despite being projected to lose nearly a hundred seats, we were comfortably in second place. The Lib Dems were way down on their post-debate peak, and were predicted to end up with about the same number of seats as in 2005. No party would have an overall majority. I spent the whole night watching the results, running on adrenalin like everyone else in the war room. In a series of broadcast appearances I pointed out that we, rather than the Lib Dems, were still Britain's one real progressive alternative, and that the message from the election was that no party had been given a ringing endorsement or a clear mandate to govern. In fact, I thought that David Cameron would probably end up heading a minority administration, and that we would have to get our act together quickly in case there was another election before too long.

The mood at Labour HQ was surprisingly upbeat. The results, though bad, were less dire than we had expected, and it was apparent that the Tories would not get the majority that had been predicted for so long. I think we were all determined as well that the atmosphere should not be funereal after the tough campaign. As the results came in, there were even cheers around the room as we held on to a number of seats we had expected to lose. It was little surprise that it was some of our hardest-working local MPs who were the ones that triumphed against the odds.

Gordon arrived at Victoria Street before dawn. He addressed the staff with gratitude and grace, and then I went with him and Andrew Adonis to the room where I'd held my daily morning meetings. As soon as we sat down, he tore a sheet from my yellow pad and started stabbing, rather than writing, rows of figures. When he looked up, he said straight away that there were two possible scenarios. If the Conservatives did scrape a majority, or got near enough to it to govern as a minority, we were out. But then, with real anticipation in his voice, he said: 'If not, we put together a Labour and Liberal majority.' Andrew, a former Lib Dem, had spent the best part of the past week in contact with friends in the party, and he was to be a driving force in talks with them in the coming days. He and Gordon now seemed to compete with each other in their excited calculation of how we could make what Gordon called 'an arrangement with the Liberals' happen: either a loose deal in which we agreed to some form of electoral reform and they agreed to support us on the Queen's Speech and confidence motions, or a fully fledged coalition with a fixed term. 'If you're serious,' I joked, 'perhaps you should stop calling them "the Liberals", and get their name right.'

I was, if not sceptical, at least cautious about whether it would work. Any way you juggled the figures, we had lost this election. We were heading for a result that put us at under 30 per cent of the vote, down from 36 per cent in 2005, and 43 per cent in 1997. It looked as if even the combined total of our seats and the Lib Dems' would not add up to an overall majority. And although Nick Clegg had been a bit more judicious in his comments in the latter part of the campaign, he had made it clear at the height of his post-debate popularity that he would find it very hard to be part of any arrangement that kept Gordon, who he had found patronising in the Commons and in their personal dealings, in Downing Street. 'The Lib Dems will fear being hoovered up by us if they do a deal,' I said to Gordon. He was certain, however, that this would be outweighed by the attraction of their Holy Grail: a new voting system.

The final results were still not in. Every few minutes we would hear cheers or groans as the latest constituency count was declared. But Gordon was determined that if the election result left any mathematical chance of bringing the Liberal Democrats on board to form a government, he would make a deal possible. Yes, we had come second. 'But that is not the final word,' he kept saying. As Prime Minister, he would have the first attempt at forming an administration. In fact, the final count would make the Tories, with 306 seats, the largest party, but twenty seats short of an overall majority. We had won 258 seats, ninety-one down on our 2005 total. The Lib Dems, despite their earlier surge in the polls, won fifty-seven, which was actually five fewer than in 2005.

I left shortly after 7.30 on the Friday morning to do a round of interviews, beginning with John Humphrys on the *Today* programme. All my political life I have started my day by listening to *Today*. I have particularly enjoyed being interviewed by Jim Naughtie or, more recently, Evan Davis, because I sense they relish the chance to put me on the spot. I once treated Jim to the sight of me changing my trousers during a live interview at a Labour Party conference. In my hurry to get to the interview I had put on the wrong suit trousers to go with my jacket, and Jim now shared my sartorial progress with *Today* listeners. John, I suspect, doesn't enjoy interviewing me as much, although I always try to answer him directly, even bluntly, and take some pleasure in not living up to my reputation as the master of spin. Now, as he set out the likely constitutional and coalition mechanics given the likelihood of a hung Parliament, I remarked that he had explained it all better than I could have done, which was hardly surprising as I hadn't slept for nearly thirty-six hours. My purpose in this and other interviews that morning was to keep our options open, and give us time to digest the results and act on them if the chance arose. I almost persuaded myself that we actually had a chance of forming a government, even though we had won far fewer seats than the Tories. As to whether the country would warm to the idea of a defeated party clinging on to power, I was much less convinced.

By the time I got back to party HQ, Andrew had spoken to Nick Clegg's chief of staff, Danny Alexander, who I knew from his earlier incarnation, as director of the cross-party Britain in Europe organisation which I had helped set up to build momentum towards joining the single currency. Danny had been in his late twenties then: warm, friendly, efficient and unabashedly enthusiastic about Europe. But what had most struck me was that he was refreshingly non-tribal, and good at working with people outside his own party. That would be a useful skill in the present circumstances, as he assumed the role of the Lib Dems' lead negotiator. They would clearly have to reflect on their own disappointing result before deciding their next move. Danny had ruled nothing in or out in his conversation with Andrew, but he seemed not to share Gordon's urgency about exploring prospects for a deal.

Tony phoned next. He was down about the result, and sounded truly sad for Gordon. He was firmly opposed to even thinking about a deal with the Lib Dems. It would be a serious error, he said, echoing my concern about what the voters would think if we tried to hang on. He, like almost everyone else, thought the Tories would form a government, either alone or in some loose arrangement with other parties, and that a new election would follow before too long. 'There will be an outcry if we stay on,' he said. 'There's going to be another election, and we'll be smashed if we don't make the right judgements.'

Gordon had meanwhile gone back to Number 10 – it was his constitutional duty to stay on in these circumstances until a new government could be formed. He and Andrew began working the phones. Gordon called Vince Cable, Paddy Ashdown and Menzies Campbell to try to rally them behind the idea of some form of Lab–Lib arrangement. He felt we were in a race to get to the bargaining table first, and was visibly deflated when TV news bulletins revealed that the Tories were already talking to Clegg's party. 'That's fine,' I told him. 'We should make a statement welcoming it, and saying it's entirely natural for them to talk to the party that got the largest number of seats.' I said that the main point to make was that Britain needed a government that reflected the wishes of the voters, and reassured him that this would legitimise our holding talks with the Lib Dems as well. He was further buoyed by a message, through Andrew, from Danny Alexander: 'Don't take this as suggesting we're only interested in talking to the Tories, but that it is only right the first discussion is with them.' I told Gordon, however, that we had to be careful how we handled ourselves. 'If we seem to be machinating to stay in office after having lost the election, if we act as if we've won when we haven't, we'll turn the public against us.'

I also knew that before long we would have to deal with an issue that would be difficult for all of us, but above all for Gordon: the likelihood that even if some deal with the Lib Dems looked conceivable, it would be at the price of his stepping aside. I wanted to test this, and I texted Danny shortly after noon: 'Between us (pl protect) ask Nick how big an obstacle is GB for LDs.' I talked to Gordon too. I said he had to be prepared to deal with Clegg's pretty obvious wariness about him, and that in any case a coalition with him at the top might be difficult to sell. I also raised the wider issues. We had the weekend at least, but if there was no resolution much beyond Monday, I felt that both he and we would run out of political rope. He did not disagree, but I could see that this was Gordon in full-focus mode, a bit like in the run-up to the G20 a year earlier, when nothing mattered but the issue at hand and his own judgement of what had to be done. I felt that he wasn't really listening; he just wanted to man the phones.

I spoke to Danny that afternoon, and got a clearer idea of the Lib Dems' plans for 'twin-track' talks, beginning with the Conservatives.

He also said that while 'personnel' – meaning Gordon – would be part of any talks, it was policy that would matter most for the Lib Dems. I was still concerned about how that would work – and concerned, too, for Gordon. If his staying on in Number 10 did turn out to be a deal-breaker, it was better that he was prepared for it. I phoned David Owen, who had told me on my return to government that at all costs I must stay loyal and supportive of Gordon. He was a friend, and a hugely experienced politician, and I valued his judgement. He was blunt. He thought that we were right to signal our openness to a deal with the Lib Dems, but that the mathematics of the result – the combined number of Labour and Lib Dem seats would not quite amount to an overall majority – and the mood in the country meant it was unlikely to work. With Gordon still in charge, he felt, there would be no chance at all. The Liberal Democrats would be 'toast' if they seemed to be propping him up. He added that I might be toast as well: 'You've done everything you could for Gordon. It was the right thing to do, but now you must stand apart and let him go. You cannot hang on to him. If you continue to lump yourself in with him, it will rebound on you.'

I do not deny that this had an effect on me, but I could not simply 'stand apart' from Gordon now. I had been with him at the start, and I would be with him at the end. If there was any real prospect of a Lab–Lib arrangement, I owed it to him, and to the party, at least to establish if it was possible, what it would look like, and if it would work. As I think Gordon must have sensed, I thought a deal between us and the Lib Dems was highly unlikely. When David Cameron went public with an extraordinarily forthright and open declaration of willingness to seek a policy compromise and a governing coalition with the Lib Dems, I was almost alone in our ranks in being impressed. Gordon and his team told me they felt it was a mistaken show of weakness, given the fact that the Tories had won the largest number of seats. To me, it sounded like the new politics, and I thought the public might welcome the idea of the Tories being willing to moderate their manifesto and make common cause with Nick Clegg. In the past, I had felt that Cameron was not bold enough about changing his party. More than anything else, in my view, that was what had cost him an overall majority. But now he was acting boldly, and if he pulled off a deal with the Lib Dems, the alliance would offer him a renewed prospect of delivering a changed perception of his party.

Our private talks with the Lib Dems began late on Friday afternoon, when Gordon, at Danny's request, called Nick Clegg at home. I was listening in on another phone, as I would throughout the informal back-and-forth until the real negotiations began. 'Nick,' Gordon began, 'the only issue is a majority of seats in the Commons.' In other words, no matter how disappointingly both our parties may have done, if we had the numbers, we could form a government that would both look and be legitimate. 'We need to agree on public expenditure and economic recovery. If we do this, everything else will fall into place.' He said that electoral reform, too, would be part of any agreement, but because the details would take time to work out, we would need a deal for a fixed four-year term. He even touched, glancingly, on the issue of his own role: 'We can talk personnel when we meet.' Perhaps he had been listening to me after all. They agreed to talk the following day. When the call was over, I was a little worried that Gordon might have come across a bit too heavily, telling Nick what he should think rather than asking him what he thought. I told him this, but he was excitedly focusing on the negotiating team he wanted to handle the detailed talks with the Lib Dems. I would be in charge, he said, partnered by Andrew Adonis, Alistair Darling and Ed Miliband.

When I awoke on Saturday morning, my mobile was clogged with messages from Gordon and Andrew telling me to call Danny Alexander. We spoke a little before 8.30. He was friendly, but absolutely straight. He said the Lib Dems were anxious not to appear to be playing us and the Tories off against each other, as if it were some kind of auction. No one would benefit from that. But the realities, as he saw them, were that while the Lib Dems were politically more natural partners with Labour, the Tories were being remarkably open-minded about the contours of a deal. While we agreed that our teams should meet for informal, preliminary talks later in the day, I sensed that Danny was sceptical about reaching a workable arrangement with us. And not chiefly because of Gordon, whom he didn't mention at this stage. He asked about the possibility of our implementing the alternative vote system without holding the referendum promised in our manifesto, as a first step towards a fully proportional system. I replied that I was a bit surprised by the question, to which he said that their worry was that the referendum would be lost because voters might see a Lab–Lib pact as a self-interested stitch-up on both sides, so it might be better to avoid such a test. Besides, would we be able to carry our backbenchers behind a deal with the Lib Dems, and also on electoral reform? These were all understandable concerns, unanswerable at this stage, but bound to come up if we were to get even close to a deal – and bound to unsettle Gordon.

Gordon was furious with the Lib Dems by the time I met him in Number 10 shortly after noon. His view was that we should let the Tories and 'the Liberals' talk until Monday, but then we should call time, say they were dragging their feet, and press for a deal of our own. In the meantime he was starting to feel that it looked bad for him to be holed up in Downing Street, and that it would be better for him to take the family to Scotland and return to London on Sunday morning. I said that sounded like an excellent idea, but added, 'Why don't you go to Chequers? It's nearer.' He seemed about to jump out of his chair at the mere mention of Chequers. 'God, no,' he said. 'It's a country house!'

As Sarah was packing, Gordon again warmed to the idea that a deal might be possible, and even began speculating about possible Lib Dem members of a coalition cabinet. He envisaged Nick being in charge of constitutional reform, Chris Huhne at Energy, David Laws at Culture, Media and Sport, and Paddy Ashdown as Defence Secretary. We discussed the prospect of Vince Cable as Chancellor. Gordon said it wouldn't work to have a Prime Minister and a Chancellor from different parties, but that Vince would be given an economic portfolio. What was apparent was that if there was any chance of a deal, Gordon was not about to let it slip. His overriding concern was keeping Labour in government, and keeping Cameron out. With the old, fiercely tribal, Brown passion, he said, 'Once the Tories are in government, with their hands on the levers, we'll never get them off.'

We held our first informal talks with the Lib Dems, at Portcullis House, across from the Commons, on Saturday afternoon. The make-up of our delegation was slightly different from what Gordon had first suggested. Alistair wasn't there, but Ed Balls and Harriet Harman were – I assumed because Gordon felt they might go off-message if they were excluded. In my opening remarks, I said that for any deal to have a hope of political legitimacy we would have to form a genuinely new government, not just a broadly unchanged Labour administration with the Lib Dems tacked on. It had to be, and it had to be seen as, a real departure. On policy, we had to recognise the need for compromise: neither side would get everything it wanted. Our starting point had to be an awareness of what was best for the country, and what voters would expect of a new government.

When we began getting into detail, Danny said there was a range of priorities for them: tax cuts for the lowest-paid, tackling the deficit, education subsidies for disadvantaged pupils, breaking up the big banks, and electoral reform. On none of these did a workable compromise policy seem impossible. The Lib Dems also appeared to be softening their line on our holding a referendum on a new electoral system. In a series of meetings that began when Gordon got back from Scotland late on Sunday morning and finally ended on Tuesday, they ended up basically agreeing with us that we should hold a referendum on the alternative vote system, but with a proportional system also as a choice on the ballot paper.

The policy specifics were not really the problem. The viability of a deal was always going to rest on whether it would look as if the Lib Dems were propping up a defeated Labour Party, and how that would play with the voters. Gordon had a preliminary meeting with Nick soon after getting back from Scotland. It seemed to go fairly well, but from the outset the Lib Dem leader raised his concern about the legitimacy, and saleability, of a coalition with Labour. And while they agreed to defer any detailed discussion about Gordon's own role until a later stage, we all knew that the matter would have to be addressed if there was to be any chance of an agreement. In fact, quite apart from our own talks with the Lib Dems, I was increasingly concerned about the personal price Gordon might pay if he were seen to be hanging on too long in Downing Street. Andrew, Sue and Ed Balls all shared my concern. We agreed that it was paramount that Gordon retain his dignity whatever happened over the coming days. Gordon himself recognised that he would probably have to go fairly soon as the price of a deal with the Lib Dems. The problem was going to be how, and when. He quite understandably wanted to avoid giving the impression that he was being pushed out. He said that he was ready to sacrifice his own position for a deal that would be good for Labour, and good for the country. But leaving with dignity was also important. 'I have been humiliated enough,' he told me.

On Sunday night, Gordon, Nick, Danny and I met in Gordon's room behind the Speaker's chair in the Commons. To avoid being seen, Gordon and I walked through the underground tunnel from Number 10 to the Ministry of Defence, where a car was waiting for us. Nick did not hide the fact that his team was still talking to the Conservatives, who, he repeated, were being much more forthcoming than they had expected. As we went through broad policy issues – a referendum on the electoral system, action on the deficit – there was obviously scope for agreement. But then, 'personnel' came up. Nick raised the issue first. 'Please understand I have no personal animosity whatsoever,' he told Gordon, 'but it is not possible to secure the legitimacy of a coalition and win a referendum unless you move on in a dignified way. You have said you don't want to be a barrier. You've been an incredible catalyst in reshaping politics, but we cannot persuade the public of renewal unless you go in time.'

Gordon did not object, but he did say that he would want to make sure the referendum worked out, and the economic recovery was in place, before he went. When Nick asked him if he envisaged simply staying until the referendum was held in the autumn, Gordon said he would need to be there to make sure of getting support for electoral reform within Labour. They went back and forth for some time, Nick explaining the 'massive political risk' of being seen to legitimise Gordon as Prime Minister after the election result, and Gordon saying he would announce that he was leaving, but that he felt he could not go until he had successfully dealt with 'the tasks in hand'. I found their exchanges impressive: firm, but with sensitivity on both sides. I tried to steer Nick away from pushing too hard at this meeting, pointing out that a Labour leadership election in the midst of implementing an ambitious early coalition programme was surely the last thing either side needed. But Danny said that no deal would work if Gordon stayed on past a referendum. Nick and Gordon had the last, if still inconclusive, word: Nick saying that Gordon's early departure was essential if we were to show that we had understood the 'fundamental desire for change' in the country, and Gordon recognising that they would have to talk it through further.

In fact, pressures beyond Gordon's control were beginning to make it ever more difficult to see a deal happening. From soundings among members of the cabinet, Sue reckoned that half a dozen or so wanted the coalition, principally Harriet and Ed Miliband. A similar number, including David Miliband and Alistair, were against. The remainder, including Ed Balls and Tessa, were doubtful or ambivalent. Ed Balls later commented to me that the PLP were similarly divided. One part wanted a coalition, a second thought that going for a deal would make us look idiotic, and the rest thought that a coalition might be workable, but only if Gordon were to go as Prime Minister – a view that, as long as it was organised so that Gordon himself announced a 'transition' timetable, Ed himself now shared.

So did Tony. Now that the talks were under way, he said that the idea of a genuinely new kind of left-of-centre coalition government seemed perfectly good in principle. But Gordon could not stay: 'As I've told him, the difference from when we were having these talks with the Lib Dems in 1997 is that we won then. Now we've lost.' Tony told him, and me, that the public simply would not accept Gordon remaining as Prime Minister in those circumstances. They would view it as a constitutional outrage. He also felt that the issue was absolutely crucial to the way Labour would be seen in future by the voters. But he had not lost his impish humour. When I had texted him to say I was free to speak, and that 'GB is going to church', he texted back, 'He'll find that a tougher negotiation.'

Danny phoned me first thing on Monday morning. 'Personnel' was now clearly becoming central to any prospect of a deal. He said Nick had felt the message about Gordon's leaving wasn't getting through to him. Gordon would have to go by mid-October at the very latest. Next, Paddy Ashdown phoned, with what I assumed was a brief to reinforce Danny's message. He began by saying that personalities mattered in negotiations like this. While Nick felt he was being treated well by Cameron, he found Gordon 'lecturing, bullying, uncongenial'. Though Paddy did not know Gordon well, I am sure he recognised that this was largely a matter of style. I had been in the room during the talks, and my own view was that while Gordon had been firm, he had broadly been in listening mode. This was tough for him. It would have been tough for anyone in his position. I hoped the Lib Dems would understand that. Paddy assured me that it was not about 'humiliating Gordon or dictating to Labour'. He recognised that Gordon should go with dignity, even with praise. But if he stayed on, there was no way a deal could be sold to the Lib Dems or to the country: 'You have got to know that Gordon staying on longer is a deal-breaker.'

When I spoke at length to Gordon, he said he was determined not to be an obstacle to a deal, if one looked possible. He now suggested that he would agree, privately, to go at the beginning of October. The only issue was what to say about it publicly. He proposed saying that he would not cling on to power, and would leave in due course. He then held a further private meeting in his Commons room with Nick Clegg. This time, it was agreed that I would wait outside as they spoke, and then join them to take an agreed note of their conclusions. When I entered the room they were standing, and I sat down in an armchair, opening my hardback notebook, pen in hand. 'This is a rare sight, a historic sight,' Gordon said. 'People at last seeing what Peter Mandelson actually does.' 'Yes,' I replied. 'He's a stenographer.'

Nick said he had told Gordon that he was going to put three options before his MPs. The first was a deal with the Tories. It still fell short of what they wanted on Europe, and left the Tories free to oppose voting reform at the time of the referendum, so he said that he would not be recommending it. The second was a 'confidence and supply' arrangement with David Cameron, under which the Tories would adopt some Lib Dem manifesto policies, but nothing on electoral reform. 'All very sub-optimal,' Nick said. That left the option of opening serious, formal talks with us. Gordon said he had told Nick that he expected a new Labour leader to be in place by the start of October. There was agreement that formal talks would begin. But the second Tory option, the weaker 'supply' option, would remain on the table.

Gordon made a statement that afternoon in front of Number 10. He said that while we understood that the Lib Dems would continue to talk to the Tories as well, he and Nick had agreed to the opening of formal discussions with Labour. He added that while he would form a new Lab–Lib Dem government if agreement was reached, he recognised that the election had been in part a verdict on him, and that he was asking Labour to begin preparations for a contest to elect a new leader by the autumn. Gordon was going – and going not only with dignity, I felt, but with statesmanship, and with class. I was inside Number 10 with one of my oldest friends in politics, Sue, who had lived through the ups and downs of New Labour's journey with me from the very beginning. Suddenly it felt as if all my years with Tony and Gordon rushed towards me and hit me in the solar plexus. I was momentarily overcome. When Gordon came back inside he tried to thank me for my support, but I couldn't speak to him. I knew tears would flow. I sensed that this would make a difficult situation more difficult for both of us, and that this was a moment each of us would best deal with alone.

Even in his going, Gordon was still setting the political weather. His statement dramatically changed the context of Nick's negotiations with both of the major parties. For the first time, it seemed possible – though still not likely – to me that a coalition between Labour and the

Lib Dems might actually work. When Nick phoned Downing Street later in the afternoon, he said that his MPs had made it clear they were not interested in the watered-down deal with the Tories. They wanted a full coalition. It was now down to a straight choice for Nick and his party: a full coalition with us, or with Cameron. I took the negotiating team for further talks with the Lib Dems that evening. There were differences of detail, but nothing big, certainly nothing irresolvable.

But from Tuesday morning onwards, the mood changed. Some newspapers were reporting that the Lib Dems thought our negotiating team were negative and even disengaged. I did not think this was the case, but when we met again at 10 a.m. there seemed to be sharper differences on a range of issues. What was most striking, however, was a new attitude of prickliness, even truculence, from the Lib Dems. Halfway through, I inconspicuously texted Danny. If this atmosphere continues, I said, we'll get nowhere. And we didn't. I felt now that the tide, on all sides, was running away from us. Cameron's team was being surprisingly generous on a whole range of Lib Dem policy priorities. My sense was that, despite Gordon's rather heroic statement of the previous day, the Lib Dems were responding to this, and were no longer seriously pressing for agreement with us. It was also becoming clear to both sides that there were strains within Labour over whether a coalition would be tenable, or would make political sense. Quite aside from private reservations within the cabinet, a number of former ministers, notably David Blunkett and John Reid, had gone public about their opposition to such a deal.

Gordon tried to rescue the situation. When he next spoke to Nick by phone, he said voices like David's and John's were a side issue. Still, by this point, I think even he was beginning to worry that the game was probably up and that he needed to focus on a dignified departure. Later in the afternoon the Queen's Private Secretary, Christopher Geidt, came to Number 10 to discuss with him how developments might unfold. I was due to go to Buckingham Palace myself at 5.30 p.m. for a meeting of the Privy Council, and I asked Christopher if it was still happening. He confirmed that it was. When I remarked that the waiting was becoming intolerable for Gordon, he said that he understood, but that things would have to become clearer before Gordon resigned.

After I returned from the Privy Council there was one last push. Gordon spoke several times with Nick by phone, as virtually all the team from his years in Downing Street grouped around him in his office. But it was becoming obvious that we had been reduced to waiting for the inevitable news that Clegg and Cameron had come to terms. Finally, Nick phoned to say he had reluctantly concluded that Labour could not deliver on a coalition agreement. Even then, Gordon was reluctant to acknowledge that the chances for a Lab–Lib deal were over. He told Nick that if he joined with the Tories, the progressive realignment Tony and Paddy had so wanted would be lost for at least a generation. He said there was a historic deal to be done, adding that the reason he had offered to stand down as leader was because he felt strongly that a deal was both important and possible. But Nick said the question was whether the very idea of a coalition with Labour was really workable, and whether the voters would ever buy it. 'The reality,' he said rather brutally, 'is that your party is knackered after thirteen years in power.'

There was one final twist. Nick and Gordon spoke again forty-five minutes later. Nick now said that he was still seeing how far he could push the Tories on Europe. By implication, a deal with us was still in play. Now it was Gordon's turn to be firm. Commendably, and rightly, he told Nick that he had decided the process could go on no longer. I am sure this was partly a matter of injured pride: he knew by this time that we were being used as a negotiating lever with the Tories. But the main reason was that he felt the continuing spectacle was bad for the country, bad for the image of politics and politicians, and bad for him personally. I had been urging him to call time on the process since the beginning of this latest series of conversations with Nick – not only because it was clear that the Lib Dems were going to come to some arrangement with Cameron, but out of my old, Walworth Road media instincts. I was fearful that if the dénouement was delayed much longer, Gordon would have to leave Downing Street after dark. That was not the image I wanted for his leave-taking, nor the one I felt that his lifetime in politics and public service deserved.

Gordon now told Nick that it was too late for further talking. It was over. He was resigning. 'You can't,' Nick replied. He said he still couldn't be sure a Tory coalition would work. Gordon's resignation could end up leading to a minority Cameron government. Gordon was serene in his reply. 'The public has run out of patience. And so have I,' he said. 'I have served the country as best I can. I know the country's mood. They will not tolerate me waiting another night. I have no option. You are a good man and you have to make a decision. I have made mine. It is final. I am going to the Palace. Goodbye.'

Gordon said a last farewell to his team in Number 10. As he did so, his sons and Sarah joined us. There was a mixture of jokes, tears and laughter. I accompanied him to the front door, as he went outside to make his final statement. It was upright and statesmanlike, and his deep personal commitment to public service rang out from it. Then, with Sarah and the children, he left for the Palace to resign from the job he had wanted for so long, initially found so thrilling, and then so very difficult. I could not help thinking that nothing had so dignified him, or so summed up what was best and strongest in him, as those final words.

One of the more brutal, but ultimately compassionate, features of the British system of government is that when you're out, you're out. Quickly. I went back to the Cabinet Office to gather my things, and said an emotional goodbye to my team, which I had grown so fond of, in the Private Office. We all embraced, and then I was gone. I went to Labour HQ, where Gordon thanked the party staff. He singled out certain individuals, describing me as 'the rock upon which the stability of the Labour Party had been built for so many years'. It was an emotional moment as we said goodbye not only to Gordon's time in Number 10, but to New Labour's thirteen years in government. I did some television interviews. I said that we had much to be proud of from our years in government. The country was a better, kinder, stronger place for our time in office. We had denied the Conservatives their wish to waltz unchallenged into

Downing Street, and we could be pleased with what our campaign had achieved.

By the next day, Vince Cable had moved into my office at the business department. Nick was in residence in the Cabinet Office room where I had spent months planning for the campaign that brought an end to Labour's longest-ever period in power. For me, of course, the arrival of the Cameron–Clegg government also marked the end of, or at least a punctuation mark in, a journey of reform and modernisation that began not years, but decades, earlier.

I felt neither sad nor relieved that our period in government had come to an end for now. I could understand why, if only because we had been navigating the worst economic crisis in memory, so many voters had concluded that the government had come to its natural end, and that we had begun to look as if we were better at managing the status quo than challenging it. The voters' verdict was especially cruel for Gordon: he had steered Britain through the economic storm, but was being denied a just reward for his endeavours.

On a personal level, I obviously had regrets. I would have liked to have served my country for a more prolonged period as a cabinet minister than I did. My return to government for a third time did help me to overcome some of the deep frustration that had remained with me to a much greater degree than I had recognised during my hugely invigorating time in Brussels. In galvanising my newly created department for the industrial activism and growth strategy I believed were so important to rebalance the economy, I felt energised, and well into my stride, when the electorate called time on New Labour. That is the problem with government. No sooner have you worked out exactly what your policies are, pointed everyone in the right direction and started to make them work, than it is someone else's turn. Still, public service remains in my view the highest calling of all. Rising to the task of helping Britain deal with its unprecedented economic and financial crisis had been the most challenging, and fulfilling, period of my time in national politics. It had also given me the chance to heal the breach with Gordon, and to forge a new relationship with the party to which I had devoted my life. All that was something for which I would be eternally grateful. My regret was that my efforts were not sufficient to take us to a fourth election victory.

There was another, more trivial, defeat as well. Ever since my very first encounters with Gordon in the 1980s, when he was a young modernising MP and I was Labour's media-manager-in-chief, I had been intrigued, and frustrated, by a sartorial mystery. No matter how I tried, he could somehow never master a basic presentational rule: appearing in public, or on television, with his tie properly done up and centred. His move into Downing Street had done nothing to improve the situation. For years, Sue Nye and I had conducted a good-natured sparring match over this. Surely it was not beyond the ability of Gordon's staff to make sure his tie was done up correctly before he went before the cameras? Sue invariably replied that his tie was 'jinxed'. No matter how many times she or others put it back in place, it would invariably have loosened or uncentred itself by the time the TV moment arrived. As Gordon was preparing to step out in front of Number 10 to deliver his final words as Prime Minister, I took things into my own hands, and made sure that this time, at least, his tie would be perfectly centred. Alas, Sue turned out to be right. By the time he began speaking, it had moved, just slightly, out of place again.

Still, despite that parting regret – and the many more serious New Labour errors or oversights which I have chronicled in these pages – I left the stage of national politics with an overriding sense of pride in what we had achieved. The positive side of the ledger seemed to me far longer than the negative. Despite the policies not fully implemented, the opportunities missed, despite even the soap-opera interludes in the three-way relationship at the centre of New Labour, I had no doubt that our accomplishments in government greatly outweighed the disappointments. We had delivered a decade of solid economic growth, with all the employment and business success that came with that. We had helped rebuild our health service, schools and other public services. Britain had become a less divided, more harmonious place, more at ease with itself and the diversity of its society than it had been when we were first elected. We had stronger universities, a well-resourced science base and more investment in the Midlands and the north than before, and much else besides. If I needed a reminder of how much stronger the country had become, I got it when I went back to my former constituency of Hartlepool shortly before the election campaign to receive the honour of Freeman of the Borough. It was a town that had changed hugely for the better as a result of the Labour government. It had also changed my life for the better, in giving me the privilege of being its MP for twelve years.

It had been a privilege, too, to be at the centre of political change in Labour, and in Britain, for a quarter of a century. Being the Third Man alongside the sometimes fraught political double act of Gordon Brown and Tony Blair had its inevitable frustrations. But the way in which our relationship ultimately survived – and, of course, my most unlikely return for our final period in government – has helped me place the more difficult moments in their proper perspective. It has reminded me that however important personalities are in politics, in the end it is the policies, the driving political vision, the leadership and the tough decisions taken that really matter, and we had not ducked these.

I know that all three of us have one central regret: that had we worked together after 1994 as we had in the initial crusade that made New Labour possible, we would have accomplished even more, and far more happily. But years ago, after my first cabinet resignation, I remarked, a bit defensively, to friends that my strengths as a politician and as a person were an inseparable result of both my 'good bits' and the not-so-good ones. While I hope I have managed to reduce the second group over time, I still believe that to be true. I am convinced as well that it has been true of both Tony and Gordon throughout. All three of us, at our strongest, retained an ability to bring out the best in one another. We did that often enough to transform Labour into a natural and enduring party of government. While there are many things I might have done differently along the way, there is one thing of which I have no doubt: that for all the ups and downs in my political career, my life as New Labour's Third Man has been worth it.

Epilogue

When the exhaustion of the election campaign, and the disappointment of losing, had begun to pass, I naturally cast my mind back to the years leading up to the landslide of 1997, and the final march by a reformed Labour Party from eighteen years of opposition into thirteen years in government.

It was, in a way, a comforting comparison. Yes, it was a reminder of how far we had fallen. But to paraphrase my comment to the party conference a few months earlier, one obvious implication was that if we had come back from the wilderness once, it should not be impossible for us to do so again. It was tempting, too, to console myself with the fact that the defeat could have been worse. We had kept David Cameron from winning an overall majority in the Commons, and had outpolled the Liberal Democrats by a large margin. But, perhaps because my own Labour history went back much further – to Michael Foot and Tony Benn, to Neil Kinnock and John Smith – I also knew that to grab at these crumbs of comfort was dangerous. The first steps towards recovering our poise and purpose as a party, and certainly towards returning to power, required learning the lessons of what had gone wrong, and facing up to the true scale of our defeat.

We had lost nearly a million votes since the least convincing of New Labour's three election victories, five years previously. With barely 8.5 million votes, and a mere 29 per cent of the total, our result was worse than in 1992 under Neil, worse than the 'brilliant defeat' I orchestrated from Walworth Road in 1987. In fact, it was only just better than the comprehensive battering we suffered in 1983. The brutality of that defeat had at least acted as a kind of shock therapy. It was what gave Neil the ability to take on Militant and begin the process of rescuing the party from irrelevance and almost certain death. Ultimately, it was what made New Labour possible. Yet as I surveyed the Labour landscape, talked and listened to colleagues after this latest defeat, the situation struck me as much more like the aftermath of 1992. We were paying lip-service to the need to 'learn lessons', but there seemed to be an expectation that, with one heave, we would be back in government, quite possibly at the next election, and certainly at the one after that.

There was some reason for optimism, and not merely because the Tories had done worse than the polls had predicted a few months earlier, or than they themselves had expected. The very nature of Cameron's rebranding of the Conservatives, and the political platform he negotiated with his Lib Dem partners, were reflections of perhaps the greatest achievement of the political project Gordon, Tony and I had begun two decades earlier. New Labour shifted the centre of gravity of British politics. National elections could now be won only by appealing to a broad constituency of voters in the centre ground, with policies that combined a commitment to social justice with respect and support for individual aspiration. But – and it was a critically important but – we also had to recognise that we had lost the trust of vital parts of that broad constituency. It was not just the overall election result that mattered. Although we had done fairly well in London, our support had collapsed in many areas of the south and south-east of England, and we had seen depressing drops in support among the skilled workers whose aspirations we had spoken to in 1997. Most seriously of all, as in the aftermath of the 1983 débâcle, large numbers of voters throughout the country seemed simply to have stopped listening to us, because they felt that we had stopped listening to them.

Partly, of course, this was because people had tired of New Labour after thirteen years in power. Going into the campaign of 2010, we had to contend with the build-up of grievances that any government accumulates after three terms in office, and with the inevitable desire for change. Some voters clearly found it hard to endorse five more years of Gordon. I am sure that 'the election that wasn't' in 2007 undermined his reputation for strength in a way than neither he, nor we, fully recovered from. But as I tried, and ultimately failed, to construct an election message around a vision of our own to meet the electorate's appetite for change, my sense was that the challenge went well beyond the mechanics of the campaign, and the occasional internal tensions surrounding it.

The real problem was that over a long period, voters had come to feel that we had moved away from the key New Labour instincts that first attracted them to us. We had ceased to sound and feel like New Labour, for example on taxation and public service reform, and therefore there was a sense in which the government was drawing to a natural close. When we talked of being the party of fairness – offering 'a future fair for all' – the message appealed to people in so far as it went. But where in 1997 we had been in touch with their broader ideas of fairness, by 2010 we were perceived to be on a different wavelength. In our final years of office, when economic times were tough, too many voters thought that while they were working hard and paying their dues, the government was working for others: bankers, immigrants, benefit recipients, or those we were helping in far-off foreign conflicts. What these voters meant by fairness was fair rules on immigration, welfare and housing – issues on which they felt we were either now speaking a different language than we had in 1997, or no longer had anything to say at all. In fact, in the final years of Tony's time in power, and under Gordon as well, we had made real headway in sharpening up our policies on immigration, social housing and – to a more limited extent – welfare reform. But this had come too late for voters who saw us as out of step with their instincts for fairness.

We had also stopped addressing the aspirations of people who made their own way in life, and wanted to retain more of their income to do so. Yes, we had provided much-improved public services, and in previous elections, when times were good, this was a core attraction of New Labour. But when the growth stopped we were left without a credible vision of how we would meet people's concerns about their families' economic future. This was what made the difference in many of the Midlands seats that we won in 1997, retained in the next two elections, but had now lost. Real disposable incomes were either stagnant or falling by the end of the Parliament. The economy was not delivering sufficient numbers of decently paid, skilled jobs. In my view, we should have been operating a far more active industrial policy since 1997 rather than being forced into it after the global crisis of 2008.

Our failures to meet people's aspirations went deeper. In my introduction to a new edition of *The Blair Revolution* in 2002 I wrote: 'The government needs principally to concentrate on the future by addressing the conditions for people to get on in life, to make the most of themselves, instead of such opportunities being dependent on the privileges of birth, of wealth, who you know and the contacts that well-connected families and friends can provide. For me, the goal of social democracy is to create the sort of society in which the daughter of a Hartlepool shop assistant has as much chance of becoming a High Court judge as the daughter of a Harley Street doctor. We are a long way from creating such a society.'

Reflecting on our defeat in 2010, I could not help but feel that this last sentence still rang true. We had made real strides towards a fairer, more meritocratic society during our years in government, whether in the way that Gordon's tax credits had helped those at the bottom of the economic ladder, or through the unprecedented opening up under Tony's educational reforms of opportunities for young people to benefit from the learning and skills they needed to make the most of their lives. But we did not go far enough. During my last year in office, when I assumed responsibilities for higher and further education, I was especially driven to use reform in higher education as an engine to accelerate social mobility in Britain. I placed this aim at the root of my 'Higher Ambitions' universities White Paper in November 2009, which reflected the reality that while there had been a significant rise in the number of disadvantaged young people in higher education since the mid-1990s, the figures for the least advantaged at the most selective universities had not changed. I had hoped that remedying this would be a central mission of a fourth-term Labour administration, and I still hope that the reforms I began to set in train in this area will not become a casualty of the change of government.

We also failed collectively to go further and faster in other areas to promote social mobility during our time in government. For a range of reasons that I have set out in this book, we did not make a sufficiently early start on our public service reforms. When we did, they worked. Our NHS reforms – combined with our reversal of years of Tory under-investment – immeasurably strengthened the health service. The schools reforms which we introduced in our third term were genuinely pioneering, and the diversity of schools provision they ushered in will be a lasting legacy of New Labour's time in government. Still, I never felt that our final period in office built on these reforms, or took them forward, sufficiently. Too often we gave the impression that we were soft-pedalling on reform, or worse, were minded to reverse it.

Part of this reflected a failure to develop further a vision of the role of the state in society – what government should do more of, and what it should do less of. If we had done so, I believe we would have been able to offer a more coherent and compelling vision for the future in an election that was inevitably dominated by the economic crisis. The Tories' 'Big Society' was a vacuous offering, but we could, and should, have countered it with our own idea of what the twenty-first-century state should look like, rather than attacking it in the purely negative terms we did.

We had become trapped in the success of our 'investment versus cuts' dividing lines of the 2001 and 2005 elections. I have no doubt that we were right to remedy the huge under-investment in our public services during the years of growth, and to fight back hard against the banking crisis. But by 2010 we had allowed a caricature to become established in the public mind that we had abandoned fiscal responsibility in pursuit of reviving a familiar electoral tactic. To have failed to take the action we did in fighting the recession – which necessitated the extra borrowing – would have been catastrophic in human, business and financial terms. But when we were faced with a huge deficit as a consequence, we would have been in a stronger position politically if we had been seen to face up earlier and more credibly to the necessity of greater public spending cuts and tax increases once recovery was secure.

During our final days in power, as I led our party's coalition negotiations with the Lib Dems, I also inevitably thought back to the ambitions for a progressive political realignment that had animated us in the early years of New Labour. Looking back at the many discussions we had with Paddy Ashdown, Roy Jenkins and others, I did not see them so much as a missed opportunity as an opportunity that was never really there to be grasped. The forces against it at the time, in both of our parties, were too strong, and the circumstances were never propitious enough to overcome them. But that was not sufficient excuse for our failure to keep working towards cooperation since that time. As Nick Clegg remarked to me a month after the election, in May 2010 we were scrambling to put something together which could have been assembled at any time during the previous thirteen years. When the circumstances changed with the hung Parliament in 2010, both the electoral arithmetic and the lack of an established rapport between our parties and their leaderships militated against any serious prospect of a progressive alliance. Still, the fact that the Lib Dems opted to join a coalition with the Conservatives seems to me no reason for us to abandon the ambition of a more progressive realignment in future. I have no doubt that a plural, open and progressive politics still offers the best prospect of a fairer, more vibrant twenty-first-century Britain. Certainly the opposite route – a descent into angry, tribal trench warfare – would guarantee Labour a prolonged period out of power.

My feeling is that, with the re-emergence of the Lib Dems as a party of government, coalition politics might well be here to stay. I sense that the old pattern of two-party pendulum politics may be breaking down. I have always supported the alternative vote electoral system, because I believe it forces candidates of all parties to work harder to gain every vote in their constituency. It is important that, unlike many Tories, we should campaign for it in the proposed referendum on the issue. I make a distinction between this reform and introducing proportional representation, which in my view would tempt the Labour Party to abandon centrist policies in favour of ideological 'purity', on the assumption that its share of the left-wing vote would be protected by a proportional system.

But in pursuit of a more plural, more open politics, the condition of the Labour Party itself clearly also needs to be brought back onto the agenda. Within days of the election, Tony's successor as MP for Sedgefield, Phil Wilson, lamented that after New Labour came into government on 1 May 1997, serious efforts at party reform stopped the following day. He was right, and the success of some of those Labour MPs who bucked the national trend and won or retained their seats in 2010 bore out his message. MPs who put themselves at the front of genuinely campaigning movements, directly in touch with the public, rather than relying on the familiar Old Labour structures and methods, reaped the benefits, and more than countered the financial muscle of the Ashcroft Tory marginals campaigns.

All of these issues will have to be addressed, debated and thrashed out as we contemplate our future not in government, but in opposition. I realise that it may seem odd for someone who is still in his fifties, and is not giving up politics forever, to say that it is time for a new generation of New Labour to write the next chapter in our governing project. But in writing this book, I have become ever more convinced that it is true. I know that my two very different founding partners of New Labour, Tony and Gordon, recognise it as well. The verdict of the voters on 6 May 2010 marked the end of a long, and I still believe overwhelmingly positive, period of New Labour in government. I do not for a minute believe that the founding ideas and ethos of New Labour have reached an end. Although we have shifted the political and social geography of Britain over the past thirteen years, there are still real differences between the two main parties, on issues that will matter hugely in the next few years. In the wake of the worst economic crisis of our lifetimes, how can we best ensure that our country is equipped to create jobs, and nurture innovation and enterprise?

With the pain that will come from a period of budgetary austerity, how can we protect the most vulnerable, and help them to recover and prosper? How can we reconnect politics with people, and government with the governed? What is the proper role of government, and the state? These are only a few of the questions that will need answering. This will require listening, and some hard thought as well.

Whoever becomes the next leader of the Labour Party will require intelligence, reflectiveness, a readiness to take tough decisions on both policy and politics, an ability to speak and inspire, and a capacity to engage at an emotional level with the British public, and not just the party faithful. There also needs to be a recognition that both parts of the title that we gave to our modernising project still matter. We have to be Labour: true to values of social justice. We also need to be New Labour. Not as some branding exercise. Not as an eye-catching label. But in the sense that we have to ask ourselves constantly how we can best apply those values, make them real for people's lives, in a country and a world that have changed and are still changing.

For New Labour, as for me and the two very different but remarkable partners with whom I joined forces to create it two decades ago, a new chapter has begun.

Index

567